Cultural Anthropology

Third Canadian Edition

Barbara D. Miller
George Washington University

Penny Van Esterik
York University

John Van Esterik
York University

PEARSON

Toronto

Library and Archives Canada Cataloguing in Publication

Miller, Barbara D., 1948–
       Cultural anthropology / Barbara D. Miller, Penny Van Esterik,
John Van Esterik. — 3rd Canadian ed.

Includes bibliographical references and index.

ISBN 0-205-46516-1

       1. Ethnology—Textbooks.   I. Van Esterik, John   II. Van Esterik,
Penny   III. Title.

GN316.M34 2007   306   C2005-906270-3

ISBN 0-205-46516-1

Vice President, Editorial Director: Michael J. Young
Executive Acquisitions Editor: Christine Cozens
Executive Marketing Manager: Judith Allen
Developmental Editor: Matthew Christian
Production Editor: Söğüt Y. Güleç
Copy Editor: Lisa Berland
Proofreader: Susan McNish
Production Manager: Wendy Moran
Photo and Permissions Research: Jane McWhinney
Composition: Gerry Dunn
Illustrations: LMY Studios
Art Director: Julia Hall
Interior Design: Anne Flanagan, Susan Thomas
Cover Design: Julia Hall
Cover Image: © Jim Erikson/CORBIS

1 2 3 4 5   11 10 09 08 07

Printed and bound in the USA.

BRIEF CONTENTS

CONTENTS

PART I
INTRODUCTION TO CULTURAL ANTHROPOLOGY

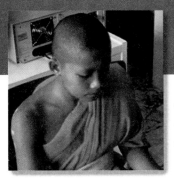

1
Anthropology and the Study of Culture   1

2
Methods in Cultural Anthropology   25

PART II
ECONOMIC AND DEMOGRAPHIC FOUNDATIONS

3

Economies and Their Modes of Production 49

4

Consumption and Exchange 75

5

Birth and Death 101

6

Personality, Identity, and Human Development 123

PART III
SOCIAL ORGANIZATION

7
Illness and Healing · 145

8
Kinship Dynamics · 169

9

Domestic
Groups 191

10

Social Groups
and Social
Stratification 209

PART IV
SYMBOLIC SYSTEMS

11
Politics, Conflict, and Social Order 233

12
Religion 259

13

Communication 285

14

Expressive Culture 307

PART V
CONTEMPORARY CULTURAL CHANGE

15
People on the Move 329

16
Development Anthropology 349

BOXED FEATURES

Lessons Applied

Critical Thinking

Multiple Cultural Worlds

PREFACE FROM BARBARA MILLER

Why would anybody write an introductory cultural anthropology textbook? Such a project requires years of research, writing, and rewriting, and is a humbling task as one continually faces how much material there is yet to read and how much more rethinking of categories and questions must be done. One catalyst for my undertaking the writing of this book was that over the three years of my teaching large classes in introductory cultural anthropology each spring semester at the University of Pittsburgh, my enrollments went from 100 in 1991 to 200 in 1992 to 300 in 1993. I figured that I must have been doing something right.

On top of that experience, throughout the many years of my teaching introductory cultural anthropology—from my first course in 1979 to now—it became clear to me what I find dissatisfying in other cultural anthropology textbooks: They mainly treat the topic of social inequality and diversity in just one chapter (usually on "social stratification"), rather than considering it as woven into every topic in cultural anthropology. Thus, their treatment of material about economies, kinship, politics, religion, and language involves little attention to how these topics relate to social inequality and diversity. While I appreciate cultural similarities worldwide, I find differences important, too, since they often divide people in ways that are dangerous, hurtful, and yet also changeable.

I am also aware of how "dead" many of the long-standing subjects in cultural anthropology have become. I have found it difficult to teach many of cultural anthropology's core topics, such as kinship and language. The material seemed irrelevant to cultural anthropology's goal of understanding why people do what they do and think the way they do.

Last, I found that my strong interest in culture change was poorly presented in the available books. I live and teach in Washington, D.C., a highly politicized and policy-focused environment. This niche impresses on me every day the need for cultural anthropology to be relevant to the contemporary world of power, policy, and change. My academic appointment at the George Washington University is located within the Elliott School of International Affairs and the Department of Anthropology. This double focus is important in terms of helping me to integrate cultural anthropology into international affairs and promoting concerns with international policy debates within anthropology. Many of my students, both undergraduates and graduates, find paid or unpaid work at various governmental and non-governmental institutions at some point during their training. I hope that *Cultural Anthropology* conveys a sense, either directly or indirectly, of the importance of anthropological research and learning for the understanding and potential amelioration of world problems such as poverty, hunger, violence, and illness. The threads of these issues, and a sense of policy relevance in cultural anthropology, run throughout the book.

I set out to write a textbook that would reshape and enliven the teaching and learning of cultural anthropology along all of these lines. Whether you are interested in environmental studies, peace studies, international business, or health studies, knowing about the world's cultures is a crucial foundation for shaping a vision of what is both possible and appropriate in terms of goals and actions. *Cultural Anthropology,* to this end, presents interesting and informative material about "exotic" and distant cultures as well as paying substantial attention to contemporary "Western" cultures (primarily European and European-American). Readers coming from diverse cultural perspectives will be able to "make the strange familiar and the familiar strange," to use the powerful words of Melford Spiro (1990).

Barbara Miller

PREFACE TO THE THIRD CANADIAN EDITION

We are pleased with the reception of the first and second editions of this textbook in Canadian schools from British Columbia to the Maritimes. The book entered the marketplace as the first Canadian edition of an introductory textbook in anthropology. In addition to updating or adding the work of more Canadian anthropologists in this third revised edition, we have streamlined the text, reducing the number and types of boxes used to illustrate key points. The key questions that open and close each chapter help students focus on the most important issues in each chapter. A new map has been added at the beginning of the text to help students locate the peoples and places referred to in the book. We hope we have done justice to the work of the many colleagues whose work has inspired us, and to the generations of students taking courses in introductory anthropology.

In the 1960s, we were introduced to anthropology as students at the University of Toronto through American textbooks. As the subject was new to us, the content and approach seemed normal. Later, when we taught anthropology in Thai universities, we saw the same textbooks translated into Thai. In the 1970s we both taught Introduction to Anthropology at universities in the United States, so American texts fit the teaching contexts and indeed were normal. In the 1980s we returned to Canada and to teaching introductory anthropology. American textbooks were still being used, but their use seemed more problematic. By the 1990s we were teaching other courses in anthropology using texts by British, American, and Canadian anthropologists that reflected the diversity of the discipline. Our colleagues still used American textbooks for teaching introduction to cultural anthropology, but with growing dissatisfaction. It is appropriate to begin the new millennium with an anthropology textbook that includes Canadian experiences, research, and personalities.

Miller's text is an excellent choice for adaptation as it contains up-to-date materials on complex societies. Its strengths complement the interests of many Canadian anthropologists, and include a strong gender balance and focus, emphasis on the themes of social inequality and diversity, and a clear demonstration of the application of anthropology to contemporary issues such as health systems, migration, and development. Population and other statistical information now include Canadian data.

The practice and teaching of anthropology is shaped by context, both institutional and national. It matters to students and professors that Canadian anthropology is not the same as American anthropology. Its foundations were set in its long association with museums, First Nations research, anglophone and francophone dialogue, and ethnohistorical studies. In the first chapter we have made some adjustments to the theoretical stance of the book in keeping with the British, European, and American roots of Canadian anthropology. To orient the students to the unique history of anthropology in Canada, we have added material on the development of Canadian anthropology and sought out Canadian case studies—both new and classic—that may be more familiar to Canadian teachers and students, including references to First Nations groups, where appropriate. We have not included Canadian material gratuitously, nor have we removed all American examples. Rather, we have recontextualized American examples to become cross-cultural comparisons; American examples are no longer the benchmark defining "us" or "we." The suggested readings at the end of each chapter include the work of some Canadian anthropologists who have contributed to the field. In short, we have tried to highlight the significant contributions Canadians and Canadian institutions have made to the discipline and practice of anthropology.

Frank Manning (1983:2) began a volume reviewing Canadian ethnology by referring to a mythical plan that would see Canada incorporating British politics, American technology, and French culture, but, by accident, the country was left with French politics, British technology, and American culture. That story reveals something of the ironic and irreverent Canadian style, both self-deprecating and ambivalent toward our ancestors. A number of American anthropologists say they regularly participate in Canadian anthropology meetings because they enjoy the civility and the intellectual style of Canadian anthropology. This style is what makes the *Royal Canadian Air Farce* and *This Hour Has 22 Minutes* and the Degrassi series recognizable as Canadian television entertainment. It helps explain why clowns and magicians have been known to perform at Canadian anthropology meetings over the years. But, like all attempts at cultural generalization, this elusive sense of style is perhaps best conveyed by the Canadian anthropologists we hope will enjoy teaching from this book.

DISTINCTIVE FEATURES OF THE THIRD CANADIAN EDITION

The world has changed in the six years since the publication of the first Canadian edition of *Cultural Anthropology*, and anthropology has changed with it. The need for understanding the relation between social inequality and globalization has never been greater. This third edition makes these connections between the global and the local even clearer. Much more attention is given to **globalization** as a force of change worldwide and how **localization** of global forces can be seen in various domains of change, including making a living, marriage and family, and religion. Each chapter contains material on such change as well as boxes discussing, for example, transnationalism, migration, cyberspace communities, and cultural pluralism.

To begin with, this textbook emphasizes the importance of studying **social inequality** and **social diversity** (including class, race, ethnicity, gender, and age) and we present material on these topics throughout the book with more in-depth attention in particular places. The major social categories of class, race, ethnicity, age, and gender are introduced in Chapter 1 as analytical categories, examined in Chapter 2 in terms of how they affect research methods and strategies, revisited in most chapters, and explored in greater depth in Chapter 10 ("Social Groups and Social Stratification").

Second, examples from **contemporary Canada** (and the "West") are integrated into the text, including the gender division of labour in Canadian farm households

(Chapter 3), the use of credit cards in "middle-class" consumption patterns (Chapter 4), an examination of Western medical training (Chapter 7), "outlaw" motorcycle clubs and other countercultural groups (Chapter 10), play and leisure as forms of expressive culture (Chapter 14), and the variety of experiences of recent immigrants (Chapter 15).

Third, an up-to-date and lively chapter on **language** and **communication** (Chapter 13) is innovative in that it de-emphasizes more "formal" aspects of linguistic anthropology such as phonetics and phonemics and gives more material on everyday language in use: children's disputes, adolescent girls' "fat talk," and dress and looks as forms of communication. We also include current research on mass media and how it is culturally shaped: for example, an in-depth study of bias in news reporting. This enhanced treatment will make teaching about language more interesting for instructors and more exciting and engaging for students. It also offers more relevance to students who are interested in careers in the many areas of communication.

Fourth, a unique chapter on **medical anthropology** (Chapter 7) is included. Students in general and especially the large numbers of pre-med students or students interested in some sort of health career will find much of interest in this chapter.

Fifth, a chapter on migration, called "People on the Move" (Chapter 15), provides updated material on this important subject. Students will learn about risks and opportunities facing various categories of migrants and gain insight from detailed cases of "new immigrant" groups in North America.

Finally, the pedagogy of this book is unique in the many ways that it promotes a **critical thinking approach** to the information provided. Instead of simply accepting what we hear or read, a critical thinking approach prompts us to ask questions. It establishes a dynamic relationship between the material and the reader rather than merely allowing for a passive form of information transferral. By providing a sense of engagement with the material, this approach promises to advance student thinking more effectively than traditional forms of learning.

HOW THIS BOOK IS ORGANIZED

Cultural Anthropology pursues its goal of promoting learning about the world's cultures in two ways, one that will be more familiar (the delivery of information) and another that may be unsettling and disturbing (asking questions about the information at hand that will make readers unsure of what they thought they knew).

In the first place, readers will encounter abundant, up-to-date *information* about what is known about cross-cultural lifeways: How do people in different parts of the world obtain food, conceive of their place in the universe, and deal with rapid cultural change? This substantive material of cultural anthropology begins with two chapters that establish a foundation for understanding what the discipline of anthropology in general is about, how cultural anthropology fits with it, and what the concept of *culture* means.

In the book's first section, Chapter 1 ("Anthropology and the Study of Culture") establishes the importance of the themes of social diversity and inequality that will accompany us throughout the book, especially class, race, ethnicity, gender, and age. Chapter 2 ("Methods in Cultural Anthropology") takes us to the question of how one does research in cultural anthropology and how findings are analyzed and presented. Students will be able to link what they already know about general research concepts (for example, inductive versus deductive approaches, qualitative versus quantitative data) with what they learn here about how cultural anthropologists have used such concepts in their research and also come up with distinct approaches to data collection, analysis, and presentation.

Following these two chapters, the book moves into a consideration of cross-cultural ways of behaving and thinking in many domains from economics to religion. All aspects of life are interrelated and it is often difficult, in real life as well as in scholarly analysis, to separate them. Chapter 3 ("Economies and Their Modes of Production") and Chapter 4 ("Consumption and Exchange") appear at the beginning of the topical chapters as the foundation of culture. Reproduction, or "making people," can be usefully paired with the topic of production, "making a living." Therefore, treatment of reproduction is placed in Chapter 5, "Birth and Death," which immediately follows the two chapters on economics. The book proceeds to the subject of the human life cycle in cross-cultural perspective (Chapter 6, "Personality and Human Development"), presenting material from the exciting subfield of psychological anthropology. This chapter connects with the introductory psychology courses that many students will have taken. The next chapter in this cluster about "making people" is Chapter 7, "Illness and Healing." A rare chapter in introductory cultural anthropology textbooks, this one will be particularly interesting to the many students who are considering careers in health-related fields.

The third major section of the book, which includes chapters dealing with various aspects of "people in groups," or social structures, begins with Chapter 8, "Kinship Dynamics." This chapter incorporates up-to-date research that has enlivened the traditional core area of cultural anthropology. Although traditional categories and definitions are presented, the emphasis is on kinship in action, and on bringing kinship into a more relevant place in cultural anthropology. Chapter 9, "Domestic Groups," looks at how people are arranged into groups

for everyday living. Chapter 10, "Social Groups and Social Stratification" widens the lens to examine social groups beyond the domestic situation, including clubs and cooperatives. It also addresses how, in different societies, groups may be arranged hierarchically in relation to one another (for example, in India's caste system). Chapter 11, "Politics, Conflict, and Social Order," presents cross-cultural material on the various forms of political organization and includes more than the usual amount of material on contemporary state-level societies. It also explores the subfield of legal anthropology, an area of interest to preprofessional students considering careers in law and law enforcement.

The chapters in the fourth section explore the topics of ideology, belief systems, and values. All the previous chapters have related to belief systems and values in one way or another, but here the focus becomes explicit, addressing three important subjects: Chapter 12, "Religion"; Chapter 13, "Communication," including verbal language, non-verbal language, and mass media; and Chapter 14, "Expressive Culture," which includes the arts, the representation of culture in museums, play, and leisure.

The final two chapters bring together many of the topics addressed in Chapters 3–14 in their examination of two of the most important aspects of contemporary cultural change: migration and international development. Chapter 15, "People on the Move," provides insights about categories of migrants and detailed information on the "new immigrants" in North America. Chapter 16, "Development Anthropology" shows how cultural anthropologists have contributed to making international development projects and processes more culturally appropriate and less harmful to local people, especially marginalized indigenous peoples and minorities. Both Chapters 15 and 16 highlight the "action" aspect of cultural anthropology and underline how it can be relevant to policy issues in the contemporary world.

BOXED FEATURES

The pedagogical goals of this book are advanced through the use of distinctive and original boxes. These features show the interconnection of anthropology to other disciplines and to career opportunities.

New to this edition, **Lessons Applied** boxes provide in-depth examples of how research in cultural anthropology can be applied to real-world problems. They highlight different anthropological roles in applied work, such as in conducting social impact assessments, in advocacy anthropology working with indigenous peoples, or as a cultural broker. For example:

- "Multiple Methods in a Needs Assessment Study"
- "The Global Network of Indigenous Knowledge Resource Centres"

Lessons Applied

MULTIPLE METHODS IN A NEEDS ASSESSMENT STUDY

THE UNITED WAY of Canada, a philanthropic agency, wanted to find out what the highest priorities were for their funding operations in Saskatoon, Saskatchewan (Ervin et al. 1991; van William 1993:206–207). Anthropologist Alexander Ervin led a team of researchers from the University of Saskatchewan's Department of Anthropology and Archaeology to respond to the United Way's request. At the time of the study in 1990, the city's population was about 200 000. The economy includes agriculture, mining, forestry, and some manufacturing. The unemployment rate was 10 percent, and food banks and soup kitchens were being increasingly used.

The team designed its research to provide baseline data on perceived social needs to assist the United Way in decision making. The assessment included six data collection activities: reviewing available written reports relevant to Saskatoon's needs, analyzing economic and social indicators, organizing 3 public forums, conducting 135 interviews with key informants from community agencies, holding 6 focus groups, and interviewing 28 United Way agency executive directors. These activities provided breadth and depth about community opinion and agency priorities and interests.

The research team produced a report that included a list of over 200 needs identified. The list was organized into 17 sectors, among them general health, mental health, the senior population, First Nations issues, racism and discrimination, and immigrant and refugee resettlement. The report also included a set of recommendations for the United Way.

FOOD FOR THOUGHT

Conducting a community needs assessment entails a research approach quite different from traditional fieldwork in cultural anthropology. What are some of the pros and cons of anthropologists conducting such applied research?

anthropology, field notes have been the basic way to record observations. Field notes include daily logs, personal journals, descriptions of events, and notes about those notes. Ideally, researchers should "write up" their field notes each day. Otherwise, a backlog piles up of daily "scratch notes," or rough jottings made on a small pad or note card carried in the pocket (Sanjek 1990:95–99). Trying to capture, in the fullest way possible, the events of a single day is a monumental task and can result in dozens of pages of handwritten or typed field notes each day. The bulk of an anthropologist's time in the field is probably spent taking rough notes by hand. The invention of the laptop computer now allows anthropologists to enter many of these notes directly into the computer.

Tape Recording, Photography, Videos, and Films

Tape recorders are an obvious aid to fieldwork because they allow the accurate recording of much more information than taking notes by hand. However, tape recording may raise problems such as informants' suspicions about a machine that can capture their voices, and the ethical issue of maintaining anonymity of informants whose actual voices are preserved on tape. Maria Cátedra

(1992) reports on her use of tape recording during research in rural Spain in the 1970s.

At first the existence of the "apparatus," as they called it, was part wonder and part suspect. Many had never seen one before and were fascinated to hear their own voice, but all were worried about what I would do with the tapes. ... I tried to solve the problem by explaining what I would do with the tapes: I would use them to record correctly what people told me, since our memory was not good enough and I could not take notes quickly enough. ... One never helped people to accept my integrity in regard to the "apparatus." In the second *brana* [small settlement] I visited, people asked me to play back what the people of the first *brana* had told me, especially some songs sung by a group of men. At first I was going to do it, but then I instinctively refused because I did not have the first people's permission. ... My initial was quickly known in the first *brana* and commented on with approval. (21–22)

A problem with tape recordings is that they have to be transcribed (typed out), either partially or completely. Each hour of recorded talk takes between five to eight hours to transcribe, on average. Even more time is needed if the recording is garbled, many interviews are heard at once, or complications in translation arise.

Like tape recordings, photographs, films, or videos may catch and retain more detail than rough notes. Any

40 PART I ■ Introduction to Cultural Anthropology

 Multiple Cultural Worlds

RESEARCHING A HAKKA COMMUNITY IN CYBERSPACE

COMPUTER-MEDIATED communication (CMC), such as email, allows people who have never met to communicate with each other (Cheung 1998). It allows people to remove opinions and shore information in a participatory rather than "top-down," way as in the case with television or journalism. CMC creates virtual social networks and contributes to the formation of new cultural patterns. Eriberto Lozada, a doctoral dissertation student at Harvard University, studied a "Hakka community in cyberspace" (1998:148). Many years ago, the Hakka people of southern China were mainly village-dwelling agriculturalists. Now, Hakka communities can be found in many countries, including Canada, the United States, Indonesia, and Malaysia. Lozada has done participant observation in a Hakka village in China in addition to studying the Hakka Global Network (HGN).

Hakka people worldwide are actively building websites about Hakka culture and promoting transnational communication at levels that would not have been imagined 10 years ago. Lozada conducted what he calls participant observation over the internet for nearly two years. Using a search engine (WebCrawler), he searched for websites that had the word "Hakka" and found five listings. He joined one website and soon began receiving numerous messages. Over the years, he collected many email messages, which form his data set. His analysis was of the messages themselves, not the people, since he had little data on the people other than that they tend to be highly educated people scattered around the world.

Thus, this is a study of discourse and its possible meanings for the people involved. Lozada's analysis of the messages involved the search for persistent themes. Overall, he found that the procedures drew to reconstitute of Hakka culture in the face of global forces of change. Many of the messages provided announcements about television or radio broadcasts carrying items about Hakka culture; others included discussions of the Hakka language, origins, and customs. Many people requested information, such as the person who wrote about his grandfather who had immigrated to Borneo and died in a certain village; he asked if anyone knew the location of that village (158).

What can a cultural anthropologist learn about cyberspace Hakka culture from studying these websites and discussions and exchanges taking place between people who have never met? One conclusion of Lozada's is that through HGN, the Hakka are creating a "local global community," a new form of cultural organization that helps them deal with the present and shape the future in ways that no one can predict.

FOOD FOR THOUGHT

How does traditional participant observation differ from the participant observation that Lozada conducted?

What ethical problems might Lozada face in conducting this research?

opinion." Ideally, the researcher should have enough familiarity with the study population to be able to design a formal questionnaire or survey that makes cultural sense. One anthropologist (Beyene 1989) dedicated time to an exploratory research phase in order to obtain background information before beginning formal interviews in her comparative study of women's reproductive experiences in Mexico and Greece:

During this initial phase of participant observation, I obtained data on women and their roles and activities, conducting unstructured and informal interviews with persons in the communities. Unstructured interviews were conducted with key informants such as older women, traditional healers, midwives, and medical personnel in the health services and clinics that served the villages. As the

process of participant observation and informal interviewing unfolded, a more efficient relevant categories and information was developed around the issues of the menopausal experiences of women in the villages, which became the topics for the formal interviews. (6)

Researchers who take ready-made questionnaires to the field with them should, at the minimum, ask another researcher who knows the field area to review the instrument to see if it makes cultural sense. Additional revisions of the questionnaire may be required in the field to make it more appropriate to local conditions. A pilot survey, or trial run, before proceeding with a formal survey will reveal areas that need to be changed before the final version is used and should be considered an essential step.

36 PART I ■ Introduction to Cultural Anthropology

 Critical Thinking

FAMILY PLANNING PROGRAMS IN BANGLADESH

BEGINNING IN the 1980s, criticism of Western family planning programs in relation to reproductive rights emerged from several directions. In the United States, the conservative brought the practitioners chance to grow control at home and abroad. (In November 1999, the United States government again refused to pay its estimated $1.5 billion in unpaid United Nations dues, because of Republican demands for conditions that ban spending any U.S. funds to support family planning clinics offering abortions in other countries.) At the same time, critics on the left claimed that the Western-supported and Western-styled family planning programs in developing countries were a form of neo-colonialism. Areas of concern included sterilization of women and the use of incentives such as cash payments, radios, or clothing to attract people to being sterilized.

Betsy Hartmann, a vocal critic of Western family planning promotion in developing countries, wrote an influential book called *Reproductive Rights and Wrongs* (1987). In the mid-1970s, she did fieldwork in a village in Bangladesh. Two key lessons about women's reproductive freedom emerged. First, in one area, there were women who were satisfied with the number of children they had, and they wanted to adopt some form of "modern" contraception, but none was available. Second,

In other areas of Bangladesh, population control programs were vigorously promoting various methods including the pill, the injectible Depo-Provera, and IUDs without

A family planning clinic in Egypt. Throughout much of the world, provision of Western-style family planning advice is controversial because it may conflict with local religious and other beliefs about the value of having many children and women's duty to be child bearers.

Fertility Control

All cultures throughout history have had ways of influencing fertility, including ways to increase it, reduce it, and regulate child spacing. Some ways are direct, such as using certain herbs or medicines that induce abortion. Others are indirect, such as long periods of breastfeeding, which reduce chances of conception. In Indonesia, for example, breastfeeding probably accounts for more child spacing than all other forms of contraception combined (Rohde 1992).

Hundreds of indigenous fertility control methods are available cross-culturally. One study conducted in Afghanistan in the 1980s found about 500 fertility-regulating techniques in just one region of the country (Hunte 1985). In Afghanistan, as in most pre-industrial

adequate medical screening, supervision, or follow-up. Many women experienced negative side-effects and became disillusioned with family planning. The government's response was not to reform the program to meet women's needs, but instead to further intensify its population control efforts by promoting female sterilization. In both contexts, women were denied control over their reproduction. (x–xi)

cultures, it is women who possess this information. Specialists, such as midwives or herbalists, provide further guidance and expertise. Of the total number of methods in the Afghanistan study, 72 percent were aimed at increasing fertility, 22 percent were contraceptives (preventing fertilization of the ovum by the sperm), and 6 percent were used to induce abortion. These methods involve plant and animal substances prepared in different ways. Herbs are made into tea and taken orally, some substances are formed into pills, some steamed and inhaled as vapours, some vaginally inserted, and others rubbed on the woman's stomach.

Contemporary medical research reveals the efficacy of many indigenous fertility-regulating methods. For example, experiments on animals show that some 450 plant species worldwide contain natural substances that prevent

108 PART II ■ Economic and Demographic Foundations

■ "Anthropology and Community Activism in Papua New Guinea"

Given the book's underlying and pervasive theme of cultural variation and social inequality within and between cultures, **Multiple Cultural Worlds** boxes are used to present material that demonstrates cultural variation and, often, but not always, inequalities by class, race, ethnicity, gender, and age. For example:

■ "Globalization and Tomato Production"

■ "Code-Switching in Martinique"

■ "Human Rights versus Animal Rights: The Case of the Grey Whale"

The book's commitment to giving students practice in how to think critically is carried out in each chapter through a **Critical Thinking** box. In most of these boxes, students will read about an issue and how it has been interpreted from two different, conflicting perspectives. The students are then asked to consider how the researchers approached the issue, what kind of data they used, and how their conclusions are influenced by their approach. Many of the boxes carry through on the three theoretical issues presented in Chapter 1 as characterizing contemporary cultural anthropology (biological determinism versus cultural constructionism, interpretive anthropology versus cultural materialism, and individual agency versus structure). For example:

■ "Adolescent Stress: Biologically Determined or Culturally Constructed?"

In other boxes, students are asked to reflect on "received wisdom" from a new angle:

■ "Was the Invention of Agriculture a Terrible Mistake?"

New categories of analysis are introduced and old ones are reassessed:

■ "Assessing One's Own Entitlement Bundle"

■ "Photography and Anthropology"

IN-TEXT PEDAGOGY

We have included many pedagogical tools in the book to help students learn and to help teachers teach. Each chapter opens with an outline of the main topics to be covered, including the boxed features. Chapter introductions include a "preview" paragraph that outlines the broad strokes of each chapter so students see how topics are connected and can navigate through the material more easily.

"Key Questions" is a feature located at the beginning of each chapter that identifies the three "key questions" students should keep in mind as they read the chapter. Each chapter concludes with "Key Questions Revisited," a section that reviews concepts and provides answers to "Key Questions" in a summary format. This new feature makes key concepts clearer and more accessible to students.

Another exciting new feature of the third edition is the maps. A new two-page map opens the text. In addition, locator maps within the text, integrated with the discussions of indigenous peoples and ethnographic material, enable students to locate the cultures discussed within their appropriate geographical contexts.

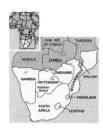

A list of key concepts can be found at the end of each chapter. Each concept is listed along with the page number on which it appears. Concepts appear in boldfaced text throughout the chapter. Finally, each chapter ends with a list of suggested readings, which come with a brief annotation to guide students who may be looking for books to read for a class project or term paper. New for this edition is a glossary providing students with precise definitions of terms used in the text.

SUPPLEMENTS FOR INSTRUCTORS

Accompanying this text is an array of supplements that will assist instructors in using the book. Contact your local Pearson Education Canada sales representative to obtain copies of the following items.

Instructor's Resource CD-ROM

This resource CD (ISBN 0-205-48347-X) includes the following instructor supplements:

- *Instructor's Manual.* Revised by Brian Myhre for the new edition, this manual includes teaching tips and classroom exercises that can be used to teach cultural anthropology, as well as suggestions on how to teach the many cases and examples included in the book.

- *Pearson TestGen.* This computerized test bank, revised for the new edition by Koumari Mitra of the University of New Brunswick, includes over 1000 questions in

multiple-choice, true/false, fill-in-the-blank, short answer, and essay format. TestGen is a testing software that enables instructors to view and edit the existing questions, add questions, generate tests, and distribute the tests in a variety of formats. Powerful search and sort functions make it easy to locate questions and arrange them in any order desired. TestGen also enables instructors to administer tests on a local area network, have the tests graded electronically and have the results prepared in electronic or printed reports. TestGen is compatible with Windows and Macintosh operating systems and can be downloaded from the TestGen website located at www.pearsoned.com/testgen.

- *PowerPoint Presentations.* These presentations combine graphics and text into chapter-based teaching modules.

Some of the supplements on the Instructor's Resource CD-ROM are also available for download from a password-protected section of Pearson Education Canada's online catalogue (vig.pearsoned.ca). Navigate to this book's catalogue page to view a list of those supplements that are available. Contact your local sales representative for details and access, or call Pearson's Faculty and Sales Service Department at 1-800-850-5813.

Allyn & Bacon Video Library

Qualified adopters may select from a wide variety of high-quality videos from such sources as Films for the Humanities and Sciences and Annenberg/CPB. Contact your Pearson Education Canada sales representative for a complete list of videos.

The Blockbuster Approach: A Guide to Teaching Anthropology with Video

This guide (ISBN 0-205-38159-6) to using videos can be downloaded from Pearson Education Canada's online catalogue at vig.pearsoned.ca.

Pearson Advantage

For qualified adopters, Pearson Education is proud to introduce the *Pearson Advantage*. The Pearson Advantage is the first integrated Canadian service program committed to meeting the customization, training, and support needs for your course. Our commitments are made in writing and in consultation with faculty. Your local Pearson Education sales representative can provide you with more details on this service program.

Content Media Specialists

Pearson's Content Media Specialists work with faculty and campus course designers to ensure that Pearson technology products, assessment tools, and online course materials are tailored to meet your specific needs. This highly qualified team is dedicated to helping schools take full advantage of a wide range of educational technology, by assisting in the integration of a variety of instructional materials and media formats.

SUPPLEMENTS FOR STUDENTS

Cultural AnthroNotes Study Chart

Packaged with all new copies of *Cultural Anthropology*, this laminated chart, created by Douglass St. Christian of the University of Western Ontario, is a handy study aid that covers key terms and concepts.

Companion Website
(www.pearsoned.ca/miller)

This Companion Website, revised for the new edition by Brian Schwimmer of the University of Manitoba, allows students to test their understanding of the material in the book. It offers a variety of exercises and opportunities to monitor their own learning and prepare for class tests. The exercises are self-scoring, giving students instant feedback and results for each quiz.

VangoNotes

Study on the go with VangoNotes. Just download chapter reviews from your text and listen to them on any mp3 player. Now wherever you are—whatever you're doing—you can study by listening to the following for each chapter of your textbook:

- **Big Ideas:** Your "need to know" for each chapter
- **Practice Test:** A gut check for the Big Ideas—tells you if you need to keep studying
- **Key Terms:** Audio "flashcards" to help you review key concepts and terms

VangoNotes are **flexible**; download all the material directly to your player, or only the chapters you need. And they're **efficient**. Use them in your car, at the gym, walking to class, wherever. So get yours today. And get studying. **VangoNotes.com**

Reader and Ethnographies

The following texts may be of interest to users of *Cultural Anthropology*. Instructors should contact a Pearson Canada sales representative for packaging information.

Reader

Conformity and Conflict: Readings in Cultural Anthropology, Twelfth Edition, by James Spradley and David W. McCurdy (ISBN 0-205-44970-0)

Canadian Ethnography Series

Volume I: "Only God Can Own the Land": The Attawapiskat Cree, by Bryan D. Cummins and John L. Steckley (ISBN 0-13-177065-9)

Volume II: From American Slaves to Nova Scotian Subjects: The Case of the Black Refugees, 1813–1840, by Harvey Amani Whitfield, Bryan D. Cummins, and John L. Steckley (ISBN 0-13-177066-7)

Volume III: Ta'n teli-ktlamsi Tasit (Ways of Believing): Mi'kmaw Religion in Eskasoni, Nova Scotia, by Angela Robinson, Bryan D. Cummins, and John L. Steckley (ISBN 0-13-177067-5)

Cultural Survival Studies in Ethnicity and Change Series

Ariaal Pastoralists of Kenya: Studying Pastoralism, Drought, and Development in Africa's Arid Lands, Second Edition, Elliot M. Fratkin (ISBN 0-205-39142-7)

AlterNatives: Community, Identity, and Environmental Justice on Walpole Island, Robert M. Van Wynsberghe (ISBN 0-205-34952-8)

Indigenous Peoples, Ethnic Groups, and the State, Second Edition, David Maybury-Lewis (ISBN 0-205-33746-5)

Aboriginal Reconciliation and the Dreaming: Warramiri Yolngu and the Quest for Equality, Ian S. McIntosh (ISBN 0-205-29793-5)

Ethnicity and Culture Amidst New "Neighbors": The Runa of Ecuador's Amazon Region, Theodore Macdonald (ISBN 0-205-19821-X)

Defending the Land: Sovereignty and Forest Life in James Bay Cree Society, Ronald Niezen, (ISBN 0-205-27580-X)

Gaining Ground?: Evenkis, Land, and Reform in Southeastern Siberia, Gail A. Fondahl (ISBN 0-205-27579-6)

Forest Dwellers, Forest Protectors: Indigenous Models for International Development, Richard Reed (ISBN 0-205-19822-8)

Malaysia and the "Original People": A Case Study of the Impact of Development on Indigenous Peoples, Robert Knox Dentan, Kirk Endicott, Alberto G. Gomes, and M.B. Hooker (ISBN 0-205-19817-1)

IN THANKS—FROM BARBARA MILLER

This book has evolved out of my long relationship with cultural anthropology, which began with the first anthropology course I took as an undergraduate at Syracuse University in 1967. Agehananda Bharati was an important figure in my undergraduate training as was Michael Freedman and cultural geographer David Sopher. Beginning with the writing of my dissertation, my theoretical perspectives were most deeply influenced by the work of anthropologists Marvin Harris, Jack Goody, G. William Skinner, and economist Ester Boserup. My research in India was enriched especially by the work of Pauline Kolenda, Stanley Tambiah, Gerry Berreman, and Sylvia Vatuk. The list of my favorite writers within and beyond anthropology today is too long to include here, but much of their work is woven into the book.

Four anthropologists carefully reviewed drafts of the first edition of the book, and I will always be grateful to them for their contribution: Elliot Fratkin (Pennsylvania State University), Maxine Margolis (University of Florida), Russell Reid (University of Louisville), and Robert Trotter II (University of Arizona). Their words of praise were just as welcome. By pointing out positive features of the book, they helped a sometimes discouraged author regain strength and continue writing and revising. Several other anthropologists offered comments about how I should revise the second and third editions: Ann E. Kingsolver, University of South Carolina; Charles R. de Burlo, The University of Vermont; Corey Pressman, Mt. Hood Community College; Diane Baxter, University of Oregon;

Ed Robbins, University of Wisconsin; Elizabeth de la Portilla, University of Texas at San Antonio; G. Richard Scott, University of Nevada, Reno; Jason Antrosio, Albion College; Katrina Worley, Sierra College; Leslie Lischka, Linfield College; Peter Brown, University of Wisconsin, Oshkosh; Howard Campbell, University of Texas, El Paso; Wesley Shumar, Drexel University; William M. Loker, California State University, Chico; and William W. Donner, Kutztown University. I have tried my best to incorporate their advice without sacrificing the original spirit of the book.

During my years of research and writing, many anthropologists have provided invaluable comments, encouragement, and photographs for this book, including Lila Abu-Lughod, Vincanne Adams, Catherine Allen, Joseph Alter, Donald Attwood, Christopher Baker, Nancy Benco, Marc Bermann, Alexia Bloch, Lynne Bolles, John Bowen, Don Brenneis, Alison Brooks, Judith K. Brown, D. Glynn Cochrane, Jeffery Cohen, Carole Counihan, Liza Dalby, Loring Danforth, Patricia Delaney, Timothy Earle, Elliot Fratkin, Martin Fusi, David Gow, Curt Grimm, Richard Grinker, Daniel Gross, Marvin Harris, Michael Herzfeld, Barry Hewlett, Danny Hoffman, Michael Horowitz, Robert Humphrey, Anstice Justin, Laurel Kendall, David Kideckel, Stuart Kirsch, Dorinne Kondo, Conrad Kottak, Ruth Krulfeld, Joel Kuipers, Takie Lebra, David Lempert, Lamont Lindstrom, Samuel Martinez, Catherine McCoid, Leroy McDermott, Jerry Milanich, Kirin Narayan, Sarah Nelson, Gananath Obeyesekere, Ellen Oxfeld, Hanna Papanek, Deborah Pellow, Gregory Possehl, David Price, Joanne Rappaport, Jennifer Robertson, Nicole Sault, Joel Savishinsky, Nancy Scheper-Hughes, Richard Shweder, Chunghee Soh, Martha Ward, James (Woody) Watson, Rubie Watson, Van Yasek, and Kevin Yelvington.

Several others, who are not anthropologists, also made important contributions to this book: Elson Boles, Nathan Brown, Cornelia Mayer Herzfeld, Edward Keller III, Qaiser Khan, and Roshani Kothari. These people, and no doubt many more whom I have failed to name, were helpful in a variety of ways, including providing critiques of sections and sending material and photographs. Harry Harding, Dean of the Elliott School of International Affairs at the George Washington University, has helped my involvement with this book from its beginning by counting it as a valid research activity for a faculty member in his School. Over the years since the first edition, several assistants have tracked down library material and done reference checking: Joseph Mineiro, Han Quyen Thi Tran, Hena Khan, Omar McDoom, and Carolyn Walkley.

My students are always a major source of inspiration. Many students in my introductory cultural anthropology classes have offered corrections and additions. They enjoy and benefit from looking at cultural anthropology from a "critical thinking" perspective, thus giving me hope that this approach does indeed work. I thank them for their support and interest.

Sylvia Shepard, my development editor for the first edition, was a crucial factor in making this book happen. I can say with surety that, without Sylvia, this book would not exist. For this edition, I was fortunate in being able to work with truly excellent people in conceptualizing and implementing the revision plan. Series editor Jennifer Jacobson is everything an author could hope for—smart, strong, and also lots of fun. Her assistant, Amy Holborow, was always there at the right time with the right ideas. My development editor for this edition is Monica Ohlinger, who heads Ohlinger Publishing Company in Columbus, Ohio. She led the process with great skill, care, and enthusiasm. Her attention to detail helped tremendously. Joanne Vickers, another member of the Ohlinger development team, provided many helpful insights throughout the process. Kathleen Deselle, in New Hampshire, took over when we got to the copyediting and proofreading stage. Kathleen also managed additions and revisions to the artwork. She and her team added yet another extremely pleasant stage to the work. Back at Allyn & Bacon headquarters in Boston, Susan Brown coordinated the research for new photographs. In Washington, I was ably assisted in reviewing the Instructor's Manual and student Study Guide by Jessica Gibson, my program assistant in the CIGA (Culture in Global Affairs) Research and Policy Program, in the Elliott School of International Affairs. This team, dispersed as we were, nonetheless shared a single vision of making this edition even more current, compelling, and coherent. Please let me know if we succeeded and how we might do better.

Bernard Wood is a source of perspective, with his wry sense of humor, on my writing and on life in general. I also thank "the Millers"—my parents, siblings, aunts and uncles, and nieces and nephews—for their interest and support throughout the years of the writing and revising. The same applies to "the Heatons"—my former in-laws, including parents-in-law, brothers- and sisters-in-law, and nieces and nephews. I thank my son, Jack Heaton, for being an inspiration to my writing, a superb travelling companion on our trip around the world with the Semester at Sea Program in 1996, and a delicately effective critic of my (occasional) excesses in thinking. This book is dedicated to him.

Barbara D. Miller
Washington, DC

IN THANKS—FROM PENNY AND JOHN VAN ESTERIK

The task of Canadianizing *Cultural Anthropology* was made possible by our being situated in York University's very vibrant department of anthropology. Students and colleagues generously provided references, suggestions, words of wisdom, and warning; we thank them all, and are particularly grateful for the assistance of Naomi Adelson, Kate Arcus, Saul Cohen, Ruth King, Ken Little, David Lumsden, Kathy M'Closkey, Margaret MacDonald, Lynne Milgram, Lynne Phillips, Nadine Quehl, Margaret Rodman, Andrea Walsh, and Daphne Winland.

At Pearson Education Canada, we would like to thank Michael Young, Editorial Director, for pursuing this project and selecting us for the undertaking. We thank Matthew Christian, Developmental Editor, for his patient efforts to keep us on schedule and focused; Lisa Berland for her careful copy editing; Susan McNish, for her meticulous proofreading; Söğüt Güleç, Production Editor, for integrating all the pieces into an outstanding product; and Heather McWhinney for her help in planning the revision. We would also like to thank Judith Allen, Senior Marketing Manager, for directing our marketing campaign, and the members of the sales team, who have given this project such support.

We are most grateful to the reviewers who made valuable suggestions during the process of preparing the third Canadian edition. Thank you to Anna de Aguayo of Dawson College, Constance deRoche of Cape Breton University, Mathias Guenther of Wilfrid Laurier University, Victor Gulewitsch of the University of Guelph, Bruce Granville Miller of the University of British Columbia, Koumari Mitra of the University of New Brunswick, and Josephine Smart of the University of Calgary. We regret the inevitable errors of omission and commission. Some of these we have been able to correct in this third Canadian edition.

Penny and John Van Esterik
Toronto

AFGH. = Afghanistan
ALB. = Albania
ARM. = Armenia
AUS. = Austria
AZER. = Azerbaijan
BANG. = Bangladesh
BEL. = Belgium
BELA. = Belarus
B & H. = Bosnia and Herzegovina
BUL. = Bulgaria
BURK. FASO = Burkina Faso
C. AFR. REP. = Central African Republic
CAM. = Cameroon
CAMB. = Cambodia
CRO. = Croatia
C. V. = Cape Verde
CYP. = Cyprus
CZE. = Czech Republic
DEN. = Denmark
EQ. GUINEA = Equatorial Guinea
EST. = Estonia
GAM. = Gambia
G.-B. = Guinea-Bissau
GER. = Germany
GUI. = Guinea
HOND. = Honduras
HUN. = Hungary
ISR. = Israel
KRYG. = Kyrgyzstan
LAT. = Latvia
LEB. = Lebanon
LITH. = Lithuania
LUX. = Luxembourg
MAC. = Macedonia
MOL. = Moldova
MYAN. = Myanmar
NETH. = Netherlands
POL. = Poland
REP. OF THE CONGO = Republic of
   the Congo
ROM. = Romania
RUS. = Russia
SER. & MON. = Serbia & Montenegro
SLO. = Slovakia
SLOV. = Slovenia
SWITZ. = Switzerland
SYR. = Syria
TAJIK. = Tajikistan
THAI. = Thailand
TURK. = Turkmenistan
UZBEK. = Uzbekistan
U.A.E. = United Arab Emirates

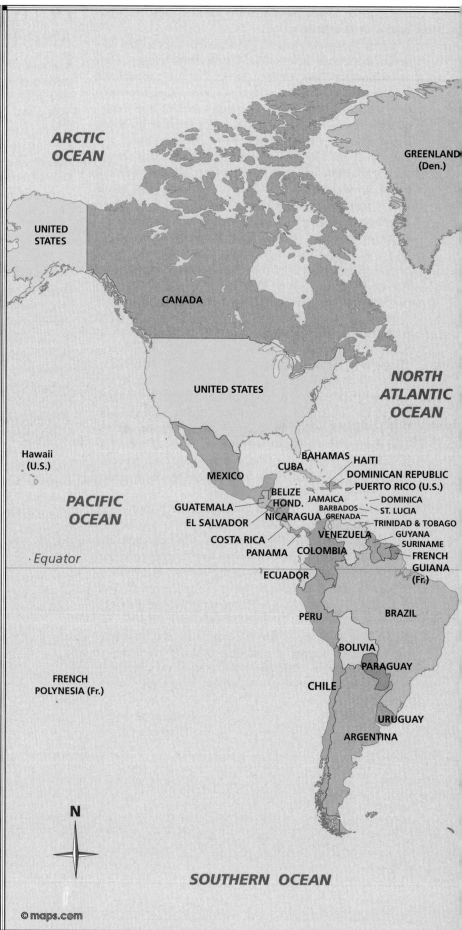

STATES OF THE WORLD

KEY QUESTIONS

- **WHAT** is anthropology?
- **WHAT** is cultural anthropology?
- **WHAT** is culture?

1

ANTHROPOLOGY AND THE STUDY OF CULTURE

Education for Buddhist monks and novices in Thailand now involves learning to use a computer in addition to studying religious scriptures.

The Maasai, a people of East Africa, make their living mainly by tending cattle. Although many Maasai interact increasingly with international tourists, their knowledge of the outside world is limited. Some villages lack electricity, so there are no televisions. Recently, in one community located in a remote area of Kenya, most people hadn't heard about the attacks on the United States on September 11, 2001; others had gained a vague idea of what had happened from radio announcements aired soon after the attacks occurred (Lacey 2002). Thus, when Kimeli Naiyomeh returned to his village from his medical studies at Stanford University, he told them stories that stunned them. He told of huge fires in buildings that stretched high into the clouds and of men with special equipment who entered the buildings to save people's lives. The villagers couldn't believe that a building could be so tall that people jumping from it would die.

These stories saddened the villagers, and they decided they should do something to help the victims. Cows are the most precious objects among the Maasai. As Kimeli Naiyomeh comments, "The cow is almost the center of life for us. . . . It's sacred. It's more than property. You give it a name. You talk to it. You perform rituals with it" (p. A7). In June 2002, in a solemn ceremony, the villagers gave 14 cows to the United States. After the cows were blessed, they were transferred to the deputy chief of the U.S. embassy in Kenya. He expressed his country's gratitude and explained that transporting the cows to the United States would be difficult, so he would sell them and buy Maasai jewellery to take instead.

Old bones, *Jurassic Park,* cannibalism, hidden treasure, *Indiana Jones and the Temple of Doom.* In North America, the popular impression of anthropology is based mainly on movies and television shows that depict anthropologists as adventurers and heroes. Many anthropologists do have adventures, and some discover treasures such as ancient pottery, medicinal plants, and jade carvings. But most of their research is less than glamorous, involving repetitive and often frustrating activities. What do anthropologists do, and why do people study anthropology?

This chapter offers an overview of general anthropology, an academic discipline devoted to the study of human life throughout history and in all its variations. General anthropology encompasses several fields or subfields. After a brief overview of each subfield, we turn to the field that is the focus of this book: cultural anthropology, the study of **culture**, learned and shared patterns of behaviour and beliefs. We then examine cultural differences and ways to understand such differences. This chapter also explains the various characteristics of culture, and how culture relates to nature but is not the same as nature. Class, race, gender, and other bases of cultural identity are introduced as important factors that will receive attention throughout this book.

THE FOUR FIELDS OF GENERAL ANTHROPOLOGY

Most anthropologists agree that the discipline of anthropology, or general anthropology, is divided into four fields:

- archaeology (or prehistory);
- physical anthropology (or biological anthropology);
- linguistic anthropology; and
- cultural anthropology (or socio-cultural anthropology).

Many anthropologists would say that training in anthropology should involve knowledge in all four fields and awareness of the linkages between them because of anthropology's broad goal of understanding human behaviour and cultural change. In Canada and in much of the world where anthropology reflects a more European heritage, the term *anthropology* often refers to socio-cultural anthropology.

Thus, many anthropologists contend that the four-field approach is no longer relevant and should be abandoned. The sheer amount of knowledge in the various fields has increased over time, and apparently greater differences in theory, methods, and subject matter have emerged, making interchange across fields less frequent or useful. At least two Canadian universities have split their departments into anthropology and archaeology. Only about one-third of the departments of anthropology in Canada include the four subfields within one department. Linguistics is most likely to be omitted, reflecting the British university pattern of considering linguistics outside the scope of anthropology (Darnell 1998). The distinctly Canadian triad of archaeology, ethnology, and folklore may have its roots in government-supported museums rather than U.S. departments of anthropology (Preston 1983:288).

In recent decades, anthropology has developed in universities around the world and is acquiring local characteristics. For instance, in much of Latin America and Africa, anthropology is more explicitly political. Anthropologists in post-colonial settings raise questions such as "Anthropology for what, for whom, and by whom?" Increasingly, anthropologists trained and working in the West are entering into creative dialogue with anthropologists in post-colonial contexts. For example, some anthropologists writing on Mayan people's activist movements have been criticized by the emerging new generation of Mayan anthropologists, who are themselves Mayan, for perpetuating outsiders' views of Mayan cultures (Warren 1998; Fischer 2001). This kind of global interchange is helping to move the discipline in new directions away from its Western roots and perspectives.

Archaeology

The field of archaeology is devoted to studying the lifeways of past cultures by examining material remains. Data include stone and bone tools, skeletal material, remains of buildings, and refuse such as pot shards (broken pieces of pottery) and coprolites (fossilized fecal matter). Since its beginnings in the mid-eighteenth century, archaeology has contributed knowledge about towns and villages, as well as the emergence of the great early states of Egypt, Phoenicia, the Indus Valley, and Mexico. New research is questioning some previous conclusions about "kingdoms." For example, excavations at a royal burial site of the Old Silla Kingdom of Korea, which extended from 57 BCE (Before Common Era) to 668 CE (Common Era), reveal that queens were often the rulers (Nelson 1993). This finding challenges the earlier generalization that centralized state systems always involve male political dominance.

An example of a relatively new area of research is archaeologists' examination of European colonialism and its impact on pre-colonial states (Graham 1998). In the Maya area, for example, where an interest in the civilization of the Classic Maya period has dominated research, archaeologists have documented intensive occupation from the time of the so-called Maya collapse, in the ninth century, to the end of the seventeenth century (Pendergast, Jones, and Graham 1993). This long sequence has enabled them to chart the changes that took place as the Spanish administrators and priests colonized the Maya world, and the result has been documentation of the continuity of cultural, social, and technological traditions from the ancient past to the modern times.

The archaeology of the recent past is another new research direction; an example is the "Garbage Project," which is being conducted by archaeologists at the University of Arizona at Tucson (Rathje and Murphy 1992). The "Garbage Archaeologists" are excavating the Fresh Kills landfill on Staten Island, near New York City. Its mass is estimated at over 90 million tonnes and its volume at 82 million cubic metres. Thus, it is one of the largest human-made structures in North America. Through excavation of artifacts such as pop-top can tabs, disposable diapers, cosmetic containers, and telephone books, the Garbage Archaeologists are learning about recent consumption patterns. These findings also provide lessons for the future. They reveal how long it takes for contemporary goods to decompose. Urban planners and other people interested in recycling may be surprised to learn that the kinds of garbage that people often blame for filling up landfills, such as fast-food packaging, polystyrene foam, and disposable diapers, are less serious problems than paper. Paper, especially newspaper, is the major culprit because of sheer quantity. This kind of information can help improve recycling efforts in North America.

Physical or Biological Anthropology

In seeking to understand human variation, adaptation, and change, physical anthropologists study many forms of life, human and non-human, past and present. This field deals with topics ranging from evolutionary theory to the human fossil record and the identification of human skeletal remains from crime scenes and accidents (Park 1996:vii). Genetics, anatomy, animal and human behaviour, ecology, nutrition, and forensics are subject areas included in this field. Many physical anthropologists do research on animals other than humans in order to understand human origins or to use them as models for understanding contemporary human behaviour.

Within physical anthropology, the subfield of primatology focuses on studies of non-human primates and how their behaviour compares with that of human primates. Primatologists are well known for their pioneering work in studying non-human primates in their natural habitats. Jane Goodall's (1971, 1986) research on Tanzanian chimpanzees revealed rich details about their social relationships. Linda Fedigan (1992) has shown how females play significant roles in the social structure of primate groups, and provided a feminist critique of theories of primate and human evolution.

Primatologist Dian Fossey interacts with a gorilla during fieldwork in Rwanda.

Physical anthropologists share many research interests with archaeologists, given their study of evidence from the past. One such area is the question of when human beings first emerged as *Homo sapiens*. An early population named the Neanderthals, dated about 130 000–30 000 years ago, are at the centre of this question. Some experts consider them the earliest humans ever discovered. Others say that they should not be considered *Homo sapiens*. The fossils are from a skull cap found in 1856 in Germany's Neander Valley (Park 1996:233). Key features that support the "humanness" of Neanderthals include large cranial capacity (skull size); evidence of tool making and tool use; and the ability to think symbolically, as suggested by burial of the dead, sometimes with offerings such as animal bones, tools, and maybe flowers. But differences are also notable. The Neanderthals' foreheads are sloped, the back of the skull is bulging, and brow ridges are large. Arguments about "humanness" rest on which features are more important and should carry more weight. One conclusion is that it is impossible to draw a hard-and-fast line between humans and prehumans because humans evolved gradually over millions of years: There was no "moment in time" when "modern humans" sprang forth from our primate ancestors.

Another area linking physical anthropology with archaeology is *paleopathology*, the study of diseases in prehistory. Analysis of trace elements in bones, such as strontium, provides surprisingly detailed information about the diets, activities, and health of prehistoric people, including whether they were primarily meat eaters or vegetarians and how their diets affected their health. Stress marks on bones provide information on work patterns—for example, skeletons of nineteenth-century voyageurs from a fur trade post in Alberta show evidence of arthritis of the spine, shoulder, and elbow, and robust muscle attachments compatible with paddling heavy freight canoes (Lovell and Lai 1994). We can also learn age at death, age at birth of first child for a woman, and birth rate per woman. Data from several time periods provide clues about how the transition to agriculture altered people's health and longevity (M. N. Cohen 1989; Cohen and Armelagos 1984; Cohen and Bennett 1993).

Linguistic Anthropology

Linguistic anthropology explores the relation between culture and language, mainly, but not exclusively, among humans. It is integral to cultural anthropology since language is the primary means for transmitting culture. How we classify relatives, honour our ancestors, and describe beauty make visible beliefs and values. Descriptive linguistics examines the structure of languages, while historical linguistics traces the origin and development of related languages, and how they change through time. Sociolinguistics explores the relation between language and social interaction.

Early philologists such as Horatio Hale (1817–1896), who worked with the elders in the Six Nations Reserve near Brantford, Ontario, in the 1870s, recorded and analyzed disappearing First Nations languages, concluding, for example, that Tutelo was related to Siouan language stock, that Mohawk was the senior language of the original Five Nations, and that Huron was nearer proto-Iroquoian than Mohawk. Today, most "disappearing" languages have either been recorded or lost, and most previously unwritten languages have been transferred into written form. Because language change goes on all the time, anthropologists document and analyze what kinds of changes are occurring and why. Many changes are related to politics and conflict worldwide. For example, in Moldova, a former Soviet republic, speakers of Russian and Ukrainian in eastern Moldova have been in conflict since 1992 over the official language policy of Moldova. Instead of having a shrinking area of study, linguistic anthropology is broadening its scope to include many aspects of communication such as the media, electronic mail, popular music, and advertising. These new research directions connect linguistic anthropology with psychology, journalism, television and radio, education, and marketing.

Cultural Anthropology

Cultural anthropology decentres us from our own cultures, teaching us to look at ourselves from the "outside" as somewhat "strange." Melford Spiro (1990) aptly asserts that the work of anthropology is to "make the strange familiar and the familiar strange." A good example of "making the familiar strange" is the case of the Nacirema, who were first described in 1956:

> They are a North American group living in the territory between the Canadian Cree, the Yaqui and the

Tarahumare of Mexico, and the Carib and the Arawak of the Antilles. Little is known of their origin, though tradition states that they came from the east. According to Nacirema mythology, their nation was originated by a culture hero, Notgnihsaw, who is otherwise known for two great feats of strength—the throwing of a piece of wampum across the river Pa-To-Mac and the chopping down of a cherry tree in which the Spirit of Truth resided. (Miner 1965:415)

The anthropologist goes on to describe the Nacirema's unusually intense focus on the human body, its beauty, and their wide variety of private and personal rituals. He gives a detailed account of one ritual that is performed daily within the homes at a specially constructed shrine area:

> The focal point of the shrine is a box or chest which is built into the wall. In this chest are kept the many charms and magical potions without which no native believes he could live. These preparations are secured from a variety of specialized practitioners. The most powerful of these are the medicine men, whose assistance must be rewarded with substantial gifts. Beneath the charm box is a small font. Each day every member of the family, in succession, enters the shrine room, bows his head before the charm box, mingles different sorts of holy water in the font, and proceeds with a brief rite of ablution. (415–416)

If you don't know this tribe, try spelling its name backwards! (Note Miner's use of the masculine pronoun, an outdated convention.)

Cultural anthropology encompasses all aspects of human behaviour and beliefs. Its subject matter includes making a living and distributing goods and services, reproduction and group formation, political patterns, religious systems, forms of communication, and expressive aspects of culture such as art, dance, and music. In addition, cultural anthropologists consider how change occurs in all of these areas.

Applied Anthropology: Separate Field or Crosscutting Focus?

Applied anthropology, or practising anthropology, involves the use or application of anthropological knowledge to help solve social problems. Richard Salisbury (1983), who developed applied anthropology at McGill University in Montreal, saw applied work as the growth point of anthropology in Canada, and trained many Canadian anthropologists to put their research to practice in fields such as Native land claims, health care, and ethnic diversity. Active engagement with First Nations peoples and rural communities characterized the work of francophone anthropologists in the 1960s. Many anthropologists in small colleges and universities engaged in community-based applied research. One of the defining features of Canadian anthropology is the integration of

basic and applied research. From the earliest work of nineteenth-century ethnologists to the expert witnesses in current land claim issues, we find the widely shared assumption that anthropological research should not be morally or ethically neutral (Darnell 1998:155). Advocacy roles, however, require sensitivity to complex moral and political contexts.

Application of knowledge to help solve particular social problems is, and should be, part of all four fields. Just like theory, application is a valid aspect of every branch of the discipline. Many archaeologists in Canada are employed, for example, in cultural resource management (CRM), undertaking professional assessments of possible archaeological remains before construction projects such as roads and buildings can proceed. Physical anthropology has many applied aspects. For example, forensic anthropologists participate in criminal investigations through identifying bodily remains. Others work in the area of primate conservation (see the Lessons Applied box). Applied linguistic anthropologists consult with educational institutions about how to improve standardized tests for bilingual populations, or they may do policy research for governments. Development anthropology refers to an aspect of applied anthropology concerned with how so-called developing countries change and how knowledge in anthropology can play a role in formulating and implementing more appropriate kinds of change.

Many anthropologists are concerned that applied anthropology should be addressing more directly and with greater force the effects of globalization, particularly some of its negative consequences such as the increasing wealth gap between powerful industrialized countries and less powerful, less industrialized countries (Hackenberg 2000). This need takes anthropologists in a challenging direction since it involves the study of global-local interactions and change over time, both important parts of cultural anthropology's focus. Moreover, it asks that cultural anthropologists abandon an attitude of non-involvement in change. One anthropologist goes so far as to ask, "Can anthropology in the 21st century be anything except applied anthropology?" (Cleveland 2000:373).

INTRODUCING CULTURAL ANTHROPOLOGY

This section provides a brief history of the field of cultural anthropology in order to examine its theoretical and methodological roots. We then turn to a discussion of the central concept of *culture*. Last, we consider several distinctive features of cultural anthropology that will appear repeatedly throughout this book.

Lessons Applied

ORANGUTAN RESEARCH LEADS TO ORANGUTAN ADVOCACY

Biruté Galdikas in Indonesia. She has been studying the orangutans for over three decades and is an active supporter of conservation of their habitat.

PRIMATOLOGIST BIRUTÉ GALDIKAS first went to Indonesia to study orangutans in 1971 (Galdikas 1995). She soon became aware of the threat to the orangutans from local people who, as a way of making a lot of money, capture them for sale to zoos around the world. These poachers separate the young from their mothers, often killing the mothers in the process. Sometimes local police locate and reclaim these captured orphans. They try to return them to the rainforest, but the transition into an unknown niche is extremely difficult and many do not survive.

Orangutan juveniles are highly dependent on their mothers, maintaining close bodily contact with them for at least two years and nursing until they are eight. Because of this long period of orangutans' need for maternal contact, Galdikas set up her camp to serve as a way station for orphans and she became the maternal figure. Her first "infant" was an orphaned orang, Sugito, who clung to her for years as if she were its own mother.

Now, the survival of orangutans on Borneo and Sumatra (their only habitats worldwide) is seriously endangered by massive commercial logging and illegal logging, population resettlement programs, cultivation, and other pressures on the forests where the orangutans live. Biruté Galdikas is focusing her efforts on preventing this from happening. She says, "I feel like I'm viewing an animal holocaust and holocaust is not a word I use lightly. . . . The destruction of the tropical rainforest is accelerating daily. And if orangutans go extinct in the wild, paradise is gone" (Dreifus 2000:D3).

Galdikas is world-renowned as the leading expert on orangutans and their environment. She has studied orangutans longer than anyone else and in as close contact as these solitary creatures allow. She links her knowledge of and love for the orangutans with applied anthropology and advocacy on their behalf. She is work-

ing at many levels—local, national, and international—in a variety of ways to help prevent orangutan extinction.

Since the beginning of her fieldwork in Borneo, she has maintained and expanded the Camp Leakey fieldsite and research centre (named after her mentor, Louis Leakey, who inspired her research on orangutans). In 1986 she co-founded the Orangutan Foundation International (OFI), which now has several chapters worldwide. She has published scholarly articles and given public talks around the world on her research. Educating the public about the imminent danger to the orangutans is an important part of her activism. She believes that public awareness will help promote programs to protect and regenerate the forests that are the life support of the orangutans.

The parks employ many local people in diverse roles, including anti-poaching guards. OFI sponsors study tours for international students and opportunities for them to contribute to conservation efforts by working on infrastructure around the orangutan parks and reserves. At the global policy level, she and other orangutan experts are lobbying international institutions such as the World Bank to promote forest conservation as part of their loan agreements.

The success of Galdikas's activism depends on her deep knowledge of orangutans. Over the decades, she has filled thousands of notebooks with her observations of orangutan behaviour, along with such details about their habitat as the fruiting times of different species of trees. She hasn't yet had time to analyze these rich data. A kind donor recently gave software and funding for staff to analyze the raw data (Hawn 2002). The findings will indicate, for example, how much territory is needed to support a viable orangutan population. In turn, these findings will facilitate conservation policy and planning. Here, as often happens, research and advocacy go hand in hand.

FOOD FOR THOUGHT

Some people claim that social science should not be linked with advocacy and activism because that will create biases in research. Others say that researchers have an obligation to use their knowledge for the human good. Where do you stand in this debate and why?

A Brief History of the Field

We can trace aspects of cultural anthropology all the way back to writers such as Herodotus, Marco Polo, and Ibn Khaldun, who travelled extensively and wrote reports about "other" cultures that they encountered. More recent conceptual roots can be found in writers of the French Enlightenment, such as philosopher Charles Montesquieu (1689–1755). His book *The Spirit of the Laws,* published in 1748, discussed the temperament, appearance, and government of people around the world and explained the differences among them in terms of the differing climates in which people lived (Barnard 2000, 22ff). European colonial expansion increasingly exposed Western thinkers to cultural differences and prompted them to question the biblical narrative of human prehistory. The Bible, for example, does not mention the existence of people in the New World, and Enlightenment thinkers were forced to ponder how such people came to be.

In the latter half of the nineteenth century, the discovery of principles of biological evolution by Charles Darwin and others had a strong impact on anthropology and resulted in the overturn of Western biblical explanations for the human condition and human variation. Biological evolution says that early forms evolve into later forms through the process of natural selection, whereby the most biologically fit organisms survive to reproduce while those that are less fit die out. Darwin's model is thus one of continuous evolutionary connections. It also promotes the idea that change occurs through struggle among competing organisms.

Several founding fathers of cultural anthropology, such as Lewis Henry Morgan in the United States and Sir Edward Tylor (1832–1917) and Sir James Frazer (1854–1941) in England, invoked the concept of evolution to explain apparent cultural differences, mainly the differences between Euro-American culture (considered as "civilization") and non-Western peoples (considered as "primitive"). They assumed that Western culture was the most evolved form and that other cultures would eventually catch up or die out. Their models of kinship evolution, for example, said that early forms of kinship centred on women, with inheritance passing through the female line, whereas more evolved forms centred on men, with inheritance passing through the male line. Regarding belief systems, they said that magic comes before religion and that religion is then replaced by science. In all these models, there is a sense that the later forms are better, more advanced.

In terms of research methods, most thinkers of the nineteenth century were "armchair anthropologists." They read reports by travellers, missionaries, and explorers and then wrote a summary of these materials. Thus they wrote about culture without the benefit of close-up study. Lewis Henry Morgan (1818–1881), a lawyer in Rochester, New York, diverged from armchair anthropology by conducting field research over many years with the Iroquois of central New York (Patterson 2001:26). Morgan was interested in the main question of the day: Were all contemporary people descended from one line or from several lines? He undertook a comparative study of Native American kinship terms and Asian kinship terms. He concluded that Native American and Asian kinship systems were essentially similar and proved that Native Americans were related to people in Asia. Morgan was thus a strong supporter of the unity of humankind. He explained apparent differences across cultures in terms of their economic systems. He viewed agriculture and private property as the most highly evolved system. Through borrowing by one group from another, cultural evolution to a higher stage would occur.

Polish-born Bronislaw Malinowski (1884–1942) is considered one of the main founding figures of contemporary anthropology. He established a major theoretical approach called functionalism: the view that a culture is similar to a biological organism, wherein various parts work to support the operation and maintenance of the whole. Thus, a culture's kinship system or religious system contributes to the functioning of the whole culture of which it was a part. Functionalism is linked to the concept of holism, the view that one must study all aspects of a culture in order to understand the whole culture. Malinowski is also considered the father of cultural anthropology's cornerstone method of fieldwork (discussed in Chapter 2).

Another major figure of the early twentieth century is Franz Boas (1858–1942). Born in Germany and educated in physics and geography, Boas went to the United States in 1887 (Patterson 2001:46ff). He brought with him a skepticism toward Western science gained from a year's study with the Inuit of Baffin Island where he learned that a physical substance such as "water" can be very differently perceived in different cultures. Boas recognized the plural validity of different cultures and introduced the concept of cultural relativism, or the position that each culture must be understood in terms of the values and ideas of that culture and should not be judged by the standards of another. In his view, no culture is more advanced than another—a position that was a radical rejection of evolutionism.

Boas promoted the detailed study of individual cultures within their own historical contexts as the only way to understand them. This approach is called historical particularism, or the view that individual cultures must be studied and described on their own terms and that cross-cultural comparisons and generalizations ignore the realities of individual cultures.

Boas made an enormous contribution in the United States to building the discipline of anthropology through his role as a professor at Columbia University. He trained

Franz Boas is an important figure in the history of anthropology for many reasons, including his emphasis on a four-field approach and the principle of cultural relativism.

involved in policy research, and his socially progressive philosophy embroiled him in controversy.

One of his most renowned studies, commissioned by U.S. President Theodore Roosevelt, was on the effects of the environment (in the sense of where one lives) on immigrants and their children. He and his research team measured 17 821 people and found substantial differences in measurements between the older and younger generations. He concluded that head size changes quickly in response to environmental change, thus being culturally shaped rather than biologically ("racially") determined. The U.S. Immigration Commission dismissed his findings, and Congress passed the Immigration Restriction Act in 1924. Boas referred to the act as "Nordic nonsense" (Patterson 2001: 49). Boas's legacy to anthropology includes a strong critique of racism and the view that culture, not biology, determines behaviour. The biology–culture (or nature–nurture) debate is still vigorous in anthropology; it is discussed in greater detail at the end of this chapter.

The roots of Canadian anthropology are anchored in both the British/European tradition of social anthropology and American cultural anthropology. Canadian anthropology was shaped by ethnohistorical and advocacy work with First Nations peoples and strong relations with museums (see Figure 1.1). Many people contributed to the institutional development of a distinguished independent anthropological tradition in Canada.

One very interesting figure was Sir Daniel Wilson, a Scottish archaeologist appointed professor of English literature and history at University College, Toronto, in 1853. He introduced the term "prehistory" into the English language, and offered courses in comparative societies (what we discuss later as ethnology) as early as 1855.

The question of how to define culture has intrigued anthropologists for over a century. Even now, spirited discussions take place between animal scientists and cultural anthropologists about whether non-human animals have culture and, if so, how it resembles or differs from human cultures (McGrew 1998). This section reviews approaches

many students who became prominent anthropologists. He founded several professional organizations in cultural anthropology and archaeology, and he supported the development of anthropology museums. He was also

FIGURE 1.1   Canadian Museum Timeline

Canadian anthropology developed in close relationship to its national and regional museums.

1841	1877	1910	1927	1968	1986
Queen Victoria granted £1500 for a geological survey of the provinces of Canada.	The Geological Survey was mandated to make botanical, zoological, and ethnological collections.	The Geological Survey began a linguistic and ethnological survey of First Nations communities in Canada.	The National Museum of Canada was established.	The National Museum of Man was established as an amalgamation of other museums of natural sciences and technology.	The National Museum of Man became the Canadian Museum of Civilization, and opened to the public in 1989.

Sir Daniel Wilson of the University of Toronto, the first lecturer on ethnology in Canada.

to defining culture in cultural anthropology, characteristics of culture, and several bases for cultural identity formation.

Definitions of Culture

Culture is the core concept in cultural anthropology, so it seems likely that cultural anthropologists agree about what it is. This may have been the case in the early days of the discipline when there were far fewer anthropologists. In the 1950s, two anthropologists, Alfred Kroeber and Clyde Kluckhohn (1952), gathered 164 definitions of culture that had appeared in anthropological writings since the 1700s. Tensions still remain in the use of the term *culture,* with some people using *culture* to refer to a means for attaining certain goals while others stress culture as ideas.

The first definition was proposed by British anthropologist Edward Tylor in 1871. He said that "Culture, or civilization . . . is that complex whole which includes knowledge, belief, art, law, morals, custom, and any other capabilities and habits acquired by man as a member of society" (Kroeber and Kluckhohn 1952:81). The phrase "that complex whole" is the most longstanding feature of this proposition. It has contributed to commitment to the perspective of holism, which emphasizes the importance of looking at cultures as complex systems that cannot be fully understood without attention to their different components —including economics, social organization, and ideology. Two other features of Tylor's definition have not stood the test of time. First, most anthropologists now avoid the use

of *man* to refer generically to all humans and instead use generic words such as *humans* and *people.* While you may argue that the word *man* can be used generically according to its linguistic roots, many studies indicate that this usage can be confusing. Second, most anthropologists no longer equate culture with civilization. The term civilization implies a sense of "highness" versus non-civilized "lowness" and sets up an invidious distinction placing "us" (the so-called civilized nations of Europe and North America) in a superior position to "them"—the other societies.

In contemporary cultural anthropology, the theoretical positions of interpretive anthropologists and cultural materialists correspond to two different definitions of culture. Interpretive anthropologists argue that culture includes symbols, motivations, moods, and thoughts. This definition focuses on people's perceptions, thoughts, and ideas, and does not focus on behaviour as a part of culture but, rather, seeks to explain behaviour. Interpretive anthropologists stress the idea that culture is contested and negotiated, and not always shared or imposed. Cultural materialist Marvin Harris states that "A culture is the total socially acquired life-way or life-style of a group of people. It consists of the patterned repetitive ways of thinking, feeling, and acting that are characteristic of the members of a particular society or segment of society" (1975:144). Like Tylor's definition of over 100 years ago, Harris's definition pays attention to both behaviour and ideas (beliefs). The definition of culture used in this book follows this more comprehensive approach.

Culture, as all learned and shared behaviour and ideas, is found universally among human beings. Thus, it exists in a general way as something everyone has. Some anthropologists have referred to this universal concept of culture as Culture with a capital C. Culture also exists in a more specific way because all cultures are not the same. **Local culture** refers to distinct patterns of learned and shared behaviour and ideas found in localized regions and among particular groups. These may include ethnic groups, racial groups, genders, and age categories. **Macroculture** refers to learned and shared ways of behaving and thinking that cross local boundaries, such as a sense of national culture that some governments seek to promote to enhance unity, or the global consumer culture that pervades upper-middle and upper-class groups transnationally.

Characteristics of Culture

Getting a clear idea of what culture is and how it affects our lives cannot come simply from a short definition. This section provides some characteristics of culture in order to help you get closer to this elusive concept. Major characteristics include culture as adaptive, culture as related to nature but not the same as nature, culture as based on symbols, culture as something that is learned, culture as integrated, and culture as something that changes.

Culture Is Adaptive The concept of **adaptation**, which derives from the Darwinian biological evolutionary model, refers to a process of adjustment that plants and animals make to their environments that enhances their survival and their reproduction. According to Darwinian theory, the process of evolution proceeds through the selective survival of plants and organisms, with the most successful patterns of adaptation leading over time to improvements in the population. This occurs through changes, often interrelated, in human biological characteristics and human culture.

Fossil and archaeological evidence have revealed some of the changes in human physical and cultural characteristics that have occurred over the millions of years of human evolution. For instance, cranial capacity has increased, allowing for enhanced symbolic thought and communication abilities. Bipedalism, or two-footed movement, replaced walking on all fours and freed the upper arms for other activities. These physical changes are related to cultural changes such as the evolution of verbal language that depends on certain physical formations in the larynx and certain forms of tool use that depend on having an "opposable thumb" (meaning that the thumb can touch the little finger).

Human economic systems (ways of making a living) are a primary form of cultural adaptation. The earliest forms of subsistence were most directly dependent on the physical environment. While hunting certain animals could be done only where those animals existed, for example, many economic strategies now are independent of context. For example, a computer software specialist is able to work in a wide variety of geographical settings. However, other occupations are still environmentally limited; being a ski instructor requires the presence of snow or a snowmaking machine and some hills. Besides ways of making a living and providing food and shelter, human cultures that promote certain forms of social organization, intergroup communication, and even leisure behaviour are adaptive within their contexts. In many ways, culture can be viewed as humanity's most powerful strategy for survival.

Culture Is Not the Same as Nature The relationship between nature and culture is of basic interest to cultural anthropologists in their quest to understand people's behaviour and thinking. Cultural anthropology emphasizes the importance of culture over nature, while recognizing that in some instances, nature shapes culture. For example, biological traits that affect people's behaviour and lifestyles are aspects of physiology, including certain diseases such as sickle-cell anemia or hemophilia. But even in these cases, it is not easy to predict how a person possessing them in Culture A will resemble or differ from a person possessing them in Culture B.

Two Ethiopian women dining at an Ethiopian restaurant. The main meal consists of several meat and vegetable dishes, cooked with special spices and laid out on *injera* bread, a soft, flat bread that is torn into small pieces and used to wrap bite-sized bits of meat and vegetables. The entire meal can be eaten without utensils.

Another way of seeing how culture diverges from nature, even though related to it, is to see how basic "natural" demands of human life are met in different ways because of culturally defined variations. The universal human functions that everyone must perform to stay alive are eating, drinking, sleeping, and eliminating. (Requirements for shelter and clothing vary, depending on the climate. Procreation is not necessary for individual survival, although it is for group survival, so it is not included in this discussion.) In all cultures, people will eat, drink, sleep, and eliminate. But beyond this, we cannot predict how, when, or where these functions will be fulfilled. Nor can we say much about the meanings that they all have in various cultures without in-depth study.

Eating Culture shapes what one eats, how one eats, and when one eats, and influences ideas about eating. The human body requires certain nutrients for survival, but they can be provided in many ways. For example, eating meat is not a necessity for survival. Many vegetarian societies have avoided eating meat of any sort for centuries.

Preferences about what tastes good vary markedly, and many examples exist of foods that are acceptable in one culture and not in another. In China, most people think that cheese is disgusting, but in France, most people love cheese. One distinction exists between eating animals that are alive and animals that are dead. In a few cultures, consumption of live, or nearly live, creatures is considered a gourmet specialty; for example, a Philippine dish includes ready-to-be-born chicks. In many cultures where hunting and fishing are dominant ways of procuring food, people believe that the freshness of the catch is important. They consider canned meat or fish highly undesirable. Although some scientists and anthropologists have attempted to delineate universal taste categories into four basic types (sweet, sour, bitter, and salty), cross-cultural research disproves these as universals. Among the Weyéwa people of the highlands of Sumba, an island in Eastern Indonesia, categories of flavours are sour, sweet, salty, bitter, tart, bland, and pungent (Kuipers 1991).

How to eat is also an important area of food behaviour. Rules about eating are one of the first things you will confront when entering another culture. Proper dining manners in India require that a person eats using only the right hand because the left hand is reserved for elimination purposes. A clean right hand (one that has been rinsed in water, preferably) is believed to be the cleanest dining implement, since silverware, plates, and glassware that have been touched by others, even though washed, are never truly pure.

Drinking   The cultural elaboration of drinking is as complex as for eating. Every culture defines the appropriate substances to drink, when to drink, and with whom. French culture allows for consumption of relatively large amounts of table wine with meals. In Canada, water is commonly consumed during meals, but in India one takes water only after the meal is finished. Different categories of people drink different beverages. In cultures where alcoholic beverages are consumed, men tend to consume more than women. Coffee is the liquid of choice among "housewives" in North America, while martinis might be the choice for male corporate executives. The meaning of particular drinks and the style of drinking and serving them are heavily influenced by culture. If you were a guest and the host offered you water, you might think it odd. If your host then explained that it was "sparkling water from France," you might be more impressed. Social drinking, whether the beverage is coffee, beer, or vodka, creates and reinforces social bonds.

Sleeping   Going without sleep for an extended period would eventually lead to insanity and even death. Common sense might say that sleep is the one natural function that is not shaped by culture, because people tend to do it every 24 hours, everyone shuts their eyes to do it, everyone lies down to do it, and most everyone sleeps at night. But there are many cultural aspects to sleep, including the question of who sleeps with whom. Cross-cultural research reveals varying rules about where infants and children should sleep: with the mother, with both parents, or by themselves in a separate room. Among indigenous cultures of the Amazon, mothers and babies share the same hammock for many months, and breastfeeding occurs whenever the baby is hungry, not on a schedule. Culture also shapes the amount of time a person sleeps.

In rural India, women sleep fewer hours than men since they have to get up earlier to start the fire for the morning meal. In fast-track, corporate North America, "A-type" males sleep relatively few hours and are proud of that fact—to have slept too much is to be a wimp.

Elimination   This subject takes the discussion into more private territory. How does culture affect the elimination process? Anyone who has travelled internationally knows that there is much to learn about elimination when you leave familiar territory. The first question is: Where to eliminate? Differences emerge in the degree to which elimination is a private act or can be done in more or less public areas. Public options include street urinals for males but not for females, as in Paris. In most villages in India, houses do not have interior bathrooms. Instead, early in the morning, groups of women and girls leave the house and head for a certain field where they squat and chat. Men go to a different area. No one uses toilet paper; instead everyone carries in their left hand a small brass pot full of water with which they splash themselves clean. This practice has ecological advantages because it adds fertilizer to the fields and leaves no paper litter. Westerners may consider the village practice unclean, but village Indians would think that the Western system is unsanitary because paper does not clean one as well as water.

In many cultures, the products of elimination (urine and feces) are considered dirty, polluting, and disgusting. People do not try to keep such things, nor do they in any way revere them. In Papua New Guinea, in the South Pacific, people take great care to bury or otherwise hide their fecal matter. They fear that someone will find it and use it for magic against them. A negative assessment of the products of elimination is not universal, however. In some cultures, these substances are believed to have positive effects. Among First Nations cultures of the Pacific Northwest, urine, especially women's urine, was believed to have medicinal and cleansing properties and was considered the "water of life" (Furst 1989). In certain death rituals, it was sprinkled over the corpse in the hope that it might rejuvenate the deceased. People stored urine in special wooden boxes for ritual use, including the first bath that a baby was given (the urine was mixed with water for this purpose). Under the influence of Ayurvedic medical beliefs of Hindu India, many people both in India and North America believe in the beneficial effects of drinking their own urine.

Culture Is Based on Symbols   Making money, creating art, and practising religion all involve symbols. A **symbol** is an object or other sign that has a range of culturally significant meanings. Symbols are arbitrary (bearing no necessary relationship with that which is symbolized), unpredictable, and diverse. Because symbols

In India, a white sari (women's garment) symbolizes widowhood. To these women, the Western custom of a bride wearing white would seem inauspicious.

are arbitrary, we cannot predict how a particular culture will symbolize any particular thing. Although we might predict that people who are hungry would have an expression for hunger involving their stomach, no one could predict that in Hindi, the language of much of northern India, a colloquial expression for being hungry says that "rats are jumping in my stomach."

Culture Is Learned Because culture is based on arbitrary symbols, it cannot be predicted or intuited, but must be learned. Cultural learning, or **enculturation**, begins from the moment of birth, if not before (some people think that an unborn baby takes in and stores information through sounds heard from the outside world). A large but unknown amount of people's cultural learning is unconscious, occurring as a normal part of life through observation. Schools, in contrast, are a formal way to learn culture. Not all cultures throughout history have had formal schooling. Instead, children learned appropriate cultural patterns through guidance from elders and observation and practice. Hearing stories and seeing performances of rituals and dramas are other longstanding forms of enculturation.

Cultures Are Integrated To state that cultures are internally integrated is to assert the principle of holism. Thus, studying only one or two aspects of culture provides

understanding so limited that it is more likely to be misleading or wrong than more comprehensively grounded approaches. Consider what would happen if a researcher were to study intertribal warfare in Papua New Guinea and focused only on the actual practice of warfare without examining other aspects of culture. A key feature of highland New Guinea culture is the exchange of pigs at political feasts. To become a political leader, a man must acquire many pigs. Pigs eat yams, which men grow, but pigs are cared for by women. This division of labour means that a man with more than one wife will be able to produce more pigs and rise politically by giving more feasts. Such feasting enhances an aspiring leader's status and makes his guests indebted to him. With more followers attracted through feasting, a leader can gather forces and wage war on neighbouring villages. Success in war brings gains in territory. So far, this example pays attention mainly to economics, politics, and marriage systems. But other aspects of culture are involved, too. Supernatural powers affect the success of warfare. Painting spears and shields with particular designs helps increase their power. At feasts and marriages, body decoration, including paint, shell ornaments, and elaborate feather headdresses, is an important expression of identity and status. It should be obvious that looking at just warfare itself will yield a severely limited view of its wider cultural dimensions.

The fact of cultural integration is also relevant to applied anthropologists who are involved in analyzing cultural change. Attempting to introduce change in one aspect of culture without giving attention to what its effects will be in other areas is irresponsible and may even be detrimental to the survival of a culture. For example, Western missionaries and colonialists in parts of Southeast Asia banned the practice of headhunting. This practice was embedded in many other aspects of culture, including politics, religion, and psychology (a man's sense of identity as a man sometimes depended on the taking of a head). Although stopping headhunting might seem like a good thing to readers of this book, it had disastrous consequences for the cultures in which it had been a practice. This book will consider such controversial issues and examples.

Cultures Interact and Change Cultures interact with and affect each other in many ways, through trade networks, telecommunications, education, migration, and tourism. Interaction and change can occur from the local level to the global, a process called **globalization**. Also, global trends can be transformed within the local context to something new, a process called **localization**. When Jamaican reggae singer Bob Marley started singing in Jamaica, he was first popular locally, in Kingston, and then on the entire island. Subsequently, his popularity expanded to the regional (Caribbean) level, and finally he gained international fame. From the international level,

Multiple Cultural Worlds

GLOBALIZATION AND TOMATO PRODUCTION

EVERY FOOD ITEM creates complex relations of production and consumption. Consider the tomato. The Tomasita Project (Barndt 1999) traced the journey of a tomato from the Mexican field to a Canadian fast food restaurant. The tomato was chosen as a symbol of globalization and the shifting roles of women as producers and consumers of food. With collaborators from Canada, Mexico, and the United States, women told their stories about making and producing food. One story told of the members of a Canadian family working at McDonald's, often on different shifts, so that they seldom ate together; other stories tell of the peasant and indigenous labourers working on

tomato plantations in Mexico, making C$3.50 a day, barely able to afford their traditional tortillas and beans. These stories bring out a North–South contradiction: while fresh tomatoes come north, fast food restaurants like McDonald's are moving south, at a faster rate since NAFTA was implemented in January 1994. Tomatoes have complex metaphorical meanings and fit into culturally constructed recipes and meals. When multinational corporations control food production, tomatoes also become commodities.

Source: Barndt 1999.

reggae and Bob Marley have filtered down into localities where they have been subject to reinterpretation.

The culture of dominant groups often serves as the "index culture" for other groups. Index cultures are found at all levels: a village elite, a city compared to a rural area, and global capitals, which influence cultures in the periphery. In Bolivia, many indigenous Aymara women migrate from the rural highlands to the capital city of La Paz, where they work as domestic servants for the wealthy (Gill 1993). In the city, they stop wearing their traditional dress and adopt the urban styles of skirts, hats, and haircuts. In Kathmandu, Nepal, the index culture for hairstyles among some upper-class women is Parisian (Thompson 1998).

Global cultural dominance, or hegemony, as a driving force of international change is influenced by the material and political interests of the powerful nations and international business corporations. The spread of American merchandise, including well-known items such as Coca-Cola and Marlboro cigarettes and less well-known but economically important items such as pharmaceuticals, is part of conscious marketing. Many cultural anthropologists question the value of much of this marketing since it often does more to enhance the profits of Western businesses than to improve human health and welfare. The promotion of American cigarettes to adolescents in the United States and in developing countries, as a compensation for the declining adult market in America, is an alarming case of cultural hegemony and inhumane mercantilism. Defenders of these practices argue that global marketing simply increases people's choices and stress that ultimately it's up to individuals to decide whether to purchase a particular item.

Food has culturally endowed meaning. Everyday food patterns and ceremonial food use may express ethnic and religious identity, promoting in-group cohesion and setting boundaries in relation to other groups. Adhering to cultural rules about food preparation and consumption can be a defining feature of who is a "good" member of a particular group. Eating is also shaped by economic and political forces (see the Multiple Cultural Worlds box).

Multiple Cultural Worlds

As mentioned earlier in this chapter, numerous local cultures exist within every macroculture. Much of this internal cultural differentiation is structured by the categories of class, race, ethnicity, gender, age, region, and institutions. A particular individual fits into several categories, but may identify more or less strongly with one, say a teenager, a woman, a member of a visible minority. Memberships may overlap or they may be related to each other hierarchically. The contrast between difference and hierarchy is important. People and groups can be considered different from each other on a particular criterion, but not unequal. For example, people with blue or brown eyes might be recognized as different, but this difference does not entail unequal treatment or status. In other instances, such differences do become the basis for inequality.

Class

Definitions of class depend on one's theoretical perspective. **Class** refers to a category based on people's economic position in society, usually measured in terms of income

A view into the yard of a house of a low-income neighbourhood of Kingston, Jamaica. People in these neighbourhoods prefer the term *low-income* to *poor*.

or wealth and exhibited in terms of lifestyle. Class societies may be divided into upper, middle, and lower classes. An earlier definition of class associated with Karl Marx and Friedrich Engels says that class membership is determined by a group's relationship to ownership of the means of production, or how groups of people make a living. Separate classes are, for example, the working class (people who trade their labour for wages) and the landowning class (people who own land on which they or others labour). In either sense, classes are related in a hierarchical system, with certain classes dominating others. According to Marx and Engels, class struggle is inevitable as those at the top seek to maintain their position while those at the bottom seek to improve theirs. People at the bottom of the class structure may attempt to improve their class position by gaining access to resources and by adopting aspects of upper-class symbolic behaviour such as speech and dress, leisure and recreation.

Class is a key basis of cultural differentiation and stratification in most contemporary states, but it is a relatively recent social development in human history. For example, in precontact tribal groups in the Amazonian region, all members had roughly equal wealth. In complex and large capitalist states, however, classes are prominent forms of cultural differentiation. Some scholars say that global systems of cultural integration now mean that indigenous tribal groups, which themselves have little internal class

differentiation, have become part of a global class structure, with their position being at the bottom.

Race

Race is a pervasive, though not universal, basis for social differentiation. However, race is a culturally constructed category, not a biological reality. In South Africa, race is mainly defined on the basis of skin colour. In pre-twentieth-century China, however, the basis of racial classification was body hair (Dikötter 1998). Greater amounts of body hair were associated with "barbarian" races and the lack of "civilization." Chinese writers described male missionaries from Europe, with their beards, as "hairy barbarians." Even in the twentieth century, some Chinese anthropologists and sociologists divided humans into evolutionary stages on the basis of their body hair. One survey of humankind provided a detailed classification on the basis of types of beards, whiskers, and moustaches.

Physical features do not explain or account for behaviour or ideas, as Boas proved a century ago. Instead, the fact of being placed in a particular racial category and the status of that category in society are what explain "racial" behaviours and ideas. Rather than being a biological category, race in the anthropological view is a cultural or social category just like class. People's perceptions about race and their use of racial differences may result in discrimination and marginality of certain groups. Racial differentiation has been the basis for some of the most invidious oppression and cruelty throughout history. A concept of racial purity inspired Hitler to pursue his program of exterminating Jews and others who were not of the Aryan "race." Racial apartheid in South Africa denied citizenship, security, and a decent life to all those labelled non-White (including, for example, "Blacks" and "Coloureds").

Ethnicity

Ethnicity refers to a sense of group affiliation based on a distinct heritage or worldview as a "people," for example, Caribbean Canadians or Italian Canadians, the Croats of Eastern Europe, and the Han people of China. This sense of identity can be vigorously expressed through political movements or more quietly stated. It can be a basis for social ranking, claimed entitlements to resources such as land or artifacts, and a perceived basis for defending or retrieving those resources.

Compared to the term *race, ethnicity* is often used as a more neutral or even positive term. But ethnicity has often been a basis for discrimination, segregation, and oppression. The "ethnic cleansing" campaigns conducted in the early 1990s by the Serbs against Muslims in the former Yugoslavia are an extreme case of ethnic discrimination. Expression of ethnic identity has been polit-

First Nations Pow Wows provide an opportunity for socializing and celebrating. Here, men of the Mystic River Nation compete in the drumming competition at the Heartbeat of Nations Pow Wow at Red River Park in Winnipeg.

ically suppressed in many cultures, such as the Tibetans in China. Tibetan refugees living outside Tibet are struggling to keep their ethnic heritage alive. Among First Nations groups in contemporary Canada, a shared ethnicity is one basis for cultural and spiritual revival.

Gender

Gender refers to patterns of culturally constructed and learned behaviours and ideas attributed to males, females, or sometimes a blended or "third gender." Thus gender variability can be contrasted to sex, which uses biological markers to define the categories of male and female. Sex determination relies on genital, chromosomal, and hormonal distributions and thus depends on Western science to determine who is male or female. Cultural anthropology shows that a person's biological makeup does not necessarily correspond to gender. A simple example is that in the West, people tend to associate the activity of sewing with women, but in many other areas of the world, sewing (or tailoring) is mainly men's work. The task, in other words, has nothing to do with biology. Only a few tasks are related to biology, such as nursing babies. Crossculturally, gender differences vary from societies in which male and female roles and worlds are largely shared, with few differences, to those in which genders are sharply differentiated. In much of rural Thailand, males and females are about the same size, their clothing is quite similar, and their agricultural tasks are complementary and often interchangeable (P. Van Esterik 2000). Among the Hua of the

New Guinea Highlands, extreme gender segregation exists in almost all aspects of life (Meigs 1984). The *rafuri*, or men's house, physically and symbolically separates the worlds of men and women. The men live in strict separation from the women, and they engage in rituals seeking to purge themselves of female influences and substances: nose or penis bleeding, vomiting, tongue scraping, sweating, and eye washing. Men possess the sacred flutes, which they parade through the village from time to time. If women dare to look at the flutes, however, men have the right to kill them for that transgression. Strict rules also govern the kinds of food that men and women may eat.

In many cultures, the lives of gay and lesbian people are adversely affected by discrimination based on gender identity and sexual preferences. Other societies are less repressive, such as Thailand and Indonesia, and First Nations.

Age

The human life cycle, from birth to old age, takes a person through a range of cultural stages that change dramatically and for which appropriate behaviour and thinking must be learned anew. Special rituals marking physical maturation, marriage, or the end of a period of learning are found in all societies, with varying degrees of elaboration. Depending on the cultural context, each life stage places a person in a new position within the culture. Age categories intersect with other categories, such as class and gender, to define a person's status in relation to other people and groups. In many African herding societies, elaborate age categories for males define their roles and status as they move from being boys with few responsibilities and little status, to young men who are warriors and live apart from the rest of the group, to finally becoming adult men who are allowed to marry, have children, and become respected elders.

In many cultures, adolescents are in a particularly powerless category since they are neither children, who have certain well-defined rights, nor adults. Given this "threshold" position, many adolescents behave in ways of which the larger society disapproves and defines as deviance, crime, or even psychopathology (Fabrega and Miller 1995). Youth gangs in North America are an example of a situation in which adolescents have a marginal social position associated with signs of psychological deviance. Concerning women, cross-cultural research shows that in many preindustrial societies, middle-aged women have the highest status in their life cycle if they are married and have children (J. Brown 1982).

Region

Region refers to a distinct spatial area with a name and cultural characteristics that separate it from other areas. These characteristics may include the more obvious ones, such as speech, dress, and food, as well as deeper patterns of social interaction, political behaviour, and religious values. Environmental features often play an important role in defining the boundaries of a region, such as the Tibetan plateau of inner Asia or the Andean region of Latin America.

The study of regional cultures has been somewhat neglected by cultural anthropologists in their pursuit of holistic understanding of small, bounded communities. Two pioneers in this endeavour are William Skinner and Jack Goody. Skinner (1964) did work on how the role of markets and trade shaped regional integration in China. His work showed that people who live in seemingly isolated rural villages in fact may have far-reaching contacts. Jack Goody (1976, 1977, 1993) formulated generalizations about regional cultures of Europe, Asia, and Africa and how they compare to each other in terms of economic systems, marriage, food culture, and even the cultivation and use of flowers. His work, for example, revealed the more prominent role of women in crop production in Africa than in Europe and Asia. Regional studies may have to sacrifice local depth for comparative breadth (although they are based on in-depth local studies in generating their wider pictures), but their findings provide meaning to localized studies by placing them in a wider context.

Institutions

Institutions, or enduring group settings formed for a particular purpose, have their own cultural characteristics. Institutions include hospitals, boarding schools and universities, and prisons. Anyone who has entered such an institution has experienced that feeling of strangeness, of not "knowing the ropes." Until you gain familiarity with the often unwritten cultural rules, you are likely to make mistakes that offend or perplex people, that fail to get you what you want and make you feel marginal, just as if you went to a land where people are speaking a language that you don't know and are doing things that you don't understand.

Hospitals are excellent examples of institutions with their own cultural rules. Melvin Konner, an anthropologist who had studied among a group of indigenous hunting-gathering people of southern Africa and had taught anthropology for many years, decided to become a doctor. In his book *Becoming a Doctor* (1987), he reports on his experience in medical school, providing an anthropologist's insights about the hospital as a particular kind of cultural institution. One of his most striking conclusions is that medical students undergo training that in many ways functions to dehumanize them, numbing them to the pain and suffering that they will confront each day. Medical training involves, for example, the need to memorize massive amounts of material, sleep deprivation, and the learning of a special form of humour

and vocabulary that seems crude and even cruel. Some special vocabulary items are *boogie*—a verb meaning to move patients along quickly in a clinic or emergency room (as in "Let's boogie!"); a *dud*—a patient with no interesting findings; and a *gomer*—an acronym for Get Out of My Emergency Room, referring to an old, decrepit, hopeless patient whose care is guaranteed to be a thankless task, usually admitted from a nursing home.

Relationships of power and inequality exist within institutions and between different institutions. These relationships crosscut other criteria, such as gender. Recent claims by women prisoners in North America of rape and abuse by prison guards are an example of intra-institutional inequality linked with gender inequality. Within and between universities, rivalries are played out in the area of competition for large research grants as well as in athletics. Within the classroom, studies document that many professors are not egalitarian in the way they call on and respond to students, depending on their gender, race, or "looks." In the Kilimanjaro region of north Kenya, a lesson about proper sexual behaviour directed to secondary school students advised boys to "preserve your bullets" and girls to "lock your boxes" (Stambach 2000:127–30). The surface message is that boys should learn to control their mental processes and girls should look after their possessions, which they keep in a metal trunk beneath their bed. The underlying message is that boys should learn to control their sexual desire and that girls should protect their bodies. The separate metaphors, bullets and boxes, for the boys and the girls, reflect and reinforce gender differences in moral codes and expected behaviour.

Distinctive Features of Cultural Anthropology

Several features of cultural anthropology have traditionally distinguished it from other disciplines. Scholars in other disciplines, however, have been adopting anthropological approaches. Thus, while cultural anthropology's traditional characteristic features may no longer be unique to the field, they are still part of its identity and character.

Ethnography and Ethnology

Cultural anthropologists approach the study of contemporary human life in two basic ways. The first is in-depth study of one culture. This approach, **ethnography,** meaning "culture writing," provides a first-hand, detailed description of a living culture based on personal observation. Ethnography is usually presented in the form of a full-length book. It is based on experiences gained by going to the place of study and living there for an extended period. As cultural anthropologist Richard Shweder says,

An ethnography begins with an ethnographic experience: with your eyes open you have to go somewhere. . . . The first thing that strikes an anthropologist in the field are details that seem alien. It is April 5, 6 a.m., 90 degrees Fahrenheit [32 degrees Celsius], and I'm in a remote region of India on a tennis court fashioned out of the earth of termite mounds. Music, cacophonous to a foreign ear, is blaring over a loudspeaker. In India, the gods and ancestral spirits, who are not hard of hearing but are sometimes a long way off, not only like to eat food offerings, they also like to be entertained. To a foreigner for whom the gods don't exist, in the midst of a tennis match at six in the morning on a very hot day, the magnified blare is a nuisance. After two sets my Indian doubles partner finally takes off his heavy wool sweater. (1986:1, 38)

In the first part of the twentieth century, ethnographers wrote about "exotic" cultures located far from the homes of European and North American anthropologists. Classics of this phase of ethnography include A. R. Radcliffe-Brown's *The Andaman Islanders* (1922), a study of people living on a group of small islands off the coast of Burma; Bronislaw Malinowski's *Argonauts of the Western Pacific* (1922), concerning a complex trade network linking several islands in the South Pacific; and Reo Fortune's *Sorcerers of Dobu* (1932), which describes a culture in the Western Pacific islands, with a focus on its social and religious characteristics. Although early Canadian ethnographies were not considered classics, it is interesting that the mammoth ethnography, *The Bella Coola Indians* by T. F. McIlwraith, the first professional anthropologist to hold an academic position at a Canadian university, was ready in draft form in 1925, but not published until 1948 because the editors judged the material to be obscene (Barker 1987).

For several decades, ethnographers tended to treat a particular tribal group or village as a bounded unit. The era of "village studies" in the ethnography of India, extending from the 1950s through the 1960s, is an example of this trend. Dozens of anthropologists went to India for fieldwork, and each typically studied in one village and then wrote an ethnography describing that village. These anthropologists were inspired by the perspective of **holism**, the view that says cultures consist of integrated features, such as economy and religion, and one must study all of the features to have a complete picture. Examples of village studies include Adrian Mayer's *Caste and Kinship in Central India* (1960), S. C. Dube's *Indian Village* (1967), and Gerald Berreman's *Hindus of the Himalayas* (1963). The topics of concern were caste, agricultural practices, kinship, and religion. Little attention was given to exploring links between villages, or to determining the effects of world forces such as nineteenth-century colonialism or twentieth-century post-colonialism on the villagers' lives. Berreman's book is an exception. It

includes a detailed chapter on "The Outside World: Urban Contact and Government Programs."

Recent ethnographies, from 1980 onward, differ from earlier ethnographies in several ways. First, they are more likely to treat local cultures as embedded within regional and global forces. Francis Henry's *Victims and Neighbors: A Small Town in Nazi Germany Remembered* (1984) examines social relations between Jews and Christians in a town in Germany where Henry grew up during the 1930s. The ethnography combines intensive interviews in 1979 about events in the 1930s to document acts of kindness in the context of state-encouraged hatred. This study demonstrates the importance of local context in understanding events of global importance such as World War II. Second, many contemporary ethnographies are focused on one topic of interest and avoid a more holistic approach. Cultural anthropologists in this category feel that holism is an impossible goal, since no one can perceive cultures from all their complex angles. A third trend is incorporating history into ethnography. Philip Gulliver and Marilyn Silverman's *Merchants and Shopkeepers: A Historical Anthropology of an Irish Market Town* (1995) examines a town in southeast Ireland that has been a site of commerce for nearly 800 years. As a regional trade centre, the location provides an opportunity to analyze shopkeeping and entrepreneurial strategies over a long duration. A fourth trend is for an increasing number of ethnographic studies to be situated in Western, industrialized cultures. Philippe Bourgois's research in East Harlem in New York City for his book *In Search of Respect: Selling Crack in El Barrio* (1995) explores how people in one neighbourhood cope with poverty and dangerous living conditions. Daniel Wolf's research on a biker gang in Alberta, *The Rebels: A Brotherhood of Outlaw Bikers* (1991), provides another example of urban ethnographic work close to home.

While these topics may superficially resemble something that a sociologist might study, the approach of a cultural anthropologist provides a unique perspective that is more richly detailed from the everyday perspective of the people.

Many factors explain these new trends in ethnography, including the expanded number of anthropologists seeking research topics and areas of theoretical importance; social changes in the world that provide new topics for study; varying strengths and interests of anthropology doctoral programs that shape the theoretical and regional focus of their students; and trends in funding institutions' interests and budgetary priorities.

In contrast to ethnography, **ethnology** is cross-cultural analysis, or the study of a particular topic in more than one culture using ethnographic material. Ethnologists have compared such topics as marriage forms, economic practices, religious beliefs, and child-rearing practices in order

Penny Van Esterik interviewing the manager of a Thai tourist park in Suphanburi Province, Thailand.

to examine patterns of similarity and variation and possible causes for them.

Cultural Relativism

Most people grow up thinking that their culture is *the* way of life and that other ways of life are strange, perhaps even inferior. Other cultures may even be considered less than human. Cultural anthropologists have labelled this attitude **ethnocentrism**: judging other cultures by the standards of one's own culture rather than by the standards of that particular culture. Ethnocentric views have fuelled centuries of efforts at changing "other" people in the world, sometimes in the guise of religious missionizing and sometimes in the form of secular colonial domination. Looking back to the era of European colonial expansion beginning in the fifteenth century, it is clear that exploration and conquest were intended to extract wealth from the colonies. In addition to plundering their colonies, the Europeans also imposed their culture on indigenous groups. The British poet Rudyard Kipling reflected the dominant view when he said that it was "the white man's burden" to spread British culture throughout the world. Christian missionaries played a major role in European attempts to transform non-Christian cultures into a European model. Many contemporary Western powers hold similar attitudes, making foreign policy decisions that encourage the adoption of Western economic, political, and social systems.

The opposite of ethnocentrism is **cultural relativism**, the idea that each culture must be understood in terms of the values and beliefs of that culture and should not be judged by the standards of another culture. Cultural relativism assumes that no culture is better than any other. How does a person gain a sense of cultural relativism? Besides living with other people, ways to develop a sense of cultural relativism include travelling, especially extended periods of study abroad, taking a course such as this, eating different foods, listening to music from Appalachia or Brazil, reading novels by authors from other cultures, making friends who are "different" from you, and exploring the multicultural world on your campus. In sum, exposure to "other" ways, with a sympathetic eye and ear to appreciating differences, is the key.

Can a person ever completely avoid being ethnocentric? The answer is probably no, because we start learning about other cultures from the position of the one we know first. Even the most sensitive person who has spent a long time living within another culture still carries an original imprint of her or his native culture. As much as we might say that we think we are viewing Culture B from the inside (as if we were natives of Culture B), that is a logical impossibility because everything about Culture B— the language, dress, food habits, social organization, work habits, leadership patterns, and religion—was learned in relation to or in comparison with what we already knew about Culture A.

One way that some anthropologists have interpreted cultural relativism is to use **absolute cultural relativism**, which says that whatever goes on in a particular culture must not be questioned or changed because no one has the right to question any behaviour or idea anywhere—it would be ethnocentric to do so. The position of absolute cultural relativism can lead, however, in dangerous directions. Consider the example of the Holocaust during World War II in which millions of Jews and other minorities in much of Eastern and Western Europe were killed as part of the German Nazis' Aryan supremacy campaign. The absolute cultural relativist position becomes boxed in, logically, to saying that since the Holocaust was undertaken according to the values of the culture, outsiders have no business questioning it. Can anyone feel truly comfortable with such a position?

Critical cultural relativism offers an alternative view that poses questions about cultural practices and ideas in terms of who accepts them and why, and who they might be harming or helping. In terms of the Nazi Holocaust, a critical cultural relativist would ask, "Whose culture supported the values that killed millions of people on the grounds of racial purity?" Not the cultures of the Jews, Gypsies, and other victims. It was the culture of Aryan supremacists, who were one subgroup among many. The situation was far more complex than a simple absolute cultural relativist statement takes into account because there was not "one" culture and its values involved. Rather, it was a case of cultural imperialism, in which one dominant group claims supremacy over minority cultures and proceeds to change the situation in its own interests and at the expense of the other cultures.

By taking a close look at a practice or value attributed to a "culture," critical cultural relativism recognizes oppressors and victims, winners and losers, and struggles over practices and values within particular cases. Critical cultural relativism is situated within the general framework of cultural relativism in which we try to view all cultures empathetically from the inside. A growing number of cultural anthropologists seek to critique (meaning to probe underlying power interests, not just to come up with negative comments as in the general usage of the term *criticism*) the behaviour and values of groups from the standpoint of some set of more or less generally agreed-on human rights. As prominent French anthropologist Claude Lévi-Strauss commented, "No society is perfect" (1968:385), even when considered from what that society claims as moral values. While considering the "imperfections" of any and all cultures, cultural anthropologists should examine and discuss their own biases, and then try to treat all cultures equally. This means looking equally critically at all cultures—their own and those of "others."

Valuing and Sustaining Diversity

Most anthropologists value and are committed to cultural diversity just as environmentalists value and are committed to biological diversity. Anthropologists contribute to the preservation of cultural diversity and knowledge by describing cultures as they have existed, as they now exist, and as they change. Many have become activists in the area of cultural survival. Since 1972, an organization named Cultural Survival has been working with indigenous people and ethnic minorities to deal as equals in their interactions with industrial society. As printed on the inside cover of their publication *Cultural Survival Quarterly*, Cultural Survival's guiding principle is as follows:

> We insist that cultural differences are inherent in humanity; protecting this human diversity enriches our common earth. Yet in the name of development and progress, native peoples lose their land, their natural resources, and control over their lives. The consequences often are disease, destitution, and despair—and war and environmental damage for us all. The destruction is not inevitable.

To that end, Cultural Survival sponsors programs to assist indigenous peoples and ethnic minorities to help themselves in protecting and managing natural resources, claiming and reclaiming land rights, and diversifying their means of livelihood. We will return to these issues in the last chapter of this book.

CONTEMPORARY DEBATES

Within cultural anthropology, enduring theoretical debates both divide the discipline and provide threads that give it coherence. Contemporary theoretical approaches include interpretive, symbolic, political ecology, political economy, and postmodernism. Although different departments of anthropology in Canada often have specific theoretical orientations, Canadian anthropologists in general tend to avoid extremely deterministic interpretations of human behaviour. They seek to explain difference as well as similarity, and address questions that crosscut theoretical (and national) borders. Three important contemporary debates, explained briefly here, will resurface throughout the book. Each is concerned with cultural anthropology's basic question of why people behave and think the way they do.

Biological Determinism versus Cultural Constructionism

Biological determinism gives priority to such biological features as people's genes and hormones in explaining human behaviour and ideas. Thus, biological determinists search for the gene or hormone that might lead to certain forms of behaviour such as homicide, alcoholism, or adolescent stress (see the Critical Thinking box). They also examine cultural practices in terms of how they contribute to the "reproductive success of the species," or how they contribute to the gene pool of subsequent generations through promoting the numbers of surviving offspring produced in a particular population. Behaviours and ideas that have reproductive advantages logically are more likely than others to be passed on to future generations. Biological determinists, for example, have provided an explanation for why human males apparently have "better" spatial skills than females. They say that these differences are the result of evolutionary selection because males with "better" spatial skills would have an advantage in securing both food and mates. Males with "better" spatial skills impregnate more females and have more offspring with "better" spatial skills.

Cultural constructionism, in contrast, is a position that says that human behaviour and ideas are best explained as products of culturally shaped learning. In terms of the example of "better" male spatial skills, cultural constructionists would provide evidence that such skills are passed on culturally through learning, not genes. They would say that parents socialize their sons and daughters differently in spatial skills and that boys are more likely to gain greater spatial skills through learning than girls, in general. Anthropologists who favour cultural construction and learning as an explanation for behaviours such as

Critical Thinking

ADOLESCENT STRESS: BIOLOGICALLY DETERMINED OR CULTURALLY CONSTRUCTED?

MARGARET MEAD, one of the first trained anthropologists of North America, went to eastern Samoa in 1925 to spend nine months studying child-rearing patterns and adolescent behaviour. She sought to answer these questions: "Are the disturbances which vex our adolescents due to the nature of adolescence itself or to the civilisation? Under different conditions does adolescence present a different picture?" (1961:24). She observed and interviewed 50 adolescent girls of three different villages. Her conclusion, published in the famous book *Coming of Age in Samoa* (1961 [1928]), was that, unlike the typical experience in the United States, children in Samoa grew up in a relaxed and happy atmosphere. As young adolescents, they made a sexually free and unrepressed transition to adulthood. These findings had a major impact on thinking about child rearing in North America, prompting attempts at more relaxed forms of child rearing in the hope of raising less-stressed adolescents.

In 1983, five years after Mead's death (at which point she had no chance for response), Derek Freeman, an Australian anthropologist, published a strong critique of Mead's work on Samoa. Freeman said that Mead's findings on adolescence were wrong. Freeman, a biological determinist, believes that, universally, adolescents are driven by hormonal changes that cause social and psychological upheavals. He claims that Mead's work was flawed in two major ways. First, he says her fieldwork was inadequate because she spent a relatively short time in the field and she had insufficient knowledge of the Samoan language. Second, he says that her theoretical bias against biological determinism led her to overlook or under-report evidence that was contrary to her interests. In addition, he marshals statistical evidence against Mead's position. He compares rates of adolescent delinquency in Samoa and England and finds that they are similar in both cultures. On the basis of this result, he argues that sexual puritanism and social repression also characterized Samoan adolescence. In other words, Samoa is not so different from the West with its supposedly pervasive adolescent problems.

Because of Mead's reputation, Freeman's critique prompted a vigorous response from scholars, mostly in

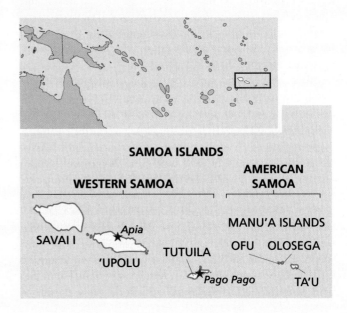

defence of Mead. One response in defence of Mead came from Eleanor Leacock, an expert on how colonialism affects indigenous cultures. Leacock (1993) claimed that Freeman's position failed to take history into account: Mead's findings apply to Samoa of the 1920s while Freeman's analysis is based on data from the 1960s. By the 1960s, Samoan society had gone through radical cultural change due to the influence of World War II and intensive exposure to Western influences, including Christian missionaries. Freeman's data, in her view, do not contradict Mead's because they are from a different period.

CRITICAL THINKING QUESTIONS

Mead felt that finding one "negative case" (no adolescent stress in Samoa) was sufficient to disprove the view that adolescent stress is a cultural universal. Do you agree that one negative case is sufficient?

If an anthropologist found that a practice or pattern of behaviour was universal to all cultures, does that necessarily mean that it is biologically driven?

homicide and alcoholism also point to the role of childhood experiences and family roles as being more important than genes or hormones. Most cultural anthropologists are opposed to biological determinism and support cultural constructivism. They feel that cultural anthropology makes an important contribution to the understanding of human nature by showing how important human culture is!

Interpretive Anthropology versus Cultural Materialism

Interpretive anthropology considers how people use symbols to make sense of the world around them, and how these meanings are negotiated. Interpretive anthropologists view culture as a contested domain, not a given. They favour an approach to ethnography that constructs a rich, complex description emerging from the insider's point of view. Interpretive anthropology tries to communicate this complexity, and rejects approaches that are reductionistic. For example, if Hindus in India say they don't eat cows because cows are sacred, interpretive anthropologists would explore the meaning of food and eating within the Hindu religion. Similarly, an interpretive anthropologist like Mary Douglas argues that pigs cannot be eaten by Jews because of their taxonomical definition in Jewish belief as defined in the rules of Leviticus. The pig is a hoofed animal that does not chew its cud, unlike cows and sheep, and is categorized as anomalous and thus impure. Materialists have rejected such reasoning because the rules of Leviticus are untestable (Harris and Ross 1987:60).

Cultural materialism, on the other hand, is the theoretical school in cultural anthropology that emphasizes the importance of material conditions in studying and explaining human behaviours and ideas. Cultural materialists take as basic the material features of life, such as the environment, natural resources, and ways of making a living. **Infrastructure** is the term that refers to these crucial material factors. Infrastructure largely shapes the other two domains of culture: **structure** (social organization, kinship, and political organization) and **superstructure** (ideas, values, and beliefs). Cultural materialists seek explanations for behaviour and ideas by looking first and primarily at infrastructural factors. For example, a materialist explanation for a taboo restricting the eating of a particular animal first considers the possibility that such an animal plays a more important role alive, such as cows' utility in agricultural work in India.

The debate between interpretive anthropology and cultural materialism has a long history in cultural anthropology, and its philosophical roots can be traced back to Plato (who emphasized that the only reality is ideas) and Aristotle (who emphasized that there is some sort of reality that can be learned about through observation). These days, most cultural anthropologists take an approach that combines the best of interpretive anthropology and cultural materialism.

Agency versus Structure

The agency versus structure debate concerns the question of how much individual will, or **agency**, has to do with why people behave and think the way they do, versus the power of forces, or "structures," that are beyond individual control. Western philosophical thought gives much emphasis to the role of agency. The individual is supposed to be able to choose how to behave and think. In contrast, analysts who emphasize structures argue that "free choice" is an illusion since choices are structured by larger forces, such as the economy, social and political institutions, and ideological systems. Explaining why people are poor, unemployed, or on welfare has been approached from both positions by cultural anthropologists and others. Some observers who emphasize the power of agency in explaining behaviour and ideas say, for example, that people are poor, unemployed, or on welfare because of their own choices. On the other hand, agency could mean individuals and groups can manipulate, resist, and negotiate around structures. The poor or marginalized can develop a voice and agency and need not be the passive victims of welfare bureaucracies or large corporations. Emphasizing structure, one would say that the poor and unemployed are trapped by larger forces and cannot escape these traps. One would argue that the people at the bottom of the economic ladder have, in reality, little opportunity to exercise choice. The tensions between structure and agency are visible in contemporary ethnographies because many anthropologists are concerned that their work not be read as either denying agency or ignoring structures.

Beyond the Debates: Holism at Heart

Anthropologists often take different theoretical positions. Some apply their work while others follow academic pursuits. Lying somewhere between "pure" science and "pure" art, anthropology seeks to understand why we all do what we do. There is no other discipline with this goal.

WHAT is anthropology?

Anthropology is an academic discipline, like history or economics. It comprises four interrelated fields in its attempt to explore all facets of human life from its very beginnings until the present: archaeology, physical or biological anthropology, linguistic anthropology, and cultural anthropology. Each field contributes a unique but related perspective. Each has a capability of making both theoretical and applied contributions. Cultural anthropology is mainly concerned with describing and analyzing contemporary people's learned and shared behaviours and beliefs.

WHAT is cultural anthropology?

Cultural anthropology is the field within general anthropology that focuses on the study of contemporary human culture—that is, on patterned and learned ways of behaving and thinking. It has several distinctive features that set it off from both the other fields of general anthropology and other academic endeavours. It uses ethnographical and ethnological approaches, supports the view of cultural relativism, and values cultural diversity.

WHAT is culture?

Culture is the key concept of cultural anthropology. Some anthropologists define culture as both shared behaviour and ideas, while others equate culture with ideas alone and exclude behaviour as a part of culture. Important characteristics of culture are that it is adaptive, related to nature but not the same as nature, based on symbols, and learned. Cultures are integrated within themselves. They also interact with other cultures and thereby change. Culture is found at different levels and people participate in cultures of different levels, including global macrocultures and local cultures shaped by such factors as class, race, ethnicity, gender, age, and institutions.

KEY CONCEPTS

absolute cultural relativism, p. 18
adaptation, p. 10
agency, p. 21
biological determinism, p. 19
class, p. 13
critical cultural relativism, p. 18
cultural constructionism, p. 19
cultural imperialism, p. 19
cultural materialism, p. 21
cultural relativism, p. 18
culture, p. 2
enculturation, p. 12
ethnicity, p. 14
ethnocentrism, p. 18
ethnography, p. 16

ethnology, p. 17
gender, p. 15
globalization, p. 12
holism, p. 17
infrastructure, p. 21
institutions, p. 16
interpretive anthropology, p. 21
local culture, p. 9
localization, p. 12
macroculture, p. 9
race, p. 14
region, p. 15
structure, p. 21
superstructure, p. 21
symbol, p. 11

SUGGESTED READINGS

William I. Adams, *The Philosophical Roots of Anthropology*. Stanford, CA: CSLI Publications, 1998. This book considers five ideas as roots of North American anthropology: progressivism, primitivism, natural law, Indianology (the study of First Nations), and German idealism. These ideas help explain why North American anthropology, compared with British anthropology, for example, retained the four-field structure.

Stanley Barrett, *Anthropology: A Student's Guide to Theory and Method*. Toronto: University of Toronto Press, 1996. This helpful handbook for undergraduate anthropology students provides a useful overview of the development of the discipline, and links methods to past and present theories.

Robert Borofsky, ed., *Assessing Cultural Anthropology*. New York: McGraw-Hill, 1994. This collection includes over 30 essays by prominent cultural anthropologists representing diverse views of the discipline and its concept of culture, the value of the comparative perspective, contemporary priorities for research and theory, and the application of anthropological perspectives to world problems.

Merryl Wyn Davies and Piero, *Introducing Anthropology*. Cambridge: Icon Books, 2002. This book offers snappy insights on key thinkers, developments, and arguments in anthropology. Each page is illustrated with cartoon-like drawings that make for lively reading.

Marvin Harris, *Our Kind: Who We Are, Where We Came From and Where We Are Going*. New York: HarperCollins, 1989. This book contains 100 thought-provoking essays on topics in general anthropology's four fields, including early human evolution, tool making, Neanderthals, food preferences, sex, sexism, politics, animal sacrifice, and thoughts on the survival of humanity.

F. Manning, ed., *Consciousness and Inquiry: Ethnology and Canadian Realities*. Ottawa: National Museum of Man, 1983. CES paper 89e. In this edited volume, eminent Canadian anthropologists present overviews or historical perspectives on their areas of specialization, including applied anthropology in Canada.

Pearl T. Robinson and Elliott P. Skinner, eds., *Transformation and Resiliency in Africa: As Seen by Afro-American Scholars*. Washington, DC: Howard University Press, 1983. Framed by an introductory essay on Black scholarship on Africa and a conclusion that looks toward the future, nine chapters explore different areas of African culture, including labour migration in Kenya, politics and government in Nigeria, religion in the Ivory Coast, religion and popular art in urban Africa, and the transformation of African music.

George W. Stocking, Jr., *The Ethnographer's Magic and Other Essays in the History of Anthropology*. Madison: University of Wisconsin Press, 1992. This book provides a detailed examination of the emergence of cultural anthropology from Tylor through Boas and Mead, with a summary chapter on major paradigms in the history of general anthropology.

Eric R. Wolf, *Europe and the People without History*. Berkeley: University of California Press, 1982. This book examines the impact since 1492 of European colonial expansion on the indigenous cultures with which they came into contact. It also traces various phases of trade relationships, including the slave trade and goods such as fur and tobacco, and the emergence of capitalism and its effects on the movement of people and goods between cultures.

WEBLINKS

The Companion Website (www.pearsoned.ca/miller) that accompanies *Cultural Anthropology*, Third Canadian Edition, includes a destinations module containing links to many websites relevant to the content of this chapter. Use it to investigate the Web and expand your understanding of anthropology.

KEY QUESTIONS

- **HOW** do cultural anthropologists conduct research on culture?
- **WHAT** does fieldwork involve?
- **WHAT** are some special issues in cultural anthropology research?

2

METHODS IN CULTURAL ANTHROPOLOGY

During the course of winter travels with the Hare Indians in Canada, anthropologist Joel Savishinsky holds a 11-kilogram lake trout. His dog team is resting behind him.

Tau, Manu'a

March 24, 1926

This will be my last bulletin from Manu'a and very probably the last from Samoa. I'll probably leave Manu'a in about three weeks. . . .

At dawn on March 8th, a boat arrived from Ofu and lured by thoughts of ethnological gain I decided to go back with the boat—a 15-foot [4.5-metre] rowboat . . . I decided it would be expensive but pleasant. So we set out in the broiling sun with a crew of some nine Samoans. The girls were desperately seasick but I rested my head on a burlap bag of canned goods, and . . . enjoyed the three-hour pull in the open sea. The swell is impressive when viewed from such a cockleshell of a boat. The Samoans chanted and shouted. . . .

The whole conduct of the malaga [ceremonial visiting party] was charming. My two companions were my talking chiefs, functionally speaking. They made all the speeches, accepted and dispersed gifts, prepared my meals, etc. . . . And these were merry companions. Even when they went to wash my clothes, one carried the clothes but the other carried the ukelele. . . . There were some slight difficulties. Once I killed 35 mosquitoes *inside* my net *in the morning*, and all had dined liberally. (Mead 1977:55–57)

There are many important differences between being a tourist and doing research in cultural anthropology, as this excerpt from one of Margaret Mead's letters from Samoa demonstrates. Most cultural anthropologists gather data by doing **fieldwork**—that is, going to "the field," which includes any place where people and culture are found (Robson 1993). A cornerstone method of fieldwork in cultural anthropology is participant observation, in which an anthropologist simultaneously lives in and studies a culture for a long period of time.

Compared to the other three fields of general anthropology, cultural anthropology is most associated with participant observation as its primary technique for gathering data. Because archaeologists work mainly with artifacts from bygone cultures, they cannot truly participate in the cultures they study. Primatologists live in natural habitats for long periods of time, but the limited degree to which humans and non-human primates can communicate with each other constrains true participation. Linguistic anthropologists who work with contemporary populations most resemble cultural anthropologists in their use of fieldwork. They are able to both observe and participate in the same ways that cultural anthropologists do.

In this chapter we explore how cultural anthropologists learn about culture through fieldwork and participant observation. The entire process of fieldwork is considered, from coming up with an idea for research to leaving the field, analyzing the data, and writing up one's findings. Later on in the chapter, we consider some special topics, such as the importance of ethics and doing fieldwork in dangerous situations. Throughout this chapter, you might try to keep in mind the similarities and differences between research in cultural anthropology and research in other areas of study, such as psychology, economics, or history.

CHANGING METHODS IN CULTURAL ANTHROPOLOGY

Methods in cultural anthropology have changed dramatically since the nineteenth century. This section presents a brief historical overview of research approaches and then introduces the key method of participant observation.

From the Armchair to the Field

Research in the early years of cultural anthropology was not based on fieldwork and participant observation. Referred to as "armchair anthropology," it involved reading reports from travellers, missionaries, and explorers and then providing an analysis. Edward Tylor (1871), who proposed the first definition of culture, was an armchair anthropologist. So was Sir James

Frazer, another famous founding figure of anthropology, who wrote *The Golden Bough* (1890), a multi-volume collection of myths, rituals, and symbols from around the world compiled from reading other people's reports. In the second stage of the late nineteenth and early twentieth centuries, some anthropologists moved out from their homes and libraries and travelled to foreign countries, where they spent time living near, but not with, the people they were studying. This pattern is nicknamed the "verandah anthropology" because typically the anthropologist would send out for "native" informants to come to the verandah for interviewing. Verandah anthropology was practised by many anthropologists who worked for colonial governments. They lived within colonial settlements, not with the indigenous people. The third stage is the current one of fieldwork and participant observation.

The field can be anywhere: a school, a rural community, a corporation, a clinic, an urban neighbourhood, in any part of the world. In some ways, the field is equivalent to a scientist's lab. A cultural anthropologist, however, does not perform experiments, but follows a less obtrusive approach.

Participant Observation: An Evolving Method

The first lessons about the value of participant observation came from nineteenth-century observations of Iroquoian groups by Lewis Henry Morgan, and lesser-known Horatio Hale. Both were nineteenth-century lawyers who lived near Iroquoian groups in New York State and Brantford, Ontario, respectively. Neither did participant observation in the sense of living for a long time, say a year or two, with the people, but both made field trips to Iroquois settlements. This experience, though brief, provided important insights into the lives of the Iroquois and formed the basis for Morgan's book, *The League of the Iroquois* (1851), and Hale's *Iroquois Book of Rites* (1883). The books helped dismantle the prevailing Euro-American perception of the Iroquois as "dangerous savages."

Bronislaw Malinowski is considered the "father" of participant observation because he first placed it in the centre of cultural anthropology methods while studying the people of the Trobriand Islands in the South Pacific during World War I. "For two years, he set his tent in their midst, learned their language, participated as much as he could in their daily life, expeditions, and festivals, and took everything down in his notebooks" (Sperber 1985:4). Malinowski made the crucial step of learning the local language, and therefore was able to dispense with interpreters. Direct communication brings the researcher much closer to the lived reality of the people being studied, as is evident in his ethnography about the Trobrianders, *Argonauts of the Western Pacific* (1922).

Bronislaw Malinowski during his fieldwork in the Trobriand Islands, 1915–1918.

In the late 1800s and early 1900s, a primary goal was to record as much as possible of a people's language, songs, rituals, and social life because many cultural anthropologists believed that cultures were disappearing. Given the assumption that small, localized cultures could be studied in their totality, early cultural anthropologists focused on gaining a holistic view of a single group. Today, few isolated cultures remain to be studied. The integration of most cultures into wider economic and political spheres has prompted new research topics and revised methods of study that can take in both local and global factors.

Several examples of contemporary ethnographies demonstrate the simultaneous attention to local patterns and wider cultural links. Harriet Rosenberg's *A Negotiated World: Three Centuries of Change in a French Alpine Community* (1988) examines 300 years of changes in a small Alpine village in southwestern France, tracing its shifting position in the political and economic transformations of French state formation. She combined historical study with ethnographic observations to explain contemporary social life and the complexity of social change.

Margaret Lock explored the cultural construction of menopause in *Encounters with Aging: Mythologies of Menopause in Japan and North America* (1993). In it she combines individual narratives about the aging symptoms associated with the end of menstruation, medical discourses about female mid-life, and the politics of aging in Japan and North America. This combination of popular and professional accounts is a powerful ethnographic approach in medical anthropology.

A methodological innovation that helps cultural anthropologists take globalization, complexity, and change into account is **multi-sited research**, or fieldwork in more than one location. Cultural anthropologists are beginning to use this approach particularly in studies of migrant populations. Studying migration has challenged traditional cultural anthropology's focus on one village or neighbourhood and created the need to take into account national and global economic, political, and social forces (Lamphere 1992; Basch, Glick Schiller, and Szanton Blanc 1994). Anthropologists study why people move and analyze their adjustments to living in a new place, especially the challenges and opportunities of maintaining their culture or constructing a new cultural identity.

Camilla Gibb (2002) studied the Harari, a dispersed community of Muslim Ethiopians, in the city of Harar and in Toronto. Since a third of the Harari are scattered across the globe, a key component of her study included discussions taking place on H-Net, an email–based discussion group where aspects of community and identity were defined and debated. Use of this new media revealed differences among diasporic generations about eventual return to Ethiopia.

Another anthropologist conducted research among Chinese Americans in the San Francisco Bay area and then in the Pearl River Delta region in Guangdong Province in the People's Republic of China (Louie 2000). The research in China focused on a youth festival that attracts young Chinese Americans seeking to find out about their homeland. At the same time, the festival allows the Chinese people to reframe and restate their sense of national identity. These studies reveal the importance of **transnationalism,** or national identity that crosses nation-states and is created through the flow of people, goods, and ideas.

DOING RESEARCH IN CULTURAL ANTHROPOLOGY

Conducting research in cultural anthropology is challenging, exciting, sometimes frustrating, and full of surprises. No doubt all cultural anthropologists would agree that their fieldwork experiences have altered their own lives immeasurably. Here we explore all the stages of a fieldwork research project, from the initial planning to the concluding analysis and writing up of the findings.

Beginning the Fieldwork Process

Two important activities characterize the first stage of cultural anthropology research: project selection and funding, and preparing for the field.

Project Selection and Funding

The first step is deciding on the research topic, since no one goes to the field without an idea of what they want to learn.

Cultural anthropologists often find a topic to research by reviewing reports on what has been done already. Through library research, also called *secondary research,* they may find a gap that needs to be filled. For example, in the 1970s, many cultural anthropologists began to focus on women because they realized that little previous research had addressed women's lives (Miller 1993). Other topics have emerged because of historical events. The discovery of the AIDS virus and its social dimensions stimulated interest from cultural anthropologists, many working within the subfield of medical anthropology. The recent rise in the numbers of immigrants and refugees in North America prompted studies of the adaptation of these groups of people. The fall of state socialism in Russia and Eastern Europe shifted attention to that region. Conflicts in Ireland, Rwanda, former Yugoslavia, and other places have spurred cultural anthropologists to ask what keeps states together and what makes them fall apart. Even luck can lead to a research topic. While conducting fieldwork in southwestern Ontario on contemporary Mennonite efforts to articulate a renewed vision of peoplehood, Daphne Winland came across a small congregation of Hmong refugees from Laos who had been sponsored by the Mennonite community in Kitchener-Waterloo, Ontario. These refugees, who had decided to convert to Christianity (specifically Mennonitism), not only provided a fascinating example of the role of religion in refugee adjustment but also a perfect case study through which to examine the central theme of her research, Mennonite struggles over their long-established identity as an ethno-religious enclave (Winland 1992).

"Restudies" are another way to design a research project. Decades of previous anthropological field studies provide us with a base of information. In 2001 and 2005, John and Penny Van Esterik returned to their fieldsite, a village in Central Thailand, to see how the community

John Van Esterik continues his restudy in a Thai village. Here he is asking his informant about pictures taken at a housewarming ritual.

had changed in 30 years. It makes sense for contemporary anthropologists to go back to a place that had been studied earlier to examine the changes that have occurred, or to look at the culture from a new angle.

A lasting contribution of Malinowski's ethnography, *Argonauts of the Western Pacific* (1922), is its detailed examination of the *kula*, a trading network linking many islands in the region in which men have longstanding partnerships with other men for the exchange of goods, such as food, and highly valued necklaces and armlets. More than half a century later, Annette Weiner (1976) travelled to the Trobriand Islands to study woodcarving. She settled in a village not far from where Malinowski had done much of his research and began making startling observations: "On my first day in the village, I saw women performing a mortuary [death] ceremony in which they distributed thousands of bundles of strips of dried banana leaves and hundreds of beautifully decorated fibrous skirts. Bundles of banana leaves and skirts are objects of female wealth with explicit economic value" (xvii).

She decided to investigate women's activities and exchange patterns. Weiner discovered a world of production, exchange, social networks, and influence that existed among women, but that Malinowski and other earlier (male) observers had overlooked. Men, as Malinowski described, exchange shells, yams, and pigs. Women, as Weiner discovered, exchange bundles of leaves and intricately made skirts. Power and prestige derive from both. Reading Malinowski alone informs us about the dramatic and exciting world of men's status systems. But that is only half the picture. Reading Weiner's *Women of Value, Men of Renown* (1976) provides an account of the linkages between domains of male and female power and value. Weiner shows how understanding of one domain requires understanding of the other.

Over the past several decades, the regional focus of research in cultural anthropology has shifted. These changes are not random, but occur in response to underlying factors such as funding sources or security interests (Shankman and Ehlers 2000). Some funding sources support domestic research by applied anthropologists on issues such as homelessness and HIV/AIDS. But when the research site is more "foreign" and "exotic," the researcher gains more status and prestige (Gupta and Ferguson 1997). Nevertheless, some of the most significant and policy-relevant anthropological research in Canada is conducted "at home." (See, for example, Scott 2001; Asch 1997; Glasser and Bridgeman 1999; Winland 1992; Davis 1989; Culhane Speck 1987; and Adelson 2000.) Private or government foundations provide research funding on a competitive basis. A research proposal is usually required for consideration by the funding source. It describes the project; explains why it is important; and provides information about how the

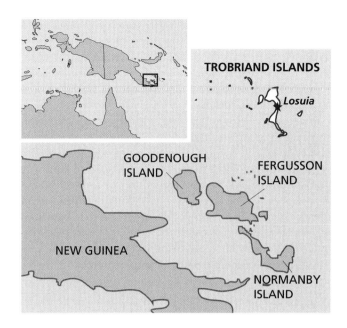

research will be conducted, how much it will cost, and what the results will be—a book, scholarly papers, a film, or a detailed report. Canadian funding for anthropological research comes primarily from the Social Science and Humanities Research Council (SSHRC), Canadian International Development Agency (CIDA) awards programs, and area-specific foundations, such as the Shastri Indo-Canadian Institute and the Japan Foundation.

Preparing for the Field

Once the project is defined and funding secured, it is time to begin preparing to go to the field. Visas, or formal research permission from the host government, may be required and may take a long time to obtain. On the other hand, they may not be needed if the research is conducted in one's native country. The government of India, for example, is highly restrictive about research by foreigners, with "sensitive" topics such as "tribal people" or family planning being off limits. Some nations have been completely closed to anthropological research for decades and are only now relaxing their restrictions. China's restrictions against allowing foreign anthropologists to do research there have been lifted only in the past 15 years or so, and Russia's restrictive policies have changed even more recently.

Preparation may involve buying equipment, such as a tent, arctic sleeping bag, or special clothing. Health preparations may involve having a series of shots for immunization against contagious diseases such as yellow fever. For research in malaria-endemic areas, individuals are advised to start taking anti-malaria pills weeks before arrival to build up immunity. If the project is to take place in a remote area far from adequate medical care, a well-stocked medical kit is essential. Research equipment and supplies are other important aspects of preparation. Cameras, video recorders, tape recorders, and laptop computers are becoming basic field equipment, reflecting technological changes in doing fieldwork from the days of the simple notebook and pen.

If a researcher is unfamiliar with the local language, intensive language training before going into the field is a necessity. If a particular language is not taught anywhere in the anthropologist's home country, intensive language study should be started on arrival in the country where the research will be done. Even with language training in advance, cultural anthropologists often find that they need to learn the local version of the more standardized language they studied in a classroom. Many cultural anthropologists rely on help from a local interpreter.

Working in the Field

Fieldwork in cultural anthropology is a difficult and lengthy social process that involves the researcher's coming to terms with an unfamiliar culture. The anthropologist attempts to learn the language of the people, live as they do, understand their lives, and often be a friend.

Site Selection

The researcher often has a basic idea of the area where the fieldwork will occur—for example, a *favela* (shanty town) in Rio de Janeiro or a village in Scotland—but it is difficult to know exactly where the project will be located until after arriving. Selecting a research site depends on many factors. For example, it may be necessary to find a large village if the project involves looking at social class differences in work patterns and food consumption, or a clinic if the study concerns health care behaviour. Locating a place where the people welcome the researcher and the project, which offers adequate housing, and which fits the requirements of the project, may not be easy.

Jennifer Robertson's (1991) selection of Kodaira as a research site in Japan for her study of urban residents and immigrants was based on a combination of good advice from a Japanese colleague, available housing, a match with her research interests, and the happy coincidence that she already knew the area:

> I spent my childhood and early teens in Kodaira [but] my personal past did not directly influence my selection of Kodaira as a fieldsite and home. . . . A colleague, Matsumura Mitsuo of the Institute for Areal Studies in Tokyo, suggested that the Mutashine region in central Tokyo prefecture would be an ideal locus for a historical anthropological study of village-making (*mura-zakuri*), the substance of my initial research proposal. That I wound up living in my old neighborhood in Kodaira was

determined more by the availability of a suitable apartment than by a nostalgic curiosity about my childhood haunts. As it turned out, I could not have landed at a better place at a better time. (6)

Gaining Rapport

Rapport refers to the relationship between the researcher and the study population. In the early stages of research, the primary goal is to establish rapport, probably first with key leaders or decision makers in the community who may serve as gatekeepers (people who formally or informally control access to human or material resources to the group or community). Gaining rapport involves trust on the part of the study population, and their trust depends on how the researcher presents herself or himself. In many cultures, local people will have difficulty understanding why a person would come to "study" them, since they may not know about universities and research and cultural anthropology. They may provide their own often inaccurate explanations, based on previous experience with outsiders whose goals differed from those of cultural anthropologists, such as tax collectors, missionaries, family planning promoters, and law enforcement officials.

Much has been written about the problem of how the anthropologist presents herself or himself in the field and how the local people interpret "who" the anthropologist is and why the anthropologist is there at all. Stories about such role assignments can be humorous. Richard Kurin (1980) reports that in the earliest stage of his research among the Karan in the Punjab region of northwest Pakistan, the villagers thought he was a spy—from the United States, Russia, India, or China. After he convinced them that he was not a spy, the villagers came up with several other acceptable roles for him—first as a "teacher" of English because he was tutoring one of the village boys, then as a "doctor" because he was known to dispense aspirin, then as a "lawyer" who could help villagers in negotiating local disputes because he could read court orders. Jean Briggs was adopted as a daughter in an Inuit community in the Canadian Arctic. This role raised the problems of losing her outsider status, depletion of her supplies, and loss of privacy.

Gift Giving and Exchange

Giving gifts to local people can help the project proceed, and they are sometimes an expected part of exchange relationships in the culture. Gifts should be culturally and ethically appropriate. Many cultural anthropologists working in developing countries have provided basic medical care, such as wound dressing, as a regular part of their interactions. Some have taught in the local school part time. Others have helped support individuals in obtaining a higher education degree outside their homelands.

Learning the local rules of exchange is important, including what constitutes an appropriate or inappropriate gift, how to deliver the gift (timing, in private or public, wrapped or unwrapped), and how to behave as a gift giver (for example, should one be modest and emphasize the smallness of the gift?). Richard Lee, who conducted fieldwork among the !Kung San Bushmen (Ju/wasi), wrote a classic article on the complexities of gift giving and reciprocity. After a year in the field, he used the custom of slaughtering a huge, fat ox at Christmas to repay in part the community for their hospitality. Because of the disparity between his inventory of canned food and the Bushmen's scant supplies of food, he fell open to accusations of being stingy, a hard-hearted miser:

> The Christmas ox was to be my way of saying thank you for the cooperation of the past year; and since it was to be our last Christmas in the field, I determined to slaughter the largest, meatiest ox that money could buy, insuring that the feast and transcendence would be a success. (Lee 1969:26)

Following his purchase of a huge ox, community members began complaining about the scrawny, bony animal he had chosen. Even after the carcass was cut open, the complaints continued:

> "Hey /gau," I burst out, "that ox is loaded with fat. What's this about the ox being too thin to bother eating? Are you out of your mind?" "Fat?" /gau shot back, "You call that fat? The wreck is thin, sick, dead!" And he broke out laughing. So did everyone else. They rolled on the ground, paralyzed with laughter. Everybody laughed except me; I was thinking. (28)

Following two days of feasting, Lee was still troubled by people's response to his generosity. He asked:

> "Why did you tell me the black ox was worthless, when you could see that it was loaded with fat and meat?"
>
> "It is our way," he said smiling. "We always like to fool people about that. Say there is a Bushman who has been hunting. He must not come home and announce like a braggart, 'I have killed a big one in the bush!' He must first sit down in silence until I or someone else comes up to his fire and asks, 'What did you see today?' He replied quietly, 'Ah, I'm no good for hunting. I saw nothing at all [pause] just a little tiny one.' Then I smile to myself," /gaugo continued, "because I know he killed something big."
>
> "But," I asked, "why insult a man after he has gone to all that trouble to track and kill an animal and when he is going to share the meat with you so your children will have something to eat?"
>
> "Arrogance," was his cryptic answer.
>
> "Arrogance?"
>
> "Yes, when a young man kills much meat he comes to think of himself as a chief or a big man, and he thinks of the rest of us as his servants or inferiors. We can't accept this. We refuse one who boasts, for someday his pride will make him kill somebody. So we always speak of his meat as worthless. This way we cool his heart and make him gentle." . . .

The pieces now fell into place. I had known for a long time that in situations of social conflict with Bushmen I held all the cards. I was the only source of tobacco in a thousand square miles [2500 square kilometres], and I was not incapable of cutting an individual off for non-cooperation. Though my boycott never lasted longer than a few days, it was an indication of my strength. People resented my presence at the water hole, yet simultaneously dreaded my leaving. In short I was a perfect target for the charge of arrogance and for the Bushmen tactic of enforcing humility. I had been taught an object lesson by the Bushmen; it had come from an unexpected corner and had hurt me in a vulnerable area. For the big black ox was to be the one totally generous, unstinting act of my year at /ai/ai, and I was quite unprepared for the reaction I received.

As I read it, their message was this: There are no totally generous acts. All "acts" have an element of calculation. One black ox slaughtered at Christmas does not wipe out a year of careful manipulation of gifts given to serve your own ends. After all, to kill an animal and share the meat with people is really no more than Bushmen do for each other every day and with far less fanfare. (29)

(Excerpt from Richard Borshay Lee, "Eating Christmas in the Kalahari." Reprinted from *Natural History*, Dec. 1969, © Natural History Magazine, Inc., 1969.)

Factors Influencing Fieldwork

An anthropologist's class, race, gender, and age all affect how he or she will be interpreted by local people. An anthropologist who is a young, unmarried female studying child-rearing practices may not be taken seriously since she is not herself a mother. In the rest of this section, we offer some examples of how class, race/ethnicity, gender, age, and other factors can influence the rapport an anthropologist is able to achieve with the population.

Class   In most fieldwork situations, the anthropologist is more wealthy and powerful than the people studied. This difference is obvious to the people. They know that the anthropologist may have spent hundreds or thousands of dollars on education and travel to the research site. They see the expensive equipment (camera, tape recorder, video recorder, even a vehicle) and valuable trade items (stainless steel knives, cigarettes, flashlights, canned food, medicines). This class difference affects how people in the field relate to the researcher. When Ernestine Friedl (1986) and her husband did fieldwork in a Greek village, their status as "professors" influenced people's behaviour. Village men would refrain from telling sexual jokes or swearing when the professor was present (213).

This pattern of the anthropologist having more wealth and status than the people being studied has typified cultural anthropology throughout its history. Laura Nader (1972) has urged a departure from this pattern. She says that some anthropologists should "study up" by doing research among powerful people such as business elites, political leaders, and government officials. Cultural anthropologists who "study up" find themselves in research situations in which they are less wealthy and less powerful than their informants. Dorinne Kondo's (1997) research on the high-fashion industry of Japan placed her in touch with many members of the Japanese elite, influential people capable of taking her to court if they felt she wrote something defamatory about them. "Studying up" has contributed to awareness of the need, in all fieldwork situations, for a recognition of the anthropologist's accountability to the people being studied. Some anthropologists deal with this need through collaborative forms of research, which helps ensure that the research "subjects" are part of the research process themselves.

Race For most of its history, cultural anthropology has been dominated by Euro-American White researchers who have studied "other" cultures, most often non-White and non-Euro-American. The effects of "Whiteness" on role assignments range from the anthropologist being labelled as a god or ancestor spirit to his or her being reviled as a representative of a colonialist past. While doing research in Jamaica, Tony Whitehead (1986) learned how race and status interact. For Whitehead, an African American, being essentially the same "race"—of African descent—did not automatically create solidarity between him and the African-descent residents of Haversham, Jamaica. The people of Haversham have a complex status system that relegated Whitehead to a higher social status position that he did not predict. Similarly, David Murray working in Martinique recognized that his "presence as a 'white' man may have censured the expression of other beliefs, feelings or opinions among both gay and straight Martinican men as the white/black racial dyad has a major structuring influence on Martinican social life" (Murray 2002:12).

Gender The literature on the impact of gender on fieldwork is large and growing (for example, Golde 1986; Whitehead and Conway 1986). Generally, if a female researcher is young and unmarried, she is likely to face more difficulties than a young unmarried male or an older female, married or single, because a young unmarried female who is on her own is often an anomaly (Warren 1988:13–15). Rules of gender segregation may dictate that a young unmarried woman should not move about freely without a male escort, and her status may prevent her from attending certain events or being in some places. Gender boundaries exist cross-culturally to varying degrees, and a researcher probably can never fully overcome them. A woman researcher who studied a secretive male gay community in the United States comments:

> I was able to do fieldwork in those parts of the setting dedicated to sociability and leisure—bars, parties, family

gatherings. I was not, however, able to observe in those parts of the setting dedicated to sexuality—even quasi-public settings such as homosexual bath houses. . . . Thus my portrait of the gay community is only a partial one, bounded by the social roles assigned to females within the male homosexual world. (Warren 1988:18)

Gender segregation limits male researchers from gaining access to a full a range of activities as well, especially in the domestic domain. In an unusual study, Liza Dalby (1983) lived with the geishas of Kyoto, Japan, and trained to be a geisha. Through this, she learned more about the inner workings of this local culture than a man ever could.

Age Typically, adult anthropologists are responsible for studying people in all age categories. Although some children and adolescents readily welcome the participation of a friendly adult in their daily lives and respond to questions openly, others are much more tentative. Margaret Mead (1986) commented that "Ideally, a three-generation family, including children highly trained to understand what they experience, would be the best way to study a culture" (321). She recognized that each age category has its own cultural rules and age-specific language, and needs to be studied on its own terms. Although Mead paid a great deal of attention to children and adolescents, few contemporary anthropologists consider children except in discussions of the family and motherhood. Recently a number of Canadian anthropologists have explored the complexity of children's lives, including the media depiction of children, the intimacy of children's play, and the cultural politics revealed in post-war parliamentary debates about family allowances and "the right kind of children" (Helleiner 2001). Virginia Caputo (2001) studied children's musical practices in Toronto and showed how their play allowed them to resist adult definitions of childhood. When Pamela Downe asked children to choose a research name for themselves, she learned about how important names are to children's identity. Seven-year-old Kizzy from Bridgetown, Barbados, explains: "Sometimes I feel very tiny . . . Like I [could] fit in a thimble, like the tooth fairy—but all's I gotta do is imagine someone calling my name and I be feeling big again. That is why I like thinking about what name you should call me in your notes" (Downe 2001:167).

Ethnographies of children also demonstrate how clichés like "the innocent child" mask differences among children according to age, gender, race, class, and location.

Other Factors The fieldworker's role is affected by many more factors than the characteristics listed above, including language, dress, and religion. Being the same religion as the elderly Jewish people at the Aliyah Center in

Liza Dalby in full geisha formal dress in the person of Ichigiku.

California helped Barbara Myerhoff (1978) in establishing rapport in her first meeting with members of the Center. This is evident in her conversation with one elderly woman named Basha:

"So, what brings you here?"

"I'm from the University of Southern California. I'm looking for a place to study how older Jews live in the city."

At the word *university*, she moved closer and nodded approvingly. "Are you Jewish?" she asked.

"Yes, I am."

"Are you married?" she persisted.

"Yes."

"You got children?"

"Yes, two boys, four and eight," I answered.

"Are you teaching them to be Jews?" (14)

Myerhoff was warmly accepted into the lives of people at the Center, and her plan for one year of research grew into a longstanding relationship.

In a study of women who were denied the *get*, or Jewish divorce document, Lisa Rosenberg (1996) was aware that although she was a Jewish woman, as a non-Orthodox woman she might be perceived as an outsider by those within the Orthodox community. She was often subject to scrutiny that was, at times, quite overt. More than once she was asked, "What synagogue do you belong to?" It was also common for her to have to speak about her Jewish education and her knowledge of Jewish law.

Culture Shock

Culture shock consists of persistent feelings of uneasiness, loneliness, and anxiety that often occur when a person has shifted from one culture to a different one. The more "different" the two cultures are, the more severe the shock is likely to be. Culture shock happens to many cultural anthropologists, no matter how much they have tried to prepare themselves for the field. Culture shock can happen to students who study abroad, overseas volunteers (CUSO, WUSC), or anyone who spends a significant amount of time living and participating in another culture. It can range from problems with food to the language barrier. Food differences were a major problem in adjustment for a Chinese anthropologist who came to the United States (Shu-Min 1993). American food never gave him a "full" feeling.

For Martha Ward (1989), who went to an island in the Pacific named Pohnpei to study the interactions between social modernization and high blood pressure, language caused the most serious adjustment problems. She spent much time in the early stages of her research learning basic phrases and vocabulary, and she reports on the frustration she felt:

. . . when even dogs understood more than I did. . . . The subtleties and innuendo I wanted to express (and could in English) were impossible. For months, I sweated profusely when I had to carry on a full conversation in Pohnpeian. It was no gentle perspiration, either; it was the sweat of hard, dirty work. Nonetheless, I will never forget the elation of deciphering and using relative clauses and personal pronouns. Nor will I forget the agony of stepping on a woman's toes. Instead of asking for forgiveness, I blurted out, "His canoe is blue." (14)

A psychological aspect of culture shock is the feeling of reduced competence as a cultural actor. At home, the anthropologist is highly competent. Everyday tasks like shopping, talking with other people, mailing a letter, or sending a fax can be done without thinking. In a new culture, the most simple task becomes difficult and one's sense of self-efficacy is undermined. In extreme cases, an anthropologist may have to abandon a project because of an inability to adapt to the fieldwork situation. For most, however, culture shock is a temporary affliction that subsides as the person becomes more familiar with the new culture.

"Reverse culture shock" can occur on returning home. Alan Beals (1980) describes his feelings on returning to San Francisco after a year of fieldwork in a village in India:

> We could not understand why people were so distant and hard to reach, or why they talked and moved so quickly. We were a little frightened at the sight of so many white faces and we could not understand why no one stared at us, brushed against us, or admired our baby.
>
> We could not understand the gabble of voices on the television set. When we could understand people, they seemed to be telling lies. The trust and warmth seemed to have gone out of life to be replaced by coldness and inhumanity. People seemed to have no contact with reality. All of the natural human processes—eating, sleeping together, quarreling, even playing—seemed to be divorced from earth and flesh. Nowhere could we hear the soft lowing of cattle or the distant piping of the shepherd boy. (119)

Fieldwork Techniques

Fieldwork is devoted to collecting data for subsequent analysis. The main approaches to data collection, **quantitative research** and **qualitative research**, provide different kinds of data and follow different analytical routes (Bernard 1995; Hammersley 1992). Quantitative data and analysis include numerical information, counting, and the use of tables and charts in presenting results. Qualitative methods generate detailed descriptions rather than counting or quantifying. Some researchers concentrate on quantitative data, some rely on qualitative data, and others use a combination of both. Regardless of these variations, participant observation is the basic research method through which the data are collected.

Varieties of Participant Observation

Once in the field, cultural anthropologists use particular **research methods** or strategies and techniques to learn about culture. Within the overall approach of participant observation, many different methods are available. The choice of methods for data gathering and the subsequent interpretation and analysis of the data depend on the anthropologist's theoretical perspective.

Deductive research methods involve posing a research question or hypothesis, gathering data related to the question, and then assessing the findings in relation to the original hypothesis. Thus, fieldwork should be devoted to the collection of detailed observational and interview data in order to learn what people do as well as how people explain what they do and why they do it. Data analysis also involves interpreting the disjuncture between what people say and their actions, as well as cross-cultural comparison.

Inductive research approaches avoid hypothesis formation in advance of the research and instead take their lead from the culture being studied. An important source of detailed information on insiders' views is **discourse**—people's talk, stories, and myths. People's discourse reveals their perceptions of important themes and concepts. Cross-cultural comparison is less significant since each system of local knowledge makes sense only in itself. Understanding other people's subjective meanings is an important part of inductive research strategies. In this view, cross-cultural comparison is extremely complex and of limited use, because each system of local knowledge makes sense only in itself.

Cultural anthropologists use two terms that are related to deductive research and inductive research, respectively. **Etic** (pronounced like the last two syllables of *phonetic*) refers to data gathering and analysis by outsiders that will yield answers to particular questions about the culture posed by the outsider. In contrast, **emic** (pronounced like the last two syllables of *phonemic*) refers to descriptive reports about what insiders say and understand about their culture.

Being a participant means that the researcher tries to adopt the lifestyle of the people being studied, living in the same kind of housing, eating similar food, wearing similar clothing, learning the language, and participating in the daily round of activities and in special events. Participation over a long period improves the quality of the data. The more time the researcher spends living a "normal" life in the field area, the more likely it is that the people being studied will also live "normal" lives. In this way, the researcher is able to overcome the Hawthorne effect, a phenomenon first discovered in the 1930s during a study of an industrial plant in the United States, in

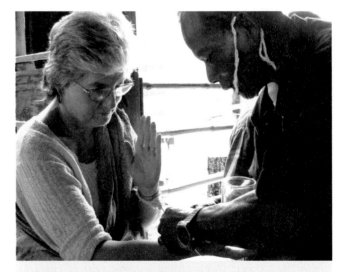

Anthropologist Penny Van Esterik participates in a "spirit calling" ceremony in Northern Laos.

which informants altered their behaviour in ways that they thought would please the researcher.

No matter how well accepted into everyday life the anthropologist becomes, however, the very nature of anthropological research and the presence of the anthropologist will have an effect on the people involved. Since the 1980s, anthropologists have increasingly considered how their presence affects their fieldwork and their findings, an approach called reflexive anthropology or reflexivity. An emphasis on reflexivity involves "constant awareness, assessment, and reassessment by the researcher of the researcher's own contribution [to and] influence [on] intersubjective research and the consequent research findings" (Salzman 2002:806). This approach is certainly a good corrective to the assumption that an anthropologist can go to the field and conduct research just as a scientist can in a lab. Working closely with real people in their everyday lives is a highly interactive and mutually influencing process: Everyone is changed in some way through the anthropological enterprise because it is a social process itself.

While participating in everyday life, the researcher carefully and thoroughly observes everything that is going on: who lives with whom, who interacts with whom in public, who are leaders and who are followers, what work people do, how people organize themselves for different activities, and far more. Obviously, not everything can be covered. Unstructured observations form the basis for a daily fieldnote diary in which the researcher attempts to record as much detail as possible about what has been observed. This process generates masses of qualitative data.

More formal methods of gathering quantitative data involve planned observations of a particular activity. One type of quantitative observational research is time allocation study, which can be an important tool for understanding people's behaviour: work and leisure patterns, social interactions and group boundaries, and religious activities. This method relies on using Western time units as the basic matrix and then labelling or coding the activities that occur within certain time segments (Gross 1984). Each coding system corresponds to its particular context. For example, activity codes for types of "garden labour" designed for a horticultural society—burning, cutting, fencing, planting, soil preparation, weeding, and harvesting—would not be useful in a time allocation study in a retirement home. Observation may be continual, at fixed intervals (for instance, every 48 hours), or on a random basis. Continuous observation limits the number of people who can be observed because it is so time-consuming. Spot observations may inadvertently miss important activities. In order to increase coverage, time allocation data can be collected by asking people to keep daily logs or diaries. Of course, self-reporting may include intentional or unintentional biases, but observations by the researcher can help correct some of these.

A philosophically interesting question arises about whether a truly emic ethnographic representation of a culture can be provided by anyone—either insider or outsider—because the very concept of ethnography is etic. Ethnography, even of the most descriptive kind, necessarily involves the abstraction of selected aspects of a culture. Even when an insider (or native) of a culture writes an ethnography about it, etic categories are likely to appear, such as "kinship" or "social inequality." No pure etic exists, either. A cultural anthropologist's etic framework logically is part of that particular person's emic world. Nevertheless, these two terms are "shorthand" reminders of different ways to understand what people do and think, and why.

Whether an anthropologist adopts an emic or etic approach, or uses more deductive or inductive methods during fieldwork, all cultural anthropologists seek to know about a culture from multiple perspectives. A cultural anthropologist circles around a culture, moving from person to person and context to context. The researcher sees the culture from multiple viewpoints and has the privilege, later, of sitting back from the data and analyzing how it all fits together. Most individuals, in their normal lives, do not have the opportunity of doing such intensive research and analysis of their own lives and cultures.

Interviews and Questionnaires

In contrast to observing and recording events as they happen, an **interview**, or the gathering of verbal data through questions or guided conversation, is a more purposeful approach to research. An interview involves at least two people, the interviewer and the interviewee, and more during "group" interviews. Cultural anthropologists use varying interview styles and formats, depending on the kinds of information they seek, the amount of time they have, and their language skills (for an alternative to the usual interview method see the Multiple Cultural Worlds box). The least structured type of interview is called "open-ended." In an open-ended interview, the respondent (interviewee) takes the lead in setting the direction of the conversation, the topics to be covered, and the amount of time to be spent on a particular topic. The interviewer does not interrupt or provide prompting questions. In this way, the researcher discovers what themes are important to the respondent.

Surveys and questionnaires administered during an interview session, in contrast, are more formal since they involve structured questions. Structured questions limit the range of possible responses, for example, by asking informants to rate their positions on a particular issue as very positive, positive, negative, very negative, or "no

Multiple Cultural Worlds

RESEARCHING A HAKKA COMMUNITY IN CYBERSPACE

COMPUTER-MEDIATED communication (CMC), such as email, allows people who have never met to communicate with each other (Cheung 1998). It allows people to express opinions and share information in a participatory, rather than "top-down," way as in the case with television or journalism. CMC creates virtual social networks and contributes to the formation of new cultural patterns. Eriberto Lozada, a doctoral dissertation student at Harvard University, studied a "Hakka community in cyberspace" (1998:148). Many years ago, the Hakka people of southern China were mainly village-dwelling agriculturalists. Now, Hakka communities can be found in many countries, including Canada, the United States, Indonesia, and Malaysia. Lozada has done participant observation in a Hakka village in China in addition to studying the Hakka Global Network (HGN).

Hakka people worldwide are actively building websites about Hakka culture and promoting transnational communication at levels that would not have been imagined 10 years ago. Lozada conducted what he calls participant observation over the internet for nearly two years. Using a search engine (WebCrawler), he searched for websites that had the word "Hakka" and found five listings. He joined one website and soon began receiving numerous messages. Over the years, he collected many email messages, which form his data set. His analysis was of the messages themselves, not the people, since he had little data on the people other than that they tend to be highly educated people scattered around the world.

Thus, this is a study of discourse and its possible meanings for the people involved. Lozada's analysis of the messages involved the search for persistent themes. Overall, he found that the prominent theme is preservation of Hakka culture in the face of global forces of change. Many of the messages provided announcements about television or radio broadcasts carrying items about Hakka culture; others included discussions of the Hakka language, origins, and customs. Many people requested information, such as the person who wrote about his grandfather who had immigrated to Borneo and died in a certain village; he asked if anyone knew the location of that village (158).

What can a cultural anthropologist learn about cyberspace Hakka culture from studying these websites and discussions and exchanges taking place between people who have never met? One conclusion of Lozada's is that through HGN, the Hakka are creating a "local global community," a new form of cultural organization that helps them deal with the present and shape the future in ways that no one can predict.

FOOD FOR THOUGHT

How does traditional participant observation differ from the participant observation that Lozada conducted?

What ethical problems might Lozada face in conducting this research?

opinion." Ideally, the researcher should have enough familiarity with the study population to be able to design a formal questionnaire or survey that makes cultural sense. One anthropologist (Beyene 1989) dedicated time to an exploratory research phase in order to obtain background information before beginning formal interviews in her comparative study of women's reproductive experiences in Mexico and Greece:

> During this initial phase of participant observation, I obtained data on women and their roles and activities, conducting unstructured and informal interviews with persons in the communities. Unstructured interviews were conducted with key informants such as older women, traditional healers, midwives, and medical personnel in the health services and clinics that served the villagers. As the

process of participant observation and informal interviewing unfolded, a series of culturally relevant categories and information was developed around the issues of the menopausal experiences of women in the villages, which became the topics for the formal interviews. (6)

Researchers who take ready-made questionnaires to the field with them should, at the minimum, ask another researcher who knows the field area to review the instrument to see if it makes cultural sense. Additional revisions of the questionnaire may be required in the field to make it more appropriate to local conditions. A pilot survey, or trial run, before proceeding with a formal survey will reveal areas that need to be changed before the final version is used and should be considered an essential step.

Marjorie Shostak (right) during fieldwork among the Ju/wasi of Botswana in 1975. Shostak focused her research on women's lives and wrote about Nisa, a Ju/wasi woman.

Combining Watching and Asking

Many cultural anthropologists agree that formal interviews and questionnaires must be complemented by observational data on what people actually do (Sanjek 2000). Consider this example of a study that relied on interview data alone to examine the relationship between personal characteristics and participation in a fishing cooperative in Newfoundland (Jentoft and Davis 1993). The Canadian and Norwegian researchers conducted formal interviews with a questionnaire among 51 members of the fishing cooperative. Questions probed such issues as whether members were willing to donate their time to cooperative projects, and what they valued most about the cooperative. On the basis of their responses, the researchers categorized the members into two basic groups: "rugged individualists" and "utilitarians." The people in the first group tended to be older and less educated than those in the latter group. According to the questionnaire responses, the rugged individualists were more willing to donate time to cooperative activities compared to the utilitarians. Since observational studies were not conducted, however, there is no way to know whether the respondents' self-reported participation in the cooperative corresponded to their actual involvement. Other research on the Canadian fishing industry examines the discourse of fishing. Adlam's study of "fish talk" among Mi'kmaq fishers of the Miramichi River, New Brunswick (2002), contrasts the traditionalist with the modernist conception of the rapidly changing fishing economy.

Other Data-Gathering Techniques

Besides participating, observing, and asking questions of various types, cultural anthropologists use many other methods to gather data to fit their project goals. This section provides a sample of some of these methods.

Kinship Data One of the oldest field methods in cultural anthropology involves collecting data on **kinship**, or people's knowledge and beliefs about who is related to whom and how. In most cases, kinship information can be obtained through structured interviews. But it is sometimes difficult to obtain accurate information. When Judith Okely (1993) was doing research on Gypsies in England, a Gypsy friend warned her during her research that she "could be burned" for writing down a family history (4). Kinship information can be useful for examining systems of inheritance, marriage choices, and even political relationships.

Life History A **life history** is a qualitative, in-depth portrait of a single life experience as narrated by that person to the researcher. A life history provides the most intimate possible perspective on a culture. For example, in *Life Lived Like a Story* (Cruikshank 1990), three First Nations women living in the Yukon recount their life experiences through family genealogies, personal recollections, and traditional stories.

Anthropologists differ in their views about the value of the life history as a method in cultural anthropology, however. Early in the twentieth century, Franz Boas rejected this method as too unreliable since informants might lie or exaggerate (Peacock and Holland 1993). One of his students, Paul Radin, disagreed, however. He believed that "personal reminiscences and impressions" would throw light on the "workings of the mind" (1963 [1920]:2). Radin's publication of the autobiography of a Winnebago Indian of Wisconsin, referred to only by his initials S.B., reveals much about how his life course was affected by involvement in the Peyote Cult that was active in Nebraska. He provides vivid descriptions of the visions and feelings he had while under the influence of the drug peyote: "Now this is what I felt and saw. The one Earthmaker (god) is a spirit and that is what I felt and saw. All of us sitting there, we had all together one spirit or soul; at least that is what I learned. I instantly became the spirit and I was their spirit or soul. Whatever they thought of, I (immediately) knew it" (59).

Current understanding of cultural variation throws into question the possibility of ever finding people who are representative of an entire culture. Thus, some anthropologists seek informants who occupy a particular social niche; for example, Gananath Obeyesekere's book *Medusa's Hair: An Essay on Personal Symbols and*

Religious Experience (1981) presents the life histories of four Sri Lankan people, three women and one man. Each one became a religious devotee and ascetic, physically distinguished by their thickly matted hair, which became mysteriously twisted in a snake-like fashion. According to these four people, they cannot comb out their hair: It is permanently matted. The devotees explain that the god's presence is in their hair. Using material in the life histories of these people, Obeyesekere provides an interpretation suggesting that they all suffered deep psychological afflictions, including sexual anxieties. Their matted hair symbolizes this suffering and provides them with a special status as holy and thus outside the bounds of normal married life and sexual relations.

Alternatively, life histories of several people within one social category can be collected to provide a picture of both shared experiences and individual differences. James Freeman's book *Hearts of Sorrow* (1989) is an example of this approach. It presents "cuts" from several life stories of Vietnamese refugees living in southern California. Together, the story cuts portray both a shared sadness of the refugees about the loss of their homeland and a range of adaptive experiences of the different individuals.

The ability of informants to "present" a story of their lives varies, depending on the cultural context. An attempt to gather life histories from women on Goodenough Island of Papua New Guinea was difficult because telling one's life story is a masculine style of presentation and the women were reluctant to adopt it (M. Young 1983). Marjorie Shostak (1981), in contrast, found a willing and extremely expressive informant for a life story in Nisa, an indigenous woman of the Ju/wasi of the Kalahari Desert in southern Africa. Nisa's book-length story, presented in her voice, includes rich details about her childhood and several marriages.

Texts Many cultural anthropologists, especially interpretive anthropologists, emphasize the value of collecting and analyzing texts. The category of "text" includes written or oral stories, myths, plays, sayings, speeches, jokes, and transcriptions of people's everyday conversations. In the early twentieth century, Franz Boas collected thousands of pages of texts from First Nations groups of the Northwest Coast of Canada, including myths, songs, speeches, and accounts of how to perform rituals. These texts are useful records of cultures that have changed since the time of his fieldwork. More recently, First Nations communities have made use of early ethnohistorical texts to assist them in recovering forgotten aspects of their culture.

Historical Sources History is culture of the past, and it therefore has much relevance to understanding contemporary cultures. Ann Stoler (1985, 1989) made excel-

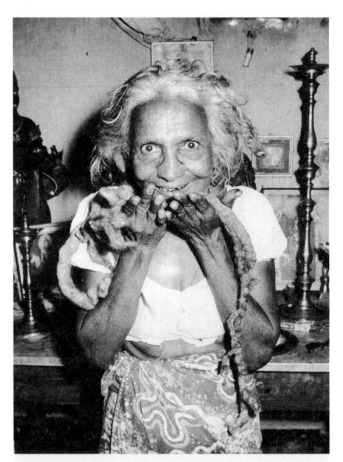

One of the Sri Lankan women whose life story Gananath Obeyesekere analyzed, a priestess to the deity Kataragama, stands in the shrine room of her house holding her long, matted hair.

lent use of archival resources in her study of Dutch colonialism in Java. Her research has exposed rich details about colonial strategies, the culture of the colonizers themselves, and their impact on indigenous Javanese culture. Most countries have libraries and historical archives in which written records of the past are maintained. Local official archives are rich sources of information about land ownership, agricultural production, religious practices, and political activities. London, Paris, and Amsterdam contain records of colonial contact and relations. The National Archives of Canada, provincial archives, and mission reports provided valuable evidence on the development of residential schools for Native peoples in Canada (D. Smith 2001). Meticulous record keeping in France meant that Harriet Rosenberg (1988) had access to information about dowries, wills, marriage contracts, court cases, land survey registers, tax rolls, and family histories for reconstructing the history of a village in the French Alps.

Fieldwork among living people can also yield rich historical information. Several methods exist to help the anthropologist delve into the cultural past. When investigating the recent past of Native American culture in New England, William Simmons (1986) knocked on doors of houses where the mailboxes had names that seemed of possible Native American heritage. He sometimes discovered long-forgotten diaries and family memorabilia tucked away in the closets and attics of these homes. Interviewing older informants about what they remember can often reveal not only events about their earlier lives but also history that they were told by their parents and grandparents.

Anthropologists study patterns of what people remember and what they don't, how culture shapes their memories, and how their memories shape their culture. Information on how memory is shaped exists in collections of letters, diaries, and family photograph albums. The importance of memory, not simply as a record of history but as interpretive reconstruction, is increasing in anthropology (Antze and Lambek 1996) and in the public domain.

Multiple Research Methods and Team Projects Most cultural anthropologists use several different methods for their research, since just one would not provide all the kinds of data necessary to understand a given problem. For example, a small survey of 40 households provides some breadth of coverage, but adding some life histories (of five men and five women, perhaps) provides depth. **Triangulation** is a technique that involves obtaining information on a particular topic from more than one angle or perspective (Robson 1993:290). Asking only one person something provides information from only that person's viewpoint. Asking two people about the same thing doubles the information and often reveals that perspectives differ. The researcher may then want to check other sources on the same topic, such as written records or newspaper reports for additional perspectives.

In Canada, team research may also involve several anthropologists and students working together with members of First Nations communities to document land claims or assess the consequences of new hydroelectric development projects for their communities. The James Bay Cree Project, which began in 1971 at McGill University in Montreal, trained graduate students in anthropology to do research for local agencies representing indigenous groups, providing information useful in settling the James Bay land claim (Trigger 1997; Salisbury 1986). (See the Lessons Applied box for another example of team research in Canada.)

Another way of gaining a more complex and complete view is through team projects that involve cultural anthropologists and researchers from other disciplines who provide additional skills. A research project designed to assess the effects of constructing a dam on the agricultural and fishing practices of people in the Senegal River Valley, West Africa, included cultural anthropologists, hydrologists, and agronomists (Horowitz and Salem-Murdock 1993). In another project, a cultural anthropologist and a nutritionist worked together to study the effects of adopting new agricultural practices in the Amazon (Gross and Underwood 1971).

Recording Culture

Imagine the cultural anthropologist in the field—participating, observing, conducting interviews, and using other techniques such as asking people to keep records of their time allocation. How does the anthropologist keep track of all this information and record it for future analysis? As with everything else about fieldwork, things have changed since the early times when a typewriter, index cards, and pencils were the major recording tools. Still, there is continuity: Taking copious notes is still the trademark method of recording data for a cultural anthropologist. This section begins with a discussion of note taking, a process that you may think is simple and needs no elaboration. But when you are in the field for a year—even for a month—you will find that "just" taking notes is quite complicated. After discussing note taking, we turn to other forms of recording data, including tape recording, photography, and video.

Field Notes

The classic impression of anthropological research is that of the cultural anthropologist observing a ritual, with notebook and pen in hand. From the beginning of cultural

A multidisciplinary team consisting of anthropologists, engineers, and agricultural experts from North America and Senegal meet to discuss a resettlement project.

Lessons Applied

MULTIPLE METHODS IN A NEEDS ASSESSMENT STUDY

THE UNITED WAY of Canada, a philanthropic agency, wanted to find out what the highest priorities were for their funding operations in Saskatoon, Saskatchewan (Ervin et al. 1991; van Willigen 1993:204–205). Anthropologist Alexander Ervin led a team of researchers from the University of Saskatchewan's Department of Anthropology and Archaeology to respond to the United Way's request. At the time of the study in 1990, the city's population was about 200 000. The economy includes agriculture, mining, forestry, and some manufacturing. The unemployment rate was 10 percent, and food banks and soup kitchens were being increasingly used.

The team designed its research to provide baseline data on perceived social needs to assist the United Way in decision making. The assessment included six data collection activities: reviewing available written reports relevant to Saskatoon's needs, analyzing economic and social indicators, organizing 3 public forums, conducting 135 interviews with key informants from community agencies, holding 6 focus groups, and interviewing 28 United Way agency executive directors. These activities provided breadth and depth about community opinion and agency priorities and interests.

The research team produced a report that included a list of over 200 needs identified. The list was organized into 17 sectors, among them general health, mental health, the senior population, First Nations issues, racism and discrimination, and immigrant and refugee resettlement. The report also included a set of recommendations for the United Way.

FOOD FOR THOUGHT

Conducting a community needs assessment entails a research approach quite different from traditional fieldwork in cultural anthropology. What are some of the pros and cons of anthropologists conducting such applied research?

---

anthropology, field notes have been the basic way to record observations. Field notes include daily logs, personal journals, descriptions of events, and notes about those notes. Ideally, researchers should "write up" their field notes each day. Otherwise, a backlog piles up of daily "scratch notes," or rough jottings made on a small pad or note card carried in the pocket (Sanjek 1990:95–99). Trying to capture, in the fullest way possible, the events of a single day is a monumental task and can result in dozens of pages of handwritten or typed field notes each day. The bulk of an anthropologist's time in the field is probably spent taking rough notes by hand. The invention of the laptop computer now allows anthropologists to enter many of these notes directly into the computer.

Tape Recording, Photography, Videos, and Films

Tape recorders are an obvious aid to fieldwork because they allow the accurate recording of much more information than taking notes by hand. However, tape recording may raise problems such as informants' suspicions about a machine that can capture their voices, and the ethical issue of maintaining anonymity of informants whose actual voices are preserved on tape. María Cátedra

(1992) reports on her use of tape recording during research in rural Spain in the 1970s:

> At first the existence of the "apparatus," as they called it, was part wonder and part suspect. Many had never seen one before and were fascinated to hear their own voice, but all were worried about what I would do with the tapes. . . . I tried to solve the problem by explaining what I would do with the tapes: I would use them to record correctly what people told me, since my memory was not good enough and I could not take notes quickly enough. . . . One event helped people to accept my integrity in regard to the "apparatus." In the second *braña* [small settlement] I visited, people asked me to play back what the people of the first *braña* had told me, especially some songs sung by a group of men. At first I was going to do it, but then I instinctively refused because I did not have the first people's permission. . . . My stand was quickly known in the first *braña* and commented on with approval. (21–22)

A problem with tape recordings is that they have to be transcribed (typed up), either partially or completely. Each hour of recorded talk takes between five to eight hours to transcribe, on average. Even more time is needed if the recording is garbled, many voices are heard at once, or complications in translation arise.

Like tape recordings, photographs, films, or videos may catch and retain more detail than rough notes. Any

---

researcher who has watched people doing a ritual, taken rough notes, and then tried to reconstruct the details of the ritual later on in more detailed field notes knows how much of the sequencing and related activity is lost to memory within just a few hours. Reviewing photographs or a video recording of the ritual provides a surprising amount of forgotten, or missed, material. But there is a trade-off. Using a camera or video recorder precludes taking notes simultaneously. Since field notes are invaluable, even if the video is also available, it is best to use a team approach. Kirsten Hastrup (1992) provides an insightful description of her use of photography—and its limitations—in recording the annual ram exhibition in Iceland that celebrates the successful herding in of the sheep from mountain pastures. Hastrup took many photographs. After they were developed, she was struck by how flat they were and how little of the totality of the event they conveyed. Photographs and films, just like field notes and other forms of recorded culture, provide only partial images of a cultural event.

Rosalind Morris (1994a) examined ethnographic films of the Northwest Coast of Canada. From the earliest films made of the Northwest Coast (1914), the Kwakwaka'wakw, Nootka, Tsimshian, and Haida, in addition to other First Nations peoples, have been represented by outsiders who made films that drew attention to potlatches, feasts, totem poles, and wood carvings. More recently, films have been made by and for First Nations communities, and they focus more on land-claim disputes and other struggles with provincial and federal governments (Morris 1994a:118). Clearly, films are no more objective than any other form of recorded culture since it is the researcher who selects what the camera will capture. (See the Critical Thinking box for a discussion of the interpretation of ethnographic photographs.)

Data Analysis

During the research process, a vast amount of data in many forms is collected. The question is how to use these data to increase our understanding of human societies. Ethnographic research mostly entails qualitative, prose-based analysis, in combination with quantitative (numeric) data where appropriate. Qualitative data can be rendered in quantitative terms, and reporting on quantitative results necessarily requires descriptive analysis of local conditions to accompany graphs, charts, and computations.

Analyzing Qualitative Data

Qualitative data include descriptive field notes, informants' narratives, myths and stories, and songs and sagas. Relatively few set guidelines exist for undertaking qualitative analysis of qualitative data. One general procedure of qualitative analysis is to search for themes, or regularities, in the data. This approach involves exploring the data, or "playing" with the data, either "by hand" or with the use of a computer. Jennifer Robertson's analysis of her Kodaira data was inspired by writer Gertrude Stein's approach to writing "portraits" of individuals, such as *Picasso* (1959). Robertson says that Stein was a superb ethnographer who was able to illuminate the nature of her subjects and their worlds through a process that Stein referred to as "condensation." To do this, "she scrutinized her subjects until, over time, there emerged for her a repeating pattern of their words and actions. Her literary portraits . . . were condensations of her subjects' repeatings" (Robertson 1991:1). Like Stein, Robertson reflected on all that she had experienced and learned in Kodaira, beginning with the years when she lived there as a child. Emerging from all this was the dominant theme, *furusato*, which literally means "old village." References to *furusato* appear frequently in people's accounts of the past, conveying a sense of nostalgia for a more "real" past.

Many qualitative anthropologists use computers to help sort for **tropes** (key themes). Computer scanning of data offers the ability to search vast quantities of data more quickly and perhaps more accurately than is possible using the human eye. The range of software available for such data management, for example ETHNO and The Ethnograph, is expanding. Of course, the quality of the results depends on, first, careful and complete inputting of the data and, second, an intelligent coding scheme that will tell the computer what it should be scanning for in the data.

The ethnographic presentation of qualitative data relies heavily on the use of quotations of informants—their stories, explanations, and conversations. Although most ethnographies also include analytical commentary, some provide just the informants' words. Lila Abu-Lughod followed this approach in her book, *Writing Women's Worlds* (1993). She presents Bedouin women's stories and conversations within a light authorial framework that organizes the stories into thematic clusters such as marriage, production, and honour. Although she provides a rather traditional, scholarly introduction to the narratives, she offers no conclusion. In her view, a conclusion would give a false sense of authorial control over the narratives. She prefers to prompt readers to think for themselves about the meanings of the stories and what they say about Bedouin life.

Some anthropologists question the value of interpretive analyses on the ground that they lack verifiability or reliability: Too much depends on the individual selection process of the anthropologist, and too much is built around too few cases. Most anthropologists would respond that

Critical Thinking

PHOTOGRAPHY AND ANTHROPOLOGY

SINCE BOOKS were first written in anthropology, many authors illustrated their ethnographies with black and white photographs of their "subjects." *Anthropology and Photography 1860–1920* (Edwards 1992) examines the parallel development of anthropology and photography as cameras enabled "exotic" peoples to be viewed by an external audience. Contemporary ethnographies continue this practice, hopefully with more sensitivity and reflection about the representation of others.

Textbooks in anthropology also use illustrations to draw the eyes and interests of students (and to break up the text), to illustrate abstract principles in the discipline, and to provide visual images of the people discussed in the text. Photographs relate to textual arguments in distinctive ways; they may supplement, complement, or even contradict written accounts. They may be arranged in groups to suggest comparison, or juxtaposed in a striking manner to illustrate change. They often document a technical process or a material object that may be unfamiliar to the reader and difficult to describe in words.

Photographs may be "worth a thousand words," but they never speak for themselves. Their meanings are shaped by the interaction between the producer of the image, the subject of the image, and the viewer. You may have a personal response to a photograph that may be quite unlike the response the photographer intended. The choice of photograph to be inserted into the text is determined by the authors and publishers; thus, the set of photographs in a textbook already represents a selection of what others think is instructive. Even captions draw attention to how you are expected to analyze photographs. Thus, the photograph is never a snapshot of reality, but something that must be interpreted.

CRITICAL THINKING QUESTIONS

To improve your "visual literacy," consider each of the photographs used in this textbook:

What questions does the photograph raise for you?

How might the presence of the camera alter the event recorded in the photo?

How do you think the community or subject of the photograph would react to the use of the photo in a textbook of anthropology?

What ethical issues are raised by the use of this photograph?

Select a photograph that illustrates rapport, ethnocentrism, gender inequity, racism, globalization, acculturation, or other concept.

Suggest an alternative caption for the photograph.

What does the photograph say about the culture portrayed and the representing culture?

verifiability in the scientific sense is not their goal and it is not a worthwhile goal for cultural anthropology in general. Instead, they seek to provide a plausible interpretation, an evocation, or new understanding that has detail and richness as its strengths rather than replicability. They would criticize purely quantitative research for its lack of richness and depth of understanding, even though it has the appearance of validity.

Analyzing Quantitative Data

Analysis of quantitative, or numeric data, can proceed in several directions. Some of the more sophisticated methods require knowledge of statistics, and many require the use of a computer and a software package that can perform statistical computations. In Barbara Miller's (1987a) research on low-income household budgeting patterns in Jamaica, she used computer analysis first to divide the sample households into three income groups (lower, medium, higher). She then used the computer to calculate percentages of expenditures in the three categories on individual goods and groups of goods, such as food, alcohol, dry goods, housing, and transportation (see Table 2.1). Because the number of households in the study was relatively small (120), the analysis could have been done "by hand." However, using the computer helped the analysis proceed more quickly and more accurately.

Writing about Culture

Ethnography, or writing about culture, is one of the main projects of cultural anthropology. Ethnographies range across a continuum from realist to reflexive. Realist and reflexive ethnographies both provide insights about culture, and both are valid presentations of something about culture by someone from another culture who is participating in the culture being described. In realist ethnographies, authors include less material about themselves directly in the text. In a realist ethnography, a single author typically narrates the findings in a dispassionate, third-person voice. The ethnography includes attention to the behaviour of members of the culture, theoretical analysis of certain features of the culture, and usually a brief account of why the work was undertaken. The result is a description and explanation of certain cultural practices. Realist ethnographies appear to follow a more scientific approach and attempt to present findings that more than one person would be able to discover about another culture. Most early works by such anthropologists as Malinowski, Mead, and Radcliffe-Brown are in the category of realist ethnography, which is still the predominant form of ethnography. For example, Katherine Verdery's study of economic and political change in Romania, *What Was Socialism, and What Comes Next?* (1996), is a realist ethnography. In this book she presents both description and analysis about how Romanian socialism operated politically and economically and how its effects are now being felt in terms of Romanian nationalism and nationalist sentiments in the post-socialist era. A clear argument threads through the descriptive material: Verdery says that socialism did not cause the current conflicts and senti-

ments about Romanian nationhood, but it did contribute to them by perpetuating and intensifying them.

In contrast, reflexive ethnographies explore the research experience itself, in addition to generating or presenting wider theoretical arguments and analysis: "The story itself . . . is a representational means of cracking open the culture and the fieldworker's way of knowing it" (Van Maanen 1988:103). Reflexive ethnographies are distinguished by the degree to which the authors include their fieldwork experience as an important part of the ethnography. They are thus characterized by highly personalized styles and findings. In contrast to realist ethnographies, reflexive ethnographers frequently use the word *I* in their writings. Reflexive ethnographers offer more poetically insightful perspectives that might not be perceived or grasped by anyone except the particular anthropologist involved. An example in this category is Vincent Crapanzano's (1980) classic study, *Tuhami*, which explores the life history of a Moroccan man who believed he was possessed by spirits. Crapanzano interweaves the effects of his own presence and perspectives into an understanding of the ethnography. Crapanzano explains, "As Tuhami's interlocutor, I became an active participant in his life history. . . . Not only did my presence, and my questions, prepare him for the text he was to produce, but they produced what I read as a change of consciousness in him. They produced a change of consciousness in me, too" (11).

TABLE 2.1 Mean Weekly Expenditure Shares (Percentage) in Eleven Categories by Urban and Rural Expenditure Groups, Jamaica, 1983–1984

Item	Urban				Rural			
	Group 1	Group 2	Group 3	Total	Group 1	Group 2	Group 3	Total
Number of Households	26	25	16	67	32	30	16	78
Food	60.5	51.6	50.1	54.7	74.1	62.3	55.7	65.8
Alcohol	0.2	0.4	1.5	0.6	0.5	1.1	1.0	0.8
Tobacco	0.8	0.9	0.9	0.9	1.1	1.7	1.2	1.4
Dry Goods	9.7	8.1	8.3	8.7	8.8	10.2	14.3	10.5
Housing	7.3	11.7	10.3	9.7	3.4	5.7	3.9	4.4
Fuel	5.4	6.0	5.0	5.6	3.7	3.9	4.1	3.9
Transportation	7.4	8.2	12.4	8.9	3.0	5.3	7.6	4.9
Health	0.3	0.6	0.7	0.5	1.5	1.4	1.7	1.5
Education	3.5	2.8	3.1	3.2	1.2	2.1	3.0	1.9
Entertainment	0.1	0.9	1.1	0.6	0.0	0.1	0.3	0.2
Other	5.2	8.3	6.9	6.8	2.1	6.0	6.9	4.6
Total*	100.4	99.5	100.3	100.2	99.4	99.8	99.7	99.9

*Totals may not add up to 100 due to rounding.

Source: From "Social Patterns of Food Expenditure Among Low-Income Jamaicans" by Barbara D. Miller in *Papers and Recommendations of the Workshop on Food and Nutrition Security in Jamaica in the 1980s and Beyond*, ed. by Kenneth A. Leslie and Lloyd B. Rankine (Kingston, Jamaica: Caribbean Food and Nutrition Institute, 1987).

SPECIAL ISSUES IN FIELDWORK

This section considers some enduring and emerging issues in anthropological fieldwork. The first topic is the important matter of fieldwork ethics. No one should undertake any kind of research without training in ethical principles and careful consideration of how to protect people involved in the project from harm. The second topic is that of danger to the researcher while conducting fieldwork. Last is a topic of emerging importance: accountability in cultural anthropology. Our discussion of this topic includes questions of who benefits from the research and how, and in what way the research can be relevant to the people studied.

Fieldwork Ethics

Anthropology was one of the first disciplines to devise and adopt a code of ethics. Two major events in the 1950s and 1960s led American anthropologists to reconsider their role in research in relation to both the sponsors (or funders) of their research and the people whom they were studying. The first was the infamous "Project Camelot" of the 1950s. Project Camelot was a plan of the United States government to influence political leadership and stability in South America (Horowitz 1967). To further this goal, the United States government employed several anthropologists, who were to gather detailed information on political events and leaders in particular countries without revealing their purpose, and then report back to their sponsor (the United States government) about their findings. It is still unclear whether the anthropologists involved were completely informed about the purposes to which their data would be put.

The second major event was the Vietnam War (or the American War, as it is called in Vietnam). This brought to the forefront conflicts about government interests in ethnographic information, the role of the anthropologist, and the protection of the people studied. American anthropologists were recruited and funded to provide information that could help subvert communism in Vietnam and Thailand (Wakin 1992). The Vietnam War affected Canadian anthropology, as many anthropologists participated in teach-ins and anti-war protests, and many departments of anthropology absorbed American draft resistors as graduate students and professors, aligning some Canadian departments more closely with American ones.

In 1970, a standard code of ethics was adopted by the American Anthropological Association (AAA). This code states that the anthropologist's primary responsibility is to ensure the safety of the people being studied. A related principle is that cultural anthropology does not condone covert or "undercover" research. The people being studied should be informed that they are being studied and the purposes for which they are being studied. Long a practice in biomedical research, the principle of **informed consent** requires that the researcher fully inform the research participants of the intent, scope, and possible effects of the study and seek their consent to be in the study. Anthropologists have adapted the concept of informed consent to make it applicable to the varied contexts in which cultural anthropologists work (Fluehr-Lobban 1994).

Canadian anthropologists face new ethical demands as they must now conform to the ethics policies of cross-disciplinary research agencies, in addition to meeting university and anthropology standards. Many anthropologists say that the nature of anthropological research often makes it difficult to apply the strict standards of informed consent that are used in medical settings. For example, people in non-literate societies may be frightened by being asked to sign a typed document of consent that they cannot read. Given that the intent of informed consent is a good one—people should be aware of the purpose and scope and possible effects of a study involving them—each anthropologist should consider some way to achieve this goal. Holding a "town meeting" with all community members present and explaining the research project is one approach.

In presenting the results of one's research, whether in a book or a film, all efforts should be made to protect the anonymity of the people in the study unless they give permission for their identities to be revealed. The usual practice in writing ethnographies has been to change the name of the specific group, area, or village, blur the location, and use made-up names for individuals mentioned.

Some topics are more sensitive than others, and some topics are sensitive to some groups and not others (Lee and Renzetti 1993). Governments may decree that certain subjects are simply off limits for research by foreigners. Strictly speaking, an anthropologist should abide by the ethical guideline stating that rulings of host governments are to be respected. Sometimes, such rules can be highly restrictive. For example, the Indian government allows no foreigners to visit the Nicobar Islands, and it has strict regulations that limit how long foreigners—tourists or anthropologists—can spend in the Andamans (only 30 days). Major factors influencing the extreme sensitivity of the Indian government about foreigners in the Andaman and Nicobar Islands include the islands' strategic location near Myanmar (Burma) and Indonesia, and the need to protect the indigenous peoples from unwanted contact.

Anthropologists researching First Nations communities in Canada must follow stringent guidelines and be approved by band councils, as well as obtaining the usual ethics approvals discussed above. Research is conducted in partnership with the council and community, and the results of research are expected to be shared with the community, although individuals retain the right to privacy.

Sexual behaviour is another important example of a potentially sensitive research topic, more from the point of view of informants than host governments. Sexual practices and ideas cannot be researched in depth without excellent rapport. In most cultures, homosexuality is even more difficult to research than heterosexuality because it may contravene mainstream norms or even laws.

Danger in the Field

Fieldwork can involve serious physical and psychological risks to the researcher and to members of his or her family if they are also in the field. A pervasive value on "the anthropologist as hero" has muffled, to a large degree, both the physical dangers and psychological risks of fieldwork. An inquiry into the hazards faced by anthropologists while conducting fieldwork—including mental health problems—has brought more attention to fieldwork safety. Based on the fieldwork experiences of anthropologists, specific recommendations were made about how fieldworkers can prepare themselves more effectively for risks they might face (Howell 1990). Some departments (including many in Canada) require students to submit a form indicating that they are aware of possible risks in the field and have taken precautions to ensure that their fieldwork will be as safe as possible.

Dangers from the physical environment can be fatal. The slippery paths of the highlands of the Philippines caused the death in the early 1980s of Michelle Zimbalist Rosaldo, one of the major figures in contemporary cultural anthropology. Disease is another major risk factor. Many anthropologists have contracted contagious diseases, such as malaria and typhoid, which stay with them throughout their lives. Bernard Deacon, a young British anthropologist who went to Malekula, a South Pacific island, was a victim of tropical disease (Gardiner 1984). His memoir, composed of letters he wrote from the field and published after his death by the woman he would have married on his return, records his observations of the prevalence of disease among the Malekulans:

> I am terribly overstrained, my work here seems all to be going to bits. There seems nothing here but Death—a man was dead in the village this morning of dysentery. . . . In one village of 20, 9 died in one week. . . . It's not like death in war or crisis—it is the final death, the death of a people, a race, and they know it more clearly than we do. . . .

Spanish influenza has wiped out whole villages in Santo, Pentecost & Malekula, one might say districts. As for work, I despair & despair again. (34–35)

A few days before he was to leave the field, Deacon caught blackwater fever, which caused his death at the age of 24.

Social violence in the field figures prominently in some recent ethnographic research experiences. During the five years that Philippe Bourgois lived in East Harlem, he witnessed a shooting outside his window, a bombing and machine-gunning of a numbers joint, a shoot-out and police car chase in front of the pizza parlour where he was eating, the aftermath of a fire-bombing of a heroin house, a dozen serious fights, and "almost daily exposure to broken-down human beings, some of them in fits of crack-induced paranoia, some suffering from delirium tremens, and others in unidentifiable pathological fits of screaming and shouting insults to all around them" (1995:32). He was rough-handled by the police several times because they could not believe that he was "just a professor" doing research, and he was mugged for the sum of $8. Bourgois's research placed him in physical danger as well as psychological risk. Nevertheless, it also enabled him to gain understanding of oppression from the inside.

Accountability and Collaborative Research

The freedom of a cultural anthropologist to represent a culture as she or he perceives it is a power issue that is increasingly being brought into question, especially by indigenous peoples who read about themselves in Western ethnographies. The people that anthropologists have traditionally studied—the non-elites of rural India, Ireland, and Papua New Guinea—are now able to read English, French, and German. They can therefore critique what has been written about their culture. Annette Weiner (1976) learned from people in the Trobriand Islands that some Trobrianders who had read sections of *Argonauts of the Western Pacific* thought that Malinowski had not gotten things right (xvi).

One of the newest directions in cultural anthropology fieldwork is the attempt to involve the study population in actively shaping the data collection and presentation. This change reflects an interest on the part of anthropologists to refrain from treating people as "subjects" and to consider them more as collaborators in writing culture. However, anthropologists must continue to take full responsibility for the effects that their work may have on the communities they study.

HOW do cultural anthropologists conduct research on culture?

Cultural anthropologists conduct research by doing fieldwork and using its characteristic method, called participant observation. Fieldwork and participant observation became the cornerstones of cultural anthropology research after Malinowski's fieldwork in the Trobriand Islands during World War I. These methods emphasize the importance of living for an extended period of time with the people being studied and learning the local language.

WHAT does fieldwork involve?

Some basic steps in doing fieldwork have been established since the time of Malinowski. They include site selection, gaining rapport, and dealing with culture shock. Depending on one's theoretical perspective, specific research techniques may emphasize quantitative or qualitative data gathering. Cultural materialists tend to focus on quantitative data while interpretive anthropologists gather more qualitative data. Taking notes by hand has always been the hallmark of data recording, but now it is complemented by other methods, including laptop computers, photography, and audio and video recording. Data

analysis and presentation, like data collection, are guided by the anthropologist's theoretical orientation and goals. Emphasis on quantitative or qualitative techniques of data collection shape the way the data are organized and presented, for example, whether statistics and tables are used.

WHAT are some special issues in cultural anthropology research?

Questions of ethics have been paramount to anthropologists since the 1950s. American anthropologists developed a set of ethical guidelines for research in 1970 to address their concern about what role, if any, anthropologists should play in research that might harm the people being studied. The first rule listed in the AAA (American Anthropological Association) code of ethics states that the anthropologist's primary responsibility is to maintain the safety of the people involved. Thus, anthropologists should never engage in covert research and should always endeavour to explain their purpose to the people in the study and maintain anonymity of the location and individuals. Other special issues include the role, responsibility, and safety of anthropologists who are conducting research in dangerous conditions.

KEY CONCEPTS

culture shock, p. 33
deductive research, p. 34
discourse, p. 34
emic, p. 34
etic, p. 34
fieldwork, p. 26
inductive research, p. 34
informed consent, p. 44
interview, p. 35
kinship, p. 37

life history, p. 37
multi-sited research, p. 27
participant observation, p. 26
qualitative research, p. 34
quantitative research, p. 34
rapport, p. 30
research methods, p. 34
transnationalism, p. 28
triangulation, p. 39
tropes, p 41

SUGGESTED READINGS

H. Russell Bernard, *Research Methods in Cultural Anthropology: Qualitative and Quantitative Approaches*. 2nd edition. Newbury Park, CA: Sage Publications, 1995. This is a sourcebook of anthropological research methods—from how to design a research project to data analysis and presentation.

Sidney C. H. Cheung, *On the South China Track: Perspectives on Anthropological Research and Teaching*. Hong Kong: Hong Kong Institute of Asia-Pacific Studies, 1998. Thirteen chapters explore aspects of anthropological research and teaching in Chinese cultures including Hong Kong, China, Taiwan, and Singapore.

S. Cole and L. Phillips, *Ethnographic Feminisms*. Ottawa: Carleton University Press, 1995. This book of readings explores how feminist anthropologists have approached ethnography, and includes experimental approaches to writing ethnography in innovative ways.

Kathleen M. DeWalt and Billie R. DeWalt, *Participant Observation: A Guide for Fieldworkers*. New York: AltaMira Press, 2002. This book is a comprehensive guide to doing participant observation. It covers research design, taking field notes, data analysis, and theoretical issues.

Peggy Golde, ed., *Women in the Field: Anthropological Experiences*. 2nd edition. Berkeley: University of California Press, 1986. This text provides 15 chapters on fieldwork by women anthropologists, including Margaret Mead's fieldwork in the Pacific, Laura Nader's fieldwork in Mexico and Lebanon, Ernestine Friedl's fieldwork in Greece,

and Jean Briggs's fieldwork among the Inuit of the Canadian Arctic.

Bruce Grindal and Frank Salamone, eds., *Bridges to Humanity: Narratives on Anthropology and Friendship*. Prospect Heights, IL: Waveland Press, 1995. The 14 chapters of this text explore the "humanistic" dimension of fieldwork, in which the anthropologist reflects on the friendships established in the field, how they contributed to the fieldwork, and how or if they can be continued once the anthropologist leaves the field.

Joy Hendry, *An Anthropologist in Japan: Glimpses of Life in the Field*. London: Routledge, 1999. This book is a first-person account of the author's third research project in Japan, including information on her original research design, how the focus changed, and how she reached unanticipated conclusions.

Carolyn Nordstrom and Antonius C. G. M. Robben, eds., *Fieldwork under Fire: Contemporary Studies of Violence and Survival*. Berkeley: University of California Press, 1995. After an introductory chapter discussing general themes, examples are provided of fieldwork experiences in dangerous situations including Palestine, China, Sri Lanka, United States, Croatia, Guatemala, and Ireland.

Roger Sanjek, ed., *Fieldnotes: The Makings of Anthropology*. Ithaca: Cornell University Press, 1990. This text includes 16 chapters by cultural anthropologists on taking and using field notes in ethnographic research in diverse settings.

WEBLINKS

The Companion Website (www.pearsoned.ca/miller) that accompanies *Cultural Anthropology*, Third Canadian Edition, includes a destinations module containing links to many websites relevant to the content of this chapter. Use it to investigate the Web and expand your understanding of anthropology.

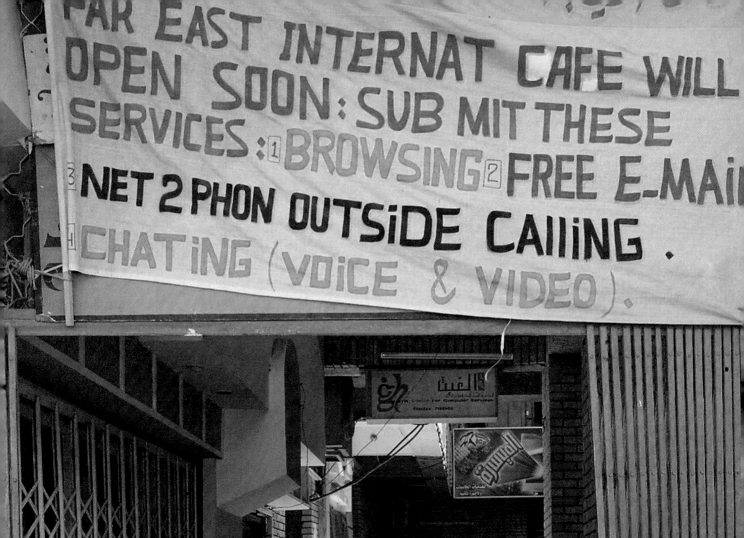

- **WHAT** is the scope of economic anthropology?
- **WHAT** are the characteristics of the five major modes of production?
- **WHAT** are some directions of change in the five modes of production?

3

ECONOMIES AND THEIR MODES OF PRODUCTION

After the war, residents of Baghdad had no running water, but many new businesses with international connections sprang up, including this internet café.

For thousands of years of human life, people made their living by gathering food and other basic necessities from nature. Everyone had equal access to life-sustaining resources. We now live in a rather different cultural world. A woman in Florida recently established the name of the Yanomami, an Amazonian tribe who live in the rainforest in Venezuela, for a Web site address. She was auctioning *www.yanomami.com*, for $25 000. When leaders of the 26 000 Yanomami people heard about this, they were not happy. In order to use their own tribal name for their site they would have to buy it. Private property has moved into the virtual realm.

Cultural anthropologists have long studied economic systems cross-culturally. In this globalizing world, they have to study that and much more: the new global economy, e-commerce, and how these changes affect economic systems that have existed for thousands of years.

In this chapter we explore how people make a living. This topic fits within the scope of the subfield of economic anthropology, which is the cross-cultural study of **economic systems**. Economic systems include three major areas: **production**, or making goods or money; **consumption**, or using up goods or money; and **exchange**, or the transfer of goods or money between people or institutions. This chapter looks at the first area. We review the characteristics of the five major **modes of production**, or the dominant way of making a living in a society, and we consider examples of change in each of these modes.

CULTURAL ANTHROPOLOGY AND ECONOMIC SYSTEMS

This section discusses two basic features of the study of production in cultural anthropology. The first is a brief introduction to the important modes of production, along with a discussion of how they are useful as categories, though, like all categories, they are not perfect. These categories provide the conceptual foundation for all the material that appears in subsequent chapters of this book, so you must know them well. Second, this section raises the question of whether people in all cultures make a sharp conceptual distinction between "culture" and "nature" as most people in Western/European cultures do. It appears that whether or not people do this is related to the kind of economic system in which they live.

Typologies: Modes of Production

In their study of production cross-culturally, cultural anthropologists have gathered rich data that are then placed into analytical categories, called modes of production. Categorizing a certain society as having a particular mode of production implies an emphasis on that type of production and does not mean that it is the only kind of production undertaken. In a given society, not everyone will necessarily be involved in the dominant mode of production. Also, a particular individual may be involved in more than one; for example, a person could be both a farmer and a herder. In most cultures, however, a dominant mode of production exists that analysts use as a basis for classification. These categories blend with and overlap each other, but they are nonetheless useful as broad generalizations.

The modes of production are discussed in order of their historical appearance in the human record. Please note, though, that this continuum does not mean that a particular mode of production evolves into the one following it—for example, foragers do not necessarily transform into horticulturalists—and so on, across the continuum. Nor does this ordering imply any kind of judgment about level of sophistication or superiority of the more recent modes of production. Even the oldest system involves complex and detailed knowledge about the environment that a contemporary city dweller, if transported to a rain forest, would find difficult to learn as a basis for survival. Furthermore, none of these systems of production is "frozen in time," for they have all undergone change and indeed are still changing.

Links: Globalization and the World Economy

The emergence and evolution of capitalism in recent centuries has had far-reaching effects on all modes of production it meets. The intensification of global trade created a global division of labour or world economy in which countries complete unequally for a share of the wealth (Wallerstein 1979). The modern world-system is stratified into three major areas: core, peripheral, and semi-peripheral. Core areas monopolize the most profitable activities of the division of labour, such as the high-tech service, manufacturing, and financial activities, and they have the strongest governments, which play a dominating role in the affairs of other countries. Peripheral areas are stuck with the least profitable activities, including the production of raw materials, foodstuffs, and labour-intensive goods, and import high-tech goods and services from other areas. They tend to have weak governments and are dominated, either directly or indirectly, by core country governments and policies. Semi-peripheral areas stand in the middle with a mixture of wealth and power. According to this analysis, all areas are equally interdependent in the division of labour, but the benefits that accrue from their specialized roles are highly unequal. Core states, with about 20 percent of the system's population, control 80 percent of the system's wealth and put out 80 percent of world pollution. In the political sphere, the core states have increased their economic power and influence through international organizations such as the World Trade Organization (WTO), which forces "free trade" policies on peripheral countries and appears to be yet another mechanism that intensifies the unequal division of labour and wealth.

This chapter examines several modes of production that, over many centuries, have been variously but increasingly affected by the capitalist logic of commodity production for markets for ceaseless capital accumulation.

MODES OF PRODUCTION

While reading this section, bear in mind that most anthropologists are uneasy about typologies because they often don't reflect the rich reality that ethnographic research presents. This scheme is presented as a way to help you organize the vast amount of ethnographic information this book will present to you.

Foraging

Foraging is based on using food that is available in nature, provided by gathering, fishing, or hunting. It is the oldest economic system, having existed since the appearance of *Homo sapiens* around 100 000 years ago, perhaps earlier. Foraging has thus survived as the predominant mode of production for 90 percent or more of human existence. Foraging is now in danger of extinction. Very few people—roughly a quarter of a million people—support themselves predominantly by foraging. European colonialism and contemporary economic globalization have drastically changed foragers' life-ways. Foragers now are mostly located in what are considered marginal areas, such as deserts, the circumpolar region, and dense tropical forest regions.

Successful foraging requires sophisticated knowledge of the natural environment: how to find particular roots buried deep in the ground, how to follow animal tracks and other signs, and how to judge the weather and water supply. It also relies on a diverse set of tools to aid in the processing of wild foods, including nutcrackers, seed-grinders, and cooking containers. Depending on the environment, the main activities of foraging include gathering such food as nuts, berries, roots, honey, insects, and eggs; trapping or hunting birds and animals; and fishing. Tools include digging sticks for removing roots from the ground and for penetrating the holes dug by animals in order to get the animals out, bows and arrows, spears, nets, and knives. Baskets are important for carrying foodstuffs. For processing raw materials into edible food, foragers use stones to mash, grind, and pound. Meat can be dried in the sun or over fire, and fire is used for cooking either by boiling or by roasting. Obtaining and processing food requires few nonrenewable fuel sources beyond wood or other combustible substances for cooking

In contrast to foragers of temperate climates, those of the circumpolar regions of North America, Europe, and Asia have to devote most time and energy to food procurement and providing shelter. The specialized technology of circumpolar peoples includes making spears, nets, and knives as well as building sleds and using domesticated animals to pull them. Sled dogs or other animals

THE DENE OF COLVILLE LAKE

THE COLVILLE LAKE community consists of 75 members of a First Nations people, the Dene (Savishinsky 1974). To distinguish them from other Dene, outsiders arbitrarily call them the Hare Indians because they hunt hares. They survive by hunting, trapping, and fishing in one of the harshest environments in the world. Joel Savishinsky's major research interest was to analyze the experience of stress, tension, and anxiety among this isolated group and observe how they cope with it. Ecological stress factors include "extreme temperatures, long and severe winters, prolonged periods of isolation, hazardous weather and travel conditions, an often precarious food supply, and the constant need for mobility during the harshest seasons of the year" (xiv). Social and psychological stress factors also exist, including contact with White people: fur traders and missionaries.

Savishinsky discovered the importance of dogs in relation to the economy and psychological well-being:

> [L]ater in the year when I obtained my own dogteam, I enjoyed much greater freedom of movement, and was able to camp with many people whom I had previously not been able to keep up with. Altogether I travelled close to 600 miles [1000 kilometres] by dogsled between mid-October and early June. This constant contact with dogs, and the necessity of learning how to drive, train and handle them, led to my recognition of the social and psychological, as well as the ecological significance of these animals in the lives of the people. (xx)

Among the 14 households, there are a total of 224 dogs. Some households have as many as 4 teams, with an average of 6.2 dogs per team, corresponding to people's estimation that 6 dogs are required for travel. More than being only economically useful, dogs play a significant role in people's emotional lives. They are a frequent topic of conversation: "Members of the community constantly compare and comment on the care, condition, and growth of one another's animals, noting special qualities of size, strength, color, speed, and alertness" (169). Emotional displays, not generally common among the Hare, are significant between people and their dogs:

Hare First Nation children use their family's sled and dogs to haul drinking water to their village from Colville Lake, Northwest Territories.

The affectionate and concerned treatment of young animals is participated in by people of all ages, and the nature of the relationship bears a striking resemblance to the way in which people treat young children. Pups and infants are, in essence, the only recipients of unreserved positive affect in the band's social life, all other relationships being tinged with varying degrees of restraint and/or negativism. (169–170)

FOOD FOR THOUGHT

Do you know of another culture in which animals are a focus of such intense human interest? Or a culture in which people have no interest in animals?

that are used to pull sleds are an important aspect of circumpolar peoples' economic technology, just as tractors are for contemporary farmers (see the Multiple Cultural Worlds box). Considerable amounts of labour are needed to construct durable igloos or permanent log houses, which are necessary adaptations to the cold temperatures. Protective clothing, including warm coats and boots, is another feature of circumpolar economic adaptation.

Division of Labour

Among foraging peoples, occupational specialization (assigning particular tasks to particular people) exists to varying degrees and depends mainly on gender and age. Among foraging cultures located in temperate climates, a minimal gender-based division of labour exists. Most people get the majority of their food by gathering roots, berries, grubs, small birds and animals, and fish. One difference is that, when hunting is done, men are more likely to be involved in long-range expeditions to hunt large animals. However, hunting large animals provides only a small portion of the diets of temperate-climate foragers. In contrast, hunting large animals, including seals, whales, and bears, and capturing large fish is an important part of food provision in circumpolar groups, and gender-based specialization is therefore more marked.

Many anthropologists have emphasized a "Man the Hunter" model for prehistoric humans and contemporary foragers in general (for example, R. B. Lee 1979). This view takes men's hunting roles in some foraging groups and uses them as the model for all foraging groups, both now and in the past. These roles were also used as the basis for theories about social patterns of male dominance in the past and the present. Comparative studies of foragers around the world indicate that greater male involvement in hunting is found in more depleted and resource-limited environments (Hiatt 1970). The implication is that men's hunting of large game is an adaptation to increasing resource scarcity in recent times and thus was not necessarily a predominant practice throughout the long history of foraging.

In contrast to the "Man the Hunter" model, some cultural anthropologists have proposed a "Woman the Gatherer" model (Slocum 1975). This model makes more sense, since the bulk of everyday food in most foraging systems came from gathering, the primary work of women. Among the Ju/wasi, for example, women's gathering provides 75 to 80 percent of the diet, while large game provided by men accounted for the rest. In some cultures, women have roles in hunting game similar to those of men, as among the Agta of the Philippines (Estioko-Griffin 1986; Estioko-Griffin, Goodman, and Griffin 1985). The Agta pattern is that some of the women go out hunting while other women stay at the camp caring for the small children, thus disproving the proposition that women's

maternal roles universally prevent them from hunting. Most cultural anthropologists would now agree that the "Man the Hunter" model is an example of male bias in interpretation. However, the "Man the Hunter" model is still strong in much popular thinking and is perpetuated through textbook images and museum displays of gender-specific roles in human evolution (Wiber 1997).

Age is a basis for task allocation in all societies since children and the aged generally spend less time in food provision. In foraging societies, both boys and girls perform various tasks that North Americans would label as "work," particularly gathering food. Among the Ju/wasi, young boys begin practising hunting skills through the games they play with small bows and arrows. They gradually take on more adult skills as they mature. Among the Agta of the Philippines, women hunt and both girls and boys learn to hunt along with their mothers.

Property Relations

The concept of private property in the sense of owning something that can be sold to someone else is not found in foraging societies. Instead, the term **use right** is more appropriate. It means that a person or group has socially recognized priority in access to particular resources, such as gathering regions, hunting and fishing areas, and water holes. This access, however, is willingly shared with others by permission. Among the Ju/wasi, certain family groups are known to control access to particular water holes and the territory surrounding them (R. B. Lee 1979:58–60). Visiting groups are welcome and will be given food and water. In turn, the host group, at another time, will visit other camps and be given hospitality there. In the Andaman Islands, family groups each control known offshore areas for fishing. Again, sharing is a common practice if permission has been given. Encroaching on someone else's area without permission is a serious misdemeanour that could result in violence. While some instances of conflict between foraging groups over territory and other resources have been documented by anthropologists, the level of conflict is less intense and less likely to be lethal than in settled groups with rules of private property. In foraging groups, use rights are generally invested in the collective group and passed down equally to all children who are members of the group.

Foraging as a Sustainable System

When untouched by outside influences and with abundant land available, foraging systems are sustainable, meaning that crucial resources are regenerated over time in balance with the demand that the population makes on them. Evidence of the sustainability of foraging systems comes from many places, but the Andaman Islands provide the clearest case because their island habitats have been "closed" systems with little, if any, out-migration from specific areas of habitation in recent centuries. The few hundred Andamanese living on Sentinel Island, which has never been entered by outsiders, seem to have been able to maintain their lifestyle within a fairly limited area since earliest observations of them (from a distance) by the British in the late nineteenth century.

One reason for the sustainability of foraging is that foragers' needs are modest. Some anthropologists have typified the foraging lifestyle as the "original affluent society" because needs are satisfied with minimal labour efforts. This term is used metaphorically to signal the fact that foraging economies should not be dismissed as poor and inadequate attempts at making a living. That is an ethnocentric judgment made from the perspective of a consumer culture with different economic and social values. Highly industrialized societies may be maladaptive in the long run because they promote overconsumption of non-renewable resources. In the 1960s, when the Ju/wasi of the Kalahari Desert were still using a foraging system, the major food source was the mongongo nut, which was so abundant that there was never a shortage (Howell 1986). In addition, hundreds of species of plants and animals were considered edible. Yet the people were very thin and often complained of hunger, year round. Their thinness may be an adaptation to seasonal fluctuations in food supply. Rather than maximizing food intake during times of plenty, they minimize it. Mealtime is not an occasion for stuffing oneself with treats until there is no room for anything more. Ju/wasi culture taught that one should have a hungry stomach, even in the midst of plentiful food.

Since foragers' needs for goods are not great, minimal labour efforts are required to satisfy them. They would typically work fewer hours a week than the average employed North American. In traditional (undisturbed) foraging societies, people spend as few as five hours a week "working," so they have more leisure time that they spend in activities like storytelling, playing games, and resting. Foraging populations also traditionally enjoyed good health records. During the 1960s, the age structure and health status of the Ju/wasi compared to that of the United States of around 1900—without any modern medical facilities (R. B. Lee 1979:47–48). They were described as a "healthy and vigorous population with a low incidence of infections and degenerative diseases." The high level of needs satisfaction and general health and well-being of foragers is the basis of their being called the "original affluent societies."

Horticulture

Both horticulture and pastoralism emerged only within the last several thousand years of human existence. They both involve an emerging dependence on the **domestication** of

During a time of food shortage in 1999, a Sudanese mother and her daughter collect edible leaves.

plants and animals, or their control by humans in terms of both their location and reproduction. No one is sure as to when and where domestication first occurred, and whether the domestication of plants and animals occurred at the same time or sequentially. Some evidence indicates that plant domestication came first.

Horticulture is a mode of production based on the cultivation of domesticated crops in gardens using hand tools. It emerged first around 12 000 BCE in the Middle East, China, and Africa. A horticultural economy is based mainly on food crops that people plant and harvest. The food grown in gardens is often supplemented by foraging for wild foods and trading with pastoralists for animal products. Horticulture is still practised by many thousands of people mainly in sub-Saharan Africa; South and Southeast Asia, including the Pacific island of Papua New Guinea; Central and South America; and some parts of the Caribbean islands. Prominent horticultural crops include yams, corn, beans, grains such as millet and sorghum, and several types of roots, all of which are rich in proteins, minerals, and vitamins.

Horticulture involves the use of hand-held tools, such as digging sticks, hoes, and carrying baskets. Rain is the sole source of moisture. Horticulture requires rotation of garden plots in order to allow used areas to regenerate and thus is also termed "shifting cultivation." Average plot sizes are less than one-half hectare, and one hectare can support a family of five to eight members for a year. Yields are sufficient to support semi-permanent village settlements of 200 to 250 people. Overall population density per square kilometre is low because horticulture, like foraging, is a land-extensive strategy. But horticulture is more labour-intensive than foraging because of the energy required for plot preparation and food processing. Horticulturalists supplement their diets by fishing or hunting, or both, and they may trade with nearby foragers.

Anthropologists distinguish five phases in the horticultural cycle:

- *Clearing:* A section of the forest is cleared, partially or completely, by cutting down trees and brush and then setting the area on fire to burn off other growth. This burning creates a layer of ash that is rich fertilizer. Thus "slash and burn cultivation" refers to these two stages of cutting and burning.

- *Planting:* This is accomplished either with a digging stick to loosen the soil into which seeds or slips of plants are placed or through the broadcasting method of simply scattering the seeds by hand over the surface of the ground.

- *Weeding:* Weeds are a relatively minor problem because of the ash cover and somewhat shady growing conditions.

- *Harvesting:* This phase requires substantial labour mainly to cut or dig crops and carry them to the residential area.

- *Fallowing:* After cultivating the same garden plot for a certain number of years (which varies depending on the environment and the type of crop grown), the land has to be left unused, or fallow, for a period of time before it regains its fertility.

Crop yields from horticulture can be great and can support denser population levels than foraging. Surpluses in food supply emerge as a new element of this mode of production. These surpluses enable trade relationships to increase and cause greater affluence for some people. In some cases, horticulture was the foundation for complex civilizations; for example, in Central Africa and in the Mayan civilization of Central America.

Division of Labour

As with foraging groups, no class differences exist in terms of work in horticultural societies. A family of husband, wife, and children forms the core work group for cultivation, but groups of men form for hunting and fishing expeditions, and women often work in collective groups for food processing. Gender is the key factor structuring the organization of labour, with male and female work roles often being clearly differentiated. Male and female roles fall into three general patterns (Martin and Voorhies 1975). Most commonly, men do the clearing, and men and women plant and tend the staple crops that are the basis of the people's everyday diets. This pattern exists in Papua New Guinea, much of Southeast Asia, and parts of West and East Africa. In the second pattern, men do the clearing and women cultivate the staple crops; men cultivate prestige crops (used in ceremonies and for exchange) and may also hunt. Many horticultural societies of East Africa fit this pattern. This pattern is, however, reversed in some cultures, notably the precontact Iroquois of upstate New York. Iroquois women were in charge of cultivating maize, the most important crop, and their economic importance was reflected in the overall social and political importance accorded to women (J. K. Brown 1975). In the third pattern, which is the least common, men do both the clearing and the cultivating. The Yanomami of the Amazon (Chagnon 1992) are an example of this male-dominated horticultural production system. Yanomami men clear the fields, plant and maintain the gardens, and harvest the crops. Yanomami women are not idle, however. They work, on average, more hours than men because they are responsible for performing the arduous and time-consuming tasks involved in processing manioc. Manioc, the main food source, is a starchy root poisonous to humans unless put through a lengthy process of soaking in water, which is carried from the river by teams of women. Once soaked, the manioc is grated by hand and cooked before it is ready for consumption.

While no simple explanation exists for why different divisions of labour in horticulture emerge, their differences have clear implications for gender status (Sanday 1973). Cross-cultural, comparative analysis of many horticultural societies shows that women's contribution to food production is a necessary but not sufficient basis for status. In other words, if women do not contribute to producing food, their status will be low. If they do contribute, their status may be high—but it may not be. The critical factor appears to be control over the distribution of what is produced, perhaps especially its public distribution beyond the family. Slavery is a prime illustration of a contribution to production that does not bring high status because a slave has no control over the product.

Children do much productive work in horticultural societies, perhaps more than in any other type of economy. A comparative research project, the "Children of Six Cultures" study (Whiting and Whiting 1975), examined children's roles in different modes of production. The Gusii of Kenya were the most dependent on horticulture. Compared to children in the other five cultures, Gusii children were assigned more tasks at younger ages. Both young boys and girls were responsible for caring for siblings, fetching fuel, and hauling water. The reason horticultural societies involve children in "responsible" adult-like tasks more than other societies has to do with the fact that in most horticultural societies, adult women's time allocation to work is very high and children's labour serves as a replacement in the domestic domain.

Property Relations

As in foraging societies, the concept of private property as something that an individual can own and sell is not operable in horticultural societies. Use rights are important and more clearly defined than in foraging societies. By clearing and planting an area of land, an individual puts an indisputable claim on it and its produce. With the production of surplus goods, the possibility of social inequality in access to goods and resources emerges. Rules about group sharing may decline or even disappear as some people gain access to higher status.

Horticulture as a Sustainable System

Crop rotation and fallowing are crucial factors in the sustainability of horticulture. Crop rotation varies the demands made on the soil. Fallowing allows the plot to rest completely and recover its nutrients. It also promotes soil quality and helps prevent compaction by allowing the growth of weeds, whose root systems help keep the soil loose. Once the fallow period is over, the weeds are burned off, providing a layer of ash that serves as a rich source of natural fertilizer. The benefits of a well-managed system of shifting cultivation are clear.

A major constraint in horticulture is the time required for fallowing in situations of pressure on the land. In general, seven years or more of fallow time are required for a year of cultivation. Reducing fallowing time quickly brings negative consequences, including soil nutrient depletion and soil erosion. Several factors contribute to reusing plots that should be left fallow (Blaikie 1985):

- Reduced access to land due to incursions from ranchers, miners, farmers, tourists;
- Government pressure on horticulturalists to intensify production for cash in order to pay taxes and other fees;
- Interest of horticulturalists in boosting production for cash in order to buy manufactured commodities; and
- Pressure from population growth when out-migration is not an option.

The last factor, population growth, is often blamed as the sole culprit, but often it is not involved at all. For example, in one case in eastern India, the major causes of land degradation were heavy government taxes and fees and growing indebtedness to merchants in the plains:

Up to thirty years ago, the hill area occupied by the Sora was covered by dense jungle, while today the hillsides are near-deserts of raw red soil. Shifting agriculture is practised with only three to four year fallow periods, as opposed to over ten years some generations ago. The population has grown only slowly, and certainly at a much slower rate than the rapidly increased destruction of the environment might suggest. (Blaikie 1985:128)

Pastoralism

Pastoralism is a mode of production based on the domestication of animal herds and the use of their products, such as meat and milk, for 50 percent or more of the pastoral society's diet. Pastoralism has long existed in the "old world"—Europe, Africa, and Asia, especially in regions where rainfall is limited and unpredictable. In the Western hemisphere, before the arrival of the Spanish in the fifteenth century, the only indigenous herding system existed in the Andean region and involved llamas. Sheep, goats, horses, and cattle became prominent after the Spanish conquest (Barfield 2001). Some First Nations groups, especially in the southwestern United States, still rely on herding animals. Pastoralists raise a limited variety of animals. The six most popular species are sheep, goats, cattle, horses, donkeys, and camels. Three others have more restricted distribution: yaks at high altitudes in Asia, reindeer in northern sub-Arctic regions, and llamas in highland South America. Many pastoralists keep dogs for protection and for help with herding. Pastoralism can succeed in a variety of environments, depending on the animal involved. For example, reindeer herding is popular in the circumpolar regions of Europe and Asia, and cattle and goat herding is common in India and Africa.

Pastoralism is geared to providing daily food, primarily milk. Thus, this mode of production is limited in what

Among the Ariaal, herders of Kenya, men are in charge of herding camels. Here, an Ariaal herder watches over two baby camels.

it can provide, so pastoralist groups forge trade links with settled groups. In this way, they can secure food and other goods they cannot produce themselves, particularly grains and manufactured items like cooking pots, in return for their animals, hides, and other animal products. Pastoralism may seem to resemble contemporary large-scale ranching operations, but in fact, ranches resemble modern industry more than traditional pastoralism (Fratkin, Galvin, and Roth 1994; Loker 1993). The primary purpose of ranching is to provide meat for sale, whereas pastoralism provides many animal products. Also, pastoralism involves the movement of animals to pasture, while ranching moves the fodder to the animals.

A common problem for all pastoralists is the continued need for fresh pasture for their animals. This need makes pastoralism, like foraging and horticulture, an extensive form of economic adaptation. Herds must move or else the pasture area will become depleted. A useful distinction is made between pastoralists depending on whether they move their herds for short or long distances (Fratkin, Galvin, and Roth 1994). The Nuer are an example of short-distance herders. E. E. Evans-Pritchard's (1947) classic study describes the Nuer, cattle herders of Sudan, in the late 1930s. Depending on the availability of water, the Nuer would spend part of the year in settled villages and part in temporary camps. Cows provided food for the Nuer from their milk, meat, and blood (the Nuer, and other pastoralists, extract blood from the cow's neck, which they then drink). Cattle also furnished hides, horn, and other materials for everyday use and were the medium of exchange for marriage and payment of fines. The economic and social importance of cattle is reflected in the Nuer's detailed vocabulary for naming types of cattle on the basis of their colours and markings.

Pastoralist systems vary greatly in terms of their level of wealth and the degree of political organization among groups. Environmental setting seems to explain much of this variation. The Qashqai of Iran are long-distance sheep herders and camel drivers (Beck 1986). This area of the Middle East is relatively lush, with a rich and varied natural resource base that supports agriculture and urban centres, including the important city of Shiraz. The nomadic pastoralism of the Qashqai involves seasonal migration to remote pastures, separated by about 500 kilometres. Long-distance herding makes the Qashqai vulnerable to raids and requires negotiation with settlements along the way for permission to cross their land. This vulnerability prompted them to develop a confederacy of tribes into a centralized political organization for protection. The Qashqai thus show how ecology, economy, and political organizations are linked within an environment well-endowed with resources and with many settled communities. In areas with fewer resources and sparser settlements, such as Mongolia in Central Asia or the circumpolar region, pastoralist groups are less politically organized and less wealthy than the Qashqai.

Labour

The pastoralist division of labour is not structured by class differences. Families and clusters of related families are the basic unit of production. Gender is an important factor in the allocation of work. In many pastoralist cultures, little overlap exists between male and female tasks. Men are often in charge of the herding activities—moving the animals from place to place. Women tend to be responsible for processing the herd's products, especially the milk. A cultural emphasis on masculinity characterizes many herding populations. Traditional reindeer herding among the Sami of Finland was connected to male identity (Pelto 1973). The definition of being a man was to be a reindeer herder. As traditional herding practices declined and many men no longer made their living from herding, they had to redefine their sense of identity.

In contrast, women are the predominant herders among the Navajo of the American Southwest. Navajo men generally had little to do with herding the sheep. Instead, their major role is crafting silver jewellery.

The size of the animal involved appears to be a factor in the gender division of labour. Women are often the herders of smaller animals, perhaps since smaller animals need to graze less widely and can be kept penned near the house. Men tend the animals that are pastured at longer distances. This difference suggests the emergence of a distinction between men's wider spatial range than women's, something that becomes further accentuated in many agricultural systems.

Children often play important roles in tending herds. Among the cattle-herding Maasai of Kenya and Tanzania, parents prefer to have many children so that they can help with the herds. Before boys in these pastoralist societies advance to the "warrior" stage, beginning around adolescence, their main task is herding.

Property Relations

The most important forms of property among pastoralists include animals, housing (such as tents, or yurts), and domestic goods (rugs, cooking ware). Use rights regulate pasture land and migratory routes. Some sense of private property exists with the animals since they may be traded by the family head for other goods. A family's tent, or yurt, is also theirs. However, no private rights in land or travel routes exist; instead, these are generally accepted informal agreements. Many pastoral societies emphasize male ownership of the herds, and sons inherit herds from their fathers. In other societies, such as the shepherding Navajo of the southwestern United States, women are the primary herders and the herds pass from mother to daughter.

These girls are in charge of herding water buffaloes to the Ganges River, at Banaras, India.

Pastoralism as a Sustainable System

Pastoralism is a highly extensive system, requiring the ability of groups to range widely with their herds in search of grass and water. Pastoralists have been able to develop successful and complex cultures in extremely limited environments; an example is the Mongolian herders, who created a vast and powerful empire. As such, pastoralism can be a highly successful and sustainable economic adaptation that functions complementarily with other economic systems. As with horticulture, however, when outside forces begin to squeeze the space available for migration, overexploitation of the environment results and pastoralism then becomes accused of depleting the environment. Many forms of outside pressure, including national interests to "sedentarize" (settle down) pastoralists so that they will be easier to tax, and commercial interests in pastoralists' land, threaten the sustainability of pastoralism.

Agriculture

Compared to horticulture, agriculture is an **intensive strategy** of production. Intensification involves new techniques that allow the same land to be used repeatedly without losing its fertility. Key inputs include more labour power for weeding, use of natural and chemical fertilizers, and control of water supply. The earliest agricultural systems are documented from the time of the neolithic period, beginning around 10 000 BCE in the Tigris-Euphrates valley, India, and China. Agricultural systems now exist on all continents except Antarctica.

Agriculture involves the use of domesticated animals for plowing, transportation, and organic fertilizer—manure or composted materials. It also relies on irrigation as a source of water and on the construction of elaborate terraces and other ways of increasing the amount of land available for cultivation. Like the modes of production already considered, agriculture involves complex local forms of knowledge about the environment, including plant varieties, pest management, precipitation patterns, and soil types. Anthropologists refer to this knowledge as indigenous knowledge to distinguish it from Western, scientific knowledge. As longstanding agricultural traditions are increasingly displaced by methods introduced from the outside, indigenous knowledge is threatened. It is in danger of becoming extinct, along with the cultures and languages associated with it. Many anthropologists are now actively involved in recording indigenous knowledge as a resource for the future.

Permanent homes, investment in private property, and increased yields all promote larger family size as a way of further increasing production through the use of household labour. Population density increases substantially in agricultural societies, and urban centres of thousands of people develop. Occupational specialization increases. Instead of people repairing their own tools and weapons, some people take on this work as a full-time job and no longer grow their own food but become dependent on trading their skills for food with farmers. Other specializations that emerge as full-time occupations are political leaders, religious leaders or priests, healers, artisans, potters, musicians, and traders. Four major types of agriculture are described here.

Family Farming

Over one billion people, or about one-fourth of the world's population, belong to households involved in family farming (what cultural anthropologists formerly termed "peasant agriculture"). In family farming, farmers "produce much of their own subsistence as well as some food or fibre to sell, supplying labour largely from their own households, and possessing continuing, heritable rights to their own resources" (Netting 1989:221). Family farming is always part of a larger market economic system (E. Wolf 1966:8). It is found throughout the world but is more prevalent in primarily agrarian countries such as Mexico, India, Poland, and Italy than in more industrialized countries. Family farmers exhibit much cross-cultural variety: They may be full-time or part-time farmers, they may be more or less closely linked to urban markets, and they may or may not grow cash crops such as coffee or sugar cane. Major tasks include plowing, planting seeds and cuttings, weeding, caring for terraces and irrigation systems, harvesting, and processing.

Division of Labour   The family (or household) is the basic unit of production. Gender and age are important factors around which productive roles are organized. A marked gender-based division of labour characterizes most family farm economies. Cross-cultural analysis of gender roles in 46 cultures revealed that men perform the "bulk" of the labour in more than three-fourths of the sample (Michaelson and Goldschmidt 1971). The few societies in which females predominate in agriculture were located in Southeast Asia. In general, men work more hours in agricultural production than in the previous systems considered, and women's work tends to be more devoted to activities near the home, such as food processing and child care (Ember 1983). This division of labour is the basis of the **public/private dichotomy** in family farm societies, in which men are more involved with the public world and women are increasingly involved in activities in or near the home.

Analysis of time allocation data for men and women in horticultural and agricultural societies reveals that both men's and women's work hours are substantially higher in agricultural economies, but in differing proportions to inside and outside work (Ember 1983). Women's contribution to production is not less in agriculture. Instead, the shares of time devoted to particular activities shift. Women's inside work hours increase absolutely and relatively (compared to men's), and their outside work hours increase absolutely, but decline relative to those of men.

Why do many family farm agricultural systems increase men's workloads and increase women's involvement in the domestic domain? One hypothesis is based on the importance of plowing fields in preparation for planting, and the fact that plowing is almost exclusively a male task (Goody 1976). This fact has led some anthropologists to argue that men plow simply because they are stronger than women or have the advantage of greater "aerobic capacity" (the ability of the circulatory system to nourish the blood through processing air). In south-central India, weather patterns require that plowing be accomplished in a very narrow time band (Maclachlan 1983). Assigning the task to the physically stronger gender ensures that it can be done more quickly and is thus an adaptive strategy because it optimizes chances for a good crop. Another hypothesis says that women are not involved with plowing and other fieldwork because such tasks are incompatible with child care (J. K. Brown 1970).

Yet another view emphasizes that agriculture increases the demand for labour within and near the house (Ember 1983). Winnowing, husking, grinding, and cooking of agricultural products such as rice are extremely labour-intensive. The high demand for family labour in agriculture prompts people to want many children, so child care becomes a more demanding task that is relegated to women. As women become isolated within their households, they are less able to depend on labour contributions from other women than in modes of production where women live and work collectively.

In some farming systems, females play an equal or even more important role in agricultural production and distribution than males. Such "female farming systems" are numerically fewer than male farming systems. Most are found in Southeast Asia, a region where **wet rice agriculture** is practised. This is a highly labour-intensive way of growing rice that involves starting the seedlings in nurseries and transplanting them to flooded fields. Males play a role in the initial plowing of the fields, but this work is less arduous than in dry-field agriculture, since the earth is wet. Women's labour and decision making are the backbone of the operations. Why women predominate in wet rice agriculture is a question that has intrigued anthropologists and economists (Bardhan 1974; Goody 1976; Winzeler 1974), but no one has provided a solid explanation for this pattern yet. Its consequences are clearer than its causes: Where female farming systems exist, women are more likely to have access to rights to land ownership, a greater role in household decision making, more autonomy, and higher status in general (Dyson and Moore 1983; Stivens et al. 1994).

A third variation in the gender division of labour in family farming involves complementary and balanced task allocations between males and females, with males involved in agricultural work and females involved in food processing and marketing. This form of gender division of labour is common among highland communities of Central and South America. For example, among the Zapotec Indians of southern Mexico's state of Oaxaca (pronounced "wah-haka"), men grow maize, the staple crop, and cash crops—bananas, mangoes, coconuts, and sesame (Chiñas 1992). Zapotec women contribute substantially to household income by selling produce in the town markets and by making tortillas and selling them from their houses. The farming household thus derives its income from the labour of both

Lessons Applied

THE GLOBAL NETWORK OF INDIGENOUS KNOWLEDGE RESOURCE CENTRES

IN 1992 the United Nations Conference on Environment and Development, held in Rio de Janeiro, first promoted global awareness of the complementary relationships between indigenous knowledge (IK) about the environment and biodiversity (Warren 2001). Scholars had long recognized the links (Scott 1998), but its official recognition in 1992 led to action directed at preserving and promoting IK in order to prevent loss of biodiversity. Cultural anthropologists have documented IK about agriculture in matters such as emic classification of soil types, what kinds of foods grow best in what contexts, how to mix crop plantings effectively, and how to prevent pests from destroying crops.

Studies also reveal that IK is culturally variable: Men know some things, women know other things, and the young and old have different kinds of IK, as do members of different economic niches within the same cultural area. All these varying "knowledges" should be documented as part of indigenous cultural/agricultural heritage, because they have local specificity and validity that outside systems often lack.

An effort is now under way to link universities and agricultural research laboratories worldwide in order to support IK data collection and documentation. Over 30 IK resource centres exist, housing computerized databases of case studies and ethnographic reports. Coordination among the centres is leading to improved guidelines and recommendations about data recording, archiving, and sharing. All of these practices are aimed at both preserving the knowledge for the future and providing wider access to it. Although the primary goal of the project is to support biodiversity, it will have the effect of supporting cultural diversity as well.

FOOD FOR THOUGHT

This global information network will clearly help inform agricultural policy-makers, but how will it benefit the people whose knowledge is being recorded and preserved in the databanks?

---

genders working interdependently on different aspects of the production process. Male and female status is also relatively balanced.

Children's roles in agricultural societies range from being prominent to rather minor, depending on the context (Whiting and Whiting 1975). The "Children of Six Cultures" study found lower rates of child work in the North Indian and Mexican agricultural villages, compared to the horticultural village in Kenya. But in some agricultural societies, children's work rates are very high, as shown through detailed observations of children's activities in two Asian villages, one in Java and the other in Nepal. In these villages, an important task of children, even as young as six to eight years old, was tending the farm animals (Nag, White, and Peet 1978), and children spent more time caring for animals than adults did. In both villages, girls aged six to eight spent more time than adults in child care. Some of the Javanese children in the six- to eight-year-old group worked for wages. In general, girls did more hours of work daily than boys at all ages.

Property Relations The investments in land that agriculture requires, such as clearing, terracing, and fencing,

are linked to the development of firmly delineated and protected property rights. Rights to land, the most important resource, can be acquired and sold. Clear guidelines exist about inheritance and transfer of rights to land through marriage. Social institutions such as law and police emerge to protect private rights to resources. The more marked gender division of labour in many family farming systems often means that men have access to the more highly valued tasks and to goods that have value in the outside world. The women are more involved with food processing, child bearing and child rearing, and family maintenance, tasks that generate no income and have no exchange value (see the Lessons Applied box about the different indigenous knowledge men and women have).

In family farming systems where male labour and decision making predominate, women and girls tend to be excluded from land rights and other forms of property control. Conversely, in female farming systems, inheritance rules tend to regulate the transmission of property rights more often through females. In Malaysia, gender inequality was less severe than in many parts of the world. Daughters traditionally inherited land equally with sons. In terms of labour force participation, women again

---

ranked high. Women's economic rights produced a significant degree of autonomy for rural women. Over time, however, this has changed. Both colonialism and international development programs have brought disadvantages to Malay women that did not exist before. For example, British colonial officials registered land in the name of men only, regardless of whether the property was owned by a woman or jointly owned by a husband and wife. With independence from British colonial rule, agricultural development programs in Malaysia, as elsewhere, have been aimed at males. The Green Revolution promoted mechanized rice farming and displaced thousands of female workers from their jobs. Rodolphe De Koninck (1992) studied the impact of the Green Revolution in Malaysia and reports how men have become entrepreneurs, borrowing money and purchasing mechanized harvesters. One man used land owned by his sisters and mother without compensation to support his harvester rental business (128). In 100 years, the gender division of labour and women's economic rights and status have been steadily transformed from one in which women had high status to one in which men now have dominant roles.

Industrial Agriculture

Industrial agriculture produces crops through means that are "capital-intensive, substituting machinery and purchased inputs such as processed fertilizers for human and animal labor" (Barlett 1989:253). It is mostly practised in the United States, Canada, Germany, Russia, and Japan and is increasingly adopted in developing nations such as India and Brazil as well as in socialist countries such as China.

Corporate Farming in Canada In Canada the rural population continues to dwindle. In 2001, approximately 725 000 Canadians or only about 2.4 percent of the total population lived on farms (Statistics Canada 2004). The use of new technology has contributed to this decline. For example, in Quebec in the 1930s the advent of the motor car allowed farm labourers to leave farming communities and cut ties with farmer employers (Verdon 1980:120). The growing involvement of farmers in the market economy also meant that farmers and labourers no longer exchanged labour as kin within the community.

On many farms in Canada, there is a clear gender division of labour. The husband is usually primarily responsible for daily farm operations, usually involving extensive use of machinery, while wives' participation ranges from equal to that of husbands to minimal (Barlett 1989: 271–273). Wives are generally responsible for managing the domestic domain. Because of their domestic and farm duties, women's daily work hours are 25 percent more than those of men. A new trend is for farm women to take salaried jobs off the farm to help support the farm. In

This farmer works near a highly urbanized area of Kyoto. In Japan, farming now often combines elements of industrial mechanization and intensive labour.

Canada, 50 percent of farm wives, in addition to their domestic and farm chores, also work off the farm (Bollman and Smith 1988; Kubik and Moore 2003:27). Children are not formally employed in farm work, but many family farms rely on children's contributions on weekends and during summer vacations. Amish farm families rely to a significant extent on contributions from all family members (Hostetler and Huntington 1992).

Industrial agriculture has brought the advent of a new subcategory of **corporate farms**, huge enterprises that produce goods solely for sale and that are owned and operated by companies that rely entirely on hired labour. Studies reveal four aspects of the evolution of industrial agriculture over the past 150 years:

- The increased use of complex technology, including machinery, chemicals, and genetic research on new plant and animal varieties.

- The increased use of **capital** (wealth used in the production of more wealth—in the form of either money or property). Industrial agriculture uses the most capital per unit of production of any farming system (Barlett 1989:260). The high ratio of capital to labour has enabled farmers to increase production, but it reduces flexibility. If a farmer invests in an expensive machine to harvest soybeans and then the price of soybeans drops, the farmer cannot quickly change from growing soybeans to potatoes.

- The increased use of energy—primarily fossil fuels to run the machinery and provide nitrates for fertilizer—to grow crops, often exceeds the calories of food energy yielded in the harvest. Calculations of how many calories of energy are used to produce a calorie of food in industrial agricultural systems reveal a very high ratio of perhaps 2.5 calories of fossil fuel to harvest 1 calorie of food, and more than 6 calories are invested when processing, packaging, and transport are counted (Barlett 1989:261). In this sense, industrial agriculture is a less efficient mode of production than foraging, horticulture, and pastoralism.

■ The decline of the family farm. In Canada, family farms were the predominant pattern until a few decades ago. Now, experts speak of "the death of the family farm." Increasing numbers of family farms have fallen into debt and cannot compete with industrial farms. In Canada, foreclosure notices to family farms tripled between 1984 and 1990 (Young and Van Bers 1991).

A key difference between corporate farms and family farms is that corporate farms depend completely on hired labour rather than on family members. Much of the labour demand in industrial agriculture is seasonal, creating an ebb and flow of workers, depending on the task and time of year. Large ranches hire seasonal cowboys for round-ups and fence mending. Crop harvesting is another high-demand point. Leo Chavez (1992) studied the lives of undocumented (illegal) migrant labourers from Central America who work in the huge tomato, strawberry, and avocado fields owned by corporate farms in southern California. Many of these migrants are Indians from Oaxaca, Mexico. They sneak across the border to work in the United States as a way of making ends meet. In the San Diego area, they live temporarily in shantytowns, or camps that Chavez describes as resembling Third World living conditions (63). Here is what a camp, where all male workers live, is like on Sunday when the men do not go out to work in the fields:

> On Sundays, the campsites take on a community-like appearance. Men bathe, and wash their clothes, hanging them on trees and bushes, or on lines strung between the trees. Some men play soccer and basketball, using a hoop someone has rigged up. Others sit on old crates or tree-stumps as they relax, talk, and drink beer. Sometimes the men talk about fights from the night before. With little else to do, nowhere to go, and few outsiders to talk to, the men often drink beer to pass the time on Saturday nights and Sundays. Loneliness and boredom plague them during nonworking hours. (65)

Another recent change in corporate agriculture has been the introduction of genetically engineered crops. A few large agribusiness corporations and government agencies encouraged this change in Canada. This process has been largely hidden from the bulk of the Canadian population, who are now consuming great quantities of genetically altered food, especially in processed items using canola and soybeans. Brewster Kneen, a former farmer and food activist, has been concerned about the consequences of industrial agriculture in Canada for many years. He argues

that there are substantial differences between the ways farmers selected plants and animals in the past, and the use of genetic technology. He argues that farmers were not imposing genetic uniformity, but rather required diversity. He writes:

> We were not violently forcing plants or microorganisms to conform to our model of what they should be in order to maximize our profits. We were encouraging transformations to be sure, but they were gradual, subtle ones that we could only observe after the fact. . . . we do not really know what the long-term consequences of genetic engineering will be, and are not prepared to move slowly and take the time to find out, [this] means that a grand experiment is taking place, and the outcome is anyone's guess. (Kneen 1999:5–8)

Industrial Collectivized Agriculture Industrial collectivized agriculture is a form of industrialized agriculture that involves nonprivate control of land, technology, and goods produced. Collectivism is inspired by the work of social theorists Marx and Engels (1848), whose call, "Workers of the world unite" in *The Communist Manifesto,* inspired many social movements. Collectivism's basic goal was to provide for greater economic equality and a greater sense of group welfare than is possible under competitive capitalism. A variety of collective agriculture arrangements have been used in places such as Russia and Eastern Europe, China, Vietnam, Laos, Cambodia, Tanzania, Ethiopia, and Nicaragua. David Kideckel (1993) conducted one of the few anthropological studies on collectivization in a Romanian community in two periods: first, in 1974 during a period of optimism for socialism, and later in 1990, after the revolution that brought socialism's end.

Socialism in Romania involved an extensive state plan with the most comprehensive and centralized system in Eastern Europe. The state oversaw nearly every aspect of society, from university enrollments to the production of steel and tractors. With the completion of agricultural collectivization in the early 1960s, about 30 percent of the land was in state farms, 60 percent in collectives, and 10 percent privately held. Workers on state farms were employees and were paid wages. They received a small garden for their own use. The state farm provided services such as child care facilities and shopping centres. Collective farms, in contrast, were ostensibly "owned" and controlled by their members, who pooled land, labour, and resources. Their earnings were determined by total farm production, and their wages tended to be lower than state farm worker wages. Collective farm workers were entitled to a "use plot" of the collective land. These plots could provide up to three-fourths of subsistence needs. Most of the private land existed in mountain zones where ecology limited the feasibility of collectivization.

This Romanian collective farm work team is sorting potatoes. Note the feminization of agricultural labour. Teams were composed of close friends, relations, and neighbours so that farms could take advantage of local social relations to satisfy their labour needs.

In spite of the socialist rhetoric proclaiming equality between all workers, there were economic distinctions between males and females. Women were relegated to agricultural and reproductive labour, while rural men moved into industry. Women were the mainstay of collective farm labour, but they were under-represented among the leadership. Nevertheless, women's increased involvement in wage-earning, and their roles in cultivating household use plots, strengthened their influence in the household and the community. Overall, the gender division of labour involved substantial overlap between male and female roles in the rural sector.

The 1980s brought serious economic decline to Romania, and in December 1989, the Romanian revolution began. By 1991, about 80 percent of the farm land had reverted to private ownership. The transition to private land was not easy. State farms gave up land reluctantly, and many collective farmers had second thoughts about private agriculture:

> One couple in their early forties were horrified when they heard a rumor that people were to be required to take back the land. . . . They had no desire to work in agriculture, and to them the half hectare to which they were entitled was a burden. (Kideckel 1993:221–222)

The Sustainability of Agriculture

Agriculture requires more in the way of labour inputs, technology, and the use of nonrenewable natural resources than the other systems discussed earlier. The ever-increasing spread of corporate agriculture is dis-placing other longstanding economic systems, including foraging, horticulture, and pastoralism. It is resulting in the destruction of important habitats, notably rainforests, in its search for agricultural land (along with commercial ranching and other aspects of industrialism, discussed next), and for water and other energy sources to support its enterprises. Intensive agriculture itself is nonsustainable. It is also undermining the sustainability of other systems. Anthropologists have pointed to some of the social costs of agriculture as well (see the Critical Thinking box).

Industrialism and Post-Industrialism

Industrialism is the production of goods through mass employment in business and commercial operations. In industrial capitalism, the form of capitalism found in most industrialized nations, the bulk of goods are produced not to meet basic needs but to satisfy consumer demands for nonessential goods. Employment in agriculture decreases while jobs in manufacturing and the service sector increase. In some industrialized countries, the number of manufacturing jobs is declining, with more people being employed in service occupations and in the growing area of "information processing" (such as computer programming, data processing, communications, and teaching). Some experts feel that Canada, for example, is moving out of the industrial age and into the "information age."

Within industrial capitalism an important distinction exists between the **formal sector**, which is salaried or wage-based work registered in official statistics, and the **informal sector**, which includes work that is outside the formal sector, not officially registered, and sometimes illegal. If you have done babysitting and were paid cash that was not formally recorded by your employer (for tax deduction purposes) or by you (for income tax purposes), then you have participated in the informal sector. Informal sector activities that are illegal are referred to as being part of the "underground economy."

The Formal Sector

The formal sector comprises a wide array of occupations, ranging from stable and lucrative jobs in what has been labelled the "primary labour market" to unstable or part-time and less lucrative jobs in the "secondary labour market" (Calhoun, Light, and Keller 1994). Cultural anthropologists conduct research in any number of domains, ranging from huge multinational corporations to neighbourhood beauty parlours. Some anthropologists have pursued the former direction, but the tendency has been to focus on small-scale organizations, especially factories. Factory studies are an important genre in cultural anthropology. They apply the tools and insights of

Critical Thinking

WAS THE INVENTION OF AGRICULTURE A TERRIBLE MISTAKE?

MOST EURO-AMERICANS have a "progressivist" view that agriculture is a major advance in cultural evolution because it brought with it so many things that Westerners admire—cities, centres of learning and art, powerful state governments, and monumental architecture:

> Just count our advantages. We enjoy the most abundant and varied foods, the best tools, and material goods, some of the longest and healthiest lives, in history. . . . From the progressivist perspective on which I was brought up, to ask "Why did almost all our hunter-gatherer ancestors adopt agriculture?" is silly. Of course they adopted it because agriculture is an efficient way to get more food for less work. (Diamond 1994:106)

Another claim about the advantage of agriculture is that it allows more leisure time, so art could flourish. Why would one rather be a hunter-gatherer, struggling every day to make ends meet?

On the other hand, many scholars raise serious questions about the advantages of agriculture. These "revisionists" argue that agriculture may be "the worst mistake in the history of the human race, . . . a catastrophe from which we have never recovered" (Diamond 1994:105–106). Some of the "costs" of agriculture include social inequality; disease; despotism; and destruction of the environment from soil exhaustion and chemical poisoning, water pollution, dams and river diversions, and air pollution from tractors, transportation, and processing plants. With agriculture, life did improve for many people, but not all. Elites emerged with distinct advantages, but the gap between the haves and the have-nots increased. Health improved for the elites, but not the landless poor and labouring classes. With the vast surpluses of food created by agricultural production, elaborate state systems developed with new forms of power exercised over the common people.

CRITICAL THINKING QUESTIONS

What is your definition of the "good life"?

Given your definition, how does life in pre-agricultural societies compare to life in contemporary agricultural and industrial societies?

What are the benefits and costs of achieving the good life among the Ju/wasi compared to contemporary agricultural and industrial societies?

Who gets the good life in each type of economy?

---

anthropology into the domain of a work-focused institution. Fieldwork techniques in factory studies include conducting interviews with workers and managers in the plant and in their homes, and observing plant operations. Findings shed light on how people adapt to this environment and on the stresses that arise.

In one factory study, a team of cultural anthropologists and graduate students focused on the role of ethnicity in shaping social relationships in a Miami clothing factory (Grenier et al. 1992). The clothing plant, a subsidiary of the largest U.S. clothing manufacturer, employs about 250 operators, mainly women. The majority of employees are Cuban women who immigrated to Miami many years ago. The workers are organized into a union, but members of the different ethnic groups have more solidarity with each other than with the union. Interethnic rivalry exists around the issue of management's treatment of members of different groups. Many non-Cuban workers claim that there is favouritism toward Cuban employees. Some supervisors and managers expressed ethnic stereotypes, but not always consistent ones: "Depending on whom one listens to, Haitians are either too slow or too fast; Cubans may talk too much or be extraordinarily dedicated workers" (75). Managers see ethnic-based competition and lack of cooperation as a key problem that they attempt to deal with by enforcing an environment that downplays ethnicity. For example, management banned workers from playing personal radios and installed a system of piped-in music by a radio station that supposedly alternates between "American" and "Latin" songs.

The Informal Sector

Studying the informal sector presents several challenges. People who work in the informal sector may not be "organized" in one location, like a factory. Often, workers are involved in illegal activities, which means they are even less willing than other people to be "studied." In general, it is easier to do research on aspects of people's lives

---

of which they are proud. Informal economy work may yield a sense of pride less often than formal economy work. On the other hand, some research advantages also arise. People involved in the informal economy, compared to a CEO of a multinational corporation, may have more time to share with the anthropologist. This is not always the case, however, since many informal sector workers are involved in more than one enterprise in an attempt to make ends meet, as well as being responsible for child care.

The illegal drug industry is an important part of the globalized informal economy. Neither international drug dealers nor street sellers pay income tax on their profits, and their earnings are not part of the official GNP of any nation. In the United States and Canada, many young males are drawn into the drug economy as sellers. Their lives are fractured with danger and violence. Some anthropologists have undertaken research in such settings, including Philippe Bourgois (1995), who reports on his findings about Hispanic crack dealers in Harlem:

Child labour is prominent in many modes of production. In this photograph, a girl picks coffee beans in Guatemala.

> Regular displays of violence are necessary for success in the underground economy—especially at the street-level drug-dealing world. Violence is essential for maintaining credibility and for preventing rip-off by colleagues, customers, and hold-up artists. Indeed, upward mobility in the underground economy requires a systematic and effective use of violence. . . . Behaviour that appears irrationally violent and self-destructive to the middle class (or the working class) outside observer, can be reinterpreted according to the logic of the underground economy, as a judicious case of public relations, advertising, rapport building, and long-term investment in one's "human capital development." (29)

In many parts of the world, prostitution is illegal but exists as part of the informal sector. In Thailand, the sex industry, although illegal, is the leading sector of the economy (Skrobanek, Boonpakdee, and Jantateero 1997). In 1990, Thailand's sex industry accounted for about 10 percent of Thailand's GNP, following closely behind income from all agricultural imports. Much of the income derives from Thailand's international popularity as a place for "sex tourism," which is travel that includes a "sex package." Thai prostitutes are also part of the international "export" sex industry. Over 200 000 Thai prostitutes live in Europe, while many others live in Japan, Hong Kong, Taiwan, Singapore, Canada, the United States, Saudi Arabia, and Kuwait.

Child sex work in Thailand is an increasingly important part of this informal economy. The number of child prostitutes under 16 years old is estimated to be about 800 000, or 40 percent of the total prostitute labour force. Recent changes, especially the fear of AIDS, have stepped up the demand for ever-younger prostitutes, since people associate child sex with safe sex. Health risks are high for prostitutes. In Thailand, statistics show that AIDS is increasing rapidly among child prostitutes. Many international organizations have become involved in focusing attention on the issue of child prostitution in Thailand.

An anthropological study of child prostitutes in a tourist community in Thailand sought to elicit the voices and views of the children themselves (Montgomery 2001). The study found that the children themselves do not feel that they fit the uniform view of child prostitutes that international organizations have. Their stories are varied, complicated, and full of internal contradictions, questions, and struggles. They believe that the work they do is moral because it is carried out mainly in support of their family. The child sex workers and their pimps, also children, exercise some choice in deciding which clients to accept and which to reject. This more complex view of child prostitution does not deny that the child sex workers are exploited and often seriously harmed, but it does show that the simple model of "victim" does not easily apply either.

This study and other research on various kinds of child labour raises universal questions about what childhood is, what a good childhood is, and what child rights are (Panter-Brick and Smith 2000). Surely, the voices and views of the children must be heard. But scholars and activists alike must look beyond the children's life decisions to the global, macroeconomic structures that generate and support the people who pay for sex with children and the poverty in the communities that send children into sex work.

CHANGING MODES OF PRODUCTION

This section draws attention to the changes that have occurred in recent times in each of the modes of production. Contemporary economic globalization is only the latest force of outside change to be exerted on local economies. European colonialism had major effects on indigenous economies, mainly by introducing cash cropping in place of production for household use.

In the later part of the twentieth century, major economic growth in Asia, the demise of socialism in the former Soviet Union, and the increasing economic power of the United States throughout the world combined to create the current "global economy" or economic globalization. The term *global economy* refers to the interconnectedness of all aspects of international, transnational, national, and local economies: raw materials, labour supply, transportation, finance, and marketing (Robins 1996). This interconnectedness is also characterized by its instantaneity—electronic forms of communication mean, more than ever, that when a world economic power centre sneezes, the rest of the world will catch a cold. Social scientists vigorously debate the effects of economic globalization on poverty and inequality (Ravaillon 2003). Economists, who tend to rely on national figures about changing income levels and distribution, have often espoused the view that economic globalization is beneficial overall, because it increases economic activity. Cultural anthropologists, who work with localized data and a more "on the ground" view, tend to emphasize the negative effects of capitalist expansion into noncapitalist settings (Blim 2000). They point to three major transformations:

- Increases in commercial production in local and periphery regions in response to the demands of a global market

- Recruitment of former foragers, horticulturalists, pastoralists, and family farmers to work in the industrialized sector and their exploitation in that setting

- Dispossession of local people of their land and other resource bases and substantial growth in the numbers of unemployed, displaced people

Although there are instances in which local cultural groups have selectively taken advantage of outside economic influences and remade them to fit their own interests, in many other cases, local economies have been almost completely transformed and local knowledge abandoned.

Foragers: The Tiwi of Northern Australia

The Tiwi live on two islands off the north coast of Australia (Hart, Pilling, and Goodale 1988). As foragers, the Tiwi gathered food, especially vegetables (such as yams) and nuts, grubs, small lizards, and fish. Women provided the bulk of the daily diet with their gathered vegetables and nuts that were ground and cooked into a porridge. Occasionally men hunted kangaroos, wildfowl, and other game such as *goanna*, larger lizards. Vegetables, nuts, and fish were abundant year-round. The Tiwi lived a more comfortable life than Aboriginal groups of the mainland, where the environment was less hospitable.

The Tiwi have long been in contact with different foreign influences, beginning in the 1600s with the arrival of the Portuguese, who were attracted to the islands as a source of iron. Later, in 1897, an Australian buffalo hunter named Joe Cooper came to the islands and kidnapped two native women to train as mainland guides in the Tiwi language. Cooper and his group greatly changed the Tiwi by introducing a desire for Western goods, especially tobacco. Later, Japanese traders arrived, offering Tiwi men manufactured goods in return for Tiwi women. In the early 1900s, the French established a Catholic mission on one island. The mission disapproved of the traditional Tiwi marriage pattern of polygamy (multiple spouses, in this case a man having more than one wife) and promoted monogamy instead. The year 1942 brought World War II to the Tiwi as the Japanese bombed and strafed a U.S. airstrip. Military bases were prominent on

the islands. Tiwi dependency on Western manufactured goods increased.

Tiwi residence patterns have changed substantially. The Tiwi have become settled villagers living in houses built of corrugated iron sheets. Tiwi men now play football (soccer) and water polo and engage in competitive javelin throwing. Tiwi art, especially carving and painting, is widely recognized in Australia and, increasingly, internationally.

The Tiwi are active in public affairs and politics, including the Aboriginal rights movement. Another major factor of change is international tourism, a force that the Tiwi are managing with dignity and awareness. One Tiwi commented that tourism may mean "that white people too will learn to live with and survive in the country" (Hart, Pilling, and Goodale 1988:144–145).

Horticulturalists: The Mundurucu of the Brazilian Amazon

Outside economic and political factors have major effects on horticultural societies. The rubber industry's impact on indigenous peoples of the Amazon ranges from maintenance of many aspects of traditional life to the complete loss of traditional life-ways. Like the Tiwi, the Mundurucu illustrate the complexities of change that are neither complete cultural retention nor complete loss (Murphy and Murphy 1985). After the arrival of Brazilians who were commercial rubber producers in the Amazon in the late nineteenth century, many Indians began to work for the Brazilians as latex tappers. For over a century, Mundurucu men combined their traditional horticultural life with seasonal work in the rubber area collecting latex. Marked cultural change occurred when many Mundurucu opted to leave their traditional villages, migrating to live in the rubber area year-round.

In the traditional villages, men still live in a separate house at one side of the village, with husbands visiting wives and children in their group houses. In the rubber settlement, husbands and wives live in their own houses and there is no separate men's house. In the traditional villages, women's communal work groups shared water-carrying tasks. Such groups do not exist in the rubber settlement villages. The husbands have taken over the task of carrying the water, so men work harder than in the traditional village. Although women in the settlement area work more hours per day than men, they believe that life is better because they like living in the same house with their husbands.

Pastoralists: Herders of Mongolia

In the early 1990s, cultural anthropologist Melvyn Goldstein and physical anthropologist Cynthia Beall

Aboriginal artist Eymard Tungatalum retouches a traditional Tiwi carving in an art gallery in Australia's northern territory. Tungatalum's carvings, along with songs and poems, are an important part of the Aboriginal people's efforts to revive their culture.

(1994) were allowed to do fieldwork among herders in Mongolia, a landlocked and mountainous country located between Russia and China. The Mongolian rural economy has long been, and still is, heavily dependent on animal herds. The "big five" animals are sheep, goats, cattle (mostly yak), horses, and camels. As one herder said, "The animals are our food and money. They give us our dairy products and meat to eat, dung to warm our *ger* [tent], and wool and skins to make our felt and clothes . . ." (38). Sheep and goats provide meat and clothing and some milk, yaks are most important for dairy products because they give milk all year, and horses and camels provide transportation. Goldstein and Beall wanted to study how the transformation from a socialist, collectivized, pastoral economy to a capitalist, market system was affecting the people.

Since the 1950s, the then USSR ruled Mongolia and sought to transform it into an agricultural and industrial state. As urban centres were established, the urban population began to grow and the rural population declined. The state provided all social services, such as health and education. There was no homelessness or unemployment.

The official policy regarding pastoralism was to ban private ownership and collectivize the herds. The transition was not smooth or easy. Collectivization resulted in a 30 percent reduction of livestock, as owners chose to slaughter animals rather than collectivize them (Barfield 1993). Subsequently, policy was altered and the people were allowed to control some of their own animals.

Starting in the late 1980s, the transition away from socialist economic policies spread to Mongolia. By the early 1990s, **privatization**, a process of transferring the collective ownership and provision of goods and services to a

In parts of Mongolia and Siberia, many pastoralists continue to herd reindeer as a major part of their economy.

system of private ownership, was the government's policy guideline. Collective ownership of herds was abandoned, and family-organized production was reinstated.

Goldstein and Beall (1994) selected a more traditional region for their research: the Moost district in the Altai Mountain area in the southeastern part of the country. The district includes over 26 000 square kilometres (10 000 square miles) of mountain and valley land, of which 99.9 percent is pasture. The area contains about 4000 people and about 115 000 head of livestock. Goldstein and Beall set up their *ger* and were immediately welcomed by an invitation to have milk-tea, a hot drink made of tea, water, milk, butter, and salt. During their stay, they spoke with many of the nomads, participated in their festivals, and learned about perceptions of economic change.

Changes in the wider Mongolian economy during privatization created serious problems for the herders. Their standard of living declined markedly in the early 1990s. Goods such as flour, sugar, candy, and cooking oil were no longer available. Prices for meat fluctuated widely, and the herders, who had become accustomed to the security of state-controlled prices, had to adjust to market fluctuations. Lower meat prices meant fewer herd animals were slaughtered. Larger herd sizes exceeded the carrying capacity of the grasslands.

External political and economic policies and events have had major effects on Mongolian herders' lifestyle. They have had to adjust to dramatic restructuring of their economy, from private family herding to collectivized herding and then back to private herding, in the space of a few decades. Along with these changes, social services such as health care and schools, which were relatively easy to access during the collective period, became less readily

available with privatization. We can only wonder how individual agency and choice have played a part within these massive structural changes. One scholar of central Asian pastoralists comments in an upbeat way that the cultural identity and pride of the descendants of Genghis Khan will endure (Barfield 1993:176) even though their numbers have dwindled, their standard of living has declined, and their herding practices are now part of the global economy.

Family Farmers: The Maya of Chiapas, Mexico, and the French of Abriès

Some applied anthropologists and other development specialists have said that family farmers in closed communities are "risk averse" because they avoid adopting innovations such as new techniques for cultivation, new seed varieties, and new forms of fertilizer. Economic anthropologists have shown, in contrast, that such conservatism may be adaptive. Family farmers have intimate knowledge of the systems within which they work, and they are capable of assessing costs and benefits of innovations. These two perspectives both emphasize the farmers' agency as decision makers, determining whether they should change in certain directions. In contrast, development projects such as the construction of roads, global patterns in demand for certain products, and labour opportunities shape the options that farmers have to consider.

Economic anthropologist Frank Cancian first studied production among the Mayan Indians of Zinacantán, located in the Chiapas region of Mexico's far south, in 1960. He returned in 1983 to conduct a restudy and thus gained insight into changes that had taken place in the intervening 20 years (1989). At the time of his first research, most Zinacantecos earned their livelihood by growing corn and selling some of their crops in a nearby city. They were largely independent of outside forces in terms of their own food supply. The community was closely knit, its social boundaries defined by people's commitment to community roles and ceremonies. Twenty years later, both the local economy and the social system had changed, reflecting the much greater effects of the world system economy on the region. Zinacantán's economy had become much more connected with forces beyond its borders.

The major direct cause of change was the massive increase in public spending by the government in the 1970s. This spending supported the construction of roads, dams, schools, and housing throughout the Chiapas region. The government also sponsored outreach programs to promote agricultural change, mainly crop diversification and ways to increase production. Another important factor was the oil boom in northern Chiapas and nearby

Tabasco province, which brought huge amounts of cash into the local economy.

By 1983, 40 percent of the households had no land at all and planted no corn. The majority of the population had become involved in wage work, and unemployment, rather than a bad farming season, was the major threat to food security. Wage work included the new opportunities in road construction, government jobs, transportation (of people, food goods, and flowers), and full-time trading in urban markets reachable by the new roads.

This story, in its general outlines, is similar to that of many family farmers throughout the world, especially in developing countries. It involves transformation from production for own-use to production for sale within a monetized system of trade for profit. Having sold the family farm, self-employed farmers enter the wage economy and become dependent on it for their livelihood. Many Zinacantecos raised their income level substantially during this period, and a clear income gap emerged among different categories of people. Being able to buy one or more trucks and take advantage of the new opportunities for urban trade created by the new roads was the most reliable way to become richer. In contrast, households with the least access to cash were left behind; these households were characteristically headed by a woman on her own.

Overall, the area became more prosperous, more monetized, and more dependent on the outside economy. Internally, social differentiation increased, and social solidarity within the community declined.

Harriet Rosenberg's (1988) study of Abriès village in the French Alps also reveals how external economic changes and opportunities affected a family farm system. Two hundred years ago, Abriès supported a population of close to 2000 people based on an economy of sheep raising. Villagers made a good living trading sheep and selling ewes' milk, butter, and cheese. "Women played an active decision-making role in family economic enterprises and were expected to know about agricultural matters" (H. Rosenberg 1988:27). The worldwide depression of the 1930s hit the village hard. The Swiss corporation Nestlé paid low prices for the farmers' milk and people attempted to peddle milk products directly to lowlanders. After World War II, the villagers were encouraged to adopt mechanized agriculture by the French government, but the continued unprofitability of agriculture forced people to move away until the village supported only 200 people. In the 1990s, winter tourism had come to the village, but local people are employed at the bottom of the pay scale and reap few benefits from tourism. "Decisions made around the world influence life in Abries but the Abriesois have no control over them. The policies of the European Economic Community are not negotiated with villages; neither are the budgets of multinational corporations such as Nestle" (H. Rosenberg 1988:210). The people com-

ment that their children must leave the village because they have no future if they stay.

Industrialists: Taiwanese in South Africa

In South Africa during the 1990s, after the dismantling of apartheid, political leaders adopted a neoliberal economic policy (Hart 2002). Links with Taiwanese industry were forged, and several Taiwanese industries were established outside major urban areas. There is no simple explanation for the Asian economic "miracle," but one component was the family model of production in which age and gender hierarchies ensure compliance. Inclusion of women in production was another key factor.

Taiwanese managers tried to use such a family system in South Africa as a way of ensuring a smoothly functioning labour force. An anthropologist who studied Taiwanese knitwear factories in two locations in KwaZulu-Natal province, South Africa, learned of substantial worker resentment against management. Women workers were especially vocal. Taiwanese patterns of negotiating with women workers by using an idiom of kinship and family did not work at all. The South African women frequently commented that they felt as though they were being treated like animals. The Taiwanese industrialists were separated by a wide racial, economic, and social divide from the factory workers. They lived far from the townships, which they considered dangerous. Imposing hierarchical kinship metaphors in such a context failed to create a viable workforce, and ultimately, many of the Taiwanese industrialists found themselves a focal point of local political conflict. In one town, a Chinese welcome monument was removed.

Industrial Workers: Barberton

Increased mechanization is another major aspect of change in industry worldwide, and it has marked impacts on labour. Unemployment and manufacturing declines in the U.S. "Rust Belt" are well-known trends in industrial lifeways. Gregory Pappas (1989) studied unemployment in Barberton, a working-class Ohio town. A tire company that had been the town's major employer closed in 1980, eliminating 1200 jobs. Pappas lived in Barberton for a year, interviewing many people and sending a questionnaire to over 600 displaced workers for further information. His work sheds light on how unemployed workers cope either by migrating or by finding new ways to spend their time in Barberton. These people are faced with having to construct a new identity for themselves: "For factory workers the place of employment is crucial; their identities are bound up in a particular place, and plant shutdowns compromise their ability to understand themselves" (83). As one unemployed man commented, "I don't know who I am anymore." In this context of decline, levels of stress and mental disorder have increased for many people.

Anthropologists and other experts question the current and future sustainability of a mode of production that relies so heavily on the use of nonrenewable resources and creates high levels of pollution. Others suggest that new forms of energy will be discovered and planets besides Earth will be able to provide resources and places of human habitation. Given the global interconnections of industrialism—its demand for raw materials, markets, and labour, and its social and environmental effects—cultural anthropologists are being challenged to devise new theories and methods to study such complexity and contribute to policies that will have positive social effects.

Capitalism Goes Global

Over 150 years ago, Karl Marx claimed that capitalism was on its last legs and a worldwide proletarian revolution would overthrow this industrial mode of production. However, in its most recent form, global incorporation, capitalism's effects are ever more powerfully felt in localities worldwide. Marx would be interested to observe how the Tiwi are developing international tourism, how Mayans in Chiapas took up road construction for cash and their abandoned corn farming declined, how French farmers tried to adapt to mountain tourism, and how Taiwanese knitwear manufacturers in KwaZulu-Natal encountered problems in cross-cultural labour management.

WHAT is the scope of economic anthropology?

Like the discipline of economics, economic anthropology encompasses the study of production, consumption, and exchange. But economic anthropology approaches these processes from a cross-cultural perspective and does not assume that Western economic patterns and values are universal. Economic anthropologists study a wider range of modes of production, or ways of making a living through goods or money, than economists study. The five modes of production anthropologists address are foraging, horticulture, pastoralism, agriculture, and industrialism. Anthropologists propose that the Western dualist notion of nature as separate from culture, with culture dominant, fits with capitalist economics and the economic exploitation of nature.

WHAT are the characteristics of the five major modes of production?

The five modes of production involve the factors of labour, property relations, and sustainability. In foraging societies, the division of labour is based on gender and age, with temperate foragers having more gender overlap in tasks than circumpolar foragers. Property is shared, with all people having equal rights to resources such as land and water holes. These resources are managed by family groups and shared with others as needed. With its strategy of limited exploitation of local resources in combination with seasonal migration, foraging has long-term sustainability when not affected by pressure from the outside world.

Horticulture and pastoralism are also extensive strategies, requiring the sequential fallowing of plots in horticulture and migration of animals to fresh pastures in pastoralism. We cannot easily generalize about the division of labour in these modes of production because they include those in which men do most of the work, those in which women do most of the work, and those in which workloads are shared more evenly. As with foraging peoples, use rights are the prominent form of property relations, but increased levels of production through the domestication of plants and animals yield more food and goods as well as heightened interest in protecting group

rights to land. Given the mobile strategies of shifting use of plots in horticulture and shifting use of pasture land in pastoralism, these modes of production have long-term sustainability when not affected by encroachments from other economic systems.

Early agriculture, like many agricultural contexts now, was family-based in terms of labour. Most family farming systems involve more male labour in the fields and more female labour in the domestic domain, although some examples of dominant female roles in field labour exist. Plantation agricultural systems, which are quite recent, involve the use of hired labour, both male and female, as does corporate farming. Socialist states created another form of labour organization for farming through the collective, which organized workers into teams regardless of family affiliation or gender. In collectivized agriculture, men and women were supposed to have equal roles, but women tended to have lower status positions than men. With settled agriculture came the emergence of private property, and social control and laws to protect private interests. Social inequality in access to the primary means of production, land, emerged along with gaps between the rich landed people and the poor landless people. Agriculture's sustainability is limited by the need to replenish the land, which is used continuously for crops and animals.

In industrialism, labour is highly differentiated by class in addition to gender and age. Widespread unemployment is found in many industrial economies. In capitalist industrial societies, private property is the dominant pattern, with high rates of imprisonment for people who violate the rules. Socialist industrial societies have attempted to distribute property among all people, but most such attempts have not been successful. Given its intensive and ever-expanding exploitation of nonrenewable resources, industrialism lacks long-term sustainability.

WHAT are some directions of change in the five modes of production?

Foragers are being incorporated into more settled economies as their access to large amounts of land is decreased by outside economic forces. Many former foraging people now work, for example, as farm labourers, jobs typically of low status in the mainstream cash

economy. Others are participating in the revitalization of their culture in the new global economy, producing art for sale on the world market or developing cultural tourism opportunities for outsiders. While horticulture and pastoralism exist on a larger scale than foraging, these land-extensive systems are also under great pressure from the competing economic forms of agriculture and industrialism. Many former horticulturalists have migrated to plantations or urban areas and become part of the cash economy. States have pressured pastoralists to settle down or to become collectivized in some contexts and then de-collectivized. In many parts of the world, family farms are declining in number as corporate farms increase. The labour force changes from being family-based to being dependent on migrant labourers who are often transnationals. A possible sixth mode of production is emerging with the information age and economic processes being carried out via the internet. E-commerce is creating new ways of making a living, new labour patterns, new forms of property, and new questions about sustainability. Cultural anthropologists are just beginning to address this latest stage in economic change.

KEY CONCEPTS

agriculture, p. 58
capital, p. 61
consumption, p. 50
corporate farms, p. 61
domestication, p. 54
economic systems, p. 50
exchange, p. 50
foraging, p. 51
formal sector, p. 63
horticulture, p. 54
industrial agriculture, p. 61

industrial collectivized agriculture, p. 62
industrialism, p. 63
informal sector, p. 63
intensive strategy, p. 58
modes of production, p. 50
pastoralism, p. 56
privatization, p. 67
production, p. 50
public/private dichotomy, p. 59
use right, p. 53
wet rice agriculture, p. 59

SUGGESTED READINGS

Anne Allison, *Nightwork: Sexuality, Pleasure and Corporate Masculinity in a Tokyo Hostess Club*. Chicago: University of Chicago Press, 1994. Based on the author's participant observation, this book explores what it is like to work as a hostess in a club that caters to male corporate employees and discusses how that culture is linked to men's corporate work culture.

Jans Dahl, *Saqqaq: An Inuit Hunting Community in the Modern World*. Toronto: University of Toronto Press, 2000. This ethnography of Saqqaq, a hunting community located on Disko Bay, eastern Greenland, is based on fieldwork carried out at several times since 1980 in order to provide a diachronic perspective. Hunting beluga is a central community activity and still forms the basis of community identity, even though commercial fishing and other economic activities have gained importance in recent times.

Frances Dahlberg, ed., *Woman the Gatherer*. New Haven: Yale University Press, 1981. These path-breaking essays examine the role of women in four different foraging societies, provide insights on human evolution from studies of female chimpanzees, and give an overview of women's role in human cultural adaptation.

Elliot Fratkin, *Ariaal Pastoralists of Kenya: Surviving Drought and Development in Africa's Arid Lands*. Boston: Allyn and Bacon, 1998. Based on several phases of ethnographic research among the Ariaal beginning in the 1970s, this book provides insights about pastoralism in general and the particular cultural strategies of the Ariaal, including attention to social organization and family life.

John G. Galaty and Pierre Bonte, eds., *Herders, Warriors, and Traders: Pastoralism in Africa*. Boulder, CO: Westview Press, 1991. This collection of readings examines the ability of pastoralists in Africa to maintain their way of life despite years of droughts and war.

David Uru Iyam, *The Broken Hoe: Cultural Reconfiguration in Biase Southeast Nigeria*. Chicago: University of Chicago Press, 1995. Based on fieldwork among the Biase people by an anthropologist who is a member of a Biase group, this book examines changes since the 1970s in the traditional forms of subsistence—agriculture, fishing, and trade—and related issues such as environmental deterioration and population growth.

Richard Lee and Richard Daly, eds., *The Cambridge Encyclopaedia of Hunters and Gatherers*. Cambridge: Cambridge University Press, 1999. This comprehensive book, written by recognized leaders in the field, outlines and evaluates anthropological knowledge on hunters and gatherers worldwide.

Heather Montgomery, *Modern Babylon? Prostituting Children in Thailand*. New York: Bergahn Books, 2001. The author conducted fieldwork in a tourist community in Thailand where parents frequently commit their children to prostitution. She sought to gain a view of this system from the perspective of the children and the parents. She found that these insiders' views are far more complex than the monolithic "victim" picture painted by international agencies.

Brian Morris, *The Power of Animals: An Ethnography*. New York: Berg, 1998. This book is an ethnography of Malawi, southern Africa. It is based on in-depth fieldwork in one region, supplemented by travel and study throughout the country. It focuses on men's roles in animal hunting and women's roles in agriculture as crucial to understanding wider aspects of Malawian culture, including diet and food preparation, marriage and kinship, gender relations, and attitudes about nature.

Katherine S. Newman, *Falling from Grace: The Experience of Downward Mobility in the American Middle Class*. New York: The Free Press, 1988. This book provides ethnographic research on the downwardly mobile of New Jersey as a "special tribe," with attention to loss of employment by corporate managers and blue-collar workers, and the effects of downward mobility on middle-class family life, particularly among women.

Richard H. Robbins, *Global Problems and the Culture of Capitalism*. Boston: Longman, 1999. Robbins takes a critical look at the role of capitalism and global economic growth in creating and sustaining many world problems such as poverty, disease, hunger, violence, and environmental destruction. The last section includes extended case studies to support the argument.

WEBLINKS

The Companion Website (www.pearsoned.ca/miller) that accompanies *Cultural Anthropology*, Third Canadian Edition, includes a destinations module containing links to many websites relevant to the content of this chapter. Use it to investigate the Web and expand your understanding of anthropology.

KEY QUESTIONS

- **HOW** are modes of production related to consumption?
- **HOW** are modes of production related to exchange?
- **WHAT** are some examples of how contemporary economic change affects consumption and exchange?

4

CONSUMPTION AND EXCHANGE

A member of the Kayapo tribe of Brazil eats a Popsicle during a break in a meeting of indigenous peoples to protest a dam-building project. Changing worldwide consumption patterns are increasing the incidence of tooth decay, diabetes, and obesity among indigenous people.

Imagine that it is the late eighteenth century and you are a member of a Kwakwaka'wakw village in British Columbia. Along with the rest of your local tribal group, you have been invited to a **potlatch**, a grand feast in which guests are invited to eat and to receive gifts from the hosts (Suttles 1991).

Be prepared to eat a lot because potlatch guests are given abundant helpings of the most honourable foods: eulachon oil (oil from the eulachon fish, which has high fat content), high-bush cranberries, and seal meat, all served in ceremonial wooden bowls. The chief will present the guests with many gifts: hand-embroidered blankets, canoes, and carefully crafted household articles such as carved wooden boxes and woven mats, and food to be taken back home.

The more the chief gives, the higher his status will rise, and the more his guests will be indebted to him. Later, when it is the guests' turn to hold a potlatch, they will try to give away as much as—or more than—their host did, thus shaming him into giving the next potlatch.

Before the arrival of the Europeans, peoples throughout the Pacific Northwest were linked with each other through a network of potlatching relationships. The Europeans tried to stop potlatching because they thought it was "wasteful," and because it contained elements that offended Christian principles they were trying to promote. In spite of the fact that the Canadian government banned potlatching and the Winter Ceremonials in 1884, potlatches continued to be held furtively and openly among some groups, and are being revived by others.

Potlatches figure prominently in ethnographic descriptions of the Northwest Coast. Some anthropologists argue that potlatch networks provided a food safety net for people in the region (Piddocke 1969). Because of local annual fluctuations in food supply, a particular group might have a substantial surplus of fish, berries, and nuts during one year, but a deficit in the next year. Foodstuffs could not be saved for long enough to deal with this unevenness. Instead of saving food, people "banked" food through potlatching: A group experiencing an abundant season would be inspired to potlatch its neighbours and distribute its surplus to others. In the future, a former host group would be the guests at a neighbouring group's potlatch when they had a surplus.

This sketch of potlatching demonstrates how closely linked production, consumption, and exchange are. Potlatches are related to levels of production; they are opportunities for consumption; and they involve exchange of goods among groups. This chapter considers the areas of economic anthropology that deal with **modes of consumption**, or the predominant patterns within a culture of using up goods and services, and **modes of exchange**, or the predominant patterns within a culture of transferring goods, services, and other items between and among peoples and groups (see Figure 4.1).

Villagers assemble gifts in preparation for a potlatch, held before 1914 in Alert Bay, Vancouver Island.

FIGURE 4.1 Modes of Production, Consumption, and Exchange

FORAGING	HORTICULTURE	PASTORALISM	AGRICULTURE	INDUSTRIALISM (CAPITALIST)
Mode of Consumption Minimalism Finite needs				*Mode of Consumption* Consumerism Infinite needs
Social Organization of Consumption Equality/sharing Personalized products are consumed				*Social Organization of Consumption* Class-based inequality Depersonalized products are consumed
Primary Budgetary Fund Basic needs				*Primary Budgetary Fund* Rent/taxes, luxuries
Mode of Exchange Balanced exchange				*Mode of Exchange* Market exchange
Social Organization of Exchange Small groups, face-to-face				*Social Organization of Exchange* Anonymous market transactions
Primary Category of Exchange The gift				*Primary Category of Exchange* The sale

CULTURE AND CONSUMPTION

In this section, we examine the concept of consumption and review various modes of consumption in relation to modes of production (see Chapter 3). We look at several consumption funds, or areas to which people devote resources, such as basic needs and social needs.

What Is Consumption?

Consumption has two senses: First, it is a person's "intake" in terms of eating or other ways of using things; second, it is a person's "output" in terms of spending or using resources. Thus, consumption includes eating habits and household budgeting practices. People consume many things: Food, drink, clothing, and shelter are the most basic consumption needs. Beyond that, they may acquire and use tools, weapons, means of transportation, computers, books and other items of communication, art and other luxury goods, and energy for heating and cooling their residence.

In order to consume, one must have something to consume or to trade for something consumable. In a market economy, most consumption depends on having cash, and a person's ability to consume would thus be measured in terms of cash income. Economists who study consumption in cash-based market economies often use data on people's cash income or expenditures as measures of consumption. However, cultural anthropologists are interested in all economic systems, not just market economies, so we broaden our analysis to include non-cash forms of income or expenditure. In non-market economies, instead of spending cash, people "spend" time, labour, or trade goods in order to provide for their needs. While it may seem odd to consider time or labour as equivalent to cash, this conceptual framework allows for cross-cultural comparison of people's access to resources and their consumption and exchange patterns.

The relationship between the processes of consumption and exchange differs in non-market and market systems. In non-market economies, many consumption needs are satisfied without any exchange at all, or only to a limited degree. In market economies, most consumption items are not self-produced and must be purchased. When a horticulturalist grows food for home consumption using seeds saved from the previous year, no exchange is involved in providing for consumption. If a farmer purchases seeds and fertilizer to grow food, then exchange is an essential part of providing for consumption needs. In non-market

A granary in West Africa allows for saving food crops for several months. Raising it above ground protects the food from being eaten by animals and from damage by moisture.

consumption that emphasizes simplicity and is characterized by few and finite (limited) consumer demands and an adequate and sustainable means to achieve them. At the other end of the continuum is **consumerism**, in which people's demands are many and infinite and the means of satisfying them are therefore insufficient and become depleted in the effort to meet demands. Minimalism is most clearly exemplified in (free-ranging) foraging societies, while consumerism is the distinguishing feature of industrial cultures (of the capitalist variety). In between these two extremes are blended patterns, with a decreasing trend toward minimalism and an increasing trend toward consumerism as one moves from left to right. Changes in the mode of production influence the transformation in consumption. Notably, the increase of surpluses and the ability to store wealth for long periods of time allow for a more consumerist lifestyle to emerge.

The social organization of consumption also changes as one moves across the continuum. As we noted in Chapter 3, social inequality in access to resources increases as one moves from foraging to agricultural and industrial (especially capitalist) societies. In foraging societies, everyone has access to all resources. Food, land, water, and materials for shelter are usually communally shared, as among the traditional Ju/wasi of southern Africa:

> Food is never consumed alone by a family; it is always (actually or potentially) shared out with members of a living group or band of up to 30 (or more) members. Even though only a fraction of the foragers go out each day, the day's return of meat and gathered foods are divided in such a way that every member of the camp receives an equitable share. The hunting band or camp is a unit of sharing, and if sharing breaks down it ceases to be a camp. (R. B. Lee 1979:118)

The distribution of personal goods, such as clothing or "leisure" items such as musical instruments or smoking pipes, is also equal. In horticultural and pastoral societies, group sharing is still a prevalent ethic, and it is the duty of leaders to make sure that everyone has food and shelter.

At the other end of the continuum, we find the leading consumerist cultures of the world. Consumption levels in North America, since the 1970s, have been the highest of any society in human history. Consumerism is widely promoted as a good thing, a path to happiness. Increasing one's consumption level and quality of life is a primary personal goal of most people, and of the government, too. Many other nations around the world have growing economies that allow some of the population to demand consumer goods and have the energy capabilities to support a luxury lifestyle (cars, air conditioning, and other appliances). These countries include the rapidly developing nations of Asia, such as China, the Republic of Korea, and Vietnam, and many countries in Africa and Latin America. For example, Ghana's economy grew at about

economies, few goods are obtained through exchange, while in market economies most goods are obtained this way.

Modes of Consumption

Using cross-cultural evidence on consumption, we can construct a general picture of modes of consumption, or dominant patterns of using things up or spending one's resources in order to satisfy demands. Modes of consumption correspond generally with the production continuum (see Figure 4.1 on page 77). At the opposite ends of the continuum, two contrasting modes of consumption exist, defined in terms of the relationship between demand (what people want) and supply (the resources available to satisfy demand) (Sahlins 1972). **Minimalism** is a mode of

A view of Toronto. The demand for electricity in urban centres worldwide has prompted the building of many high dams to generate power. Food must be shipped to urban markets. In general, cities have high energy costs compared with rural areas.

5 percent a year in the 1990s. At the same time, electricity consumption increased almost 11 percent a year in the nation and in Accra, the capital, it grew at over 13 percent a year. The increase is the result of both industrial growth and increased consumer demand for electrical appliances, including fans, refrigerators, televisions, stereos, air conditioners, VCRs, computers, and fax machines.

In all, the amount of goods that the world's population consumed in the past fifty years equals what was consumed by all previous generations in human history. Minimalism was sustainable over hundreds of thousands of years.

Some industrialized nations, such as Sweden, have taken steps to control consumerism and its negative environmental effects, especially through reducing the use of cars.

[Stockholm] is laid out to encourage walking, bicycling, and, in the long winter, cross-country skiing. Continuous paths through parklands encircle many of the islands on which the city is built, and Stockholm's commercial district is laced with bicycle routes, wide sidewalks, and pedestrian zones. Buses move swiftly through the metropolis, and the national bus and railway depot is in the heart of the city. People commute not only by foot and cycle, but also by kayak through the city's dozens of channels and waterways. (Durning 1993:23)

In small-scale societies, such as those made up of foragers, horticulturalists, and pastoralists, consumption items are typically produced by the consumers themselves. If not, they are likely to be produced by people with whom the consumer has a personal, face-to-face relationship. We can refer to this kind of consumption as personalized. Everyone knows where products come from and who produced them. This pattern contrasts markedly with consumption in much of the contemporary, globalized world, which we might call radically depersonalized consumption. Multinational corporations manage the production of most of the goods that people in industrialized countries consume. Many of these products are multi-sourced, with parts assembled in diverse parts of the world by hundreds of unknown workers.

Depersonalized consumption is linked with mass production, which ensures a high level of production—the production of infinite goods to satisfy infinite needs. Even in the most industrialized contexts, though, depersonalized consumption has not completely replaced personalized consumption. The popularity of farmers' markets in urban centres is one example of personalized consumption in which the consumer buys apples from the person who grew them and with whom the consumer is likely to have a friendly conversation, perhaps while eating one of the apples.

Consumption Funds

A **consumption fund** is a category of a person's or household's budget used to provide for their demands. Cross-cultural analysis of expenditures (including time or labour and cash) reveals that expenditure patterns differ according to the mode of production and the amount of surplus goods available in the society. In looking at a typical set of consumption funds, it is important to remember that people in nonmonetized contexts "spend" time or labour, not cash.

In a forager's "budget," the largest share of expenditures goes into the **basic needs fund**, which includes food, beverages, shelter, fuel, clothing, and the tools needed to obtain these items. In other words, foragers "spend" the largest proportion of their "budget" on fulfilling their basic needs, including repair and maintenance of tools and baskets, weapons, and shelter. Smaller amounts of expenditure are made to the **entertainment fund**, for personal leisure, and the **ceremonial fund**, for public events beyond

Critical Thinking

ASSESSING ONE'S OWN ENTITLEMENT BUNDLE

DO YOU own land on which you grow your own food? If yes, then a basic part of your entitlement bundle consists of direct entitlements to food.

Or do you buy your food? If so, where do you get the money to buy food? If parents or other relatives give you money to buy food, then your entitlement bundle consists of indirect entitlements of two sorts: cash transfers from other people and then exchange of cash for food. Maybe you work for someone who pays you cash in return for your labour. That's an indirect entitlement, too.

What would you do if every cafeteria, restaurant, and grocery store declared that they no longer would accept money in exchange for food?

Do you have any other entitlements in your bundle that you could use to get food? You might take some of

your personal goods, such as your bicycle or computer, to trade for food. You might see if some of your friends or relatives have some stored-up supplies that they would give you or lend you. If you own land, you might start planting food crops, but that would not help in the short run. In an extreme situation in which none of these options worked, you might be driven to stealing food, but theft is not considered an entitlement because it is illegal.

If none of these strategies succeeds, you have experienced "entitlement failure" and the end result could be starvation.

---

the immediate group such as a potlatch. No funds go to the **tax/rent fund**, which are payments to a government or landowner for civic responsibilities or use of land or housing.

Consumption budgets in consumerist cultures differ in the overall size of the budget and in the proportions allocated to particular funds. First, the budget size is larger. People in agricultural and industrial societies work longer hours (unless they are unemployed); thus, they "spend" more time and labour than foragers. However, the very poor may simply not be able to meet their basic needs. This change follows a well-known economic principle that budgetary shares for food and housing decline as income rises. People with higher incomes may spend more on food and housing in an absolute sense than people with lower incomes, but the proportion of their total budget devoted to food and housing is less. For example, someone who earns a total of $1000 a month and spends $800 on food and housing, expends 80 percent of his budget in that category. Someone who makes $10 000 a month and spends $2000 a month on food and housing, expends only 20 percent of her budget in this category, even though she spends more than twice as much as the first person, in an absolute sense. People living in agricultural and industrial cultures devote the largest proportion of their budget to the tax/rent fund. In some agricultural contexts, tenant farmers and share-croppers provide one-third or one-half of their crops to the landlord as rent. Income taxes constitute over 50 per-

cent of income in countries such as Japan, Sweden, the Netherlands, and Italy (Pechman 1987). Consumers in industrial countries are also placing increasing importance on the entertainment fund, which is used for recreation such as attending movies and sports events, travel, and buying home entertainment appliances.

Consumption Inequalities

Amartya Sen (1981), an economist and a philosopher, developed the concept of **entitlements**, which are socially defined rights to life-sustaining resources, in order to explain why some groups suffer more than others during a famine. We can extend the use of the concept of entitlements to nonfamine situations as well, as a way of looking at consumption inequalities in everyday life. Also, Sen's original use of the entitlement concept was in terms of intrasocietal patterns, but we will use it at three levels: global, national, and household. The concept of entitlements helps us understand how social inequality works and can change.

According to Sen, a person possesses a set or "bundle" of entitlements. A person may own land, earn cash from a job, be on welfare, or live off an inheritance, for example. Through these entitlements, people provide for their consumption needs. Some kinds of entitlements, however, are more secure and more lucrative than others, and thus they provide more secure and luxurious levels of consumption (see the Critical Thinking box). **Direct entitlements** are the most secure form of entitlement. In an agricultural society, for example, owning land that produces food is a direct entitlement. **Indirect entitlements** are ways of gaining subsistence that depend on exchanging something in order to obtain consumer needs—for example, labour, animal hides, welfare cheques, or pension benefits. Indirect entitlements entail dependency on other people and institutions and are thus riskier bases of support than direct entitlements. For example, labour or animal hides may drop in value or no longer be wanted, and welfare cheques may cease to be awarded. People who have no direct entitlements and only one or two forms of indirect entitlements in their bundle are in the most vulnerable position during times of economic decline, scarcity, or disaster.

In foraging societies, everyone has the same entitlement bundles and, except for infants and the very aged, the bundles are direct (infants and the aged are dependent on sharing from members of the group for their food and shelter and so could be said to have indirect entitlements). In industrial capitalist societies, entitlement bundles, in terms of access to food and resources, are preponderantly indirect. The few people who still grow their own food are a small proportion of the total population, and even they are dependent on indirect entitlements for electricity and other aspects of maintaining their lifestyle. In the highly monetized economies of industrialized societies, the most powerful entitlements are those that provide a high and steady cash income such as a good job, savings, and a retirement fund.

Entitlements at Three Levels

Applied globally, entitlement theory enables us to distinguish nations that have more or less secure and direct access to life-supporting resources from those that have not. Countries with high rates of food production have more secure entitlement to food than nations that are dependent on imports, for example. Growing cash crops rather than food crops puts a nation in a situation of indirect entitlement to food. The same applies to access to energy sources that may be important for transportation to work or for heating homes. Direct access to energy resources is preferable to indirect access. The current structure of the world economy, as noted in Chapter 3, places some countries in far more secure positions than others.

In a parallel way, the entitlement concept can be applied at the level of the household to examine within-household entitlement structures. In contemporary industrial societies, having a job, owning a business or farm land, owning a home, or having savings and investments puts a person in a more secure position. This means that adults, and often males more than females in most industrial societies, have more secure entitlements than other household members. Depending on the cultural context, inheritance

Civil war in southern Sudan in 1998 contributed to the spread of famine. Here a sister and brother await medical treatment in a Doctors Without Borders relief compound.

practices may ensure that certain children receive entitlements to certain assets (the family business, for example) while other children are left out.

Famine offers us a way of examining how entitlement theory works out in practice. **Famine** is massive death resulting from food deprivation in a geographically widespread area. It tends to reach a crisis point and then subside. Famines have been recorded throughout history for all parts of the world, including Europe (Dando 1980:113). Between the year 10 and 1850, 187 famines were recorded in what is now the United Kingdom. India, Russia, and China experienced major famines in the twentieth century. Most recently, famines have occurred mainly in Africa: the Sahelian famine of 1969–1971, the Ethiopian famine of 1982–1984 and 2000, and the Sudan and Somalian famines of 1988–1992. The North Korean famine (or near-famine) of the late 1990s is one of the few cases that have occurred outside Africa in recent times.

Most people think that famines are caused by "too many people to feed," or by natural disasters such as droughts and floods. Neither overpopulation nor natural disasters are sufficient explanations for famine (Sen 1981). First, calculations of world food supply in relation to population indicate that there is enough food produced every year to feed the world's population. Second, natural factors are often catalysts of famines, but natural disasters happen in many parts of the world and are not necessarily followed by famine. For example, Florida's devastating Hurricane Andrew did not cause a statewide famine. The answer to what causes famine lies in entitlement failures at three levels: global, national, and household.

The Global Level Throughout history, many countries that were colonized by external powers are now more resource-depleted than before and more dependent on food imports. Colonization changed local production from that of food crops for the farmers themselves to cash crops for sale. Thus, massive replacement of direct entitlements to food by indirect entitlements occurred. International relations in contemporary times often involve the "politics of food." As a journalist reported on the Sudan in 1988: "There is, cruelly, food to be had. The land is fertile, the rains were good, and this year's harvest will be the best in a decade. But four million people are starving because of a civil war. . . . On both sides the terrible weapon is increasingly food, not bullets" (Wilde 1988:43). The northern army blocked the delivery of food aid to the south, and the food that did get through was often diverted by the southern rebel troops. Norway donated substantial amounts of maize, but the United States was slow to get involved because it did not want to upset its diplomatic relationship with the Sudanese government.

Global politics were a key causal factor in the Bengal famine of 1943–44. This massive famine was related to British efforts during World War II to stop the Japanese forces from advancing into India from Burma. The region of Bengal at that time included what is now a state of India (named West Bengal) and the nation of Bangladesh (called East Bengal when it was part of British India). Bengal was a lush food-producing region located adjacent to Burma. As the Japanese moved closer to India, the British devised and implemented a plan to destroy food supplies in Bengal that could be used by the advancing enemy. The British burned standing crops and seeds that were being stored, and they destroyed fishing boats as well (Greenough 1982; Sen 1981). This policy succeeded in stopping the Japanese, but at a terrible cost of thousands of Bengalis' lives.

The National Level Within countries, entitlement inequalities lead to particular patterns of suffering. In no famine has everyone in the affected area starved. Instead, many people grow wealthy by hoarding food and selling it at inflated prices. During the Bengal famine, the people who were most affected were those who lacked direct entitlements to food: the landless poor who normally worked as labourers for the landowners and were paid in cash food shares, and fishing people who could not fish without boats (Sen 1981). In the meantime, rich landowners and merchants bought up the rice that existed and secretly stored it. As food prices rose astronomically during the famine, they grew even richer by selling hoarded rice.

The Household Level Within households, famine conditions force decisions about how to allocate scarce resources or deal with the absence of any resources at all.

No cultural anthropologist was on the scene during the Bengal famine, studying intrahousehold decision making. However, indirect historical evidence of how decisions were made can be found in records kept by the Bengal Relief Committee about people who came to relief centres for food, medicine, and clothing (Greenough 1982). One finding is that the famine caused the breakup of households. In Bengali culture, males are valued over females and adults are valued over children. In the household, the senior male is the head of household and has the highest authority and responsibility. These values are reflected in resource allocation choices during times of scarcity.

During the famine, spouses frequently separated, with the husband either leaving the wife behind or sending her away. The relief records show a high number of abandoned married women. Women who were interviewed said that "their husbands were unable to maintain them at the present moment and asked them to go elsewhere to search for food" (Greenough 1982:220). Many of these women migrated to cities, such as Calcutta, where their options for survival were limited to dependency on relief handouts, begging, or prostitution. Some women and girls were sold by their families into prostitution. Children were sold by desperate families either in hope that someone else could give them food or for the immediate purpose of obtaining cash. Many children were simply abandoned by the roadside. The pre-eminence and importance of the male head of household and the emphasis on preservation of the family line through males in Bengal shaped this pattern of decision making that differentially deprived women and children from household support.

Consumption Categories

People's consumption patterns are also shaped by class, gender, race, and age. These intersecting categories influence entitlement bundles and ways of consuming resources. People's consumption patterns are rarely the consequences of just one factor but, rather, are shaped by affiliation with multiple and intersecting groups that determine entitlement bundles and ways of consuming resources.

Class Class differences, which are defined in terms of levels of income and wealth, are reflected in class-specific consumption patterns. In societies with class structures, upper-class people spend more on consumption than the poor. The poor, however, spend a higher percentage of their total income on consumption than the rich, especially on basic needs such as food, clothing, and shelter. Class differences in consumption in contemporary industrial societies may seem so obvious that they are scarcely worth studying. A team of French researchers, however, undertook a national sample survey with over 1000

Homeless children rest by a storefront grate in Ho Chi Minh City, Vietnam. The transition from socialism to capitalism has altered people's entitlement bundle in Vietnam.

responses to study class differences in consumer preferences and tastes (Bourdieu 1984). The results revealed strong class patterns in, for example, choice of favourite painters or pieces of music, most closely associated with people's level of education and their father's occupation. An overall pattern of "distance from necessity" in tastes and preferences characterized members of the educated upper classes, who were more likely to prefer abstract art. In comparison, the working classes, given their economic position, were closer to "necessity" and their preference was for realist art. Bourdieu provides the concept of the "game of distinction," in which people of various classes take on the preferences of higher-income people in order to enhance their own standing. Education, according to Bourdieu, provides the means for lower-class people to learn how to play the game of distinction according to upper-class rules.

Gender In many societies, especially those where males and females have highly demarcated roles and status, consumption patterns are clearly gender marked as well. Specific foods may be thought to be "male foods" or "female foods." In places where alcoholic beverages are consumed, the overwhelming pattern is that males drink more than females. Following is a vivid example of differences in food consumption between males and females in highland Papua New Guinea, where males generally have higher status than females. This example begins with the eruption of a mysterious disease, with the local name of *kuru*, among the Fore (pronounced "for-ay"), a high-

land foraging group (Lindenbaum 1979). Between 1957 and 1977, about 2500 people died of *kuru*, but the victims were mostly women. A victim of the disease would first have shivering tremors, followed by a progressive loss of motor ability along with pain in the head and limbs. People afflicted with *kuru* could walk unsteadily at first but would later be unable to get up. Death occurred about a year after the first symptoms appeared.

The Fore believed that *kuru* was caused by sorcery, but a team of medical researchers and cultural anthropologist Shirley Lindenbaum showed that *kuru* was a neurological disease caused by the consumption of the flesh of deceased people who were themselves *kuru* victims. Who was eating human flesh, and why? Among the Fore, it was considered acceptable to cook and eat the flesh of a deceased person, although it was not considered a preferred form of food. Some Fore women were turning to eating human flesh because of the increased scarcity of the usual sources of animal protein in the region. Population density had increased, areas under cultivation had increased, forest areas had decreased, and wild animals as a protein source were scarce in the Fore region. This scarcity acted in combination with the Fore's strongly male-preferential system of consumption: Preferred protein sources go to men. Women, therefore, turned to consumption of less-preferred foods and thereby contracted *kuru,* and died.

Race/Ethnicity Racial apartheid was a matter of national policy in South Africa until 1994 and is a clear example of explicit racial inequalities in consumption. Whites owned property, had wealth, and lived prosperous lives that included good food, housing, and educational opportunities for their children. Blacks were denied all of these things. The current government in South Africa is still attempting to redress decades of deprivation linked to racial categories and now has to face the additional burden of widespread HIV/AIDS.

In the United States, as in Canada, racial differences in consumption and welfare exist. One area in which racial discrimination affects consumption is access to housing, a subject that has been studied by cultural anthropologists and other social scientists (B. Williams 1988; Yinger 1995; Hacker 1992). Access by Blacks to housing in integrated neighbourhoods in American cities is limited by the tendency of Whites to move out as more Black families move in. A 1992 survey conducted in Detroit found that most Blacks prefer to live in an integrated neighbourhood, but nearly half of the Whites surveyed said they would move out if the neighbourhood were one-third Black (Farley 1993, cited in Yinger 1995:7).

Nova Scotia's Black population arrived in the late 1700s and following the war of 1812. Segregated on small farm lots on rocky, marginal land, the settlers formed Canada's earliest and largest Black settlement, Africville. The community had no plumbing, sewage, running water, or paved roads, and was identified as early as 1917 as a slum requiring clearance. It was cleared in the 1960s, with property owners compensated or rehoused. Today the descendants of Africville view the destruction of their community as racially motivated and seek redress for the injustices of community destruction and relocation (Millward 1996). On July 5, 2002, Africville was designated a national heritage site as a reminder of the need for racial respect.

Age   Age categories often have characteristic consumption patterns that are culturally shaped. Certain foods are believed appropriate for infants, young children, adolescents, adults, or the aged. Consider the category of "the aged." Biologically, the elderly have "more critical and unique nutritional needs" than other age groups (Shifflett and McIntosh 1986–1987). In spite of these special needs, in many cultures the very old fall into a category with declining entitlements and declining quality of consumption. In North America, the elderly tend to decrease their physical activities, and they tend to omit important food groups, especially fruits and vegetables. Little exercise and inadequate diet lead to increased obesity and reduced resistance to disease. Elderly men or women living alone may eat junk food and meals prepared with the least effort.

Aging affects everyone, regardless of class level, but wealth can protect the elderly from certain kinds of marginalization and deprivation. The class effects of aging are somewhat reduced in Canada by community care programs that gear community-based care and long-term institutionalized care to income and the Canada Pension Plan, as well as universal access to health care.

Forbidden Consumption: Food Taboos

Anthropologists have a longstanding interest in trying to explain culturally specific food **taboos**, or rules of prohibition. This interest has generated several conflicting theories, with the strongest difference between cultural materialists and those who favour symbolic or meaning-centred theories.

Marvin Harris and Food Taboos

Marvin Harris (1974) asks why there are Jewish and Muslim taboos on eating pig when pig meat is so enthusiastically consumed in many other parts of the world. He says, "Why should gods so exalted as Jahweh and Allah have bothered to condemn a harmless and even laughable beast whose flesh is relished by the greater part of mankind?" (36). Harris proposes that we consider the role of environmental factors during early Hebrew times and

Preparations for a feast in the highlands of Papua New Guinea, where people place much value on consuming high-status foods such as roasted pig meat.

the function of this prohibition in terms of its fit to the local ecology:

> Within the overall pattern of this mixed farming and pastoral complex, the divine prohibition of pork constituted a sound ecological strategy. The nomadic Israelites could not raise pigs in their arid habitats, while for the semi-sedentary and village farming populations, pigs were more of a threat than an asset. . . . The pig has a further disadvantage of not being a practical source of milk, and of being notoriously difficult to herd over long distances. . . . Above all, the pig is thermodynamically ill-adapted to the hot, dry climate of the Negev, the Jordan Valley, and the other lands of the Bible and the Koran. Compared to cattle, goats, and sheep, the pig has an inefficient system for regulating its body temperature. Despite the expression "To sweat like a pig," it has recently been proved that pigs can't sweat at all. (41–42)

Raising pigs in this context would be a luxury. On the other hand, in "pig-loving" cultures of Southeast Asia and the Pacific, climatic factors including temperature, humidity, and the presence of forest cover (good for pigs) promote pig raising. There, pigs offer an important protein source in people's diets that complements yams, sweet potatoes, and taro. In conclusion, Harris acknowledges that not all religiously sanctioned food practices can be explained ecologically, and he allows that food practices do have a social function in promoting social identity. But first and foremost, analysis of food consumption should consider ecological and material factors of production.

Food Taboos as Systems of Meaning

Mary Douglas (1966) argues that what people eat has to do with the value of food as a way of communicating symbolic meaning as well as with the material conditions of life, including hunger. For Douglas, people's mental categories provide a psychological ordering of the world. Anomalies, or things that don't fit into the categories, become reminders to people of moral problems or things to avoid.

She uses this approach of ordered categories and disordered anomalies in her analysis of food prohibitions in the Old Testament book of Leviticus. One rule is that people may eat animals with cloven hoofs and that chew a cud. Several tabooed animals are said to be unclean, such as the camel, the pig, the hare, and the rock badger. Among a pastoral people, she says, it is logical that the model food animal would be a ruminant (a cloven-hoofed, cud-chewing, four-footed animal such as a cow, bison, goat, and sheep). In contrast, a pig is a four-footed animal with cloven hoofs, but it does not chew a cud; thus the pig is an anomaly and taboo as food. In this way, Leviticus sets up a system that contrasts sacred completeness and purity (the animals one can eat) with impurity and sinfulness (the animals one cannot eat) to remind people of God's holiness and perfection and people's responsibility toward God.

Anthropologists studying food systems try to consider both the material aspects of food practices and the communicative, symbolic meaning of food in order to explain food prohibitions and preferences, acknowledging that there is more to food than just eating.

CULTURE AND EXCHANGE

Cultural anthropologists have done much research on gifts and other forms of exchange, starting with the early twentieth century studies by Malinowski of the *kula* of the Trobriand Islands (described later in this chapter) and Boas's research on the potlatch of the Pacific Northwest. In all economic systems, individuals and groups exchange goods and services with others, so exchange is a cultural universal. But cultural variations arise in several areas: in what is exchanged, in how exchange takes place, and in when exchange takes place (see the Multiple Cultural Worlds box).

What Is Exchanged?

Exchange involves the transfer of something that may be material or immaterial between at least two persons, groups, or institutions. The items exchanged may be purely utilitarian or they may carry meanings and have a history, or "social life," of their own (Appadurai 1986). In contemporary industrial societies, money is a key item of exchange. In non-market economies, money plays a less important role, and valued items such as time, labour, and goods are prominent exchange items.

But non-monetary exchange exists in contemporary industrial societies, too. Hosting dinner parties, exchanging gifts at holiday times, and sharing a bag of potato chips with a friend are examples of common forms of non-monetary exchange. Some scholars would even include giving caresses, kisses, loyalty, and glances (Blau 1964).

Material Goods

Food is one of the most common exchange goods in everyday life and on ritual occasions. Marriage arrangements often involve complex stages of gifts and countergifts exchanged between the groom's family and the bride's family. Wedding exchanges among the Nias of northern Sumatra, Indonesia, provide a good illustration. From the betrothal onward to the actual marriage, there is a scheduled sequence of events at which gifts are exchanged between the families of the bride and groom (Beatty 1992). At the first meeting, the prospective groom expresses his interest in a betrothal. He and his party visit the bride's house and are fed: "The guests are given the pig's lower jaw (the portion of honour) and take away with them raw and cooked portions for the suitor's father" (121). Within the next week or two, the groom brings a gift of three to twelve pigs to confirm the betrothal. He also returns the container used for the pig meat given to him on the previous visit, filled with a certain kind of nut. The groom gives pigs and gold as the major gift that seals the marriage. Gifts will continue to be exchanged between the two families over many years. Exchanges of food are important in signalling and reaffirming friendships.

Exchanging alcoholic beverages is an important feature of many communal, ritual events in Latin America. In an Ecuadorian village called Agato, the San Juan fiesta is the high point of the year (Barlett 1980). The fiesta consists of four or five days during which small groups of celebrants move from house to house, dancing and drinking. The anthropologist reports on the event:

> I joined the groups consisting of the president of the community and the elected *alcaldes* (councilmen and police), who were accompanied by their wives, a few friends, and some children. We met each morning for a hearty breakfast at one house, began drinking there, and then continued eating and drinking in other homes throughout the day and into the evening. . . . Some people drink for only one or two days, others prefer to make visits mainly at night, while some people drink day and night for four days. . . . The host or hostess greets the group with a bucket of chicha (home-made corn beer) and a dipper or

Multiple Cultural Worlds

FAVOURS AND GIFTS IN CHINA

WHILE DOING fieldwork in urban China, Mayfair Yang (1994) learned about the pervasive importance of *guanxixue* (pronounced "guan-shee-shwe"), or the exchange of gifts, favours, and banquets in order to cultivate mutual obligation and indebtedness. Yang went to China with the intention of doing research in a factory, but she was never given clearance to do that work. In the process of trying to gain permission, she learned about the many levels of bureaucracy that were involved in getting permission for the fieldwork. In order to pass through each of these stages, simple and straightforward requests would not be enough: Much *guanxixue* would be needed. Given the importance of *guanxixue* in Chinese social relationships, Yang decided to shift her research focus to that topic. She writes that "Guanxixue is a ubiquitous theme; it appears in economic transactions; in political and social relationships; in literature, newspapers, academic journals, theater, and film. . . . Compared with other social practices, there also seems to be a greater cultural elaboration of vocabulary, jokes, proverbs, and etiquette surrounding guanxixue" (6).

Guanxixue involves getting what one wants through giving. If you give someone a gift and they accept it, or if you invite someone to dinner, then—later—you can ask a favour of the person and the rules of *guanxixue* prescribe that your favour will be granted. *Guanxixue* is not the same as bribery because it is indirect and usually handled discreetly. Yang describes one interaction that is less discreet since the first, discreet, attempt failed:

> A worker wanted to get a few authorized days off from work to attend to some personal business. He first tried to give presents in private to the factory manager, but the latter declined. So he cunningly worked out a way to make the manager accept. He waited for an opportunity when the manager was in the presence of many other workers to give the gift to him. . . . He said to the manager, "Here is the gift which my father, your old comrade-in-arms . . . asked me to deliver to you. Please accept it so his feelings are not hurt." Both the worker and the manager knew that the story about his father being an old friend of his was made up, so the real aim of the gift was apparent to the manager. In front of so many people, however, the manager was in danger of losing face if he refused to accept the gift unless he could come up with a good reason." (133–134)

The manager did not want to say in public that he would not accept the gift because that would appear to be ungenerous. And he did not want to call the worker a liar because the worker would lose too much face. The manager was forced to accept the gift. Later, when the inevitable request for authorized days off work arrived, he would have to say yes or else the factory people would talk about his lack of generosity.

---

bottle of trago (purchased cane liquor) and a shotglass. One member of the group, often the oldest man, accepts the liquor and distributes drinks to the entire party. Participants are urged to "do their share" to consume the liquor, but refusals are also accepted easily. After several rounds of drink, the server returns the empty bottle or bucket to the host, the group choruses goodbyes and hurries into the street. (118–119)

Guests who drink at someone's house will later serve their former hosts alcohol in return. In this way, social ties are reinforced.

Symbolic Goods

Intangible valuables such as myths (sacred stories) and rituals (sacred practices) are sometimes exchanged in ways similar to material goods. In lowland areas of Papua New Guinea, men trade myths, rituals, dances, flutes, costumes, and styles of body decoration for the pigs of highland men (Harrison 1993). Certain secret spells were some of the most prestigious trade items. In the Balgo Hills region of Australia, longstanding exchange networks transfer myths and rituals among groups of women (Poirier 1992). Throughout the region, the women may keep important narratives and rituals only for a certain time and then must pass them on to other groups. One such ritual is the *Tjarada*, a love-magic ritual with an accompanying narrative. The *Tjarada* came to the women of Balgo Hills from the north. They kept it for about 15 years and then passed it on to another group in a ceremony that lasted for three days. During the time that the Balgo Hills women were custodians of the *Tjarada*, they incorporated some new elements into it. These elements are retained even after its transfer to the next group. Thus, the *Tjarada* contains bits of local identity of each group that has had it.

A Guatemalan woman works at her hand loom. Maya weaving is closely linked with identity and ethnicity. This association is especially evident in women's embroidered blouses, *huipiles* (pronounced "hu-wee-PEEL-es"), which convey messages about the wearer's wealth, age, and home region. Three decades of civil war have threatened Maya culture in Guatemala, but many Maya groups are now revitalizing their traditions, including weaving.

A sense of linked community and mutual responsibility thereby develops and is sustained among the different groups that have held the *Tjarada*.

Labour

In labour-sharing groups, people contribute labour to other people on a regular basis (for seasonal agricultural work such as harvesting) or on an irregular basis (in the event of a crisis such as the need to rebuild a barn damaged by fire). Labour-sharing groups are part of what has been called a "moral economy," since no one keeps formal records on how much any family puts in or takes out.

Instead, accounting is socially regulated. The group has a sense of moral community based on years of trust and sharing. In Amish communities of North America, labour sharing is a major factor of production, infrastructure maintenance, and social cohesion. When a family needs a new barn or faces repair work that requires group labour, a barn-raising party is called. Many families show up to help. Adult men provide manual labour, and women provide food for the event. Later, when another family needs help, they call on the same people.

Money

The term **money** refers to things that can be exchanged for many different kinds of items (Godelier 1971:53). Besides being a medium of exchange, money can be a standard of value and a store of value or wealth (Neale 1976). Money can be found in such diverse items as shells, salt, cattle, furs, cocoa beans, and iron hoes. Compared to other exchange items, money or currency is a relatively recent innovation. Although no one knows when money first appeared, one of the earliest forms of coined money was in use by the Greeks in Asia Minor (Turkey) in the seventh century BCE. Pre-coin money undoubtedly existed well before that time.

Items that can be exchanged for only a few other items are called **limited-purpose money**. Canadian Tire "money," for example, can only be used to buy goods in Canadian Tire stores. Raffia cloth serves as limited-purpose money among the Lele of central Africa (Douglas 1962). Raffia cloth, made from the fibres of a certain kind of palm, is a medium of payment for certain ritual and ceremonial events, such as a marriage, and as a payment of compensation for wrongdoing. It is not used for commercial transactions such as buying food or houses or for renting or buying land.

Modern money is **multi-purpose money**, or a medium of exchange that can be used as payment for all goods and services available. In addition to its substitutability (money can be exchanged for goods and other money), modern money is distinguished by its portability, divisibility, uniformity, and recognizability (Shipton 2001). On the other hand, modern money is vulnerable to economic changes, such as inflation, which reduce its value. Early anthropologists who proposed evolutionary models of culture thought that modern money is more rational than limited-purpose money and that it would replace other forms of money as well as non-monetized exchanges such as barter. Modern money is indeed spreading throughout the world. Non-monetary cultures often adopt modern money in limited ways, prohibiting its use in religious exchanges, for example, or in life-cycle rituals such as marriages. Even the most monetized cultures place limits on what may be bought and sold for money.

All kinds of money are symbolic—they have meaning to the user, and they are associated with the user's identity and sense of self. Credit cards may be a positive sign of modernity or may be associated with overspending and wastefulness. They have "class" levels signified by cards of different colours.

Rights in People

Throughout history, some people have been able to gain control of other people and treat them as objects of exchange, as in systems of institutionalized slavery and in underground, criminal activities. The particular topic of women as "items" of exchange in marriage is a puzzling one in anthropology and has occasioned much debate. Lévi-Strauss proposed many years ago that the exchange of women between men is one of the most basic forms of exchange in human culture. His argument about exchange is based on the universality of some sort of "incest taboo," which he defines as a rule preventing a man from marrying or cohabiting with his mother or sister (1969). Such a rule, he says, is a logical motivation for equal exchange: "the fact that I can obtain a wife is, in the final analysis, the consequence of the fact that a brother or father has given her up" (62). According to this theory, men are thus impelled to develop exchange networks with other men. This process increases social solidarity between groups. For Lévi-Strauss, the incest taboo is the basis of the original form of exchange and thereby the emergence of an important aspect of culture.

Other anthropologists say that this theory, while intriguing, is male-centred and denies agency to the women involved. In an influential essay called "The Traffic in Women," Gayle Rubin (1975) says that it disregards the many foraging societies in which men do not have rights in women and in which women choose their own male partners. Evidence from horticultural and agricultural societies of Southeast Asia further refutes Levi-Strauss's universal model of men exchanging women (Peletz 1987). In these systems, the focus of marriage arrangements is on the exchange of men and control of their labour power and productivity. Adult women arranged their daughters' marriages, selecting the groom themselves.

Modes of Exchange

All societies devise systems for the exchange of resources that are not consumed by producers. The most common modes of exchange include reciprocity (generalized and balanced), redistribution, and the market system. While generalized reciprocity occurs in all societies, it is the dominant mode of exchange within foraging, horticultural, and pastoral societies. Market exchange becomes increasingly important in agricultural societies when surplus is produced, and in industrial economies where production for sale is the primary goal.

Reciprocity

Reciprocity is the mutual exchange of goods and services, or gifts and favours. **Generalized reciprocity** is a transaction that involves the least conscious sense of interest in material gain or thought of what might be received in return. When, or if, a possible return might be made is not calculated. Such exchanges often involve goods and services of an "everyday" or mundane nature, such as a cup of coffee. Generalized reciprocity is the predominant form of exchange between people who know each other well and have a high degree of trust in each other. It is the predominant form of exchange in foraging societies and it is also found among close kin and friends cross-culturally.

The Pure Gift A **pure gift** is something given with no expectation or thought of a return. The pure gift could be considered an extreme form of generalized reciprocity. Examples of a pure gift may include donating money for a food drive, in which the giver never knows or sees the receiver, or donations to famine relief, blood banks, and religious organizations. Some people say that a truly pure gift does not exist since one always gains something, no matter how difficult to measure, in giving—even if it is just the good feeling of generosity. Parental care of children is often considered a pure gift since most parents do not consciously calculate how "much" they have spent on their children with the intention of "getting it back" later on. In Thailand, expectations for reciprocity between parents and children are made explicit in the ordination ritual; a son is ordained as a monk to pay for the gift of his mother's milk (J. Van Esterik 1996). Those who do not consider parental care a pure gift say that even if the "costs" are not consciously calculated, parents have unconscious expectations about what their children will "return" to them, whether the return is material (care in old age) or immaterial (making the parent feel proud).

Balanced reciprocity is the exchange of approximately equally valued goods or services, usually between people of roughly equal social status; the exchange may occur simultaneously from both parties, or an agreement or understanding may exist that stipulates the time period within which the exchange will be completed. This aspect of the timing contrasts with generalized reciprocity, in which there is no fixed time limit for the return. In balanced reciprocity, if the second party fails to complete the exchange, the relationship will break down. Balanced reciprocity is less personal than generalized reciprocity and, according to Western definitions, more "economic." The form of exchange whereby the giver tries to "one up"

Shell ornaments are important items to be worn at ceremonial events, as shown on this man of the Sepik River area of Papua New Guinea.

out the importance of women's exchanges of food, bundles of banana leaves, and woven skirts for mortuary ceremonies.

Redistribution

Redistribution is a form of exchange that involves one person collecting goods or money from many members of a group, then, at a later time, "returning" the pooled goods to everyone who contributed. In comparison to the two-way pattern of reciprocity, redistribution involves some sort of "centrality." It contains the possibility of institutionalized inequality since what is returned may not always equal what was contributed. The pooling group may continue to exist in spite of inequality because of the leadership skills of the person who mobilizes contributions.

In the New Guinea Highlands, political leadership involves redistribution in a system of contributions and ritual feasts called *moka* that may take several years to organize. Formal taxation systems of industrial societies can be considered a form of redistribution. People pay taxes to a central institution, and they receive services from the government in return. Depending on the context, the return may or may not appear to be satisfactory to the contributors. In Canada, the federal government redistributes tax revenues to the provinces in the form of equalization payments that favour the poorest provinces. The degree of personal contact in different redistributive systems varies just as with forms of reciprocity. Similarly, the contexts in which greater personal interaction is involved tend to be more egalitarian and less exploitative than the impersonal forms.

Unbalanced Exchange

Market exchange is the buying and selling of commodities under competitive conditions in which the forces of supply and demand determine value (Dannhaeuser 1989:222). In market transactions, the people involved may not be related to or know each other at all. They may not be social equals, and their exchange is not likely to generate social bonding. Many market transactions take place in a marketplace, a physical location in which buying and selling occur. Markets evolved from other, less formal contexts of **trade**, a formalized exchange of one thing for another according to set standards of value. In order for trade to develop, someone must have something that someone else wants.

Specialization in producing a particular good promotes trade between regions. Particular products are often identified with a town or region. In Oaxaca, Mexico, different villages are known for blankets, pottery, stone grinders, rope, and chili peppers (Plattner 1989:180–181). In Morocco, the interior city of Fez is famous for its blue-

or get the better of the exchange at the expense of the partner is sometimes referred to as *negative reciprocity*.

The *kula* is an example of a system of balanced reciprocity. Men of many different Trobriand groups participate in the exchange of necklaces and armlets, giving them to their partners after keeping them for a while. The trading includes local trading partners who are neighbours and people in faraway islands who are visited via long canoe voyages on high seas. Men are distinguished by the particular armlets and necklaces that they trade, since certain armlets and necklaces are more prestigious than others. However, the *kula* social code dictates that "to possess is great, but to possess is to give." Generosity is the essence of goodness, and stinginess is the most despised vice. The higher the man's social rank, the more he must give. *Kula* exchanges should involve items of equivalent value. If a man trades a very valuable necklace with his partner, he expects to receive in return a very valuable armlet as a *yotile* (equivalent gift). At the time, if one's partner does not possess an equivalent item, he may have to give a *basi* (intermediary gift). The *basi* stands as a token of good faith until a proper return gift can be given. The *kudu* ("clinching gift") will come later and balance the original gift. The equality of exchange ensures a tight social bond between the trading partners and a statement of social equality and mutual trust. When a man sails to an area in which there may be danger because of previous raids or warfare, he can count on having a friend to receive him and give him hospitality. Although most attention has been on men's *kula* exchanges, Annette Weiner (1976) pointed

Moroccan pottery is for sale here in a regular market in Marrakech.

of such localized markets can be seen in the number of neighbourhood shops in the city of Shanghai (Lu 1995). Shanghai is the most Westernized city in China, but in the back streets and neighbourhoods, small-scale and personalized marketing still prevails, with shops selling sesame cakes, hot water, wine, traditional Chinese medicine, coal, tobacco, paper, soy sauce, and locally produced groceries.

More contemporary, less personalized forms of permanent marketplaces in North America include shopping malls and stock exchanges. The internet and "eBay" is the least personalized way to shop.

Other Forms of Unbalanced Exchanges

Several forms of unbalanced exchange exist that involve the transfer of goods from one person or institution to another without an equivalent return. In extreme instances, no social relationship is involved; in others, sustained unequal relationships are maintained over time between people. These forms range from the extreme example of giving something with no expectation of return to taking something with no expectation of return. These forms of unbalanced exchange can occur anywhere along the continuum of economic systems, but they are more likely to be found in large-scale or culturally complex societies where more options for other than face-to-face, balanced exchange exist.

Gambling   Gambling, or gaming, is the attempt to make a profit by playing a game of chance in which a certain item of value is staked in hopes of acquiring the much

glazed pottery, whereas the Berber people of the southern mountain region are known for their fine blankets, rugs, and other woven goods. Specialization also develops with illegal commodities, such as Jamaican marijuana or B.C. bud. Such market exchanges may be based on the exchange of goods or money.

The periodic market, a site for market transactions that is not permanently set up but occurs regularly, emerged with the development of agriculture and urban settlements. A periodic market, however, is more than just a place for buying and selling; it is also a place of social activity. Government officials drop in on the market, religious organizations hold services, long-term acquaintances catch up with each other, and young people may meet and fall in love.

Worldwide, permanent markets situated in fixed locations have long served the everyday needs of villages and neighbourhoods. Permanent markets throughout China, for example, have long provided for the everyday needs of local people (Skinner 1964). The persistence of the role

In China, many marketers are women. These two women display their wares in a regular neighbourhood food market in a city about an hour from Shanghai.

Lessons Applied

ASSESSING THE SOCIAL IMPACT OF NATIVE AMERICAN CASINOS

A FEW scattered "impact studies" on Native American casinos were carried out in the 1990s, but they were not based on a large number of casinos, nor did they include in-depth study of particular establishments. Thus their results were not solid enough to provide a foundation for policy-makers. One study found that, in terms of effects on the surrounding community, the presence of a Native American casino is much like having a new, large enterprise of any sort: Local employment and income rise, business opportunities are created, and local services such as law enforcement are strained (Lake and Deller 1996). Another study that examined the impact of several casinos over a four-year period found the following positive effects: young adults moving back to the reservation, increased adult employment, and a decline in the mortality rate (Evans and Topoleski 2002). Negative changes included a 10 percent increase in auto thefts, larceny, violent crime, and bankruptcy in the surrounding counties. The authors caution that their findings cannot be applied to policy formation without further study, because the issues are so complex. For example, many of the people employed in the casinos are not Native Americans.

Given the lack of comprehensive studies of the effects of Native American gaming, USET sought to provide high-quality, policy-relevant information as a tool for tribal leaders. The study is being led by anthropologist Kate Spilde, who works with the Harvard Project on American Indian Economic Development (HPAIED). It is being conducted in collaboration with tribal officials and casino managers. The study seeks to assess impacts on both the Native American gaming tribes and the surrounding communities. Initiated in 2003, it will take two and a half years and will involve on-site research with 100 gaming tribes throughout the United States. The study will also include eight in-depth case studies of individual tribes, chosen to represent the diversity of tribal gaming in terms of market size, tribal population, scope of gaming, profitability, and other factors. The research findings will be presented in a final report to be used by tribal policy makers and United States gaming policy-makers.

A report on the pilot project for the national study, carried out in Oklahoma, can be downloaded at *www.ksg.harvard.edu/hpaied/publ.htm.*

FOOD FOR THOUGHT

Consider the development of Native American casinos from the theoretical perspective of structure versus agency. (Recall the discussion of these perspectives in Chapter 1.)

---

larger return that one receives if one wins the game. If one loses, that which was staked is lost. Gambling is an ancient practice and is common cross-culturally. Ancient forms of gambling involved games such as dice throwing and card playing. Risky investing in the stock market can be considered a form of gambling, as can gambling of many sorts through the internet. Although gambling may seem an odd category within unbalanced exchange, its goals of making a profit seem to justify its placement here. The fact that gambling within "high" capitalism is on the rise justifies anthropological attention to it. In fact, some scholars have referred to the present stage of Western capitalism as "casino capitalism," given the propensity of investors to play very risky games on the stock market.

Native American gambling establishments in the United States and Canada have mushroomed in recent years. The state of Michigan alone has nearly 20 Native American casinos. Throughout the country, Native American casinos are so financially successful that they are perceived as an economic threat to many state lotteries. The Pequot Indians of Connecticut, a small tribe of around 200 people, now operate the most lucrative gaming establishment in the world, Foxwoods Resort and Casino, established in 1992 (Eisler 2001). The story of this success hangs on the creativity of one man: Richard "Skip" Hayward. An unemployed shipbuilder in the 1970s, he granted his grandmother's wish that he revive the declining tribe. Hayward used the legal system governing Native Americans to his advantage, forged links with powerful people such as Malaysian industrialist Lim Goh Tong and Bill Clinton (to whose campaign the Pequot donated half a million dollars), made powerful enemies such as Donald Trump, and became the chief of his now-rich tribe.

The Pequots, and many other Native American groups, have become highly successful capitalists. Anthropologists and other social scientists are asking what impact these casinos will have on their Native American owners and the surrounding area and what such newly rich groups will do with their wealth (see the Lessons Applied box). In 1992, 24 Native American tribes formed an intertribal organization called USET (United South and Eastern Tribes), which is supporting a nationwide study in the U.S. of the social and economic impacts of Native American gaming.

Theft Theft is taking something with no expectation or thought of returning anything to the original owner for it. It is the logical opposite of a pure gift. The study of theft has been neglected by anthropologists, perhaps because it might involve danger. One insightful analysis considers food stealing by children in Africa (Bledsoe 1983). During fieldwork among the Mende of Sierra Leone, Caroline Bledsoe's research focus was on child fostering (placing a child in the care of friends or relatives, usually so they can receive apprenticeship training or education in a city school). She learned that children who are fostered out, especially older ones, receive less food at meal times than children living with a biological parent, specifically less meat and leafy green sauces. The nutritional status of fostered children, however, was not as low as their limited food shares would indicate. Further investigation revealed a widespread pattern of children foraging for wild food and a "clandestine economy" of food stealing. Bledsoe at first dismissed cases of food stealing as rare exceptions, "But I began to realize that I rarely walked through town without hearing shouts of anger from an adult and cries of pain from a child being whipped for stealing food" (2). Since her goal was to assess children's nutritional status, she needed to know about how much food children were gaining from foraging and stealing. Her discussion of methods for this kind of research is illuminating:

> I focused on eliciting information primarily from children themselves. This required careful effort, because children wanted to avoid getting in trouble. Most were reluctant at first to divulge their strategies. However, as children saw that I regarded their efforts as they themselves did—as almost an art—they disclosed some of their more creative techniques of "tiefing" ("TEEF-ing") as petty stealing is referred to in Sierra Leone Creole . . . Another technique I tried was meal simulations in which people showed me how children "tiefed" even at meal time, both when the food was being prepared as well as while groups of children were seated together, eating rice and sauce with their hands out of a communal bowl, as most people eat. Since this was simulation, people greatly enjoyed demonstrating the subtleties of "tiefing" and bad etiquette. (2)

Bledsoe had the children participate in simulations of meal preparation and meal serving. In both situations, children revealed to her subtle methods of "tiefing." She also asked them to keep diaries to elicit information on "tiefing." At first, children wrote about more legitimate ways they acquired food, such as doing errands for small tips, playing soccer games for stakes, soliciting relatives for "munch-ing" money, asking friends to share snacks with them, and visiting friends at meal times. From an analysis of these diaries, she found that fostered children and children temporarily placed in the care of friends or relatives participate more in food stealing than children living with their natal families. Food stealing can be seen as children's attempts to compensate for their less-than-adequate food shares at home. They do this by claiming food that is not part of their rightful entitlement, by "tiefing."

Stealing as a conscious attempt to alter an unfair entitlement system underlies an analysis of the "looting" that occurred in Los Angeles in 1992 following the Rodney King verdict (Fiske 1994). This looting can be seen to be rooted in the economic inequities faced by the African American community of South Central Los Angeles at the time of the Rodney King decision.

> Between 1982 and 1989, 131 factories closed in LA with the loss of 124,000 jobs. . . . The jobs that were lost were ones that disproportionately employed African Americans . . . in the four years before 1982, South Central, the traditional industrial core of LA, lost 70,000 blue-collar jobs. In Black eyes, this pattern is produced not by a raceless free market, but by racism encoded into economics: To them the 50 percent Black male unemployment in South Central does not look like the result of neutral, let alone natural, economic laws. (469–470)

The North American culture of consumption presumes equality among all consumers. In South Central Los Angeles, this is not the case: "For the deprived, shopping is not, as it is for the wealthy, where success in the sphere of production is materially rewarded: It is an experience of exclusion and disempowerment. Shopping is painful" (481). How does all of this relate to exchange? The "looting" during the Los Angeles uprising can be seen as an expression of deep-seated resentment about economic discrimination. "Looting" could instead be termed "radical shopping" in the sense that it was political protest, just as consumer boycotts are protests of a different sort. The politics of language emerge: The media's use of the word "looting" linked the uprising to the domain of crime, leaving prison as the only solution. Framing the uprising as a law-and-order issue only diverted the public's attention from its roots in severe economic discrimination.

Obviously, much theft that occurs in the world is motivated by greed, not economic deprivation or oppression. The world of theft in expensive commodities such as gems, drugs, and art has not been extensively researched by cultural anthropologists, nor has corporate financial malpractice yet been examined as a form of theft.

Exploitation Exploitation is getting something of greater value for less in return; it is extreme and persistent unbalanced exchange. Slavery is a form of exploitation in which people's labour power is appropriated without their consent and with no recompense for its value. Slavery is rare among foraging, horticultural, and pastoral societies. Social relationships that involve sustained unequal exchange do exist between members of different social groups that, unlike pure slavery, involve no overt coercion and a certain degree of return by the dominant member to the subdominant member. Some degree of covert compulsion or dependence is likely to be present, however, in order for relationships of unequal exchange to endure.

Relationships between the Efe, who are "pygmy" foragers, and the Lese, who are farmers, in Congo (formerly Zaire) exemplify sustained unequal exchange (Grinker 1994). The Lese live in small villages located along a dirt road. The Efe are semi-nomadic, and they live in temporary camps near Lese villages. Men of each group maintain long-term hereditary exchange partnerships with each. Members of the two groups describe their relationship simply: The Lese give cultivated foods and iron to the Efe, and the Efe give meat, honey, and other forest goods to the Lese.

Each Efe partner is considered a member of the "house" of his Lese partner, although he lives separately. Their main link is the exchange of food items, a system conceptualized by the Lese not as trade, per se, but as sharing of co-produced goods, as though the two partners were a single unit with a division of labour and a subsequent division or co-sharing of the goods produced. Yet there is evidence of inequality in these trading relationships, with the Lese having the advantage. The Efe provide much-wanted meat to the Lese, but this role gives them no status, for it is the giving of cultivated foods by the Lese to the Efe that conveys status. In fact, the Lese claim that the Efe are *their* dependents, denying that their interest in Efe meat supplies actually makes them dependent. Another area of inequality is in marital and sexual relationships. Lese men may marry Efe women, and sometimes do, and the children are considered Lese. Efe men cannot marry or have sexual intercourse with Lese women.

Theories of Exchange

Here we look at two theories that seek to explain why people participate in patterned processes of exchange. The first is a functional view that sees exchange as creating social and economic safety nets for people, along the lines of the potlatch explanation provided at the beginning of the chapter. The second is a critical theory that points to how patterns of exchange create and sustain social inequality.

Exchange and Risk Aversion

At the beginning of this chapter, the potlatch system was presented as an exchange network with an economic security function. Linking together with other groups smoothes out the unevenness of a particular local economy to a certain extent. Many more such examples can be found cross-culturally.

Carol Stack (1974) was perhaps the first cultural anthropologist to study how exchange patterns among kin and friends in the urban United States serves as a social safety net. She did research in "The Flats," the poorest section of a Black community in a Midwestern city that she calls Jackson Harbor. Jackson Harbor is marked by racial inequality with, for example, a much higher proportion of Blacks than Whites living in deteriorating or severely dilapidated housing. Stack's approach differed from earlier studies of the Black family in the U.S. by avoiding negative comparisons with middle-class White lifestyles. She instead looked at the Black family members' strategies for dealing with poverty and uncertainty.

> I found extensive networks of kin and friends supporting, reinforcing each other—devising schemes for self-help, strategies for survival in a community of severe economic deprivation. Their social and economic lives were so entwined that not to repay an exchange meant that someone else's child would not eat. People would tell me, "You have to have help from everybody and anybody," and "The poorer you are, the more likely you are to pay back." (28)

Stack spent nearly three years in The Flats, studying the complex exchange system. She also became involved in the system: "If someone asked a favor of me, later I asked a favor of him. If I gave a scarf, a skirt, or a cooking utensil to a woman who admired it, later on when she had something I liked she would usually give it to me. Little by little as I learned the rules of giving and reciprocity, I tried them out" (28). Timing is important in the "swapping system." The purpose is to obligate the receiver over a period of time; thus, swapping rarely involves simultaneous exchange. The swapping system of The Flats lies between the categories of generalized and balanced reciprocity, both of which are related to the maintenance of social bonds.

Exchange and Social Inequality

In addition to strengthening social relations, exchange may also support and perpetuate social inequalities. Paul Bohannan (1955), an early economic anthropologist, studied the economy of the Tiv, horticulturalists of Nigeria, before European monetary systems entered their economy. He learned that, besides gift exchange, three spheres of market exchange existed in which items of equivalent value are traded for each other. Each of the three spheres carried different levels of prestige. The lowest-ranking sphere is the arena of women's trade. It includes chickens, hoes, baskets, pots, and grain. This domestic sphere has the most frequent activity, but no prestige.

The second ranking category included brass rods, special white cloth, guns, cattle, and slaves. Slavery had been abolished at the time of Bohannan's research and the brass rods were increasingly rare, but the Tiv still talked about the relative value of these items. For example, one brass rod was equivalent to one large piece of white cloth, and five rods or pieces of cloth were equal to a bull, while ten equalled a cow. Young men seeking marriage would accumulate such goods in order to enhance their prestige and to impress elder males.

The top-ranking exchange sphere contains only one item: rights in women. This category ranks highest in the Tiv moral sphere since a male's highest goal is to gain and maintain family dependents (wife and children). As Bohannan (1955) says, "The drive toward success leads most Tiv, to the greatest possible extent, to convert food into prestige items; to convert prestige items into dependents—wives and children," a process of up-trading he terms "conversion." Subsequent analyses have pointed out that the Tiv spheres of exchange, like those of many other African cultures, support the power structure of elder males (Douglas and Isherwood 1979). They maintained dominance over the entire social system by keeping tight control over marriageable women. This forces younger males into competition for marriage and for eventual entry into the ranks of the elders.

Bohannan's analysis dealt with how exchange relationships within one culture strengthen the power position of certain social groups and keep others in subordinate positions because they cannot participate in the highest form of exchange. At the global level, many examples of exchange between powerful and nonpowerful groups show how the powerful groups use exchange to maintain their position and how difficult it is for the nonpowerful groups to escape their position of subordination. Few Canadians may be familiar with the stories about the whalers who harvested the once abundant beluga whales in Hudson's Bay to satisfy the lucrative European market for whale oil; the street lamps of England were lit with the rendered fat of these whales no longer available to Cree hunters (Adelson 2000:38).

Anyone who has grown up in North America has probably heard the tales of European colonialists trading a string of glass beads for the island of Manhattan, and of the colonialists' plying Native Americans with "fire water," alcoholic drinks, and thus creating their dependency and acquiescence. The current heavy alcohol consumption among many indigenous peoples worldwide is testimony to the continuing power of alcohol as part of the mode of exchange of colonialism and its modern forms. The introduction of alcohol to the indigenous people of Australia, for example, has created a culture—especially among men—of binge drinking and depletion of cash earnings to buy alcohol (Saggers and Gray 1998).

Before the coming of outsiders to Australia, the Aborigines had nothing like alcohol. It arrived with the British. Despite much effort in recent decades to reduce alcohol consumption among Aboriginal peoples, no decline is apparent. One interpretation is that economic marginalization and social discrimination support continued high levels of alcohol consumption, along with the assurance of a continued supply of alcohol from the global market.

CHANGING PATTERNS OF CONSUMPTION AND EXCHANGE

Several trends are notable in the transformation of consumption and exchange. The powerful market forces of the first world are the predominant shapers of global change. At the same time, local cultures variously adopt and adapt to global patterns of consumption and exchange, and sometimes resist them outright.

Cash Cropping and Declining Nutrition

Increasing numbers of horticultural and agricultural groups have been persuaded to change over from growing crops for their own use to cash crop production. Intuition might tell you that cash cropping should lead to a rising standard of living. Some studies show, to the contrary, that often people's nutritional status declines with the introduction of cash cropping. A carefully documented analysis of how people's nutritional status was affected by introducing sisal (a plant that has leaves used for making rope) as a cash crop in Brazil is one such case (Gross and Underwood 1971). Around 1950, sisal was widely adopted in arid parts of northeastern Brazil. The traditional economy was based on some cattle raising and subsistence farming. Many poor subsistence farmers gave up farming and took up work in the sisal processing plants. They thought that steady work would be preferable to being dependent on the unpredictable rains in this dry region.

Processing sisal leaves for rope is an extremely labour-consuming process. One of the most demanding jobs is being a "residue man," whose tasks include shovelling soggy masses of fibre, bundling fibre, and lifting bundles for weighing. In families that contained a "residue man," the amount of money required for food was as much as what the sisal worker earned. In one case-study household, the weekly budget was completely spent on food. The greatest share of the food goes to the sisal worker himself because of his increased energy output in his work. Analysis of data on the nutritional status of several hundred children in sisal-processing areas showed that: "Some sisal workers in northeastern Brazil appear to be forced systematically to deprive their dependents of an adequate diet . . . if they did not they could not function as wage earners. In those cases where the workers' dependents are growing children, the deprivation manifests itself in attenuated growth rates" (736).

The Lure of Western Goods

There is now scarcely any human group that does not engage in exchanges beyond its boundaries to acquire new consumer goods (Gross et al. 1979). The northern Cree have embraced many technological changes in the last few decades: "Satellite dishes, fax machines, computers and websites are as much a part of northern living as skidoos, rifles, and the ubiquitous Northern Stores (formerly the Hudson's Bay Company Posts)" (Adelson 2000:11). Forest-living foraging groups in the Brazilian Amazon also embraced manufactured goods with amazing enthusiasm. They appreciated the efficacy of a steel machete, axe, or cooking pot. In the early decades of the twentieth century, when the Brazilian government sought to "pacify" Amazonian groups, they used manufactured goods. They placed pots, machetes, axes, and steel knives along trails or hung them from trees. Once the Indians have grown accustomed to these new items, the next step is to teach them that these gifts will not be repeated. The Indians are now told that they must work to earn money or must manufacture goods for trade so that they can purchase new items. Unable to contemplate returning to life without steel axes, the Indians begin to produce extra arrows or blowguns or hunt additional game or weave baskets beyond what they normally need so that this new surplus can be traded. Time that might, in the past, have been used for other tasks—subsistence activities, ceremonial events, or whatever—is now devoted to production of barter goods (Milton 1992:40).

Adoption of Western foods has negatively affected the nutrition and health of indigenous peoples. Cree health and strength is intimately connected to eating Cree bush food. Now that there is a greater variety of processed foods available for sale, it is often consumed to excess (Adelson 2000:103). In the Amazon, "The moment manufactured foods begin to intrude on the indigenous diet, health takes a downward turn" (Milton 1992:41). The Amazonian Indians have begun to use table salt, which they have been given by outsiders, and refined sugar. Previously, they consumed small quantities of salt made by burning certain leaves and collecting the ash. The sugar they consumed came from wild fruits, in the form of fructose. Sucrose tastes "exceptionally sweet" in comparison, and the Indians get hooked on it. As a result, tooth decay, obesity, and diabetes become new health risks.

Cases of locally produced beer, "333," are unloaded near the port of Ho Chi Minh City, Vietnam, where logos of many Western products are familiar sights in the growing capitalist economy.

The White Bread Takeover

A cross-cultural analysis of food cultures, with attention to contemporary change, revealed an enduring and growing distinction between bread and porridge (Goody 1977). Bread is associated with dominant, colonizing cultures, and porridge is associated with dominated and colonized cultures.

An illustration of this dichotomy comes from rural Ecuador (Weismantel 1989). In the village of Zumbagua, bread has been a high-status, special-occasion food for many years. Recently, children have begun pressuring parents to serve bread regularly to replace the usual barley gruel for breakfast. Children prefer bread. The anthropologist reports, "Many of the early morning quarrels I witnessed in Zumbagua homes erupted over the question of bread. This conflict arises between young children and their parents. Pre-school children, especially, demand bread as their right" (93). But "Zumbagua adults do not feel that bread is appropriate for everyday meals because it is a part of a class of food defined as *wanlla*. Wanlla is anything that is not part of a meal . . . bread is the wanlla par excellence. It is the universally appropriate gift" (95). Importantly, bread consumption requires cash income. The husband (more frequently than the wife) works for wages in the city. He often returns with a gift of bread for the family, while the wife provides the traditional boiled grain soups or gruels.

Children's demands for bread increase the role of purchased foods. This in turn leads to increased dependence on the cash economy and on male wages rather than on traditional female provisioning.

Privatization's Effects in Russia and Eastern Europe

As the countries of the former Soviet Union dismantle socialism and enter the market economy, income inequality is rising. The new rich are enjoying unprecedented levels of comfortable living. The influx of Western goods, including sugared soft drinks and junk food, nicknamed "pepsistroika" by an anthropologist who did fieldwork in Moscow (Lempert 1996), allows people to change their traditional diets in ways that nutritional guidelines in North America would advise against.

At the same time, consumption levels have fallen among the newly created poor. Historically, average reported levels of food intake in what is now Russia and Eastern Europe have exceeded those of most middle-income countries (Cornia 1994). Between 1961 and 1988, consumption of average calories, proteins, and fats rose and were generally higher than those recommended by the World Health Organization. These countries were also characterized by full employment and low income inequality, so the high consumption levels were shared by everyone. This is not to say that diets were perfect. Characteristic weaknesses, especially in urban areas and among low-income groups, were low consumption of good-quality meat, fruits, vegetables, and vegetable oils, while people tended to overconsume cholesterol-heavy products (eggs and animal fats), sugar, salt, bread, and alcohol.

An upscale car dealer in Moscow uses a cell phone to communicate with customers. His car lot stands on what was a sports ground during the Soviet era.

In China, a market vendor weighs her produce and calculates the price using a laptop computer.

Now, there are two categories of poor people: "the ultra-poor" (those whose incomes are below the subsistence minimum, or between 25 and 35 percent of the average wage) and "the poor" (those whose incomes are above the subsistence minimum but below the social minimum, or between 35 and 50 percent of the average wage). The largest increases in the number of ultra-poor occurred in Bulgaria, Poland, Romania, and Russia where, in 1992, between 20 to 30 percent of the population could be classified as ultra-poor and another 20 to 40 percent as poor. Overall calorie and protein intake diminished significantly. People in the ultra-poor category are substituting less expensive sources of nutrients, so now they consume more animal fats and starch, and less milk, animal proteins, vegetable oils, minerals, and vitamins. These changes are affecting the growth rates of children. In Bulgaria, the prevalence of growth stunting among infants rose from under 2 percent in 1989–1990 to 17 percent in 1991. Rates of low-birthweight babies rose in Bulgaria and Romania, reflecting the deterioration in maternal diets. The rate of childhood anemia has also risen dramatically in Russia.

Credit Card Debt

Throughout the world, certain markets have long allowed buyers to purchase goods on credit. Such informal credit purchasing was usually based on personal trust and face-to-face interaction. It is only recently, however, that the credit card has made credit purchasing a massive, impersonal phenomenon in North America and many other parts of the world: "New electronic technology in the 1970s and deregulation in the 1980s offered retail bankers exciting opportunities to experiment with credit as a commodity, and they did experiment, wildly, at 'penetrating the debt capacity' of varied groups of Americans" (B. Williams 1994:351). Among middle-class people in North America, the use of credit cards is related to their attempts to maintain a middle-class lifestyle:

> The primary users of installment credit appear to be those between ages twenty-five and forty-four whose incomes are stagnant or falling. Many have relied on credit to shape an appropriately classed life course: to attend college, purchase durables and set up households, meet the needs of kin, and launch children. . . . They have served like domestic partners to some who cannot live on one income. Thus, for the last ten years, many normative middle-class people have not been able to support the households they want when they want them, or to organize their lives, without loans and liens. (B. Williams 1994:353)

People's attitudes about their credit card debts vary. Some people express feelings of guilt similar to having a drug dependency. One woman reported, "Last year I had a charge-free Christmas. It was like coming away from drug abuse" (354). Others who are in debt feel grateful: "I wouldn't be able to go to college without my credit card" (355). Williams suggests that, no matter what people's attitudes are, credit cards are sinking many people deeply into debt. The cards buy a lifestyle that is not actually affordable, and therefore they "mask" actual economic decline in North America. The culture of electronic credit is a subject that cultural anthropologists will no doubt be devoting more attention to in the future, since credit card use is expanding around the world.

Continuities and Resistance: The Enduring Potlatch

Potlatching among Native peoples of the Northwest Coast was subjected to decades of opposition from Europeans (D. Cole 1991). The missionaries opposed potlatching and other "un-Christian" activities. The governments thought it was wasteful and excessive, out of line with their goals for the "economic progress" of the Native peoples. In 1885 the Canadian government outlawed the potlatch. Among all the Northwest Coastal groups, the Kwakwaka'wakw resisted this prohibition most strongly and for the longest time throughout the sporadically enforced ban. Potlatching among the Haida and Tlingit, in contrast, disappeared with relatively little resistance. Potlatches are no longer illegal, but a long battle was required to remove restrictions.

Contemporary reasons for giving a potlatch are similar to those in past times: naming children, mourning the dead, transferring rights and privileges, marriages, and the raising of totem poles and houses. However, the length of time devoted to planning a potlatch has shortened. Elders recall that several years were involved in planning a proper potlatch. Now about a year is enough. Still, much property must be accumulated to make sure that no guest goes away empty-handed, and the guest list may include between 500 and 1000 people. The kinds of goods exchanged are different today: Typical potlatch goods now include crocheted items (such as cushion covers, afghans, and potholders), glassware, plastic goods, manufactured blankets, pillows, towels, articles of clothing, and sacks of flour and sugar (Webster 1991).

A dance during a potlatch in the memory of a Tshimshian elder. The potlatch was held on the island of Metlakatla, southeast Alaska.

HOW are modes of production related to consumption?

Anthropologists contrast modes of consumption in non-market versus market-based systems of production. In the former, minimalism is the dominant mode of consumption, with finite needs. In the latter, consumerism is the dominant mode of consumption, with infinite needs. Foraging societies typify the minimalist mode of consumption. Industrial capitalist societies typify the consumerist mode of consumption. The modes of production that emerged between foraging and industrialism exhibit varying degrees of minimalism and consumerism.

HOW are modes of production related to exchange?

The mode of exchange corresponds to the modes of production and consumption. In foraging societies, the dominant mode of exchange is reciprocity, with the goal of keeping the value of the items exchanged roughly equal over time. This balanced mode of exchange involves people who have a social relationship with each other. The relationship is reinforced through continued exchange. In the context of market exchange, the goal of making a profit through exchange overrides social relationships. In market exchange, the people involved in the transaction are less likely to know each other or to have a social relationship. In fully marketized economies, most transactions are anonymous, that is, no social relationship is involved at all, as in e-commerce.

WHAT are some examples of how contemporary global economic change affects non-market modes of consumption and exchange?

Globalizing capitalism appears to be shaping most of the changes in consumption and exchange occurring around the world. Cultural anthropologists critique this process as being better for capitalism than it is for the people of non-market cultures being swept into the global economy. Western-inspired goods, such as steel axes and white bread, are now in high demand by people in non-Western, non-industrialized contexts. Such goods must be purchased, a fact that impels people to work for cash so that they can buy things. Nutritional status of many non-industrial groups has fallen with the adoption of Western-style foods containing large amounts of sugar and salt. The demand for cash has prompted many people to switch from growing food for their own use to growing crops for sale. This transition means that farmers have relinquished a direct entitlement for an indirect entitlement, thus putting themselves at risk when the market price drops for the crop they grow. Throughout post-Soviet countries, average health and nutrition levels dropped after perestroika, and they continue to decline.

KEY CONCEPTS

balanced reciprocity, p. 88
basic needs fund, p. 79
ceremonial fund, p. 79
consumerism, p. 78
consumption fund, p. 79
direct entitlements, p. 80
entertainment fund, p. 79
entitlements, p. 80
famine, p. 81
generalized reciprocity, p. 88
indirect entitlements, p. 81
limited-purpose money, p. 87
market exchange, p. 89

minimalism, p. 78
modes of consumption, p. 76
modes of exchange, p. 76
money, p. 87
multi-purpose money, p. 87
potlatch, p. 76
pure gift, p. 88
reciprocity, p. 88
redistribution, p. 89
taboos, p. 84
tax/rent fund, p. 80
trade, p. 89

SUGGESTED READINGS

Jane I. Guyer, ed., *Money Matters: Instability, Values and Social Payments in the Modern History of West African Communities*. Portsmouth, NH: Heinemann/James Currey, 1995. A collection of chapters by historians and cultural anthropologists examining topics such as why people in rural Gambia do not save money in banks, money as a symbol among the Yoruba, and the impact of colonial monetization in Nigeria and elsewhere.

Betsy Hartmann and James Boyce, *Needless Hunger: Voices from a Bangladesh Village*. San Francisco: Institute for Food and Development Policy, 1982. Evidence from fieldwork in rural Bangladesh shows that poverty and hunger in Bangladesh are primarily caused by severe class inequalities in economic entitlements. The text includes a critique of the role of foreign aid in perpetuating inequalities, as well as suggestions for change.

Dwight B. Heath, *Drinking Occasions: Comparative Perspectives on Alcohol and Culture*. New York: Taylor & Francis, 2000. This book provides an ethnological review of drinking. The author focuses on several questions: When do people drink alcohol? Where do people drink? Who drinks and who doesn't? How do people drink? What do people drink? And why do people drink? He asks, in conclusion, where do we go from here with this topic?

Grant McCracken, *Culture and Consumption*. Bloomington: Indiana University Press, 1988. This book examines consumption in history, theory, and practice in relation to different consumer goods, including a consideration of clothing as language.

Daniel Miller, *The Dialectics of Shopping*. Chicago: University of Chicago Press, 2001. First delivered as the Lewis Henry Morgan lecture series at the University of Rochester, the chapters in this book reflect the author's interest in studying shopping as a clue to social relations. He discusses how shopping is related to kinship, community, ethics and identity, and the political economy. He draws on his own ethnographic research in several locations.

Sidney W. Mintz, *Sweetness and Power: The Place of Sugar in Modern History*. New York: Penguin Books, 1985. Combining historical and anthropological techniques, this book traces an important part of the story of world capitalism— the transformation of sugar from a luxury item to an omnipresent item of consumption worldwide.

Lidia D. Sciama and Joanne B. Eicher, eds., *Beads and Bead Makers: Gender, Material Culture and Meaning*. New York: Berg, 1998. Over a dozen articles on beads including early international trade in Venetian beads, the relationship between beads and ethnicity in Malaysia, beads and power at the New Orleans Mardi Gras, and rosaries in the Andes, all providing insights about gender roles and meanings.

James L. Watson, ed., *Golden Arches East: McDonald's in East Asia*. Stanford: Stanford University Press, 1997. This book contains five case studies, preceded by an introduction written by the editor and an afterword by Sidney Mintz, noted cultural anthropologist of food and foodways. Case studies are located in China, Taiwan, Korea, and Japan, and address topics such as how McDonald's American culture becomes localized, dietary effects on children, eating etiquette, and how food choices relate to national identity.

WEBLINKS

The Companion Website (www.pearsoned.ca/miller) that accompanies *Cultural Anthropology*, Third Canadian Edition, includes a destinations module containing links to many websites relevant to the content of this chapter. Use it to investigate the Web and expand your understanding of anthropology.

KEY QUESTIONS

- **HOW** is reproduction related to modes of production?
- **HOW** does culture shape fertility in different contexts?
- **HOW** does culture shape mortality in different contexts?

5

BIRTH AND DEATH

A mother and her infant, South Africa.

- A common belief among Hindus in India is that men are weakened by sexual intercourse because semen is a source of strength, and it takes a long time to replace even a drop. Yet India has a high rate of population growth.
- The Chinese government policy of urging parents to have only one child significantly decreased the population growth rate. It also increased the death rate of female infants to the extent that there is now a shortage of brides.
- The highest birth rates in the world are found among the Mennonites and Hutterites in the United States and Canada. In these Christian groups, women on average bear nine children.

Such "population puzzles" can be understood using anthropological theories and methods. Population dynamics, along with many other examples of human variation in births and deaths, are an important area of life that is culturally shaped and that changes over time in response to changing conditions. This chapter provides a glimpse into some aspects of **demography**, or the study of population dynamics, and how it is culturally regulated.

While demographers compile statistical reports, cultural anthropologists contribute understanding of what goes on behind the numbers and provide insights about the causes of demographic trends. For example, demographers may find that fertility rates are falling more rapidly in one nation than in another. They may be able to correlate certain factors with it, such as changing literacy rates or economic growth. Cultural anthropologists studying these issues would take a closer look at the causes and processes involved in the declining birth rates, including some that might not be included in official censuses or other statistical sources. They would gather information on household-level, and also individual-level, behaviour and attitudes.

Demography includes three areas: **fertility** (births, or rate of population increase from reproduction), **mortality** (deaths, or rate of population decline in general or from particular causes), and **migration** (movement of people from one place to another). When cultural anthropologists examine these processes, they often focus on small populations and samples and examine the relationships between population dynamics and other aspects of culture, such as gender roles, sexual beliefs and behaviour, marriage, household structure, child care, and health and illness.

This chapter starts by discussing how the modes of production (see Chapter 3) relate to reproduction. It then examines how and to what extent culture shapes the important natural processes of birth and death in different contexts.

CULTURE AND REPRODUCTION

Every human population, at all times, has had culturally constructed ways to either promote or limit population growth. Archaeologists and cultural anthropologists have enough data to allow the construction of general models of **reproduction** (the predominant patterns of fertility in a culture) corresponding roughly with different means of livelihood. Three general models of reproduction are proposed. The foraging model of reproduction, which lasted for most of human prehistory, had low population growth rates because of a combination of moderate birth rates and moderate death rates. The agricultural model emerged with sedentarization (permanent settlement). As increased food surpluses became available to support more people, birth rates increased over death rates, and high population densities were reached in agricultural societies such as India and China. Children's labour was highly valued. Horticulturalists and pastoralists exhibit some features of the foraging and agricultural models of reproduction, depending on specific conditions. In the industrialized model of reproduction, exemplified by Europe, Japan, and North America, population growth rates declined because of falling birth rates and declining death rates.

Reproduction in Foraging Societies

Archaeological evidence about prehistoric populations, from about six million years ago to the Neolithic era of agricultural development around

12 000 years ago, indicates that population growth rates among foragers remained low over millions of years. Foraging societies' daily and seasonal spatial mobility calls for a relatively small number of children to facilitate movement. It is difficult for adults to carry more than one infant. The low population growth rates over thousands of years were likely the result of several factors: high rates of spontaneous abortion because of heavy workloads of women, the seasonality of diets that created reproductive stress on women, long breastfeeding durations (which suppressed ovulation), induced abortion, and **infanticide** (deliberate killing of offspring). Low birth rates appear to be more important than mortality in leading to population stability, or *homeostasis.*

Nancy Howell (1979) conducted research on the demography of the Ju/wasi that sheds light on how population homeostasis is achieved. Her data show that birth intervals (the time between one birth and a subsequent birth) among the Ju/wasi are often several years in duration. What accounts for the long birth intervals? Two factors emerge as most important among the Ju/wasi: breastfeeding and women's low levels of body fat. Frequent and long periods of breastfeeding inhibit progesterone production and suppress ovulation. Also, a certain level of body fat is required for ovulation (Frisch 1978). Ju/wasi women's diets contain little fat. Their body fat level is also kept low through the physical exercise their foraging work entails. The combination of diet and exercise maintained Ju/wasi women's body fat at low levels, suppressing ovulation.

Thus, ecological factors (food supply, breastfeeding, and diet) and economic factors (women's workloads) are basic determinants of Ju/wasi demography. This model of reproduction can be interpreted as highly adaptive to the Ju/wasi environment and sustainable over time. Among the Ju/wasi who have given up foraging and become sedentarized farmers or labourers, fertility levels have increased, because of higher consumption levels of grains and dairy products and less physical activity.

Reproduction in Agricultural Societies

Settled agriculture promotes and supports the highest fertility rates of any model of production. **Pronatalism**, an ideology promoting many children, emerges as a key value of farm families. It is prompted by the need for a large labour force to work the land, care for animals, process food, and do marketing. In this context, having many children is a rational reproductive strategy related to the model of production. Thus, people living in family farming systems cross-culturally have their own "family planning"— which is to have many children. Examples include the Mennonites and Hutterites of the United States and Canada (Stephenson 1991).

Members of an Amish household sit around their kitchen table.

In rural North India, sons are especially important, given the gender division of labour. Men provide the crucial work of plowing the fields and protecting the family in the case of village quarrels over land rights and other matters. When Western family planning agents first visited the village of Manupur in northern India in the late 1950s to promote small families, the villagers did not see the value of their ideas (Mamdani 1972). They equated a large family with wealth and success, not poverty and failure. Western family planning agents made the mistake of thinking that rural Indians had no thoughts of their own about what constitutes the desired family size and that they could simply provide modern contraceptive techniques to an interested market. Having many children in a family farming system "makes sense." When mechanization is introduced, cheap hired labour becomes widely available, or socialized agriculture is established, then farm families change their approach to reproduction and opt for smaller numbers of children because it makes less sense to have many children.

Reproduction in Industrial Societies

In industrial societies, either capitalist or socialist, reproduction tends to decline to the point of **replacement-level fertility** (the number of births equals the number of deaths, leading to maintenance of current population size) or **below-replacement-level fertility**, when the number of births is fewer than the number of deaths, leading to population decline. Below-replacement-level societies include Canada; Japan; several European countries such as Austria, Belgium, Hungary, Denmark, and Norway; and some countries that the United Nations categorizes as "developing." The 2000 World Population

Data Sheet (Washington D.C. Population Reference Bureau) lists 48 developed and developing countries with below-replacement-level fertility. Children are considered less useful in production because of the changing labour demands of industrialism. Furthermore, children are required to attend school and cannot work for their families as much. Parents respond to these changes by having fewer children and by "investing" more resources in the fewer children they have.

Changes during the industrial mode of reproduction correspond to what demographers call the **demographic transition**, a model of change from the high fertility and high mortality in agricultural societies to the low fertility and low mortality of industrialized societies. This model proposes two phases. First, mortality declines as a result of improved nutrition and health, leading to high rates of population growth. The second phase is reached when fertility also declines, resulting in low rates of population growth. Cultural anthropologists have critiqued the demographic transition model as being too narrowly focused on the role of industrialism and not allowing for alternative models (Ginsberg and Rapp 1991). They claim that industrialism, with its reduced need for labour, is not the only factor that reduces pronatalism. China, for example, began to reduce its population growth rate before widespread industrialism (Xizhe 1991). Instead, strong government policies and a massive family planning program were key factors: "China's transition has been, by and large, not a natural process, but rather an induced one" (281) because its motivation came mainly from the government rather than from couples themselves.

One prominent characteristic of capitalist industrial states is their socially stratified demographies. Middle- and upper-class people tend to have few children, with high survival rates. Among the poor, both fertility and mortality rates are unusually high. Brazil, a newly industrializing state with the most extreme inequality of income distribution in the world, also has extreme differences in demographic patterns between the rich and the poor.

Another characteristic of industrial countries is population aging. In Japan, for example, the total fertility rate declined to replacement level in the 1950s, and subsequently reached the below-replacement-level (Hodge and Ogawa 1991:vii). Japan is currently experiencing a decline in population growth of about 15 percent per generation. At the same time, Japan is experiencing a rapid aging of the population. Many people are moving into the senior category, creating a population bulge not matched by population increases in younger age groups.

A third distinguishing feature of industrial demographies is the high level of involvement of scientific (especially medical) technology in all aspects of pregnancy: preventing it, achieving it, and even terminating it (Browner and Press 1995, 1996). The growing importance of the "new reproductive technologies" (NRTs) such as in vitro fertilization is a major part of a growing market in scientific reproduction. This technologization of reproduction is accompanied by increasing levels of specialization in providing the new services.

SEXUAL INTERCOURSE AND FERTILITY

Cultures shape human reproduction from its very beginning, sexual intercourse itself. Cultural practices and beliefs about pregnancy and birth affect the viability of the fetus during its gestation as well as the infant's fate after birth.

Sexual Intercourse

Anthropological research on sexuality and sexual practices is particularly difficult to undertake. Sexuality involves private, sometimes secret, beliefs and behaviours. The ethics of participant observation disallow intimate observation or participation, so data can be obtained only indirectly. Biases in people's reports to an anthropologist about their sexual beliefs and behaviour are likely for several reasons. They may be too shy to talk about sex in the first place, too boastful to give accurate information, or simply unable to answer questions such as "How many times did you have intercourse last year?" If people do provide detailed information, it might be inappropriate for an anthropologist to publish it because of the need to protect confidentiality. Malinowski (1929) wrote the first anthropological study of sexuality, based on his fieldwork in the Trobriands. He discusses the sexual lives of children; sexual techniques; love magic; erotic dreams; husband-wife jealousy; and a range of topics related to kinship, marriage, exchange, and morals. Since the late 1980s, cultural anthropologists have paid more attention to the study of sexuality, given the increase in cases of sexually transmitted diseases (STDs), including HIV/AIDS.

When to Begin Having Intercourse?

Sexual intercourse between a fertile female and fertile male is normally required for human reproduction, although artificial insemination is an option in some contexts. Biology also defines the time span within which a female is fertile: from menarche (the onset of first menstruation) to menopause (the final cessation of menstruation). Globally, average age at menarche is between 12 and 14 years, with earlier ages found in the industrial nations and later ages in developing nations, presumably because of different diets and activity patterns. Average age at menopause varies more widely, from the 40s to the 50s, with later ages in industrialized societies. The higher fat content of diets in industrialized nations may account for this difference.

Cultures socialize children about the appropriate time to begin sexual intercourse. Guidelines for initiating sexual intercourse may differ by gender, class, race, and ethnicity. In many societies, menarche marks the beginning of adulthood for a girl. She should marry soon after menarche, and she should become pregnant as soon as possible in order to demonstrate her fertility.

Cross-culturally, rules more strictly forbid premarital sexual activity of girls than boys. In Zawiya, a traditional Muslim town of northern Morocco, as in much of the Middle East, the virginity of the bride—but not the groom—is highly valued (Davis and Davis 1987). The majority of brides conform to the ideal. Some unmarried young women do engage in premarital sex, however, and if they choose to have a traditional wedding, then they must somehow deal with the requirement of producing blood-stained wedding sheets. How do they do this? If the bride and the groom have been having premarital sexual relations, the groom may assist in the deception by nicking a finger with a knife and bloodying the sheets himself. Another option is to buy fake blood in the drugstore.

In many societies, a high value is placed on a woman becoming pregnant soon after she reaches menarche, making "teenage pregnancy" a desired condition instead of a "social problem," as perceived by many experts in North America (Ginsberg and Rapp 1991:320). The concept of a 30-year-old first-time mother would shock villagers in Bangladesh, for example, as to both its physical possibility and its social advisability. Commonly in South Asia, Africa, and elsewhere, a married woman's status depends on her having children. The longer she delays, the more her spouse and in-laws might suspect her of being infertile. In that case, they might send her back to her parents or bring in a second wife.

A bride wearing traditional wedding clothing in the city of Meknès, Morocco.

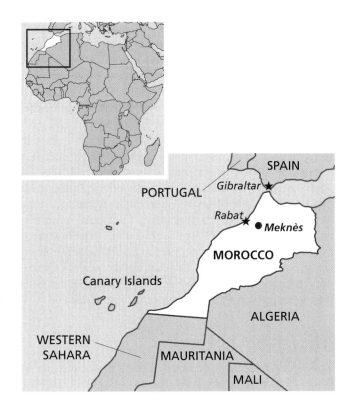

How Often Should One Have Intercourse?

Cross-cultural studies indicate a wide range in frequency of sexual intercourse, confirming the role of culture in shaping sexual desire. However, the relationship between sexual intercourse frequency and fertility, the subject of this section, is not simple. A common assumption is that people in cultures with high rates of population growth must have sexual intercourse frequently. Without "modern" birth control, such as condoms, birth control pills, and the IUD, intercourse frequency would seem to lead to high rates of fertility.

A comparison of reported intercourse frequency for Euro-Americans in the United States and Hindus in India reveals that Indians had intercourse far less frequently (less than twice a week) than the Euro-Americans did (two to three times a week) in all age groups (Nag 1972). Several features of Indian culture limit sexual intercourse. The Hindu religion teaches the value of sexual abstinence, thus providing ideological support for limiting sexual intercourse. Hinduism also suggests that one should abstain from intercourse on many sacred days: the first night of the new moon, the first night of the full moon, and the eighth day of each half of the month (the light half and the dark half), and sometimes on Fridays. As many as 100 days each year could be observed as non-sex days. A more subtle psychological factor may be what Morris Carstairs (1967) termed the "lost semen complex" to explain the beliefs of Gujerati men in North India: "Everyone knew that semen was not easily formed; it takes forty days and forty drops of blood to make one drop of semen. . . . Semen of good quality is rich and viscous, like the cream of unadulterated milk. A man who possesses a store of such good semen becomes a super-man. . . . Celibacy was the first requirement of true fitness, because every sexual orgasm meant the loss of a quantity of semen, laboriously formed" (83–86, quoted in Nag 1972:235).

The fact remains, however, that fertility is higher in India than in many other parts of the world where such restrictions on sexual intercourse do not exist. Obviously, sheer frequency of intercourse is not the explanation. It takes only one act of sexual intercourse at the right time of the month to create a pregnancy. The point of this discussion is to show that "reverse reasoning" (assuming that high fertility means that people have nothing better to do than have sex) is wrong. The cultural dynamics of sexuality in India function to restrain sexual activities and thus may keep fertility lower than it otherwise would be.

The Politics of Fertility

This section explores decision making about fertility at three levels: the family level, the national level, and the global level. Within the family, decision makers weigh factors influencing why and when to have a child. At the national level, governments seek to plan their overall population objectives on the basis of particular goals that are sometimes pronatalist (favouring many births) and sometimes antinatalist (opposed to many births). At the global level, we can see that powerful economic and political interests are at work influencing the reproductive policies of individual nations and, in turn, of families and individuals within them.

Family-Level Decision Making

At the family level, parental and other family members' perceptions about the value and costs of children influence their reproductive decision making (Nag 1983). Assessing the value and costs of children is a complex matter involving many factors. Four variables are most important in affecting the "demand" for children in different cultural contexts: children's labour value, children's value as old-age support for parents, infant and child mortality rates, and the economic costs of children.

In the first three, the relationship is positive: When children's value is high in terms of labour or old-age support, fertility is likely to be higher. When infant and child mortality rates are high, fertility rates also tend to be high in order to "replace" offspring who do not survive. Costs—including direct costs (for food, education, clothing) and indirect costs (employment opportunities that the mother gives up)—have a negative relationship. Higher costs promote the desire for fewer children. Industrial society alters the value of children in several ways: "Industrialization,

improvement in income, urbanization, and schooling are likely to reduce the labour value of children" (Nag 1983:58) and greatly increase their costs. Provision of old-age security and pension plans by the state may reduce that fertility incentive, although few developing countries have instituted such policies thus far.

In a highland village in the Oaxacan region of southern Mexico, men and women have different preferences about the number of children they wish to have (Browner 1986). Men are more pronatalist than women. Among women with only one child, 80 percent were content with their present family size. Most men (60 percent) who were satisfied with their present family size had four or more children. One woman said, "My husband sleeps peacefully through the night, but I have to get up when the children need something. I'm the one the baby urinates on; sometimes I have to get out of bed in the cold and change both our clothes. They wake me when they're sick or thirsty, my husband sleeps through it all." (714)

Depending on the gender division of labour and other social features related to gender, sons or daughters may be relatively more valued. Son preference is widespread, especially in Asia and the Middle East, but it is not a cultural universal. In some societies, people prefer a balanced sex ratio in their offspring, while in others daughters are preferred. Daughter preference is found in some Caribbean populations, in Venezuela, and some parts of Africa south of the Sahara. Longitudinal research conducted from 1956 to 1991 among the Tonga of Gwembe District, Congo, documents a female-biased population system that has persisted since at least the second half of the twentieth century (Clark et al. 1995). At most ages, men's death rates are higher than those of women. Differences in mortality are especially great for the very young and the elderly, among whom males die at twice the rate of females the same age. The kinship system of the Tonga influences this female-survival advantage. Among the Tonga, property is passed down from mother to daughter. Also, at marriage, the groom makes valuable payments to the bride's father. Thus daughters, not sons, bring wealth into the family, and their preferential care and enhanced survival reflect their value.

In Tokugawa, Japan, during the eighteenth and nineteenth centuries, husbands and wives had different fertility preferences based on the different value to them of sons versus daughters (Skinner 1993). Tokugawa wives, as is still common in Japan, preferred to have "first a girl, then a boy." This preference is related to the benefit in having a girl to help the mother in her work and to care for subsequent children, especially the boy it was hoped would come next. Husbands prefer a son-first strategy since a son helps them with their work. Husbands and wives each tried to achieve their goals with the one method available: **sex-selective infanticide**, or the killing of offspring on the basis of sex. Depending on their relative power, either the husband or wife would be able to dominate the decision making about whether a child born would be kept. But how could one assess the relative power of spouses? Age differences in Japan are a key status index. Seniority commands deference, respect, and obedience. Three categories of marital power can be defined, based on age differences at the time of marriage: low husband power (when the wife is older than the husband), intermediate husband power (when ages are about equal), and high husband power (when the husband is older than the wife). Over one-third of the marriages involved men who were at least 10 years older than their wives, about 60 percent were in the intermediate category, and less than 6 percent were in the low husband-power category. Was the gender of children related to marital power relations? Results in Figure 5.1 clearly show that parental preferences about having a girl or boy did exist and were acted on, depending on whose values won out.

Girls participating in the Guelaguetza festival, Oaxaca. Oaxaca is a distinctive cultural region and the scene of a vigorous movement for indigenous people's rights.

At the National Level

National governments play major roles in decreasing or increasing rates of population growth within their boundaries. Governments are concerned about providing employment and public services, maintaining the tax base, filling the ranks of the military, maintaining ethnic and regional proportions, and dealing with population aging. The former Soviet Union faced significant planning challenges created by the contrasts between the below-replacement fertility of the "European" areas and high

fertility rates in the Central Asian and Muslim regions such as Tajikistan and Kyrghizstan. Some countries, including Japan and France, are concerned about declining population growth rates. Their leaders have urged women to have more babies. The Quebec government is aware of the province's low birth rate and has developed policies to provide extra supports for families, including subsidies and low-cost child care. Israel is openly pronatalist, given its interest in boosting its national population level as a political statement of strength.

At the Global Level

The broadest, most far-reaching layer that affects decision making about fertility occurs at the international level, where global power structures such as the World Bank, pharmaceutical companies, and religious leaders influence national and individual priorities about fertility. In the 1950s, there was a wave of enthusiasm among Western nations for promoting family planning programs of many types. Recently, the United States has adopted a more restricted policy for limited advocacy for family planning and has withdrawn support for certain features such as abortion. The policy of the Canadian International Development Agency (CIDA) is to support women's reproductive health programs in developing countries in the context of family health, safe motherhood, women's nutrition, and quality family-planning services. Population policies of the governments of donor countries affect the welfare of people in developing countries since funding for particular programs may wax or wane depending on political currents. (See the Critical Thinking box.)

FIGURE 5.1 Gender of First-Born Child According to Spouse Power in the Household, Tokugawa, Japan

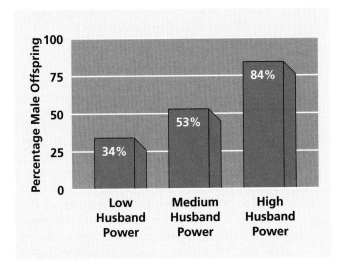

Note: Under normal conditions, one would expect roughly equal percentages of male and female births.

Source: From "Conjugal Power in Tokugawa Japanese Families: A Matter of Life or Death" by William G. Skinner, in *Sex and Gender Hierarchies*, edited by Barbara D. Miller. Copyright © 1993. Reprinted by permission of Cambridge University Press.

Critical Thinking

FAMILY PLANNING PROGRAMS IN BANGLADESH

BEGINNING IN the 1980s, criticism of Western family planning programs in relation to reproductive rights emerged from several directions. In the United States, the conservative Reagan administration opposed support of abortion and other forms of population control at home and abroad. (In November 1999, the United States government again refused to pay its estimated $1.5 billion in unpaid United Nations dues, an estimated 80 percent of all unpaid dues, because of Republican demands for conditions that ban spending any U.S. funds to support family planning clinics offering abortions in other countries.) At the same time, critics on the left claimed that the Western-supported and Western-styled family planning programs in developing countries were a form of neo-colonialism. Areas of concern included sterilization of women and the use of incentives such as cash payments, radios, or clothing to attract people to being sterilized.

Betsy Hartmann, an early critic of Western family planning promotion in developing countries, wrote an influential book called *Reproductive Rights and Wrongs* (1987). In the mid-1970s, she did fieldwork in a village in Bangladesh. Two key lessons about women's reproductive freedom emerged. First, in one area, there were women who were satisfied with the number of children they had, and they wanted to adopt some form of "modern" contraception, but none was available. Second,

> In other areas of Bangladesh, population control programs were vigorously promoting various methods including the pill, the injectible Depo-Provera, and IUDs without

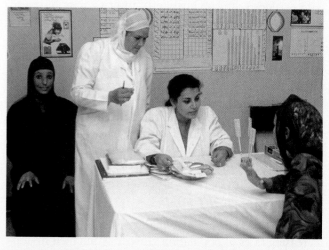

A family planning clinic in Egypt. Throughout much of the world, provision of Western-style family planning advice is controversial because it may conflict with local religious and other beliefs about the value of having many children and women's duty to be child bearers.

adequate medical screening, supervision, or follow-up. Many women experienced negative side-effects and became disillusioned with family planning. The government's response was not to reform the program to meet women's needs, but instead to further intensify its population control efforts by promoting female sterilization. In both contexts, women were denied control over their reproduction. (x–xi)

Fertility Control

All cultures throughout history have had ways of influencing fertility, including ways to increase it, reduce it, and regulate child spacing. Some ways are direct, such as using certain herbs or medicines that induce abortion. Others are indirect, such as long periods of breastfeeding, which reduce chances of conception. In Indonesia, for example, breastfeeding probably accounts for more child spacing than all other forms of contraception combined (Rohde 1982).

Hundreds of indigenous fertility control methods are available cross-culturally. One study conducted in Afghanistan in the 1980s found about 500 fertility-regulating techniques in just one region of the country (Hunte 1985). In Afghanistan, as in most pre-industrial

cultures, it is women who possess this information. Specialists, such as midwives or herbalists, provide further guidance and expertise. Of the total number of methods in the Afghanistan study, 72 percent were aimed at increasing fertility, 22 percent were contraceptives (preventing fertilization of the ovum by the sperm), and 6 percent were used to induce abortion. These methods involve plant and animal substances prepared in different ways. Herbs are made into tea and taken orally, some substances are formed into pills, some steamed and inhaled as vapours, some vaginally inserted, and others rubbed on the woman's stomach.

Contemporary medical research reveals the efficacy of many indigenous fertility-regulating methods. For example, experiments on animals show that some 450 plant species worldwide contain natural substances that prevent

In addition, Hartmann became involved in exposing the United States' involvement in sterilization abuse in Bangladesh, arguing that sterilization was targeted at the poorest women and involved "coercive" incentives. The incentive given to a man or woman for sterilization was Taka 175, equivalent to several weeks' wages. Women also received a *sari* (women's clothing worth about Taka 100), and men received a *lungee* (men's clothing worth about Taka 50). In some cases, food incentives were given. Poor women who approached local government officials for wheat as part of a special food aid program were told that they would get wheat if they had the "operation." Food aid was withheld from women who refused. The number of sterilizations increased during the autumn months when food was scarcest. Doctors and clinic staff received a bonus for each sterilization. Some family planning workers who failed to meet the sterilization quota for the month suffered pay cuts. However, others have argued that the "compensation payment does not appear to be an important influence on the decision as to whether or not to get sterilized" (Pillsbury 1990:181).

In the mid-1980s, over 60 health advocacy groups formed a coalition to block the approval of the injectable hormone Depo-Provera for use as a contraceptive in Canada. An effective contraceptive when injected every three months, activists were concerned that Depo-Provera had been used for years in family planning programs in developing countries and refugee camps before having been approved for use in Canada. They raised concerns over safety issues, including considerations of risk-benefit for women, and informed consent, since Depo-Provera had been administered to mentally handicapped women, women with disabilities, First Nations women, addicted women, and women prisoners, often without informed consent, screening, or follow-up care. Because of the potential for abuse and concerns about safety, the coalition managed to delay approval of the drug's use as a contraceptive in Canada until 1997 (Tudiver 1997). It is currently used successfully in Canada and in overseas programs but in 2005, new warnings suggested that it should be used as a last resort and for a short period of time.

CRITICAL THINKING QUESTIONS

How might anthropological fieldwork provide more information on the role of agency and individual decision making concerning family planning choices?

If you were a population policy-maker for CIDA, would you support family planning programs using incentives such as cash payments or the use of Depo-Provera without informed consent? How would you justify your position?

Was the delay in approving Depo-Provera use as a contraceptive in Canada justified considering its widespread and effective use today in Canada and in developing countries?

ovulation, block fertilization, stop implantation, or reduce fertility in some other way. In the history of Tibet, the population was stable for long periods of time. The Tibetans subsisted mainly on barley and peas. When mice were fed a diet of 20 percent peas, litter sizes dropped by half. At 30 percent peas, the mice failed to reproduce at all.

The following section considers two areas of family planning, the one that may be considered the old form of family planning—induced abortion—and the "new reproductive technologies" developed mainly in the West and now being increasingly exported to other contexts.

Induced Abortion

Direct intervention in a pregnancy may be resorted to in order to prevent fetal development and lead to abortion (expulsion of the fetus from the womb). Induced abortion, in its many forms, is probably a cultural universal. A review of ethnographic literature on about 400 societies indicates that it was practised in virtually all societies (Devereaux 1976). It is usually done either by the woman herself or with assistance from another woman, perhaps a midwife. Attitudes toward abortion range from acceptability to conditional approval (abortion is acceptable under specified conditions), to tolerance (abortion is regarded with neither approval nor disapproval), to opposition and punishment for offenders. Methods of inducing abortion include hitting the abdomen, starving oneself, taking drugs, jumping from high places, jumping up and down, lifting heavy objects, and doing hard work.

Economic and social factors largely explain why people induce abortion (Devereaux 1976:13–21). Nomadic

Afghan women waiting for their turn at the clinic in Bazarak. Throughout Afghanistan, patriarchal norms prevent women from going to clinics, or the geographical terrain and distance make it impossible to get to a clinic in cases of emergency. Rates of maternal mortality in remote areas of Afghanistan are perhaps the highest in the world.

women, for example, work hard and have to carry heavy loads, sometimes for long distances. This lifestyle does not allow women to care for many small children at one time. Poverty is another motivating factor: When a woman is faced with another birth in the context of limited resources, abortion may appear to be the best option. Culturally defined "legitimacy" of a pregnancy, along with possible social penalties for bearing an illegitimate child, has been a prominent reason for abortion in Western societies.

Some governments have intervened in family decisions to regulate access to abortion in varying ways, sometimes promoting it, and other times forbidding it. Since the late 1980s, China has pursued one of the most rigorous campaigns to limit population growth (Greenhalgh 2003). Its One-Child per Couple Policy, announced in 1978, allowed most families to have only one child. It involved strict surveillance of pregnancies, strong group pressure toward women pregnant for the second time or more, and forced abortions and sterilizations. This policy inadvertently led to an increase in female infanticide, as parents, in their desire for a son, opted to kill or abandon any daughters born to them.

Religion and abortion are often related, but there is no simple relationship between what a particular religion teaches about abortion and what people actually do. Catholicism forbids abortion, but thousands of Catholic women have sought abortions throughout the world. Islamic teachings forbid abortion and female infanticide, yet sex-selective abortion of female fetuses is practised covertly in Pakistan and by Muslims in India. Hinduism teaches *ahimsa*, or nonviolence toward other living beings, including a fetus whose movements have been felt by the mother ("quickening"). Yet thousands of Hindus seek abortions every year, and many are specifically to abort a female.

In contrast, Buddhism provides no overt rulings against abortion. In fact, Japanese Buddhism teaches that all life is fluid and that an aborted fetus is simply "returned" to a watery world of unshaped life and may, some time later, come back to live with humans (LaFleur 1992). This belief fits well with the fact that abortion has, in recent years, been the most commonly used form of birth control in Japan.

The New Reproductive Technologies

Women's reproductive rights are an important and contentious contemporary issue in all societies. These rights may involve the choice of seeking abortion in some societies, while in another (such as China), the right to bear

People in Japan regularly visit and decorate statues in memory of their aborted or "returned" fetuses.

a child. They include the issue of the right to decide the gender or other characteristics of an unborn child. Since the early 1980s, new forms of reproductive technology have been developed and been made available in many places around the world.

One development is the ability to gain genetic information about the fetus, which can be used by parents in decision making about whether to continue or stop the pregnancy. In North America and some European countries, amniocentesis is a legal test used to reveal certain genetic problems in the fetus, such as Down syndrome or spina bifida. Anthropologists have begun to question the social equity involved in this testing and the ethical issues related to the growing role of technology in birth and reproduction. For example, Rayna Rapp's research (1993) among poor women on Medicare in New York City demonstrated that new technology such as amniocentesis overpowered rather than empowered women.

In 1989, the federal government of Canada appointed a commission to explore the social, ethical, and medical implications of the new reproductive technologies. After four years of research and public hearings, the Royal Commission on New Reproductive Technologies released its report in November 1993. The committee recommended banning surrogate motherhood; sex-selection procedures for non-medical purposes; the buying and selling of human eggs, sperm, embryos, and fetal tissue; and genetic alteration such as the creation of human–animal hybrids. Procedures such as artificial insemination and in vitro fertilization should only be performed in public, non-profit clinics. The commission also upheld the rights of a pregnant woman over the rights of her fetus; no woman should face civil liability for harm done to her fetus during pregnancy.

In vitro fertilization (IVF) procedures are another important feature of the new reproductive technologies. Rather than being a population control technology for limiting fertility, IVF is designed to bypass infertility in a woman or couple and thus promote fertility. This technique is highly sought after by many couples in Western countries, especially middle- and upper-class couples, among whom infertility is inexplicably high. It is also increasingly available in urban centres around the world (Inhorn 2003). As this new technology spreads throughout the world, people reframe it within their own cultural logics. In much of North America and the United Kingdom, where in vitro fertilization first became available, people tend to view it as "reproduction gone awry," because it is non-natural and a sign of one's natural inadequacy and failure (Jenkins and Inhorn 2003). Research on local cultural understandings of NRTs is emerging. In Athens, Greece, women who seek in vitro fertilization see it as natural because it helps them realize a key aspect of their feminine nature through pregnancy and birth (Paxson 2003). Many of these middle-class urban women commented that becoming a mother is the purpose of a woman's life, so IVF allows a woman's natural destiny to unfold. Husbands felt less positive about IVF because they believe that their important role in conception is bypassed by the process.

Medical institutional culture also varies worldwide in terms of its attitudes toward IVF. In the United States and Canada, it is medically acceptable to provide IVF services, and some, in Canada, are covered by medical insurance. In Japan, a doctor who performed an IVF procedure was expelled by the leading obstetric society there in 1998 (M. Jordan 1998). Japanese societal values in relation to reproduction are complicated: They oppose surgery because it cuts the body, but they support abortion. There is, however, growing public demand in Japan for new reproductive techniques—a demand that is opposed by the medical profession. Religious institutions are also reacting to the NRTs, including in vitro fertilization, and formulating policies. Debate and diversity exist among global religions. Within Islam, for example, Sunnis allow IVF if the woman is fertilized with her husband's semen and recognize the resulting offspring as the legal child of the couple. Shiites, however, do not (*Women's Health Weekly* 2003).

The globalization of IVF is driven by many factors, including pronatalism, the stigma of childlessness, and adoption restrictions. Behind all these factors lurks the fact of rising infertility in both men and women, conditions more likely to go untreated among poorer populations. Infertility does seem to have class distributions, as does access to infertility treatment, including IVF. Estimates are that infertility affects 8 percent to 12 percent of couples worldwide (Inhorn 2003). Sub-Saharan Africa, referred to as the "infertility belt," has the highest rate of infertility in the world; about one-third of couples are unable to conceive. Given the poverty of this region, infertility services are also least available there.

CULTURE AND DEATH

Cultural anthropologists have done many studies on fertility, but their research on mortality is relatively scant (Bledsoe and Hirschman 1989). This difference is partly because mortality is more difficult to research in a typical fieldwork period in the traditional fieldwork setting of a village or urban neighbourhood. In a year, several births might occur in a village of 1000 people, while fewer infant deaths will occur and perhaps no murders or suicides. (Of course, if one did fieldwork in a home for the aged, then death would be far easier to study than birth.) Another reason for the difference in research emphasis between fertility and mortality is the greater availability of funding for fertility studies, given the worldwide concern with population growth and family planning.

Death may occur randomly and from biological causes that impair the body's functioning. However, cultural factors often put certain people more at risk of dying from a certain cause and at a particular age than others. Consider statistics on deaths from car accidents. According to many studies, the rate of severe accidents is higher among men, and men exhibit more high-risk driving behaviour, such as driving at high speeds and driving under the influence of alcohol (Hakamies-Blomqvist 1994). A study of fatal accidents in older male and female drivers in Finland finds a clear increase among older female drivers. The analysis found that older women drivers had substantially less driving experience in terms of mileage and conditions, compared to older men drivers. The lower experience level of women drivers, in turn, was related to more men having held jobs to which they commuted. Women's relative lack of driving experience places women at a disadvantage when it comes to coping with the effects of aging on driving. If the division of labour were to change and more women had jobs to which they commuted, the accident pattern of older women drivers might also change.

Causes of death can be analyzed on several levels. For example, if an infant living in a poor, tropical country dies of dehydration, what might be the cause? Levels of causality considered in population studies are *proximate, intermediate,* and *ultimate* causes. A proximate cause is the one that is closest to the actual outcome. In the case of the infant death, dehydration was the proximate cause of death and one that might be written on the death certificate. Why was the baby dehydrated? A closer look into the situation might show that the baby was malnourished. Malnutrition leads to diarrhea and subsequent dehydration. Malnutrition could be considered the intermediate cause of death. Why was the baby malnourished? This question takes us down a complex pathway of inquiry—perhaps the baby was not breastfed, and the family was poor and tried to bottle feed using expensive breast milk substitutes that were over-diluted with dirty water (P. Van Esterik 1989); perhaps the baby died during a period of extreme food scarcity in the area; or maybe the baby was an unwanted third daughter and was fed less than she needed in order to thrive. The question of ultimate causation entails an analysis of the deeper economic, political, and social factors that put a particular individual at increased risk of dying. In the next sections, we review how culture shapes death.

Infanticide

Deliberate killing of offspring has been widely documented, although it is not usually a frequent or common practice in any particular society. **Direct infanticide** is the death of an infant or child resulting from actions such as beating, smothering, poisoning, or drowning. **Indirect infanticide**, a more subtle process, may involve prolonged practices such as food deprivation, failure to take a sick infant to a clinic, or failure to provide warm clothing in winter. The most frequent motive for direct infanticide reported in the cross-cultural record is that the infant was "deformed" or very ill (Scrimshaw 1984:490–91). Other motives for infanticide include sex of the infant, an adulterous conception, an unwed mother, the birth of twins, too many children in the family already, and poverty. Psychologists Martin Daly and Margo Wilson (1984) offered a sociobiological explanation for 148 cases of infanticide in Canada from 1961 to 1979, arguing that mothers convicted of killing their offspring were likely to be young and unmarried, and may thus have had fewer supportive resources to help them.

Family Resource Constraints and Child "Fitness"

In all cultures, parents have expectations for their children—what roles they will play as children, their future marital status, and their roles as adults. If an infant appears to be unable to meet these expectations, parental disappointment and detachment may occur. As yet, no general theory has been formulated to explain precisely the relationship between resource constraints and perceived child "fitness." Not all people living in poverty practice infanticide, nor do all people practice infanticide when a child is born with certain disabilities.

Culturally accepted infanticide has long existed among the Tarahumara, a group of about 50 000 indigenous peoples living in a rugged mountainous area of northern Mexico (Mull and Mull 1987). Most live in log houses with dirt floors and no running water or electricity. They grow corn and beans and raise sheep and goats, mainly for their own use. Human strength is valued in adults as well as in children, since children begin helping with herding and child care early in their lives. Dorothy and Dennis Mull first learned of the possible existence of culturally sanctioned infanticide when Dennis was working as a volunteer physician in a hospital. A 12-month-old girl who had been admitted several months earlier developed a complication necessitating the amputation of half her foot. During her recovery in hospital, her mother's visits became less frequent. In conversations with the medical staff, the mother expressed a restrained but deep anger about the fact that her daughter had lost half her foot. After the child had been released from the hospital, she reportedly "failed" and died. One member of the community interpreted her death this way: "Well, after all, with only half a foot she'd never be able to walk right or work hard. She might never find a husband" (116–117).

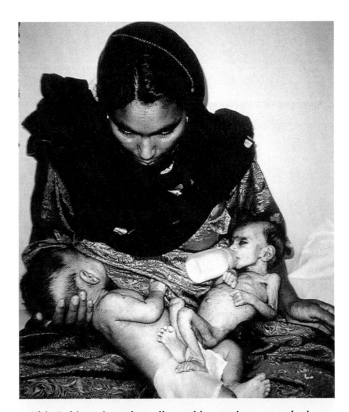

This Pakistani mother allowed her twin son exclusive access to her breast milk, while not breastfeeding her twin daughter. The girl died the day after this photo was taken. The mother told her doctor to use the picture if it would help others avoid making the same mistake.

Among the poor of urban Brazil, there exists a similar pattern of indirect infanticide driven by poverty (Scheper-Hughes 1993). Life is hard for the poor residents of the shantytown called Bom Jesus. Life expectancy is low, although precise information on mortality is not available for these shantytown dwellers (116–117). Available data on infant and child mortality rates in Bom Jesus since the 1960s led anthropologist Nancy Scheper-Hughes to coin the ironic phrase "the modernization of mortality." The modernization of mortality in Brazil refers to a deep division between mortality patterns of the rich and the poor. Recent economic growth in Brazil has brought rising standards of living for many. The national **infant mortality rate** (deaths of children under the age of one year per 1000 births) has declined substantially in recent decades, but the declines have been unevenly distributed. High infant death rates are concentrated among the poorest classes of society. Poverty forces mothers to selectively (and unconsciously) neglect babies that seem sickly or weak, sending them to heaven as "angel babies" rather than trying to keep them alive with the inadequate resources available. The people's religious beliefs, a form of Catholicism, pro-

vide ideological support for this practice of indirect infanticide since it allows mothers to believe that their dead babies are now safe in heaven.

When the infant's sex is the basis for infanticide, females tend to be the target (Miller 1997:42–44). Among foraging groups, sex-selective infanticide is rare, being found mainly among some Inuit groups. While early ethnographers such as Boas and Rasmussen attribute high rates of female infanticide to the need to reduce the number of non-food producers, more recent reports emphasize the decline in infant mortality rates among the Inuit as health care improved (Frideres 1998:401). Among horticultural societies, a correlation exists between the level of inter-group warfare and the practice of female infanticide (Divale and Harris 1976). Warfare puts a premium on raising males, to the detriment of investing care and resources in females.

Indirect female infanticide exists in contemporary times in much of China, the Republic of Korea, Hong Kong, India, Pakistan, and parts of the Middle East (see the Multiple Cultural Worlds box). In these countries, female infanticide is related to a complex set of factors, including the gender division of labour and marriage practices and costs.

Suicide

Suicide is known in all societies, but the degree to which it is viewed as a positive or negative act varies. In some cultures, suicide is legally or religiously defined as a crime. Catholicism defines suicide as a sin, and suicide rates tend to be lower in Catholic countries than in Protestant countries (Durkheim 1951:152). However, martyrdom has a long history in the Christian tradition. Buddhism does not condone suicide, nor does it consider attempted suicide a punishable crime. Indeed, Buddhists have sometimes resorted to suicide as a political statement, as in the suicides of Buddhist priests and nuns by self-immolation during the Vietnam War.

Suicide terrorism is a term that has become prominent in the United States since the September 11, 2001, attacks. Those attacks, as well as many others carried out in the Middle East and elsewhere by people of several different religious and political persuasions, involve the suicide of one or more people with the intention of killing other people as well (Andriolo 2002). Many religions put a positive value on martyrdom, or a person facing and accepting death for a sacred cause. Linking personal martyrdom with killing others is also found in some religions and secular political movements. The young Tamil woman who in 1991 blew herself up, along with India's former prime minister Rajiv Gandhi (Indira Gandhi's eldest son), is an example of a political martyr–assassin. Her cause was ethnic Tamil separatism in Sri Lanka. Islam condemns

Multiple Cultural Worlds

FEMALE INFANTICIDE IN INDIA

THE INDIAN population has 55 million fewer females than males. Much of this gap is caused by indirect female infanticide and sex-selective abortion. Most of the scarcity of girls is located in northern India, where baby girls are breastfed less often and for a shorter period of time than baby boys, and they are taken to clinics for treatment of illnesses less frequently. Hospital admissions in the North are 2:1 boys to girls, and that is not because more boys are sick than girls, but because parents and grandparents are more willing to allocate time and money for the health of boys than girls (Miller 1997).

Why is discrimination against daughters and in favour of sons in terms of household allocations of food, health care, and even attention more marked in northern India than in its southern and eastern regions? This pattern corresponds with two features of the economy: production and marriage exchanges. The northern plains are characterized by dry-field wheat cultivation, which requires intensive labour inputs for plowing and field preparation and then moderate amounts of field labour for sowing, weeding, and harvesting, with women assisting in the latter tasks as unpaid family labour. Production in southern and eastern India relies more on wet rice cultivation, in which women form the bulk of the paid agricultural labour force. In much of southern India, women of the household may even participate on an equal footing with men in terms of agricultural planning and decision making.

Paralleling this regional difference in labour patterns is a contrast in costs related to marriage. In the North, marriage typically requires, especially among the propertied groups, **groomprice** or **dowry**—the transfer of large amounts of cash and goods from the bride's family to the groom's family (Miller 1997). Marriage costs in the South among both propertied and unpropertied groups were more likely to emphasize **brideprice**—the transfer of cash and goods from the groom's side to the bride's father, along with a tradition of passing gold jewellery through the female line from mother to daughter. From a parent's perspective, the birth of several daughters in the northern system is a financial drain. In the South, a daughter is considered a valuable labourer and source of wealth. Importantly, much of northern dowry and southern bridewealth circulates: An incoming dowry can be used

to finance the marriage of the groom's sister, and bridewealth received in the South at the marriage of a daughter can be used for the marriage of her brother. Logically, in the North, the more sons per daughter in the household the better, since more incoming dowries will allow for a "better" marriage of a daughter.

The economic costs and benefits to a household of having sons versus daughters in India also vary by class. This variation relates to both work patterns and marriage patterns. Middle- and upper-class families, especially in the North, tend to keep girls and women out of the paid labour force more than the poor. Thus, daughters are a greater economic liability among the better-off than among the poor where girls, as well as boys, may earn money in the informal sector, for example, doing piecework at home. This class difference is mirrored in marriage costs. Among the poor, marriage costs are less than among the middle and upper classes, and sometimes involve balanced exchange between the bride's and groom's families. Thus, marital costs of daughters are lower and the benefits of having sons are not that much greater than those of having daughters.

Poverty is therefore not the major driving factor of son preference and daughter disfavour in India. It is more related to a desire to maximize family status and wealth by having sons and avoiding having daughters: If one has two sons and one daughter in the North Indian marriage system of huge dowries, then two dowries will come in with the brides of the sons and only one dowry will be expended. Incoming dowries can be used to finance the dowry of one's own daughter, so one can provide a huge outgoing dowry that will attract a "high quality" husband. If, on the other hand, one has two daughters and one son, the ratio of incoming to outgoing wealth changes significantly. This situation would impoverish a family rather than enrich it.

FOOD FOR THOUGHT

Have you experienced, or has anyone you know experienced, a feeling of being less valued as a child than other children in the family? If you are an "only child," you will need to ponder experiences you may have heard from friends.

suicide and teaches that hell awaits those who commit it. But certain reinterpretations, among Philippine Muslims, for example, see purposeful suicide killings as being outside Islamic teachings but nonetheless justifiable on other grounds. A few pages in the manual that the September 11 hijackers had with them related their actions to raids that the prophet Muhammad conducted to consolidate his position, thus portraying their actions as acceptable and even heroic and the end for them as entry into paradise instead of hell. Many Islamic scholars, however, do not accept the validity of this reasoning.

Throughout much of Asia and the South Pacific, suicide is considered a noble and honourable act. When Cheyenne Brando, daughter of Marlon Brando and Tahitian actress Tarita, committed suicide in Tahiti, the local mayor called her suicide "a beautiful gesture" (Gliotto 1995:70). Honourable suicide is also found in Japan, where it seems to result from a strong commitment to group goals and a feeling of failure to live up to those goals (Lebra 1976). In this way, suicide is a way of "saving face."

Sati (pronounced "SUT-TEE"), or the suicide of a wife upon the death of her husband, has been practised in parts of India for several hundred years and, on occasion, into the present. According to Hindu scriptures, a woman whose husband dies does an act of great personal and group honour if she voluntarily joins his corpse on the funeral pyre and thus burns to death. No one knows for sure how common this was in the past, but its ideal is still upheld by conservative Hindus. The most recent reported *sati* occurred in the northern state of Rajasthan in 1987 by a young widow named Roop Kanwar. Historians and social scientists have debated the degree of voluntarism involved in such suicides, as there is evidence of direct coercion in some cases—the widow was drugged, or physically forced onto the pyre. Indirect coercion is also culturally embedded in the belief that a woman whose husband dies is to blame for his death. Perhaps she didn't serve him with enough devotion, pray or fast for him enough, or she ate too much and didn't give him enough food. The life of surviving widows is difficult, involving loss of status, shame, and material deprivation. Knowing this, a new widow may decide she would be better off dead.

In terms of sheer numbers, suicide is more prevalent in the industrialized, urbanized societies of Europe than elsewhere. However, in several developing nations, such as Sri Lanka and Samoa, suicide rates have risen steeply in recent decades. The general explanation proposed for the cross-cultural variation in suicide rates is that the rapid social changes brought about by industrialism, the spread of education, and global change in consumer values are often not matched by people's ability to satisfy these new aspirations. French sociologist Émile Durkheim (1897) used the term *anomie* to refer to the feelings of disloca-

A temple in Rajasthan, northern India, dedicated to women who have committed *sati*.

tion and dissatisfaction caused by rapid social change and thwarted ambitions. The concept of anomic suicide seems to apply well to the rising trend of youth suicide worldwide. In Canada, the suicide rate for adolescent males between 15 and 19 years has risen fourfold since 1960, from 5 to 19.9 per 100 000 in 1997. Suicide rates among First Nations youth are six times higher than the rates in the rest of Canada (Frideres 1998:182).

Epidemics

The chapter on medical anthropology (Chapter 7) will discuss disease in more depth, but for our purposes here, it is important to introduce the massive impact of HIV/AIDS on mortality in the past two decades as a primary example of epidemic-related death. At the present time, sub-Saharan countries have been the most affected by the HIV epidemic (Nyambedha, Wandibba, and Aagaard-Hansen 2003). Most of the deaths have occurred among adults of parent age. These deaths are tragic in themselves, and they also leave behind them huge numbers of orphaned children. Global estimates are that 10 million children under the age of 15 years have lost their mother or both parents to AIDS. In Kenya alone, it is likely that there will be 1.5 million orphaned children by 2005. Some families in Kenya are now headed by children as

RESEARCH ON LOCAL CULTURAL PATTERNS FOR IMPROVED ORPHAN CARE IN KENYA

THE DRAMATIC increase in the numbers of orphans in Africa—an increase attributable to the AIDS epidemic—calls for new thinking about how to care for these children, because traditional mechanisms are inadequate. Child care patterns in many parts of the world, and especially in many African kinship systems, involve grandparents and other family members. But now, even this social safety net is not enough.

Many non-governmental agencies have become involved in helping to design community-based services for AIDS orphans. Cultural anthropologists can help make these services more effective by offering insights about local cultural practices and beliefs so that programs can be tailored to fit particular communities. Anthropologists have long known that "one-size-fits-all" programs, designed by outsiders without attention to local culture, may operate less effectively than they could or, at worst, fail disastrously.

One anthropological study undertaken to provide such needed cultural information was conducted in western Kenya in an area bordering Lake Victoria (Nyambedha, Wandibba, and Aagaard-Hansen 2003). The Luo are the predominant ethnic group in the region. The area is poor, and most Luo practise small-scale farming and obtain some additional income from fishing, migrant labour, and informal gold mining. Recurrent droughts lead to frequent crop failures. Children are important in the local economy: They work on farms planting, weeding, and harvesting and do such other important tasks as collecting firewood, herding animals, fetching water, and fishing. Clean water is scarce. Health services provided by a Christian mission and the government are of poor quality and not affordable for most people.

The Luo define an orphan as someone under the age of 18 years who has lost either one or both parents; thus they refer to single and double orphans. (The Luo definition differs from the usual international definition: someone under the age of 15 years who has lost both parents.) The Luo say that the neediest are double orphans.

The research involved both quantitative and qualitative data-gathering techniques (review Chapter 2). Questionnaires were administered to a random sample of households, and then in-depth interviews were conducted with a sub-sample of 20 orphans and orphan caretakers from the first survey. Other interviews were conducted with key informants in a range of social roles, such as village elders, teachers, members of women's groups, and staff of the local children's home. Fourteen focus group discussions (FGDs) were held with a cross-section of people to explore further the main themes of the study. Last, five households where orphans lived were monitored for six months to obtain longitudinal information on household resources, changes in household membership, coping mechanisms, and outside support.

Analysis of the data reveals many useful findings. First, they provide information on the population of orphans.

young as 10 to 12 years old. Community-based interventions to help these disadvantaged children suffer from several weaknesses, including lack of attention to local cultural factors (see the Lessons Applied box).

Violence

Violent death can be the result of private, interpersonal conflict or it can occur in a public arena, either through informal conflict between individuals or groups, such as gang fights, or through formal conflict, such as war. Throughout history, millions of people have died from private and public violence. Often their deaths have culturally defined patterns.

Private Violence: Spousal Abuse

Throughout the world, private violence resulting in death is all too common. One example, infanticide, was discussed earlier. Lethal spousal violence is known to exist throughout most of the world in varying degrees, although it is difficult to pinpoint cross-cultural rates because statistics are undependable or unavailable. In the case of spouses, far more women are killed by husbands or male partners than vice versa. Anecdotal evidence suggests that in much of the Middle East, a husband may kill his wife or daughter with a fair amount of impunity, as if it is within his rights in terms of protecting family honour. In Canada in 1997, one in eight women living with a man was abused at some time, according to the Canadian

About one out of three children (34 percent) had lost one or both parents. Of these, about half had lost their father, about 20 percent had lost their mother, and 30 percent were double orphans.

Second, the study provided information on the orphans' needs. The main problems the orphans faced were food shortage, lack of money for school fees, and inadequate medical care and clothing. In Luo culture, fathers are responsible for paying children's school fees. Thus paternal orphans tended to drop out of school. Maternal orphans are considered more vulnerable than paternal orphans, because their father is likely to remarry and his new wife will favour her own biological children. About half of the orphans remained with one parent. Others moved in with relatives, especially grandparents, whose resources were already stretched but who felt they could not refuse to take in their grandchild. Many orphans taken in by better-off relatives ended up providing free labour for that family. Alternatively, they took on wage work for non-relatives. In either case, their school participation suffered.

The large and sudden increase in the number of orphans creates larger strains on the community as people come to realize that their traditional pattern of caring for orphans within the kinship structure is not adequate. The traditional generosity of kin seems to be declining. At the same time, a longstanding pattern of spending a lot of money on funerals means that resources that could go to orphans go to burial and after-burial rituals instead.

Community-based organizations such as churches and women's groups in this region are doing little to help the orphans, although in other areas they are more active. The study provides a baseline of the population of orphans, information about their specific needs and coping strategies, and insights about community views of the problem. It points to the particular needs of different types of orphans and the varying strengths of different family structures in caring for orphans.

The authors reject the idea of constructing an orphanage as a way of dealing with the problem. They offer no specific suggestions for community-based programs, but it is easy to see that the following would help: financial support to single-parent and grandparent caretakers, waiving or community funding of the school fees for orphans, and a social movement to divert some of the money used for funerals to orphan care.

FOOD FOR THOUGHT

Has the issue of AIDS orphans in Africa come to your attention before? If so, how—television, newspapers, or what? How was the issue presented? If it had not come to your attention, what might explain its relative invisibility as a globally significant issue?

Department of Justice. Anthropological studies of the dynamics of domestic violence cross-culturally are discussed later in this book. The United States has high rates of lethal spousal violence with Kentucky having the highest reported rates of wife killing.

In India, beginning in the 1980s, many cases of an apparently new form of **femicide**, or murder of a person based on the fact of being female, were reported in the media. Called *dowry death*, such murders were characteristically committed by a husband, often in collusion with his mother, and carried out by throwing a flammable substance over the victim and then lighting her on fire. These murders are especially prevalent in northern cities, among the middle and upper classes. They are spurred by an obsessive material interest in extracting wealth from the wife's family through first her dowry and later, a continuing stream of demanded gifts. If the bride's family cannot comply with these demands, the bride is harassed, and her life is endangered. This form of femicide is related to the overall low value of women in India, especially in the North and among the status-aspiring middle and upper classes.

Public Violence

Two forms of lethal public violence that anthropologists study are warfare and genocide. These topics are discussed in greater depth in Chapter 11. In this section, we focus on their effects on mortality. The few studies that have addressed mortality from warfare cross-culturally reveal that, among horticultural societies, warfare accounts for the highest proportion of male deaths and functions as a major mechanism of population control (Divale and Harris 1976). Horticulture's requirement for large territories puts many groups in conflict with one another. In recent decades, conflicts with outsiders have increased; for example, the Yanomami of the Brazilian and Venezuelan Amazon region are squeezed by outsiders such as cattle ranch developers and miners (R. Ferguson 1990). This external pressure impels them to engage in intergroup raids that often result in the deaths of male fighters, but also sometimes women, who may be captured and then killed. In some especially vulnerable groups of Yanomami, it has been reported that up to one-third of all adult males die as a result of intergroup raids and warfare.

In contrast, in industrialized societies, the death rates of males actively involved in warfare constitute a much smaller proportion of total death rates, being replaced by such causes as automobile accidents or heart disease. Canadian casualties totalled 138 166 in World War I, 53 145 in World War II, and 516 in the Korean War. Since then, most Canadian military casualties, numbering less than 150, have come during UN and NATO Peacekeeping operations, according to the Department of National Defence. The Vietnam–American War of the 1960s and 1970s resulted in the death of about 60 000 Americans in Vietnam (mostly males) and of many times that number of Vietnamese.

Some scholars distinguish **ethnocide**, destruction of a culture without physically killing its people, from **genocide**, the destruction of a culture and its people through physical extermination. The Chinese occupation of Tibet, the Khmer Rouge's massacres in Cambodia, the Serbian-Bosnian conflict, the Hutu-Tutsi conflict in Rwanda, and

Refugees from the late 1990s violence in Rwanda on their way to neighbouring Democratic Republic of Congo (Zaire). Many refugees did not survive the ordeal, although adequate statistics are not available to assess the mortality rate of refugees.

Shanawdithit, the last known Beothuk, captured in 1823. She died of tuberculosis in St. John's, Newfoundland.

the Indonesian government's actions in East Timor are examples of politically motivated genocide.

The history of Native American demography can also be interpreted as one of genocidal destruction and has been called "the American holocaust." It is likely that well over 50 million Amerindians died as a result of contact with the Europeans from 1492 through the seventeenth century (Stannard 1992). For example, the European presence in Central America had the following results:

> Before the coming of the Europeans, central Mexico, radiating out from the metropolitan centers over many tens of thousands of square miles, had contained about 25 million people—almost ten times the population of England at that time. Seventy-five years later hardly more than one million were left. And central Mexico, where 60 out of a hundred people perished, was typical. . . . In western and central Honduras 95 percent of the native people were exterminated in half a century. In western Nicaragua the rate of extermination was 99 percent—from more than one million people to less than 10,000 in just sixty years. (430)

The indigenous population of the Caribbean islands was also exterminated. Only archaeological evidence and Spanish archival documents recording fragments of the original peoples' culture remain.

In another example of genocidal destruction, the Beothuk, the Aboriginal inhabitants of Newfoundland, were actively hunted and killed primarily by British farmers, fishers, and trappers who settled on the bays that had been the Beothuk's summer camps. The Beothuk had been pushed further inland, away from their resources, from the time of the island's discovery in 1497. With no intermediaries such as traders or missionaries interested in interacting with them, and weakened by diseases such as bubonic plague, smallpox, and tuberculosis, the population decreased from approximately 345 in 1768, to 72 in 1811; the "last" Beothuk, Shanawdithit, was captured and brought to St. John's in 1823, where she died of tuberculosis in 1829 (J. Price 1979; I. Marshall 1996).

Genocide against indigenous peoples has been occurring for centuries as imperialist powers and profit-seeking explorers and settlers have intentionally brought about the extinction of entire peoples (Maybury-Lewis 2002). During the nineteenth century, British settlers in Tasmania carried out an overt campaign to exterminate the indigenous Tasmanians. In other cases, mass killings were used as means of terrorizing survivors into performing forced labour, as, for example, in the rubber plantations of Peru and the Congo. These historical examples of "imperialist genocide" were driven by greed and supported by a racist ideology that considered indigenous people less than human. Today, greed-driven and carelessly planned development projects such as large dams (Chapter 16) often prove to be an indirect form of genocide when they completely disrupt where indigenous people live, force them to resettle, and subject them to new diseases and suicidal despair.

Politically motivated examples of genocide of indigenous peoples also can be easily found. Since the middle of the twentieth century, the government of India has waged a campaign of terror against many groups in its states bordering Burma to prevent separatist movements from gaining strength. One tribe, the Nagas, numbers about two and a half million; the Indian government has placed 200 000 troops in their area to quell the tribe's attempts to join with Nagas in Burma to form a separate Naga country. The Naga people voted overwhelmingly for independence in 1951, and India invaded the region in 1954. There are no mortality data available for this situation, but one can only assume that the casualties are far higher on the Naga side than on the government side.

KEY QUESTIONS REVISITED

HOW is reproduction related to modes of production?

Reproduction, or the dominant ways in a society that people come into the world and leave the world, are everywhere shaped by culture. More specifically, the various modes of production are basic structures to which reproduction responds. For thousands of years, foragers maintained a balanced level of population through direct and indirect means of fertility regulation. As sedentarization increased and food surpluses became more available and storable, population increased as well, culminating in the highest rates of population growth in human history among settled agriculturalists.

HOW does culture shape fertility in different contexts?

Cross-culturally, many techniques exist for increasing fertility, reducing it, and regulating its timing. Anthropological studies of indigenous fertility-regulating mechanisms reveal hundreds of different methods, including the use of herbs and other natural sources for inhibiting or enhancing fertilization, and for inducing abortion if an undesired pregnancy occurs. In non-industrial societies, the knowledge and practice of fertility regulation was largely unspecialized and available to all women. Early specializations included midwives and herbalists. In the industrial mode of reproduction, scientific and medical specialization abounds, and most knowledge and expertise is no longer in the hands of women themselves. Class-stratified access to fertility-regulating methods exists globally and within nations.

HOW does culture shape mortality in different contexts?

Population growth and change are also affected through the cultural shaping of death. The practice of infanticide is of ancient origin, and it still exists today. It may be done in response to familial resource limitations, perceptions of "fitness" of the child, or preferences about the gender of offspring. Deaths from suicide, and from public and private violence, also reflect particular cultural patterns that "target" certain people or groups. In a specific mode of production, death at a certain age or from a particular cause is more likely than it would be in a different mode of production. Thus, far from being random, natural events, birth and death are cultural events to a large extent.

KEY CONCEPTS

below-replacement-level fertility, p. 103
brideprice, p. 114
demographic transition, p. 104
demography, p. 102
direct infanticide, p. 112
dowry, p. 114
ethnocide, p. 118
femicide, p. 117
fertility, p. 102
genocide, p. 118

groomprice, p. 114
indirect infanticide, p. 112
infant mortality rate, p. 113
infanticide, p. 103
migration, p. 102
mortality, p. 102
pronatalism, p. 103
replacement-level fertility, p. 103
reproduction, p. 102
sex-selective infanticide, p. 106

SUGGESTED READINGS

Kamran Asdar Ali, *Planning the Family in Egypt: New Bodies, New Selves*. Austin: University of Texas Press, 2002. This ethnographic study, conducted by a Pakistani doctor and anthropologist, examines the policies and practices of family planning programs in Egypt to see how this elitist, Western-influenced state creates demographically compliant citizens. His findings reveal the dilemma created for women as family planning programs pressure them to think of themselves as individual decision makers acting in their own and the nation's interest by limiting their fertility, even though they are still bound by their wider families and religion to pronatalism.

Caroline Bledsoe and Barney Cohen, eds., *Social Dynamics of Adolescent Fertility in Sub-Saharan Africa*. Washington, D.C.: National Academy Press, 1993. An anthropologist and a demographer examine national survey data on cultural factors related to high fertility rates among adolescents in sub-Saharan Africa. Attention is given to patterns of adolescent sexuality, attitudes toward marriage, women's status, knowledge and practice of contraception, and the role of education in change.

John D. Early and Thomas N. Headland, *Population Dynamics of a Philippine Rain Forest People: The San Ildefonso Agta*. Gainesville: University of Florida Press, 1998. This comprehensive study of population dynamics of an Agta group living on Luzon Island in the Philippines draws on a 44-year quantitative database on fertility, mortality, and migration from the time when the Agta were forest foragers to the present (they are now small-scale farmers in rural Philippine society). It profiles a minority people without economic and political power and documents the impact of international logging interests on their lives.

Thomas E. Fricke, *Himalayan Households: Tamang Demography and Domestic Processes*. New York: Columbia University Press, 1994. An example of demographic anthropology, this is a local study of population patterns and change in one region of Nepal. The book includes chapters on the subsistence economy, fertility and mortality, the life course, household dynamics, and recent changes.

W. Penn Handwerker, ed., *Births and Power: Social Change and the Politics of Reproduction*. Boulder, CO: Westview Press, 1990. An overview chapter by the editor is followed by 11 case studies, including studies of the Inuit of Canada, the Bariba of West Africa, the Mende of Sierra Leone, teen pregnancies in the United States, and people who have AIDS in Africa.

Nancy Howell, *Demography of the Dobe !Kung*. New York: Academic Press, 1979. This classic book describes the demography of a group of South African foragers before they were sedentarized. The text considers how anthropological methods contribute to demographic analysis of small-scale societies, causes of illness and death, fertility and sterility, and population growth rates.

Marcia C. Inhorn, *Infertility and Patriarchy: The Cultural Politics of Gender and Family Life in Egypt*. Philadelphia: University of Pennsylvania Press, 1996. Based on fieldwork in Alexandria, this book uses narratives from several infertile Egyptian women to show the different ways these women and their families deal with cultural pressures to bear children.

Leith Mullings and Alaka Wali, *Stress and Resilience: The Social Context of Reproduction in Central Harlem*. New York: Kluwer Academic, 2001. Documenting the daily efforts of African Americans to contend with oppressive conditions, this ethnography focuses on the experiences of women especially during pregnancy and details the strategies they use to address the strains that their economic and social context place on them.

Nancy Scheper-Hughes, *Death without Weeping: The Violence of Everyday Life in Brazil*. Berkeley: University of California Press, 1993. This book is a landmark "ethnography of death," based on fieldwork in a Brazilian shantytown over several periods of time. The author argues that poverty drives a demographic system of very high infant mortality rates and high fertility.

Nancy Scheper-Hughes and Carolyn Sargent, eds., *Small Wars: The Cultural Politics of Childhood*. Berkeley: University of California Press, 1998. Following an introduction by the co-editors, 18 chapters explore aspects of infant and child mortality and health in a wide array of contexts, including Japan, Ecuador, the United States, Israel, Mexico, Portugal, the Dominican Republic, Cuba, England, Croatia, and Brazil.

Soraya Tremayne, ed., *Managing Reproductive Life: Cross-Cultural Themes in Sexuality and Fertility*. New York: Bergahn Books, 2001. Twelve chapters are organized under three headings: agency and identity, fertility and parenthood, and policy and vulnerable groups. Cases are from India, Thailand, the United Kingdom, Burkino Faso, Peru, Nigeria, and Hong Kong, and topics include motherhood among prostitutes, the stigma of infertility, how male migration affects fertility, and the reproductive health of refugees.

WEBLINKS

The Companion Website (www.pearsoned.ca/miller) that accompanies *Cultural Anthropology*, Third Canadian Edition, includes a destinations module containing links to many websites relevant to the content of this chapter. Use it to investigate the Web and expand your understanding of anthropology.

KEY QUESTIONS

- **HOW** does culture shape personality during infancy and childhood?
- **HOW** does culture shape personality during the transition from childhood to adulthood?
- **HOW** does culture shape personality during adulthood?

6

PERSONALITY, IDENTITY, AND HUMAN DEVELOPMENT

Young boys of the Shan people, Thailand, participating in the Poi Sang Long festival. This annual event culminates in the initiation of young boys into the Buddhist monkhood for a minimum of two years.

The Mehinaku are peaceful horticulturalists of the Brazilian Amazon whose society, thus far, is mainly intact (Gregor 1981). Nonetheless, the Mehinaku are aware of the presence and power of other Brazilians.

An analysis of 385 dreams of the Mehinaku indicates that they have deep anxieties about the outsiders. Of the total set of dreams, over half contained indications of some level of anxiety. In 31 of the dreams, Brazilians were central characters, and of these, 90 percent of the dreams were tinged with fear, evidencing a clear focus of anxiety on the outsiders. Recurrent themes in the dreams with outsiders as key characters were fire, assault, and disorientation. Although the Mehinaku's land and culture are still intact, their inner tranquility is gone.

The study of people's dreams in different cultural contexts is just one of the many approaches that psychological anthropologists pursue in their attempt to understand psychological processes.

Psychological anthropology addresses many of the topics of contemporary Western psychology: learning, perception, cognition, memory, intelligence, the emotions, sexuality and gender, personality, identity, and mental health problems. Studying these topics cross-culturally reveals the ethnocentrism involved in applying Western psychological concepts universally, including definitions of what is "normal." An enduring question in psychological anthropology is whether and how much human psychology is the same cross-culturally or whether variation overrides universals.

This chapter provides background on how cultural anthropology has approached the study of the individual within culture—particularly how cultures shape **personality**, an individual's patterned and characteristic way of behaving, thinking, and feeling. We also consider how cultures create people's sense of identity: who they think they are in relation to others, their sense of self. The material is presented in terms of general stages of the life cycle, from birth through death in old age.

The subject matter of this chapter is referred to as *ethnopsychology*, the study of how various cultures define and create personality, identity, and mental health. This chapter focuses on "normal" human development, as defined culturally. Problematic aspects of human development, including what Western psychology defines as mental illness, are discussed in Chapter 7.

CULTURE, PERSONALITY, AND IDENTITY

Most cultural anthropologists assume that personality is formed through **enculturation**, or socialization, the process of transmitting culture to infants and other new members of society. They seek answers to these questions: Do different cultures enculturate their members into different personalities? If so, how and why?

The Culture and Personality School

The U.S.-based Culture and Personality School began in the 1930s and persisted through the 1970s. Culture and personality studies began with Franz Boas's interest in the individual, developed through his fieldwork on the Northwest Coast and the Central Arctic. The school was further developed through his students. Members of the school adopted some aspects of Freudian theories, including the importance of childhood experiences in shaping personality and identity, and the symbolic analysis of dreams. Boas's student Edward Sapir shared his interest in the relation between language and culture. In spite of Boas and Sapir's important role in institutionalizing Canadian anthropology, culture and personality as a "school" was never strongly developed in Canada, partly because of the influence of British social anthropology in the country. American influence in Canadian anthropology was most visible in the 1960s when many American professors taught in Canadian anthropology departments. By that time, culture and personality was no longer an important theoretical orientation in the United States. Meanwhile, Canadian anthropologists began collaborating with psychologists and psychiatrists to explore transcultural psychiatry. In 1955, transcultural psychiatric studies was established at McGill University to explore the effects of culture on psychiatric disorders.

Two directions that the Culture and Personality School took were, first, understanding how child-rearing practices affect personality and, second, describing national-level personality patterns. The first of these is still accepted, whereas the second is largely discredited.

Personality and Child Rearing

In the early 1930s, Margaret Mead went with her husband, anthropologist Reo Fortune, to the Sepik River area of northern New Guinea. Her subsequent publication, *Sex and Temperament in Three Primitive Societies* (1935), revealed striking differences in how male and female roles and personalities were defined and acted out. Once again, Mead's findings seemed to prove that nature is subservient to culture—that culture, not nature, dictates what is male and what is female. Among the Arapesh, the first group she studied, both men and women had nurturant and gentle personalities. Both valued parental roles and both participated equally in child care. Arapesh males and females all behave according to what is stereotypically defined as "feminine" in Western cultures. Among the Mundugumor, in contrast, both males and females corresponded to the Western stereotype of "masculine" behaviour. Adults in general were assertive, aggressive, loud, and even fierce. Children were treated indifferently by their parents, with neither mothers nor fathers expressing nurturance. The situation among the Tchambuli was equally surprising to Mead and her readers: The men fussed about their looks, gossiped with each other most of the day, and did little in the way of productive work. The women were competent and responsible, providing most of the food through fishing and gardening, and managing the household. Among the Tchambuli, women played a dominant role in the culture, and their personalities reflected this importance. These findings suggest that gender is an arbitrary matter, defined culturally and shaped through child-rearing patterns. Mead's detailed analysis of variations

Margaret Mead, during some of her later years of fieldwork, observes children's interactions in Sicily.

in child care, including differences in degrees of tenderness or neglect during breastfeeding, provide evidence of how children in different contexts learn patterns of personality and behaviour.

Cultural Patterns and National Character

Ruth Benedict, a leading figure of the Culture and Personality School, argued that cultures promote distinct personality types. In her book *Patterns of Culture* (1959), she proposed that descriptions of cultures might be integrated around the unconscious selection of a few cultural traits from the "vast arc" of potential traits. For example, one culture may emphasize monetary values while another overlooks them. The selected traits "interweave" to form a cohesive pattern, a **cultural configuration**, characteristic of the thoughts and behaviours of everyone in that culture. Benedict first formulated her theories while doing research on Native American cultures. In her view, the Pueblo Indians of the American Southwest had personalities that exemplified a "middle road," involving moderation in all things and avoiding excess and violence. She termed the Pueblo an "Apollonian" culture, after the Greek deity Apollo. In contrast, she labelled the Kwakwaka'wakw (the group Boas called Kwakiutl) of the Pacific Northwest "Dionysian," after the Greek god of revelry and excess, because of their individualism and high levels of expressive emotionality, mainly evident in their potlatches.

Benedict's portrait of the Kwakwaka'wakw has been criticized for its over-reliance on Boas's data on just one group of southern nobility after European contact; its selective ignoring of the amiable, playful side of their life; and for ignoring ecological factors. Similar criticisms have been levelled against Ruth Landes, a student of Boas and Benedict, for her portrayal of the Ojibwa of northwestern Ontario. Her work stressed the extreme individualism and atomistic behaviour of the Ojibwa, their lack of political organization, and severe anxiety neuroses manifested in cannibalism and violence. Anthropologists have criticized her work for questionable ethnographic accuracy and for failing to place the Ojibwa in historical context by noting their changed economic conditions after government suppression of political and religious organizations (Lovisek, Holzkamm, and Waisberg 1997).

During World War II, the United States Office of War Information commissioned Benedict to analyze Japanese personality structure and submit reports to the government to help defeat the Japanese. During the war, she could not do fieldwork, and so she consulted secondary sources (newspapers, magazines, movies) and interviewed Japanese Americans. Her resulting book, *The Chrysanthemum and the Sword* (1946), presents a set of essential features of Japanese character: importance of *on* (obligation, the necessity to repay gifts and favours), the concept of virtue, the value of self-discipline, keeping one's name "clear" or honourable, and rules of etiquette.

Following Benedict's work on Japan, **national character studies** that defined personality types and core values of nations declined in importance and are now criticized for three main reasons: (1) they are ethnocentric, classifying cultures according to Western psychological values and features; (2) they are reductionist, emphasizing only one or two features; and (3) they are totalizing, obscuring intranational variation in their construction of a single national character (e.g., *the* French, *the* English, *the* Japanese).

Class and Personality

Two cultural anthropologists of the mid-twentieth century proposed theories about how poverty shapes personality. George Foster (1965), who did research among small-scale farmers in Mexico, proposed a model called the **image of the limited good**. People who have this world view believe that the resources or wealth available within a particular social group are finite. If someone increases his or her wealth, other people necessarily lose out. The pie analogy illustrates how the image of the limited good works. If a group of eight people equally divides a pie into eight pieces, everyone gets the same share. But if one person takes two pieces, only six pieces remain for everyone else to divide. One person's gain is another's loss. The image of the limited good, according to Foster, is found along with a "status quo" mentality that prevents people from trying to improve their economic condition. Major personality traits associated with the image of the limited good are jealousy, suspiciousness, and passivity.

Oscar Lewis (1966) proposed a related concept, the **culture of poverty**, to explain the personality and behaviour of the poor and why poverty persists. He typified poor Mexican people as, among other things, "improvident," lacking a future time-orientation, and sexually promiscuous. He argued that because of these personality traits, poor people are trapped in poverty and cannot change their situation.

Nearly 50 years after the writing of Foster and Lewis, the prevailing view of their theories is that they were ethnocentric, reflecting the position of Foster and Lewis as privileged people living in the context of mid-twentieth-century capitalist growth in the United States. The prevailing values of economically successful people in that context included self-assertion, aggressive competitiveness, and a belief that resources are infinite. Opposite traits and values were attributed to the poor as negative features to explain why poverty persisted. These scholars considered neither structure nor human agency to try to understand people's lifestyles in poverty. In spite of the limits of their theories, Lewis is remembered for his many rich ethnographies of poor people's lives in Mexico, Puerto Rico, and the United States, and Foster contributed valuable work in medical anthropology.

Recent ethnopsychiatry studies have tried to be less ethnocentric in their interpretations. Some new work considers the many cases of revolution and resistance among poor and marginalized people, completely reversing the models proposed by Foster and Lewis about passivity.

At the opposite end of the class spectrum, psychological anthropologists are beginning to "study up" the class structure. Allison's examination (1994) of how corporate culture shapes personality of middle- and upper-class urban "salarymen" in Japan shows how child-care patterns based on total control by mothers fit with the demands of the corporate business world to create compliant male workers.

Person-Centred Ethnography

The newest direction in psychological anthropology is called *person-centred ethnography*; it is research that focuses on the individual and how the individual's psychology and subjective experience both shape and are shaped by her or his culture (Hollan 2001). In terms of its methods, person-centred ethnography relies heavily on what people say about their perceptions and experiences. Thus, like Western psychology and psychiatry, it is fundamentally discourse-based rather than observation-based.

Gaining an emic view about individual people and their perceptions is the paramount goal. Yet most person-centred ethnographies situate details about individuals and what they say about their experience within the wider cultural context, because individuals and cultures are interactive.

One such contextualized study considers notions of the self and selfhood in a mountainous village in Nepal (Hardman 2000). The context provided is mainly about family relations, religion and concepts of the ancestors, and rituals, but some discussion is provided of land rights and the egalitarian principle of exchange. The emphasis, however, is on the local conception of *niwa*, or individuality and personality in terms of desires and wishes. In opposition to many broad statements from non-anthropologists about "Asian mentalities" and the lack of a concept of an autonomous self in "Asian societies," this study found clear evidence of a concept of individuality and interpersonal difference in *niwa*. As one villager commented, there are as many different *niwa* as there are faces. Interestingly, individual *niwa* is generally not to be expressed in public. With increasing social change, however, it is exhibited more often. Women are demonstrating their initiative and agency by selling beer and liquor. Young people are expressing opinions in public. According to the values of wider society, individuality should not go so far as to upset socially shared views of propriety, which include frugality, charitable giving, and feelings of conscience and shame. The self and individualism can exist but must do so within cultural bounds.

As many psychological anthropologists direct their attention to the details of individual perceptions and experience, others insist that the comparative method cannot be abandoned (Moore and Mathews 2001). For example, how does the Nepali villager's concept of *niwa* compare to notions of the self in other societies? Are there private/public notions of self elsewhere, and, if so, how does that distinction play out? We see here the fruitful tension between ethnography (analysis of a single group of people) and ethnology (placing detailed local cases into a wider comparative frame).

PERSONALITY AND IDENTITY FORMATION FROM INFANCY THROUGH ADOLESCENCE

In North America, commonly accepted life stages include infancy, childhood, adolescence, middle age, and old age (psychologists and other experts concerned with human development construct even finer substages). Western life-cycle stages are based on biological features such as the ability to walk, puberty, and capacity for parenthood (Bogin 1988). However, these stages are not cultural universals. Whereas the biological model assumes that all its life-cycle markers should form the basis of universal stages, cultural anthropologists find striking variation in how different cultures construct life stages and how such stages may be quite unrelated to biology (Johnson-Hanks 2002). The cultural construction of life stages thus can ignore or override what Western biology would dictate.

Birth and Infancy

This section on how culture shapes personality and identity considers first the social context of birth itself. We then consider the issue of parent–infant co-sleeping patterns and how they may shape personality and identity. Last, we take up the topic of gender identity formation at this early stage of the life cycle.

The Birth Context

Cultural anthropologists have asked whether the event of birth itself has psychological effects on the infant. Cross-cultural research does in fact reveal that variations in the birth experience affect an infant's psychological development. Brigitte Jordan (1983), a pioneer in the cross-cultural study of birth, conducted research on birth practices in Mexico, Sweden, Holland, and the United States. She studied the birth setting, including its location and who is present, the types of attendants and their roles, the birth event, and the post-partum period. Among Mayan women in Mexico, the midwife is called in the early stages of labour. One of her tasks is to give a *sobada* (massage) to the mother-to-be. She also provides psychological support by telling stories, often about other women's birthing experiences. The husband is expected to be present during the labour, so that he can see "how a woman suffers." The woman's mother should be present, along with other female kin such as her mother-in-law, godmother and sisters, and her friends. Compared to many other birthing contexts, the Mayan mother is surrounded by a large group of supportive people.

The Western medical model of birth and non-Western practices contrast sharply—and sometimes come into serious conflict. In a Western hospital birthing situation where immigrant families have views on proper infant care, providing an anthropological perspective on their culture may serve to mediate conflict between the medical culture and the immigrant people's culture (see the Lessons Applied box).

A study exploring natural childbirth in Toronto, including Lamaze preparation as an alternative to medical control, showed that mothers wanted more control over the childbirth experience and less dependence on

Lessons Applied

THE ROLE OF CULTURAL KNOWLEDGE IN CONFLICT MEDIATION IN A U.S. HOSPITAL NURSERY

MANY NORTH AMERICAN hospitals are concerned about how to provide services for their rapidly growing immigrant populations. In a new suburban hospital that Deitrick (2002) studied, most of the nurses on staff were long-time residents of the community and had graduated from a local community college, where their training included no attention to cultural differences.

Cultural conflict arose upon the birth of a baby to a Turkish immigrant family. The infant had not yet been brought to the mother's room, and members of her family arrived to welcome the new baby. Along with them came a Muslim religious leader to administer the usual honey blessing to the infant before his first feeding. This ritual ensures a sweet life for the baby.

The nurse in charge denied the family access to the baby, saying that he first must have a medical examination and that unpasteurized honey could not be given to him. The baby's father was upset and claimed that the blessing must be administered because whatever the baby first tastes determines the quality of its life.

Fortunately, a nurse who also had training in cultural anthropology, Lynn Deitrick, entered into the discussions and was able to act as a cultural broker, a person—often but not always an anthropologist—who is familiar with the practices and beliefs of two different cultures and can promote cross-cultural understanding to prevent or mediate conflicts. She listened to the views of the Turkish family and learned that only a tiny amount of honey would be placed on the baby's tongue for the blessing. She suggested a compromise to the medical staff whereby the baby would be taken for 10 minutes to the mother's room, where the family would be present and the Muslim cleric could administer the blessing. The attending physician agreed, saying that she was not "on record" as approving the blessing but that she understood its importance. Deitrick took the baby to the family and returned 10 minutes later to find a smiling mother and father. The baby then underwent blood tests and other medically mandated procedures and was discharged in good health—*and* assured of a sweet life—two days later.

FOOD FOR THOUGHT

Did Lynn Deitrick do the right thing by acting as a cultural broker in this case, or should the medical model have been followed with no compromise?

---

technological interventions such as induced labour, anesthesia, episiotomies, and fetal heart monitoring (Romalis 1981). Although most births in Canada take place in hospitals, out-of-hospital births are increasing in number. In hospitals and birth centres, the newborn infant is generally taken to a nursery where it is wrapped in cloth, placed in a crib under bright lights, and fed with sugar water rather than being left with the mother to be fed. Critics argue that the Western hospital-based system of highly regulated birth is extremely technocratic and "too managed," alienating the mother—and the father as well as other members of the family and the wider community—from the birthing process and the infant (Davis-Floyd 1992).

Criticism of the Western birth process and the subsequent physical separation of the infant from the mother has led to consideration of how to improve the way birth is conducted and the condition it sets for maternal support and infant bonding. For example, the Baby-Friendly Hospital Initiative supported by UNICEF, WHO, and many non-governmental organizations (NGOs) identifies hospital practices that will encourage mother-infant bonding and successful breastfeeding, including initiating breastfeeding immediately after birth, allowing mothers and infants to room together, discouraging the use of pacifiers, and refusing monetary donations and free supplies from the infant formula industry. In 1999, the Brome-Missisquoi-Perkins Hospital in Cowansville, Quebec, became the first Canadian hospital to be designated as "Baby-Friendly," joining over 19 000 Baby-Friendly Hospitals worldwide.

Bonding

Many Western psychologists argue that early parent–infant contact and bonding at the time of birth is crucial for setting in motion parental attachment to the infant. Western specialists say that if this bonding is not established at the time of the infant's birth, it will not develop later. Explanations for juvenile delinquency or other unfavourable

---

child development problems often include reference to lack of proper infant bonding at birth. In spite of these theories, many Western-based hospital practices separate infants from mothers immediately after birth.

Nancy Scheper-Hughes (1992), whose research in a Brazilian shantytown was discussed in Chapter 5, questions Western bonding theory. She argues that bonding does not necessarily have to occur at birth to be successful. Her observations in Brazil show that many mothers do not exhibit bonding with their infants at birth. Bonding occurs later, if the child survives infancy, when it is several years old. She proposes that this pattern of later bonding is related to the high rate of infant mortality among poor people of Brazil. If women were to develop strong bonds with their infants, they would suffer untold amounts of grief. Western bonding is adaptive in low-mortality/low-fertility societies in which strong maternal attachment is reasonable because infants are likely to survive.

Sleeping Patterns

Related to bonding theory is the question of where and with whom the infant sleeps. The practice of infants and children sleeping beside their parents is found in most societies. Recent research by physical anthropologist James McKenna (1993) demonstrates the advantages of sleeping in close contact with at least one other person, including possible protection against SIDS (sudden infant death syndrome). His research demonstrates the importance of a co-sleeping environment, rather than a solitary environment, for infant well-being.

The Basque people of northern Spain favour long periods of co-sleeping (Crawford 1994). Interviews with 217 Basque mothers probed topics such as their attitudes about parenting, religious beliefs, dreams, personality characteristics, and the mother's childhood sleeping patterns. Of these women, 167 had slept in their parents' room for two to three years. Compared to the women who had not been co-sleepers as children, women who had been co-sleepers had both greater ego strength and a greater sense of connectedness. This study suggests that co-sleeping does not necessarily prevent the development of a strong ego.

Gender and Infancy

As noted in Chapter 1, cultural anthropologists distinguish between sex and gender. In the view of Western science, sex has three biological markers: genitals, hormones, and chromosomes. Males are defined as people who have a penis, more androgens than estrogens, and the XY chromosome. Females have a vagina, more estrogens than androgens, and the XX chromosome. Increasingly, however, scientists know that these two categories are not definitive. In all populations, some people are born with indeterminate genitals, similar proportions of androgens

In Bom Jesus, a shantytown in northeastern Brazil, this mother was told by a doctor at the local clinic that her son was dying of anemia and that she needed to feed him red meat. The mother said, "Now where am I going to find the money to feed my hopeless son rich food like that?" Western mother–infant bonding theory does not appear to apply in all cultures.

and estrogens, and chromosomes with more complex distributions than simply XX and XY. Thus, continuum models of sex and gender might be more accurate than strictly binary models.

Gender refers to the learned behaviour and beliefs associated with maleness and femaleness, and thus is culturally constructed. Individuals acquire their gender identity, roles, and status through learning, much of which is unconscious. From the moment of birth, an infant's life course is shaped by whether it is labelled male or female and what the defined roles and status of "male" and "female" are in that society. Most cultural anthropologists acknowledge the high degree of human "plasticity," as demonstrated by Mead's early work on gender roles and personality in New Guinea, and that gender socialization can to a large extent "override" sex-linked features such as hormones.

Many other researchers continue to insist that a wide range of supposedly sex-linked personality characteristics are innate. A major problem arises in how to test for innate characteristics. First, one needs data on infants before they are subject to cultural influences. But culture starts shaping the infant from the moment of birth through handling and treatment by others (some scholars say that socialization could begin even in the womb through exposure to sound and motion). Second, studying and interpreting the behaviour of infants is fraught with potential bias.

Studies of infants have focused on assessing the potential innateness of three major Euro-American personality stereotypes: whether infant males are more aggressive than infant females, whether infant females are more social than infant males, and whether males are more independent. Boy babies cry more than girl babies, and some people believe this is evidence of higher levels of inborn aggression in males. An alternative interpretation is that baby boys on average tend to weigh more than girls. They therefore are more likely to have a difficult delivery from which it takes time to recover, so they cry more, but not out of aggressiveness. In terms of sociability, baby girls smile more often than boys. Does this mean girls are born to be people pleasers? Evidence of caretakers smiling more at baby girls shows that the more frequent smiling of girls is a learned, not innate response. In terms of independence or dependence, studies thus far reveal no clear gender differences in how upset babies are when separated from their caretakers.

Overall, studies seeking to document innate gender differences through the behaviour of infants are not convincing. However, some anthropologists continue to explore the possibilities of innate neurophysiological differences in the central nervous systems of male and female infants in pre- and perinatal development as one of many factors explaining differences in violent aggression/nurturance and spatial acuity/verbal acuity polarities (Laughlin 1989). Two questions continue to be important. First, if gender differences are innate, why do cultures go to so much trouble to instill them? Second, if gender differences are innate, then they should be similar throughout history and cross-culturally, which they aren't. Throughout the rest of this chapter, we explore cultural constructions of gender at various stages of the life cycle.

Socialization during Childhood

The concept of "the child" as a special age category may have emerged first in Europe in the last few centuries. In art, portraits of children became commonplace only in the seventeenth century. Other changes occurred at the same time: new interests in children's habits, more elaborate terminology about children and childhood, and special clothing for children instead of small-sized versions of adult clothing. The special focus on "the child" is associated with the emergence of industrial capitalism's need for an ever-expanding market. "The child" becomes a new niche for sales, which allows for the production and sale of clothes, books, and toys specifically for that niche. In less industrialized cultures, "the child" is not regarded as having such specialized needs. In these societies, children are expected to take on adult tasks at an earlier age. These different expectations about what a child should do and be have implications for personality formation.

Mode of Production and Child Personality

The "Six Cultures Study" is a renowned cross-cultural study designed to provide comparative data on children's personalities in relation to their activities and tasks (Whiting and Whiting 1975). Researchers observed a total of 67 boys and 67 girls between the ages of 3 and 11 years. They recorded many forms of behaviour, such as being supportive of other children; hitting other children; and performing tasks such as child care, cooking, and errands. These behaviours were analyzed in the following personality dimensions: "nurturant-responsible" or "dependent-dominant." Nurturant-responsible personalities are characterized by more caring and sharing acts toward other children. The dependent-dominant personality involves fewer acts of caring and sharing toward other children, and more acts that asserted dominance over other children. Six teams of researchers were trained in the methodology and conducted intensive research in six contexts (see Table 6.1).

The Gusii children of Kenya had the highest prevalence of a nurturant-responsible personality type, while the children in Orchard Town had the lowest. Orchard Town children had the highest prevalence of the dependent-dominant personality type. The range of variation in the prevalence of these dimensions followed a general pattern related to the economy. The six cultures fit into two general groups, economically and in terms of child tasks and personality development. "Group A" cultures (Kenya, Mexico, Philippines) all had more nurturant-responsible children. Their economies are similar: They are more reliant on horticulture and other forms of less intensive production. The economies of "Group B" cultures (Japan, India, and the United States) were based on either intensive agriculture or industry.

How does the mode of production influence child tasks and personality? The key underlying factor is differences in women's work roles. In Group A cultures, women are an important part of the labour force and spend much time working outside the home. In these cultures, children take on more family-supportive tasks and thereby develop personalities that are nurturant-responsible. When women

TABLE 6.1 Modes of Production and Child Personality: Six Cases

Culture	Location	Nurturant-Responsible (High Scores)/ Dependent-Dominant (Low Scores) Personality
Group A: Horticulture, Small-Scale Family Farming		
Gusii	Kenya	+1.14
Oaxaca	Mexico	+0.54
Tarong	Philippines	+0.48
Group B: Intensive Agricultural or Industrial		
Taira	Japan	−0.24
Rajputs	India	−0.75
Orchard Town	United States	−1.04

Source: From B. B. Whiting and J. W. M. Whiting, *Children of Six Cultures: A Psycho-Cultural Analysis*, p. 71. Copyright © 1975 by the President and Fellows of Harvard College. Reprinted by permission of Harvard University Press, Cambridge, MA.

work mainly in the home, as in Group B cultures, children have fewer tasks and less responsibility. They develop personalities that are more dependent-dominant. Gusii children were responsible for the widest range of tasks and at earlier ages than in any other culture in the study, often performing tasks that an Orchard Town mother does. While some children in all six cultures took care of other children, Gusii children (both boys and girls) spent the most time doing so. They also began taking on this

Sibling caretaking, as shown here in Ghana, is a common task of older children cross-culturally, but especially so in pre-industrial societies.

responsibility at a very young age, between five and eight years old.

This study has implications for Western child development experts. In one direction, we can consider what happens when the dependent-dominant personality develops to an extreme level—into a narcissistic personality. A **narcissist** is someone who constantly seeks self-attention and self-affirmation, with no concern for other people's needs. The Western consumer-oriented economy supports the development of narcissism through its inculcation of identity formation through ownership of self-defining goods (clothing, electronics, cars) and access to self-defining services (vacations, therapists, fitness salons). The Six Cultures Study's findings suggest that involving children in more household responsibilities might result in less self-focused personality formation.

Informal Learning

Most of the world's children under age five spend these years within the family, learning informally from family members. In recent years, institutionalized care in daycare centres has increased in many parts of the world. Parents send their child to preschool as a substitute for family care while they are working, for social enrichment, or as a way to "fast-track" the child intellectually. Children enrolled in daycare and early childhood programs in Canada in 1994–1995 were found to have a head start in school, including having better communication, learning, and math skills regardless of family income or mother's education level, according to a Statistics Canada study.

Toys and games also shape children's personalities. Among hunting peoples such as the Yanomami, young boys learn to be future hunters by shooting small arrows from small bows at small targets such as beetles. They learn to kill animals without sentimentality. In contrast, caring for animals as pets is a prominent part of child

Left: A Yanomami boy acquires skills necessary for hunting and warfare through play. Right: An American boy playing a video game.

socialization in the West, where many animals are taboo as food. Some games, such as chess, teach strategic thinking that appears to be correlated with social-political patterns of hierarchy and obedience.

Charles James Nowell is a Kwakwaka'wakw man born in 1870 at Fort Rupert, in what is now British Columbia. He was interviewed in English in 1940. He recalls:

> When I was a boy we used to give potlatches of small canoes to imitate the potlatches of older people. I had small canoes made for me just the shape of the big ones. My second brother made some of them, and I paid other older people tobacco and things to make some others for me. When I have enough to give my potlatch, I go around to all the boys of the other tribes at Fort Rupert. I call my own tribe boys to come in front of my house and to count these small canoes and put them in rows according to the rank of the fathers of the boys. . . .
>
> Our fathers and brothers teach us to give these potlatches, and help us do it, telling us all about what we should do to do it right. That is just like teaching what we should do when we get grown up and give real potlatches. My older brothers were the ones who taught me, but they didn't come and watch us while we gave them.

They only heard about it and how we did afterwards. When I come home, they tell me that is fine. They are the ones that started it—I wouldn't have done it if they hadn't started it—and they helped me all the time with my play potlatches. (Hirschfelder 1995:103–104)

The media is another important area for child socialization and personality acquisition. Generations of Canadian children watched the *Polka Dot Door* and *Mr. Dressup,* shows that attempt to break down gender and racial stereotypes. American cartoon shows are also aired on Canadian television. One study considered children's cartoon shows aired on American television in the 1980s (B. Williams 1991). Content analysis reveals two types of shows, one featuring interpersonal relationships aimed at little girls and one featuring battles that toy companies intended for little boys.

Formal Schooling

Universal primary education exists in most nations, but not all. For example, in Mali, one of the world's poorest countries, only 25 percent of children attend primary school (United Nations Development Programme 1994). Poorer children cross-culturally face more problems enrolling and remaining in school. In some countries, the school system is inadequate, with too few local schools available. In poor families, children are needed to work. The schooling experience is also diminished for the poor because malnourished and exhausted children have more difficulty concentrating during class. Their level of achievement is likely to be lower than that of better-off children because of economic factors. Teachers, however, may interpret their performance as a sign of "bad attitude," apathy, and laziness.

In Malawi, a poor nation of southern Africa, all children face obstacles in completing primary education, but it is especially difficult for girls (Davison and Kanyuka 1992). An ethnographic study of this situation included 80 students (40 boys and 40 girls) at two grade levels. It was conducted in four poor rural districts where girls' school participation rates were among the lowest and their drop-out rates the highest. Most of the children came from agricultural families. Both boys and girls face the same constraints in terms of the quality of the schools and teachers. Girls also have to contend with negative attitudes from male teachers about the value of schooling for them. This discouragement of their academic achievement in the schools is mirrored by their home situation, where parents indirectly discourage girls from valuing schooling and instead instill in them the values of domesticity. Girls are supposed to learn to assume the traditional roles of wife and mother.

School systems that offer little in the way of creative learning experiences, home situations that are unsupportive of girls' achievement, and conservative political elements in the wider society combine to constrain both cognitive achievements and the attainment of independent, autonomous personalities among women. "Tracking" female students into domestic roles characterizes formal education throughout much of the world, especially in conservative societies. The students in these situations may experience conflicts about such tracking and resist it to varying degrees.

In school, children learn much about how they should behave and think, both formally through the curriculum and informally through clubs, peer pressure, and sports. Illustrations in textbooks may further socialize children into particular roles and personality patterns.

Adolescence and Identity

Puberty is a time in the human life cycle that occurs universally and involves a set of biological markers. In males, the voice deepens and facial and body hair appear; in females, menarche and breast development occur; in both males and females, pubic and underarm hair appear and

Schoolchildren in Japan exhibiting eagerness to participate in class.

sexual maturation is achieved. **Adolescence**, in contrast, is a culturally defined period of maturation from around the time of puberty until adulthood is attained, usually marked by becoming a parent, getting married, or becoming economically self-sufficient.

Is Adolescence a Universal Life-Cycle Stage?

Some scholars say that all cultures define a period of adolescence. One comparative study using data from 186 societies indicated the universality of a culturally defined phase of adolescence (Schlegel 1995; Schlegel and Barry 1991). Cultures as diverse as the Navajo and the Trobriand Islanders, among others, have special terms comparable to the term *adolescent* for a person between puberty and marriage. Sociobiologists have generated a theory that views adolescence as a response to the biological onset of reproductive capacity and as biologically adaptive because it provides "training" for becoming a parent (Schlegel 1995:l6).

In contrast to the sociobiological view, other anthropologists view adolescence as culturally constructed. They dispute the claims of universal adolescence and its function as reproductive training. In many cultures, there is no recognized period of adolescence. In others, recognition of an adolescent phase is recent. Moroccan anthropologist Fatima Mernissi (1987), for example, states that adolescence was not a recognized life-cycle phase for females in Morocco until the late twentieth century. "The idea of an adolescent unmarried woman is a completely new idea in the Muslim world, where previously you had only a female child and a menstruating woman who had to be married off immediately so as to prevent dishonorable engagement in premarital sex" (xxiv).

In different cultures, the length of the period of adolescence, or whether it exists at all, is related to the constructions of gender roles. In many horticultural or pastoral societies where men are valued as warriors, as among the Maasai, a lengthy period between childhood and adulthood is devoted to training in warfare and developing solidarity among males. Females, on the other hand, move directly from being a girl to being a wife. For example, a Maasai girl learns her adult roles while she is a child, assisting in the care of cattle and doing other tasks. In other cultures, females have long periods of separation between girlhood and womanhood, marked by seclusion from general society, during which they learn special skills and lore, and then re-emerge into society as marriageable (J. K. Brown 1978). Such evidence of variation seems to speak against any theory of universality.

The fact that adolescence is found in many pre-industrial societies puts into question the explanation that adolescence is a by-product of industrial economies. Cultural materialist approaches suggest that there is a relationship between adolescence and the mode of production; a prolonged period of adolescence is likely to be preparation for culturally valued adult roles as workers, warriors, or reproducers. For example, the definition of adolescence for females in many pre-industrial societies, accompanied by years of training and seclusion, is found where adult females have high rates of participation in food production (J.K. Brown 1978). This relation can be explained by the need to train young women for their adult roles. Similarly, certain areas of employment in industrialized societies, especially professions such as medicine and law and the upper echelons of the corporate world, require a university education. The many years of study can be considered a key part of the adolescent period preceding the assumption of adult roles.

During the latter half of the twentieth century, industrialization and economic globalization were accompanied by the spread of Western notions of adolescence among the middle and upper classes in countries around the world. The age at marriage has risen as young people attempt to finish their educations and find employment before starting a family (Xenos 1993). At the same time, class differences exist. Those who are poor tend to have shorter adolescent phases; they spend less time in formal education, and they are likely to become parents at younger ages.

Coming of Age and Gender Identity

Margaret Mead made famous the phrase "coming of age" in her book *Coming of Age in Samoa* (1928). It can refer generally to the period of adolescence or specifically to a ceremony or set of ceremonies that marks the boundaries of a period of adolescence. What are the psychological aspects of this phase of life when children become adults?

Among the Sambia, a highland New Guinea group, people do not believe that a young boy will "naturally" grow into a man (Herdt 1987). Instead, a boy's healthy maturation requires that he join an all-male initiation group. In this group, he becomes a partner of a senior male, who regularly transfers his semen to the youth orally. The Sambia believe that ingesting semen nourishes the youth and provides for his healthy growth. After a period in this initiation group, the youth will rejoin society and take up a heterosexual relationship and raise children.

Ceremonies that provide the transition from youth to adulthood often involve marking the body in some way to impress the person undergoing it with a clear sense of gender and group identity. Such marking includes scarification, tattooing, and genital surgery. In many societies, adolescent males undergo genital surgery that involves removal of part of the skin around the tip of the penis. Without this operation, the boy would not be considered a full-fledged male. A young Maasai male, in a first-person account of his initiation into manhood, describes the "intolerable pain" he experienced following the circumcision, as well as his feeling of accomplishment two weeks later when his head was shaved and he became a warrior: "As long as I live, I will never forget the day my head was

A Maasai warrior's mother shaves his head during part of his initiation ceremony into adulthood.

shaved and I emerged a man, a Maasai warrior. I felt a sense of control over my destiny so great that no words can accurately describe it" (Saitoti 1986:71).

For girls, the physical fact of menstruation is marked by rituals in some cultures; in others it is not noted publicly at all. In rural areas of Turkey, and elsewhere in the Middle East, menstruation is not even mentioned to young girls, who are thus surprised and shocked at menarche (Delaney 1988:79). These girls may therefore feel ashamed and embarrassed by menstruation. Their Islamic culture teaches them that menstruation is the result of Eve's disobedience against Allah. Eve allowed herself to be persuaded by Satan to eat a forbidden fruit, and so was punished by being made to bleed monthly. In contrast, Hindus have elaborate feasts and celebrations for girls on their first menstruation in South India, though not in the North (Miller 1997). In the absence of studies on the psychological impact of these differences, one can only speculate at this point that being made the person of honour at a celebration would have positive effects on a girl's sense of self-esteem, whereas ignoring or linking menstruation with shamefulness would have the opposite effect.

The term **female circumcision**, or female genital cutting, refers to a range of genital cutting practised on females, including the excision of part or all of the clitoris, part or all of the labia, and the least common practice, infibulation, stitching together of the vaginal entry leaving a small aperture for drainage of menstrual blood (Shell-Duncan and Hernlund 2000). These procedures are performed when the girl is between 7 to 15 years of age. Some form of genital cutting is most common in the Sahelian countries of Africa, from the west coast to the east coast. It is also found in Egypt, in some groups of the Middle East (particularly among Bedu tribes), and among some Muslim groups in South and Southeast Asia. Genital cutting occurs in many groups in which female labour participation is high, but also in others where it is not. In terms of religion, genital cutting is often, but not always, associated with people who are Muslim. In Ethiopia some Christian groups practise it. Scholars have yet to provide a convincing explanation for the regional and social distribution of female genital cutting.

Many young girls have been reported to look forward to the ceremony so that they will then be freed of having to do childhood tasks and can take on the more respected roles of an adult woman. In other cases, anthropologists have reported hearing statements of resistance. Among the Ariaal, pastoralists of northern Kenya, a new bride undergoes circumcision on the day of her wedding (Fratkin 1998:60). The Ariaal practice involves removal of the clitoris and part or all of the labia majora. At one wedding, a bride-to-be was heard to say: "I don't want to do this, I don't even know this man, please don't make me do this." The older women told her to be strong and that it would soon be over. The bride-to-be is expected to emerge in a few hours to greet the guests and join the wedding ceremony. In 1999, Senegal joined Sudan, Somalia, Kenya, Togo, Ghana, and Burkina Faso in banning female genital cutting. Few issues have forced the questioning of cultural relativism more than female genital cutting (see the Critical Thinking box).

Sexual Identity

Puberty is the time when sexual maturity is achieved and sexual orientation becomes more apparent. Anthropologists, unlike psychologists, have tended to avoid arguments about whether sexual preferences are biologically determined (somehow mandated by genetic or hormonal factors) or culturally constructed and learned. Biological anthropologist Melvin Konner (1989) argues that both factors play a part, but simultaneously warns us that no one has a simple answer to the question of "who becomes gay":

> Neither science nor art has yet produced a single answer. Yet perhaps that in itself is the answer: that anything so complicated and various and interesting could have a single origin seems wrongheaded. Socrates and Tennessee Williams, Sappho and Adrienne Rich, to take only four people, representing only two cultures, seem so certain to have come to their homosexuality in four such different ways as to make generalizations useless. (60)

Lesbian feminist poet Adrienne Rich's (1980) approach combines attention to both biology and culture in her view that all people are biologically bisexual, but that patriarchal cultures try to mould them into being heterosexual. This "compulsory heterosexual project," she says, will never be completely successful in overcoming innate bisexuality, and so some people will always opt out of the heterosexual mould and become either homosexual or bisexual. (See the Multiple Cultural Worlds box on page 137.)

Anthropologists generally examine how cultural context shapes the form, interpretation, and expression of same-sex sexuality, emphasizing socialization and childhood experiences as the most powerful factors shaping sexual orientation. Support for this position comes from a study in the United States that later-born children are more likely to be homosexual than earlier-born children (Blanchard et al. 1995). For lesbians, fewer studies are available, but those that are indicate that lesbians tend to be later-born and to have more sisters than heterosexual women. A hypothesis worth investigating is whether parents unconsciously promote "girl-like" behaviour in the last-born when they have a string of sons in order to have a child to fulfill female roles, and the "boy-like" behaviour in a last-born girl who follows several sisters.

Another indication of the importance of culture in sexual identity is that many people change their sexual

Critical Thinking

CULTURAL RELATIVISM AND FEMALE CIRCUMCISION

INDIGENOUS VIEWS supporting female genital cutting say that it is a necessary step toward full womanhood (Ahmadu 2000). It is required for a woman to be considered marriageable in societies in which marriage is the normal path for women. Fathers say that an uncircumcised daughter is unmarriageable and will bring no brideprice. Aesthetically, supporters claim that removal of the labia makes a woman beautiful and removing "male" parts makes her a complete woman.

The Western view, which is increasingly shared by many people who traditionally practised female genital cutting, is that it is both a sign of low female status and an unnecessary cause of women's suffering.

Female circumcision has been linked with a range of health risks, including those related to the surgery itself (shock, infection), and future genito-urinary complications. Infibulation causes scarring and malformation of the vaginal canal that obstruct delivery and cause lacerations to the mother and even death of the infant and mother. The practice of having a new bride's husband "open" her, using a stick or knife to loosen the aperture, is both painful and an opportunity for infection. After giving birth, a woman is usually re-infibulated, and the process begins again. Health experts have suggested that the repeated trauma to the woman's vaginal area could increase the risk of contracting HIV/AIDS. The Western view argues that the effects of both clitoridectomy and infibulation on a woman's sexual enjoyment are highly negative, and that clitoral orgasm, for one thing, is no longer possible. Some experts have also argued that FGC is related to the high level of infertility in many African countries (Chapter 5). A recent study of fertility data from the Central African Republic, Côte d'Ivoire, and Tanzania, however, found no clear relationship between FGC and fertility levels.

This widespread and enduring practice (though no one knows its precise beginnings) has all too often become viewed in oversimplified terms, with emphasis on its most extreme forms. What are the views of insiders? Is there any evidence for agency? Or is it all structure and should anthropologists support movements to end the practice?

One new voice that transcends insider/outsider divisions is that of Fuambai Ahmadu, born and raised in Washington, D.C. She is descended from a prominent Kono lineage in Sierra Leone, and is getting a doctorate in anthropology for research on female circumcision in Gambia. In 1991, she travelled to Sierra Leone with her mother and several other family members for what she refers to as her "circumcision." In a powerful and insightful essay, she describes Kono culture as gender-complementary, with strong roles for women. She also describes her initiation and subsequent reflections. While the physical pain was excruciating (in spite of the use of anesthetics), "the positive aspects have been much more profound" (Ahmadu 2000:306). Through the initiation she became part of a powerful female world. Her discussion addresses the effects of genital cutting on health and sexuality and argues that Westerners have exaggerated these issues by focusing on infibulation (which she says is rarely practised) rather than the less extreme forms. If, however, global pressures against the practice continue, she will go along with it and support "ritual without cutting" (308).

CRITICAL THINKING QUESTIONS

Why is female circumcision, in the eyes of many human rights groups, a more controversial practice than male circumcision?

Where do you stand on this issue and why?

What information on female circumcision, other than the material presented in this chapter, have you gathered in order to form your opinion?

orientation more than once during their lifetime. In the Gulf state of Oman, the *xanith* is a male who becomes more like a female, wearing female clothing and having sex with other men, often for several years, but then reverting to a standard male role by marrying a woman and having children (Wikan 1977). Similar fluidity during the life cycle between homosexuality and heterosexuality occurs among Sambia males (Herdt 1987). These examples indicate that a person can assume different sexual identities over time.

No matter what theoretical perspective one takes on the causes of sexual preferences, it is clear that homosexuals are discriminated against in many cultural contexts where heterosexuality is the norm of mainstream society. Homosexuals in North America have frequently been victims of violence, housing discrimination, and legal biases.

Multiple Cultural Worlds

NEW LEGAL RIGHTS FOR GAY AND LESBIAN COUPLES IN CANADA

AFFIRMING EQUAL rights for gays and lesbians in provincial and federal law has been a long process. Gay and lesbian organizations emerged in the 1960s, promoting varied agendas including legal reforms, civil rights through human rights codes, and social support. In 1969, the federal government amended the Criminal Code to exempt from prosecution two consenting adults engaged in sexual activity. Decriminalization was accompanied by Prime Minister Trudeau's comment that "the state has no place in the bedrooms of the nation." Nevertheless, in the more right-wing climate of the 1970s and 1980s, bathhouses were raided in Toronto, and their occupants arrested and charged as "found-ins." In 1986, the Ontario government added "sexual orientation" to its human rights code.

In October 1999, the Ontario legislature granted new rights to gay and lesbian couples. Bill 5 gives same-sex couples the same rights and responsibilities as heterosexual common-law couples. The new law follows a Supreme Court decision that ordered the province to end discriminatory treatment of gays and lesbians under the Family Law Act. The law amends 67 provincial statutes to add the new category of same-sex partner to every statute that refers to common-law spouses, without changing the legal definition of marriage or spouse. Critics of the bill argue that gay and lesbian couples should have been included in the definition of "spouse"—not separated into a new class. In July 2002, the Ontario courts ordered the provincial government to recognize same-sex marriage. In 2005, after most other provinces had also recognized same-sex marriage, the federal government legalized gay and lesbian marriage, making Canada the fifth country to recognize same-sex marriage.

FOOD FOR THOUGHT

What effect do you think legal changes will have on attitudes toward same-sex relationships and sexual identity in your community?

They often suffer from being stigmatized by parents, other students, and the wider society. The psychological damage done to their self-esteem is reflected in the fact that homosexual youths in North America have substantially higher suicide rates than heterosexual youths.

Some cultures explicitly allow for more than two strictly defined genders and permit the expression of varied forms of sexual orientation without societal condemnation. Most "third genders" are neither purely "male" nor "female," according to a particular culture's definition of male and female. There are ways for "males" to cross gender lines and assume more "female" behaviours, personality characteristics, and dress.

The *berdache* constitutes an accepted and admired third gender role in many First Nations groups. A **berdache** is a male (in terms of genital configuration) who opts to wear female clothing, may engage in sexual relations with a man as well as a woman, and performs female tasks such as basket-weaving and pottery-making (W. Williams 1992). A particular person may become a berdache in a variety of ways. Some people say that parents, especially if they have several sons, choose one to become a berdache. Others say that a boy who shows interest in typically female activities or who likes to wear female clothing is allowed to become a berdache. Such a child is a focus of pride for the family, never a source of disappointment or stigma. Throughout decades of contact with Euro-American colonizers, including Christian missionaries, the institution of the berdache became a focus of disapproval and ridicule by the outsiders (Roscoe 1991). Under the influence of the negative reactions of the Euro-Americans, many Native American cultures began to suppress their berdache traditions in favour of mainstream White values and practices that promote less gender fluidity. In the 1980s, as Native American cultural pride began to grow, the open presence of the berdache and the **amazon** (a woman who takes on male roles and behaviours) has returned. Native American cultures in general remain accepting of gender role fluidity and the contemporary concept of being gay: "Younger gay Indians, upon coming out to their families, will sometimes have an elderly relative who takes them aside and tells them about the berdache tradition. A part-Choctaw gay man recalls that his full-blooded Choctaw grandmother realized he was gay and it was totally acceptable . . . This respectful attitude eliminates the stress felt by families that harbor homophobia" (p. 225). First Nations in general continue to be more tolerant of homosexuality than mainstream Euro-American society. They have recently coined the term *Two Spirit* to refer to gay, lesbian, bisexual, transgendered, and

A Zuni berdache, We'wha, wearing the ceremonial costume of Zuni women and holding a pottery bowl with sacred cornmeal.

as dancers or musicians. Given this public role and the hijira's association with prostitution, people in the mainstream do not admire or respect hijiras, and no family would be delighted to hear that their son has decided to become a hijira. In contrast to the berdache among First Nations peoples, the hijiras form a separate group from mainstream society.

In Thailand, three basic gender categories have long co-existed: *phuuchai* (male), *phuuying* (female), and *kathoey* (transvestite/transsexual/hermaphrodite) (Morris 1994b; P. Van Esterik 2000). Like the berdache and hijira, a kathoey is "originally" a male who crosses into the body, personality, and dress defined as female. Kathoeys represent a "third gender," and may be heterosexual, homosexual, or bisexual in orientation. In contemporary Thailand, sexual orientation does not confer a fixed gender identity, nor is it legally regulated. The discourse on HIV/AIDS is shaping the way sexual identities are talked about and labelled, and terms derived from English are appearing. For example, the words for lesbian include *thom* (from the word *tomboy*) and *dee* (from *lady*). As in many parts of the world, reflecting the widespread presence of patriarchal norms, lesbianism is a more suppressed form of homosexuality than male homosexuality, and there has been less research on women's same-sex relationships.

PERSONALITY AND IDENTITY IN ADULTHOOD

Adulthood for most of the world's people means the likelihood of some form of marriage (or long-term domestic relationship) and having children. This section discusses how selected aspects of adulthood, such as parenthood and aging, affect mature people's psychological status and identity.

Becoming a Parent

More studies have been done of how cultures shape maternal roles than paternal roles. Biologically, a woman becomes a mother when she gives birth to an infant: She is transformed from a pregnant woman to a mother. Like adolescence, the cultural definition of motherhood varies in terms of its beginning, duration, and meaning. In some cultures, a woman is transformed into a mother as soon as she thinks she is pregnant. In others, she becomes a mother and is granted full maternal status only when she delivers an infant of the "right" sex, a male in much of northern India.

Among the Beti people of Southern Cameroon, West Africa, motherhood is not merely or clearly defined by

transsexual people. However, Two Spirit is not primarily a description of one's sexual orientation, but rather a term to emphasize the spiritual nature of non-binary gender identities.

In India, the counterpart of the berdache is termed a **hijira**. Hijiras dress and act like women, but are neither truly male nor truly female (Nanda 1990). Many hijiras were born with male genitals, or with genitals that were not clearly male or female. Hijiras have the traditional right to visit the home of a newborn, inspect its genitals, and claim it for their group if the genitals are neither clearly male nor female. Some evidence exists that hijiras may forcibly claim or steal babies in order to increase their population. Hijiras born with male genitals may opt to go through an initiation ceremony that involves cutting off the penis and testicles. Hijiras roam large cities of India, earning a living by begging from store to store (and threatening to lift their skirts if not given money). Because women rarely sing or dance in public, the hijiras play an important role as performers in public events, especially having a child (Johnson-Hanks 2002). The Beti are both an ethnic group and a social status group of educated professionals within the wider society. "School girl" is one category of young Beti women. If a school girl becomes pregnant, this is a matter of great shame, and the girl is not considered to have entered a phase of motherhood even though she has borne a child. In this case, a biological marker does not bring about movement into a new life stage but instead contributes to ambiguity in categories.

In non-industrial societies, becoming a mother occurs in the context of supportive family members. Some cultures promote prenatal practices such as abiding by particular food taboos. Such rules make the pregnant woman feel that she has some role in helping to make the pregnancy turn out right. In the West, medical experts during the twentieth century have increasingly defined the prenatal period as an important phase of becoming a mother, and they have issued many scientific and medical rules for potential parents, especially mothers (Browner and Press 1995, 1996). Pregnant women are urged to seek prenatal examinations; be under the regular supervision of a doctor who monitors the growth and development of the fetus; follow particular dietary and exercise guidelines; and undergo a range of tests such as ultrasound scanning. Some anthropologists think that such medicalized pregnancies lead to the greater likelihood of post-partum depression among mothers as a result of their lack of control in the birthing process.

Becoming a father is usually less socially noted than becoming a mother. The practice of **couvade** is an interesting exception to this generalization. Couvade refers to "a variety of customs applying to the behaviour of fathers during the pregnancies of their wives and during and shortly after the births of their children" (Broude 1988:902). The father may take to his bed before, during, or after the delivery. He may also experience pain and exhaustion during and after the delivery. More common is a pattern of couvade that involves a set of prohibitions and prescriptions for male behaviour. For example, an expectant father may not hunt a certain animal, eat certain foods, cut objects, or engage in extramarital sex. Early theories of why the couvade exists relied on Freudian interpretations that men were seeking cross-sex identification (with the female role) in contexts where the father role was weak or fathers were absent. Cross-cultural examination of the existence of couvade indicates the opposite: Couvade occurs in societies where paternal roles in child care are prominent. This interpretation views couvade as one phase of men's participation in parenting: Their good behaviour as expectant fathers helps ensure a good delivery for the baby. Another interpretation of couvade is that it offers support for the mother. In Estonia, a folk belief is that a woman's birth pains will be less if her husband helps by taking some of them on himself (Oinas 1993).

Most cultural anthropologists agree that child care is predominately the responsibility of women worldwide—but not universally. While breastfeeding is exclusively a female act of nurturance and care, other aspects of child care can be taken over by caretakers besides the biological mother. In many cultures of the South Pacific, child care is shared across families, and women breastfeed other women's babies. Paternal involvement varies as well. Among the Aka pygmy hunter-gatherers of Central Africa, paternal child care is prominent (Hewlett 1991). The Aka are an exceptional case, perhaps even unique, in comparison with other societies because of the high involvement of fathers in child care. Aka fathers are intimate, affectionate, and helpful, spending about half of their time each day holding or within arm's reach of their infants. While holding their infants, they are more likely to hug and kiss them than mothers are. Good fatherhood among the Aka means being affectionate toward children and assisting the mother when her workload is heavy. Among the Aka, a prevailing ideology of gender equality exists and violence against women is unknown; the high level of paternal involvement in child care probably helps explain this pattern.

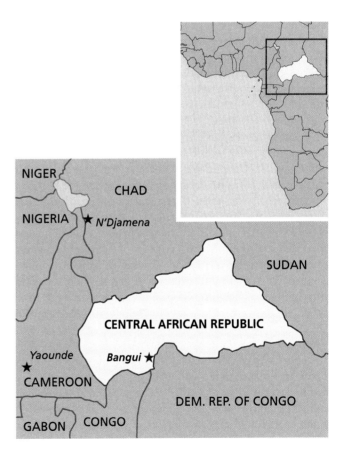

An Aka father and his son. Aka fathers are affectionate caretakers of infants and small children. Compared to mothers, they are more likely to kiss and hug children.

Middle Age

Perceptions of the boundaries of "middle age" have changed in industrial countries as the life span has increased. A generation ago, people in their 30s were considered middle aged, while now a turning point is more likely to be the fortieth birthday. One possible reason behind this relatively new emphasis on 40 as a turning point is that it reflects the current midpoint of a "typical" life span for a middle-class North American. In cultures with shorter life spans, a "midlife" crisis would necessarily occur at some point other than the age of 40 years, if it were to happen at all. Such a "crisis" seems strongly embedded in contemporary North American culture and its pervasive fear and denial of death (Shore 1998:103).

Menopause is a significant aspect of middle age for women in some, but not all, cultures. A comparative study examined differences in perception and experience of menopause among Mayan women of Mexico and rural Greek women (Beyene 1989). Among the Mayan women, menopause is not a time of stress or crisis. They associate menstruation with illness and look forward to the time when they no longer have menses. Menopause among these women is not associated with physical or emotional symptoms. In fact, none of the women reported hot flashes or night sweats. Among the Mayan women, menopause brought no associated role changes. In contrast, Greek women in the village of Stira recognized menopause as a natural phenomenon that all women experience and one that causes temporary discomfort, *exapi*, which is a phase of hot flashes especially at night, that may last about a

year. The women did not think *exapi* was terribly serious, certainly nothing worthy of medical attention. Postmenopausal women emphasized the relief and freedom they felt. Postmenopausal women can go into cafés by themselves, something they would never do otherwise, and they can participate more fully in church ceremonies. In Japan, also, menopause is a minimally stressful experience and is rarely considered something that warrants medical attention (Lock 1993).

In Canada, debates about surgical menopause and the safety of hormone replacement therapy confirm the medicalization of an event that is physiologically universal, but that carries diverse cultural meanings. Patricia Kaufert (1986) studied the transition to menopause in women in Manitoba, and found that the rate of estrogen use was low, and that it was used intermittently and possibly with reluctance. These variable findings raise the question of how much perceived suffering from menopause in North America is **iatrogenic**, that is, an affliction caused by medical definition or intervention.

The Senior Years

The "senior" life cycle stage may be a particular development of contemporary human society because, like most other mammals, our early ancestors rarely lived beyond their reproductive years (Brooks and Draper 1998). The category of the aged, like several other life-cycle stages discussed, is variably recognized, defined, and valued. In many cultures, elders are highly revered, and their life experiences are valued as the greatest wisdom. In others, aged people become burdens to their families and to society. In general, the status and well-being of the elderly cross-culturally is higher where they continue to live with their families (Lee and Kezis 1979). This pattern is more likely to be found in non-industrial societies than in highly industrialized ones, where the elderly are increasingly experiencing a shift to "retirement homes." In such age-segregated settings, people have to create new social roles and ties and find new ways of gaining self-esteem and personal satisfaction. Being allowed to have pets seems to have a positive effect on people's adjustment to retirement homes (Savishinsky 1991).

The Final Passage

It may be that no one in any culture welcomes death, unless he or she is in very poor health and suffering greatly. Contemporary North America, with its dependence on medical technology, appears to be particularly active in resisting death, often at very high financial and psychological cost. In many other cultures, a greater degree of acceptance prevails. A study of attitudes toward death and dying among Alaskan Inuit revealed a pervasive feeling that people are active participants in their death rather than passive victims (Trelease 1975). The usual pattern for a person near death is that the person calls friends and neighbours together, is given a Christian sacrament, and then, within a few hours, dies. The author comments, "I do not suggest that everyone waited for the priest to come and then died right away. But the majority who did not die suddenly did some degree of planning, had some kind of formal service or celebration of prayers and hymns and farewells" (35).

In any culture, loss of a loved one is accompanied by some form of sadness, grief, and mourning. The ways of expressing such emotions vary from extended and public grieving that is expressively emotional to no visible sign of grief being presented. The latter pattern is the norm in Bali, Indonesia, where people's faces remain impassive at funerals and no vocal lamenting occurs (Rosenblatt, Walsh, and Jackson 1976). No one knows how different modes of expression of loss might affect the actual experience of loss itself (Brison and Leavitt 1995). Does highly expressive public mourning contribute to a "faster" healing process, or does a quietly repressed sense of grief play an adaptive role, as Scheper-Hughes (1993) argues for the poor of Brazil? The domain of emotional suffering surrounding death is a relatively new area of study for psychological anthropologists, one that promises to provide intriguing insights. The expression of grief surrounding death is also of interest to anthropologists who study religion (Bowen 1998). Research shows that beliefs about the dead, and how the dead may affect the living, shape people's experience of death and mourning.

HOW does culture shape personality during infancy and childhood?

Human psychological development begins from the moment of birth, if not before. Margaret Mead was a pioneer in showing how infant care practices, such as breastfeeding, how the baby is held, and how much contact the infant has with others, can affect personality formation, including gender identity. Her study of the Arapesh, Mundugumor, and Tchambuli peoples of New Guinea indicates that gender is a largely "plastic" (or malleable) aspect of human personality. Cross-cultural studies show that children's work roles and family roles correspond to personality patterns. Informal and formal learning, depending on cultural context, shapes young people's sense of identity.

HOW does culture shape personality during the transition from childhood to adulthood?

Adolescence, a culturally defined time around puberty and before adulthood, varies cross-culturally from being nonexistent to being long in duration and involving detailed training and elaborate ceremonies. "Coming of age" ceremonies sometimes involve bodily cutting, which denotes membership of the initiate in a particular gender. In contrast to the sharp distinction between "male" and "female" laid out in Western science and folk belief, many cultures

have longstanding traditions of third gender identities, most prominently for males or people of indeterminate biological sex markers, to become more like females in those cultures.

HOW does culture shape personality during adulthood?

Reflecting the fact that women tend to be more involved in child care than males, cultures generally provide more in the way of enculturation of females for this role. In non-industrial societies, learning about motherhood is embedded in other aspects of life, and knowledge about birthing and child care is shared among women. In industrialized cultures, science and medicine play a large role in defining the maternal role. This change reduces women's autonomy and fosters their dependence on external, non-kin–based structures.

The senior years in non-industrialized societies are shorter, in general, than in industrialized societies in which lifespan tends to be longer. Elder men and women in non-industrial cultures are treated with respect, considered to know the most, and retain a strong sense of their place in the culture. Increasingly in industrialized societies, elderly people are removed from their families and spend many years in age-segregated institutions. This transition tends to have negative implications for their psychological well-being.

KEY CONCEPTS

adolescence, p. 133
amazon, p. 137
berdache, p. 137
couvade, p. 139
cultural configuration, p. 125
culture of poverty, p. 126
enculturation, p. 124
female circumcision, p. 135

hijira, p. 138
iatrogenic, p. 140
image of the limited good, p. 126
narcissist, p. 131
national character studies, p. 126
personality, p. 124
puberty, p. 133

SUGGESTED READINGS

Evalyn Blackwood, ed., *The Many Faces of Homosexuality: Anthropological Approaches to Homosexual Behavior.* New York: Harrington Park Press, 1986. This text contains chapters on anthropological writings about lesbianism, and case studies of ritualized male homosexuality in Irian Jaya, the berdache in North America, hijiras of India, lesbian relationships in Lesotho, and Mexican male homosexual interaction patterns in public.

Jean Briggs, *Never in Anger.* Cambridge, MA: Harvard University Press, 1970. This classic study explores the ethnographer's experience with the Inuit of the Canadian Arctic through a perceptive and reflective examination of family life.

Jean Briggs, *Inuit Morality Play.* New Haven, CN: Yale University Press, 1998. A wonderful introduction to the use of psychoanalytic anthropology, this book details the "dramas" in the life of a three-year-old Inuit girl. (Winner of the Boyer Prize in psychoanalytic anthropology for 1999).

Sally Cole, *Ruth Landes: A Life in Anthropology.* Omaha: University of Nebraska Press, 2003. In this book, Canadian anthropologist Sally Cole reconsiders the life and work of Ruth Landes, whose work among the Ojibwa is considered today an early and exemplary study of gender relations.

Ellen Gruenbaum, *The Female Circumcision Controversy: An Anthropological Perspective.* Philadelphia: University of Pennsylvania Press, 2001. The author draws on her more than five years of fieldwork in Sudan, and discusses how change is occurring through economic development, the role of Islamic activists, health educators, and educated African women.

Charlotte E. Hardman, *Other Worlds: Notions of Self and Emotion among the Lohorung Rai.* New York: Berg, 2000. The author conducted fieldwork in a mountainous region of Nepal to learn about one community's perception of what it means to be a person.

Judith Schachter Modell, *Ruth Benedict: Patterns of a Life.* Philadelphia: University of Pennsylvania Press, 1983. This biography of a prominent psychological anthropologist provides insights into Benedict's development as an anthropologist, her research and writings, and her role in the Culture and Personality School.

Michael Moffatt, *Coming of Age in New Jersey: College and American Culture.* New Brunswick, NJ: Rutgers University Press, 1991. Based on a year's participant observation in a college dormitory in a university in the eastern United States, this study presents insights on sexuality, race relations, and individualism.

Mimi Nichter, *What Girls and Their Parents Say about Dieting.* Cambridge, MA: Harvard University Press, 2000. The author collected and analyzed interview data with adolescent girls in the United States, focusing on girls' perceptions of their weight, their attachment to dieting, and influences of their mothers' views and comments on weight.

Richard Parker, *Bodies, Pleasures, and Passions: Sexual Culture in Contemporary Brazil.* Boston: Beacon Press, 1991. This ethnographic study of contemporary sexual culture in Brazil addresses such topics as sexual socialization, bisexuality, sadomasochism, AIDS, prostitution, samba, the symbolism of breasts, courting, and the Carnaval.

Joel S. Savishinsky, *Breaking the Watch: The Meanings of Retirement in America.* Ithaca, NY: Cornell University Press, 2000. Fieldwork in a nursing home in a small town in central New York state sheds light on the retirees themselves through vivid portraits of several, along with their own words on friendship in the home, finding purpose in life, and dealing with finances.

Joseph J. Tobin, David Y. H. Wu, and Dana H. Davidon, *Preschool in Three Cultures: Japan, China, and the United States.* New Haven: Yale University Press, 1989. This book offers comparative insights about parents' reasons for sending children to preschool, including a shared concern for learning cooperation in all three contexts and a contrast between the emphasis on academic learning in the United States and on social learning in Japan.

WEBLINKS

The Companion Website (www.pearsoned.ca/miller) that accompanies *Cultural Anthropology,* Third Canadian Edition, includes a destinations module containing links to many websites relevant to the content of this chapter. Use it to investigate the Web and expand your understanding of anthropology.

- **WHAT** does medical anthropology contribute to understanding illness cross-culturally?

- **WHAT** does medical anthropology contribute to understanding healing systems cross-culturally?

- **HOW** are illness and healing changing during globalization?

7

ILLNESS AND HEALING

Mentawai healers treat a woman suffering from a toothache on Siberut Island, Indonesia.

Primatologist Jane Goodall witnessed a polio epidemic among the chimpanzees she was studying in Tanzania (Foster and Anderson 1978:33–34). A group of healthy animals watched a stricken member try to reach the feeding area, but did not help him. Another badly paralyzed chimpanzee was simply left behind when the group moved on.

Humans also sometimes resort to isolation and abandonment, as seen in the traditional Inuit practice of leaving aged and infirm people behind in the cold; the stigmatization of HIV/AIDS victims; and the ignoring of the homeless mentally ill in North American cities. Compared to our non-human primate relatives, however, humans have created more complex and variable ways of interpreting health problems and highly creative methods of preventing and curing them.

Since the 1970s, medical anthropology has been one of the fastest growing areas of research in all of anthropology's four fields. This chapter presents a selection of findings from this exciting subfield. We first learn about ethnomedicine, or the health systems of particular cultures. This section describes various cultural approaches to health, illness, and healing from an emic perspective. In the second section, we consider three important theoretical approaches in medical anthropology, each with a distinctive view of how to study and interpret health systems and health problems. In the last section, we address contemporary change, including new health challenges and how healing has changed, especially as indigenous systems increasingly interact with Western medicine.

ETHNOMEDICINE

Medical anthropologists have long been interested in studying **ethnomedicine**, or cross-cultural health systems. A health system encompasses many areas: perceptions and classifications of illness, prevention measures, diagnosis, healing (magical, religious, scientific, healing substances), and healers. In addition to these core topics, ethnomedicine has recently expanded its focus to new topics such as the anthropology of the body, culture and disability, and change in indigenous or "traditional" healing systems, especially change resulting from the effects of globalization and the growth of multiple and mixed healing systems.

In the 1960s when the term *ethnomedicine* first came into use, it referred only to non-Western health systems and was synonymous with *folk medicine, popular medicine,* and even the abandoned term *primitive medicine*. Two major problems exist with using the term *ethnomedicine* in this way. First, it is "totalizing"—that is, excessively generalizing. Labelling all non-Western medicine as "folk" or "popular," in contrast to "scientific" or "professional" Western medicine, overlooks such highly developed and specialized non-Western systems as those of India and China, to name just two examples. It is also totalizing in terms of implying that all Western health systems are "professional" and thus overlooks much thinking and practice in the West that could well be labelled "folk" or "popular." Second, the early meaning of *ethnomedicine* is ethnocentric, because Western medicine is an ethnomedical system too, intimately bound to Western culture and its values. We must nonetheless recognize that, especially since the 1950s and the increasing spread of Western culture and science globally, Western

South African healer Magdaline Ramaota speaks to clients in Durban. In South Africa, few people have enough money to pay for AIDS drugs. The role of traditional healers in providing psychological and social support for victims is extremely important.

biomedicine is more appropriately termed a global or "cosmopolitan" system.

The current use of the term *ethnomedicine* thus embraces all health systems. Within any of them, a range of variations may exist—from more local practices and beliefs held by laypeople to more widespread practices that require skills that must be learned over many years of training available only to a few.

Perceptions of the Body

Cultural perceptions of the body have implications for how people maintain health, respond to illness, and approach healing. The highland Maya of Chiapas, southern Mexico, have a detailed vision of the exterior body, but do not focus much attention on internal organs, a fact related to the absence of surgery as a healing technique among them (Berlin and Berlin 1996). Western logic of mind–body dualism has long pervaded popular and sci-

entific thinking about health and illness. Thus, Western medicine has a special category called "mental illness," which addresses certain health problems as if they were located only in the mind. In many cultures where such a mind–body distinction does not exist, there is no category of "mental illness."

Cross-cultural variation exists in perceptions of which bodily organs are most critically involved in the definition of life versus death. In the West, a person may be declared dead while the heart is still beating if the brain is judged "dead." In Japan, organ transplant from a brain-dead donor remains an unacceptable medical practice (Lock 1996). The definition of *brain-dead* is not accepted in Japan, perhaps an indication of the relatively great value accorded to the brain in Western culture (Ohnuki-Tierney 1994).

In Japan, negative attitudes about cutting the body explain the much lower rates of surgery there than in North America. The Japanese concept of *gotai* refers to the value of maintaining bodily intactness in life and death to the extent that even ear piercing is devalued. "Newspapers reported that one of the qualifications of a bride for Crown Prince Naruhito was that she not have pierced ears" (Ohnuki-Tierney 1994:235). An intact body ensures rebirth. Historically, the warrior's practice of beheading the victim was the ultimate form of killing because it violated the integrity of the body and prevented the enemy's rebirth. *Gotai* is also an important reason for the widespread popular resistance to organ transplantation in Japan.

Another area of interest for medical anthropologists is the relationship between the physical body and the social body in matters of health, illness, and healing. Western biomedicine typically treats only the physical body or only the mind, as they are thought to be completely separate from each other and from the social and cultural milieu of the patient. In contrast, many non-Western healing systems encompass the social context within which an individual's body is situated.

Health is also closely related to the body politic. The Cree from northern Quebec translate *miyupimaatisiiu* as "being alive well." The term encompasses practices of Cree daily living such as hunting, eating the right foods, keeping warm, and balancing human relationships. Naomi Adelson's research (2000) with the Whapmagoostui Cree living along the Great Whale River demonstrated that understanding health means understanding what it means to be Cree in a rapidly changing political and economic environment.

Most medical systems recognize a relationship between mind and body, and between individuals and their social contexts. Strained social relations—including those with supernatural beings—may cause illness; healing is intended to address and alleviate problems in the social body as

People in Laos gathered around an offering to the spirits in preparation for a *sukhwan* ritual.

well as the physical body. A cure is brought about by holding a family or community ritual that seeks to regain correct social relations or that will appease the deities. For example, the Lao residing in Laos and those who settled as refugees in North America perform a communal ritual called *sukhwan* to "tie" the 32 components of an individual's spirit essence permanently into the body with sacred strings tied around the wrist. This ritual draws the individual, who may have been ill or frightened, more tightly into the community (P. Van Esterik 1992).

Defining Health Problems

Medical anthropologists, like philosophers, devote much attention to defining concepts and delineating the object of study. Because medical anthropologists have conducted many studies of emic perceptions of health and health problems, they have found that their own (usually Western) concepts do not fit well with other cultural definitions. Cross-cultural knowledge forces us to broaden our own definitions. Consider, for example, the term *dore* as used by the Desana people of the Colombian rainforest, a group of forager–horticulturalists (Reichel-Dolmatoff 1971 cited in Hahn 1995:23). This term refers to a complex set of symbols related to the verb "to order" or "to send." Among the Desana, falling sick is the result of an order, a mandate, sent by or through a supernatural agent—a rather different definition from any found in Western biomedicine.

An approach commonly used in medical anthropology to help sort through the richness of cultural labels and perceptions is the disease/illness dichotomy. This dicho-

tomy is parallel to etic and emic understandings of health problems. The term *disease* refers to a biological pathology that is objective and universal (Kleinman 1995:31). A virus is a virus no matter where it lands. Disease is thus a scientific, etic concept. In contrast, the term *illness* refers to the culturally specific understandings and experiences of a health problem or some more generalized form of suffering. A viral infection may be differently understood and experienced in different societies. In some it may not be perceived as a health problem at all or may be thought of as "sent" by a supernatural force. Culture thus provides the framework within which disease and other forms of suffering become illness. Medical anthropologist and physician Arthur Kleinman suggests that Western biomedicine focuses narrowly on disease and neglects illness (1995). He urges medical anthropologists to continue to do research on illness and bring its importance to the attention of biomedicine.

Another important concept reflects the attempt of medical anthropologists to broaden our understanding of health problems to include structural suffering, or structural affliction. The term *structural* refers to certain devastating forces that cause suffering, such as economic and political conditions of war, famine, forced migration, and poverty. These conditions affect health in many ways, inducing effects that range from depression to death. They also include the negative effects of disruption of one's family life, livelihood, and sense of home and security. The usual approaches in Western biomedicine are not designed to deal with the effects of structural suffering. Western disease classifications do not encompass structural suffering.

Medical anthropologists study how people of different cultures label and classify illness and suffering. The term *nosology* refers to the classification of health problems. The term *ethno-nosology* refers to cross-cultural systems of classification of health problems. Western biomedicine defines and labels diseases according to its diagnostic criteria and sets these guidelines down in thick manuals used by physicians when treating patients. In non-state societies, verbal traditions are the repository of such information. The basis for classifications cross-culturally often include causal agent, vector (the means of transmission, such as mosquitoes), the body part that is affected, symptoms, the pathological process itself, the stage of the disease, the victim's behaviour, and combinations of any of these.

Locally specific disorders not easily assigned to Western disease categories are sometimes referred to as **culture-bound syndromes** (see the Multiple Cultural Worlds box). A culture-bound syndrome is a collection of signs and symptoms that is restricted to a particular culture or a limited number of cultures (Prince 1985:201). Culture bound syndromes are one way of looking at the cultural interpretation of disease or illness. Many culture-bound syndromes are caused by psychosocial factors, such as stress or shock, but they may also have biophysical symptoms. For example, *susto*, or "fright disease," is a widely distributed culture-bound syndrome of Latino cultures. People afflicted with *susto* attribute it to shock, such as losing a loved one or experiencing a frightening accident (Rubel, O'Nell, and Collado-Ardón 1984).

In the Chiapas area of Mexico, a woman reported that her *susto* was brought on by an accident in which pottery she had made was broken on its way to market, and a man said that his *susto* came on after he saw a dangerous snake. *Susto* symptoms include appetite loss, loss of motivation, breathing problems, generalized pain, and nightmares. Analysis of many cases of *susto* in three villages showed that the people most likely to be afflicted were those who were socially marginal or experiencing a sense of role failure. The woman whose pottery had broken, for example, had also suffered two spontaneous abortions and was worried that she would never have children. People with *susto* have higher mortality rates than the unafflicted population. This finding indicates that a deep sense of social failure places a person at a higher risk of dying.

Medical anthropologists first studied culture-bound syndromes in non-Western cultures, and this focus has led to a bias in thinking that all culture-bound syndromes are found in "other" cultures. Now it is recognized that some afflictions of the West could also be interpreted as culture-bound syndromes, such as *agoraphobia*, or an obsessive fear of leaving one's home and going to public places, or eating disorders such as anorexia nervosa and bulimia.

Anorexia nervosa and a related condition called bulimia used to be considered culture-bound syndromes found predominantly among Euro-American adolescent girls of North America. More recently, cases have also been documented among African American girls, and a small number of cases have appeared in Japan, Hong Kong, South Africa, Argentina, and urban India (Fabrega and Miller 1995; Nasser, Katzman, and Gordon 2001). Anorexia nervosa's cluster of symptoms include aversion to food, distorted body image, hyperactivity, and, as it progresses, continuous wasting of the body and often death. Fat phobia or self-perceptions of fatness are often absent in Asian patients, a reminder that there are many routes to anorexia.

No one has found a biological cause for anorexia nervosa, and thus it can be interpreted as a culturally constructed affliction. Eating disorders are difficult to cure with either medical or psychiatric treatment (Gremillon 1992). Pinpointing the cultural causes has not proved easy. Many experts cite the societal pressures on young girls in North America toward excessive concern with their looks, especially body weight. Others feel that anorexia is related to girls' unconscious resistance to overcontrolling parents. To such girls, food intake may appear to be the one thing they control. This need for self-control through food deprivation becomes addictive and entrapping. The highly controversial Montreux Clinic in Victoria, B.C., proposed a causal model of psychological negativity that "forbade" sufferers to eat. Although the primary cause of anorexia may be rooted in culture, the affliction becomes intertwined with the body's biological functions. Extreme fasting leads to the body's inability to deal with ingested food. A starving anorexic literally may no longer be able to eat and derive nourishment from food. Some medical treatments therefore include in-hospital monitored feeding or intravenous feeding to override the biological block. Other interventions by Canadian hospitals and advocacy groups include the following: support groups for parents of children with eating disorders; out-patient treatment programs to develop coping strategies and improve self-acceptance; individual psychotherapy focusing on issues such as control or body image; family counselling; publicity concerning the early signs of eating disorders; public education such as National Eating Disorders Week (first week of February) and internet resources.

Preventive Practices

Many different practices based in either religious or secular beliefs exist cross-culturally for preventing misfortune, suffering, and illness. Among the Maya of Guatemala, one major illness is called *awas* (Wilson 1995). Children born with *awas* show symptoms such as lumps

Multiple Cultural Worlds

CULTURE-BOUND SYNDROMES

SOME MEDICAL anthropologists have been concerned about labelling locally specific complaints as culture-bound syndromes or culturally interpreted disorders because the label may reinforce stereotypes and result in dismissing the complaints of women, refugees, or First Nations patients. A focus on static categorization may also obscure how meanings are linked to larger social and political contexts, and how diseases and disorders may be a form of resistance. The following work relevant to Canadian medical anthropology demonstrates some of the debates about whether a label names a unique cultural product or a local manifestation of a more general disease process.

- **"Old Hag"—Newfoundland:** The "Old Hag" is a local term for a condition of sleep paralysis and hallucinations accompanied by the feeling that a great weight is pressing on the chest. Attacks of the "Old Hag" are not considered manifestations of mental illness, but rather normal occurrences, possibly caused by occupationally derived sleeplessness related to the demands of family fishing in Newfoundland (Firestone 1985).

- *Anfechtung*—**Hutterites in Manitoba:** *Anfechtung* is identified as a culture-bound syndrome characterized by a withdrawal from social contact, a feeling of having sinned, and concerns with religious unworthiness. Through the Hutterite baptism of blood, disciples experience the suffering of Christ as an inner suffering of doubt and despair (Stephenson 1991:28). Stephenson reminds us that the stereotypes of Hutterites as dour, sober-faced authoritarians struggling under religious oppression influence the way illnesses are interpreted by health professionals.

- *Pibloktoq* **(Arctic hysteria)—Inuit:** Arctic hysteria is widely cited as a culture-bound syndrome characterized by brooding, depressive silences followed by convulsive hysterical seizures, followed by collapse and recovery with amnesia for the experience. Possible explanations for the syndrome include the ecology of long, dark, cold days; crowded conditions in confined houses; shamanistic beliefs; and dietary conditions such as calcium and vitamin D deficiency, and hypervitaminosis A. Marine animals contain high, toxic concentrations of vitamin A in their livers, kidneys, and fat, which are then consumed in large quantities by Inuit (Landy 1985). Landy argues that biological and cultural factors are inseparable, and taken together, may offer a biocultural approach to explaining emotional disturbances.

- **Windigo—Cree and Ojibwa:** "Windigo psychosis," long identified as a classic culture-bound syndrome, is described as a condition characterized by depression, nausea, distaste for usual foods, and feelings of being possessed by a cannibalistic spirit. The condition is attributed to the Cree, Ojibwa, and other subarctic First Nations groups in northeastern Canada. Early reports hypothesized that the condition developed as a result of the stress of a diminishing or uncertain food supply. Landes's (1938) description of Ojibwa Windigo as a severe anxiety neurosis manifested as obsessive cannibalism has been criticized. However, others argue that the more significant question is, Under what conditions is a person likely to be accused of being a Windigo (Marano 1982)? While Windigo beliefs may structure how anxieties and psychoses are talked about, as reflected in the analysis of Cree "cannibalistic" myths, actual cases of cannibalistic psychotic behaviour are absent or very few in number. More significant questions concern how concepts like the Windigo relate to the mental health of First Nations peoples (Waldram 2004).

- **Evil eye (***mal ojo***)—Mediterranean and Latin American Hispanic groups:** Fitful sleep, crying without apparent cause, diarrhea, vomiting, and fever in a child or infant may be attributed to a fixed stare from an adult. An adult, usually female, may also be harmed by the evil and envious eye of another. Migliore (1983) looked at evil eye beliefs among Sicilian immigrants in Ontario, arguing that the term may refer to causes of general misfortune or specific illness. Carroll (1984) has linked evil eye beliefs to the weaning conflict and the loss of the maternal breast, setting up an emotional pattern that carries into adult life.

- **Nerves (***Nervios, Nevra***)—widespread in Euro-American contexts:** "Nerves" is a general term to refer to a culturally acceptable way of describing psychosocial distress to family and health professionals. Symptoms include headaches, dizziness, chest pain, trembling, disorientation, fatigue, lack of appetite, and feelings of melancholy and despair. Dona Davis (1984) reported cases of middle-aged women from the outports of Newfoundland complaining of bad nerves to their doctors and being given prescriptions for tranquilizers. In the local fishing communities, "woman the worrier" is a noble role and carries a wide range of meanings. Similarly, the narratives of first-generation Greek immigrant women in Montreal stressed their experiences of isolation, discrimination, and marital discord expressed through complaints of *nevra* (Lock and Wakewich-Dunk 1990). In both cases, nerves may be thought of as a form of communication about living with stress, poverty, and deprivation.

under the skin, marks on the skin, or albinism. Causes of *awas* are related to events that happen to the mother during her pregnancy: She may have been denied food that she desired or was pressured to eat food she didn't want, or she may have encountered a rude, drunk, or angry person (usually a male). In order to help prevent *awas* in babies, the Mayas go out of their way to be careful around pregnant women. A pregnant woman, like land before the planting, is considered sacred and treated in special ways. She is always given the food she wants, and people behave with respect in her presence. In general, the ideal is to keep a pregnant woman in a state of *kalkab'il*, or peace, contentment, and optimism.

Common forms of ritual health protection include charms, spells, and strings tied around parts of the body. After visiting a Buddhist temple in Japan, for example, one might purchase a small band to tie around the wrist to prevent future problems related to health and fertility. Wrist ties are commonly placed on infants in rural areas in India, especially by Hindus. Recall the *sukhwan* rituals among the Lao who often use protective wrist strings to strengthen children.

In Thailand, spirits (*phii*) are a recognized source of illness, death, and other misfortunes. One variety of *phii*, a widow ghost, is the sexually voracious spirit of a woman who has met an untimely and perhaps violent death. When a seemingly healthy man dies in his sleep, a widow ghost is blamed. The wooden phalluses hung on the houses were protection against a possible attack. Mary Beth Mills, an anthropologist working in Thailand, learned of the display of these carved wooden phalluses (see photo) as protection against this form of sudden death among men (Mills 1995):

> [I]nformants described these giant penises as decoys that would attract the interest of any *phii mae maai* which might come looking for a husband. The greedy ghosts would take their pleasure with the wooden penises and be satisfied, leaving the men of that household asleep, safe in their beds. (251)

In 1990, fear of a widow ghost attack spread throughout a wide area of northeastern Thailand. The fear was based on national news and radio reports of unexplained deaths among Thai migrants working in Singapore. Local people, many of whom had family and friends employed in Singapore, interpreted these sudden deaths as caused by widow ghosts. Widow ghosts are known to roam about, searching for men whom they take as their "husbands." Mary Beth Mills returned to Baan Naa Sakae village at the time of the fear:

> I returned to Baan Naa Sakae village after a few days' absence to find the entire community of two hundred households festooned with wooden phalluses in all shapes and sizes. Ranging from the crudest wooden shafts to carefully carved images complete with coconut shell testicles

Wooden phalluses in a household compound in a village in northeastern Thailand are displayed to protect men from sudden death.

> and fishnet pubic hair, they adorned virtually every house and residential compound. The phalluses, I was told, were to protect residents, especially boys and men, from the "nightmare deaths" (*lai tai*) at the hands of malevolent "widow ghosts" (*phii mae maai*). (249)

As radio and other news coverage of the deaths in Singapore diminished over several weeks, so did concerns about widow ghosts, and villagers quietly removed the protective phalluses.

Diagnosis

If an affliction has been experienced and the person with the condition decides to seek help for it, diagnosis is the first stage in treatment. Diagnosis attempts to find out what is wrong and to label the affliction in order to determine the proper form of treatment. It includes magical-religious techniques such as **divination**, in which a specialist uses techniques to gain supernatural insights, and secular techniques such as asking the ill person to supply detailed descriptions of symptoms. Among the Navajo, three types of diagnostic techniques exist: hand trembling, star gazing, and listening (W. Morgan 1977). The hand trembling diagnosis works this way: The specialist enters the home of the afflicted person and, with friends and relatives present, discusses the problem. The specialist sits facing the patient, closes his eyes, and thinks of all the possible causes. When the correct one comes to mind, the specialist's arm involuntarily shakes, revealing the diagnosis. In all three forms of Navajo diagnosis, the specialist goes into a trance-like state that lends authority to the outcome.

Among the urban poor of Bahia in Brazil, a flexible approach exists to ascertaining the cause of disease (Ngokwey 1988). In Feira de Santana, the second-largest city in the state of Bahia, illness causation theories fit into the following domains: natural, socioeconomic, psychological, and supernatural. Natural causes include exposure to the environment. Thus, "too much cold can provoke gripe; humidity and rain cause rheumatism; excessive heat can result in dehydration. . . . Some types of winds are known to provoke *ar do vento* or *ar do tempo,* a condition characterized by migraines, hemiplegia, and "cerebral congestion'" (795). Other natural explanations for illness take into account the effects of aging, heredity, personal nature (*natureza*), and gender. Heredity is a common explanation for mental retardation. Contagion is another "natural" explanation, as are the effects of certain foods and eating habits. Popular knowledge connects the lack of economic resources, proper sanitation, and health services with illnesses. "One informant said, 'There are many illnesses because there are many poor'" (796). Psychosocial factors such as emotions may contribute to disease: "Anger and hostile feelings (*raiva*), anxiety and worry are possible causes of various illnesses ranging from *nervoso,* a folk illness characterized by 'nervousness,' to heart problems and *derrame* (cerebral hemorrhage)" (796). Illness is also attributed to supernatural causes such as spirits and magical acts.

The African-Brazilian religious systems of the Bahia region encompass a range of spirits who can inflict illness, including spirits of the dead and devil-like spirits. Some spirits cause specific illnesses, while others bring general misfortune. Spells cast by envious people with the evil eye are a well-known cause of illness. People also recognize multiple levels of causality. In the case of a stomach ache, for example, they might blame a quarrel (the ultimate cause), which prompted the aggrieved party to seek the intervention of a sorcerer, who cast a spell (the instrumental cause), which led to the illness. This multiple etiology then calls for multiple treatments.

People's own (emic) perceptions of symptoms and explanations for why illness occurs often contradict the teachings of Western biomedicine. This divergence may lead, on one hand, to people's rejection of Western biomedicine and, on the other, to frustration among medical care providers who accuse such people of "noncompliance." We return to this issue in the last section of this chapter.

Ways of Healing

This section considers two ways of conceptualizing and dealing with healing: the public and participatory group healing of the Ju/wasi and the humoral system of bodily balance through food intake in Malaysia. We also consider healers and healing substances.

Community Healing Systems

A general distinction can be drawn between private and **community healing.** The former addresses individual bodily ailments in isolation and the latter emphasizes social context as crucial to healing. Compared to Western biomedicine, many non-Western systems make greater use of public healing and community involvement. Many First Nations groups in Canada make use of healing circles to restore balance in their lives. Often the medicine wheel, a symbol for the balance of spirit, heart, mind, and body is used in community healing. An example of public or community healing comes from the Ju/wasi foragers of the Kalahari Desert in southern Africa. Ju/wasi healing emphasizes the mobilization of community "energy" as a key element in the cure:

> The central event in this tradition is the all-night healing dance. Four times a month on the average, night signals the start of a healing dance. The women sit around the fire, singing and rhythmically clapping. The men, some-

A Ju/wasi healer in a trance, in the Kalahari Desert, southern Africa. Most healers are men, but some are women.

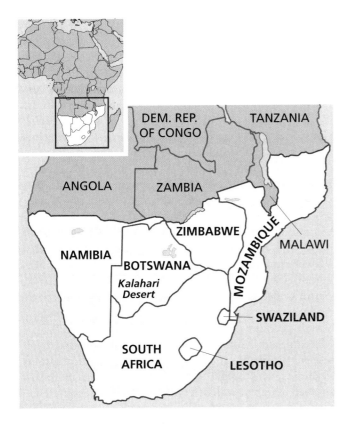

times joined by the women, dance around the singers. As the dance intensifies, *num* or spiritual energy is activated by the healers, both men and women, but mostly among the dancing men. As *num* is activated in them, they begin to kia or experience an enhancement of their consciousness. While experiencing kia, they heal all those at the dance. . . . The dance is a community event at which the entire camp participates. The people's belief in the healing power of *num* brings substance to the dance. (Katz 1982:34–36)

Thus, an important aspect of the Ju/wasi healing system is its openness—everyone has access to it. The role of healer is also open. Healers have no special privileges. In fact, more than half of all adult men and about 10 percent of adult women are healers.

Humoral Healing Systems

Humoral healing systems are based on a philosophy of balance among certain natural elements within the body (McElroy and Townsend 1996). Food and drugs have different effects on the body and are classified as either "heating" or "cooling" (the quotation marks indicate that these properties are not the same as thermal temperatures per se). Diseases are classified as being the result of bodily imbalances—too much heat or coolness, which must then be counteracted through dietary changes or medicines that will bring back balance.

Humoral healing systems have been practised for thousands of years in the Middle East, the Mediterranean, and much of Asia, and spread to the New World through Spanish colonization. They have shown substantial resilience in the face of Western biomedicine, often incorporating it into their own framework—for example, in the classification of biomedical treatments as either heating or cooling. Humoral logic persists in Euro-American public culture in advice such as "feed a cold; starve a fever."

In Malaysia, several different humoral traditions co-exist, reflecting the region's history of contact with outside cultures. Malaysia has been influenced by trade and contact between its indigenous culture and that of India, China, and the Arab-Islamic world for around 2000 years. Indian, Chinese, and Arabic medical systems are similar in that all define health as the balance of opposing elements within the body, although each has its own variations. Indigenous belief systems may have been especially compatible with these imported models because they also were based on concepts of heat and coolness.

Insights about what the indigenous systems were like comes from ethnographic accounts about the Orang Asli, Aboriginal peoples of the Malaysian interior who are relatively less affected by contact. A conceptual system of hot–cold opposition dominates Orang Asli cosmological, medical, and social theories. The properties and meanings of heat and coolness differ from those of Islamic, Indian, or Chinese humoralism in several ways. In the Islamic, Indian, and Chinese systems, for example, death is the ultimate result of too much coolness. Among the Orang Asli, excessive heat is the primary cause of mortality. Heat emanates from the sun, and it is associated with excrement, blood, misfortune, disease, and death. Humanity's hot blood makes people mortal, and their consumption of meat speeds the process. Heat causes menstruation, violent emotions, aggression, and drunkenness. Coolness, in contrast, is vital for health.

Health is protected by avoiding the harmful effects of the sun by staying in the forest shade. This belief justifies the rejection of agriculture by some groups because it exposes people to the sun. Treatment of illness is designed to reduce or remove heat. If someone were to fall ill in a clearing, the entire group would relocate to the coolness of the forest. The forest is also a source of cooling leaves and herbs. Healers are cool and retain their coolness by bathing in cold water and sleeping far from the fire. Extreme cold, however, can be harmful. Dangerous levels of coolness are associated with the time right after birth since the mother is believed to have lost substantial heat: The new mother must avoid drinking or bathing in cold water. She increases her body heat by tying sashes containing warm leaves or ashes around her waist, bathing herself and her newborn child in warm water, and lying near a fire.

Steven Benally, Jr., an apprentice medicine man, practises for a ceremony in his hogan on the Navajo Reservation near Window Rock, Arizona. An apprentice often studies for a decade or more.

Healers

In an informal sense, everyone is a "healer" since self-treatment is always the first consideration in dealing with a perceived health problem. Yet in all cultures some people become recognized as having special abilities to diagnose and treat health problems. Specialists include midwife, bonesetter (someone who resets broken bones), **shaman** (a healer who mediates between humans and the spirit world), herbalist, general practitioner, psychiatrist, acupuncturist, chiropractor, and dentist. Cross-cultural evidence indicates some common features of healers: selection (certain individuals may show more ability for entry into healing roles); training (this often involves years of observation and practice, and the training may be arduous); certification (this may be either legal or ritual); professional image (the role is demarcated through behaviour, dress, and markers such as the white coat in the West or the Siberian shaman's tambourine for calling the spirits); and expectation of payment (compensation is expected in kind or cash) (Foster and Anderson 1978:104–115).

Healing Substances

Around the world, many different natural or manufactured substances are used as medicines for preventing or curing health problems. Anthropologists have spent more time studying the use of medicines in non-Western cultures than in the West, although a more fully cross-cultural approach is emerging that examines the use of Western pharmaceuticals as well (van der Geest, Whyte, and Hardon 1996). **Ethnobotany** explores the cultural knowledge of local plants, including the use of plants as medicines. Increasing awareness of the range of potentially useful plants worldwide provides a strong incentive for protecting both biodiversity and indigenous cultural knowledge of plant uses. A family physician from Toronto visited Ojibwa elders in a Georgian Bay community, where women healers explained their use of plant products for healing, including catnip, licorice, cedar leaves, peppermint, and red sumac berries (Borins 1995). See also Walker's inventory of edible forest plants of the Northwest Territories (1984). Leaves of the coca plant have for centuries been a key part of the medicinal systems of the Andean region, although it has broader uses in ritual, in covering hunger pains, and in combatting the cold (Carter, Mamani, and Morales 1981). Coca is used for gastrointestinal problems, and next most commonly for sprains, swellings, and colds. A survey of coca use in Bolivia showed a high prevalence rate: Of the 3501 people asked if they use coca medicinally, about 85 percent answered yes. The leaf may be ingested alone (chewed), and it is frequently combined with other substances in a *maté*, or drink composed of herbs in a water base. Specialized knowledge about preparing some of the *matés* is reserved for trained herbalists. One *maté*, for example, is for treating asthma. Made of a certain root and coca leaves, it

Traditional medicines available in a shop in Toronto include dried ingredients and patent medicines from Hong Kong, Taiwan, and mainland China.

should be taken three to four times a day until the patient is cured.

Minerals are also widely used for prevention and healing. For example, bathing in sulphurous waters or water that contains high levels of other minerals has wide popularity for promoting health and curing several ailments, including arthritis and rheumatism. About 40 000 people a year go to the Dead Sea, which lies beneath sea level between Israel and Jordan, to treat skin diseases (Lew 1994). The adjacent sulphur springs and mud from the shore are believed to be helpful for people with skin ailments such as psoriasis. German studies conclude that it is more cost effective to pay for a trip to the Dead Sea than it is to hospitalize a psoriasis patient.

Western patent medicines have gained popularity worldwide. There are benefits to the use of these medicines, as well as problems, including use without prescription and overprescription. Often, sale of patent medicines is unregulated, and they are available for purchase from local markets by self-treating individuals. The popularity of capsules and even injections has led to misuse and overuse in many cases. Multinational pharmaceutical companies aggressively market medicines, and even "dump" out-of-date and recalled products not permitted for sale in North America. Medical anthropologists are assessing the distribution channels of medicines, the increased commodification of medicine, and cross-cultural perceptions of the efficacy of patent, herbal, and Western pharmaceuticals.

APPROACHES IN MEDICAL ANTHROPOLOGY

Here we consider four approaches to understanding health systems. The first emphasizes the importance of the environment in shaping health problems and their spread. The second highlights symbols and meaning as critical in people's expression of suffering and how healing occurs. The third underlines the need to look at economic and political structural factors as deep causes of health problems and as related to certain features of Western biomedicine. The fourth applies anthropological knowledge to improve health care.

The Ecological/Epidemiological Approach

The **ecological/epidemiological approach** examines how aspects of the natural environment interact with culture to cause health problems and to influence their spread throughout populations. According to this approach, research should focus on gathering information about the environmental context and social patterns that affect health, such as food distribution within the family, sexual practices, hygiene, and population contact. Research tends to be quantitative and etic, although this approach is often combined with qualitative and emic methods to provide richer results (as discussed in Chapter 2).

The ecological/epidemiological approach yields findings relevant to public health programs by revealing causal links between environmental context and health problems. It also helps by providing socially targeted information about groups "at risk" for specific problems. For example, although hookworm is extremely common throughout rural China, researchers learned that rice cultivators have the highest rates of all. This pattern is related to the fact that the disease is spread through night soil (human excrement used as fertilizer) that is applied to the fields where the cultivators work.

Settled populations living in dense clusters are more likely than mobile populations to experience certain health problems, including declining diet quality and infectious disease (M. Cohen 1989). Many contemporary studies in the ecological/environmental mode attest to the importance of this distinction. As more and more mobile populations choose, or are forced, to settle into agricultural or urban lives, it is increasingly urgent that the often negative health consequences of sedentariness be recognized and mitigated. One recent study compared the health status of two groups of Turkana people in northwest Kenya (Barkey, Campbell, and Leslie 2001). Some of the Turkana are still pastoralists, whereas others have settled into a town where they no longer keep animals.

Women working in padi fields near Jinghong, China. Agricultural work done in standing water increases the risk of hookworm infection.

The two groups differ strikingly in diet, activities, and social organization. Pastoralist Turkana eat mainly animal foods (milk, meat, and blood), spend much time in rigorous physical activity, and live in large family groups. Settled Turkana men eat mainly maize and beans. Although the study provided no information on physical activity, it is logical to assume that sedentariness means less. Settled Turkana no longer live with large family groups. Instead, they live near strangers. A comparison of the health of men in the two groups revealed that the settled men reported more eye infections, chest infections, backache, and cough/cold. This does not mean that the pastoralist Turkana men had no health problems. For example, a quarter of the pastoralist men reported eye infections, but one-half of the settled men did so. In terms of nutrition, the settled Turkana were shorter and had greater body mass than the pastoral Turkana.

Colonialism and Disease

Anthropologists have applied the ecological/epidemiological approach to the study of the impaired health and survival of indigenous peoples as a result of colonial contact. A basic question is how the introduction of European *pathogens* (disease-producing organisms) varies on the basis of size of the indigenous populations involved (Larsen and Milner 1994). Overall, findings about the effects of Western colonial contact are negative, from the worst examples being quick and outright extermination of indigenous peoples, to other groups showing resilience within drastically changed conditions.

In the Western hemisphere, European colonialism brought a dramatic decline in the indigenous populations they contacted, although disagreements exist about the numbers involved (Joralemon 1982). In coordination with archaeologists and colonial historians, medical anthropologists have tried to estimate the role of disease in depopulation compared with other factors such as warfare, harsh labour practices, and general cultural disruption, and to discover which diseases were most important. Research along these lines indicates that the precontact New World was largely free of the major European infectious diseases such as smallpox, measles, and typhus, and perhaps also syphilis, leprosy, and malaria. The exposure of indigenous peoples to these infectious diseases, therefore, was likely to have a massive impact, given the people's complete lack of resistance. One analyst compared contact to a "biological war":

> Smallpox was the captain of the men of death in that war, typhus fever the first lieutenant, and measles the second lieutenant. More terrible than the conquistadores on horseback, more deadly than sword and gunpowder, they made the conquest by the whites a walkover as compared to what it would have been without their aid. They were the forerunners of civilization, the companions of Christianity,

the friends of the invader. (Ashburn 1947:98, quoted in Joralemon 1982:112)

This quotation emphasizes the importance of the three major diseases in Latin American colonial history: smallpox, measles, and malaria. A later arrival, cholera, also had severe effects because its transmission through contaminated water and food thrives in areas of poor sanitation. In Canada, the two greatest epidemics affecting Aboriginal health were smallpox in the sixteenth and seventeenth centuries, and tuberculosis, which continues to be a major problem today (Waldram, Herring, and Young 1995). First Nations groups in Canada today also face the chronic diseases of the twentieth century, such as diabetes and heart disease. Some of these diseases may be linked to disruptions in traditional diets, a key component of maintaining health.

The Interpretive Approach

Interpretive approaches to health systems consider how people in different cultures label, describe, and experience illness and how healing offers meaningful responses to individual and communal distress. An important direction in interpretive medical anthropology has been to focus on the explanatory models and illness narratives of individual sufferers in order to understand the cultural realities of individual patients (Kleinman 1988). Illness and

A Korean mansin performs the Tale of Princess Pari, a female hero who braves the perils of the underworld in quest of an herb that will restore her dying parents. Twenty years ago, this segment of the *kut* for the dead would have been performed outside the house gate. In urban Korea, it is performed inside to avoid complaints about noise and traffic obstruction.

healing as dialectical processes involve the interaction between physical processes and social, cultural, and psychological contexts. Kleinman argued that Western biomedicine fails to recognize this, unlike many non-Western medical systems, which consider sufferers in their sociocultural context.

Interpretive approaches also pay attention to symbolic aspects of healing, such as ritual trance. Claude Lévi-Strauss, in a classic essay called "The Effectiveness of Symbols" (1967), examined how a song sung during childbirth among the Kuna Indians of Panama lessens the difficulty of childbirth. His main point was that healing systems provide meaning to people who are suffering. The provision of meaning offers psychological support and courage to the afflicted and may enhance healing through what Western science calls the **placebo effect** (a healing effect obtained through the positive power of believing that a particular method is efficacious). Anthropological research suggests that between 10 and 90 percent of the efficacy of medical prescriptions lies in the placebo effect (Moerman 1979, 1983, 1992). Several features may be involved: the power of the person prescribing a particular treatment, the very act of prescription, and concrete details about the medicine, such as its colour, name, and place of origin (van der Geest, Whyte, and Hardon 1996). For example, many international migrants prefer to obtain medicines from their homelands. In other situations, the prestige of a medicine from Sweden or Switzerland is an important factor.

Margaret Trawick (1988), in her study of Ayurvedic healing in India, examines the enduring efficacy and appeal of Ayurvedic treatments—treatments that are increasingly available in Canadian cities as well. Ayurvedic medicine is a widely used Indian health system based on texts composed from the beginning of the Christian era to about 1000 CE. Based on humoral principles, Ayurvedic diagnoses take into account bodily "channels" controlling the flow of life forces through the human body, and whether these are blocked or open and clear. Trawick transcribed an interview between an 80-year-old Ayurvedic physician and an old woman of a poor caste group. The transcription reveals the themes of channels, processes of flow, points of connection (the heart is believed to be the centre of all channels), and everyday activities that regulate the flow of life. After the interview, the doctor offers dietary prescriptions, such as avoidance of tamarind since that causes "dullness," and consumption of light food. Finally, he gently tells her that, basically, she is growing old. In this interaction, the meanings conveyed through the interview offer the client a sense that she is being taken seriously by the caregiver and give her some self-efficacy in that there are things she can do to alleviate her distress, such as carefully following a dietary regime (Trawick 1988:138–139).

Critical Medical Anthropology

Critical medical anthropology considers the way economic and political structures shape people's health status, their access to health care, and the prevailing healing systems. Critical medical anthropologists examine how economic and political systems create and perpetuate social inequality in health status. They have also exposed the power of **medicalization**, or the labelling of a particular issue or problem as medical and requiring medical treatment when, in fact, it may be economic or political.

Critical medical anthropologists examine how larger structural forces determine the distribution of illness and people's responses to it. But they are also concerned to see how individuals may, through personal agency, resist such forces. Critical medical anthropology also examines Western biomedicine itself, viewing it as a global power structure, critiquing medical training, and looking at doctor–patient relationships as manifestations of social control rather than social liberation. For example, Canadian medical anthropologist Pamela Downe (1999) analyzed how street prostitutes in Costa Rica medicalize the violence and discrimination in their lives, but resist and cope through their own brand of humour and jokes.

Many Canadian medical anthropologists favour a critical medical anthropology approach, reflecting, perhaps, their experience with national debates about universal health care and the social safety net. Margaret Lock and Gilles Bibeau (1995) link Canadian debates about language, national identity, and multiculturalism to the eclecticism and pluralism of method characteristic of medical anthropology in Canada.

The Role of Poverty

Broad distinctions exist between the most prevalent afflictions of the richer, more industrial nations and the poorer, less industrial nations. In the former, the major causes of death include circulatory diseases, malignant cancers, AIDS, alcohol consumption, and tobacco consumption (United Nations Development Programme 1994:191). For developing countries, a different profile appears: tuberculosis, malaria, and AIDS. There is substantial empirical evidence that poverty is a major cause of morbidity (sickness) and mortality (death) in both industrial and developing countries. It may be manifested in different ways, for example, by causing extreme malnutrition in Chad or Nepal, and high death rates from street violence among the poor of affluent nations.

Throughout the developing world, rates of childhood malnutrition are inversely related to income. As income increases, calorie intake as a percentage of recommended daily allowances also increases (Zaidi 1988:122). Thus, increasing the income levels of the poor may be the most direct way to influence health and nutrition. Yet, in contrast to this seemingly logical approach, many health and nutrition programs around the world have been focused on treating the outcomes of poverty rather than its causes.

The widespread practice of "treating" the health outcomes of poverty and social inequality with pills or other medical options has been documented by critical medical anthropologists. An example is Nancy Scheper-Hughes's research in Bom Jesus (1993), a poor area of northeastern Brazil mentioned in Chapter 5. People who experienced symptoms of weakness, insomnia, and anxiety were given pills by a local doctor. Her interpretation is that instead of needing pills, the people were hungry and needed food. This system serves the interests of pharmaceutical companies in the first place, and, more generally, helps to keep inequitable social systems in place. Similar critical analyses have shown how psychiatry treats symptoms and serves to keep people in their places, rather than addressing the root causes of affliction, which may be powerlessness, unemployment, and thwarted social aspirations. High rates of depression among women in Western societies, treated with a range of psychotropic drugs and personal therapists, are a notable example.

Western Medical Training Examined

Since the 1980s, critical medical anthropologists have pursued the study of Western biomedicine as a powerful cultural system. Much of their work critiques the dehumanization of medical school training and the overriding emphasis on technology. They often advocate for greater recognition of social factors in diagnosis and treatment, reduction of the spread of biomedical technology, and diversification of medical specialists to include alternative healing such as massage, acupuncture, and chiropractic (Scheper-Hughes 1990).

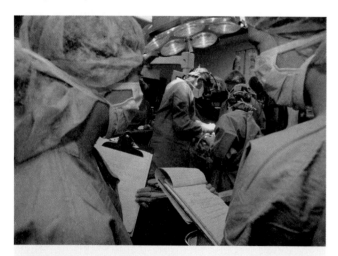

Medical students in training in a Western biomedical setting. These students are observing brain surgery.

Robbie Davis-Floyd (1987) examined the culture of obstetric training in the United States. She interviewed 12 obstetricians, 10 male and 2 female. As students, they absorbed the technological model of birth as a core value of Western obstetrics. This model treats the body as a machine (recall the discussion of the technological model of birth in Chapter 5). The physician-technician uses the assembly-line approach to birth in order to promote efficient production and quality control. One of the residents in the study explained: "We shave 'em, we prep 'em, we hook 'em up to the IV and administer sedation. We deliver the baby, it goes to the nursery and the mother goes to her room. There's no room for niceties around here. We just move 'em right on through. It's not hard to see it like an assembly line" (292). The goal is the "production" of a healthy baby. The doctor is in charge of achieving this goal, and the mother takes second place. One obstetrician said, "It is what we all were trained to always go after—the perfect baby. That's what we were trained to produce. The quality of the mother's experience—we rarely thought about that. Everything we did was to get that perfect baby" (292).

This goal involves the use of sophisticated monitoring machines. One obstetrician said, "I'm totally dependent on fetal monitors, 'cause they're great! They free you to do a lot of other things. . . . I couldn't sit over there with a woman in labor with my hand on her belly, and be in here seeing 20 to 30 patients a day" (291). In addition, use of technology conveys status: "Anybody in obstetrics who shows a human interest in patients is not respected. What *is* respected is interest in machines" (291).

How does obstetrical training socialize medical students into accepting this technological model? First, medical training involves a lengthy process of "cognitive retrogression" in which the students go through an intellectual hazing process. During the first two years of medical school, most courses are basic sciences; learning tends to be rote, and vast quantities of material must be memorized. The second phase, which could be termed dehumanization, is one in which medical school training succeeds in overriding humanitarian ideals through its emphasis on technology and objectification of the patient (Davis-Floyd 1987:299). Since midwifery was legalized in Ontario in 1994, even midwives are using more medical technology to fulfill their professional obligations and to respond to the choices of their clients (MacDonald 2001).

Medical training can offer a particular challenge to women, as Perri Klass documents in *A Not Entirely Benign Procedure: Four Years as a Medical Student* (1987). She was especially challenged in making it through the "initiation" of medical school because she was pregnant during part of it and then a mother. Cynthia Carver (1981) provides an insider's view of medical training at the University of Toronto, where she saw her fellow students become more rigid, goal-oriented, disciplined, authoritarian, and more concerned with finances. Even in innovative medical schools such as McMaster Medical School in Hamilton, students learn careful self-presentation to convince others of their developing competence and professionalization (Haas and Shaffir 1982).

Similar studies of other biomedical specialists, such as surgeons, make the same point (Cassell 1991) and show how the power of the physician is correlated with the complexity of the technology they use. Other studies reveal the problem of reliance on technology when healing requires human understanding and interaction rather than machines (Fadiman 1997).

Clinical Medical Anthropology

Clinical medical anthropology, or applied medical anthropology, is the application of anthropological knowledge to further the goals of health care providers—that is, in improving doctor–patient understandings in multicultural settings, making recommendations about culturally appropriate health intervention programs, and providing insights about factors related to disease that medical practitioners do not usually take into account. For example, making use of ethnographic work on Ojibwa concepts of disease categories, a successful treatment program for diabetes was developed for Ojibwa in Toronto. The program was effective because it acknowledged the historical and social context of the disease and emphasized personal control over lifestyle in the rapidly changing urban environment of Toronto (Hagey 1984).

Although critical medical anthropology and clinical medical anthropology may seem diametrically opposed to each other (with the first seeking to critique and even limit the power and range of the medical establishment and the second seeking to make it more effective), some medical anthropologists are building bridges between the two perspectives.

An example of a clinical medical anthropologist who combines the two approaches is Robert Trotter (1987), who conducted research on lead poisoning among children in Mexican American communities. The three most common sources of lead poisoning of children in the United States are eating lead-based paint chips, living near a smelter where the dust has high lead content, and eating or drinking from pottery made with an improperly treated lead glaze. The discovery of an unusual case of lead poisoning by health professionals in Los Angeles in the early 1980s prompted investigations that produced understanding of a fourth cause: the use of a traditional healing remedy, *azarcon,* which contained lead, by people of the Mexican American community. *Azarcon* is given for the treatment of *empacho,* which is a combination of indigestion and constipation, believed to be caused by food sticking to the abdominal wall. Trotter then investigated the availability and use of *azarcon* in Mexico, and its distribution in the United States. His work resulted in restrictions on *azarcon* to prevent its further use, recommendations about the need to provide a substitute remedy for the treatment of *empacho* that would not have harmful side effects, and ideas about how to advertise this substitute. Throughout his involvement, Trotter combined several roles: researcher, consultant, and program developer, all of which brought anthropological knowledge toward the solution of a health problem.

Much work in clinical medical anthropology involves health communication (Nichter and Nichter 1996: 327–328). Anthropologists can help health educators in the development of more meaningful messages through

- addressing local images of ethnophysiology and acknowledging popular health concerns;
- taking seriously local illness terms and conventions;
- adopting local styles of communication;
- identifying subgroups within the population that may be responsive to different types of messages and incentives;
- monitoring the response of communities to health messages over time and facilitating corrections in communication when needed; and
- exposing possible victim-blaming in health messages.

These principles helped health care officials understand local response to public vaccination programs in several countries of Asia and Africa (Nichter 1996) (see the Lessons Applied box).

Communication through audio teleconferencing has also provided support to people in more remote or rural areas. In Newfoundland, women with a history of breast cancer found teleconferencing to be invaluable in dealing with the emotional upheaval of the disease. They needed to talk with other women who knew what living with breast cancer was about, particularly long-term survivors. With teleconferencing, one participant explained, the community didn't have "to know my business" (Church, Curran, and Solberg 2000:22).

Cross-cultural communication is also important in multicultural health settings in Canada, an issue addressed in the book *Cross-Cultural Caring: A Handbook for Health Professionals in Western Canada* (Waxler-Morrison, Anderson, and Richardson 1990). The authors provide culturally sensitive advice about the cultural context of disease to help practitioners make sense of their patients' distress. However, cultural sensitivity and even ethnic matching of patients and practitioners does not guarantee good health care.

Lessons Applied

PROMOTING VACCINATION PROGRAMS

VACCINATION PROGRAMS, especially as promoted by UNICEF, are often introduced in countries with much fanfare, but they are sometimes met with little enthusiasm by the target population. In India, many people are suspicious that vaccination programs are clandestine family planning programs (Nichter 1996). In other instances, fear of foreign vaccines prompts people to reject inoculations. Overall, acceptance rates of vaccination have been lower than Western public health planners expected. What factors have limited vaccination acceptance?

Public health planners have not paid enough attention to broad reasons that certain innovations are accepted or rejected. There have been problems in supply (clinics do not always have vaccines on hand). Cultural understandings of illness and the role of inoculations have not been considered. Surveys show that many mothers have a partial or inaccurate understanding of what the vaccines protect against. In some cases, people's perceptions and priorities did not match what the vaccines were supposed

to address. In others, people did not see the value of multiple vaccinations. In Indonesia, a once-vaccinated and healthy child was not considered to be in need of another inoculation.

Key features in the overall communication strategy are promoting trust in the public health program and providing locally sensible understandings of what the vaccinations do and do not do. Another important role that applied medical anthropologists play in promoting more effective public health communication is to work with public health specialists in enhancing their understanding of and attention to local cultural practices and beliefs.

FOOD FOR THOUGHT

Are all vaccines of unquestionable benefit to the recipients? Search the internet for information on new vaccines—for example, the vaccine against hookworm—in terms of their pros and possible cons.

GLOBALIZATION AND CHANGE

Perhaps no other aspect of Western society except the capitalist market system, and the English language, has so permeated the rest of the world as Western biomedicine. As biomedicine is adopted in other contexts, it undergoes localization and change. Medical anthropologists study how and why such change occurs and what the effects are on the people involved.

Globalization trends in the past decade have brought not only economic and political changes, but also medical changes. The flow of influence has mainly gone in the direction of spreading aspects of Western biomedicine to many parts of the world. Changes have also resulted in the increasing appreciation in the West for some aspects of non-Western healing, such as acupuncture. In this section we consider new and emerging health challenges, changes in healing practices, and the growing role of applied medical anthropology.

The New Infectious Diseases

The 1950s brought hope that infectious diseases were being controlled through Western scientific advances such as antibiotic drugs, vaccines against childhood diseases, and improved technology for sanitation. In North America, deaths from infections common in the late nineteenth and early twentieth centuries were no longer major threats in the 1970s. In tropical countries, pesticides lowered rates of malaria by controlling the mosquito populations. Since the 1980s, however, confidence that infectious diseases have been controlled has been shaken. Besides the spread of HIV (human immunodeficiency virus) and AIDS (acquired immune deficiency syndrome), another challenge is presented by the fact that many infectious microbes have reappeared in forms that are resistant to known methods of prevention and treatment. New contexts for exposure and contagion are being created through increased international travel and migration, expansion of populations into previously uninhabited forest areas, changing sexual behaviour, and overcrowding in cities. Several new and re-emerging diseases are caused by unsafe technological developments. For example, the introduction of soft contact lenses has caused eye infections from the virus *acanthamebiasis*. In the early 1980s, many women in North America were diagnosed with a

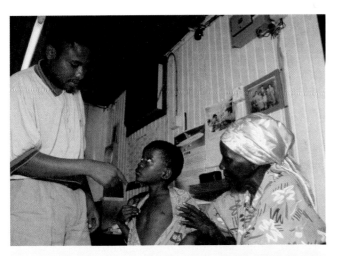

A woman takes her eight-year-old grandson who has HIV/AIDS to a clinic in Dar es Salaam, Tanzania. Throughout the world, increasing numbers of children are infected and are, at the same time, orphans because their parents have died of the disease.

new disease, toxic shock syndrome, caused by a bacterial toxin possibly related to dioxins, a by-product of the chlorine bleaching process used to bleach tampons.

Many medical anthropologists are contributing their expertise to understanding the causes for and distribution of the new infectious diseases through studying social patterns and cultural practices. Research about HIV/AIDS addresses factors such as intravenous drug use, sexual behaviour, and condom use among different groups and how intervention programs could be better designed and targeted (see the Critical Thinking box).

Diseases of Development

Diseases of development are diseases that are caused or increased by economic development activities (Hughes and Hunter 1970). Examples of diseases in this category are schistosomiasis, river blindness, malaria, and tuberculosis (Foster and Anderson 1978:27).

In many developing countries, dramatically increased rates of schistosomiasis (a disease caused by the presence of a parasitic worm in the blood system) have been traced to the construction of dams and irrigation systems. Over 200 million people suffer from this debilitating disease (Inhorn and Brown 1997:41). The larvae of this particular form of worm hatch from eggs and mature in slow-moving water such as lakes and rivers. Upon maturity, they can penetrate human (or other animal) skin with which they come into contact. People who wade or swim in infected waters are highly likely to become infected. Once inside the human body, the adult schistosomes breed in the veins around the human bladder and bowel. They

send fertilized eggs through urine and feces into the environment, which then continue to contaminate water in which the eggs hatch into larvae. Anthropologists' research has documented dramatic increases in the rates of schistosomiasis at high dam sites and artificial lakes, over the past four decades of dam construction in developing countries (Heyneman 1984). This heightened risk is caused by the dams slowing the rate of water flow. In stagnant water systems, as opposed to the undisturbed rapid flow, an ideal environment emerges for the development of the larvae. Many anthropologists have used this information to speak out against the construction of large dam projects.

Formerly unidentified diseases of development continue to appear. One of these is Kyasanur Forest disease, or KFD (Nichter 1992). This viral disease was first identified in 1957 in southern India:

> Resembling influenza, at onset KFD is marked by sudden chills, fever, frontal headaches, stiffness of the neck, and body pain. Diarrhea and vomiting often follow on the third day. High fever is continuous for five to fifteen days, during which time a variety of additional symptoms may manifest themselves, including gastrointestinal bleeding, persistent cough with blood-tinged sputum, and bleeding gums. In more serious cases, the infection progresses to bronchial pneumonia, meningitis, paralysis, encephalitis, and hemorrhage. (224)

In the early 1980s, an epidemic of KFD swept through over 30 villages in a part of Karnataka state near the Kyasanur Forest. During this time, mortality rates in hospitals ranged between 12 and 18 percent of those admitted. Investigation revealed that KFD especially affects agricultural workers and cattle tenders who were most exposed to newly cleared areas near the forest. In the cleared areas, international companies established plantations and initiated cattle raising. Ticks, which had long existed in the local ecosystem, increased in number in the cleared area and found inviting hosts in the cattle and their tenders. Thus, human modification of the ecosystem through deforestation and introduction of cattle raising caused the epidemic and shaped its social distribution.

Changes in Healing: Medical Pluralism

Contact between cultures sometimes leads to a situation in which aspects of both cultures coexist: two (or more) different languages, religions, systems of law, or health systems, for example. The term *pluralism* expresses the presence of multiple cultural options within a society; **medical pluralism** refers to a situation in which more than one medical/health system exists in a given society.

Medical pluralism provides both options and complications. First, something may be classified as a health problem in some cultures and not in others. For example, spirit

Critical Thinking

HIV/AIDS AND MEDICAL ANTHROPOLOGY

IN 2004, nearly 40 million people globally were living with HIV, and 60 percent of those infected were living in sub-Saharan Africa. In 2004, HIV took the lives of three million people worldwide. In Canada in 2004, around 56 000 people were living with HIV (UNAIDS 2004). What role do medical anthropologists play in the fight against HIV/AIDS? They bring special observational methods to HIV/AIDS research teams, often living among people with HIV/AIDS in order to understand barriers to HIV/AIDS prevention and treatment. Ultimately, medical anthropologists help make prevention and treatment programs more appropriate to the local context and language, and thus more effective. They combine qualitative and quantitative methods to explore complex and sensitive issues such as the interaction between gender, body image, and sexuality. They study the links between individual practices, cultural systems, and the larger political and economic forces shaping the disease. For example, this holistic approach has been effective in showing how AIDS relates to poverty.

The following examples show the kind of issues medical anthropologists are exploring in HIV/AIDS research, particularly on the topics of local perception of disease and on improving prevention and treatment programs.

- In the late 1980s, when HIV/AIDS was first recognized in Haiti, many Haitians thought it was a "disease of the city," contracted through sexual intercourse, or a "jealousy sickness" brought on one poor person by another through magic (Farmer 1990). The first explanation emphasizes the conventional biomedical definition of HIV/AIDS as an infectious disease; the second speaks to the Haitians' recognition of the social, political, and economic influences that render particular individuals or groups susceptible to illnesses of all kinds.
- San Jose prostitutes also recognize HIV/AIDS as an infectious disease, but locate it as part of a complex of contagion that includes drug abuse, diabetes, and violence (Downe 1997). While they are ready to embrace biomedicine—specifically "germs"—as a way to explain this contagion, they refuse to be defined as the vectors of the disease.
- A study assessing attitudes toward condom use among White, African American, and Hispanic respondents in the United States (Bowen and Trotter 1995) found that Whites were more likely to use condoms, followed by Hispanics, with lowest use among African Americans. Across all groups, people with "main partners" compared to "casual partners" were more likely to use

possession is welcomed in some cultures, but would be considered schizophrenia according to Western psychiatry. Second, the same symptoms may be classified as having different causes (such as supernatural versus germ theories) and therefore require different treatments. Third, certain treatment modalities may be rejected because they violate cultural rules. All of these issues affect how a particular culture will react to exogenous (outside) medical practices.

In some cases, we find the coexistence of alternative forms of healing that offer clients a range of choices. For example, traditional Chinese medicine, particularly acupuncture, is available in most Canadian cities as complementary treatment. In others cases, conflicting explanatory models of illness and healing result in serious misunderstandings between healers and clients.

When Explanatory Models Conflict

Many anthropologists have documented the disjuncture between biomedicine and local cultural patterns. In some instances, miscommunication occurs between biomedical doctors and clients in matters as seemingly simple as a prescription that should be taken with every meal. The doctor assumes that this means three times a day, but in some situations people do not eat three meals a day and thus unwittingly do not follow the doctor's instructions.

One anthropological study of a case in which death ultimately resulted from cross-cultural differences shows the complexity of communication across medical cultures. The F family are Samoan immigrants living in Honolulu, Hawaii (Krantzler 1987). Neither parent speaks English. Their children are "moderately literate" in English, but speak a mixture of English and Samoan at home. Mr. F was trained as a traditional Samoan healer. Mary, a daughter, was first stricken with diabetes at the age of 16. She was taken to the hospital by ambulance after collapsing, condoms, as were older people and people classified as having a higher level of personal assertiveness. Recommendations for increasing condom usage include targeted self-awareness programs and assertiveness training, especially for younger people in casual relationships.

- Dennis Willms, a medical anthropologist from McMaster University, has worked in Kenya, Uganda, Malawi, and South Africa helping to develop HIV/AIDS prevention and intervention programs based on qualitative ethnographic research. In Uganda, research demonstrated that the reasons many long-distance truck drivers have unsafe sex are related to poverty, marriage practices, and fatalism. Educational intervention on HIV/AIDS for traditional healers in Zimbabwe and Malawi helped faith communities provide more supportive care in their communities (Higginbotham, Willms, and Sewankambo 2001).
- Even preventive programs that emphasize social conditions can be ineffective in practice if bureaucracies stigmatize and target marginal groups, especially low-caste and ethnic minority sex workers. For example, in Nepal, Pigg (2001) found that groups working on AIDS prevention and treatment do not challenge power

relations that perpetuate patterns of ill health. Similarly, lack of informed consent and the need for constant attention to ethical issues in HIV/AIDS research are issues for anthropologists working in bureaucratic settings (de la Gorgendiere 2005).

Research on HIV infection among intravenous cocaine users in Montreal and Vancouver demonstrated that needle exchange programs alone cannot stem the spread of HIV. By integrating qualitative participant observation methods into the substance abuse and HIV prevention studies, anthropologist Philippe Bourgois and epidemiologist Julie Bruneau (2000) were able to show the broader social and economic context of needle exchange programs for street addicts in Montreal and Vancouver. Bourgois likens the Canadian drug policy to abusive parents who alternatively whip and pamper their children.

CRITICAL THINKING QUESTIONS

What concepts and skills have medical anthropologists brought to interdisciplinary health teams at home and internationally? Explore how HIV/AIDS could be researched from the perspective of the different approaches described in this chapter.

half-conscious, on the sidewalk near her home in a Honolulu housing project. After several months of irregular contact with medical staff, she was again brought to the hospital in an ambulance, unconscious, and she died there. Her father was charged with causing Mary's death through "medical neglect." Nora Krantzler analyzes this case from the perspectives of the Western medical providers and Samoan culture.

Mary was diagnosed with juvenile-onset diabetes mellitus and treated in a hospital. She and her family were taught how to give insulin injections and urine tests. However, Mary did not keep her appointments and returned to the hospital four months later, blind in one eye. Although told of the need for compliance, her father also insisted on preparing a potion to supplement the insulin. The medical experts increasingly judged that "cultural differences" were the basic problem, and that in spite of all their attempts to communicate with the F family, her family was basically incapable of caring for Mary.

The family's perspective, in contrast, was grounded in *fa'a Samoa,* the Samoan way. In the family's opinion, Mary never had a single physician responsible for her care and they were never given adequate explanation of her problem and its treatment. Thus, the family lost trust in the hospital and began to rely on the father's skill as a healer.

While cultural differences may cause problems of communication, they may also marginalize certain groups and deny them adequate health care services. Dara Culhane Speck's ethnography of the politics of health care in a First Nations community on Alert Bay, adjacent to the northeastern end of Vancouver Island, British Columbia, is a powerful indictment of Native–White relations and the consequences of the destruction of an indigenous health care system. *An Error in Judgement* (1987) documents the death from an undiagnosed ruptured appendix of Renee Smith, an 11-year-old Nimpkish girl. The island's sole medical practitioner was considered responsible for the girl's death through his negligence, alcoholism, and racism; nevertheless, community members were reluctant to lose access to the doctor and the community hospital.

The family and leaders of the Nimpkish band wrote to the Attorney General of British Columbia, the provincial Minister of Health, and the College of Physicians and Surgeons to complain about the quality of health care on the island and to request an inquiry into the deaths of band members. In 1974, the British Columbia Medical Association published a report on *Native Health*, stressing that Natives fail to recognize early symptoms of illness; have a higher tolerance for pain and discomfort and a fatalistic acceptance of things as they are; and present themselves in the acute and often fatal stages of an illness (Culhane Speck 1987:100).

The report perpetuated the idea that Natives were responsible for the quality of health care they received. In 1980, the Government of Canada Inquiry into Indian Health and Health Care in Alert Bay was convened. According to the Nimpkish Band Council, the community wanted to know why their rates of hospitalization and death were so high: ". . . why is our life expectancy so low? Why is our survival threatened? What is the quality of our health care services? Why have so many of our people lost confidence in the health care we have been receiving?" (Culhane Speck 1987:234). Answers to these and other questions probably lie in the complex ethnohistory of British Columbia (Kelm 1999).

Selective Pluralism

The Sherpas of Nepal offer an unusual example of a newly capitalizing context in which preference for traditional healing systems remains strong, along with the adoption of certain aspects of biomedicine (V. Adams 1988). Former pastoralist–farmers, the Sherpas are now heavily involved in providing services for international tourism. They work as guides, porters, cooks, and administrators in trekking agencies, and in hotels and restaurants. Thus, many Sherpas are well acquainted with the cosmopolitan cultures of international travellers (506). The wide variety of healing therapies available in the Upper Khumbu region fit into three general categories: (1) orthodox Buddhist practitioners, such as lamas, who are consulted for both prevention and cure through their blessings, and *amchis*, who practise Tibetan medicine, a system largely derived from India's Ayurvedic medicine; (2) unorthodox religious or shamanic practitioners, who perform divination ceremonies for diagnosis; and (3) biomedical practitioners, who initially used their diagnostic techniques and medicines for tourists, and then established a permanent medical facility in 1967.

In Khumbu, traditional healers are thriving and in no way threatened by wider economic changes brought by the tourist trade and influx of wealth. The reason is that high-mountain tourism is a particular form of capitalist

Among the many forms of medical treatment available to the Sherpa of Nepal, shamanic healing remains a popular choice.

development that does not radically change the social relations involved in production. This type of tourism brings in money but does not require large-scale capital investment from outside. Thus the Sherpas maintain control of their productive resources, their family structures remain largely the same, and wider kinship ties remain important in the organization of tourist business.

Canadian medical anthropologist Stacey Pigg (1996) found that shamanic healing is also central to experiences of modernity in Kathmandu, Nepal, where ritual healing thrives alongside biomedical services.

Since 1978, the World Health Organization (WHO) has endorsed the incorporation of traditional medicine, especially healers, in national health systems (Velimirovic 1990). This policy emerged in response to increasing levels of national pride in local medical traditions and to the shortage of trained biomedical personnel. Debates continue about the synthesis of traditional and modern biomedicine, and the relative efficacy of many traditional medical practices compared to biomedicine. For instance, opponents of the promotion of traditional medicine claim that it has no effect on such infectious diseases as cholera, malaria, tuberculosis, schistosomiasis, leprosy, and others. They insist that it makes no sense to allow for or encourage ritual practices against malaria, for example, when a child has not been inoculated against it. Supporters of traditional medicine as one aspect of a planned, pluralistic medical system, point out that biomedicine neglects a person's mind and soul while traditional medicine is more holistic. Also, indigenous curers are more likely to know clients and their families, thus facilitating therapy. Nevertheless, critical medical anthropologists point out that international health policy still has the power to define what is traditional and therefore worthy of being included in WHO training programs.

One area where progress has been made in maintaining positive aspects of traditional health care is in midwifery. WHO assists many developing country governments with training programs that equip traditional birth attendants (TBAs) with rudimentary training in germ theory and provide them with basic "kits" that include a clean razor blade for cutting the umbilical cord. The many thousands of TBAs working at the grassroots level around the world thus are not squeezed out of their work, but continue to perform their important role with some enhanced skills and tools.

WHAT does medical anthropology contribute to understanding illness cross-culturally?

The relatively young subfield of medical anthropology, within cultural anthropology, has pursued several directions of research. In the first, which emphasizes the links between ecological or environmental factors and social factors, medical anthropologists have shown how certain categories of people are at risk of contracting particular diseases, within various contexts in historical times and the present. Research on ethnomedicine reveals both differences and similarities across medical systems in perceptions of illness and symptoms. Culture-bound syndromes are illnesses that appear not to be universal in the way they cluster symptoms. The interpretive approach addresses health and illness as sets of meanings. Critical medical anthropologists reveal where social inequality and poverty contribute to certain kinds of illnesses. Clinical medical anthropologists work to apply information on cultural practices and beliefs about illness to improve how health care is provided.

WHAT does medical anthropology contribute to understanding healing systems cross-culturally?

Research in ethnomedicine shows how perceptions of the body differ cross-culturally. Ethnomedical studies of healing modalities, healers, and healing substances encompass a wide range of approaches. Community healing systems are more characteristic of non-industrial societies and they emphasize group interaction and treating the individual within the social context. In industrial societies, biomedicine emphasizes the body as a discrete unit, and treat-

ment addresses the individual body or mind. The interpretive approach places in the forefront the study of meaning in illness and healing. Medical anthropology research in this area shows how, cross-culturally, the definitions of affliction and suffering are embedded in meaning and so are methods of prevention and healing. This approach places a high value on looking at the placebo effect in different cultural contexts. Critical medical anthropology locates healing and healers in systems of control and power. They have pointed to two trends: the medicalization of problems that are social, and the exclusion of the poor from health care. In their examination of Western medicine, critical medical anthropologists show how this system, rather than being one of purely humanitarian care, is part of powerful structures that put the physician in the role of a controlling, detached, technical expert. In contrast to critical medical anthropology, clinical medical anthropology seeks to make biomedicine more effective by providing cultural information to its practitioners. Clinical anthropologists are at the forefront of helping biomedical clinicians prevent diagnostic and communication errors when dealing with people who have alternative medical models.

HOW are illness and healing changing during globalization?

Health systems everywhere are facing accelerated change from globalization and the spread of Western biomedicine, a process that has prompted reconsideration of "traditional" medicine and its potential. Along with the growth and expansion of global market economics and political structures, Western biomedicine is also spreading. One result is that most countries now are characterized by medical pluralism, through which people can choose to consult healers from one or more systems.

KEY CONCEPTS

clinical medical anthropology, p. 159
community healing, p. 152
critical medical anthropology, p. 157
culture-bound syndromes, p. 149
diseases of development, p. 161
divination, p. 151
ecological/epidemiological approach, p. 155

ethnobotany, p. 154
ethnomedicine, p. 146
humoral healing systems, p. 153
medical pluralism, p. 161
medicalization, p. 157
placebo effect, p. 157
shaman, p. 154

SUGGESTED READINGS

Elois Berlin and Brent Berlin, *Medical Ethnobiology of the Highland Maya of Chiapas, Mexico*. Princeton: Princeton University Press, 1996. This detailed report discusses the range of gastrointestinal diseases classified by the highland Maya, including the diarrheas, abdominal pains, and worms, and how the Maya use knowledge of plants to treat them within a humoral system.

Nancy N. Chen, *Breathing Spaces: Qigong, Psychiatry, and Healing in China*. New York: Columbia University Press, 2003. Taking a critical medical anthropology approach, this ethnography explores *qigong*, a charismatic form of healing based on meditative breathing exercises. The author places her study in the context of capitalist and Western psychiatric globalization, and their impacts on the lives of people in China.

Paul Farmer, *AIDS and Accusation: Haiti and the Geography of Blame*. Berkeley: University of California Press, 1992. This text combines attention to the global structures related to the spread of HIV/AIDS with in-depth study in one village in Haiti where HIV/AIDS is locally interpreted as one more phase in people's long-term exposure to afflictions and suffering.

Richard Katz, *Boiling Energy: Community Healing among the Kalahari Kung*. Cambridge: Harvard University Press, 1982. This account of the healing practices of the Ju/wasi (!Kung) of the Dobe area between Namibia and Botswana focuses on several different healers, their training, and styles.

Emily Martin, *The Woman in the Body: A Cultural Analysis of Reproduction*. Boston: Beacon Press, 1987. This text explores how Western medical texts represent women's reproductive experiences and how they compare to a sample of Baltimore women's perceptions and experiences of menstruation, childbirth, and menopause.

Carol Shepherd McClain, ed., *Women as Healers: A Cross-Cultural Perspective*. New Brunswick, NJ: Rutgers University Press, 1989. This collection of 11 studies is preceded by a general overview. Case studies include Ecuador, Sri Lanka, Mexico, Jamaica, the United States, Serbia, Korea, southern Africa, and Benin.

Sherry Saggers and Dennis Gray, *Dealing with Alcohol: Indigenous Usage in Australia, New Zealand and Canada*. New York: Cambridge University Press, 1998. This comparative study looks at structural issues such as European colonialism and interests of liquor companies in creating and sustaining high rates of alcohol consumption among many indigenous groups, and people's own understanding of their situation.

J. Waldram, A. Herring, and K. Young, *Aboriginal Health in Canada: Historical, Cultural, and Epidemiological Perspectives*. Toronto: University of Toronto Press, 1995. This volume offers very comprehensive coverage of First Nations health issues and includes discussions of current health problems, an overview of health and health care from an historical perspective, and ideas on what future changes need to be made.

WEBLINKS

The Companion Website (www.pearsoned.ca/miller) that accompanies *Cultural Anthropology*, Third Canadian Edition, includes a destinations module containing links to many websites relevant to the content of this chapter. Use it to investigate the Web and expand your understanding of anthropology.

KEY QUESTIONS

- • **HOW** do cultures define kinship through descent?
- • **HOW** do cultures define kinship through sharing?
- • **HOW** do cultures define kinship through marriage?

8

KINSHIP DYNAMICS

A wedding procession of a Minangkabau couple in Sumatra, Indonesia. The bride wears an elaborate gold headdress, typical of the Minangkabau, as is the groom's turban.

Learning another culture's kinship system is as challenging as learning another language. This was true for Robin Fox (1995) during his research among the Tory Islanders of Ireland. Some of the Irish kinship terms and categories he encountered were similar to North American English usage, but others were not. For example, the word *muintir* can mean "people" in its widest sense, as in English. It can also refer to people of a particular social category, as in "my people," that refers to close relatives.

Another similarity is with *gaolta*, the word for "relatives" or "those of my blood." In its adjectival form, *gaolta* refers to "kindness," like the English word *kin*. Tory Islanders have a phrase meaning "children and grandchildren," also like the English term *descendants*. The word for *friend* on Tory Island is the same as the word for *kin*, reflecting the cultural circumstances on Tory Island with its small population, all living close together: Everyone is related by kinship, so, logically, friends are kin.

Studying kinship systems offers surprising discoveries. In some cultures, an uncle has a closer relationship with his sister's children than with his own children. In others, a child considers his or her mother's sisters as mothers and is close to all of them. Cousins, including first cousins (offspring of one's mother's and father's siblings), are preferred as marriage partners in much of the Middle East and in parts of South Asia, where cousin marriages are both common and legal. In Canada first cousin marriage is legal but not preferred. In the United States some states allow first cousin marriage; others forbid it on the assumption that first cousin marriage may result in the birth of children with genetic defects. In some cultures, a person may have more than one spouse. Increasing numbers of people in Europe and North America choose to cohabit with a partner and never get married.

The closest and most intense human relationships often involve people who consider themselves related to each other through kinship. All cultures have ideas about what defines a kinship relationship and rules for appropriate behaviour between kin. These rules can be informal or formally defined by law, such as a law forbidding marriage between first cousins. Everyone begins learning about his or her particular culture's **kinship system** (the combination of ideas about who are kin and what kinds of behaviour kinship relationships involve) from infancy. Like one's first language, one's kinship system becomes so ingrained that it tends to be taken for granted as something "natural" rather than cultural.

Gathering data on kinship is basic to most anthropological research projects because one of the first fieldwork tasks is to learn "who is who." Areas of questioning include asking informants about who they live with, whether or not they are married, how many children they have, and who in their family may have died. In many cultures, the researcher finds that people openly provide such information. In other situations, gathering accurate kinship data may be difficult. In Canada, an example of potential bias in gathering kinship data relates to rules about the welfare system. Among low-income people on welfare, a woman is eligible for welfare payments only if she is not married (either formally or through common law). In order to protect her eligibility for welfare payments, a married woman may report herself as living alone even if she has a permanent, co-resident partner.

THE STUDY OF KINSHIP

In all cultures, kinship links modes of production, reproduction, and ideology. Depending on the type of economy, it accordingly shapes children's physical growth and personality development, influences a person's marriage options, and affects the status and care of the aged. In small-scale pre-industrial cultures, kinship is the primary, and often only, principle that organizes people into coherent and meaningful groups. In such contexts, the kinship group performs the functions of ensuring the continuity of the group through arranging marriages; maintaining social order through setting moral rules and punishing offenders; and providing for the basic needs of members through regulating production, consumption, and distribution. In large-scale industrial societies, kinship ties exist, but many other forms of social affiliation draw people together into groups that have nothing to do with kinship.

Early anthropologists documented the importance of kinship in the societies they researched. Lewis Henry Morgan and others argued that kinship was the most important organizing principle in non-state cultures. They also discovered that definitions of who counts as kin differed from those of contemporary Europe and North America. Western cultures emphasize "blood" relations as primary; that is, relations between people linked by birth from a biological mother and father (Sault 1994). Ties through marriage are secondary. This model is expressed in the English-language adage: "blood is thicker than water." Not all cultures define who is a "blood" relative in the same way. In some, males in the family are of one "blood" (or "substance"), while females are of another. This contrasts with the Euro-American definition that all biological children of the same parents share the same "blood." In yet other cultures, a more important criterion for kinship is breastfeeding: Babies who were nursed by the same woman are considered related and cannot marry each other. The popular Western view of kinship as based on "blood" relationships and its contemporary grounding in a genetic relationship with the birth mother and "procreative father" (the male who provides the semen that fertilizes the female's ovum) is so widely accepted as real and natural that understanding other kinship theories is difficult for Westerners.

Kinship Analysis

Early anthropological work on kinship tended to focus on finding out who is related to whom and in what way. Typically, the anthropologist would interview one or two people, asking questions such as: What do you call your brother's daughter? Can you (as a man) marry your father's brother's daughter? What is the term you use to refer to your mother's sister? In another approach, in an interview the anthropologist would ask an individual to name all his or her relatives, explain how they are related to the interviewee, and provide the terms by which they refer to him or her.

From this kind of reported information, the anthropologist would construct a **kinship diagram**, a schematic way of presenting data on the kinship relationships of an individual, called "ego" (see Figure 8.1). This diagram depicts all of ego's relatives, as remembered by ego and reported to the anthropologist. Strictly speaking, information gained from the informant for his or her kinship diagram is not supplemented by asking other people to fill in where ego's memory failed (as contrast to a genealogy; see below). In cultures where kinship plays a greater role in social relations, it is likely that an informant will be able to provide information on more relatives than in one where kinship ties are less important in comparison to other networks such as friendships and work groups.

In contrast to a kinship diagram, a **genealogy** is constructed by beginning with the earliest ancestors (rather than starting with ego and working outward) that can be traced and working down to the present. The Tory Islanders were not comfortable beginning with ego when Robin Fox was attempting to construct kinship diagrams. They preferred to proceed genealogically, so he followed their preference. Tracing a family's complete genealogy may involve archival research in the attempt to construct as full a record as possible. Many cultures have trained genealogists whose task is to help families discover or maintain records of their family lines. In Europe and North America, Christians often record their "family tree" in the front of the family Bible.

Decades of anthropological research have produced a mass of information on kinship terminology, or the terms that people use to refer to people they consider to be kin

FIGURE 8.1 Symbols Used in Kinship Diagrams

Characters	Relationships	Kin Abbreviations
◯ female	= is married to	**Mo** mother
△ male	≈ is cohabiting with	**Fa** father
⊘ deceased female	≠ is divorced from	**Br** brother
⩘ deceased male	≉ is separated from	**Z** sister
● female "ego" of the diagram	⊙ adopted-in female	**H** husband
▲ male "ego" of the diagram	⧌ adopted-in male	**W** wife
◼ "ego," regardless of gender	│ is descended from	**Da** daughter
	⊓ is the sibling of	**S** son

of various types. For example, in Euro-American kinship, children of one's father's sister and brother and one's mother's sister and brother are all referred to by the same kinship term: cousins. Likewise, one's father's sister (aunt) and brother (uncle) and one's mother's sister and brother have the same terms. And the terms *grandmother* and *grandfather* can refer to the ascending generation on either one's father's or mother's side. In some cultures, different terms are used for kin on one's mother's and father's side. In North India, one's father's brother is called *chacha*, and one's mother's brother *mama*; one's father's father is *baba* and one's mother's father is *nana*. Another type of system emphasizes solidarity along lines of siblings of the same gender, so that one's mother and mother's sisters all have the same term, which translates as "mother." This system is found among the Navajo, for example.

Anthropologists have classified the cross-cultural variety in kinship terminology into six basic types, named after groups that were first discovered to have that type of system; for example, there is an "Iroquois" type and an "Eskimo" type (see Figure 8.2). Cultures that have similar kinship terminology are then placed into one of the six categories. The Yanomami would, in this way, be identified as having an Iroquois naming system. (Our perspective is that memorizing these six types of terminology is not a fruitful way to promote understanding of actual kinship dynamics, the focus of this chapter, so this text avoids going into detail on them.)

Toward Kinship in Action

The formalism of early kinship studies led many students of anthropology—and some of their professors—to think that kinship is a boring subject. Fortunately, a renewed

interest in kinship is occurring that considers it in relation to other topics such as power relations, reproductive decision making, women's changing work roles, and ethnic identity (Carsten 2000). While we can leave much of the terminology behind, some of the complexity of kinship systems cross-culturally must be faced. Margaret Trawick (1992) offers these insights in her book on Tamil kinship in South India:

> Tamils and neighboring peoples have a very elegant set of ways of organizing their families and larger kin groups into patterned systems. Any person trying to understand South Indian culture must eventually come round to examining and trying to comprehend these elegant patterns of kinship organization. . . . I would argue that South Indian people create such patterns not only because they "work," not only because they perform some necessary social "function," but also because, in their beauty, they give their creators pleasure. . . . Kinship patterns can be understood as objects of artistic appreciation, in the same way that mathematical proofs or car engines are, for some people, such objects. Opening the hood of a fancy sports car, some of us will see nothing but a confusing jumble of ugly machinery. Others, who understand such things, will be perfused with bliss. It is the same with kinship patterns. (117–118)

As anthropologists attempt to study kinship as a dynamic aspect of life, they are increasingly turning to varied sources of data gathering, rather than simply interviewing informants. Participant observation is extremely valuable for learning about who interacts with whom, how they interact with each other, and why their relationship has the content it has. Observations can provide understanding, for example, of the frequency and intensity of people's kinship interactions and the degree to which they have supportive social networks. Another

FIGURE 8.2 Two Kinship Naming Systems

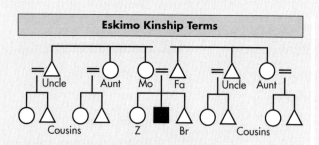

Eskimo kinship terminology, like that of most Euro-Americans, has unique terms for kin within the nuclear family that are not used for any other relatives: mother, father, sister, brother. This fact is related to the freestanding aspect of the nuclear family. Another feature is that the same terms are used for relatives on both the mother's and father's sides, which is related to bilateral descent.

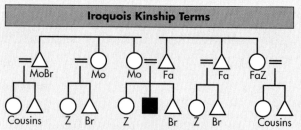

Iroquois kinship terminology operates in unilineal systems. One result is that there are different terms for relatives on the mother's and father's sides and distinctions between cross- and parallel cousins. Another feature is the "merging" of one's mother with one's mother's sister (both are referred to as "mother") and one's father with one's father's brother (both are referred to as "father").

approach, the life history method (see Chapter 2), reveals changes through an individual's lifetime and the way they are related to other events such as migration, a natural disaster, or political change. Focused life histories are useful in targeting key events related to kinship, such as marriage or cohabitation, divorce, or widowhood/widowerhood. Anthropologists interested in population dynamics, for example, use focused life histories, interviews, and questionnaires to gather information on personal demographics to learn at what age a woman commenced sexual relations, how many pregnancies she had, if and when she had an abortion or bore a child, whether the child lived or died, and when she stopped having children.

DESCENT

Descent is the tracing of kinship relationships through parentage. It is based on the fact that everybody is born from someone else. Descent creates a line of people from whom someone is descended, stretching through history. But not all cultures reckon descent in the same way. Some cultures have a **bilateral descent** system, in which a child is recognized as being related by descent to both parents. Others have a **unilineal descent** system, which recognizes descent through only one parent, either the father or mother. The distribution of bilateral and unilineal systems can be correlated with different modes of production. This correspondence makes sense because economies—production, consumption, and exchange—are tied to the way people and their labour power are organized and how commodities are used and transferred. Examples of this correlation are discussed in the following section. We begin with the descent system that is the most prevalent cross-culturally.

Unilineal Descent

Unilineal descent systems are the basis of kinship in about 60 percent of the world's cultures, making some form of unilineality the most common form of descent. In general, unilineal systems characterize societies with a "fixed" resource base, such as crop land or herds over which people have some sense of ownership. Inheritance rules that regulate the transmission of property through only one line help maintain cohesiveness of the resource base. Unilineal systems thus are most associated with horticultural, pastoralist, and agricultural modes of production. Unilineal descent systems have higher frequencies of extended families than bilateral cultures (discussed in Chapter 9).

Two patterns of unilineal descent are **patrilineal descent**, in which kinship is traced through the male line alone, and **matrilineal descent**, in which, kinship is traced through

the female line alone. In both unilineal systems, children are usually considered full members of the lineage. However, in a patrilineal system, upon marriage women typically become members of their husband's lineage. In the matrilineal descent system only daughters carry on the family line. However, sons typically retain important rights in their matrilineage even after marriage. The two systems are not simple mirror images of one another.

The question of why a particular culture is matrilineal or patrilineal has not been resolved, but patrilineality and matrilineality may indicate the relative status of men and women in each system. Members of the gender that controls the resources (both productive and reproductive) tend to have higher status. Thus, in general, women have higher status in matrilineal societies and men have higher status in patrilineal societies. The question of why a particular kinship system is matrilineal or patrilineal is still a puzzle.

Patrilineal Descent

Patrilineal descent is found among about 44 percent of all cultures. It is prevalent throughout much of India, East Asia, the Middle East, Papua New Guinea, northern Africa, and some horticultural groups of sub-Saharan Africa. Cultures with patrilineal descent tend to have ideologies that are consistent with that concept. For example, theories of how conception occurs and how the fetus is formed give priority to the male role. Among the Kaliai people of Papua New Guinea, people say that an infant is composed entirely of *aitama aisuru*, the "father's water" or semen, which is channelled to the fetus. The mother is an "incubator" who contributes nothing substantial to the developing fetus. The mother's relationship with the infant develops later, through breastfeeding.

Margery Wolf's book, *The House of Lim* (1968), is a classic ethnography of a patrilineal system. She lived for two years with the Lims, a Taiwanese farming household (see Figure 8.3). In her book, she first describes the village setting and then the Lims' house, giving attention to the importance of the ancestral hall with its family altar, where the household head meets guests. She then provides a chapter on Lim Han-ci, the father and household head, and then a chapter on Lim Hue-lieng, the eldest son. She then introduces the females of the family: wives, sisters, and an adopted daughter. The ordering of the chapters reflects the importance of the "patriarch" (senior, most powerful male) and his eldest son who will, if all goes according to plan, assume the leadership position as his father ages and then dies. Daughters marry out into other families. In-marrying females (wives, daughters-in-law) are always considered outsiders, never fully merged into the patrilineage. The Lims' kinship system exemplifies strong patrilineality in that it heavily weights position, power, and property with males. In such systems, girls are raised "for other families" and are thus not fully members of their natal (birth) family; however, they never become fully merged into their marriage family, always being considered somehow "outsiders." Residence of married couples is typically **patrilocal**, with or near the husband's natal family. The world's most strongly patrilineal systems are found in East Asia, South Asia, and the Middle East (see the Multiple Cultural Worlds box).

Matrilineal Descent

Matrilineal descent exists in about 15 percent of all cultures. It traces kinship through the female line exclusively, and children belong to their mother's group. Less common than patrilineal descent, it is found among many Native North American groups; across a large band in central Africa; among many groups of Southeast Asia, the Pacific, and Australia; in parts of eastern and southern India; in a small pocket of northern Bangladesh; and in localized areas of the Mediterranean coast of Spain and Portugal. Matrilineal societies vary greatly, from foragers such as the Tiwi of northern Australia to settled ranked societies such as the Nayar of southern India (Lepowsky 1993:296). The majority, however, are found in horticultural systems where women have primacy in production and distribution of food and other goods.

Married couples tend to reside **matrilocally**; that is, with or near the wife's natal family. Often, but not always, matrilineal kinship is associated with recognized public leadership positions for women, as among the Iroquois or Hopi. In general, women's status is likely to be higher in matrilineal descent systems than in patrilineal descent systems.

In matrilineal cultures, ideologies about conception give primacy to female contributions to the fetus. Among the Malays of Langkawi Island, people say that children are created from the seed of their father and the blood of their mother (Carsten 1995:229). The seed spends 40 days inside the body of the father. The first, fifteenth, and thirtieth days of the month are the days on which "the seed falls." Then the seed "descends to the mother." There it mixes with her menstrual blood. It has only to mix with the mother's menstrual blood once in order to conceive. After that, the seed is nourished in the mother's womb from her blood.

The Minangkabau (pronounced "mee-NAN-ka-bow," the last syllable rhyming with "now") of Indonesia are the largest matrilineal group in the world (Sanday 2002; Blackwood 1995). They are primarily rural agriculturalists, producing substantial amounts of surplus rice, but many of them also participate in migratory labour, working for wages in Indonesian cities for a time, and then returning home. In their matrilineal kinship system,

FIGURE 8.3 The Lim Family of Taiwan

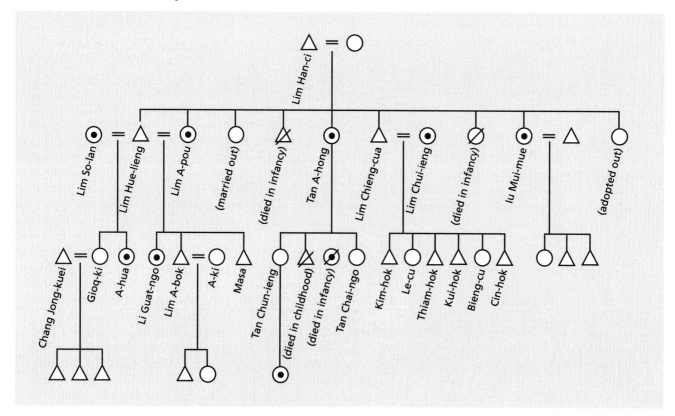

Multiple Cultural Worlds

THE NAMED AND THE NAMELESS IN A CANTONESE VILLAGE

THE VILLAGE of Ha Tsuen is located in the northwest corner of a rural area of Hong Kong's New Territories (Watson 1986). About 2500 people live in the village. All the males belong to the same patrilineage and have the same surname of Teng. They are descended from a common ancestor who settled in the region in the twelfth century. In Ha Tsuen, as in its wider region, kinship is reckoned patrilineally. Daughters of Ha Tsuen marry out of the village. Sons of Ha Tsuen marry brides who come in from other villages, and marital residence is patrilocal. In Ha Tsuen, as in most strongly patrilineal systems, women do not own property, and they have no direct control of the means of production. Few married women are employed in wage labour; rather, they depend on their husbands for financial support. Local politics is a male domain, as is all public decision making. Women's primary role is in reproduction, especially of sons. A woman's status as a new bride is low; indeed, the transition from daughter to bride can be difficult psychologically. As a woman bears children, especially sons, her status in the household increases.

The naming system reflects the greater power, importance, and autonomy of males. A child is first given a name referred to as his or her *ming* when it is 30 days old. Before that time, the mother and infant are secluded to prevent soul loss in the infant. The thirtieth-day ceremony is as elaborate as the family can afford if the baby is a boy, including a banquet for neighbours and village elders, and the presentation of red eggs to everyone in the community. For a girl, the thirtieth-day ceremony is likely to involve just a special meal for close family members. Paralleling this bias toward sons in monetary expenditure is the amount of thinking that goes into the selection of the *ming* and its meaning. A boy's *ming* is more distinctive and flattering, perhaps having a literary or classical connection. A girl's *ming* often has a negative connotation, such as "Last Child," "Too Many," "Little Mistake," or "Joined to a Brother," which implies hope

that this daughter will be a lucky charm to bring the birth of a son next. Uncomplimentary names may be given to a boy, but the goal is for protection: to trick the spirits into thinking he is only a worthless girl so that they won't take him. Thus, a precious son may be given the *ming* "Little Slave Girl."

Marriage is the next formal naming occasion. When a male marries, he is given or chooses for himself a *tzu,* or marriage name. Gaining a *tzu* is an integral part of the marriage ceremony and a key marker of male adulthood. The *tzu* is not used in everyday address, but appears mainly on formal documents. A man will have a *wai hao,* "outside name," which is his public nickname. As he enters middle age, he may also take a *hao,* or courtesy name, which he chooses and which reflects his self-aspirations and self-perceptions. In the case of a woman, her *ming* ceases to exist upon marriage. She no longer has a name, but instead her husband refers to her as *nei jen,* "inner person," since now her life is restricted to the domestic world of household, husband's family, and neighbourhood. In her new world of kin, she is referred to by **teknonyms** (names for someone based on their relationship to someone else), such as "Wife of So and So" or "Mother of So and So." Her personhood and identity are rigidly defined by the kinship system and her names will be derived from her place in that system. In old age, she becomes *ah po,* "Old Woman," like every other aged female in the village.

Throughout their lives, men accumulate more and better names than women, and they can choose them themselves. Over the course of their lives, women have fewer names than men. Women's names are standardized rather than personalized, and they have no control over them.

FOOD FOR THOUGHT

Do you know of any examples of naming biases determined by a child's gender, birth order, or other basis?

women hold power through their control of lineage land and its products and of agricultural employment on their land and through their pre-eminent position in business (especially having to do with rice). Inheritance passes from mothers to daughters, making the matrilineal line the enduring controller of property. Each submatrilineage, constituting perhaps four generations, lives together in a

lineage house or several closely located houses. The senior woman has the power—her decisions are sought in terms of all economic and ceremonial matters. She is called *Bundo Kanduang,* "womb mother" or "elder woman" or "wise woman." Her advice is respected by all, although group consensus (not dictatorial power of the senior woman) is the guiding principle in group dynamics and is shaped by all senior members. The senior male of the sublineage has the role of representing its interests to other groups, but he is only a representative, not a powerful person in his own right.

Matrilineal kinship appears to be declining worldwide in the face of globalized Western/European cultural forces, such as colonialism and neo-colonialism, which have had a strong effect in establishing patrilineal kinship norms through the spread of Western education, religion, and law. European colonial rule in Africa and Asia contributed to the decline in matrilineal kinship by registering land and other property in the names of assumed male heads of households, even where females were the heads (Boserup 1970). This process effectively eroded women's previous rights and powers. Western missionary influence throughout much of the world also transformed matrilineal cultures into more patrilineal systems (Etienne and Leacock 1980). European influences have led to the decline of matrilineal kinship among Native North Americans, which have long constituted one of the largest distributions of matrilineal descent worldwide (although not all Native North American groups were or are matrilineal). A comparative study of kinship among three diverse areas of the Navajo reservation in Arizona shows that matrilineality exists where conditions most resemble the pre-reservation era (Levy, Henderson, and Andrews 1989). In the case of the Minangkabau of Indonesia, matrilineal kinship is being undermined by the combined forces of Dutch colonialism, which promoted the image of male-led nuclear families as an ideal; the Islamic faith, which currently promotes female domesticity and male household dominance; and the modernizing Indonesian state, which insists on naming males as heads of households (see Chapter 9) (Blackwood 1995).

Double Descent

A minority of cultures have **double descent** systems (also called *double unilineal descent*) that combine patrilineal and matrilineal descent. In these systems, offspring are believed to inherit different personal attributes and property from both their father's line and their mother's line. Many early anthropologists mistook this mixed system for a patrilineal system, demonstrating once again the power of ethnocentrism in interpretation. For example, the Bangangté of Cameroon in West Africa have a double descent system, although it was first described by anthropologists as patrilineal (Feldman-Savelsberg 1995). This misrepresentation was probably the result of interviewing only men and focusing on the inheritance of land property rather than on other traits. "While Bangangté, in their conversations with inquisitive anthropologists, first list the property and titles they inherit from their

fathers, they present a much more complex picture to those who listen further" (486). Research among married women uncovered double descent. Through the maternal line, one inherits movable property (such as household goods and cattle), personality traits, and a type of witchcraft substance that resides in the intestines. Patrilineal ties determine physical resemblance and rights to land and village residence. Matrilineally related women tend to bond together and visit each other frequently, consulting on marriage partners for their children, advising on child naming choices, and supporting each other in times of trouble.

Bilateral Descent

Bilateral descent traces kinship from both parents equally to the child. Family groups tend to be nuclear, with strong bonds between father, mother, and their children. Marital residence is predominantly **neolocal**, that is, residence for the newly married couple is somewhere away from the residences of both the bride's and the groom's parents. Neolocality offers more flexibility than what is usual in unilineal systems. Inheritance of property from the parental generation is allocated equally among all offspring regardless of their gender. In bilateral descent systems, conception theories can emphasize an equal biological contribution to the child from the mother and father. For example, contemporary Western science states that the sperm contributed by the male and the ovum contributed by the female are equally important in the formation of a new person.

Bilateral descent is found in less than one-third of the world's cultures (Murdock 1965:57). The highest frequency of bilateral descent is found at the opposite ends of the production continuum. For example, the Ju/wasi have bilateral descent, and most people think bilateral descent is the prevalent pattern in North America (see the Critical Thinking box). A minority pattern of bilateral descent is called **ambilineal descent**. This system recognizes that a person is descended from both parents, but allows individuals to decide with which descent group to be more closely affiliated. Such a culture is therefore characterized by **bilocal** residence, that is, a choice is available between living near or with the family of either the groom or the bride. For example, in Tahiti, newly married couples choose to live with or near either the bride's or the groom's family, with no particular preference involved (Lockwood 1993).

Given that most of the world's people recognize some connection between a baby and both parents, it is puzzling as to why the majority of kinship systems are unilineal and thus emphasize only one parent. Evolutionists of the late 1800s claimed that in early societies, the father was not known. Bilateral kinship, they said, emerged as

Critical Thinking

HOW BILATERAL IS "AMERICAN KINSHIP"?

"AMERICAN KINSHIP" refers to a general model based on the bilateral system of Euro-Americans of the 1960s (Schneider 1968). According to this model, children are considered to be descended from both mother and father, and general inheritance rules suggest that property would be divided equally between sons and daughters. Given the rich cultural diversity of the United States and Canada, most would now consider the label "American kinship" and its characterization as bilateral to be overgeneralized. Biases are often prominent toward either patrilineality or matrilineality. Indicators of patrilineality include the prevalent practice of a wife dropping her surname at marriage and taking her husband's surname, and the use of the husband's surname for offspring. This is called *patrinomy*. Although inheritance is supposedly equal between sons and daughters, often it is not. In many business families, the business is passed from father to sons, while daughters are given a different form of inheritance, such as a trust fund. On the other hand, a certain degree of **matrifocality** (a domestic system in which the mother is the central figure) arises from another source: high rates of divorce and the resulting trend of young children living with the mother more often than the father. A matrifocal emphasis creates mother-centred residence and child-raising patterns, but may not affect inheritance patterns.

In order to explore descent patterns in Canada, each student in the class should draw his or her own kinship diagram. Students should note their ethnicity at the top of the chart, choosing the label with which they feel most comfortable. Then, each student should draw a circle around the relatives who are "closest" to "ego," including parents, grandparents, aunts, uncles, cousins—whoever fits in this category as defined by ego. As a group, students in the class should then consider the following questions about the kinship diagrams.

CRITICAL THINKING QUESTIONS

How many students drew equal circles around relatives on both parents' sides?

How many emphasized the mother's side? How many emphasized the father's side?

Do ethnic patterns emerge in terms of the circled kin?

From this exercise, what can be said about "American kinship" in Canada?

"higher civilization" and male dominance emerged, granting the male greater recognition in paternity. Thus, unilineal kinship systems are remnants of earlier times. This argument is weak on two grounds. First, it is ethnocentric to claim that contemporary bilateral cultures, especially Euro-American culture, are the only ones that recognize the father's role in paternity. Obviously, in patrilineal systems this would be readily acceptable. Second, foraging peoples tend to have bilateral kinship, suggesting that the world's earliest humans may have also had bilateral kinship, assuming that foraging was the first human mode of production.

In attempting to explain the relative scarcity of bilateral systems, some anthropologists have offered a theory that looks to the mode of production as influencing the type of kinship system. They point out that bilateral kinship systems are associated mainly with two modes of production: foraging and industrialism. Both modes of production rely on a flexible gender division of labour in which both males and females contribute, relatively equally, to production and exchange. Logically, then, a bilateral kinship system recognizes the strengths of both the mother's and father's side. Bilateral kinship is also an adaptive system for members of foraging and industrial populations because it fits with small family units that are spatially mobile. Bilateral kinship offers the most flexibility in terms of residence, keeping open opportunities related to making a living. As the world becomes increasingly urbanized and industrialized, and if the gender division of labour and resource entitlements were to become more equal, then bilateral kinship might increase in distribution.

As noted earlier, residence rules often match the prevailing "direction" of descent rules. Thus, in most patrilineal societies, marital residence is patrilocal (with or near the male's kin). In most matrilineal societies, it is matrilocal (with or near the woman's kin) or **avunculocal** (with or near the groom's mother's brother). Common in Western industrialized society is the practice of neolocality. These residence patterns have political, economic, and social implications. The combination of matrilineal descent and matrilocal residence, for example, is often found among groups that engage in long-distance warfare (Divale 1974). Strong female household structures maintain the domestic scene while the men are absent on military campaigns, as among the Iroquois of upstate New York and the Nayar of southern India. Patrilineal descent and patrilocal residence promote the development of cohesive male-focused lineages that are associated with frequent local warfare, which requires the presence of a force of fighting men on the home front.

SHARING

Many cultures give priority to kinship that is not based on biologically defined birth, but through acts of sharing and support. These relationships may be informal or formally certified, as in legalized adoption. Ritually formalized kinship also fits in this category, including *godparenthood* (kinship based on ritual ties) and *blood brotherhood* (kinship based on sharing of "blood" or some other substance).

Food Sharing

Cultural anthropologists have devoted relatively little attention to studying food-based kinship, but examples are increasing in the literature. Among the Kaliai, as noted above, fathers are said to be related to their children by descent, while mothers are related to them through breastfeeding. Sharing-based kinship is common throughout much of Southeast Asia, New Guinea, and Australia (Carsten 1995). On an island of Malaysia, the process of developing sharing-based relatedness starts in the womb and continues throughout a person's life. The first food sharing is when the fetus is fed by the mother's blood. After birth, the infant is fed from its mother's breast. Breast milk is believed to derive from the mother's blood and thus "blood becomes milk." This tie is crucial. A child who is not breastfed will not "recognize" its mother. Breastfeeding is the basis of the incest rule:

> [K]in who have drunk milk from the breast of the same woman may not marry. . . . The salience of a prohibition on marriage between milk siblings is rendered greater by the fact that many children spend a considerable part of their childhood in houses other than their maternal ones. The frequency of formal and informal fostering arrangements . . . substantially increases the possibility that a child may drink the milk of a woman who is not its birth mother. . . . It is quite easy to imagine that a child who has been casually put on the breast of a neighbor or distant kinswoman might later marry her child. This ever-present threat looms large in the minds of villagers and runs through their discourse on incest. (227)

After the baby is weaned, its most important food is cooked rice. Sharing cooked rice, like breast milk, becomes another way the kinship ties are created and maintained, especially between mothers and children. Men are often away—on fishing trips, in coffee shops, or at the mosque—and so they are less likely to have these rice-sharing bonds.

Adoption and Fostering

Fostering a child is sometimes similar to a formal adoption in terms of permanence and a developed sense of a close relationship. Or it may involve a temporary placement of a child with someone else for a specific purpose, with little development of a sense of kinship. Such "child transfers" (relocating a child's residence and primary care from one social unit to another) often fall midway between what Westerners would consider formal adoption and fostering. Given these several options for defining relations between adults and children, several questions arise for cultural anthropologists: How do different kinship systems deal with the issue of adoptive (or otherwise "transferred") offspring? Do adopted and fostered children have special problems constructing their personal identity and sense of self? Does this vary by culture? How do adopted offspring gain a sense of belonging if they are raised by people other than their birth parents? For the most part, these questions await in-depth research.

A study in two villages of East Java, Indonesia, reveals that informal child fostering, or "borrowing" is common (Beattie 2002). The initiative for a child transfer is usually out of the parents' hands. The borrower approaches the parents and tells them of a dream he or she had—of rescuing a child from a flood, for example—which, in the Javanese view, gives the parents no choice but to "lend" their child. The arrangement is quite informal when children are borrowed by non-kin, and the child takes turns spending time with both families, having a meal or nap here and there. When a child is borrowed by a kinsperson, though, the arrangement is more likely to be ritually sealed. Foster parents are renamed "mother" and "father," and the child calls the natural mother "elder sister." Whether or not a child is fostered, Javanese children have flexible living arrangements, spending time in different houses, eating and sleeping wherever they feel at home. The kinship fluidity mirrors fluidity in other aspects of life, such as gender roles and religion. No strict dichotomy in gender roles exists between "male" and "female." Rather, there is a wide spectrum of possibilities, with much room in the middle, androgynous ground. A similar flexibility exits in the realm of religion; people are either Hindu or Muslim, but not rigidly so in either case. It is possible to transfer from one to the other, depending on political circumstances. For example, many Muslims became Hindu

Lessons Applied

TRANSNATIONAL ADOPTION AND THE INTERNET

CHINA'S POPULATION policy (discussed in Chapter 5) has made children—especially girls—available for international adoption. While sons ensure the continuity of the patrilineage, girls are considered better caretakers of the elderly. Ann Anagnost (2004) explored the world of transnational adoption where North American parents adopt infants from China. She noted that many people outside China assume that baby girls there are abandoned because of Chinese cultural attitudes and government policy. However, Anagnost notes that baby girls do find adoptive homes in China. Nevertheless, many children are made available for international adoption every year.

Her research explores how adoptive parents use internet communication to articulate thoughts they might otherwise never express. Online discussions explore the best adoption agencies, the process of referral when an infant is assigned to waiting parents, the arrival of the child, and later adjustment. These informal parent networks are used to ask practical advice and share information. When they settle into the daily routine of parenting, internet participation tapers off.

Adoptive parents express concern about the possibility of "reactive attachment disorder" in their adoptions caused by the lack of nurturing contact in the early weeks and months after birth. Yet Chinese adoptions are favoured because they are secure, fast, inexpensive, and final—final because there is no danger the birth parent will try to reclaim the child. One popular topic of discussion is how to construct a cultural identity for a Chinese adoptee. For example, parents search out ethnically marked clothes and toys, particularly dolls, and send their children to special summer "culture camps."

An orphanage in Shanghai, China. Human rights activists have claimed that abuse was widespread in Chinese orphanages, especially of children with physical handicaps. Following this allegation, foreign media were invited to visit the Shanghai Children's Welfare Institute.

FOOD FOR THOUGHT

If you were conducting an applied project to improve parental and child experiences using an agency specializing in transnational adoptions, what ethical concerns would you have? Would you consider the discussion rooms "off-limits" for an applied anthropologist? How would you put your advice on policy changes at the agency into effect?

during the Suharto regime, even though a strict interpretation of Hinduism would say that one has to be born a Hindu.

Legalized Adoption in North America

Currently, about one of every ten couples in Canada is infertile, and many of these couples would like to have children. Some use fertility drugs, in vitro fertilization, or surrogate child bearing. Many people, including those who have biologically recognized children, choose to adopt

(see the Lessons Applied box). Since the mid-1800s, adoption has been a legalized form of child transfer in Canada. It is "a procedure which establishes the relationship of parent and child between persons not so related by nature" (Leavy and Weinberg 1979, v, quoted in Modell 1994:2). Judith Modell, cultural anthropologist and adoptive parent, studied people's experiences of adoptees, birth parents, and adoptive parents. According to Modell, the biological relationship of kinship is so pervasive that the legal process of adoption attempts to construct the adoptive relationship to be as much like a biological one as possible. The adopted child is given a new birth certificate. After adoption, the birth parent ceases to have any relationship with the child. This pattern is called "closed adoption." A recent trend is toward "open adoption," in which adoptees and birth parents have access to information about each other's identity and have freedom to interact with one another. Of the 28 adoptees Modell talked with, most but not all were interested in searching for their birth parents.

> A few said they were "mildly curious" about their birth-parents while others had requested birth and medical records. Ten had established some kind of relationship with a birth family. . . . No one said they thought searching was bad. Those who did not want to find any more information were convinced that all adoptees had a "right to know." Four told me they would never consider searching. "I would just never go looking for her [birth mother] or my father. It just isn't something I consider important enough for me to do—in the first place, she could have passed away." One admitted that he had a "burning curiosity," but considered it would be "a selfish move on my part" to find out anything further. Another who said she had no "desire to go looking," added, "I wish I could see a photograph of my parents without meeting them." A fourth said, in an uncertain tone of voice, "Maybe I am just not curious enough." (144–145)

For many adoptees, a search for birth parents involves an attempt to discover "who I really am." It is a search for an identity that is believed to lie in genealogical roots. For others, such a search is backward-looking and not a path toward formulating one's identity. Given this diversity of views, it is not possible to formulate firm generalizations. The momentum of the movement for open adoption signifies many people's adherence to the biological model of selfhood and identity. Thus, in North America, we could interpret the system of legal adoption as one that legalizes sharing-based kinship, but does not completely replace a sense of descent-based kinship for everyone involved. This statement also applies to many birth parents who seek to reconnect with the children they gave up for adoption.

Ritually Established Sharing Bonds

Ritually defined "sponsorship" of children descended from other people is common throughout the Christian—especially Catholic—world from South America to Europe and the Philippines. Relationships between godparents and godchildren often involve strong emotional ties and financial flows from the former to the latter. In Arembepe, a village in Bahia state in northeastern Brazil, "Children asked their godparents for a blessing the first time they saw them each day. Godparents occasionally gave cookies, candy, and money, and larger presents on special occasions" (Kottak 1992:61). In wealthier, more urbanized contexts, godparents can provide major financial support, including costs of education. They may be expected to assume the role of "adoptive" parents in the event of death of the child's birth parents (Woodrick 1995:223).

In the village of Santa Catalina in the Oaxaca Valley of southern Mexico, godparenthood is both a sign of the sponsor's status and the means to increased status (Sault 1985). A request to be a sponsor is acknowledgment of a person's ability to care for the child. The prestige of being asked to be a sponsor reflects well on one's entire family. It also gives the godparent influence over the godchild. Because the godparent can call on the godchild for labour, being a godparent of many children increases power through the ability to amass a major labour force when needed. In Santa Catalina, the majority of sponsors are male–female couples, but a notable number of sponsors were women alone, while no male alone was a sponsor. This difference is related to the relatively important role and high status of women in the Maya culture of the Oaxaca region.

MARRIAGE

The third major basis for forming close interpersonal relationships is through marriage or other forms of "marriage-like" relationships, such as long-term cohabitation. This section presents anthropological material mainly on formal marriage (other domestic arrangements are discussed in Chapter 9).

Toward a Definition

Anthropologists recognize that some form of **marriage** exists in all cultures, though it may take different forms and serve different functions. However, what constitutes a cross-culturally valid definition of marriage is open to debate. A standard definition from 1951 is now discredited: "Marriage is a union between a man and a woman such that children born to the woman are the recognized legitimate offspring of both parents" (Barnard and Good 1984, 89). This definition says that the partners must be of different sexes. It implies that a child born outside a marriage is not socially recognized as legitimate. Exceptions exist to both these features cross-culturally. Same-sex marriages are now legal in Denmark, Norway, Holland, Spain, and Canada. In the United States in 2000, the state of Vermont passed a law giving legal rights to same-sex couples. Policy debates are ongoing about whether same-sex "domestic partners" are eligible for "spousal" employment benefits. Even the question of whether marriage always involves two people is salient, given ethnographic examples of ritual marriages between people and gods and people and trees.

Marriage patterns among the matrilineal Nayars and the patrilineal Nambudiri brahmans of Kerala, in South India, have forced anthropologists to stretch their concept of what marriage is. The Nayars are well known in anthropology for their high levels of female education, female autonomy, and complex marriage patterns (Fuller 1976; Mencher 1965; Gough 1959). In the traditional pattern, no longer followed, a young Nayar woman would be married to a Nayar man according to the proper ritual rules, and the marriage would be sexually consummated after the ceremony. From then on, the wife would wear a *tali,* a gold wedding necklace. Complexity arises, however, because Nayars are of the kshatriya caste cluster (traditionally a warrior category). Nayar men, in the past, went away for many years, fighting battles in distant regions. The Nayars followed the residence rule of matrilocality (a married Nayar woman continued to live with her mother and her line of relatives, including aunts and uncles, nieces and nephews). During the husband's absence, it was considered perfectly appropriate for a married Nayar woman to enter into "side marriages" called *sambandhan* relationships with other men. These relationships were often arranged by a woman's father or brothers. *Sambandhan* relationships could include Nambudiri brahman men.

The Nambudiri brahmans were the local priestly caste and also rich landowners. In contrast to their neighbouring Nayars, they have patrilineal kinship and they practised **primogeniture**, whereby only the eldest son could inherit the family property. Another Nambudiri rule was that only the oldest son was allowed to marry a Nambudiri bride. Younger brothers' only option for marriage was through *sambandhan* relationships with Nayar women. They did not live with their Nayar wives, however, but maintained a visiting relationship with them. Any child born to a Nayar woman was said to be born from a Nayar man.

Thus, later-born Nambudiri sons were excluded from contributing reproductively to their lineage. What happened to the "surplus" of marriageable Nambudiri girls? According to Hindu cultural principles, a key parental duty is to see to the proper marriage of daughters. Spinsterhood is not a respectable option. Furthermore, Nambudiris were the highest status group in the area, and it would not have been acceptable for them to marry anyone lower than they. These rules combine to create a serious bind: A Nambudiri girl must marry, she cannot marry beneath her status, and there are not enough first sons among the Nambudiris to go around. The solution was found in ritual marriage. Many Nambudiri girls were married to a tree believed to be a deity. A marriage ceremony, complete with the bride circling the "groom" seven times

as in any Hindu marriage ceremony, was performed and she would then wear the marriage *tali.* This ritual effectively placed Nambudiri females into a position parallel to a Catholic nun who "marries" Jesus and pledges herself to lifelong celibacy. Over time, these relationships between the matrilineal Nayars and the patrilineal Nambudiris have declined, mainly because of the decline of Nayar military service and legal changes made by the national government that restrict matrilineality.

In terms of the legitimacy of children, in many cultures no distinction is made between legitimate or illegitimate children on the basis of whether they were born within a marriage. Many women in the Caribbean region, for example, do not marry until later in life. Before that, a woman has sequential male partners with whom she bears children. None of her children are considered more or less "legitimate" than any other.

Other definitions of marriage focus on rights over the spouse's sexuality. But not all forms of marriage involve sexual relations; for example, the practice of woman–woman marriage exists among the Nuer of the Sudan and some other African groups (Evans-Pritchard 1951: 108–109). In this type of marriage, a woman with economic means gives gifts to obtain a "wife," goes through the marriage rituals with her, and brings her into the residential compound just as a man would who married a woman. This wife contributes her productive labour to the household. The two women do not have a sexual relationship. Instead, the in-married woman will have sexual relations with a man. Her children will belong to the compound into which she married, however. Thus, this arrangement supplies the adult woman's labour and her children's labour to the household compound.

Given the range of practices that can come under the heading of marriage, many anthropologists have given up trying to find a working definition that will fit all cases. Others have suggested an open checklist of features, such as reproduction, sexual rights, raising children, or a ritual ceremony. Anthropologist Linda Stone has developed a definition that focuses on the kinship relationships formed upon marriage. This may be the most inclusive definition possible: She defines marriage as an intimate relation between spouses that creates culturally recognized in-law kin relations (Stone 1998:183). This definition accounts for all possible combinations of number and sex of spouses and avoids the problem of confounding marriage with more casual relations. It can also include homosexual marriage.

Selecting a Spouse

All cultures have preferences about whom one should and should not marry or with whom one should or should not have sexual intercourse. Sometimes these preferences are

Two young lesbian women in Ontario celebrate their marriage dressed in traditional white wedding dresses.

informal and implicit and other times they are formal and explicit.

Rules of Exclusion

Some sort of **incest taboo**, or a rule prohibiting marriage or sexual intercourse between certain kinship relations, is one of the most basic and universal rules of exclusion.

In his writings of the 1940s, French anthropologist Claude Lévi-Strauss dealt with the question of why all cultures have kinship systems. In his classic ethnological study, *The Elementary Structures of Kinship* (1949), he argues that incest avoidance motivated men to exchange women between families. This exchange, he says, is the foundation for social networks and social solidarity beyond the immediate group. Such networks allow for trade between areas with different resources and the possibility that peaceful relations will exist between bride-exchangers. He took bride exchange as the basis for distinguishing two types of systems: **restricted exchange systems**, in which women are exchanged only between two groups (A and B exchange with each other), and **generalized exchange systems**, in which exchange involves more than two groups and occurs in a more diffuse and delayed way (A gives to B, who gives to C, and then C gives to A). These two types of exchange determine how intensive or extensive a group's social network becomes. Restricted exchange systems build dense and tightly interwoven local networks. Generalized

exchange systems create extensive and loose systems. Why should two such different systems exist? One hypothesis is that generalized exchange is an adaptation to risky economic contexts because it offers a wider security net of social relationships.

Western genetic research suggests an alternative theory about why there is a universal incest taboo. Larger breeding pools help reduce the frequency of certain genetically transmitted conditions. Both theories are functional, in that they attribute the universal existence of incest taboos to their adaptive contribution, although in two different ways. No one has resolved the question of why incest taboos exist.

The most basic and universal form of incest taboo is against marriage or sexual intercourse between fathers and their children, and mothers and their children. In most cultures, brother–sister marriage has also been forbidden. But there are exceptions. The most well-known example of the allowance of brother–sister marriage comes from Egypt at the time of the Roman Empire (Barnard and Good 1984:92). Census data from that era show that between 15 and 20 percent of marriages were between full brothers and sisters, not just within a few royal families, as is popularly believed. In other cultures, such as the Nuer of Sudan, the incest taboo extends to the extended lineage, which may include hundreds of people. The question of cousins is dealt with in highly contrasting ways cross-culturally. Notably, incest taboos do not universally rule out marriage or sexual intercourse with cousins. In fact, some kinship systems promote cousin marriage, as discussed in the next section.

Preference Rules

In addition to incest taboos, many other rules of exclusion exist, such as prohibiting marriage with people of certain religions, races, or ethnic groups. Such exclusionary rules are often stated in the inverse—as rules of preference for marriage *within* a particular religion, race, or ethnic group.

A variety of preference rules exist cross-culturally concerning whom one should marry. Rules of **endogamy** (or marriage within a particular group) stipulate that the spouse must be chosen from within a defined pool of people. In kin endogamy, certain relatives are preferred, often cousins. Two major forms of cousin marriage exist. One is marriage between **parallel cousins**, children of either one's father's brother or one's mother's sister—the term *parallel* indicates that the linking siblings between cousins are of the same sex. The second is marriage between **cross-cousins**, children of either one's father's sister or one's mother's brother—the term *cross* indicates the different sexes of the linking siblings. Parallel-cousin marriage is favoured by many Islamic groups, especially the subform called *patrilateral parallel-cousin marriage,* which indicates a tendency for cousin marriage in the direction of the father's line rather than the mother's. That is, a child will marry a child of his or her father's brother. Hindus of southern India favour cross-cousin marriages, especially between matrilateral cross-cousins (through the mother's line). But although cousin marriage is the preferred form, it nonetheless constitutes a minority of all marriages in the region. A survey of 3527 couples in the city of Chennai (formerly called Madras; see the map) in South India showed that three-fourths of all marriages involved unrelated people, while one-fourth were between first cross-cousins (or between uncle and niece, which is considered the same relationship as cross-cousin) (Ramesh, Srikumari, and Sukumar 1989). Readers who are unfamiliar with cousin marriage systems may find them objectionable on the basis of the potential genetic disabilities from "close inbreeding." A study of thousands of such marriages in South India, however, revealed only a very small difference in rates of certain "birth defects" compared with cultures in which cousin marriage is not practised (Sundar Rao 1983).

Endogamy may also be based on location. Village endogamy is a basis of arranging marriages throughout

Males and females throughout much of Southeast Asia are approximately the same size, as is the case with this couple from Bali, Indonesia.

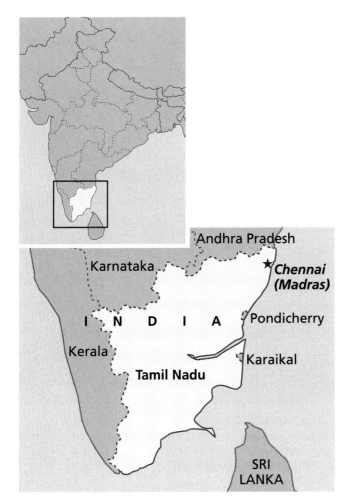

the eastern Mediterranean among both Christians and Muslims. Village endogamy is the preferred pattern among Muslims throughout India and among Hindus of southern India. Hindus of northern India, in contrast, forbid village endogamy and consider it a form of incest. Instead, they practise village **exogamy** ("marriage out"). For them, a preferred spouse should live in a far-off village or town. Thus, marriage distance is greater in the north than in the south, and brides are far less likely to maintain regular contact with their natal kin in the north. Many songs and folktales of North Indian women convey sadness about being separated from their natal families, a theme that may not make much sense in a situation of village endogamy, where the bride's parents are likely to be close by.

Status considerations often shape spouse selection. The rule of **hypergyny** requires the groom to be of higher status than the bride; in other words, the bride "marries up." Hypergyny is a strong rule in northern India, especially among upper-status groups. It is also implicitly followed among many people in North America, where females "at the top" have the hardest time finding an appropriate partner because there are so few options "above them." Women medical students are a prime population experiencing an increased marriage squeeze because of status hypergyny.

The opposite is **hypogyny**, when the female "marries down." Status hypogyny is rare cross-culturally, as is age hypogyny, in which the groom is younger than the bride. Age hypogyny, though rare as a preferred pattern, is increasing in North America because of the "marriage squeeze" on women who would otherwise prefer a husband of equal age or somewhat older.

Physical features, such as ability, looks, and appearance, are factors that may be explicitly or implicitly recognized, or both. Features such as facial beauty, skin colour, hair texture and length, height, and weight are variously defined as important, depending on the culture. Invariably, however, "looks" tend to be more important for females. Marriage advertisements placed in newspapers in India (similar to the "personal ads" in Western newspapers) that describe an available bride often mention that her skin colour is "fair" or "wheatish" and may note that she is slender and tall—although she should not be too tall, that is, taller than a potential groom. Preference for having the groom be taller than the bride is more common in male-dominated contexts. Marriages where the spouses are similar in height are common in cultures where gender roles are relatively equal and where sexual *dimorphism* (differences in shape and size of the female body compared to the male body), is not marked, as in much of Southeast Asia.

Physical ability is another feature affecting marriage options. People with physical disabilities, particularly women, face constraints in marrying nondisabled partners (Sentumbwe 1995). Nayinda Sentumbwe, a blind researcher, conducted fieldwork with participants in education and rehabilitation programs for blind people in Uganda. He realized that all of the married blind women in his study had blind spouses, but few of the married men did. In exploring the reason for this pattern, Sentumbwe considered Ugandan perceptions of blind people and gender relations, especially the housewife role. Most Ugandans consider blindness to be the worst of all physical disabilities. In their perception, blindness decreases women's competence as wives and mothers and reduces their desirability as spouses. Ugandan housewives have many roles: mother, hostess, housekeeper, homestead-keeper, provider of meals, and provider of homegrown food, among others. It is important for men to have "competent" wives, and so they avoid blind women as partners. Instead, men often choose blind women as lovers. The relationship between lovers is private and does not involve social competence in the woman.

The importance of romantic love as a requirement for marriage is a matter of debate between biological determinists and cultural constructionists. Biological determinists argue that feelings of romantic love are universal among all humans because they play an adaptive role in uniting males and females in care of offspring. Cultural constructionists, in contrast, argue that romantic love is far from universal, that it is an unusual, even "aberrant" factor influencing spouse selection (Little 1966, quoted in Barnard and Good 1984:94). In support of a cultural constructionist position, anthropologists point to variations in male and female economic roles to explain cross-cultural variations in an emphasis on romantic love. Romantic love is more likely to be an important factor in relationships in cultures where men contribute more to subsistence, and where women are therefore economically dependent on men. Sri Lankan young people in Toronto are reported to see love marriages as occurring between inexperienced or immature individuals. Arranged marriages "offered a tangible sense of security, family support and approval" (Morrison, Guruge, and Snarr 1999:151). Whatever the cause of romantic love, it is a common basis for marriage in many cultures (Levine et al. 1995).

These debates have prompted cultural anthropologists to devote more research to how romantic love is defined and constructed cross-culturally and within different cultures. For example, Dorothy Holland and Margaret Eisenhart (1990) conducted a study of young American women just entering college from 1979 to 1981 and again in 1987 after they had graduated and begun their adult lives. Their research sites were two southern colleges in the United States, one predominantly attended by White Euro-Americans and the other by African Americans. They found a contrast between the women of the two colleges. The

The Taj Mahal, located in Agra, North India, is a seventeenth-century monument to love. It was built by the Mughal emperor Shah Jahan as a tomb for his favourite wife, Mumtaz Mahal, who died in childbirth in 1631.

White women were much more firmly committed to notions of romantic love than the African American women. This pattern matched differences in career goals and expectations of future earning ability. White women were less likely to have strong and independent career goals and more likely to expect to be economically dependent on their spouse. The African American women expressed self-dependence and stronger career goals. Holland and Eisenhart suggest that the ideology of romantic love apparently "derails" many young White women from competing with men in the job market. The theme of romantic love provides young women with a model of the heroic male provider as the ideal, with her role being one of attracting him and offering the domestic context for their married life. Black women are socialized to be more economically autonomous, a pattern that stems from African practices in which women earn and manage their own earnings.

Arranged marriages, not based initially on romantic love between the bride and groom, are formed instead as a link between the two families involved and considerations of what constitutes a "good match" between the families. Arranged marriages are common in many contemporary Middle Eastern, African, and Asian countries. Some theorists have claimed that arranged marriages are "traditional" while love marriages are "modern," and thus believe arranged marriages will disappear with modernity. However, Japan presents a case of a highly industrialized economy with a highly educated population in which arranged marriages constitute a substantial proportion of all marriages, about 25 to 30 percent (Applbaum 1995). In earlier times, marriage partners would be found through personal networks, perhaps relying on an intermediary who knows both families. Now, in large cities such as Tokyo and Osaka, professional matchmakers have become important sources for finding marriage partners. One registers, pays a fee, and fills out forms about family background. The most common desirable characteristics in a spouse are the family's reputation and social standing, the absence of undesirable traits such as a case of divorce or mental illness in the family, and the potential spouse's education, income, and occupation.

Marriage Gifts

Most marriages are accompanied by gift-giving of goods or services between the partners, members of their families, or friends. As Lévi-Strauss said long ago, exchange can be considered an essential aspect of marriage. In many societies, wedding gifts are the major economic transactions in a person's lifetime (Barnard and Good 1984:114). No one has been able to calculate how much the total flow of marriage gifts and the total cost of weddings is as a percentage of a given economic system, but it is likely to be significant in most contemporary cultures.

The major forms of marital exchanges cross-culturally are dowry and brideprice (Goody and Tambiah 1973). Dowry involves the transfer of goods, and sometimes money, from the bride's side to the new conjugal unit for their use. Common throughout the northern Mediterranean, this "classic" form of dowry includes household goods such as furniture and cooking utensils and sometimes rights to a house. Dowry is the predominant form of marriage transfer in a broad region of Eurasia, from Western Europe through the northern Mediterranean and into China and India (Goody 1976). In northern India, what is called "dowry" is more appropriately termed "groomprice" since the goods and money pass not to the new couple, but rather to the groom's family (Billig 1992). In China during the Mao era, marriage gifts of any type were viewed as a sign of women's oppression and made illegal. Now, marriage gifts are becoming more common with the recent increase in consumerism (Whyte 1993).

Brideprice, or the transfer of goods or money from the groom's side to the bride's parents, is more common in horticultural and pastoral cultures, while dowry is associated with intensive agricultural societies. In cultures where dowry and brideprice are given, recent decades have brought an inflation in the required amounts, making it difficult in some cases for young people to marry. **Bride-service**, less common than brideprice, is still practised in some horticultural societies, especially in the Amazon. Bride-service involves the groom working for his father-in-law for a certain period of time before returning home with the bride. Bride-service is brideprice paid in labour rather than in goods.

Many marriages involve gifts from both the bride's and groom's sides. For example, a typical pattern in Canada is for the groom's side to be responsible for the rehearsal dinner the night before the wedding, while the bride's side is responsible for everything else.

Forms of Marriage

Creating a marriage can be accomplished merely by the couple spending a night together or with an elaborate and costly wedding ceremony that takes place over several days. Weddings vary cross-culturally and intraculturally in terms of the accompanying feasts and festivities, which may involve special food and music, secular or religious ceremonies, variation in duration, and numerous costs. The degree of simplicity or elaboration of weddings can be explained to some extent by differences in production systems and a family's economic status within socially stratified contexts. In low-consumption, foraging societies, marriage receives little formal marking and little expenditure of effort, time, or money. Marjorie Shostak (1981) describes the simplicity of first marriages among the Ju/wasi foragers as studied in the 1970s:

The marriage ceremony is quite modest, although negotiations and gift exchanges are typically begun long before the actual marriage takes place. A hut is built for the couple by members of both families, and is set apart from the rest of the village. As sunset approaches, friends bring the couple to the hut. The bride, head covered, is carried and laid down inside; the groom, walking, is led to the hut and sits beside the door. Coals from the fires of both families are brought to start the new fire in front of the marriage hut. The friends stay with them, singing, playing, and joking. The couple stay apart from each other, maintaining a respectful reserve, and do not join in the festivities. After everyone leaves, they spend their first night together in the hut. The next morning, oil is ceremonially rubbed on both of them—each by the other's mother. (130)

In contrast, in socially stratified societies, substantial local cultural variation exists in weddings across class and ethnic groups. In Canada, this variation includes "common-law marriage," an unmarked form that is achieved simply through the passage of time; secular weddings held in a court with minimal ritual; church weddings with or without much ritual and with or without expensive meals; and the fabulously expensive weddings of the very wealthy, followed by a costly honeymoon for the newlyweds.

Cultural anthropologists distinguish two basic forms of marriage on the basis of the number of partners involved. **Monogamy**, the simplest, is marriage between two people—a male and female if the pair is heterosexual, or two people of the same sex in the case of a homosexual pair. Heterosexual monogamy is the most common form of marriage cross-culturally, and in many countries, it is the only form of marriage allowed by law.

Polygamy refers to a marriage with multiple spouses, a pattern that is allowed by the majority of the world's cultures, even though the majority of people within such cultures may not practise plural marriage (Murdock 1965:24). Two forms of polygamous marriage exist. The predominant pattern is **polygyny**, marriage of one husband with more than one wife. Within cultures that allow polygyny, the majority of unions nevertheless are monogamous. **Polyandry**, or marriage between one woman and more than one man, is rare. However, it has been practised among groups as diverse as the Kaingang of the Amazon, the Todas of southern India, and the Chukchee of Siberia. One region in which polyandry occurs over a large area includes Tibet and the high Himalayas of India and parts of Nepal.

Anthropologists have asked why polygyny, marriage between one man and more than one woman simultaneously, exists in some cultures and not in others (White and Burton 1988). Evolutionary theorists of the nineteenth century suggested that polygyny constituted a middle stage. Engels's three stages, for example, went from *group marriage* (in which everyone was supposedly married to everyone else, a hypothetical situation unknown ethnographically for the past or the present), to polygyny, and then to monogamy. Biological determinists say that polygyny contributes to males' reproductive success by allowing them to maximize the spread of their genes in future generations. But neither the evolutionary nor biological determinist models offer insight into the cross-cultural variation in the distribution of polygyny. Economic theories have been proposed. One prominent economic hypothesis states that polygyny will be more likely in contexts where women's contribution to the economy is more important. Political and demographic factors have also been examined, especially the role of warfare in reducing the ratio of males to females, and the taking of female captives in warfare. Data for 142 societies show that one factor alone cannot explain the presence or absence of polygyny (White and Burton 1988). Instead, support for a set of interrelated views emerges:

- Polygyny fits with an expansionist economic strategy in homogeneous and high-quality environments.
- Polygyny is associated with warfare for plunder and/or female captives.
- Polygyny is associated with the presence of strongly bonded groups of males linked through ties between brothers.
- Polygyny is constrained in the context of plow agriculture or by high dependence on fishing.

Some support was found for the hypothesis about the effect of female contribution to subsistence, but not at such a strong level as for these factors.

A newly married husband and wife and their relatives in front of a church in Seoul, Republic of Korea.

Change in Marriage

Marriage continues to be a major basis of forming kinship bonds cross-culturally. While the institution of marriage in general remains prominent, many of its specific details are changing. Almost everywhere, the age at first marriage is rising. This change is related to increased emphasis on completing a certain number of years of education before marriage and rising aspirations about the potential spouse's economic status before contemplating marriage. Marriages between people of different nations and ethnicity are increasing, caused partly by increased rates of international migration (see Chapter 15). Migrants take with them many of their marriage and family practices. They also adapt to rules and practices in their area of destination. Pluralistic practices evolve, such as conducting two marriage ceremonies—one based on the "original" culture and the other conforming to norms in the place of destination.

Style changes in weddings abound. Globalization of Western-style "white weddings" promotes the adoption of many features that are familiar in the West: a white wedding gown for the bride, a many-layered wedding cake, and certain kinds of floral arrangements. What the bride and groom wear is an expression of both the bride's and groom's personal identity and also the cultural identity of their family and larger social group. Clothing choice reflects adherence to "traditional" values, or may reject those in favour of more "modern" values, that is, Euro-American trends. Throughout much of East and Southeast Asia, advertisements and upscale stores display the Western-style white wedding gown (but not so much in India, where white clothing for women signifies widowhood and is inauspicious). On the other hand, some resurgence of local "folk" styles is occurring in some contexts, such as in Morocco, where there is a trend for "modern" brides to wear a Berber costume (long robes and jewellery characteristic of the rural, mountain people) at one stage of the wedding ceremony.

HOW do cultures define kinship through descent?

Key differences in descent systems exist between unilineal systems, which are numerically predominant, and bilateral systems. Within unilineal systems, patrilineal systems differ from matrilineal systems in terms of property division, residence rules, and their implications for the status of males and females. The number of matrilineal kinship systems is declining in the face of Western influence, beginning with European colonial expansion in the 1500s.

HOW do cultures define kinship through sharing?

Kinship can also be created through acts of sharing and support. In cultures throughout much of Southeast Asia, women often breastfeed children of other women; this practice forms a kinship bond through the sharing of milk, in that all children who are breastfed by a woman are considered to be related. Some form of child transfers, from one primary caretaker to another, is probably a cross-cultural universal. In some societies, such as in Canada, legalized options for child transfers through adoption are common and even allow for the transfer of children from one nation to another. Ritualized sharing also creates kinship bonds as in the case of godparenthood.

HOW do cultures define kinship through marriage?

Marriage continues to be an important basis of kinship formation, even though it often results in divorce in many contexts. All cultures have rules of exclusion about which people should not be considered as a marriage partner, with some form of incest taboo found universally. All cultures likewise have preference rules stating which people would make the best choice as a marriage partner. Marriage preferences and arrangements reflect other aspects of the culture, for example, the relative importance of males or females in the economy.

KEY CONCEPTS

SUGGESTED READINGS

John Borneman, *Belonging in the Two Berlins: Kin, State, Nation.* New York: Cambridge University Press, 1992. This book considers two levels of analysis: people's changing perceptions of the family and the government's policies related to the family.

Irene Glasser and Rae Bridgman, *Braving the Street: The Anthropology of Homelessness. Public Issues in Anthropological Perspective,* vol. 1. New York: Berghahn Books, 1999. Fieldwork with homeless people reveals complexities of the problem that have been overlooked by public officials. The authors propose solutions.

Laurel Kendall, *Getting Married in Korea: Of Gender, Morality, and Modernity.* Berkeley: University of California, 1996. The ethnographic study examines preferences about desirable spouses, matchmaking, marriage ceremonies and their financing, and the effect of women's changing work roles on their marital aspirations.

Judith S. Modell, *A Sealed and Secret Kinship: The Culture of Policies and Practices in American Adoption.* New York, Berghahn Books, 2002. This books focuses on the increasing debate about adoption by reviewing case examples of parents, children, kin, and non-kin of adoptive families in the United States. The author addresses topics such as adoption reform, adoptee experiences of searching for their birth parents, current practices of placing children, and changes in welfare policy.

Nancy Tapper, *Bartered Brides: Politics, Gender and Marriage in an Afghan Tribal Society.* New York: Cambridge University Press, 1991. Based on fieldwork before the Soviet invasion, this study examines marriage among the Maduzai, a tribal society of Turkistan. The book looks at how marriage relates to productive and reproductive aspects of society and the role it plays in managing political conflict and competition.

Margaret Trawick, *Notes on Love in a Tamil Family.* Berkeley: University of California Press, 1992. This reflexive ethnography takes a close look at the daily dynamics of kinship in one Tamil (South Indian) family. Special attention is given to sibling relationships, the role of older people, children's lives, and the way love and affection are played out in a particularly Tamil way.

Michael Young and Peter Willmott, *Family and Kinship in East London.* New York: Penguin Books, 1979. This classic study of kinship relationships among the working class of "Bethnal Green" gives particular attention to the importance of married women's continued close relationships with their mothers as maintained through residential proximity and visiting.

WEBLINKS

The Companion Website (www.pearsoned.ca/miller) that accompanies *Cultural Anthropology,* Third Canadian Edition, includes a destinations module containing links to many websites relevant to the content of this chapter. Use it to investigate the Web and expand your understanding of anthropology.

KEY QUESTIONS

- **WHAT** is a household and what are major household forms?
- **WHAT** are some important economic and social features of households?
- **HOW** are household patterns changing?

9

DOMESTIC GROUPS

Some members of a Bedu household in Yemen.

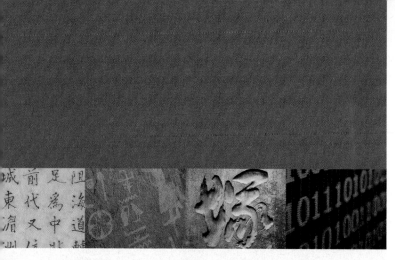

In casual conversation, North Americans might use the words *family* and *household* interchangeably to refer to people who live together. Social scientists have proposed a distinction between the two terms, both of which may refer to a domestic group, or people who live together. A **family** includes people who consider themselves related through kinship (as described in Chapter 8—descent, marriage, or sharing). In North American English, the term *family* includes both "close" or "immediate" relatives and more "distant" relatives. One may live with and see some members of one's family every day, but others only once a year on a major holiday, or less. People who are considered close family relatives may be scattered in several different residences, including grandparents, aunts, uncles, and cousins; children of divorced parents, who live with one parent and visit the other; and children of divorced parents, who may live with different parents. The notion of the family as a clearly defined unit with firm boundaries thus often misrepresents the fluidity of this category (Lloyd 1995).

In contrast to the term *family,* the term **household** refers to a domestic group that may or may not be related by kinship and that share living space, including perhaps a kitchen and certain budgetary items such as food and rent. Most households around the world consist of family members who are related through kinship. An example of a non-kin household is a group of friends who live in the same apartment. A single person living alone is also a household.

This chapter discusses anthropological findings about a variety of domestic groupings, especially in terms of how households operate as economic units. It also considers the content of the relationships of household members and factors that lead to the breakup of domestic groups.

THE HOUSEHOLD: VARIATIONS ON A THEME

In this section, we consider three major forms of households and then examine the concept of household headship. The topic of female-headed households receives detailed attention as this pattern of headship is of considerable contemporary policy interest.

Household Forms

Household organization can be categorized into several types according to how many married adults are involved. Single-person households comprise only one member, living alone. A single-parent household comprises an adult with offspring. The **nuclear household** (which many people call the **nuclear family**) contains one adult couple (married or "partners"), with or without children. Complex households include a variety of household forms based on the presence of more than two married adults. Polygynous (multiple wives) and polyandrous (multiple husbands) households are one form of complex household in which one spouse has multiple partners. They may all live together in one residence or, as is the case in many African polygynous households, each wife has a separate residential unit within the overall household compound. **Extended households** contain more than one adult married couple. These couples may be related through the father–son line (making a patrilineal extended household, such as the Lims of Taiwan who were mentioned in Chapter 8), the mother–daughter line (making a matrilineal extended household), or through sisters or brothers (making a collateral extended household).

The precise cross-cultural distribution of these various types is not known. However, some broad generalizations can be offered. First, nuclear household units are found in all cultures (Murdock 1965:2). The nuclear household as the exclusive household type is characteristic of about one-fourth of the world's cultures. Another one-fourth allows polygamous marriages. One-half of the cultures are characterized by the presence of extended households. The distribution of nuclear versus complex household forms roughly corresponds with modes of production. The nuclear form is most characteristic of economies at the two extremes of the continuum: in foraging groups and in industrialized societies. As noted in Chapter 8, the greater prevalence of nuclear households in these two modes of production reflects the need for spatial mobility and flexibility in making a living. Polygynous or polyandrous households and extended households constitute a substantial proportion of households in horticultural, pastoral, and non-industrial agricultural economies. Throughout Asia—China, Japan, India—in much of Africa, and among First Nations people, some form of complex or extended households is both the ideal and frequently the reality.

In India, where extended households are the preferred form, the household may contain 50 or more members. Property provides the material base to support many people and, in turn, large land holdings require a large labour force to work the land. In northern India, more households own property, compared to southern and eastern India where rates of landlessness are higher. In addition to property differences, the unbalanced sex ratio in the North means there are more sons available to bring in wives and establish patrilineal extended households. Logically, then, patrilineal extended households are more common in the northern part of the country (Kolenda 1968).

Some anthropologists argue that the frequency of extended households will decline with industrialization and urbanization, which are considered key factors of modernity. This argument is based on an assumed European model of reduced numbers of extended farming households and increased numbers of nuclear households. Taking the nuclear household as a key marker of modernity, though, has its problems. First, historical evidence indicates that nuclear households characterized non-industrial, premodern northwestern Europe (Goody 1996). So, the apparent transformation from extended households to nuclear households with modernity is not universally correct. Asian data clearly do not fit the model. In India, urban areas have a higher percentage of extended households than rural areas (Freed and Freed 1969). Further, data from India on literacy rates, often taken as an indicator of modernity and exposure to change, again show contradictory findings. A study in West Bengal, a state in eastern India, found that extended household heads are more likely to be literate than nuclear household heads (Dasgupta, Weatherbie, and Mukhopadhaya 1993).

Moving from India to Japan, we again find that the extended household structure has endured in the context of an industrial and urban economy. The *ie*, or "stem household," has a long history in Japan (Skinner 1993) and is still important (Bachnik 1983). A variant of an extended household, a **stem household** contains two (and only two) married couples related through the males. Thus,

In China, the stem family household system is undergoing change as many people have one daughter and no son as a result of the One-Child Policy and generally lowered fertility.

only one son remains in the household, bringing in his wife, who is expected to perform the important role of caretaker for the husband's parents as they age. In Japan and in contemporary China, the patrilineal stem household is still a widely preferred form. Yet it is increasingly difficult to achieve since the rising aspirations of children often mean that no child is willing to live with and care for the aging parents. In this context, parents sometimes exert considerable pressure on an adult child to come and live with them (Traphagan 2000). One compromise solution is for an adult child and his or her spouse to live near the parents but not with them.

These examples of the endurance of extended household formation in certain Asian contexts relate to the discussion, later in this chapter, of family businesses. It makes sense that extended households have a greater chance of survival when they function as "mini-corporations," with shared economic interests and a loyal set of managers and workers linked by kinship.

Household Headship

The question of who heads a household is often difficult to answer. This section reviews some of the approaches to this question and provides insights into how cross-cultural perceptions about **household headship** differ.

The "head" is the primary person (or people) in charge of supporting the household financially and making decisions. Cultural anthropologists realize that the concept of household head is an ethnocentric, Euro-American definition of one person who makes most of the money, controls most of the decision making, and was traditionally a man. European colonialism spread the concept of the male head of household around the world along with its male-biased legal system that vests household authority in the father.

The model of one male head has influenced the way official statistics are gathered and reported worldwide. The result is that if a household has a co-residing male and female, there will be a tendency to report the household as "male-headed," regardless of the actual internal dynamics. In Brazil, the official definition considers only a husband to be head of the household, regardless of whether he contributes to the household budget and is married to the woman. Thus, "[S]ingle, separated or widowed women who house and feed their children, grandchildren and elderly or handicapped parents are deprived of the title of head of the family. If they have a partner with them on the day when the census official arrives, he is considered to be the head of the family, whether or not he is the father of any of the children, contributes to the family income, or has been living there for years or only a few months" (de Athayde Figueiredo and Prado 1989:41). Similarly, according to official reports, 90 percent of households in the Philippines are headed by males (Illo 1985). Anthropological research shows, however, that women play a prominent role in income generation and budgetary control, and both male and female domestic partners tend to share decision making. Thus, co-headship would be a more appropriate label for many households in the Philippines and elsewhere.

Many early anthropologists were also male-biased in their assessment of household headship. They overlooked household headship patterns that did not conform to their Eurocentric view of male headship. Beginning with the work of Nancie González, awareness of the prevalence and functioning of woman-headed households has increased. González was one of the first anthropologists to define and study matrifocality, a domestic pattern in which a female (or females) is the central, stable figure around whom other members cluster (1970:233). In matrifocal households, the mother is likely to be the primary, or only, income provider. The concept of matrifocality does not exclude the possibility that men may be part of the household. That is, a matrifocal household is under the control of a woman head who may or may not have a (male) partner.

There has been much public discussion in North America recently about partnerless women as household heads. Concern has arisen because the number of such households is increasing, and they are more likely to be poorer than households containing a married couple. What causes the formation of partnerless woman–headed households? A woman-headed household can come about if a partner existed at one time, but for some reason— such as separation, divorce, or death—is no longer part of the household, or a partner exists but is not co-resident because of long-term out-migration, imprisonment, or some other form of separate residence. (Most thinking about woman-headed households assumes a heterosexual relationship and thus does not account for woman-headed households formed by a single woman with children either adopted or conceived through artificial insemination, with or without a visiting woman partner.) Three theories are often proposed to account for the absence of a male spouse or partner.

- *Slavery:* The high frequency of woman-headed households among African Americans in the Western hemisphere is often said to be the heritage of slavery, which intentionally broke up conjugal ties. This theory has several problems. First, if slavery were the cause of woman-headed households, one would predict that all peoples who experienced slavery would have this household form. In Jamaica, which is populated mainly by descendants of African slaves, percentages of woman-headed households vary between rural and urban areas (Miller and Stone 1983). Yet both urban and rural people have the same heritage. In the United States, no generic "Black household" exists, just as there is no generic "White household": "Black Americans count for more than 10 million households, ranging from young adults in condominiums to suburban couples with two children and a swimming pool" (Hacker 1992:67). Second, historically in the United States, homes with two co-residing parents were the norm among Black Americans following the Civil War through the mid-twentieth century. This makes it difficult to describe woman-headed households today as a "legacy" of slavery. It is true that the slave system denied legal standing to adult pairings since owners did not want their slaves committed to lifetime relationships. Slaves were subject to sale, and wives and husbands, parents and children were separated. While such circumstances would seem to have led to a "breakup" of a conjugal (married) household tradition, it is now clear that the slaves themselves never accepted the arrangements imposed by the owners: "Once freed, blacks sought the durable unions they had been denied" (69). Third, in the United States, percentages of woman-headed households have increased in roughly the same proportion among Blacks and Whites. These parallels indicate that similar factors may underlie the changes for both populations. Last, the distribution of woman-headed households throughout the world is more widespread than the distribution of slavery. So, other factors must be involved in promoting the formation of this pattern.

- *Poverty:* Woman-headed households are said to be adaptations to poverty, because in many societies, the poor have a higher frequency of woman-headed households. If so, it is only one of many possible adaptations since not all low-income populations worldwide are characterized by high rates of woman-headed households. Within just the United States, significant ethnic differences exist: "Low-income Chinese, Japanese, and other Asiatic peoples generally have low frequencies of single-parent households, and many Mexican-American communities have a strong predominance of dual-parent families even though experiencing relatively low incomes and considerable unemployment" (Pelto, Roman, and Liriano 1982:40). As an explanatory factor, poverty needs to be considered along with attention to male and female income-earning capabilities, other resources available, and other support systems.

In the Caribbean region and throughout Latin America, the association between poverty and woman-headed households is strong. But beneath this seemingly negative association, some positive findings appear. In the Caribbean region, about one-third of all households are woman-headed, and most of the women have never been married (Massiah 1983). Instead, they have visiting unions (involving a steady sexual relationship, but the maintenance of separate residences). Many women who were interviewed as part of a study conducted in several of the islands commented that they sometimes expect and hope for financial support from their male partner or "baby father." Numerous others emphasized the value they place on freedom from a husband or permanent partner. One woman said, "Being single fits in with my independent thinking" (41). Another commented on her visiting union: "I like freedom, so I'm keeping it like it is" (41).

In much of African-Caribbean culture, economic conditions dictate that men are not dependable sources of financial support. Women in low-income groups in the Caribbean and throughout much of Latin America have an advantage over males in earning money. Rural women earn income, for example, from gardening and marketing their produce. Urban women work in service occupations, small businesses, domestic service, and light industry. Cities offer more opportunities for such salaried employment than rural areas, and thus they attract greater numbers of female migrants. When men do get jobs, they are likely to be irregular or seasonal. On top of limited employment options, African-Caribbean men tend to withhold portions of their earnings for personal expenditures (Chant 1985).

In addition to income generation, women have an advantage over men in mobilizing supplementary household support from kin and friends. Thus, women in these contexts are less dependent on men's income than in places where they do not have access to such jobs and resources. In fact, having a non-earning male around the house who consumes and does not contribute constitutes a net economic loss. Thus, a woman-headed household can be viewed as a positive adaptation to economic and social circumstances (see

Members of a matrifocal household in rural Jamaica: two sisters and their children.

the Critical Thinking box). The differences in male and female employment opportunities affect women's preferences concerning location and household structure. In El Salvador, "a woman without a stable partner, regardless of her legal or religious marital status . . . generally preferred city to rural life; married women with working spouses like rural life" (Nieves 1979:139).

- *Unbalanced sex ratio:* Woman-headed households are said to occur in contexts of high male out-migration or in other demographic situations causing a shortage of males. The sheer availability of partners may put constraints on marriage. In Spanish Galicia, the local economy, inheritance rules, and household formation are related (Kelley 1991). This coastal region has a high percentage of households headed by unmarried women. In the village of Ezaro, for example, about one-fourth of all baptisms in the latter half of the nineteenth century were of illegitimate children. The proportion has declined in the twentieth century, but the Galician region still stands out from the rest of Spain in this respect. In Ezaro, households headed by unmarried mothers constitute over 10 percent of the total. The general Mediterranean kinship system puts high value on marriage and male honour through control of the sexuality of female family members. Yet little or no stigma is attached to unwed motherhood in Galicia. Women household heads often gain honoured positions in their villages.

What accounts for this system? The answer lies in Galicia's high rates of male emigration. The scarcity of males promotes flexible attitudes toward unwed motherhood and other adaptive features not found elsewhere in the Mediterranean region. The women have important roles in production and property relations. In

Critical Thinking

IS A FATHER-HEADED HOUSEHOLD BEST?

MUCH WESTERN popular thought places the nuclear household, comprising a co-resident adult heterosexual couple and children, as "the best" type, and as "natural." Other forms, especially woman-headed households, are often viewed as "broken" versions of the nuclear household, and are said to be less adequate structures within which to raise children. Putting the "father" back into the household is an important policy goal in North America. Given the discussion on household headship, what can be said about the household debate?

CRITICAL THINKING QUESTIONS

Why do some people argue that "putting the father back in the household" will improve lives for children?

What if there is more than one father for the children of one mother?

What if the father has no job?

What if the household has a co-resident adult couple, but they are both males or both females?

Ezaro, women are in charge of agricultural work. They inherit land and gain prestige and power from owning and managing agricultural land. Women's agricultural work is the basis of their reputation in the community: "Women's work is considered so critical to the prestige of the household in Ezaro that success at work is the single most important factor in the community's evaluation of a woman's character (and in her own self-evaluation). The good woman in Ezaro is the hardworking woman" (572). Her work is more important in this respect than her marital status.

Inheritance practices reflect the importance of women's agricultural work. The goal is to ensure continuity of the *casa*, the house, which includes both the physical structure and its members. Parents usually award one of their children with a *millora*, a larger share of the inheritance, making that child the principal heir. The rest is divided equally among siblings. Daughters are often chosen to receive the *millora*, and thus a single woman can become head of an estate. Her children ensure that the estate has continuity. In contrast, a man cannot become a household head and gain social status without being married.

The preceding theories about why woman-headed households exist can be labelled "compensatory theories." They suggest that a woman-headed household emerges as a default system when "something is wrong" or men are unavailable as spouses. This bias is based on the assumption that the heterosexual nuclear household is the "normal" pattern that occurs when everything is "okay." A Marxist view would say that a variety of household forms are expectable, depending on such factors as men's and women's economic roles, especially access to work, wages, and the distribution of productive resources such as property.

The Household as an Economic Unit

Households can be examined from a variety of perspectives: as economic units, political units, and social groups. This section discusses the economic workings of households. Three topics are addressed: work roles inside the household, households as businesses, and the financial impact of remittances (money that is sent) from non-resident members.

Gender, Labour, and Household Type

This section offers insights into how the gender division of labour in two different contexts is related to household roles and relationships. The first case is based on research in South Wales, U.K., where the "classic" nuclear household is still prevalent. The second is based on research among Tibetan peoples living in Nepal among whom polyandry is practised and households are, therefore, composed of several adult males all of whom are married to the same woman (Chapter 8).

The "Classic" Nuclear Household   The "classic" Euro-American model of the nuclear household involves a division of labour in which only one spouse (the male) works in the wage economy and the other (the female) does unpaid work in the domestic domain, including child care. This pattern is common in North America and Western Europe. An anthropological study in South Wales, U.K., addressed women's and men's perceptions of their contributions and value to the household (Murcott 1993). In South Wales nuclear households, the husband works outside the home for wages while the wife remains in the home doing work that is unremunerated, including bearing and raising children, preparing meals, and cleaning. Welsh wives defined their domestic responsibility mainly in terms of their importance in providing "home cooking." Home cooking means preparation of a "cooked meal" of meat, potatoes, vegetables, and gravy: "[A] proper meal is a cooked dinner. This is one which women feel is necessary to their family's health, welfare, and, indeed, happiness. It is a meal to come home to, a meal which should figure two, three or four times in the week and especially on Sundays" (78). In contrast, the responsible husband goes out to work. At the end of his work day, he comes home for dinner. The responsible wife has prepared a cooked meal for him. As one woman commented: "When my husband comes home . . . there's nothing more he likes I think than coming in the door and smelling a nice meal cooking. I think it's awful when someone doesn't make the effort. . . . I think well if I was a man I'd think I'd get really fed up if my wife never bothered" (79). Cooking a proper meal is a more important task for a married woman than for a single person. Cultural evaluations of the "good wife" or the "good husband" tend to fit with the prevailing economy in South Wales where the wage job market is dominated by men.

The Polyandrous Household How is the gender division of labour organized in households with multiple spouses? As noted in Chapter 8, polyandrous households are rare cross-culturally, but relatively common in some areas of Asia, especially in the Himalayan region. Among Tibetan peoples, fraternal polyandry, in which one wife has several husbands who are related as brothers, is the ideal form of marriage (Goldstein 1987). Research among Tibetan people who live in an area of Nepal near the border with Tibet reveals the following:

> Two, three, four or more brothers jointly take a wife, who leaves her home to come and live with them. Traditionally, marriage was arranged by parents, with children, particularly females, having little or no say. This is changing somewhat nowadays, but it is still unusual for children to marry without their parents' consent. Marriage ceremonies vary by income and region and range from all the brothers sitting together as grooms to only the eldest one formally doing so. . . . The eldest brother is usually dominant in terms of authority, that is, in managing the household, but all the brothers share the work and participate as sexual partners. Tibetan males and females do not find the sexual aspect of sharing a spouse the least bit unusual, repulsive, or scandalous, and the norm is for the wife to treat all the brothers equally. (39)

Tibetans say that they choose to marry polyandrously because of economic factors: It prevents division of land and animals, and helps everyone achieve a higher standard of living. Anthropological analysis reveals other economic benefits, such as the more diverse and flexible male labour force than would be available in a monogamous household. The wife works in the fields and manages food processing and other household work. Of the husbands,

The woman on the lower right is part of a polyandrous marriage, which is common among Tibetan people. She is married to several brothers, two of whom stand behind her. The older man with the blue sash in the front row is her father-in-law.

one stays and works on the land, another may be away with the herds, and another may be involved in long-distance trade. In earlier times, before Tibet became controlled by China, its pattern of feudal serfdom required regular labour contributions from one male in each household. This posed yet another demand for male labour. In a monogamous system, this requirement would have negative effects on the household economy.

Polyandry thus provides a male labour "safety net" and helps to maximize economic advantage in an ecological context that requires diversification and flexibility.

Household Businesses

The subject of household businesses is important in anthropology and many other disciplines, including sociology, economics, business, and international development. Anthropologists have found fascinating material in their studies of family businesses in areas such as the division of labour and intergenerational conflict.

Household Businesses in Chinese Culture In contemporary China, household businesses are regaining prominence, with the new economic policies that promote growth in the private sector. A study using nationwide survey data sought to assess what the role of women has been in the trend toward establishing new, nonagricultural businesses (Entwisle et al. 1995). (See the Multiple Cultural Worlds box.) The sample covered about one-third of China's provinces and included 3764 households. Results show that the number of adults and the gender composition of the adults affect whether a household enterprise will be launched. The more adults there are,

Multiple Cultural Worlds

CHINESE HOUSEHOLD BUSINESSES IN CALCUTTA

ANTHROPOLOGICAL STUDY of "overseas" Chinese households involved in the tanning industry in Calcutta, India, provides insights about the adjustments that Chinese migrants make within a new context (Oxfeld 1993). In India, Chinese migrants' success in the tanning business is largely due to the effective use of both male and female labour. The gender division of labour among Chinese migrants to India differs from that of Chinese people in Taiwan. Most notably, in rural Taiwanese household businesses, a clear division of labour between men and women is carefully maintained such that men and women do completely different tasks. Also, in Taiwan, a sharp distinction exists between the public and private domains, with men working outside the home and women working inside the home.

In Calcutta many Chinese households are involved in the tanning industry. In these households, some tasks are done only by men, but several other tasks involve contributions from both men and women. Both male and female household members perform several tasks related to processing the leather. These shared tasks include mixing chemicals and packing the finished products. Both of these tasks are performed within the domestic domain.

Men, exclusively, perform the few tasks that involve interaction with unrelated males, such as buying rawhides. Rawhides are sold in two Muslim areas of the city where one rarely sees a woman in public. Buying rawhides also involves "hard-core bargaining" and sustained interaction with men, something from which women are excluded. Selling the finished leather is also men's work. It, too, involves interactions with other males in the public domain.

During the ceremony that marks the opening of a new tannery of a Chinese household business in Calcutta, India, the male descendants of the owners carry red lanterns and walk in a procession to the new factory.

FOOD FOR THOUGHT

While the gender division of labour differs between Chinese households of Taiwan and Calcutta, what aspect of gender roles stays the same according to this description?

and the more adult men there are, the greater is the likelihood that the household will start a business: "Working-age men are almost three times as likely than women to work in the household business, and working-age women are more than twice as likely as men to work exclusively in agriculture. . . . Household businesses appear to be an opportunity for men, not for women" (47–48). Women's household roles in China have long been that of "filling in," by doing work that needed to be done while men pursue the "main" tasks. With the move toward privatization, agriculture is now secondary to business in importance. So women "fill in" while men move out of agriculture into business. However, this pattern may

change if the private sector continues to grow and the number of shops increases because women often work in shops.

Farming Family Businesses in North America   In the United States and Canada, most household farms are either sold or liquidated after the retirement or death of their founders. This pattern exists in spite of the widespread preference of owners to pass them on to their offspring. What factors promote successful succession? Most studies have looked at the relationships between fathers and sons, since they tend to be most involved in the day-to-day operation of businesses (Marotz-Baden and

Mattheis 1994). The roles of daughters are often overlooked, but some interesting findings are emerging.

In two-generation farm households, daughters-in-law have higher stress levels than other adult members. A daughter-in-law's stress level will be high if she wants to be integrated into the business and perceives that she is not. Unresolved tensions between a dissatisfied daughter-in-law and the rest of the household, especially her mother-in-law, may have more serious consequences for intergenerational continuity of the business than tensions between father and son. The prevailing gender division of labour in North America designates men mainly as the farm operators. Women are involved in bookkeeping, household organization, coordination of household and farm labour, and membership in community organizations. Transmission of the farm is usually through the male line. Because starting up a farm on one's own is costly, most young farmers or ranchers work with or for their parents. Marriage, then, means that a daughter-in-law moves from her natal home into that of her husband and his parents, which places the daughter-in-law in a vulnerable and stressful position. Role ambiguity for the daughter-in-law is closely related to the presence and power of her mother-in-law.

One might assume that, over time, the daughter-in-law and mother-in-law relationship would strengthen with shared experiences and greater sharing of decision making. A study of 54 daughters-in-law in two-generational farm households in Montana showed, instead, that daughters-in-law thought their relationship with their mother-in-law had worsened over time, especially as more children were born. The daughters-in-law who perceived their relationships to be most strained also reported more stress and were less involved in decision making (Marotz-Baden and Mattheis 1994:133).

Remittances

Remittances, or money that is sent to a household, usually by non-resident family members, constitute an important part of many household economies. Migrant labourers may leave home for a specific period of time or to earn a specific amount of money before returning. In other cases, migrants leave and do not return, but continue to send money back home. An important stream of the international flow of remittances comes from the Persian Gulf area, where men and women from many countries from Egypt to Bangladesh, Thailand, and the Philippines migrate to work; men work in the oil industry, and women work as domestic maids, nurses, and in other services.

A less well-known source of remittance income for some households is through sex work, or prostitution, of one or more of their members. Contribution to the household economy from sex work varies. In the United States, **family disaffiliation** (feeling alienated from one's family)

Cambodian sex workers seek out customers in Phnom Penh. Cambodia is also a source of illegal transfer of sex workers into neighbouring Thailand.

is a frequent motivation for a woman to enter prostitution, especially among the Euro-American population (McCaghy and Hou 1994). These girls and women tend to come from divorced homes; they frequently have been victims of familial abuse and neglect; and they have a poor relationship with their parents. They use their earnings for self-support and do not frequently send money home. However, a study of African American sex workers in Milwaukee indicated that they often maintained contact with their families, and it is more likely that they would share their income from sex work with their families. In Asia, too, family disaffiliation is uncommon for female sex workers. Instead, kin support is a prominent motivation for doing sex work. In Thailand, few sex workers had broken ties with their families. Most visited their family once a year and sent regular remittances. In general, less stigma is attached to sex work if it is done for kin support, given the strong norms of family obligation in many Asian contexts.

INTRAHOUSEHOLD DYNAMICS

How do household members interact with each other? What are their emotional attachments, rights, and responsibilities? What are the power relationships between and among members of various categories such as spouses, siblings, and those of different generations?

Kinship systems define what the content of these relationships should be. In everyday life, people may conform more or less to the ideal, as was apparent in the description of problems between mothers-in-law and daughters-in-law in extended farming households of North America. The important dimension of how people may or may not diverge from ideal roles and relationships is, oddly, one that has been neglected for a long time by cultural anthropology and has only recently gained some attention.

Spouse/Partner Relationships

Anthropologists who study relationships between spouses and partners consider a range of topics: decision making, power relationships, the degree of attachment and commitment, duration of commitment, and the possibility of intimate relationships outside the primary relationship. This section presents findings on levels of emotional satisfaction between spouses and how they might relate to extramarital relationships.

A landmark sociological study of marriages in Tokyo in 1959 compared marital satisfaction of husbands and wives in love marriages and arranged marriages (Blood 1967). In all marriages, marital satisfaction declined over time, but differences between the two types emerged. The decline was greatest for wives in arranged marriages and least for husbands in arranged marriages. In love-match marriages, husbands' satisfaction dropped dramatically and a bit later than their wives' satisfaction, but both husbands and wives had nearly equal levels of satisfaction by the time they had been married nine years and more.

However, in Japan, if satisfaction in marriage is not enough, there is a technological solution. In this case it is the multibillion-dollar "love hotel" industry (Cronin 1995). It's hard to miss some love hotels. They can be astoundingly gaudy affairs on the outside, often done up to vaguely resemble such out-of-place icons as cruise ships, wedding cakes, or the Statue of Liberty. Otherwise, love hotels are paradigms of discretion. You drive into a parking lot whose entrance is covered with long cloth fringes to foil prying eyes. Various types of pull-down or clip-on devices are available for covering up your licence plate, lest a jealous spouse take to cruising the lot in search of your car.

The most impressive concession to privacy offered by many love hotels, however, is the ability to check in and out without interacting with any staff. Just inside the entrance to the hotel is an electronic screen that tells you the numbers of the rooms that are vacant. You then make your way to one of the rooms and gain entrance by inserting yen notes (typically about $30 an hour) into a computerized lock. The door flies open, and that room number disappears from the screen at the entrance.

High-tech touches inside the neat, if small and slightly garish, rooms can include wide-screen-video karaoke and a remote-controlled sound system that offers not only dozens of music channels but also noises such as gongs and crowing roosters (hey, whatever turns you on) and even the sounds you would hear in a train station (to be played as background when you phone your boss or spouse from the room to say you're going to be late).

When you leave, maids are electronically summoned by the computerized door lock to thoroughly clean and sanitize the room. One hour and five minutes after you first walked in, the room number is back up on the board.

Sexual activity of couples can be both an indication of marital satisfaction and a cause of marital satisfaction. Anthropologists have not studied this topic much, but help from sociologists working with survey data is available. Analysis of reports of marital sex from a 1988 survey in the United States shows that frequency per month declines with duration of marriage, from an average of 12 times per month for people aged 19 to 24 years, to less than once a month for people 75 years of age and older (Call, Sprecher, and Schwartz 1995). Older married people have sex less frequently, as do those who report being less happy. Within each age category, sex is more frequent among three categories of people: those who are cohabiting but not married, those who had cohabited before marriage, and those who were in their second or later marriage. A more recent survey, conducted in 1992, revealed that the people who reported the highest levels of physical and emotional pleasure were those who, either married or cohabiting, were in relationships in which the spouse or partner had not had another sexual relationship in the past year (Laumann et al. 1994:364).

Sibling Relationships

Sibling relationships are another understudied aspect of kinship dynamics. Suad Joseph (1994) provides an example of research on this topic in her study of a working-class neighbourhood of Beirut, Lebanon, prior to the civil war. She got to know several families well and became especially close to Hanna, the oldest son in one of these families. Hanna was an attractive young man, considered a good marriage choice, with friends across religious and ethnic groups. He seemed peace-loving and conscientious. Therefore, the author reports: "I was shocked . . . one sunny afternoon to hear Hanna shouting at his sister Flaur and slapping her across the face" (50). Aged 12, Flaur was the oldest daughter. "She seemed to have an opinion on most things, was never shy to speak her mind, and welcomed guests with boisterous laughter. . . . With a lively sense of humor and good-natured mischief about her, neighbors thought of her as a live wire" (50). Further consideration of the relationship between Hanna and Flaur indicated that Hanna played a fatherly role to Flaur. He would be especially irritated with her if she lingered on the street near their apartment building, gossiping with other girls: "He would forcibly escort her upstairs to their apartment, slap her, and demand that she behave with dignity" (51). Adult family members thought nothing was wrong and said that Flaur enjoyed her brother's aggressive attention. Flaur herself commented, "It doesn't even hurt when Hanna hits me" and that she hoped to have a husband like Hanna.

An interpretation of this common brother–sister relationship in Arab culture is that it is part of the socializing process that maintains and perpetuates patriarchal family relationships: "Hanna was teaching Flaur to accept male power in the name of love . . . loving his sister meant taking charge of her and that he could discipline her if his action was understood to be in her interest. Flaur was reinforced in learning that the love of a man could include that male's violent control and that to receive his love involved submission to control" (52). This close and unequal sibling relationship persists throughout life. Even after marriage, a brother maintains a position of responsibility toward his sister and her children, as does a married sister toward her brother and his children. This loyalty can lead to conflict between husband and wife as each vies for support and resources from their respective spouses in competition with siblings.

Domestic Violence

Domestic violence can occur between domestic partners, parents and children, and siblings. Violence between domestic partners, with males dominating as perpetrators and women as victims, seems to be found in almost all cultures, although in varying forms and frequencies (J. K. Brown 1992). A cross-cultural review of ethnographic evidence of wife beating revealed that wife beating is more common and more severe in societies where men control the wealth and less common and less severe where women's work groups are prominent (Levinson 1989).

(See the Lessons Applied box.) The presence of women's work groups appears to be related to a greater importance of women in production and matrifocal residence. Both factors provide women with the means to leave an abusive relationship. For example, among the Garifuna, an African-Indian people of Belize, Central America, incidents of spouse abuse occur, but they are infrequent and not extended (Kerns 1992). Women's solidarity in this matrifocal society to a large extent limits male violence against women.

Increased domestic violence worldwide throws into question the notion of the house as a refuge or place of security. In North America, for example, evidence exists for high and increasing rates of intrahousehold abuse of children (including sexual abuse), violence between spouses or partners, and abuse of aged family members. More cross-cultural research is needed to help policymakers understand the factors affecting the safety of individuals within households.

HOUSEHOLD TRANSFORMATIONS

The composition and sheer existence of a particular household can change due to several factors including divorce, death, and possible remarriage. This section reviews some anthropological findings on these topics.

Divorce and Kinship Patterns

Divorce and separation, like marriage and other forms of long-term union, are cultural universals, even though they

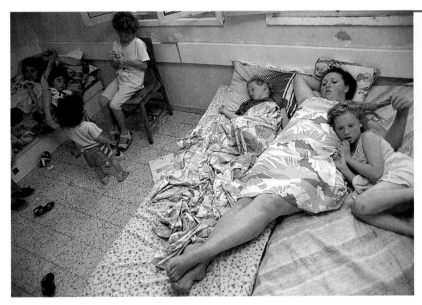

A shared bedroom in a battered woman's shelter, Tel Aviv, Israel. Many people wonder why abused women do not leave their abusers. Part of the answer lies in the unavailability and low quality of shelters throughout much of the world. Another factor is that a woman who leaves an abusive relationship is often in greater danger of serious injury (or death) than when she stays in the relationship.

Lessons Applied

WIFE ABUSE IN RURAL KENTUCKY

DOMESTIC VIOLENCE in the United States is reportedly highest in the state of Kentucky. An ethnographic study of domestic violence in Kentucky revealed several cultural factors that make it difficult to prevent wife abuse in this region (Websdale 1995). The study included interviews with 50 abused wives in eastern Kentucky as well as with battered women in shelters, police officers, shelter employees, and social workers.

Three categories of isolation exist in rural Kentucky and make domestic violence particularly difficult to prevent:

- *Physical isolation* The women reported a feeling of physical isolation in their lives. Abusers' tactics were more effective because of geographical isolation:

   The batterer's strategies, according to the women, included removing the phone from the receiver (for example, when leaving for work) . . . locking the thermostat, especially in winter, as a form of torture; disabling motor vehicles to reduce or eliminate the possibility of her leaving the residence; destroying motor vehicles; closely monitoring the odometer reading on motor vehicles (a simple yet effective form of control due to the lack of alternative means of transportation); driving recklessly to intimidate his partner; discharging firearms in public (for example, at a battered woman's pet). (106–107)

   It is difficult to leave an abusive home located many kilometres from the nearest paved road, especially if the woman has children. No public transportation serves even the paved road. Nearly one-third of households had no phones. Getting to a phone to report abuse results in delay and gives police the impression that the call is less serious.

   Physical remoteness delays response time to calls for help and increases a woman's sense of hopelessness. Sheriffs have acquired a very poor reputation among battered women in the region for not attending domestic calls at all.
- *Social isolation* Aspects of rural family life and gender roles lead to a system of "passive policing." In rural Kentucky, men are seen as providers and women are strongly tied to domestic work and child rearing. When women do work, their wages are about 50 per-

cent of men's wages. Residence is often in the vicinity of the husband's family, which creates isolation of a woman from the potential support of her natal family and restricts help-seeking in the immediate vicinity because the husband's family is likely to be non-supportive. Police officers, especially local ones, view the family as a private unit, a man's world. They are less inclined to intervene and arrest husbands whom they feel should be dominant in the family. In some instances, the police take the batterer's side, share the batterer's understandings of the situation, and have similar beliefs in a man's right to control his wife.

- *Institutional isolation* Battered women in rural areas face special problems in using the limited services of the state. The fact that abused women often know the people who run the services ironically inhibits the women from approaching them, given values of family privacy. In addition, social services for battered women in Kentucky are scarce. Other institutional constraints include less schooling for rural women than urban women, lack of daycare centres to allow mothers the option to work outside the home, inadequate health services with doctors appearing unfamiliar with domestic violence, and religious teaching of fundamentalist Christianity that supports patriarchal values, including the idea that it is women's duty to stay in a marriage, to "weather the storm."

The analysis suggests some recommendations. Women need more and better employment opportunities to reduce their economic dependency on abusive partners. Rural outreach programs should be strengthened. Expanded telephone subscriptions might decrease rural women's institutional isolation. Because of the complexity of the social situation in Kentucky, no single solution will suffice.

FOOD FOR THOUGHT

Think of some ways in which the structural conditions in Kentucky differ from or resemble those in another context where wife beating occurs.

may be frowned on or forbidden. Marriages may break up for several reasons: Voluntary separation and death of one of the partners are the most common. Globally, distinct variations exist in the legality and propriety of divorce. Some religions, such as Roman Catholicism, prohibit divorce. In some cultures, such as Islamic societies, divorce is easier for a husband to obtain than for a wife. Important questions about marital dissolution include the causes for it, the reasons rates of divorce appear to be rising worldwide, and the implications for the welfare of children of divorced parents.

Why do divorce rates vary cross-culturally? One hypothesis suggests that divorce rates will be lower in cultures with unilineal descent, where a large descent group has control over and interests in offspring (Barnard and Good 1984:119). Royal lineages, with their strong vested interests in maintaining the family line, are examples of groups especially unlikely to favour divorce, because divorce generally means losing control of offspring. When Princess Diana agreed to an uncontested divorce from Prince Charles in February 1996, she negotiated a lump-sum payment estimated at £17 million. More importantly, she asked to continue to be involved in all decisions related to her children and remain in Kensington Palace. However, she was stripped of her title of honour, a poignant decision in light of her tragic death in August 1997.

How does this theory of a relation between kinship systems and divorce hold up in the face of evidence? In bilateral foraging societies, couples generally have a fluid way of both joining and then breaking up. The same is true for contemporary North America with its (more or less) bilateral system. Patrilineal kinship systems of Pakistan and northern India seem related to the low divorce rates there.

Are separation and divorce more characteristic of some kinds of unions than others? In North America, people in cohabiting relationships are more likely to split up than people who are formally married, and the same is likely to be true in other contexts as well. In La Laja, Venezuela, a poor *barrio*, or neighbourhood in a city, three forms of marriage exist: church marriage, legal marriage, and common-law marriage through co-residence for a period of time (Peattie 1968:45). Church marriages are the least common form of marriage in La Laja. People say that they are expensive because of the costs for clothing and festivities required. Women in La Laja comment that a church marriage is bad because it permits no divorce: It is a contract with no escape clause in a society where separation often seems appropriate. Common-law marriages, the predominant form in La Laja, may be terminated by either party. For example, women said, "He left me for another woman." "He drank too much and I decided to spend the rest of my years in peace with my children" (46).

How durable are marriages with multiple spouses? Concerning the relationship between polygyny and divorce, a case study in Nigeria found that two-wife arrangements are the most stable, while unions with three or more wives have the highest rates of disruption (Gage-Brandon 1992).

Gender and Divorce

Now we consider two examples of how gender roles affect an individual's ability to obtain a divorce and the nature of the settlement, including child custody. Both the situation in Islamic law and the challenges faced in Canada by lesbian mothers indicate how the law favours males.

Throughout most of the Islamic world, the law grants men easy access to divorce. Secular Turkey is the only Muslim nation in which the law allows women and men equal access to divorce. Elsewhere, for Islamic women, divorce is difficult, expensive, and usually unsuccessful. Variations in the requirements for divorce under Islam exist according to different schools of law. The branch called *Maliki law* is the most liberal (Mir-Hosseini 1993). It provides three modes of divorce. The first and most common is separation by *khul'*, which is initiated by the husband. He secures his wife's consent and they come to an agreement about the compensation to be given to her. *Khul'* divorce does not require legal action.

The second type is the age-old form called *talaq*, or "repudiation." This form is reserved for the husband, who simply says, "I divorce you" three times, with or without the knowledge or consent of the wife. The husband needs to get the *talaq* registered by two Notary Judges. Some limitations on *talaq* exist: A man cannot divorce a wife by *talaq* when he is intoxicated, in a fit of violence or anger, or when his wife is menstruating. The husband must pay a consolation gift whenever he repudiates his wife. The amount of compensation may be contested by the wife in court. It is not based on length of marriage, but more on the degree of harm to the wife, especially if the husband repudiated her on caprice; it is less if she is at fault or gave her consent. In Morocco, in 1987, 10 percent of the 1898 divorce cases filed were initiated by men who sought to reduce the dues set by the Notary Judge when they registered their *talaq*.

The third way to obtain a divorce is *tatliq*, a form pursued by women. Grounds for divorce under *tatliq* include the husband's failure to provide maintenance, the husband having an incurable disease injurious to the wife (such as insanity or leprosy, but only if she was not aware of the condition before marriage), the husband's ill treatment of the wife, the husband's absence for a period of at least one year and its effect of causing the wife harm, and the husband's abandonment of marital relations resulting from his taking an oath of sexual abstinence (he is given a period of four months to break the oath). Divorce by *tatliq* requires extensive written proof, including medical certificates, bank statements, and reports by witnesses. Of 156 *tatliq* divorces recorded in two Moroccan cities, the husband's absence was the grounds for nearly half of the total. Success rates for divorce by *tatliq* are low, with variation according to the grounds. Divorce on the grounds of harm has the lowest rate of acceptance, because it is so difficult to prove, given the demanding requirements for written testimony from witnesses and other documentation.

Lesbian mothers face many barriers in getting a fair divorce settlement from a former heterosexual marriage. Child custody is a key issue, as revealed by an ethnographic study conducted in California: "Of the formerly married heterosexual women I interviewed, 24 percent had either experienced an actual custody action or been threatened by one. The proportion of lesbian mothers who reported such experiences rose to 41 percent" (Lewin 1993:163). Judges tend to view lesbian mothers as unsuitable custodial parents because of their sexual orientation. In Canada, judges have adopted what might appear to be a more "reasonable" approach (Arnup 2000:203). Canadian courts argued that if the lesbian mothers were discreet about their lifestyles, they would be considered suitable mothers. However, as in the United States, Canadian lesbian mothers attempting to protect themselves from custody challenges from their former husbands often adopt an "appeasement strategy." They keep a low profile—abandoning claims to marital property and to child and spousal support, and compromising on issues such as visitation. One lesbian mother gave up her share in the marital house, saying "He never really brought it into the negotiations directly. But he would like call me and harass me, and by innuendo suggest that there were many issues that he could bring up if he wanted to. . . . So basically, I traded my equity in the house for that issue not being raised at that time" (Lewin 1993:170). These strategies have negative consequences, limiting contact between father and child and reducing parental discussion about the child.

Widow(er)hood

The position of a widow or widower carries altered responsibilities and rights. Women's position as widows is often marked symbolically. In some Mediterranean cultures, a widow must wear modest, simple, black clothing, sometimes for the rest of her life. Her sexuality is supposed to be virtually dead. At the same time, her new "asexual" status allows her greater spatial freedom than before. She can go to public coffeehouses and taverns, something not done by women whose husbands are living.

Extreme restrictions on widows are recorded for parts of South Asia, where social pressures on a widow strongly enforce self-denial and self-deprivation, especially among the propertied class. A widow should wear only a plain white sari, shave her head, eat little food, and live an asexual life. Many widows in India are abandoned, especially if they have no son to support them. They are considered polluting and inauspicious. In a similar fashion, in South Africa, widows experience symbolic and life-quality changes much more than do widowers:

> A widower is encouraged to take on the challenge of picking up the pieces and to face life again. He is reminded that he must be strong and swallow his pain. His body is not marked in any significant way except to have his head shaved, as is the custom in most African communities.
>
> He also is required to wear a black button or arm band. The period of mourning for widowers is generally six months, compared to at least one year for widows. . . . The fear of the ritual danger embodied in widows is expressed in terms of "heat," "darkness," and "dirt.". . . Her body is marked in different communities by some or all of the following practices: shaving her head, smearing a mixture of herbs and ground charcoal on her body, wearing black clothes made from an inexpensive material, and covering her face with a black veil and her shoulders with a black shawl. A widow may express her liminal status in a variety of ways, [by] eating with her left hand, wearing clothes inside out, wearing one shoe, or eating out of a lid instead of a plate (Ramphele 1996:100).

Remarriage

Remarriage patterns are influenced by economic factors and gender-linked expectations that shape a person's desirability as a partner. In North America, divorce frequently is followed by remarriage for both males and females, with

A widow of Madeira, Portugal, wearing the typical modest black clothing required in some Mediterranean cultures as a sign of widowhood.

a slight edge for men (Cornell 1989). In Japan, the tendency to remarry for males is significantly greater than for women. A marked age distribution in non-remarriage for women exists: "[W]hile divorced Japanese women, up to age 40, are already about 15% more likely to remain divorced than are their U.S. white female counterparts of the same age, after age 40 their situation grows rapidly more unfavorable for remarriage. In the subsequent decade it rises to 25% more divorced at age 45, 40% more at age 48, more than half again as many at age 50, and 65% more at age 51" (460). Older women's lower rates of remarriage are the result of age-hypergynous marriage and males' greater access to economic and political resources that increase their attractiveness as marriage partners in spite of their increasing age.

Social Change and Domestic Life

Changing economic opportunities in recent times have led to rapid change in household structures and dynamics. For example, employment of daughters in electronics factories in Malaysia has changed intrahousehold power structures (Ong 1987). The girls' mothers encourage them to take up factory work and urge them to contribute a proportion of their earnings to the household economy. This frees up daughters from their father's control (as is traditional among Malaysian Muslims), while giving greater control to the mother.

International migration is another major cause of change in family and household formations (see Chapter 15). Dramatic changes can occur in one generation when members of a farming household in, for example, Taiwan or India, migrate to England, France, Canada, or the United States. In their homeland, having many children makes economic sense, but it does not in their new destination. These migrants decide to have only one or two children and live in small, isolated nuclear households.

International migration creates new challenges for relationships between parents and children. The children often become strongly identified with the new culture and have little connection with their ancestral culture, and this pattern can be a source of anxiety for their parents. Often, values in the new culture conflict with those of the culture of origin, putting children in conflict with their parents over issues such as dating, dress, and career goals.

In 1997, the people of Norway were confronted with a case of kidnapping of an 18-year-old Norwegian citizen named "Nadia," who was taken by her parents to Morocco and held captive there (Wikan 2000). The full story is a complicated one, but the core issues revolve around conflict between Moroccan family values and Norwegian ones. Nadia's parents felt that she should be under their control and that they had the right to arrange her marriage in Morocco, while Nadia held a Norwegian concept of personal autonomy. In the end, Nadia and her parents returned to Norway, where the courts granted that, for the sake of the family, the parents not be jailed on grounds of kidnapping their daughter. The case brought stigma to Nadia among the Muslim community of Norway, who viewed her as a traitor to her culture. She now lives at a secret address and avoids publicity. An anthropologist close to this case who served as an expert cultural witness during the trial of her parents reports that, in spite of her seclusion, she has offered help to other young women who have sought her out.

Cultural anthropologists and sociologists have valuable insights to offer policy-makers and concerned individuals about the current status of "the family" and future trends in family/household structure and dynamics in North America. In 2001, households in Canada numbered over 12.5 million, more than doubling in less than 40 years (Statistics Canada 2002). During the same period, household size shrank from an average of 3.9 persons to 2.4 persons. In the United States the share headed by married couples declined from 74 percent to 55 percent. The current situation contains several seemingly contradictory patterns that were first noted in the early 1980s by two sociologists (Cherlin and Furstenberg 1992): (1) the number of unmarried couples living together has more than tripled since 1970, and (2) one out of four children is not living with both parents. At current rates, half of all North American marriages begun in the 1980s will end in divorce.

What about domestic life in this new millennium? Basic outlines of the near future indicate the reduced economic dependence of women and the weakening of marriage in industrialized societies (Cherlin 1996:478–480). These changes, in turn, will lead to increased movement away from nuclear household living and increased diversity in household forms.

At the beginning of the twenty-first century, three kinds of households are most common in North America: households composed of couples living in their first marriage, single-parent households, and households formed through remarriage (Cherlin and Furstenberg 1992:3). A new fourth category is the **intergenerational household**, in which an "adult child" returns to live with his or her parents. About 45 percent of unmarried adults in Canada between the ages of 20 and 35 share a home with their mother or father or both (Boyd and Norris 1999). Currently, in North America, adult offspring spend over two hours a day doing household chores, with daughters contributing about 17 hours a week and sons 14.4 hours. The daughters spend most of their time doing laundry, cooking, cleaning, and washing dishes, while sons are more involved in yard work and car care. Even so, the parents still do three-quarters of the housework.

Domestic arrangements are certainly not a dull and static concept. Just trying to keep up to date on their changing patterns in North America is a daunting task, not to mention the rest of the world.

WHAT is a household and what are major household forms?

A household is a domestic group comprising people who may or may not be related by kinship and who share a living space and, often, budgetary responsibilities for the household. Nuclear households are defined as consisting of a mother and father and their children, but they can also be just a husband and wife without children. Nuclear households are found in all cultures, but are most clearly associated with industrial societies with their emphasis on neolocal residence upon marriage. Extended households include more than one nuclear household. Extended households are often both the ideal and the most common pattern in cultures where unilineal descent is practised and where either patrilocal or matrilocal residence upon marriage means that married children live with or near the parents of either the groom or bride. Stem households, which are especially common in East Asia, are a variant of extended households. In stem households, only one child, usually the first-born son, remains with the parents. Household headship can be either shared between two adult partners or can be borne by a single person as in woman-headed households.

WHAT are some important economic and social features of households?

Households, depending on the context, are involved to varying degrees in production, consumption, and exchange. In non-industrial societies, households often fulfill all these functions. In industrial societies, they are more concerned with consumption and exchange since most production takes place outside the household. Intrahousehold dynamics, or social relationships among members of a household, involve interactions predominantly between parents and children and among siblings. Research on intrahousehold dynamics has revealed that households are complex arenas of power conflicts as well as sharing, and security as well as occasional violence. Household breakup comes about through divorce, separation of cohabiting partners, or death of a spouse or partner.

HOW are household patterns changing?

The increasingly globally connected world in which we live has marked effects on household patterns. While marriage continues to be a prominent basis for nuclear and extended household formation, other options for household formation, such as cohabitation, continue to be important. Yet others are becoming more important in some contexts, such as single-parent or single-person households. In contradiction to theories predicting the decline of the extended household with modernization, evidence suggests continuity of extended households in India and perhaps elsewhere. In Japan, however, maintaining the stem household structure has become more difficult due to children's increasing reluctance to live with their parents. The implications of changes in household forms and dynamics for the care of dependent members, especially children and the aged, is a key question of our times.

KEY CONCEPTS

extended households, p. 192
family, p. 192
family disaffiliation, p. 199
household, p. 192
household headship, p. 193

intergenerational household, p. 205
nuclear family, p. 192
nuclear household, p. 192
remittances, p. 199
stem household, p. 193

SUGGESTED READINGS

Dorothy Ayers Counts, Judith K. Brown, and Jacquelyn C. Campbell, *Sanctions and Sanctuaries: Cultural Perspectives on the Beating of Wives*. Boulder, CO: Westview Press, 1992. This book includes 15 case studies plus an introductory overview and concluding comparative essay. One chapter considers the possible evolutionary origin of wife abuse. The wide range of cultural contexts studied include Australia, southern Africa, Papua New Guinea, India, Central America, the Middle East, and the Pacific.

Ellen Oxfeld, *Blood, Sweat, and Mahjong: Family and Enterprise in an Overseas Chinese Community*. Ithaca, NY: Cornell University Press, 1992. This ethnography addresses the Chinese immigrant community in Calcutta, India, and family involvement in the tanning industry; attention is given to the social history of the Hakka community, gender roles, and norms about family entrepreneurship.

Peter H. Stephenson, *The Hutterian People: Ritual and Rebirth in the Evolution of Communal Life*. Lanham, MD: University Press of America, 1991. This ethnography investigates how the Hutterites have maintained a vital and long-lived utopian religious community. Many of these people live in Canada's western provinces.

Debbie Taylor, *My Children, My God: A Journey to the World of Seven Single Mothers*. Berkeley: University of California Press, 1994. This narrative report by a journalist is based on interviews with seven single mothers in different countries: Uganda, Brazil, India, China, Australia, Egypt, and Scotland.

WEBLINKS

The Companion Website (www.pearsoned.ca/miller) that accompanies *Cultural Anthropology*, Third Canadian Edition, includes a destinations module containing links to many websites relevant to the content of this chapter. Use it to investigate the Web and expand your understanding of anthropology.

KEY QUESTIONS

- **WHAT** is the range of cross-cultural variation of social groups?
- **WHAT** is social stratification, and what are its effects on people?
- **WHAT** is civil society?

10

SOCIAL GROUPS AND SOCIAL STRATIFICATION

A North Indian village carpenter seated in front of his house. The status position of carpenters is middling, neither as high and powerful as landholding elites or brahman priests, nor as low as those who deal with polluting materials such as animal hides or refuse.

This chapter focuses primarily on non-kin groups and relates to the issue of cultural formation. In Chapter 1, several factors related to the formation of local cultures were defined: class, race, ethnicity, gender, age, region, and institutions such as prisons and retirement homes. Thus far, we have looked at how these factors affect fieldwork, and how they vary in different economies and in different reproductive systems. This chapter looks again at these key factors of social differentiation in order to see how they affect group formation and the relationships between groups in terms of hierarchy and power. It first examines a variety of social groups and then considers inequalities between certain key social categories.

Canada's small population in a gigantic territory with two official languages "requires a greater use of the imagination . . . [demanding] of the citizenry a more open and active imagination, a more acute sensibility. It is not a situation for lazy minds and easy emotions" (Saul 1997:57).

The United States, which the early nineteenth century French political philosopher Alexis de Tocqueville called a "nation of joiners," has been united around powerful and unifying symbols like the "stars and stripes." Some have questioned whether Canada has developed a similar sense of unity and it often seems the nation faces imminent dissolution. Yet there is no question that, for many Canadians, membership in social groups beyond the family is an important aspect of life. The questions of what motivates people to join groups, what holds people together in groups, and how groups deal with leadership and participation have intrigued many scholars for centuries.

SOCIAL GROUPS

A **social group** is a cluster of people beyond the domestic unit who are usually related on grounds other than kinship, although kinship relationships may exist between people in the group. Two basic categories exist: the **primary group**, consisting of people who interact with each other and know each other personally, and the **secondary group**, consisting of people who identify with each other on some common ground but who may never meet with one another or interact with each other personally.

Members of all social groups have a sense of rights and responsibilities in relation to the group which, if not maintained, could mean loss of membership. Because of its face-to-face nature, membership in a primary group involves more direct accountability about rights and responsibilities than secondary group membership. When discussing different kinds of groups, social scientists also draw a distinction between informal groups and formal groups (March and Taqqu 1986:5):

- Informal groups are smaller and less visible.
- Members of informal groups have close, face-to-face relationships with one another, while members of formal groups may or may not know each other.
- Organizational structure is less hierarchical in informal groups.
- Informal groups do not have legal recognition.

Modes of economies seem to affect the proliferation of social groups, with the greatest variety being found in agricultural and industrial societies. One theory suggests that mobile populations, such as foragers and pastoralists, are less likely to develop enduring social groups beyond kin relationships. It may be true that foragers and pastoralists have less variety of social groups, but they are not completely without any social groupings. A prominent form of social group among foragers and pastoralists is an **age set**, a group of people close in age who go through certain rituals, such as circumcision, at the same time.

A related hypothesis is that settled and densely populated areas have more social groups as a way to organize society. Again, this may be generally true, but important variations and exceptions exist. Cross-culturally, both informal and formal groups appear to be more varied and active in Africa and Latin America than in South Asia (Uphoff and Esman 1984). In Bangladesh, a densely populated and agrarian country of South Asia, indigenous social groups are rare. The most prominent ties beyond the household are kinship-based (Miller and Khan 1986). In spite of the lack of indigenous social groups, however, Bangladesh has gained world renown for its success in forming local credit groups for grassroots development through an organization called the Grameen Bank, which gives loans to poor people to help them start small enterprises.

In Bali, an island province of Indonesia, several formal and focused groups exist for specific purposes, including temple committees to provide for the costs of temple maintenance and collective rites; custom-law wards to cooperate in cremation ceremonies; neighbourhood groups to send food to the temple for the gods; and irrigation groups to provide water for the rice fields (Lansing 1995). Members of all households participate in several of these groups at the same time. The precise reasons that some cultures have strong and enduring social groups beyond kinship affiliations await further exploration and explanation from social scientists.

In the following sections, we will encounter a variety of social groups. We begin with the most face-to-face, primary groups of two or three people based on friendship and move to larger groups with explicit goals, such as countercultural groups and activist groups.

Friendship

Friendship fits in the category of a primary social group that is informal. One question that cultural anthropologists ask is whether friendship is a cultural universal. Two factors make it difficult to answer this question. First, insufficient cross-cultural research exists to answer the question definitively. Second, defining friendship cross-culturally is problematic. It is likely, however, that something like "friendship" (close ties between non-kin) is a cultural universal, though shaped in different degrees from culture to culture.

Social Characteristics of Friendship

Friends are chosen on a voluntary basis, but, even so, the criteria of who qualifies as a friend may be culturally structured. For instance, gender segregation will limit cross-gender friendships and promote same-gender friendships. In Thailand, "friends until death" are friends who can be trusted with intimate knowledge of one's motivations and desires (see the Multiple Cultural Worlds box for another example). Another characteristic of friendship is that friends are supportive of each other, psychologically and sometimes materially. Support is mutual, shared back and forth in an expectable way. Friendship generally occurs between social equals.

Anthropologist Thomas Dunk researched how a group of working-class men friends in Thunder Bay, Ontario, informally ensure that everyone contributes their fair share (as in balanced exchange, see Chapter 4). After a game of lob-ball (a form of softball) the men meet at a bar. In the bar after the game, everyone takes turns buying rounds. If someone is short of money one evening, someone else or several other people stand him drinks. This "just happens"; one does not need to ask. True friends, for these men, are people who give to each other without asking, and this extends beyond the walls of the bar after a game (Dunk 1991:92).

Friendships in Prison

Prisons, like colleges and universities, are social institutions with limited populations among whom relationships may develop. In the case of colleges and universities, people are there voluntarily and have a good idea about how long they will be there. It makes sense to form enduring bonds with friends and classmates. In the context of prisons, people are not there voluntarily, and the formation of social ties is limited.

One factor that affects the formation of friendship in prisons is the duration of the sentence. A study that explored this issue first had to deal with the difficulty of doing participant observation. A research team of two people included an "insider" and an "outsider" (Schmid and Jones 1993). The "insider" was an inmate serving a short-term sentence who did participant observation, conducted interviews, and kept a journal. The "outsider," a sociologist, met with him weekly to discuss findings (he also did the analysis). The inmate researcher was a male, and so this study deals only with male prisoners. Furthermore, since his was a short-term sentence, its findings concern the effects of short-term sentencing (of one or two years) on social relationships among inmates.

Three stages of short-term inmate adaptation are typical. In the first stage, inmates experience uncertainty and fear, based on their images of what life is like in prison. They avoid contact with other prisoners and guards as

Multiple Cultural Worlds

MALE AND FEMALE FRIENDSHIPS IN RURAL SPAIN

THE PREVAILING gender division of labour and spatial gender segregation found in southern Spain shape differences in men's and women's friendship patterns (Uhl 1991). Women's lives are taken up mainly with unpaid household work within the domestic domain. Men's lives involve the two activities of work and leisure outside the house. This dichotomy is somewhat fluid, however, for women's domestic roles do take them into the public domain—markets, town hall, taking children to school—with some time for visiting friends.

Women often referred to their friends either with kin terms or as *vecina*, "neighbour," reflecting women's primary orientation to family and neighbourhood. For men, an important category of friend is an *amigo*, a friend with whom one casually interacts. This kind of casual friendship is the friendship of bars and leisure-time male camaraderie. It grows out of work, school, common sports and hobbies, and drinking together night after night. Women do not have such friendships. Men also are more likely than women to have *amigos(as) de trabajo*, friendships based on work activities. Differences between men and women also emerge in the category of "true friends," or *amigo(as) de la verdad* or *de confianza*. True friends are those with whom one shares secrets without fear of betrayal. Most men claimed to have many more true friends than the women had, reflecting their wider social networks.

FOOD FOR THOUGHT

What different categories of friends do you have? Are some kinds of friends "closer" or "truer" than others?

---

much as possible. The second stage involves the creation of a survival niche. The prisoner has selective interactions with other inmates and may develop a "partnership" with another inmate. Partners hang around together and watch out for each other. Maintaining a close tie with another inmate is difficult: "I think it would be almost impossible to carry on a relationship, a real close relationship, being here for two years or a year and a half. It's literally impossible. I think that the best thing to do is to just forget about it, and if the relationship can be picked up again once you get out, that's fine. And if it can't, you have to accept that" (453). In the third stage, the prisoner anticipates his eventual release, transfers to a minimum security area, increases contact with outside visitors, and begins the transition to the outside. In this stage, partners begin to detach from each other as one of the pair moves toward the outside world.

Friendship among the Urban Poor

Carol Stack's study of how friendship networks promote economic survival among low-income African Americans is a landmark contribution (1974). Her research was conducted in the late 1960s in "The Flats," the poorest section of a Black community in a Midwestern city. She found extensive networks of friends "supporting, reinforcing each other—devising schemes for self help, strategies for survival in a community of severe economic deprivation" (28). Close friends, in fact, are referred to by kin terms.

People in The Flats, especially women, maintain a set of friends through exchange: "swapping" goods (food, clothing) needed by someone at a particular time, sharing "child keeping," and giving or loaning food stamps and money. Such exchanges are part of a clearly understood pattern—gifts and favours go back and forth over time. Friends thus bound together are obligated to each another and can call on each other in time of need. In discussing the common practice of child keeping, Stack says,

> The exchange of children, and short-term fosterage, are common among female friends. Child-care arrangements among friends imply both rights and duties. Close friends frequently discipline each other's children verbally and physically in front of each other. In normal times, and in times of stress, close friends have a right to "ask" for one another's children. A woman visiting a friend and her children may say, "Let me keep your girl this week. She will have a fine time with me and my girls. She won't want to come back home to her mama." This kind of request among kin and friends is very hard to refuse. Temporary child-care services are also a means of obligating kin or friends for future needs. Women may ask to "keep" the child of a friend for no apparent reason. But they are, in fact, building up an investment for their future needs. (82)

In opposition to theories that suggest the breakdown of social relationships among the very poor, this research documents how poor people strategize and cope through social ties.

Clubs and Fraternities

Clubs and fraternities often define membership on some sense of shared identity. Thus, they may often, but not always, comprise people of the same ethnic heritage (such as the United Empire Loyalists in Canada), occupation or business, religion, or gender. Although many clubs appear to exist primarily to serve functions of sociability and psychological support, deeper analysis often shows that these groups do have economic and political roles as well.

Women's clubs in a lower-class neighbourhood in Paramaribo, Suriname, have multiple functions (Brana-Shute 1976). Many clubs exist, each with its own name, flag, and colour. The clubs raise funds to sponsor special events and support individual celebrations, meet financial needs, and send cards and flowers for funerals. All club members attend each other's birthday parties and death rites as a group. The clubs thus offer to the women psychological support, entertainment, and financial supports. A political aspect exists, too. Club members are often members of the same political party, and core groups of club members may attend political rallies and events together. These women constitute political interest groups that can influence political outcomes: "Interviews with politicians and party workers confirmed the existence of real pressure placed on them by women individually and in groups" (175).

College fraternities and sororities are highly selective groups that serve a variety of explicit functions, such as entertainment and social service. They also form bonds between members that may help in securing jobs after graduation. Unlike sociologists, few anthropologists have studied the "Greek system" on campuses. One exception is Peggy Sanday, who was inspired to study college fra-

In a low-income neighbourhood in Rio de Janeiro, Brazil, men play dominoes and drink beer while others observe.

ternities after a gang rape of a woman student by several fraternity brothers at the campus where she teaches. In her book, *Fraternity Gang Rape: Sex, Brotherhood, and Privilege on Campus* (1990), she explores initiation rituals, the role of pornography, ritual dances, and heavy drinking at parties, and how they relate to a pattern of male bonding solidified by victimization and derision of women. Her interviews revealed the prevalence of gang rape, or a "train" in some, not all, fraternities. Fraternity party invitations may even hint at the possibility of a "train." Typically, the brothers seek out a "party girl"— a somewhat vulnerable young woman who may be especially seeking of acceptance or especially high on alcohol or other substances (her drinks may even have been "spiked"). They take her to one of the brother's rooms where she may or may not agree to have sex with one man—often she passes out. Then a "train" of men have sex with her. Rarely prosecuted, the male participants reinforce their sense of privilege, power, and unity with one another through this group ritual involving abuse of a female outsider.

Cross-culturally, men's clubs in which strong male–male bonds are created and reinforced by the objectification and mistreatment of women are common, but not universal. They are especially associated with cultures where male–male competitiveness is an important feature of society (Bird 1996) and in which warfare and group conflict are frequent. In many Amazonian groups, the men's house is fiercely guarded from being entered by women. If a woman were to trespass on male territory, she is subject to punishment by gang rape. One interpretation is that

males have a high degree of anxiety about their identity as fierce warriors and as sexually potent males (Gregor 1982). Maintaining their identity as fierce males toward outsiders involves taking an aggressive position in relation to women of their own group. Parallels of "women-hating" men's clubs among women do not exist. University sororities are not mirror images of university fraternities. Women's groups and organizations, even if vocally anti-male, do not involve physical abuse of males or ritualized forms of derision.

Countercultural Groups

Several kinds of groups are formed by people who seek consciously to resist conforming to the dominant cultural pattern, as in the "hippie" movement of the 1960s. This section considers examples of countercultural groups. One similarity among these groups is the importance of bonding through shared rituals.

Youth Gangs

The term *gang* can refer to a variety of groups, such as one's friends, as in, "I think I'll invite the gang over for pizza" (Short 1996:325). The more specific term **youth gangs** refers to a group of young people, found mainly in urban areas, who are often considered a social problem by adults and law enforcement officials (Sanders 1994:5–15).

Youth gangs vary in terms of how formally they are organized. Gangs—like clubs and fraternities—often have formalized rituals of initiation for new members, a recognized leader, and symbolic markers of identity such as tattoos or special clothing. An example of an informal youth gang with no formal leadership hierarchy or initiation rituals are the "Masta Liu," found in Honiara, the capital city of the Solomon Islands (Jourdan 1995). The primary unifying feature of the male youth who become Masta Liu is the fact that they are unemployed. Most have migrated to the city from the countryside to escape what they consider an undesirable lifestyle there: working in the fields under control of their elders. Yet, as a group, they have developed a distinct lifestyle and identity:

> Drifting in and out of jobs, in and out of hope, they are very often on the verge of delinquency. Many of them have had some brush with the law . . . songs are being written about them, people talk about them. . . . The *liu* have become a significant segment of the urban population, not only because of their sheer numbers, but because of the influence they have on the development of the urban popular culture. Their life-style, the way they dress and talk, their taste in music and films, their outlook on life, all this gives a particular direction to social change in Honiara. (202)

Some *liu* live with extended kin in the city, others organize *liu*-only households. They spend their time wandering around town (*wakabaot*) in groups of up to 10: "They stop at every shop on their way, eager to look at the merchandise but afraid to be kicked out by the security guards; they check out all the cinemas only to dream in front of the preview posters . . . not even having the $2 bill that will allow them to get in; they gaze for hours on end, and without moving, at the electronic equipment displayed in the Chinese shops, without saying a word: one can read in their gaze the silent dreams they create" (210).

"Street gangs" are a more formal variety of youth gang. They generally have leaders and a hierarchy of membership roles and responsibilities. They are named and their members mark their identity with tattoos or "colours." Much popular thinking associates street gangs with violence, but not all are involved in violence. An anthropologist who did research among nearly 40 street gangs in New York, Los Angeles, and Boston learned much about why individuals join gangs, providing insights that contradict popular thinking (Jankowski 1991). One common perception is that young boys join gangs because they are from homes with no male authority figure with whom they could identify. In the gangs studied, just as many gang members were from intact nuclear households as from families with an absent father (39).

Another common perception is that the gang replaces a missing feeling of "family" as a motive. This study, again, showed that the same number of gang members reported having close family ties as those who didn't.

What, then, might be the reasons behind joining a male urban gang? A particular personality type characterized many gang members, a type that could be called a "defiant individualist." The defiant individualist type has five

Members of the gang "18" in San Salvador, El Salvador, passing time on the street. The group's leader prohibits the use of alcohol and drugs except on Saturdays and Sundays.

traits: intense competitiveness, mistrust or wariness, self-reliance, social isolation, and a strong survival instinct. Urban poverty possibly leads to the development of this kind of personality structure. It becomes a reasonable response to the economic obstacles and uncertainty.

The global spread of urban youth gangs relates to global economic changes in urban employment. In many countries, the declining urban industrial base has created persistent poverty in inner-city communities (Short 1996:326). At the same time, aspirations for a better life have been promoted through schooling and the popular media. Urban gang members, in this view, are the victims of large structural forces beyond their control. Yet research with gangs shows that they are not just passive victims of structural forces. Many of these youths want to be economically successful, but social conditions channel their interests and skills into illegal pursuits rather than into legal pathways to achievement.

Motorcycle Gangs

Another "countercultural" group similar to the "street gangs" is the widespread North American (and growing global) phenomenon of outlaw motorcycle gangs. In the late 1940s young men who had served in the citizen armies of Canada and the United States formed clubs of motorcycle riders. Some of these developed into the "one per centers," the one percent of motorcyclists who were troublemakers according to mainstream motorcycle enthusiasts. The "outlaw" clubs are characterized by wearing colours, or club insignia, which often include pictures of skulls or weapons meant to intimidate citizens and other

Members of the Hell's Angels biker gang leave a chapel in Edmonton after the funeral of a brother who was killed in a motor vehicle accident.

gang members alike. The club member typically "chops" or modifies his "hog" (a Harley-Davidson motorcycle), and exhibits loyalty to his brothers by helping defend a particular territory by physical force, if necessary.

Daniel R. Wolf (1991), an anthropologist who managed to become a member of one such club in Edmonton, describes how and why young working-class men find identity and satisfaction in the gang. Working-class employment does not provide the sense of self or meaning that may be available to other societal roles in industrial Canada. Wolf argues that the motorcycle club provides these young alienated men with an identity and community they cannot find elsewhere (340). Riding in the wind, partying with brothers, and participating in sexual orgies with compliant women ("mamas") balance the constant threat of being hassled by the police and the dangers of physical injury both from citizens in "cages" (cars or trucks) running them off the roads and from fights with other gangs.

Body Modification Groups

Of the many non-mainstream movements in North America, one includes people who have a sense of community strengthened through forms of body alteration. James Myers (1992) did research in California among people who feel they are a special group because of their interest in permanent body modification, especially genital piercing, branding, and cutting. Myers was involved in six workshops organized especially for the San Francisco SM (sadomasochist) community by Powerhouse, a San Francisco Bay Area SM organization; the Fifth Annual Living in Leather Convention held in Portland, Oregon, in 1990; and time in tattoo and piercing studios as well as talking with students and others in his home town who were involved in these forms of body modification. The study population included males and females, heterosexuals, gays, lesbians, bisexuals, and SMers. The single largest group was SM homosexuals and bisexuals. The study population was mainly White, and most had either attended or graduated from college.

Myers witnessed many modification sessions at workshops: Those seeking modification go up on stage and have their chosen procedure done by a well-known expert. Whatever the procedure, the volunteers evidence little pain (usually a sharp intake of breath at the moment the needle passes through or the brand touches skin). After that critical moment, the audience breathes an audible sigh of relief. The volunteer stands up, adjusts clothing, and members of the audience applaud. Myers interprets this public event as a kind of initiation ritual that binds the expert, the volunteer, and the group together. Pain has long been recognized as an important part of rites of passage, providing an edge to the ritual drama. The audience in this case witnesses and validates the experience and also becomes joined to the initiate through witnessing.

Left: A Tahitian chief wears traditional tattoos that indicate his high status. Right: A woman with tattooed arms and pierced nose in the United States.

A prominent motivation for seeking permanent body modification was a desire to identify with a specific group of people, and the body marking is thus a sign of affiliation. As one informant said,

> It's not that we're sheep, getting pierced or cut just because everyone else is. I like to think it's because we're a very special group and we like doing something that sets us off from others. . . . You see all the guys at the bar and you know they are pierced and tattooed, and it gives you a good feeling to know that you're one of them. . . . Happiness is standing in line at a cafeteria and detecting that the straight-looking babe in front of you has her nipples pierced. I don't really care what her sexual orientation is, I can relate to her. (292)

Work Groups

Work groups are organized to perform specific tasks, although they also may have other functions, including sociality and friendship among members. They are found in all modes of production, but they tend to be more prominent in pre-industrialized horticultural and agricultural communities where land preparation, harvesting, or repair of irrigation canals requires large inputs of labour that exceed the capability of a single household unit. In her classic study of the Bemessi people of Cameroon, West Africa, Phyllis Kaberry (1952) describes a labour group system (called a *tzo*, translated as "working bee"):

> [A *tzo*] consists of women who are of about the same age and who are kin or friendly neighbors. For the preparation of corn beds there may be ten or twelve individuals; for weedings only three or four. About a week's notice is given and, once a woman has received help on her own plot, she is under an obligation to fulfill a similar duty to others on pain of being reported to the *Fon* (chief). The women usually work in pairs, chat, and urge each other on. Towards the end of the afternoon a small repast is provided, which includes a little fish contributed by the husband. (56)

Youth work groups are common in African regions south of the Sahara, particularly in settled, crop-growing areas. Such work groups are often composed of one or more age sets. The major responsibility of the youth groups is providing field labour. The group works one or more days in the village chief's fields for no remuneration. The group also maintains public paths and the public meeting area, constructs and maintains roads between villages, builds and repairs canals, combats brush fires, maintains the village mosque, and prevents animals from grazing where they aren't allowed (Leynaud 1961). Girls' groups exist, but in patrilocal contexts they are less durable because their marriage and relocation breaks ties with childhood companions (Hammond 1966:133). As adults, however, women in African cultures have many types of associations, such as mothers' groups, savings groups, and work groups.

Irrigation organizations are formal groups devoted to maintaining irrigation canals and dealing with the tricky issue of distributing the water. Indigenous irrigation organizations are common around the world and have been the focus of much anthropological and sociological attention. These organizations are responsible for a highly valued good, and they tend to develop leadership and membership rules and roles. Given the fact that watershed systems are connected across large regions, irrigation organizations often provide a link between local groups. Allocating the water from the systems also requires careful administration. As is often the case, water is allocated proportionally according to landholdings (Coward 1976, 1979). But farmers who are downstream are more likely to be deprived of their fair share than farmers who are upstream and can divert more water to their fields. In order to deal with conflicts that arise from this built-in inequity in one area of the Philippines, subgroups of farmers formed to meet and discuss distribution problems.

Another administrative issue relates to corruption such as water theft, in which a particular farmer will tap off water out of turn (D. H. Price 1995). In one area of Egypt, water theft was more common as distance from the main canal increased. These farmers felt they were justified because they tended to get less water through the distribution system than farmers closer to the source.

Cooperatives

Cooperatives are a form of economic group with two key features: surpluses are shared among the members, and decision making follows the democratic principle of one person, one vote (Estrin 1996). Agricultural and credit cooperatives are the most common forms of cooperatives worldwide, followed by consumer cooperatives.

We will look at two examples of cooperatives to see how human agency, within different structures, can bring about positive results. In the first case, the cooperative gives its members economic strength and checks the power of the richest farmers in one region of India. In the second case, women craft producers in Panama achieve economic position within the world market and also build social ties and political leadership skills.

Farmers' Cooperatives in Western India

In India's western state of Maharashtra, the sugar industry is largely owned and operated through farmer cooperatives (Attwood 1992). Most shareholders are small farmers, producing just one or two acres of sugar cane. Yet the sugar industry, owned and managed cooperatively, is huge, almost as large as the state's iron and steel industry. In contrast, in the northern states where sugar cane is grown, cooperatives are not prominent.

How and why are sugar cooperatives so successful in this region? The answer lies in the different pattern of social stratification. The rural social stratification system in Maharashtra is simpler than in northern India. In most villages, the Marathas are the dominant caste, but they constitute even more of a majority and they control even more village land than is typical of dominant castes. They also have stronger local ties with each other because their marital arrangements are locally centralized. Thus, they have a better basis for cooperating with each other in spite of class differences among themselves. Large farmers dominate the elected board of directors of the cooperatives. These "sugar barons" use their position to gain power in state politics. However, within the cooperatives, their power is held in check. They do not form cliques that exploit the cooperatives to the detriment of the less wealthy. In fact, large farmers cannot afford to alienate the small and mid-sized farmers, for that would mean economic ruin for the cooperative and the loss of their own profits. The technology of sugar cane processing requires wide participation of the farmers. Mechanization involves investing in expensive heavy equipment. The machinery cannot be run at a profit unless it is used at full capacity during the crushing season. If small and mid-sized farmers were displeased with their treatment, they might decide to pull out of the cooperative and put their cane into other uses. Then capacity would be underused and profits would fall. If the large farmers were to try to take advantage of the system, they would be "cutting their own throats." The success of cooperatives has much to do with the power balance between large farmers versus the mid-sized and small farmers.

Kuna Indian woman selling *molas*, San Blas Islands, Panama.

Craft Cooperatives in Panama

In Panama's east coastal region, Kuna women have long sewn beautiful *molas*, or cloth with appliquéd designs. This cloth is made for their own use as clothing (Tice 1995). Since the 1960s, *molas* have been important items for sale both on the world market and to tourists who come to Panama. Revenue from selling *molas* is now an important part of the household income of the Kuna. Some women continue to operate independently, buying their own cloth and thread and selling their *molas* either to an intermediary who exports them or in the local tourist market. But many other women have joined cooperatives that offer them greater economic security.

The cooperative buys cloth and thread in bulk and distributes it to the women. The women are paid almost the entire sale price for each *mola*, with only a small amount of the eventual sale prices being taken out for cooperative dues and administrative costs. Their earnings are steadier than what the fluctuating tourist season offers.

Beyond the initial economic reasons for joining the cooperative, other benefits include the use of the cooperative as a consumer's cooperative (buying rice and sugar in bulk for members), as a source of mutual strength and support, and as a basis for women's greater leadership skills and opportunities for political participation in the wider society.

SOCIAL STRATIFICATION

Social stratification consists of hierarchical relationships between different groups—as if they were arranged in layers or "strata." Stratified groups may be unequal on a variety of measures, including material resources, power, human welfare, education, and symbolic attributes. People in groups in higher positions have privileges not experienced by those in lower groups, and they are likely to be interested in maintaining their privileged position. Social stratification emerged late in human history, most clearly with the emergence of agriculture. Now some form of social stratification is nearly universal.

Analysis of the categories—such as class, race, gender, and age—that form stratification systems reveals a crucial difference in the degree to which membership in a given category is an **ascribed position**, based on qualities of a person gained through birth, or an **achieved position**, based on qualities of a person gained through action. Ascribed positions include one's race, ethnicity, gender, age, and physical ability. These factors are generally out of the control of the individual, although some scope for flexibility exists in gender through surgery and hormonal treatments and for certain kinds of physical conditions. Also, one can sometimes "pass" for being a member of another race or ethnic group. Age is an interesting ascribed category because an individual will pass through several different status levels associated with age. Achievement as a basis for group membership means that a person belongs on the basis of some valued attainment. Ascribed systems are thus more "closed" and achievement-based systems more "open" in terms of mobility within the system (either upward or downward). Some scholars of social status believe that increasing social complexity and modernization led to an increase in achievement-based positions and a decline in ascription-based positions.

In this section, we look at the way key social categories define group membership and varying relations of inequality among groups.

The Concept of Status Groups

Societies place people into categories—student, husband, child, retired person, political leader, or member of the Order of Canada—which are referred to as a person's **status** (position or standing in society) (C. Wolf 1996). Each status has an accompanying **role** (expected behaviour for someone of a particular status), with a "script" for how to behave, look, and talk. Some statuses have more prestige attached to them than others (the word *status* can be used to mean prestige, relative value, and worth). Groups, like individuals, have status, or standing in society. Noted German sociologist Max Weber called lower-status groups "disprivileged groups." These include, in different contexts and in different times, physically disabled people, people with certain illnesses such as leprosy or HIV/AIDS, indigenous peoples, minorities, members of particular religions, women, and others.

Within societies that have marked status positions, different status groups are marked by a particular lifestyle, including goods owned, leisure activities, and linguistic styles. The maintenance of group position by higher-status categories is sometimes accomplished by exclusionary practices in relation to lower-status groups through a tendency toward group in-marriage and by socializing only within the group.

Class: Achieved Status

Social class refers to a person's or group's position in society defined primarily in economic terms. In many cultures, class is a key factor determining a person's status, whereas in others it is less important than, for example, birth into a certain family. However, class and status do not always match. A rich person may have become wealthy in disreputable ways and never gain high status. Both status and class groups are secondary groups, because a person is unlikely to know every other member of the group, especially in large-scale societies. In most instances, they are also informal groups since there are no recognized leaders or elected officials of the "urban elite" or the "working class." Subsegments of these large categories do organize themselves into formal groups, such as labour unions or exclusive clubs for the rich and famous. Class can be both ascribed and achieved since a person who is born rich has a greater than average chance of living an upper-class lifestyle.

In "open" capitalist societies, the prevailing ideology is that mobility in the system is up to the individual. This view emphasizes the importance of human agency in the ability of an individual to overcome structural forces. Some anthropologists refer to this ideology as meritocratic individualism—the belief that rewards go to those who deserve them. This ideology would seem to be most valid for people with decent jobs rather than menial workers or the unemployed, but in fact the ideology is widely held outside the middle class (Durrenberger 2001). In the United States, the pervasive popular belief in rewards for equal opportunity and merit is upheld and promoted in schools and universities in the face of substantial evidence to the contrary.

In the United States, conservative governments and political parties have long sought to weaken labour unions, and they continue to promote the fantasy of a classless society based on meritocratic individualism to support anti-union policies. Many anthropologists point to the power of economic class position in shaping a person's lifestyle and his or her ability to choose a different one.

Obviously, a person born rich can, through individual agency, become poor, and a poor person can become rich. But in spite of exceptions to the rule, a person born rich is more likely to lead a lifestyle typical of that class, just as a person born poor is more likely to lead a lifestyle typical of that class.

The concept of class was central to the theories of Karl Marx. Situated within the context of Europe's industrial revolution and the growth of capitalism, Marx wrote that class differences, exploitation of the working class by the owners of capital, class consciousness among workers, and class conflict are forces of change that would eventually bring the downfall of capitalism.

In contrast to Marx's approach, French sociologist Émile Durkheim viewed social differences (including class) as the basis for social solidarity (1966 [1895]). He distinguished two major forms of societal cohesion: **mechanical solidarity**, which exists when groups that are similar join together, and **organic solidarity**, which prevails when groups with different abilities and resources are linked together in complementary fashion. Mechanical solidarity creates less enduring relationships because it involves little mutual need. Organic solidarity builds on need and creates stronger bonds. Durkheim placed these two concepts in an evolutionary framework, saying that in pre-industrial times, the division of labour was only minimally specialized: Everyone did what everyone else did. With increasing social complexity and economic specialization, organic solidarity developed.

Race, Ethnicity, and Caste: Ascribed Status

Three major ascribed systems of social stratification are based on divisions of people into unequally ranked groups on the basis of race, ethnicity, and **caste**, a ranked group, determined by birth, often linked to a particular occupation and to South Asian cultures. Like status and class groups, these three categories are secondary social groups, because no one can have a personal relationship with all other members of the entire group. Each system takes on local specificities depending on the context. For example, race and ethnicity are interrelated and overlap with conceptions of culture in much of Latin America, although differences in what they mean in terms of identity and status occur in different countries in the region (de la Cadena 2001). For some the concept of *mestizaje*, or racial mixture, refers to people who are disenfranchised and cut off from their Indian roots, but for others it can refer to literate and successful people who retain indigenous cultural practices. One has to know the local system of categories and meanings attached to them to understand the dynamics of inequality that go with them.

Yet systems based in difference defined in terms of race, ethnicity, and caste share with each other, and with class-based systems, some important features. First, they relegate large numbers of people to particular levels of entitlement to livelihood, power, security, esteem, and freedom (Berreman 1979:213). This simple fact should not be overlooked. Second, those with greater entitlements dominate those with lesser entitlements. Third, members of the dominant groups tend—consciously or unconsciously—to seek to maintain their position. Fourth, in spite of efforts to maintain systems of dominance, instances of subversion and rebellion do occur, indicating the potential for agency among the disprivileged.

Race

Racial stratification results from the unequal meeting of two formerly separate groups through colonization, slavery, and other large-group movements (Sanjek 1994). Europe's "age of discovery," beginning in the 1500s, ushered in a new era of global contact. In contrast, in relatively homogeneous cultures, ethnicity is a more important distinction than race. In contemporary Nigeria, for example, the population is relatively homogeneous, and ethnicity is the more salient term there (Jinadu 1994). A similar situation prevails in Rwanda and other African states.

A key feature of racial thinking is its insistence that behavioural differences among peoples are "natural," inborn, or biologically caused (in this, it resembles sexism, ageism, and casteism). Throughout the history of racial categorizations in the West, such features as head size, head shape, and brain size have been accepted as the reasons for behavioural differences. Franz Boas contributed to de-linking supposed racial attributes from behaviour. He showed that people with the same head size but from different cultures behaved differently, and people with different head sizes within the same cultures behaved similarly. For Boas and his followers, culture, not biology, is the key explanation for behaviour. Thus, race is not a biological reality; there is no way to divide the human population into races on the basis of certain biological features. Yet "social race" exists and continues to be a basis of social stratification. In spite of some progress in reducing racism in North America in the twentieth century, racial discrimination persists. One way of understanding this persistence is to see racial discrimination as linked to class formation, rather than separate from it (Brodkin 2000). In this view, racial stereotyping and discrimination functions to maintain people in less desirable jobs, or unemployed, as necessary aspects of advanced industrial capitalism, which depends on a certain number of low-paid workers and even a certain amount of unemployment.

Racial classifications in the Caribbean and Latin America are especially complicated systems of status clas-

Boys in a small town of Brazil exhibit the skin-colour diversity in the Brazilian population.

sification. This complexity results from the variety of contact over the centuries between peoples from Europe, Africa, Asia, and indigenous populations. Skin tone is one basis of racial classification, but it is mixed with other physical features and economic status as well. In Haiti, for example, racial categories take into account physical features such as skin texture, depth of skin tone, hair colour and appearance, and facial features (Trouillot, 1994). They also include a person's income, social origin, level of formal education, personality or behaviour, and kinship ties. Depending on how these variables are combined, a person occupies one category or another—and may even move between categories. Thus a person with certain physical features who is poor will be considered to be a different "colour" than a person with the same physical features who is well off. (Trouillot 1994:148–149)

An extreme example of racial stratification was the South African policy of apartheid, legally sanctioned segregation between dominant Whites and non-Whites. White dominance in South Africa began in the early 1800s with White migration and settlement. In the 1830s, slavery was abolished. At the same time, increasingly racist thinking developed among Whites (Johnson 1994:25). Racist images, including visions of Africans as lazy, uncontrolled, and libidinous, served as the rationale for colonialist domination in place of outright slavery. In spite of years of African resistance to White domination, the Whites succeeded in maintaining and increasing their control for nearly two centuries. In South Africa, Blacks constitute 90 percent of the population, a numerical majority dominated through strict apartheid by the White minority until only recently. Every aspect of life for the majority of Africans was far worse than for the Whites. Every measure of life quality—infant mortality, longevity, education—showed great disparity between the Whites and the Africans. In addition to physical deprivation, the Africans experienced psychological suffering through constant insecurity about raids from the police and other forms of violence.

Since the end of apartheid in South Africa in 1994, many social changes have taken place. One study describes the early stages of the dismantling of apartheid in the city of Umtata, the capital of Transkei (Johnson 1994). Before the end of apartheid, Umtata "was like other South African towns: all apartheid laws were in full force; public and private facilities were completely segregated; only whites could vote or serve in the town government; whites owned all the major economic assets" (viii). When the change came, Umtata's dominant Whites bitterly resisted at first. They did not want to lose their privileges, and they feared reprisals by the Africans. These things did not happen, however. The initial stages of transition brought "neo-apartheid," in which White privilege was not seriously threatened. Then members of the dominant group began to welcome the less tense, "nonracial" atmosphere.

In contrast to the explicitly racist discrimination of South African apartheid, racism exists within contexts where no public discourse about race or racism is found, where instead there is silence about it (Sheriff 2000). In such a context, the silence works to allow racial discrimination to continue in ways that are as effective as a clearly stated policy such as apartheid, or perhaps even more so since it is more difficult to critique and dismantle an institution whose existence is denied. As Canadian anthropologist Stanley Barrett says,

> Racism has been endemic in Canada. It has stretched from the early slavery at the nation's dawn down through the Fascist phase prior to the Second World War to the Paki-bashing of recent years. It has reached from the Pacific to the Atlantic, taking different forms according to the local ethnic composition, targeting Asians in Vancouver, blacks in Nova Scotia, and Jews everywhere. It has been represented in corporate and government boards and among manual labourers at construction sites. And it has appeared both visibly in the form of violent attacks and covertly in the form of variations in wages and employment opportunities based on racial criteria. Many observers might want to argue that what racism does exist in Canada has simply been the sad product of deviant individuals, or a temporary problem brought on by unemployment or some other crisis. Yet the degree, scope, and persistence of the phenomenon lead to a single conclusion; racism in Canada has been institutionalized . . . racism that is intrinsic to the structures of society. It may be overt or covert, expressed formally in the laws of the land, or less visibly in patterns of employment and the content of school textbooks. . . . What is significant about institutional racism, whether open (the reservation system for Native peoples) or hidden (ordinary white Canadians are more cautious about appearing racist), is not only that differential advantage along racial lines is embedded in society itself, but also that it perpetuates itself over time, for that is the nature of the institutional framework: independent of individual volition, relatively unconscious and unmotivated, it reproduces itself . . . institutional racism is almost synonymous with "the way things are. (Barrett 1987: 307–308)

Ethnicity

Ethnicity includes a shared sense of identity on some grounds and a set of relations to other groups (Comaroff 1987). Identity is formed sometimes on the basis of a perception of shared history, territory, language, or religion. As such, ethnicity can be a basis for claiming entitlements to resources such as land or artifacts, and a perceived basis for defending or regaining those resources.

States are interested in managing ethnicity to the extent that it does not threaten security. China has one of the most formalized systems for monitoring its many ethnic groups, and it has an official policy on ethnic minorities, meaning the non-Han groups (Wu 1990). The government lists a total of 54 groups other than the Han majority, which constitutes about 94 percent of the total. The other 6 percent of the population is made up of the 54 groups, about 67 million people. The non-Han minorities occupy about 60 percent of China's land mass and are located in border or "frontier" areas such as Tibet, Yunnan, Xinjiang, and Inner Mongolia. Basic criteria for defining an ethnic group include language, territory, economy, and "psychological disposition." The Chinese government establishes strict definitions of group membership and group characteristics, including setting standards for ethnic costumes and dances. The Chinese treatment of the Tibetan people is especially severe and can be considered an attempt at ethnocide or annihilation of the culture of an ethnic group by a dominant group. The Tibetans continue to resist the loss of their culture and absorption into the Han mainstream. The government's treatment of Tibetan traditional medicine over the past several decades illustrates how the Han majority uses certain aspects of minority cultures (see the Critical Thinking box).

People of one ethnic group who move from one place to another are at risk of exclusionary treatment from the local residents at their new location. Roma, or gypsies, are a **diaspora population**, a dispersed group living outside their original homeland, and are scattered throughout Europe and North America. Their history is one of mobility and marginality since they first left India around 1000 CE (Fonseca 1995). Everywhere they live, they are marginalized and looked down on by the settled populations. Traditional Rom lifestyle is one of movement, with temporary camps of their wagons often appearing overnight on the outskirts of a town. For decades,

Critical Thinking

THE CHINESE TAKEOVER OF TIBETAN MEDICINE

IN 1951, Tibet became part of China, and the Chinese government undertook measures to bring about the social and economic transformation of what was formerly a decentralized, Buddhist feudal regime. This transformation has brought increasing ethnic conflict between Tibetans and Han Chinese, including demonstrations by Tibetans and crackdowns from the government. Traditional Tibetan medicine has become part of the Chinese–Tibetan conflicts because of its culturally significant and religiously important position in Tibetan society (Janes 1995:7).

Several policy swings of the Chinese state toward Tibetan traditional medicine occurred in the second half of the twentieth century: Between 1951 and 1962, it was tolerated but largely ignored; by 1962, it was officially included as a component of the public health system and given funds for clinical operations and training programs; in 1966, it was delegitimized; in 1978, it was near extinction; and in 1985, it re-emerged as a legitimate sector of the government health bureaucracy, having a major role in providing primary health care in the Tibetan region, with a substantial operating budget and over 1200 physicians.

Linkage with a centralized medical system substantially transformed traditional Tibetan medicine. The training of physicians is one area of major change. Previously based on a model of apprenticeship training, it is now Westernized and involves several years of classroom-based, lecture-oriented learning followed by an internship. At Tibet University, only half of all formal lecture-based instruction is concerned with traditional Tibetan medicine. Curriculum changes have reduced the integrity of Tibetan medicine: It has been separated from its Buddhist content, and parts of it have been merged with a biomedical approach. While one might say that overall, traditional Tibetan medicine has been "revived" in China, stronger evidence supports the argument that the state has co-opted it and transformed it for its own purposes.

CRITICAL THINKING QUESTIONS

How could the Chinese government justify the suppression of Tibetan traditional medicine?

Why do you think the Chinese government eventually revived Tibetan traditional medicine?

Which form of medicine dominates Chinese government health planning and policy—biomedical or traditional medicine? Can you suggest why?

European governments have tried to force the Roma to settle down. In addition, Rom migration to cities in Eastern Europe is increasing because of the recent economic crisis, unemployment, and declining standard of living. In cities, high-status groups reside in areas segregated from others (Ladányi 1993). Low-status people must live where no one else wants to reside. In Budapest, Hungary, the Rom minority is the most disadvantaged ethnic group. Not all Roma in Budapest are poor, though. Some 1 percent has gained wealth, and they live in high-status neighbourhoods. However, the vast majority live in substandard housing, in the slum inner areas of Pest. Since the fall of state socialism, discrimination against Roma has increased. Rom houses have been torched, and their children have been harassed while going to school.

A less difficult but still not easy adjustment is being experienced by Indo-Canadians (immigrants from India to Canada). Research among a sample of nearly 300 Indo-Canadians in Vancouver, British Columbia, revealed that about half of all the respondents reported experiencing some form of discrimination in the recent past (Nodwell and Guppy 1992). The percentage was higher among men (54 percent) than among women (45 percent). The higher level for men was consistent across the four categories: verbal abuse, property damage, workplace discrimination, and physical harm. Verbal abuse was the most frequent form of discrimination, reported by 40 percent of both men and women. Indo-Canadians of the Sikh faith who were born in India say that they experience the highest levels of discrimination in Canada. Apparently, however, their actual experience of discrimination is not greater than for other Indo-Canadians. The difference is that Sikhs who were born in India are more sensitive to discrimination than others. Sikhism, as taught and practised in India, supports a strong sense of honour, which should be protected and, if wronged, avenged. This study helps explain differences in perception of discrimination among ethnic migrants. It does not explain why such high levels of discriminatory treatment exist in a nation committed to ethnic tolerance.

A Rom encampment in Romania's Transylvania region. Not all European Roma are poor, however. Some urban Roma have become wealthy and have therefore attracted the jealousy of the non-Rom population.

Caste

The caste system is a form of social stratification found in its clearest form in India, among its Hindu population, and in other areas of Hindu culture such as Nepal, Sri Lanka, and Fiji. It is particularly associated with Hindu peoples because ancient Hindu scriptures are taken as the foundational sources for defining the major social categories called *varnas* (a Sanskrit word meaning "colour," or "shade"). The four *varnas* are the *brahmans*, who were priests; the *kshatriya*, or warriors; the *vaishya*, or merchants; and the *shudras*, or labourers. Of these, men of the first three *varnas* could go through a ritual ceremony of "rebirth" and thereafter wear a sacred thread. These three categories are referred to as "twice-born," and their status is higher than that of the *shudra varna*. Beneath the four *varna* groups were people considered so low that they were outside the caste system itself (hence, the word *outcast*). Throughout history, these people have been referred to by many names in Indian languages and by the English term *untouchable*. Mahatma Gandhi, himself a member of an upper caste, renamed them *harijans* (or "children of god") as part of his attempt to raise their status into that of the level above them. Currently, members of this category have adopted the term *dalit* (meaning "oppressed" or "ground down") as their favoured name.

The *dalit* category and all of the *varnas* contain many locally named groups called *castes* or, more appropriately, *jatis*. The term *caste* is a Portuguese word meaning "breed" or "type" and was first used by Portuguese colonialists in the fifteenth century to refer to the closed social groups they encountered (Cohn 1971:125). *Jati* means "birth group," and conveys the meaning that a Hindu is born into his or her group. It is an ascribed status and cannot be changed under normal conditions. Just as the four *varnas* are ranked with each other, so are all the *jatis* within them. For example, the category of brahmans "may be subdivided into priestly and non-priestly subgroups, the priestly Brahmans into Household-priests, Temple-priests and Funeral-priests; the Household-priests into two or more endogamous circles; and each circle into its component clans and lineages; non-priestly Brahmans are superior in relation to priestly ones, and Household-priests in relation to Funeral-priests" (Parry 1966:77).

Status levels also exist among *dalits*. In western Nepal, artisans such as basket-weavers and ironsmiths are the highest tier (M. Cameron 1995). They do not touch any of the people beneath them. The second tier includes leatherworkers and tailors. The bottom tier comprises people who are "untouchable" to all other groups including other *dalits* because their work is extremely polluting according to Hindu rules: musicians (some of their instruments are made of leather and they perform in public) and sex workers.

Indian anthropologist M. N. Srinivas (1959) contributed the concept of the **dominant caste** to refer to

Only a special category of brahman priests can officiate at the Chidambaram temple in South India. Here, members of an age-mixed group of priests sit for a moment's relaxation.

the tendency for one caste in any particular village to control most of the land and, often, to be numerically preponderant as well. Although brahmans are at the top of the social hierarchy in terms of ritual purity, they are not always the dominant caste. Throughout northern India, it is common for *jatis* of the *kshatriya varna* to be the dominant village group. This is the case in Pahansu village, where a group called the Gujars is dominant (Raheja 1988). The Gujars constitute the numerical majority, and they control most of the land (see Table 10.1). Moreover, they dominate in the **jajmani system**, a patron-provider system in which landholding patrons (*jajmans*) are linked through exchanges of food for services with brahman priests, artisans (blacksmiths, potters), agricultural labourers, and other workers such as sweepers (Kolenda 1978:46–54). In Pahansu, Gujars have power and status as the major patrons, supporting many different service providers who are thus beholden to them.

Some anthropologists have described the *jajmani* service system as one of mutual interdependence (organic solidarity, to use Durkheim's term), which provides security for the less well-off. Joan Mencher (1974) and others argue that the system benefits those at the top to the detriment of those at the bottom. Mencher has done fieldwork among low-caste people. This perspective, from "the bottom up," views the patron-service system and the entire caste system as one of exploitation by those at the top. Mencher says that the benign interpretation is based on research conducted among the upper castes who present this view. A more comprehensive look reveals that while both patrons and clients have rights and responsibilities, the relationship is not equal. Patrons have more power. Dissatisfied patrons can dismiss service providers, refuse them loans, or not pay them. Service providers who are dissatisfied with the treatment they receive from their patrons have little recourse. Male patrons often demand sexual privileges from low-caste females from service-providing households.

Throughout South Asia, the growth of industrial manufacturing and marketing has reduced the need for some service providers, especially craftspersons such as tailors, potters, and weavers. With less need for their skills in the countryside, many former service providers have left the villages to work in urban areas. The tie that remains the strongest is between patrons and their brahman priests, whose ritual services cannot be replaced by machines.

The caste system involves several mechanisms that maintain it: marriage rules, spatial segregation, and ritual. Marriage rules strictly enforce *jati* endogamy. Marriage outside one's *jati,* especially in rural areas and particularly between a higher-caste female and lower-caste male, is cause for serious, even lethal, punishment by caste elders and other local power-holders. Indian newspapers frequently carry accounts of local action taken to punish offenders, who may be beaten to death or stoned. Sometimes the female's life is spared, but she may be branded, have her head shaved, and be subject to social scorn. Among urban educated elites, a trend to allow inter-*jati* marriages is perceptible, but such marriages are still not preferred.

TABLE 10.1 Caste Ranking in Pahansu Village, North India

Caste Name	Traditional Occupation	Number of Households	Occupation in Pahansu
Gujar	agriculturalist	210	owner cultivator
Brahman	priest	8	priest, postman
Baniya	merchant	3	shopkeeper
Sunar	goldsmith	2	silversmith, sugar cane press operator
Dhiman (Barhai)	carpenter	1	carpenter
Kumhar	potter	3	potter, tailor
Nai	barber	3	barber, postman
Dhobi	washerman	2	washerman
Gadariya	shepherd	4	agricultural labourer, weaver
Jhivar	water-carrier	20	agricultural labourer, basket-weaver
Luhar	ironsmith	2	blacksmith
Teli	oil-presser	2	beggar, cotton-carder, agricultural labourer
Maniharan	bangle-seller	1	bangle-seller
Camar	leatherworker	100	agricultural labourer
Bhangi	sweeper	17	sweeper, midwife

Source: Adapted from Raheja 1988:19.

Spatial segregation functions to maintain the privileged preserve of the upper castes and to continually remind the lower castes of their marginal status. In many rural contexts, the *dalits* live in a completely separate cluster; in other cases, they have their own neighbourhood sections into which no upper-caste person will venture. Ritual rules and practices also serve to maintain dominance. The rich upper-caste leaders sponsor important annual festivals, thereby regularly restating their claim to public prominence (Mines 1994).

Social mobility within the caste system has traditionally been limited, but instances have been documented of group "up-casting." Several strategies exist, including gaining wealth, affiliation, or merger with a somewhat higher *jati*, education, migration, and political activism (Kolenda 1978). A group that attempts to gain higher *jati* status takes on the behaviour and dress of twice-born *jatis*. These include men's wearing the sacred thread, vegetarianism, non-remarriage of widows, seclusion of women from the public domain, and the giving of larger dowries for the marriage of a daughter. Some *dalits* have opted out of the caste system by converting to Christianity or Buddhism. Others are becoming politically organized through the Dalit Panthers, a social movement seeking greater power and improved economic status for *dalits* (Omvedt 1995).

Discrimination on the basis of caste was made illegal by the Indian constitution of 1949, but constitutional decree did not bring an end to these deeply structured inequalities. The government of India has instituted policies to promote the social and economic advancement of *dalits*, such as reserving places for them in medical schools, seats in the government, and public sector jobs. This "affirmative action" plan has infuriated many of the upper castes, especially brahmans, who feel most threatened. Is the caste system on the decline? Surely, aspects of it are changing. Especially in large cities, people of different *jatis* can "pass" and participate more equally in public life—if they have the economic means to do so.

CIVIL SOCIETY

Civil society consists of the social domain of diverse interest groups that function outside the government to organize economic, political, and other aspects of life. It has a long history in Western philosophy, with many different definitions proposed by thinkers such as John Locke, Thomas Paine, Adam Smith, and Karl Marx (Kumar 1996:89). According to the German philosopher Hegel, civil society encompasses the social groups and institutions between the individual and the state. Italian social theorist Gramsci wrote that there are two basic types of civic institutions: those that support the state, such as the Church and schools, and those that oppose state power, such as trade unions, social protest groups, and citizens' rights groups.

Civil Society for the State: The Chinese Women's Movement

In many instances, governments seek to build civil society to further their goals. The women's movement in China is an example of such a state-created organization. Canadian anthropologist Ellen Judd conducted a study of the women's movement in China, within the constraints that the government imposes on anthropological fieldwork by foreigners. Under Mao's leadership, foreign anthropologists were not allowed to do research of any sort in China. The situation began to change in the 1980s when some field research, within strict limitations, became possible.

Judd has developed a long-term relationship with China over several decades, having lived there as a student from 1974 to 1977, undertaking long-term fieldwork there in 1986, and returning almost every year since for research or some other activity, such as being involved in a development project for women or attending the Beijing Fourth World Conference on Women. According to Judd, "These various ways of being in China all allowed me some interaction with Chinese women and some knowledge of their lives . . ." (2002:14). In her latest project to study the Chinese women's movement, she wanted to conduct research as a cultural anthropologist would normally do, through intensive participant observation over a long period of time.

But even now, the Chinese government prohibits such research, keeping foreigners at a distance from everyday life. Judd was not allowed to join the local women's organization or to speak privately with any of the women. Officials accompanied her on all household visits and interviews. She was allowed to attend meetings, however, and she had access to all the public information about the goals of the women's movement, which is called the Women's Federations. A policy goal of the Chinese government is to improve the quality of women's lives, and the Women's Federations were formed to address that goal. The government oversees the operation at all levels, from the national level to the township and village. The primary objective is to mobilize women, especially rural women, to participate in literacy training and market activities.

Judd's fieldwork, constrained as it was by government regulations and oversight, nevertheless yielded some insights. She learned, through interviews with women members, about some women who have benefited from the programs, and she discovered how important

Lessons Applied

ANTHROPOLOGY AND COMMUNITY ACTIVISM IN PAPUA NEW GUINEA

A CONTROVERSIAL issue in applied anthropology is whether or not an anthropologist should take on the role of community activist or act as an advocate on behalf of the people among whom they have conducted research (Kirsch 2002). Some say that anthropologists should maintain a neutral position in a conflict situation and simply offer information on issues—information that may be used by either side. Others say that it is appropriate and right for anthropologists to take sides and help support less powerful groups against more powerful groups. Those who endorse anthropologists' taking an activist or advocacy role argue that neutrality is never truly neutral: By seemingly taking no position, one indirectly supports the status quo, and information provided to both sides will generally serve the interests of the more powerful side in any case.

Stuart Kirsch took an activist role after conducting field research for over 15 years in a region of Papua New Guinea that has been negatively affected by a large copper and gold mine called the Ok Tedi mine. The mine releases 73 000 tonnes of mining wastes into the local river system daily, causing extensive environmental damage that in turn affects people's food and water sources. Kirsch has joined with the local community in their extended legal and political campaign to limit further pollution and to gain compensation for damages suffered. He explains his involvement with the community as a form of reciprocal exchange. The community members have provided him with information about their culture

for over 15 years. He believes that his knowledge is part of the people's cultural property and that they have a rightful claim to its use.

Kirsch's support of the community's goals took several forms. First, his scholarly research provided documentation of the problems of the people living downstream from the mine. Community activists incorporated his findings in their speeches when travelling in Australia, Europe, and the Americas to spread awareness of their case and gather international support. During the 1992 Earth Summit, one leader presented the media with excerpts from an article by Kirsch during a press conference held aboard the Greenpeace ship *Rainbow Warrior II* in the Rio de Janeiro harbour. Second, he worked closely with local leaders, helping them decide how best to convey their views to the public and in the court. Third, he served as a cultural broker in discussions among community members, politicians, mining executives, lawyers, and representatives of NGOs in order to promote solutions for the problems faced by people living downstream from the mine. Fourth, he convened an international meeting of environmental NGOs in Washington, D.C., in 1999 and secured funding to bring a representative from the community to the meeting.

In spite of official reports recommending that the mine be closed in 2001, its future remains uncertain. No assessment of past damages to the community has been prepared. As the case goes on, Kirsch will continue to support the community's efforts by sharing

---

education for women is in terms of their ability to enter into market activities. The book she wrote is largely descriptive, focusing on the "public face" of the Women's Federations in one locale. Such a descriptive account is the most that can emerge from research in China at this time. Given that the women's organizations are formed by and for the government, this example stretches the concept of civil society to—and perhaps beyond—its limits.

Activist Groups

Activist groups are groups formed with the goal of changing certain conditions, such as political repression, violence, and human rights violations. In studying activist

groups, cultural anthropologists are interested in learning what motivates the formation of such groups, what their goals and strategies are, and what leadership patterns they exhibit. Sometimes anthropologists join the efforts of activist groups and use their knowledge to support these groups' goals (see the Lessons Applied box).

Many, but certainly not all, activist groups are initiated and organized by women. CO-MADRES of El Salvador is an important, women-led social movement in Latin America (Stephen 1995). CO-MADRES is a Spanish abbreviation for an organization called, in English, the Committee of Mothers and Relatives of Political Prisoners, Disappeared and Assassinated of El Salvador. It was founded in 1977 by a group of mothers in denunciation

---

with them the results of his research, just as they have for so long shared their culture with him. Indigenous people worldwide are increasingly invoking their rights to anthropological knowledge about themselves. According to Kirsch, these claims require anthropologists to rethink their roles and relationships with the people they study. It can no longer be a relationship in which the community provides knowledge and the anthropologist keeps and controls that knowledge for his or her intellectual development alone. Although the details are still being worked out, the overall goal must be one of collaboration and cooperation.

FOOD FOR THOUGHT

Consider the pros and cons of anthropological advocacy, and decide what position you would take on the Ok Tedi case. Be prepared to defend your position.

Yonggam people gather at a meeting in Atkamba village on the Ok Tedi River to discuss legal proceedings in 1996. At the end of the meeting, leaders signed an agreement to an out-of-court settlement, which was presented to the Victorian Supreme Court in Melbourne, Australia. The current lawsuit concerns the Yonggam people's claim that the 1996 settlement agreement has been breached.

of the atrocities committed by the Salvadoran government and military. During the civil war that lasted from 1979 until 1992, a total of 80 000 people had died and 7000 more had disappeared, or one in every 100 Salvadorans.

The initial group comprised nine mothers. A year later, it had grown to nearly 30 members, including some men. In 1979, they made their first international trip to secure wider recognition. This developed into a full-fledged and successful campaign for international solidarity in the 1980s, with support in other Latin American countries, Europe, Australia, the United States, and Canada. The group's increased visibility earned it repression from the government. Its office was first bombed in 1980 and then four more times after that. In addition, a majority of the

most active CO-MADRES have been detained, tortured, and raped. Forty-eight members of the CO-MADRES have been detained since 1977; five have been assassinated. Harassment and disappearances continued even after the signing of the Peace Accords in January 1992: "In February 1993, the son and the nephew of one of the founders of CO-MADRES were assassinated in Usulutan. This woman had already lived through the experience of her own detention, the detention and gang rape of her daughter, and the disappearance and assassination of other family members" (814).

In the 1990s, CO-MADRES focused on holding the state accountable for human rights violations during the civil war, as well as some new areas, such as providing

A march of the "Mothers of the Disappeared" in Argentina. This organization of women combines activism motivated by personal causes (the loss of one's child or children to political torture and death) and wider political concerns (state repressiveness in general).

better protection for political prisoners, seeking assurances of human rights protection in the future, working against domestic violence, educating women about political participation, and developing some economic projects to help women attain financial autonomy. They are part of a coalition of women's groups that worked on the 1994 political platform to secure better rights and conditions for women. The work of CO-MADRES, throughout its history, has incorporated elements of both the "personal" and the "political," concerns of mothers and family members for lost kin and for exposing and halting abuses of the state and military. The lesson learned from the case of CO-MADRES is that activist groups formed by women can be based on issues related to the domestic domain (murdered sons and other kin), but their activities can extend to the top of the public political hierarchy.

Other activist organizations formed around the problem of the marketing of infant formula in the developing countries and the subsequent decline in breastfeeding rates. In the 1970s, activist groups in North America and Europe mobilized to expose how large multinational corporations were seeking markets for their infant formulas. Protest groups argued that selling breast milk substitutes to mothers who could not afford the cost of an adequate supply and who had limited access to clean water and fuel to sterilize bottles was causing a major health crisis, and they began consumer boycotts of companies such as Nestlé. This attention to unethical marketing practices ultimately forced debates resulting in the World Health Assembly passing the International Code on Marketing of Breast Milk Substitutes in 1981. Because of continuing flagrant violations of this code by several food and pharmaceutical corporations promoting infant formula, groups such as the International Baby Food Action Network (IBFAN) continue to monitor their compliance to the code. An umbrella organization, the World Alliance for Breast-

feeding Action (WABA), formed by activists from various countries in 1991, continues to encourage the practice of breastfeeding through worldwide campaigns. For example, the Baby Friendly Hospital initiative encourages health care providers to assist mothers to breastfeed immediately after birth, World Breastfeeding Week mobilizes grass-roots support for breastfeeding, and Mother-Friendly Workplaces assists employed women to combine breast-feeding and employment (P. Van Esterik 1995:160).

Another example of activist group formation under difficult conditions comes from urban Egypt (Hopkins and Mehanna 2000). The Egyptian government frowns on overt political action outside the realm of the government. Although Egyptian citizens are deeply concerned about environmental issues such as waste disposal, clean air and water, and noise, group formation for environmental causes is not easily accomplished. People interviewed in Cairo reported that they rarely discuss environmental issues with one another. One example of environmental concern, however, did result in the closing of a highly polluting lead smelter. In this case, the people in the affected neighbourhood banded together around this particular issue and called attention to the situation in the public media, prompting high-level officials to take up their case. They were successful partly because their target was localized—one relatively small industry—and also because the industry was so clearly guilty of polluting the environment. This effort, however, did not lead to the formation of an enduring group.

In post-socialist states, concern about the environment has prompted the emergence of many non-governmental groups. In Poland, youth activism related to the environment grew in strength beginning in the late 1980s (Glínski 1994:145). This was the first generation to come after Stalin that had not experienced martial law, so they had less fear of organizing than their parents. Furthermore, the government's policy of limited liberalization involves concessions to social groups and the interests they express, and the mass media have greater freedom of expression. In opposition to dominant values of the 1960s and 1970s, members of the early phase of the Polish green movement promoted nonviolence, distance from the political system, and an ironic and gentle way of communicating their interests. The government promoted distance between it and the youth environmental groups in several ways: It ignored environmental issues, many political elites actively sought to marginalize the youth movement, and police units were dispatched against public protests of the youth groups, (for example, demonstrations in the late 1980s and early 1990s against construction of a nuclear power plant and a dam).

The 1990s brought a second phase in youth involvement when preliminary dialogue between some organizations and the Ministry of Environmental Protection took place. The ministry established a special office and organized monthly meetings with representatives of the youth groups. The groups themselves are becoming more formally organized as NGOs, and their activities receive support from national and international foundations and ecological groups. This example of the change in the role and organization of a social movement unfolded in the post-socialist context of Poland, but it shares general features with youth movements in other places, such as increased political involvement, organizational sophistication, and global linkages

New Social Movements and Cyberpower

Social scientists have begun to use the term *new social movements* to refer to the many new groups that emerged in the late 1980s and 1990s, often as the result of post-socialist transitions, but in other contexts too (some examples are discussed in Chapter 16 in the context of international development). These groups are often constituted by disprivileged minorities—ethnic groups, women, the poor. Increasingly, they involve networks wider than the immediate social group, and most recently, they have taken advantage of cybertechnology to broaden their membership, exchange ideas, and raise funds (Escobar 2002). Cyber-enhanced social movements are important new political actors and the source of promising ways to resist, transform, and present alternatives to current political structures. The importance of cybernetworking has, of course, not been lost on formal political leaders, who are paying increased attention to their personal websites and those of their parties.

WHAT is the range of cross-cultural variation of social groups?

Groups can be classified in terms of whether all members have face-to-face interaction with one another, whether membership is based on ascription or achievement, and how formal the group's organization and leadership structure is. Thus, groups extend from the most informal, face-to-face groups, such as those based on friendship, to groups that have formal membership requirements and whose members are widely dispersed and never meet each other. All groups have some criteria for membership, often based on a perceived notion of similarity. Many groups require some sort of initiation of new members, which, in some cases, involves dangerous or frightening activities that serve to bond members to one another through a shared experience of helplessness.

WHAT is social stratification, and what are its effects on people?

Social stratification is a concept based on the fact that people are, first, formed in groups. It refers to hierarchical relationships between and among different groups. Stratified intergroup relations are commonly based on cat-egories such as class, race, ethnicity, gender, age, and ability. The degree of social inequality among different status groups is highly marked in agricultural and industrial societies, whereas status inequalities are not characteristic of foraging societies and are not significant in most pastoral and horticultural societies. India's caste-based system is an important example of a rigid structure of social inequality based on a person's birth group.

WHAT is civil society?

Civil society consists of groups and organizations that, although they are not part of the formal government, perform functions that are economic or political. Civil society groups can be roughly divided into those that support government policies and initiatives, and thus further the interests of government, and those that oppose government policies and actions, such as environmental protest groups. Some anthropologists who study activist groups decide to take an advocacy role and apply their knowledge to further the goals of the group. This direction in applied anthropology is related to the view that anthropological knowledge is partly the cultural property of the groups who have shared their lives and insights with the anthropologist.

KEY CONCEPTS

SUGGESTED READINGS

Sandra Bell and Simon Coleman, eds., *The Anthropology of Friendship*. New York: Berg, 1999. The editors provide an introductory chapter on enduring themes and future issues in the anthropological study of friendship. The nine essays that follow discuss friendship in contemporary Melanesia, historical friendship as portrayed in Icelandic sagas, friendship in the context of a game of dominoes in a London pub, how friendship creates support networks in North-East Europe, and the globalization of friendship ties revealed through an East African case.

Stanley Brandes, *Staying Sober in Mexico City*. Austin: University of Texas Press, 2002. This ethnography of Alcoholics Anonymous groups in Mexico City focuses on how these groups help low-income men remain sober through social support. Although emphasizing the role of human agency in these men's attempts to remain sober, the author reminds us that the high rate of alcoholism among poor Mexican men must be viewed in the context of structural conditions that make life very difficult.

Liliana Goldin, ed., *Identities on the Move: Transnational Processes in North America and the Caribbean Basin*. Austin: University of Texas Press, 2000. This collection offers essays on identity formation and change in the process of voluntary migration or displacement and on how states label and exclude transnationals, often in racialized ways.

Thomas A. Gregor and Donald Tuzin, eds., *Gender in Amazonia and Melanesia: An Exploration of the Comparative Method*. Berkeley: University of California Press, 2001. Two anthropologists, one a specialist on indigenous peoples of Amazonia and the other on Papua New Guinea, are the editors of this volume, which includes a theoretical overview chapter and then several chapters addressing similarities and differences between cultures of the two regions in domains such as fertility cults, rituals of masculinity, gender politics, and age-based gender roles.

Cris Shore and Stephen Nugent, eds., *Elite Cultures: Anthropological Perspectives*. New York: Routledge, 2002. This volume contains two introductory chapters and a concluding chapter framing 12 ethnographic cases from around the world. The major issues addressed are how elites in different societies maintain their positions, how elites represent themselves to others, how anthropologists study elites, and the implications of research on elites for the discipline of anthropology.

Jerome Rousseau, *Central Borneo: Ethnic Identity and Social Life in a Stratified Society*. Oxford: Clarendon Press, 1990. Based on fieldwork and archival material, this book outlines the social organization, kinship patterns, and interregional links among the peoples of central Borneo.

Karin Tice, *Kuna Crafts, Gender, and the Global Economy*. Austin: University of Texas Press, 1995. This ethnographic study looks at how the tourist market has affected women's production of *molas* in Panama and how women have organized into cooperatives to improve their situation.

Kevin A. Yelvington, *Producing Power: Ethnicity, Gender, and Class in a Caribbean Workplace*. Philadelphia: Temple University Press, 1995. This ethnography examines class, race, and gender inequalities as linked processes of social stratification within the context of a factory in Trinidad and in the wider social sites of households, neighbourhoods, and global interconnections.

WEBLINKS

The Companion Website (www.pearsoned.ca/miller) that accompanies *Cultural Anthropology*, Third Canadian Edition, includes a destinations module containing links to many websites relevant to the content of this chapter. Use it to investigate the Web and expand your understanding of anthropology.

- **WHAT** do political and legal anthropology cover?
- **WHAT** are the major cross-cultural forms of political organization and social order?
- **WHAT** are cross-cultural patterns of social conflict?

11

POLITICS, CONFLICT, AND SOCIAL ORDER

The antiglobalism movement has gained supporters worldwide. This is a scene from the Seattle demonstration during the Global Trade Meeting of 2000.

POLITICAL ANTHROPOLOGY

When cultural anthropologists consider the concept of politics, they tend to take a broader view than a political scientist because their cross-cultural data indicate that many kinds of behaviour and thought are political in addition to formal party politics, voting, and government. Cultural anthropologists offer important examples of political systems that might not look like political systems at all to people who have grown up in large states. This section explores basic political concepts from an anthropological perspective and raises the question of whether political systems are universal to all cultures.

British anthropologists, especially Bronislaw Malinowski and A. R. Radcliffe-Brown, long dominated theory-making in political anthropology. Their approach, referred to as *functionalism*, emphasized how institutions such as political organization and law promote social cohesion. Later, the students of these two teachers developed divergent theories. For example, in the late 1960s, some scholars began to look at aspects of political organization that pull societies apart. The new focus on disputes and conflict prompted anthropologists to gather information on dispute "cases" and to analyze the actors involved in a particular conflict through "processual analysis."

The approach has been countered by a swing toward a more macro view (Vincent 1996), which examines politics, no matter how local, within a global context (Asad 1973). This global perspective has prompted many studies of colonialism and neo-colonialism in political anthropology and historical anthropology. Ann Stoler's book, *Capitalism and Confrontation in Sumatra's Plantation Belt*, 1870–1979 (1985), on the history and cultural impact of Dutch colonialism in Indonesia, is a classic study in this genre. In the 1980s, the experiences of *subaltern* peoples (those subordinated by colonialism) and subaltern movements in former colonized regions attracted research attention, particularly from native anthropologists of decolonizing countries.

The history of political anthropology in the twentieth century illustrates the theoretical tensions between the individual-as-agent approach (processual approach) and the structural, political economy perspective that sees people as constrained in their choices by larger forces.

N ews events during the first decade of the twenty-first century are typified by bloodshed, conflict, and disturbing threats. Canadian troops are fighting in Afghanistan, terrorists attack public transportation in Europe, and nuclear proliferation continues in nations such as North Korea and Iran.

Political anthropology, a subfield of cultural anthropology, addresses the area of human behaviour and thought related to power: who has it and who doesn't; degrees of power; the bases of power; abuses of power; relationships between political and religious power; political organization and government; social conflict and social control; and morality and law. The subfield of legal anthropology focuses on the issues of order and conflict.

Multiple Cultural Worlds

SOCIALIZATION OF WOMEN POLITICIANS IN KOREA

PARENTAL ATTITUDES affect children's involvement in public political roles. Chunghee Sarah Soh's (1993) research in the Republic of Korea reveals how variation in paternal roles affects daughters' political leadership roles. Korean women members of the National Assembly can be divided into two categories: elected members (active seekers) versus appointed members (passive recipients). Korea is a strongly patrilineal and male-dominated society, so women political leaders represent "a notable deviance from the usual gender-role expectations" (54). This "deviance" is not stigmatized in Korean culture; rather, it is admired within the category of *yŏgŏl*. A *yŏgŏl* is a woman with "manly" accomplishments. Her personality traits include extraordinary bravery, strength, integrity, generosity, and charisma. Physically, a *yŏgŏl* is likely to be taller, larger, and stronger than most women, and to have a stronger voice than other women. Why do some girls grow up to be a *yŏgŏl*?

Analysis of the life histories of elected and appointed women legislators offers clues about differences in their socialization. Elected women legislators were likely to have had atypical paternal experiences of two types: either an absent father or an atypically nurturant father. Both of these experiences facilitated a girl's socialization into *yŏgŏl* qualities, or, in the words of Soh, into developing an androgynous personality combining traits of both masculinity and femininity. In contrast, the presence of a

Representative Kim Ok-son greets some of her constituents who are members of a local Confucian club in Seoul, Republic of Korea. She is wearing a men's style suit and has a masculine haircut.

"typical" father results in a girl developing a more "traditional" female personality that is submissive and passive.

One intriguing question that follows from Soh's findings is: What explains the socialization of different types of fathers—those who help daughters develop leadership qualities and those who socialize daughters for passivity?

FOOD FOR THOUGHT

In your experience, what socialization factors might influence boys or girls to become politicians?

Politics: The Use of Power, Authority, and Influence

What, first, do we mean by the word *politics*? The term **politics** refers to the organized use of public power, as opposed to the more private politics of family and domestic groups. **Power** is the ability to bring about desired results, often through the possession or use of force. Closely related to power are authority and influence. **Authority** implies "the right to take certain forms of action." It is based on a person's achieved or ascribed status or moral reputation. Authority differs from power in that power is backed up by the potential use of force, and power can be wielded by individuals without their having the authority in the moral sense.

Influence is the ability to achieve a desired end by exerting social or moral pressure on someone or some group. Unlike authority, influence may be exerted from a low-

status and marginal position. All three terms are relational. A person's power, authority, or influence exists in relation to other people. Power implies the greatest likelihood of a coercive and hierarchical relationship, and authority and influence offer the most scope for consensual, cooperative decision making. Power, authority, and influence are all related to politics, power being the strongest basis for action and decision making—and potentially the least moral.

Politics: A Cultural Universal?

Is politics a human universal? Some anthropologists would say no. They point to instances of cultures with scarcely any institutions that can be called political, with no durable ranking systems, and very little aggression. Foraging lifestyles, as a model for early human evolution, suggest that non-hierarchical social systems characterized human life for 90 percent of its existence. Only with the emergence of private property, surpluses, and other changes did ranking systems, government, formal law, and organized group aggression emerge. Also, studies show how dominance-seeking and aggression are learned behaviours, emphasized in some cultures and among some segments of the population, such as the military, and de-emphasized among others, such as religious leaders, healers, and child care providers. Being a good politician or a Major-General is a matter of socialization (see the Multiple Cultural Worlds box on page 235).

Other anthropologists argue that, despite a wide range of variation, politics is a human universal. Every society is organized to some degree by kinship relationships, and many anthropologists would not draw a clear boundary between how kinship organizes power and how political organization organizes power.

POLITICAL ORGANIZATION AND LEADERSHIP

Political organization refers to groups that exist for purposes of public decision making and leadership, maintaining social cohesion and order, protecting group rights, and ensuring safety from external threats. Power relationships situated in private, within the family, for example, may be considered "political" and may be related to wider political realities, but they are not considered forms of political organization. Political organizations have several features that overlap with the groups and organizations discussed in the previous chapter:

- *Recruitment principles:* Criteria for determining admission to the unit.
- *Perpetuity:* Assumption that the group will continue to exist indefinitely.
- *Identity markers:* Particular characteristics that distinguish it from others, such as costume, membership card, or title.
- *Internal organization:* An orderly arrangement of members in relation to each other.
- *Procedures:* Prescribed rules and practices for behaviour of group members.
- *Autonomy:* Ability to regulate its own affairs. (Tiffany 1979:71–72)

Cultural anthropologists cluster the many forms of political organization that occur cross-culturally into four major types (see Figure 11.1). The four types of political organization correspond, generally, to the major economic forms (see Chapter 3). Recall that the categories of economies represent a continuum, suggesting that there is overlap between the different types rather than neatly drawn boundaries; this overlap exists between types of political organization as well.

FIGURE 11.1 Economies and Political Organization

FORAGING	HORTICULTURE	PASTORALISM	AGRICULTURE	INDUSTRIALISM (CAPITALIST)
Political Organization				*Political Organization*
Band	Tribe	Chiefdom	Confederacy	State State
Leadership				*Leadership*
Band leader	Headman/Headwoman Big-man Big-woman	Chief Paramount chief		King/queen/president prime minister/emperor
Social Change				

More surpluses of resources and wealth ⟶
Increased population density and residential centralization ⟶
More social inequality/ranking ⟶
Less reliance on kinship relations as the basis of political structures ⟶
Increased internal and external social conflict ⟶
Increased power and responsibility of leaders ⟶
Increased burdens on the population to support political organization ⟶

Bands

The term **band** refers to the political organization of foraging groups. Because foraging has been the predominant mode of production for almost all of human history, the band has been the most longstanding form of political organization. A band comprises a small group of households, between 20 and a few hundred people at most, who are related through kinship. These units come together at certain times of the year, depending on their foraging patterns and ritual schedule.

Band membership is flexible: If a person has a serious disagreement with another person or a spouse, one option is to leave that band and join another. Leadership is also informal in most cases, with no one person being named as a permanent leader for the whole group at all times. Depending on events, such as organizing the group to relocate or to send people out to hunt, a particular person may come to the fore as a leader for that time. This is usually someone whose advice and knowledge about the task are especially respected.

There is no social stratification between leaders and followers. A band leader is a "first among equals." Band leaders have limited authority or influence, but no power. They cannot enforce their opinions. Social levelling mechanisms prevent anyone from accumulating much authority or influence. Political activity in bands involves mainly decision making about migration, food distribution, and interpersonal conflicts. External conflict between groups is rare since territories of different bands are widely separated and the population density is low.

The band level of organization barely qualifies as a form of political organization because groups are flexible, leadership ephemeral, and there are no signs or emblems of political affiliation. Some anthropologists argue that "real" politics did not exist in undisturbed band societies.

Tribes

A tribe is a more complex form of political organization than the band. Typically associated with horticulture and pastoralism, tribal organization developed only with the advent of these modes of production. A **tribe** is a political group that comprises several bands or lineage groups, each with similar language and lifestyle and occupying a distinct territory. These groups may be connected through a **clan** structure in which most people claim descent from a common ancestor, although they may be unable to trace the exact relationship. Kinship is the primary basis of membership. Tribes contain from a hundred to several thousand people. They are found in the Middle East, South Asia, Southeast Asia, the Pacific, Africa, and among First Nations people in North America.

A tribal headman or headwoman (most are male) is a more formal leader than a band leader. Key qualifications for this position are being hardworking and generous and possessing good personal skills. A headman is a political leader on a part-time basis only, yet this role is more demanding than that of a band leader. Depending on the mode of production, a headman will be in charge of determining the times for moving herds, planting and harvesting, and setting the time for seasonal feasts and celebrations. Internal and external conflict resolution is also his responsibility. A headman relies mainly on authority and persuasion rather than power. These strategies are effective because tribal members are all kin and have a loyalty to each other. Furthermore, exerting force on kinspersons is generally avoided.

Ethnohistorical research found that the Ojibwa of northwestern Ontario, who were previously thought to have lived in small, mutually hostile bands, participated in a tribe-wide organization called the Grand Council that involved ranked male leaders, including a grand chief, civil chiefs, war chiefs, and others. Abundant resources, especially wild rice and sturgeon, allowed the Rainy River Ojibwa in the mid-nineteenth century to control access to their territory. Seasonal gatherings in large groupings at

Chief Paul Payakan, leader of the Kayapo, a group of indigenous people living in the rainforest of the Brazilian Amazon. Payakan was instrumental in mobilizing widespread political resistance in the region against the construction of a hydroelectric dam.

maple groves (to tap for maple sugar), fishing stations, berry patches, garden sites (growing potatoes and corn), and rice fields were "the foundation for tribal government and Ojibwa military power" (Lovisek, Holzkamm, and Waisberg 1997:138). Colonial officials had to abide by the Grand Council's rules when moving through the territory, and Ojibwa religious leaders were successful in resisting Christian missionizing for a time.

Among horticulturalists of the Amazonian rain forest, tribal organization is the dominant political pattern. Each local tribal unit, which is itself a lineage, has a headman (or perhaps two or three). Each tribal group is autonomous, but recently many have united temporarily into larger groups, in reaction to threats to their environment and lifestyle from outside forces.

Pastoralist tribal formations are often linked into a confederacy, with local units or segments each maintaining substantial autonomy. The local segments meet together rarely, usually at an annual festival. In case of an external threat, the confederacy gathers together. Once the threat is removed, local units resume their autonomy. The overall equality and autonomy of each unit in relation to the others, along with their ability to unite and then disunite, is referred to as a **segmentary model** of political organization (a pattern of smaller units within larger units that can unite and separate depending on external threats).

Big-Man and Big-Woman Leadership

In between tribal and chiefdom organizations is the **big-man system** or **big-woman system**, in which key individuals devote efforts to developing a political following through a system of redistribution based on personal ties and grand feasts (as mentioned in Chapter 4). Anthropological research in Melanesia, a large region in the South Pacific, established the big-man type of politics, and most references to it are from this region (Sahlins 1963; A. Strathern 1971). Personalistic, favour-based political groupings are, however, also found elsewhere.

Big-man political organization is common in Papua New Guinea. In several tribes in the Mount Hagen region of the New Guinea Highlands, an aspiring big-man develops a leadership position through making *moka* (A. Strathern 1971). Making *moka* involves exchanging gifts and favours with individuals and sponsoring large feasts where further gift-giving occurs. A crucial factor in big-manship in the Mount Hagen area is having at least one wife. An aspiring big-man urges his wives to work harder than ordinary women in order to grow more food to feed more pigs. (Pigs are an important measure of a man's status and worth.) The role of the wife is so important that a man whose parents died when he was young is at an extreme disadvantage. He has impaired chances of getting a wife or wives since he lacks financial support from his parents for the necessary bridewealth.

Using his wife's (or wives') production as an exchange base, the aspiring big-man extends his *moka* relationships, first with kin and then beyond. By giving goods to people, he gains prestige over them. The recipient, later, will make a return gift of somewhat greater value. The exchanges go back and forth, over the years. The more one gives, and the more people in one's exchange network, the greater prestige the big-man develops.

Although big-manship is an achieved position, analysis of the family patterns of big-manship in the Mt. Hagen area shows that most big-men are the sons of big-men (see Table 11.1). This is especially true of major big-men, of whom over three-quarters were sons of former big-men. It is unclear whether this pattern results from the greater wealth and prestige of big-man families, from socialization into big-manship through paternal example, or from a combination of these aspects.

With few exceptions, the early anthropological literature about Melanesian tribal politics portrays men as dominating public exchange networks and the public political arenas. Women as wives are mentioned as important in providing the material basis for men's political careers. A study of Vanatinai, however, a Pacific island that is gender-egalitarian, reveals the existence of big-women as well as big-men (Lepowsky 1990). In this culture, both men and women can gain power and prestige by sponsoring feasts at which valuables are distributed, especially mortuary feasts (feasts for the dead). Although more Vanatinai men than women are involved in political exchange and leadership-building, some women are extremely active. These women lead sailing expeditions to neighbouring islands to visit their

TABLE 11.1 Family Background of Big-Men in Mt. Hagen, Papua New Guinea

	Father Was a Big-Man	Father Was Not a Big-Man	Totals
Major Big-Men	27	9	36
Minor Big-Men	31	30	61
Total	58	39	97

Source: From *The Rope of Moka: Big-Men and Ceremonial Exchange in Mount Hagen, New Guinea*, p. 209, by Andrew Strathern. Copyright © 1971. Reprinted by permission of Cambridge University Press.

Throughout much of the South Pacific, big-man politics has long involved the demonstration of generosity on the part of the leaders, who are expected to be able to mobilize resources for impressive feasts such as this one on Tanna Island.

exchange partners, who are both male and female, and they sponsor lavish feasts attended by many people. On Vanatinai, big-women also include powerful sorcerers, famous healers, and successful gardeners.

Contact with European colonial culture gave men a political edge that they had not had before on Vanatinai. The Europeans traded with men for goods and approached women mainly for sexual relations. Formal government councils were established. Thus far, all councillors on Vanatinai have been male. In addition, some Vanatinai men have received training in the English language, the language of government, and thus have another advantage. In other cases, European domination led to more political equality between men and women with the imposition of "pacification," which ended local warfare and thereby eliminated one of the traditional paths to power for men.

Chiefdoms

A **chiefdom** is a political grouping of permanently allied tribes and villages under one recognized leader. Compared to most tribes, chiefdoms have larger populations, often numbering in the thousands, and are more centralized and socially complex. Hereditary systems of social ranking and economic stratification are found in chiefdoms (Earle 1991), with social divisions existing between the chiefly lineage or lineages and non-chiefly groups. Chiefs and their descendants are considered to be superior to commoners, and intermarriage between the two strata is forbidden. Chiefs are expected to be generous, but they may have a more luxurious lifestyle than the rest of the people. The chiefship is an "office" that must be filled at all times.

When a chief dies or retires, he or she must be replaced. In contrast, the death of a band leader or big-man does not require that someone else be chosen as a replacement. A chief has more responsibilities than a band or tribal leader. He or she regulates production and redistribution, solves internal conflicts, and plans and leads raids and warring expeditions. Criteria for becoming a chief are more clearly defined. Besides ascribed criteria (birth in a chiefly lineage, or being the first son or daughter of the chief), achievement is still important. Achievement is measured in terms of personal leadership skills, charisma, and accumulated wealth. Chiefdoms have existed in many places throughout the world.

Anthropologists and archaeologists are interested in how and why chiefdom systems evolved as an intermediary unit between tribes and states, and what the political implications of this evolution are (Earle 1991). Several political strategies support the expansion of power in chiefdoms: controlling more internal and external wealth and distributing feasting and gift exchanges that create debt ties; improving local production systems; applying force internally; forging stronger and wider external ties; and controlling ideological legitimacy. Depending on local conditions, different strategies were employed. Internal control of irrigation systems was the most important factor in the emergence of chiefdoms in prehistoric southeastern Spain, while control of external trade was more important in the prehistoric Aegean region (Gilman 1991).

Gender and Leadership

Much evidence about leadership patterns in chiefdoms comes from historical examples. Prominent chiefs—men and women—are documented in colonial archives and missionary records. Many historic examples of women chiefs and women rulers come from West Africa, including the Queen Mother of the Ashanti of Ghana and of the Edo of Nigeria (Awe 1977).

Oral histories and archival records show that Yoruba women had the institution of the *iyalode,* or chief of the women. The *iyalode* was the women's political spokesperson in the "council of kingmakers," the highest level of government. She was a chief in her own right, with chiefly insignia, including a necklace of special beads, a wide-brimmed straw hat, a shawl, personal servants, special drummers, and bell ringers. She had her own council of subordinate chiefs. The position of *iyalode* was based on achievement. The most important qualifications were a woman's proven ability as a leader, economic resources to maintain her new status as chief, and popularity. Tasks included settling disputes via her court and meeting with women to formulate the women's stand on such policy issues as the declaration of war and the opening of new markets. Although she represented all women in the group and had massive support, she was outnumbered at the

Pocahontas played an important role in First Nations–British relations during the early colonial period.

council of kingmakers because she was the only female and the only representative of all women.

Why do women play greater political roles in some chiefdoms than others? The most successful answers point to women's economic roles as the primary basis for political power, as among the Iroquois and many African horticultural societies. In contrast, the dominant economic role of men in Native American groups of the prairies, following the introduction of the horse by the Spanish and the increased importance of buffalo hunting by men, supported male-dominated political leadership in such groups as the Cheyenne.

A marked change in leadership patterns among chiefdoms in the past few hundred years has been the decline of women's political status in many groups, mainly because of European and North American colonial and missionary influences (Etienne and Leacock 1980). For example, the British colonialists redefined the institution of *iyalode* in Nigeria. Now "she is no longer a member of any of the important councils of government. Even the market, and therefore the market women, have been removed from her jurisdiction, and have been placed under the control of the new local government councils in each town" (146).

Ethnohistorical research on chiefdoms in Hawaii provides a similar view of formerly powerful women chiefs (Linnekan 1990). Following Captain Cook's arrival in 1778, a Western-model monarchy was established. By the time the United States annexed the islands in 1898, indigenous Hawaiian leaders had been displaced from prominent economic and political roles by Westerners.

Confederacies

An expanded version of the chiefdom occurs when several chiefdoms are joined in a confederacy, headed by a chief of chiefs, "big chief," or paramount chief. Many prominent confederacies have existed: in Hawaii in the late 1700s and in North America, including the Iroquois league of five nations that stretched across New York state, the Cherokee of Tennessee, the Algonquins who dominated the Chesapeake region in present-day Virginia and Maryland, and the Huron of southern Ontario. The Huron confederacy, called *Wendat*, included five distinct groups living in the region around Lake Simcoe, Georgian Bay, and Lake Huron in southern Ontario. In the Huron confederacy, each village had a chief and there were regional and confederacy councils that brought together chiefs from all the villages. Chiefs of principal villages were the heads of councils. The confederacy council met at least once a year and decided issues of war and peace. Special pools of goods were built up as a public treasury and were administered by chiefs for long-distance trade (Trigger 1969, 1976).

States

A **state** is a centralized political unit encompassing many communities and possessing coercive power. The earliest evidence of the state form of political organization comes from Mesopotamia, China, India, and Egypt, perhaps as early as 4000 BCE. States emerged in these several locations with the development of intensive agriculture, increased surpluses, and increased population density. The state is now the form of political organization in which all people live. Band organizations, tribes, and chiefdoms still exist, but they are incorporated, to a greater or lesser degree, within state structures.

There are many theories proposed for why the state evolved (Trigger 1996). Marxist theory says that the state emerged to maintain ruling-class dominance. Demographic theory posits that population density drove the need for central mechanisms for social control. Economic theory argues that the state emerged in response to the increased surpluses of food production in the neolithic era, which produced sufficient wealth to support a permanent ruling class. Political theory says that the state arose as a necessary arbiter as competition increased for arable land and access to food surpluses. Rather than emphasizing a single causal factor, most scholars now incorporate multiple causes in their theories. Another development is that scholars have moved from the "why" question to the "how" question (Trigger 1996). New areas of inquiry include the state's increased bases for central power, such as finances and information management.

Powers of the State

Most cultural anthropologists now ask "how" states become and remain states. In this inquiry, they focus on the enhanced power that states have over their domain:

- *States define citizenship and its rights and responsibilities.* In complex nations, since early times, not all residents were granted equal rights as citizens.

- *States monopolize the use of force and the maintenance of law and order.* Internally, the state controls the population through laws, courts, and the police. Externally, the state uses force defensively to maintain the nation's borders and offensively to extend its territory.

- *States maintain standing armies and police* (as opposed to part-time forces).

- *States keep track of their citizens in terms of number, age, gender, location, and wealth through census systems that are regularly updated.* A census allows the state to maintain formal taxation systems, military recruitment, and policy planning such as population settlement, immigration quotas, and social benefits such as old-age pensions.

- *States have the power to extract resources from citizens through taxation.* All political organizations are supported by contributions of the members, but variations occur in the rate of contributions expected, the form in which they are paid, and the return that members get in terms of services. Public finance in states is based on formal taxation that takes many forms. **In-kind taxation** is a system of mandatory, non-cash contributions to the state. For example, the Inca state used the *corvée*, a labour tax, to finance public works such as roads and monuments and to provide agricultural labour on state lands. Cash taxes, such as the income tax that takes a percentage of wages, emerged only in the past few hundred years.

- *States manipulate information.* Control of information to protect the state and its leaders can be done directly (through censorship, restricting public access to certain information, and promoting favourable images via propaganda) and indirectly through pressure on journalists and television networks to present information in certain ways.

Symbols of State Power

Religious beliefs and symbols are often closely tied to the power of state leadership: The ruler may be considered to be a deity or part deity, or a high priest of the state religion, or may be closely linked with the high priest who serves as adviser. Architecture and urban planning remind the populace of the greatness of the state. In pre-Columbian Mexico, the central plaza of city-states, such as Tenochtitlán (founded in 1325), was symbolically equivalent to the centre of the cosmos and thus the locale of greatest significance (Low 1995). The most important temples and the residence of the head of state surrounded the plaza. Other houses and structures, in decreasing order of status, were located on avenues in decreasing proximity to the centre. The grandness and individual character of the leader's residence indicate power, as do monuments—especially tombs to past leaders or heroes or heroines. Egypt's pyramids, China's Great Wall, and India's Taj Mahal are a few of the world's great architectural reminders of state power.

In democratic states where leaders are elected by popular vote and in socialist states where political rhetoric emphasizes social equality, expense and elegance are

Afghanistan Prime Minister Hamed Karzai wears a carefully assembled collection of regional political symbols. The striped cape is associated with northern tribes. The Persian-lamb hat is an Uzbek style popular in the capital city, Kabul. He also wears a tunic and loose trousers, which are associated with villagers, and sometimes adds a Western-style jacket as well.

"toned down" in some ways by the adoption of more egalitarian ways of dress (even though in private, these leaders may live relatively opulent lives in terms of housing, food, and entertainment). The earlier practice of all Chinese leaders wearing a "Mao jacket," regardless of their rank, was a symbolic statement of their anti-hierarchical philosophy.

Local Power and Politics in Democratic States The degree to which the state influences the lives of its citizens varies. So-called totalitarian states have the most direct control of local politics. In most other systems, local politics and local government are granted some degree of power. In highly centralized states, the central government controls public finance and legal institutions, leaving little power or autonomy in these matters to local governments. In decentralized systems, local governments are granted some forms of revenue generation (taxation) and the responsibility of providing certain services. Local politics continue to exist within state systems, with their strength and autonomy dependent on how centralized the state apparatus is.

In Japan, relatively egalitarian systems of local power structures exist in villages and hamlets. Families subtly vie for status and leadership roles through gift-giving, as is common in local politics worldwide (R. Marshall 1985). Egalitarianism prevails as a community value, but people strive to be "more than equal" by making public donations to the *buraku*, or hamlet. The custom of "giving a gift to the community" is a way that hamlet families can improve their positions in the local ranking system. In one hamlet, all 35 households recently gave gifts to the community on specified occasions: the forty-second birthday of male family members, the sixty-first birthday of male family members, the seventy-seventh birthday of male family members, the marriage of male family members, the marriage of female family members whose husband will be the household successor, the birth of the household head or successor couple's first child, and the construction of a new house. These occasions for public gift-giving always include an invitation to a meal for members of all hamlet households:

> About a month before the meal is scheduled, the donor household notifies the hamlet head of its intentions and places with him the cash portion of its gift, from which provisions for the meal will be purchased. . . . The donor family and the hamlet head agree on a suitable date and time for the meal, usually a Sunday afternoon as a prelude to a general meeting of the hamlet as council for the discussion of hamlet affairs. . . . When the hamlet members are all seated in the hamlet hall and the meal has been placed before them . . . the hamlet head holds up the decorated envelope in which he received the cash

gift and reads from it the donor household's name, the amount of the gift, and the nature of the occasion. During the meal the envelope is circulated from hand to hand around the tables and examined without comment as it travels around the hall. (169)

Since the 1960s, it has also become common to give an item that is useful for the hamlet, such as a set of fluorescent light fixtures for the hamlet hall, folding tables, space heaters, and vacuum cleaners.

Local politics within a democratic framework reveal another type of gift-giving and exchange in the interest of maintaining or gaining power. Here we see people in elected positions of power giving favours in expectation of political loyalty in return. In these cases, various **factions** vie with each other. A faction, a more formalized aspect of local politics, is a politically oriented conflict group whose members are mobilized and maintained by a leader to whom the main ties of loyalty and affiliation are lateral—from leader to follower—rather than horizontal between members (Brumfiel 1994). Factions tend to be personalistic, transitory, lacking formal rules and meeting times, and lacking formal succession. Factional politics is not redistributive, however. It often leads to conflict and unequal resource distribution.

Gender and Leadership

Most states are hierarchical and patriarchal, excluding members of lower classes and women from equal participation. Some contemporary states are less male-dominated than others, but none are female-dominated. Strongly patriarchal contemporary states preserve male dominance through ideologies that restrict women's political power, such as *purdah* (female seclusion and segregation from the public world), as practised in much of the Muslim Middle East, Pakistan, and North India. In China, scientific beliefs that categorize women as less strong and dependable than men have long been used to rationalize the exclusion of women from politics (Dikötter 1998).

A handful of contemporary states have or have recently had women as prime ministers or presidents. Such powerful women include Indira Gandhi in India, Golda Meir in Israel, Margaret Thatcher in the United Kingdom, and Benazir Bhutto in Pakistan. Female heads of state are often related by kinship (as wife or daughter) to former heads of state. Indira Gandhi, for example, was the daughter of the popular first prime minister of independent India, Jawaharlal Nehru (she is not related to Mahatma Gandhi). But it is unclear whether these women's leadership positions can be explained by their inheriting the role or through the political socialization they may have received, directly or indirectly, as a result of being born into political families.

CHANGE IN POLITICAL SYSTEMS

In the early days of political anthropology, researchers examined the varieties of political organization and leadership and created categories such as bands, tribes, chiefdoms, and states. Contemporary political anthropologists are more interested in political dynamics and change, especially in how the pre-eminent political form, the state, affects local people's lives. This section covers selected topics in the anthropological study of political change.

Emergent Nations and Transnational Nations

Many different definitions exist for a *nation,* and some of them overlap with definitions given for a *state* (Maybury-Lewis 1997:125–132). One definition says that a **nation** is a group of people who share a language, culture, territorial base, political organization, and history (Clay 1990). In this sense, a nation is culturally homogeneous, and thus, Canada would not be considered a nation but rather a unit composed of many nations. According to this definition, groups that lack a territorial base cannot be termed nations. A related term is the *nation-state,* which some people say refers to a state that comprises only one nation, while others think it refers to a state that comprises many nations. A clear example of a nation is the Iroquois nation of central New York state.

Depending on their resources and power, nations may constitute a political threat to states. In response to this (real or perceived) threat, states seek to create and maintain a sense of unified identity. Political scientist Benedict Anderson, in his widely read book *Imagined Communities* (1991), writes about the efforts that state-builders employ to create a sense of belonging and commitment—"imagined community"—among diverse peoples. Strategies for building state identity among the many nations within a state include the imposition of one language as "the" national language; the construction of monuments and museums; and the creation of songs, poetry, and other media-relayed messages about the "motherland." More recently, anthropologists inspired by Anderson's writings have added to his thinking by, for example, including state laws and other bureaucratic practices as forms of secular ritual that seek to create a sense of unity (Bigenho 1999). State control of areas of life such as religion and language has been documented for many parts of the world.

World peace increasingly involves intrastate and cross-state ethnic politics and conflict. The Tibetans, the Chechens, the Kayapo, the Eritreans (whose war of liberation ended in 1993), the Palestinians, the Sikhs of north-

A political rally of indigenous people in Bolivia.

western India, the Kurds of Turkey and Iraq, and the Assamese of eastern India . . . the list goes on . . . are all groups building their own solidarities and political momentums. Attempts by nationalistic states to force homogenization of these and other ethnic groups will prompt resistance of varying degrees from those who wish to retain autonomy. Cultural anthropologists are becoming more involved in studying both local and global aspects of ethnic relations. Their data can contribute to the realm of "peace and conflict" studies and policy through providing case studies and theories based on comparative analysis.

Globalization and Politics

Since the seventeenth century, the world's nations have been increasingly linked in a hierarchical structure. This structure of power relations is largely regulated through international trade. In the seventeenth century, Holland was the one core nation, dominating world trade. It was then surpassed by England and France, which remained the two most powerful nations up to around 1900. In the early part of the twentieth century, challenges for world dominance were made by the United States and later by Germany and Japan. The outcome of World War II placed the United States as leader of the "core." Greater complexities in world-systems theory now allow for an

Aung San Suu Kyi is the leader of the Burmese democracy and human rights movement. The daughter of Burma's assassinated national hero, Aung San, she was under house arrest from 1989 to 1995. She was awarded the Nobel Peace Prize, making her the eighth woman to receive the award.

additional category of semi-periphery states, intermediary between the core and the periphery.

Cultural anthropology's traditional strength has been the study of small, bounded local groups, so anthropologists have had relatively little to say about international affairs. Now, more anthropologists have enlarged their focus to include the international level, studying both how global changes affect local politics and how local politics affect international affairs. Worldwide communication networks facilitate global politics. Ethnic politics, although locally initiated, increasingly has international repercussions. Migrant populations promote interconnected interests across state boundaries.

Culture exists at all levels of human interaction—local, national, international, and transnational, and even in cyberspace—and power relations are embedded in culture at all these levels. Anthropologists are now contributing to debates about the definition and use of the term *culture* by international organizations such as UNESCO: Happy as we are that organizations pay attention to culture, our wish is that they would not use outdated concepts that portray cultures as nicely bounded entities with a simple list of traits, such as language, dress, and religion (Wright 1998; Eriksen 2001).

Anthropologists are also tackling the study of powerful international organizations such as NATO (Feldman 2003). Anthropologists must "study up," as Laura Nader urged us to do over three decades ago (1972), because people, power, and culture are "up" there. Anthropologists need to examine their own culture, which tends to be power-averse, to feel empathy with the powerless—with "the village people" and not the people who wield power

at NATO. As one anthropologist urges, it is high time that anthropologists break their silence about institutions with lethal powers (Feldman 2003).

THE ANTHROPOLOGY OF ORDER AND CONFLICT

Socially agreed-upon ways of behaving shape people's everyday life in countless ways. We wait for our turn to get on a bus rather than pushing to the head of the line, and we pay for a sandwich at the deli instead of stealing it. Anthropologists in all four fields have devoted attention to the subjects of social order and social conflict. Historical archaeologists, studying cultures that had writing, have traced the development of written law through time. Other archaeologists have examined artifacts such as weapons, remains of forts, and the waxing and waning of political centres in order to understand group conflict in the past. Many primatologists study non-human primate patterns of cooperation, coalitions, and conflict. Linguistic anthropologists have done research on social conflict related to national language policies and on how communication patterns within the courtroom influence outcomes. Legal anthropology is the subfield within cultural anthropology that is most directly concerned with the study of social control and social conflict.

Over the course of the twentieth century, the direction of legal anthropology has headed away from its original foundations in functionalism (the way a particular practice or belief contributed to social cohesion) toward a view that focuses on internal divisiveness. Helping to launch the subfield through his classic book *Crime and Custom in Savage Society* (1962 [1926]), functionalist Malinowski wrote that in the Trobriand Islands, social ties themselves promoted mutual social obligation and harmony. No separate legal institutions existed throughout Melanesia; instead, law was embedded in social life. Thus, he made the important contribution that social relationships can perform the same functions as formal laws and courts.

Later, in the mid-twentieth century, Max Gluckman (1955, 1963) diverged from functionalism in studying disputes and conflict. His research in central African villages revealed how the court systems resolved conflict. Much early research on indigenous law and legal processes, including Gluckman's, was commissioned by colonial administrations. The colonialists wanted to learn about local customs in order to rule over the colonized peoples more effectively. This early work was mainly concerned with documenting how different cultures defined law, justice, and punishment.

By the 1960s, another new turn was established with the study of law in action. This transition brought an emphasis on collecting ethnographic data on the dispute event and the chain of events that followed it. June Starr's book, *Dispute and Settlement in Rural Turkey* (1978), exemplifies this approach of extended case analysis. Her book is built around 32 dispute cases, including two boys fighting at a wedding, a man's dog killing a chicken, the lighthouse keeper's wife taking a lover, and a dispute among siblings about dividing the family land. In examining each case, Starr provides information on the social relationships of the disputants, the cultural significance of the dispute, Turkish law in relation to the offence (for example, Turkish law says that it is a criminal offence to shoot a gun at a wedding), forms of resolution, and why particular resolutions emerged compared to others. This approach highlights rules of law and order, but situates them in the cultural context for interpretation.

Several new directions have emerged in legal anthropology: the study of legal discourse, especially in courtroom settings; law and transnational processes in colonial and post-colonial settings; **critical legal anthropology** (an approach that examines how the law and judicial systems serve to maintain and expand the dominant power interests rather than protecting those who are marginal and less powerful); and law and human rights in cross-cultural perspective (Merry 1992).

Systems of Social Control

The concept of social control has several meanings depending on one's theoretical perspective. A generally accepted definition in anthropology is that **social control** is "the processes which help produce and maintain orderly social life" (Garland 1996:781). Scholars of a more critical bent would emphasize the negative aspects of social control systems as supporting hierarchy and domination, either directly or indirectly. Underlying both views are two premises:

- Social control systems exist to ensure a certain degree of social conformity to agreed-upon rules.

- Some people in all cultures may violate the rules and resist conformity (what sociologists refer to as "deviant behaviour").

Social control systems include internalized social controls that exist through socialization for proper behaviour, education, and peer pressure, and formal systems of codified rules about proper behaviour and punishments for deviation. The Amish and Mennonites, Christian immigrant groups from Europe, rely on internalized social controls more than most cultural groups in the United States and Canada. These groups have no police force or legal system; the way social order is maintained is through religious teaching and group pressure. If a member veers from

correct behaviour, punishment such as ostracism ("shunning") may be applied.

Cultural anthropologists distinguish two major instruments of social control: norms and laws. **Norms** are generally agreed-upon standards for how people should behave. All societies have norms. They are usually unwritten and learned unconsciously through socialization. Norms include, for example, the expectation that children should follow their parents' advice, that people standing in line should be orderly and not try to "jump" the line, and that an individual should accept an offer of a handshake (in cultures where handshakes are the usual greeting) when meeting someone for the first time. In rural Bali, etiquette dictates certain greeting forms between people of different status: "[P]ersons of higher status and power are shown very marked respect: they are greeted submissively and treated obsequiously; if seated, then others moving past them crouch . . . so as not to loom above them" (Barth 1993:114). Enforcement of norms tends to be informal; for example, a violation may simply be considered rude and the violator avoided in the future. In others, punishment may be involved, such as asking someone who is disruptive in a meeting to leave.

The categories of norm and law form a continuum in terms of how explicitly they are stated and how strongly they are enforced. A **law** is a binding rule created through enactment or custom that defines right and reasonable behaviour. Laws are enforceable by threat of punishment. Systems of law are more common and more elaborate in state-level societies, but many non-state societies have formalized laws. Often the legitimacy and force of law are based on religion. For example, Australian Aborigines believe that law came to humans during the "Dreamtime," a time in the mythological past when the ancestors created the Aboriginal world. Contemporary Islamic states explicitly link law and religion. Secular Western states consider their laws to be religiously neutral, but in fact, much Western legal practice is heavily influenced by Judeo-Christian beliefs. Critiques of law versus norms have focused on how, in some instances, laws are less morally sound than norms.

Social Control in Small-Scale Societies

Anthropologists distinguish small-scale societies and large-scale societies in terms of prevalent forms of conflict resolution, social order, and punishment of offences. Formal laws are rare among foraging groups, although Inuit and Australian Aborigines are notable for their more formalized, although unwritten, law systems. Because bands are small, close-knit groups, disputes tend to be handled at the interpersonal level through discussion or one-on-one fights. The group may act together to punish an offender through shaming and ridicule. Emphasis is on maintaining social order and restoring social equilibrium, not hurtfully punishing an offender. Ostracizing an offending member (forcing the person to leave the group) is a common means of formal punishment. Capital punishment has been documented, but is rare. For example, in some Australian Aboriginal societies, a law restricts access to religious rituals and paraphernalia to men who have gone through a ritual initiation. If an initiated man shared secrets with an uninitiated man, the elders would delegate one of their group to kill the offender. In such instances, the elders act like a court.

In non-state societies, punishment is often legitimized through belief in supernatural forces and their ability to affect people. Among the highland horticulturalists of the Indonesian island of Sumba, one of the greatest offences is to fail to keep a promise (Kuipers 1990). Breaking a promise will bring on "supernatural assault" by the ancestors of those who have been offended by the person's misbehaviour. The punishment may come in the form of damage to crops, illness or death of a relative, destruction of the offender's house, or having clothing catch on fire. When such a disaster occurs, the only choice is to sponsor a ritual that will appease the ancestors.

Conflict resolution among horticulturalists relies on many of the same methods as among foragers, notably public shaming and ridicule. In the Trobriands of the early twentieth century, Malinowski (1961) reports,

> The rare quarrels which occur at times take the form of an exchange of public expostulation (yakala) in which the two parties assisted by friends and relatives meet, harangue one another, hurl and hurl back recriminations. Such litigation allows people to give vent to their feelings and shows the trend of public opinion, and thus it may be of assistance in settling disputes. Sometimes it seems, however, to harden the parties. In no case is there any definite sentence pronounced by a third party, and agreement is but seldom reached then and there. (60)

Village *fission* (breaking up) and ostracism are other common mechanisms for dealing with unresolvable conflict. The overall goal in dealing with conflict in small-scale societies is to return the group to harmony.

Social Control in States

In societies that are more densely populated, more socially stratified, and that have more wealth, increased stresses occur in relation to the distribution of surplus, inheritance, and rights to land. In addition, increased social scale means that not everyone knows everyone else, and face-to-face accountability may exist only in local neighbourhoods. Yet informal mechanisms also exist. In the Lessons Applied box, one activist anthropologist provides a cultural critique of them.

Specialization   The specialization of tasks related to law and order—police, judges, lawyers—increases with

A "leopard-skin chief" among the cattle-herding Nuer of the Sudan acted as an intermediary between people and groups in conflict, including instances of murder. His power, however, was limited to negotiation and the ability to threaten punishment through supernatural means.

the emergence of state organization. In pre-state societies, it is often society at large that determines right from wrong and punishes offenders, or the elders may have special authority and be called on for advice. In tribal societies, special advisers, such as the "leopard-skin chief" of the Nuer of Sudan, have had a role in decision making about crime and punishment. However, full-time professionals, such as judges and lawyers, emerged with the state. These professionals often come from powerful or elite social groups, a fact that perpetuates elite biases in the justice process itself. In North America, the legal profession is committed to opposing discrimination on the basis of gender and race, but it is nonetheless characterized by a lack of representation of women and minorities. Minority women, who face a double bind, are especially underrepresented (Chanen 1995:105).

Policing includes processes of surveillance and the threat of punishment related to maintaining social order (Reiner 1996). Police are the specific organization and personnel who discover, report, and investigate crimes. As a specialized group, police exist mainly in complex state societies.

Lessons Applied

LEGAL ANTHROPOLOGIST ADVISES RESISTANCE TO "COERCIVE HARMONY"

IN THIS example, an anthropologist uses her cross-cultural insights to provide a critique of her own culture, with an eye to producing improved social relations (Nader 2001). Laura Nader had conducted extensive fieldwork in Latin America, as well as in the World Court in Europe. Her main interest lies in cross-cultural aspects of conflict and conflict resolution. In terms of her observations of her home country, the United States, she points out that leading politicians are currently emphasizing the need for unity, consensus, and harmony among the American people. But the United States, she points out, was founded by dissenters, and democracy depends on people speaking out. Democracy, in her view, supports the right to be indignant and the idea that "indignation can make Americans more engaged citizens" (B13).

A professor of anthropology at the University of California at Berkeley, Nader fosters the expression of critique, opinion, and even indignation when she teaches. One of her students commented that "Dr. Nader is a pretty good professor, except she has opinions" (B13). She took that as a compliment.

Nader feels that Europeans are generally less concerned about social harmony than the United States is. Americans consider it bad manners to be contentious, whereas in Europe, debate—even bitterly contentious

debate—is valued. She uses the term *coercive harmony* to refer to the informal but strong pressure in the United States to agree, to be nice, to avoid digging beneath the surface, to stifle indignation at the lack of universal health care or the low voter turnout in presidential elections. The unstated, informally enforced policy of coercive harmony labels cultural critique as bad behaviour, as negative rather than positive. Nader finds it alarming that in a country that proclaims freedom as its primary feature, coercive harmony in fact suppresses contrary views and voices through the idiom of politeness, niceness, and friendliness.

How can this insight be used to improve the situation in the United States? Nader suggests one step: Make sure that critique, dissent, and indignation are supported in schools. Teachers should avoid contributing to the informal enforcement of social harmony and consensus and should instead proactively encourage critique.

FOOD FOR THOUGHT

Would you say Canadians are closer to the style of Americans or Europeans? Do you find that your teachers encourage critique, dissent, and indignation?

Trials and Courts   In societies where misdoing and punishment are defined by spirits and ancestors, a person's guilt is evidenced simply by the fact that misfortune has befallen him or her. If a person's crops were damaged by lightning, then that person must have done something wrong. In other instances, guilt may be determined through **trial by ordeal**, a form of trial in which the accused person is put through some kind of test that is often painful. In this case, the guilty person will be required to place a hand in boiling oil, for example, or to have a part of their body touched by a red-hot knife. Being burned is a sign of guilt, while not being burned means the suspect is innocent. The court system, with lawyers, judge, and jury, is used in many contemporary societies, although there is variation in how cases are presented and juries constituted. The goal of contemporary court trials is to ensure both justice and fairness. Analysis of actual courtroom dynamics and patterns of decision making in North America and elsewhere, however, reveals serious problems in achieving these goals.

Punishment   Administering punishment involves doing something unpleasant to someone who has committed an offence. Cultural anthropologists have examined forms of punishment cross-culturally, as well as the relationship between types of societies and forms of punishment. In small-scale societies, punishment is socially rather than judicially managed. The most extreme form of punishment is usually ostracism and only rarely death. Another common form of punishment is that in the case of theft or murder, the guilty party must pay compensation to members of the harmed family. The prison, as a place where people are forcibly detained as a form of punishment, has a long history. The dungeons and "keeps" of old forts and castles all over the world are vivid evidence of the power of some people to detain and inflict suffering on others (Millett 1994). In general, however, such prisoners were not detained for long periods—they were tried and punished and their cell emptied. Long-term detention of prisoners did not become common until the seventeenth century in Europe (Foucault 1977). The first

---

penitentiary in the United States was built in Philadelphia in the late 1700s (Sharff 1995), and the first in Canada in Kingston in 1835. Cross-nationally and through history, percentages of imprisoned people vary widely. The United States and Russia have high percentages compared to other contemporary Western countries: 550 and 470 prisoners per 100 000 inhabitants, respectively. The British Isles rate is about 100, Canada about 111, while the Scandinavian countries have among the lowest rates, at fewer than 60. In the United States, the prison population has tripled over the past 100 years to nearly two million people, in spite of fairly even levels of crime. In Canada, the prison populations in both federal and provincial jurisdictions dropped in the 1990s and have never attained the levels of incarceration observed in the United States.

The death penalty (capital punishment) is rare in pre-state societies because condemning someone to death requires a high degree of power. A comparison of capital punishment in the contemporary United States with human sacrifice among the Aztecs of Mexico of the sixteenth century reveals striking similarities (Purdum and Paredes 1989). Both systems involve the death of mainly able-bodied males who are in one way or another socially marginal. In the United States, most people who are executed are non-White, have killed Whites, are poor, and have few social ties. Aztec sacrificial victims were mainly male war captives from neighbouring states, but Aztec children were also sometimes sacrificed. The deaths in both contexts have a political message: They communicate a message of the state's power and strength to the general populace, which is why they are highly ritualized and well publicized as events.

Social Inequality and the Law

Critical legal anthropologists examine the role of law in maintaining power relations through discrimination against indigenous people, women, and minorities in various judicial systems around the world. While one could draw examples from many countries about how racial biases and discrimination affect legal processes, the example here comes from Canada.

First Nations peoples in Canada make up 3 percent of the total population, but account for 12 percent of federal prison admissions and 20 percent of provincial prison admissions (Ponting and Kiely 1997). Practices in the justice system in Canada result in lawyers spending less time with First Nations clients than with other clients. Accused First Nations peoples are more likely to be denied bail, and First Nations defendants are more than twice as likely to be incarcerated. In Manitoba, typical of western Canada, more than half of all inmates are from First Nations (155).

The interior scene of the Cellular Jail in India's Andaman Islands, which was so named because all prisoners had single cells, arranged in long rows, in order to prevent them from any social interaction and possible collusion to escape or rebel.

Change in Legal Systems

Law-and-order systems, like other cultural domains, change over time. European colonialism since the seventeenth century has had major impacts on indigenous systems. Legal systems of contemporary countries have to deal with social complexity that has its roots in colonialism and new patterns of migration.

European Colonialism and Indigenous Systems

Colonial governments, to varying degrees, attempted to learn about and rule their subject populations through what they termed "customary law" (Merry 1992). By seeking to codify customary law, colonial governments created fixed rules where flexibility and local variation had formerly existed. Often the colonialists overrode customary law and imposed their own laws. Homicide, marriage, land rights, and indigenous religion were frequent areas of European imposition. Colonial governments everywhere banned headhunting and blood feuds. Among the Nuer of Sudan, British legal interventions resulted in substantial confusion among the Nuer about the issue of blood feuds (Hutchinson 1996). Nuer practices involved either the taking of a life in repayment for a previous homicide or negotiated payments in cattle, depending on the relations between the victim and the assailant, what type of weapon was used, and a consideration of current rates of bridewealth as an index of value. In contrast, the British determined a fixed (non-negotiable) amount of indemnity. They imprisoned people for committing a vengeful murder. From the Nuer point of view, these changes were incomprehensible. They interpreted being put in prison as a way of protecting the person from a reprisal attack.

When European administrators and missionaries encountered aspects of marriage systems different from their own, they often tried to impose their own ways. Europeans tried in most cases to stop polygamy as un-Christian and uncivilized. In South Africa, however, British and Afrikaaner Whites tolerated the continuation of traditional marriage practices of South African peoples (D. L. Chambers 2000). So-called customary law, applying to the many diverse practices of South African Black communities, permits a number of marriage forms that, despite their variety, share two basic features. First, marriage is considered a union between two families, not two individuals. Second, bridewealth is paid in nearly all groups, though formerly in cattle and now in cash. These traditions made sense in a largely rural population in which men controlled the major form of movable wealth—cattle. In the latter part of the twentieth century, many people no longer lived in rural areas within extended families, and most of these people worked in the wage economy. In the view of South African Blacks of the 1990s, much of customary marriage law appeared inequitable to women, and so the 1994 Black-majority parliament that came to power adopted a new marriage law that eliminated a large part of the customary law. This change reflects a split between the views of "modernist" legislators, who favour gender equity in the law as provided for in the new constitution, and the views of especially rural elders, who feel that tradition has been forsaken.

Colonial imposition of European legal systems onto indigenous systems added another layer, and one that had pre-eminent power over others. **Legal pluralism** refers to a situation in which more than one kind of legal process might be applied to identical cases (Rouland 1994:50). For example, should a case of murder in the Sudan be tried according to indigenous Sudanese principles or European ones? Post-colonial nations are now in the process of attempting to reform their legal systems and develop more unified codes (Merry 1992:363).

Law and Complexity

The issue of whether Muslim girls can wear head scarves in school in non-Muslim countries is another example of group rights versus state laws (Ewing 2000). For many Muslims, the head scarf is a sign of proper Muslim society, a rejection of Western secularism, and an aspect of religious freedom. Westerners typically view the head scarf as a sign of women's oppression and as a symbol of rejection of the entire ethos of schooling and modernity. In France, beginning in 1989, disputes have erupted over girls wearing head scarves in school. In 1994, the French education director stated that head scarves would not be permitted in school, yet Jewish boys, at that point, had been allowed to wear yarmulkes (head caps). Muslim leaders responded by taking the issue to court, and as of 2004, the issue has not been settled.

Social Conflict and Violence

All systems of social control have to deal with the fact that conflict and violence may occur. This section turns to a consideration of the varieties of social conflict as studied by cultural anthropologists.

Feuding

Feuding, or long-term, retributive violence that may be lethal between families, groups of families, or tribes, is probably the most universal form of intergroup aggression.

This scene occurred in Mantes-la-Jolie, France, in 1994. Female Muslim students who wish to wear a head scarf while attending public schools in France have been banned from doing so by the government. This ban has led to protests and court disputes for over a decade.

Its practice is motivated by a concept of revenge that leads to the pattern of long-term, back-and-forth violence between two groups. Feuding has long had an important role among the horticultural Ilongot people of the Philippine highlands (Rosaldo 1980). From 1883 to 1974, Ilongot feuds were structured around headhunting as the redress for an insult or offence. Manhood was defined by the taking of a first head, and fathers were responsible for transferring the elaborate knowledge of headhunting to their sons. In 1972, the government banned headhunting and attempted to stop the Ilongot from practising shifting cultivation. The repercussion of these changes has been devastating. The banning of headhunting weakened father–son ties that had been solidified by the handing down of the elaborate techniques of headhunting. The people said they were no longer Ilongots.

Ethnic Conflict

Ethnic pluralism is a characteristic of most states in the world today. Ethnic conflict and grievances may result from an ethnic group's attempt to gain more autonomy or more equitable treatment (Esman 1996). It may also be caused by a dominant group's actions to subordinate, oppress, or eliminate an ethnic group by genocide or ethnocide. In the past few decades, political violence has increasingly been enacted within states rather than between states and constitutes the majority of "the 120-odd shooting wars in the world today" (Clay 1990). Political analysts and journalists often cite ethnicity, language, and religion as the causes of certain conflicts. Ethnic identities give people an ideological sense of commitment to a cause, but one must always look beneath these labels to see if deeper issues exist. Such deeper causes may include claims to land, water, ports, and other material resources.

The vast region of Central Asia is populated by many ethnic groups, none of whom has a pristine indigenous claim to the land. Yet, in Central Asia, every dispute appears on the surface to have an ethnic basis: "Russians and Ukrainians versus Kazakhs over land rights and jobs in Kazakhstan, Uzbeks versus Tajiks over the status of Samarkhand and Bukhara, conflict between Kirghiz and Uzbeks in Kyrghyzstan, and riots between Caucasian Turks and Uzbeks in the Fergana Valley of Uzbekistan" (Clay 1990:48).

Attributing all such problems to ethnic differences overlooks the fact that the concept of a functioning plural society is more firmly entrenched in the Central Asian states than anywhere else in the former Soviet Union. In contrast to the Baltic states, the Central Asian nations have granted citizenship to all inhabitants. This acceptance of diversity follows an old pattern: Different ethnic groups fit different economic slots. This could be called a *segmentational model,* in which different groups control significant resources and institutions, contrasted with a *stratificational model,* in which one group dominates others (Esman 1996). A more illuminating way of analyzing the basis of conflict in Central Asia is to consider the division between centres and hinterlands and their different access to crucial resources. Uzbekistan has most of the cities and irrigated farmland, but small states like Kyrghyzstan and Tajikistan control most of the water. Turkmenistan has vast oil and gas riches. "No ethnic catalyst would be needed to provoke conflict in such situations; simple need or greed would more than suffice" (51).

Revolution

A **revolution** is a "political crisis propelled by illegal and usually violent actions by subordinate groups which threatens to change the political institutions or social structure of a society" (Goldstone 1996:740). Revolutions are sometimes called "wars," but they receive separate consideration here as within-state conflicts that are considered illegal by the state. Revolutions have occurred in a range of societies, including pre-industrial monarchies, post-colonial developing countries, and totalitarian states. Scholars who have compared revolutions in modern times—England 1640, France 1789, Mexico 1910, China 1911, Russia 1917, Iran 1979—say that interrelated factors, such as a military or fiscal crisis and a weak state military machine, may begin a revolution. The process of revolutions varies in terms of the degree of popular participation, roles of radicals and moderates, and leadership.

Theorists also argue about the different role of rural versus urban sectors in fomenting revolution. Many revolutions occurred in mainly agrarian countries and were propelled by rural participants, not urban radicalism (Skocpol 1979; E. Wolf 1969). Such agrarian-based revolutions include the French, Russian, and Chinese revolutions. A rural-based movement also characterizes many national liberation movements against colonial powers, such as French Indochina, Guinea-Bissau, Mozambique, and Angola (Gugler 1988). Algeria was a somewhat more urbanized country, but it was still about two-thirds rural in 1962 when the French finally made peace there. In all of these cases, the colonial power was challenged by a rural-based guerrilla movement that controlled crop production, processing, and transport and thus could strike at the heart of the colonial political economy.

On the other hand, some revolutions have been essentially urban in character, including those in Bolivia, Iran, and Nicaragua. The case of Cuba is mixed since rural-based guerrillas played a prominent role, and the cities provided crucial support for the guerrillas. The importance of cities in these revolutions is related to the fact that the countries were highly urbanized. Thus, revolutionary potential exists where resources are controlled and where the bulk of the population is located. Given the rapid urban growth and limited resources in developing

Critical Thinking

WARFARE BETWEEN EUROPEANS AND FIRST NATIONS PEOPLES

IN THE seventeenth and eighteenth centuries in northeastern North America, several incidents of warfare occurred between the advancing European colonials or frontiersmen and groups of First Nations peoples. Warfare is a cultural phenomenon no less influenced by rules of behaviour than other cultural events. At the time of this particular conflict, Europeans had codes of behaviour during warfare different from those of the First Nations people.

Thomas Abler, an anthropologist at the University of Waterloo, compares First Nations incidents of scalping, torture, and cannibalism to the European incidents of rape during warfare (1992). He argues that many groups of First Nations people in warfare took scalps from dead enemies and displayed them on return to camp. Europeans interpreted this behaviour as deviant or strange, although it was common practice in Europe at the time to display heads of enemies on pikes or poles. Abler notes that by the end of the seventeenth century, European frontiersmen were taking and displaying native scalps, and European colonial governments were paying for them. For First Nations peoples, scalps played important roles in ritual events after the battle. To participate in colonial payment schemes, they divided a scalp in two, one part for the cash reward, the second for ritual events.

The other feature of warfare that disturbed Europeans was the torture and cannibalism of captives in war performed by First Nations peoples throughout the northeast. Of course, Europeans tortured captives, but this was done to exact confessions and as part of an execution process. Moreover, in Europe it was done by professionals in front of spectators as a form of entertainment. In the First Nations groups, all members of a community participated in the torture, which could last all night until the captive died. Then the body was typically dismembered and parts of it were eaten perhaps to obtain the essence of the enemy's power.

Not found in First Nations groups but common among Europeans at war was the practice of raping women. Abler gives evidence that many Europeans, both men and women, reported that captive women were never raped by First Nations warriors, although European men regularly raped First Nations women who were captured in war. While the Europeans adopted scalping, they did not adopt cannibalism, while First Nations in the northeast never adopted rape in warfare. "The failure of such practices to cross cultural boundaries allows each side to view the actions of the other with horror and to classify enemy behaviour as barbaric" (15).

CRITICAL THINKING QUESTIONS

Looking at warfare from a critical thinking perspective, consider what aspects of warfare are universal.

How do societies try to put limits on the excesses of war? How successful do you think these attempts are?

How would a cultural anthropologist study contemporary warfare?

countries, it is possible that the world may be entering "the age of urban revolutions" (Gugler 1988).

Warfare

Several definitions of war have been proposed (Reyna 1994). Is it open and declared conflict between two political units? This definition would rule out, for example, the U.S.–Vietnam War because it was undeclared. Is it simply organized aggression? This definition is too broad since not all organized violence can be considered warfare. Perhaps the best definition is that **war** is "organized, purposeful group action, directed against another group . . . involving the actual or potential application of lethal force" (Ferguson 1994, quoted in Reyna 1994:30). A crit-

ical point is that lethal force during war is legal if it is conducted according to the rules of battle (see the Critical Thinking box).

Cultural variation exists in the frequency and seriousness of wars. Intergroup conflicts between different bands of foragers are relatively rare. More often, they involve conflicts between individuals belonging to different groups, not group conflicts per se. Conflicts are usually fought out person-to-person, either with words or fists. The informal, nonhierarchical political organization among bands is not conducive to waging armed conflict. Bands do not have specialized military forces or leaders.

Archaeological evidence indicates that warfare emerged and intensified during the neolithic era. Plant and animal domestication required more extensive land use, and it was accompanied by increased population densities. The combined economic and demographic pressures put more and larger groups in more direct and more intense competition with each other. Tribal leadership patterns facilitate mobilization of warrior groups for raids, but not all tribes have equal levels of warfare.

Many chiefdoms are characterized by relatively high rates of warfare and casualty rates. They have increased capacity for war in terms of personnel and surplus foods to support long-range expeditions. In many chiefdoms, the chief could call on his or her retainers as a specialized fighting force as well as general members of society. Chiefs and paramount chiefs could be organized into more effective command structures (Reyna 1994:44–45). These levels of aggregation and potential for more extensive and massive campaigns continued to expand as chiefdoms and confederacies evolved into state-level organizations. In states, standing armies and complex military hierarchies are supported by the increased material resources under the control of leaders through taxation and other forms of revenue generation. Greater state power allows for more powerful and effective military structures, which in turn increase the state's power; thus, a mutually reinforcing relationship emerges between the military and the state.

Examining the causes of war between states has occupied scholars in many fields for centuries. Some experts point to common, underlying causes, such as attempts to extend boundaries, secure more resources, ensure markets, support political and economic allies, and resist aggression from other states. Others point to humanitarian concerns that prompt participation in "good wars," to defend values such as freedom or to protect human rights as defined in one nation and being violated in another

Causes of wars in Afghanistan have changed over time (Barfield 1994). Since the seventeenth century warfare increasingly became a way for kings to justify their power in terms of the necessity to maintain independence from outside forces such as the British and Czarist Russia. The last Afghan king was murdered in a coup in 1978. When the then Soviet Union invaded in 1979, there was no centralized ruling group to meet it. The Soviet Union deposed the ruling faction and replaced it with one of their own and "then engaged in a wholesale war against the population. Three million Afghans fled to Pakistan and Iran, over one million were killed, millions of others were displaced internally" (7). Yet, in spite of having no central command, divided by ethnic and sectarian differences, and outmatched in equipment by Soviet forces, a war of resistance eventually wore down the Soviets, who withdrew in 1989. Subsequently, in 2001 and 2002, the United States with its allies deposed another Afghan government, the Taliban, in the aftermath of the destruction of the World Trade Center towers in New York City.

Women near Kabul, Afghanistan, look at replicas of land mines during a mining awareness program sponsored in 2003 by the International Committee of the Red Cross (ICRC). Afghanistan is still heavily mined, and rates of injury and mortality from mines are high.

The case of Afghanistan suggests that war was a more effective tool of domination in the pre-modern period when war settled matters more definitively. "The number of troops needed after a conquest were relatively few because they were not expected to have to put down continual internal revolts, but to defend the new conquest from rival outsiders" (7). Success in the Soviet Union's attempt to hold Afghanistan would have required more extensive involvement and commitment, including introduction of a new political ideology or economic structure that would win the population over, population transfer to remove opposition, and immigration of allies into the area. Barfield notes that in contemporary times, "winning battles or wars becomes only the first stage in a much more complicated process with no guarantees of ultimate success" (10). Current events in both Iraq and Afghanistan show only too clearly that winning a war and taking over a country represent only the first stage in a process much more complicated than the term *regime change* implies. Afghanistan is now attempting to recover and rebuild after 25 years of war in the context of another foreign invasion. Its problems of national integration and security have roots that go much deeper than these intrusions (Shahrani 2002). These roots include powerful local codes of honour that value political autonomy and require vengeance for harm received, the moral system of Islam, the revitalized drug economy, and the effects of intervention from outside powers involving governments and corporations, including Unocal of California, Delta Oil of Saudi Arabia, and Bridas of Argentina. The difficulty of constructing a strong state with loyal citizens in the face of these conflicting internal and external factors is great.

Nonviolent Conflict

Mohandas K. Gandhi was one of the greatest designers of strategies for bringing about peaceful political change. Born in India, he studied law in London and then went to South Africa, where he worked as a lawyer serving the Indian community, and evolved his primary method of civil disobedience through nonviolent resistance (Caplan 1987). In 1915, he returned to India, joined the nationalist struggle against British colonialism, and put into action his model of civil disobedience through nonviolent resistance, public fasting, and strikes.

Celibacy is another key feature of Gandhian philosophy because avoiding sex helps maintain one's inner strength and purity. Regardless of whether one agrees with Gandhi's approach to food and sex, it is clear that the methods he developed of nonviolent civil disobedience have had a profound impact on the world. Martin Luther King, Jr., and his followers adopted many of Gandhi's tactics during the Civil Rights Movement in the United States,

Mahatma Gandhi (left), leader of the Indian movement for freedom from British colonial control, on his famous "Salt March" of 1930, in which he led a procession to the sea to collect salt in defiance of British law. He is accompanied by Sarojini Naidu, a noted freedom fighter.

as did members of the Peace Movement of the 1960s and 1970s in the United States and the Environmental Movement of the 1990s in North America.

Political scientist James Scott (1985) used the phrase "weapons of the weak" as the title of his book on rural people's resistance to domination by landlords and government through tactics other than outright rebellion or revolution. Most subordinate classes throughout history have not had the "luxury" of open, organized political activity because of its danger. Instead, people have had to resort to ways of living with or "working" the system. Everyday forms of resistance include "foot dragging," desertion, false compliance, feigned ignorance, and slander, as well as more aggressive acts such as theft, arson, and sabotage. Many contemporary anthropologists have followed Scott's lead and contributed groundbreaking studies of everyday resistance.

Maintaining World Order

Computer-operated war missiles, email, faxes, satellite television, and jet flights mean that the world's nations are more closely connected and able to influence each other's fate than ever before. Modern weaponry means that such influences can be even more lethal. In the face of these geopolitical realities, politicians, academics, and the public ponder the possibilities for world peace. Anthropological research on peaceful, local-level societies shows that humans are capable of living together in peace. The question is: Can people living in larger groups that are globally connected also live in peace?

International Legal Disputes

Numerous attempts have been made, over time, to create institutions to promote world peace, of which the United Nations is the most established and respected. One of the United Nations' significant accomplishments was the creation of a world court, the International Court of Justice, which is located at The Hague in Holland (Nader 1995). In 1946, two-thirds of the Court's judges were American or Western European. Now the Court has many judges from developing countries and more sympathy for such nations. Despite this more balanced representation from a wide range of countries, there has been a decline in use of the International Court of Justice and an increased use of international negotiating teams for resolving disputes between nations. Laura Nader analyzed this decline and found that it follows a trend in the United States beginning in the 1970s to promote "alternate dispute resolution" (ADR). The goal was to move more cases out of the courts and to privatize dispute resolution. In principle, ADR seems a more peaceful and more dignified option. Deeper analysis of actual cases and their resolution shows, however, that this bilateral process tends to favour the stronger party. Nader looked at several cases of international river disputes. In each example, adjudication (formal decree by a judge) would have resulted in a better deal for the weaker party than bilateral negotiation did. Overall, less powerful nations are being negatively affected by the trend to move away from using the International Court of Justice.

The United Nations and International Peacekeeping

What role might cultural anthropology play in international peacekeeping? Robert Carneiro (1994) has a pessimistic response. During the long history of human political evolution from bands to states, Carneiro says that warfare has been the major means by which political units enlarged their power and domain. Foreseeing no logical end to this process, he predicts that war will follow war until superstates become ever larger and one megastate is the final result. He also considers the United Nations powerless in dealing with the principal obstacle to world peace, which is national sovereignty interests. If the belief exists that war is inevitable, that leaves little room for hope that anthropological knowledge might be applied to peacemaking efforts.

Despite Carneiro's views, cultural anthropologists have shown that war is not a cultural universal, and that different cultures have ways of solving disputes without resorting to killing. The cultural anthropological perspective of critical cultural relativism (review this concept in Chapter 1) can provide useful background on issues of conflict and prompt a deeper dialogue between parties.

Representatives of 10 NATO countries at the World Court in The Hague. This distinguished body of legal experts exhibits a clear pattern of age, gender, and ethnicity.

One positive point emerges with regard to the possibility of world peace. The United Nations does provide an arena for airing disputes. This more optimistic view suggests that international peace organizations play a major role in providing analysis of the interrelationships among world problems and helping others see the causes of violence (Vickers 1993:132). In addition, some people see hope for local and global peacemaking through nongovernmental organizations (NGOs) and local grassroots initiatives that seek to bridge group interests.

WHAT do political and legal anthropology cover?

Political anthropology is the study of power relationships in the public domain and how they vary and change cross-culturally. Political anthropologists study the concept of power, as well as related concepts such as authority and influence. They have discovered differences and similarities between politics and political organization in small-scale societies and large-scale societies as they looked at issues such as leadership roles and responsibilities, the social distribution of power, and the emergence of the state. Legal anthropology encompasses the study of cultural variation in social order and social conflict. Legal anthropologists are increasingly examining how legal systems change. Global colonialism and contemporary globalization have changed indigenous systems of social control and law, often resulting in legal pluralism.

WHAT are the major cross-cultural forms of political organization and social order?

Patterns of political organization and leadership vary according to mode of production and global economic relationships. Foragers have a minimal form of leadership and political organization in the band. Band membership is flexible. If a band member has a serious disagreement with another person, including a spouse, one option is to leave that band and join another. Social control in small-scale societies seeks to restore order more than to punish offenders. Leadership in bands is informal. A tribe is a more formal type of political organization than the band. A tribe comprises several bands or lineage groups, with a headman or headwoman as leader. Big-man political systems are an expanded form of tribe, with leaders having influence over people in several dif-

ferent villages. Chiefdoms may include several thousand people. Rank is inherited and social divisions exist between the chiefly lineage or lineages and non-chiefly groups. A state is a centralized political unit encompassing many communities and possessing coercive power. A wide variety of types of legal specialists is more frequently associated with the state than with small-scale societies, in which social shaming and shunning are common methods of punishment. States arose in several locations with the emergence of intensive agriculture, increased surpluses, and increased population density. Most states are hierarchical and patriarchal. In states, imprisonment and capital punishment may exist, reflecting the greater power of the state. Strategies for building nationalism include imposition of one language as "the" national language, monuments, museums, songs, poetry, and other media-relayed messages about the "motherland." Ethnic/national politics have emerged within and across states as groups compete for either increased rights within the state or autonomy from it.

WHAT are cross-cultural patterns of social conflict?

Cross-cultural data on levels and forms of conflict and violence indicate that high levels of lethal violence are not universal and are more associated with the state than earlier forms of political organization. Social conflict ranges from face-to-face conflicts, as among neighbours or domestic partners, to larger group conflicts between ethnic groups and states. Solutions that would be effective at the interpersonal level are often not applicable to large-scale, impersonalized conflict. Cultural anthropologists are turning their attention to studying global conflict and peacekeeping solutions. Key issues involve the role of cultural knowledge in dispute resolution and how international or local organizations can help achieve or maintain peace.

KEY CONCEPTS

SUGGESTED READINGS

Stanley R. Barrett, *Culture Meets Power.* Westport, CN: Praeger, 2002. The author examines why the concept of power has gained ascendancy in anthropology, seeming to eclipse the concept of culture. He argues that the concept of power is no less ambiguous than that of culture and that the two concepts both need to be considered in understanding contemporary affairs, including events such as the September 11, 2001, attacks on the United States.

Jane K. Cowan, Marie-Bénédicte Dembour, and Richard A. Wilson, eds., *Culture and Rights: Anthropological Perspectives.* New York: Cambridge University Press, 2001. This collection includes three overview/theoretical chapters, seven case studies that address issues such as child prostitution and ethnic and women's rights, and a chapter that critiques the UNESCO concept of culture.

Mona Etienne and Eleanor Leacock, eds., *Women and Colonization: Anthropological Perspectives.* New York: Praeger, 1980. This classic collection examines the impact of Western colonialism and missionary intervention on women of several indigenous groups of North America, South America, Africa, and the Pacific.

Thomas Gregor, ed., *A Natural History of Peace.* Nashville: Vanderbilt University Press, 1996. This book contains essays on "What Is Peace," reconciliation among non-human primates, the psychological bases of violent and caring societies, community-level studies on Amazonia and Native America, and issues of peace and violence between states.

Phillip Gulliver, *Disputes and Negotiations: A Cross-Cultural Perspective.* New York: Academic Press, 1979. This classic analysis shows how the issues and behaviour surrounding negotiation are similar in cultures that differ widely in values, rules, and cultural assumptions.

Carolyn Nordstrom and Antonius C. G. M. Robben, eds., *Fieldwork under Fire: Contemporary Studies of Violence and Survival.* Berkeley: University of California Press, 1995. After an introductory chapter that discusses general themes, several examples of fieldwork experiences in dangerous situations including Palestine, China, Sri Lanka, United States, Croatia, Guatemala, and Ireland are given.

Dan Rabinowitz, *Overlooking Nazareth: The Politics of Exclusion in Galilee.* New York: Cambridge University Press, 1997. This book presents an ethnographic study of Palestinian citizens in an Israeli new town. It examines specific situations of conflict and cooperation and provides wider theoretical insights about nationalism and ethnicity. Biographical accounts of three Palestinians—a medical doctor, a basketball coach, and a local politician—are included.

Bruce G. Trigger, *The Huron: Farmers of the North*, 2nd ed. Belmont, CA: Wadsworth, 1990. This fascinating monograph combines archaeological, historical, linguistic, and ethnographic evidence on the Huron of southern Ontario.

Joan Vincent, *Anthropology and Politics: Visions, Traditions, and Trends.* Tucson: The University of Arizona Press, 1990. This text presents a definitive history of the emergence of political anthropology, with a detailed presentation of theories and findings through the late 1980s.

WEBLINKS

The Companion Website (www.pearsoned.ca/miller) that accompanies *Cultural Anthropology*, Third Canadian Edition, includes a destinations module containing links to many websites relevant to the content of this chapter. Use it to investigate the Web and expand your understanding of anthropology.

KEY QUESTIONS

- **WHAT** is religion and what are the basic features of religions cross-culturally?

- **HOW** do world religions reflect globalization and localization?

- **WHAT** are some important aspects of religious change in contemporary times?

12

RELIGION

A Catholic procession during Easter week in Guatemala.

Religion has been a cornerstone topic in cultural anthropology since its beginning. Over these many decades, a rich collection of material has accumulated. Early attention was focused on religions of non-state societies. More recently, anthropologists devoted attention to the major religions of state-level societies. With increasing globalization and population movements, religious traditions are also moving and changing as they adapt to new cultural contexts.

RELIGION IN COMPARATIVE PERSPECTIVE

This section sets the stage for the following sections by discussing core areas in the anthropology of religion, including how we define religion, given the cross-cultural diversity in belief systems, and theories about why religion began and why it is so pervasive. We then cover types of religious beliefs, ritual practices, and religious specialists.

What Is Religion?

Since the earliest days of anthropology, various definitions of religion have appeared. One of the simplest, offered by E. B. Tylor in the late 1800s, is that religion is the belief in spirits. The definition favoured by a cultural materialist approach is that **religion** is both beliefs and actions related to supernatural beings and forces (what Tylor referred to as "spirits"). In defining religion so that it fits the cross-cultural material, anthropologists avoid a narrow definition that says religion is the belief in a supreme deity. In many religions, no concept of a supreme deity exists, while others have multiple deities. Religion is related to but not the same as a people's **world view**, or way of understanding how the world came to be, its design, and their place in it. World view is a broader concept and does not include the criterion of concern with a supernatural realm. An atheist has a world view, but not a religious one.

Magic versus Religion

In the late 1800s, Tylor wrote that magic, religion, and science are alike in that they are different ways people have tried to explain the physical world and events in it. For Tylor, the three systems were contradictory and incompatible. Tylor thought that magical laws were false and scientific laws were true, and that religion is based on the false assumption

When studying the religious life of people of rural northern Greece, anthropologist Loring Danforth observed rituals in which participants walk across several metres of burning coals (1989). They do not get burned, they say, because their faith and a saint protect them. Experimentation has shown that anyone can walk on burning coals if they keep moving; a layer of sweat on the bottom of the feet keeps the heat from damaging the skin as long as the fire is not an open flame.

Upon his return to the United States, Danforth met an American who regularly walks on fire as part of his New Age faith and also organizes training workshops for people who want to learn how to fire-walk. Danforth himself fire-walked in a ceremony in rural Maine.

While not every anthropologist who studies religion undertakes such challenges during fieldwork, they all share an interest in enduring questions about humanity's understanding of the supernatural realm and relationships with it: Why do some religions have many gods and others just one? Why do some religions advocate animal sacrifice? Why do some religions give greater room for women's participation? How do different religions respond to changing conditions in the political economy?

that the world operates under the control of supernaturals. James Frazer (1978[1890]), writing at about the same time as Tylor, defined **magic** as the attempt to compel supernatural forces and beings to act in certain ways, in contrast to religion, which is the attempt to please supernatural forces or beings. After reviewing many practices cross-culturally that he considered magical, Frazer deduced two general principles of magic that correspond to two major categories of magic. First is the "law of similarity," the basis of what he called "imitative magic." It is founded on the assumption that if person or item X is like person or item Y, then actions done to person or item X will affect person or item Y. The most well-known example is a voodoo doll. By sticking pins into doll X that represents person Y, then person Y will experience pain or suffering. The second is the "law of contagion," which is the basis for "contagious magic." The law of contagion says that persons or things once in contact with a person can still have an effect on that person. Common items for working contagious magic are a person's hair trimmings, nail clippings, teeth, spit or blood or fecal matter left carelessly beside a pathway, or the placenta of a baby. In cultures where contagious magic is practised, people are careful about disposing of their personal wastes so that no one else can get hold of them.

Such scholars of religion as Tylor and Frazer supported an evolutionary model, with magic as the predecessor of religion. They evaluated magic as less spiritual and ethical than religion and therefore more "primitive." They assumed that, in time, magic would be completely replaced by the "higher" system of religion, and then ultimately by science as the most rational way of thinking. They would be surprised to see the widespread presence of magic in the modern world, as evidenced, for example, by a recent ethnographic study of magic and witchcraft in contemporary London (Luhrmann 1989).

In fact, magic exists in all cultures. In different situations, people turn to magic, religion, or science. For example, magic is prominent in sports (Gmelch 1997). Professional baseball players repeat actions or use charms (including a special shirt or hat) to help them win on the assumption that if it worked before, it may work again. They are following Tylor's law of contagion. Such magical thinking is most common in contexts where uncertainty is greatest. In baseball, pitching and hitting involve more uncertainty than fielding, and pitchers and hitters are more likely to use magic. Besides sports, magical practices are prominent in farming, fishing, the military, and love. Thus, we can no longer accept an evolutionary model by which religion has replaced magic, since magic is still widely practised. In a similar fashion, one cannot argue that science has replaced religion.

Christian fire-walkers in northern Greece express their faith by walking on hot coals and reaffirm divine protection by not getting burned.

Theories of the Origin of Religion

Why did religion come into being? The universal existence of some form of religion has prompted many theorists to adopt a functionalist approach. According to this view, religion provides ways of explaining and coping with universal "imponderables of life" such as birth, illness, misfortune, and death.

Tylor's theory, as proposed in his book *Primitive Culture* (1871), was based on his assumption that early people had a need for explanation, especially for the difference between the living and the dead. They therefore developed the concept of a soul that exists in all living things and departs from the body after death. Tylor named this way of thinking **animism**, the belief in souls or "doubles." Eventually, Tylor speculated, the concept of the soul became personified until, later, human-like deities were conceived. For Tylor, religion evolved from animism to **polytheism** (the belief in many deities) to **monotheism** (the belief in one supreme deity). Beliefs characteristic of animism still exist; they include, for example, beliefs about angels and visitations of the dead and the New Age religious use of crystals (Stringer 1999).

In contrast to Tylor, Frazer suggested that religion developed out of the failure of magic. Neither scholar suggested a place or time period during which these developments may have occurred, and both based their theories on speculation rather than archaeological or other empirical data.

Later, functional theories emerged. Émile Durkheim, in his book *The Elementary Forms of the Religious Life* (1966 [1895]), offered a functional explanation for how and why religion came into being. He reviewed ethnographic data on "primitive" religions cross-culturally and was struck by their social aspects: Durkheim speculated that early humans realized, through clan gatherings, that contact with one another made them feel uplifted and powerful. This positive feeling, arising from social solidarity, became attached to the clan totem, an emblem of their group that became the first of many future objects of worship. Religion therefore originated to serve society by giving it cohesion through shared symbols and group rituals. Malinowski said that rituals help reduce anxiety and uncertainty. Marx, taking a *class conflict* approach rather than a functional one, emphasized religion's role as an "opiate of the masses." By this phrase, Marx meant that religion provides a superficial form of comfort to the poor, masking the harsh realities of class inequality and thereby preventing uprisings of the poor against the rich.

A third major theoretical theme, *symbolic analysis*, informs Freud's theory of the role of the unconscious. Many anthropologists agree with Freud that religion is a "projective system" that expresses people's unconscious thoughts, wishes, and worries.

A fourth major theoretical theme, which can be seen to combine Durkheimian functionalism with symbolic analysis, comes from Clifford Geertz (1966), who proposed that religions are primarily *systems of meaning*. In this view, religion offers a conception of reality, "a model of life," and a pattern for how to live, a "model for life."

Varieties of Religious Beliefs

Religions comprise beliefs and behaviour. Scholars of religion generally address belief systems first since they appear to inform patterns of religious behaviour. Religious beliefs tend to be shared by a group, sometimes by very large numbers of people. Through the centuries, people have found ways to give their beliefs permanence. Elders teach children the group's songs and tales, artists paint the sto-

ries on rocks and walls, and sculptors create images in wood and stone that depict aspects of religious belief.

In this section, we consider cross-cultural variation in religious beliefs. We discuss major forms in which religious beliefs are transmitted from one generation to the next. We then review a range of beliefs about supernatural beings.

How Beliefs Are Expressed

Beliefs are expressed and transferred over the generations in two main formats: **myth**, narrative stories about supernatural forces or beings, and **doctrine**, direct and formalized statements about religious beliefs.

A myth is a narrative that has a plot with a beginning, middle, and end. The plot may involve recurrent motifs, the smallest units of narrative. Myths convey messages about the supernaturals indirectly, through the medium of the story itself, rather than by using logic or formal argument. Greek and Roman myths, such as the stories of Zeus, Athena, Orpheus, and Persephone, are world-famous. Some people would say that the Bible is a collection of mythology; others would object to that categorization as it suggests that the stories are not "real" or "sacred."

Myths are distinguished from folktales, which are largely secular stories, although borderline cases exist. For example, some people would classify "Cinderella" as a folktale, while others would quickly point out that the fairy godmother is not an ordinary human and so "Cinderella" should be considered a myth. These arguments are more entertaining than important.

Myths have long been part of people's oral tradition. Only with the emergence of writing were these stories

A stone sculpture at Mamallapuram, South India, dating from the eighth to ninth centuries, depicts the impending triumph of the goddess Durga (riding the lion, on the left) over the bull-headed demon. The story of her creation by the gods and her ultimate saving of the world through the killing of the demon has inspired countless works of art in India.

recorded, and then only if they were of great importance, perhaps part of a royal or priestly tradition. Many of the world's myths are still unwritten.

Anthropologists have asked why myths exist. The functionalist explanation is that myths help to maintain the society itself. Malinowski says that a myth is a "charter" for society in that it expresses core beliefs and teaches morality. French anthropologist Claude Lévi-Strauss, probably the most famous mythologist, says that myths are tribal peoples' form of philosophy, their way of explaining the world. The philosophical message does not lie on the surface of the myths. It is embedded in their underlying structure and the symbolism of key characters and events. Human beings, he says, think in terms of binary classification. He finds binary oppositions as the basic structure of all myths—for example, nature versus culture, life versus death, raw versus cooked food, wild versus tame animals, and incest versus exogamy. Such oppositions are philosophically uncomfortable for people to face—for example, the fact that life cannot exist without death. Myths help people deal with the deep puzzles and discomforts of life by presenting the oppositions along with a third position that mediates between the two extremes and provides a solution. For example, many Pueblo Indian myths juxtapose grass-eating animals (vegetarians) with predators (carnivores). The mediating third character is the raven, which is a carnivore but, unlike other creatures, does not have to kill to eat meat because it is a scavenger.

Epics are longer than myths and focus more on heroic traditions. Many epics are firmly associated with particular ethnic groups or nations, such as the *Odyssey* and the *Iliad* of Greece. Less well known in North America are India's two great Hindu epics, the *Mahabharata* and the *Ramayana*. Iceland's *eddas* of the thirteenth century are grouped into two categories: mythic (dealing with gods) and heroic (dealing with humans).

Doctrine, the other major form in which beliefs are expressed, explicitly defines the supernaturals—who they are, what they do, and how to relate to them through religious practice; the world and how it came to be; and people's roles in relation to the supernaturals and to other humans. Doctrine, which is written and formal, is close to law in some respects because it makes direct links between incorrect beliefs and behaviours and the punishments for each. Many religious scriptures incorporate both myth and doctrine.

Doctrine is more common in institutionalized, large-scale religions than with localized, small-scale "folk" religions. Thus, the major world religions discussed later in this chapter all have established doctrine to which followers should adhere. Doctrine, however, can and does change (J. Bowen 1998:38–40). Over the centuries, various popes have pronounced new doctrine for the Catholic church. A papal declaration of 1854, given with the intent of reinvigorating European Catholicism, gave authenticity to the concept of the Immaculate Conception, an idea with substantial popular support.

Muslim doctrine is expressed in the Qur'an, the basic holy text of the Islamic faith that consists of revelations made to the prophet Muhammad in the seventh century, and the *hadith*, collections of Muhammad's statements and deeds (J. Bowen 1998:38). In Kuala Lumpur, Malaysia, a small group of highly educated women called the Sisters in Islam regularly debate with members of the local *ulama* (male religious authorities who are responsible for interpreting Islamic doctrine especially concerning families, education, and commercial affairs) (Ong 1995).

Celebration of Holi, a spring festival popular among Hindus worldwide. In this scene in New Delhi, a young woman sprays coloured water on a young man as part of the joyous event.

In recent years, the debates have concerned such issues as polygamy, divorce, women's work roles, and women's clothing.

Beliefs about Supernatural Forces and Beings

In all cultures, some concept of otherworldly beings or forces exists, even though not all members of the culture believe in their existence. Supernaturals range from impersonal forces to those that look just like humans. Supernaturals can be supreme and all-powerful creators or smaller-scale, annoying spirits that take up residence in people through "possession."

The term **animatism** refers to belief systems in which the supernatural is conceived of as an impersonal power. A well-known example is *mana*, a concept widespread throughout the Melanesian region of the South Pacific. *Mana* is a force outside nature that works automatically; it is neither spirit nor deity. It manifests itself in objects and people and is associated with personal status and power since some people accumulate more of it than others. Some supernaturals are **zoomorphic** (deities that appear in the shape, or partial shape, of animals). No satisfactory theory has appeared to explain why some religions develop zoomorphic deities, and for what purposes, and why others do not. Religions of classical Greece and Rome, and ancient and contemporary Hinduism are especially rich in zoomorphic supernaturals.

Anthropomorphic supernaturals, deities in the form of humans, are common, but not universal. The human tendency to perceive of supernaturals in their own form was noted 2500 years ago by the Greek philosopher Xenophanes (who lived sometime between 570 and 470 BCE). He said, "If cattle and horses, or lions, had hands, or were able to draw with their feet and produce the worlds which men do, horses would draw the forms of gods like horses, and cattle like cattle, and they would make the gods' bodies the same shape as their own" (*Fragments* 15). But why some religions do and others do not have anthropomorphic deities is another question that is impossible to answer. Such deities are more common in sedentary societies than among foragers.

Anthropomorphic supernaturals, like humans, can be moved by praise, flattery, and gifts. They can be tricked. They have emotions: They get irked if neglected, they can be loving and caring, or they can be distant and unresponsive. Most anthropomorphic supernaturals are adults. Few are very old or very young. Humans and supernaturals have similar marital and sexual patterns. Divine marriages tend to be heterosexual. In societies where polygyny occurs, male gods also have multiple wives. Deities have sexual intercourse, within marriage and sometimes extramaritally. Gods of the Greek and Roman pantheon, the entire collection of deities, often descended to earth and kidnapped and raped human women. So far, however, legal divorce has not occurred among supernaturals, although separations have. While many supernaturals have children, grandchildren are not prominent.

In pantheons, a division of labour exists by which certain supernaturals are responsible for particular domains. This greater specialization among the supernaturals reflects the greater specialization in human society. There may be a deity of forests, rivers, the sky, wind and rain, agriculture, childbirth, disease, warfare, and marital happiness. Some gods are more effective for material wealth and others for academic success. The supernaturals have political roles and hierarchies. High gods, like Jupiter and Juno of classical Roman religion, are distant from humans and hard to contact. The more approachable deities are below them on the hierarchy. Next, one finds a miscellaneous collectivity of spirits, good and bad, often unnamed and uncounted, in the lowest tier. This discussion clearly applies to polytheistic religions, but it is also relevant to monotheistic religions, such as Islam and Christianity, that incorporate lesser supernaturals such as saints.

Deceased ancestors can also be supernaturals. In some religions, spirits of the dead can be prayed to for help, and in turn they may require respect and honour from the living (J. Smith 1995:46). Many African, Asian, and First Nations religions have a cult of the ancestors, as did religions of ancient Mesopotamia, Greece, and Rome. In contemporary Japan, ancestor veneration is the principal religious activity of many families. Three national holidays recognize the importance of the ancestors: the annual summer visit of the dead to their home and the visits by the living to graves during the two equinoxes. Important ancestors sometimes evolved into deities with wide popularity. Similarly, humans other than ancestors may also, after their death, be transformed into deities. Although not seen as deities, the Roman Catholic tradition has established a group of deceased humans who can become saints (see the Multiple Cultural Worlds box).

Beliefs about Sacred Space

Beliefs about the sacredness of certain spaces are probably found in all religions, but such beliefs are more prominent in some religions than others. Sacred spaces may or may not be marked in a permanent way. Unmarked spaces include rock formations or rapids in a river (Bradley 2000). The fact that unmarked spaces in prehistory may have been religious sites poses a major challenge to archaeologists interested in reconstructing early religion. Sometimes, though, archaeologists can find evidence of sacrifices at such sites to attest to their ritual importance.

Among the indigenous Saami people of northern Norway, Sweden, and Finland, religious beliefs were, before Christian missionary efforts, strongly associated

Multiple Cultural Worlds

THE BLESSED KATERI TEKAKWITHA: A "SAINT" FOR ALL FIRST NATIONS PEOPLES

KATERI TEKAKWITHA was a Mohawk First Nations woman born in upstate New York in 1656. She was converted to Christianity by the French Jesuit missionaries in 1676 at the age of 20 and moved to the Jesuit mission at Kahnawake near Montreal. Under the influence of the Jesuits, Kateri took a vow of virginity and practised extreme austerities such as flagellations, branding, exposure, and fasting (Holmes 2001:89). She died after only two years at the mission, but her piety was celebrated by the Jesuits, who reported she died calling out "Jesus! Mary! I love you!" Pope John Paul II beatified her in 1980. Many First Nations people hoped the Pope would canonize her on his visit to Toronto in 2002, but this did not happen.

Her devotees are found among many First Nations converts to Roman Catholicism all over North America. Holmes reports that knowledge about her reached the

Navajo and Pueblo of the Southwest United States in the 1930s. For these people, Kateri represents hope for unity among all First Nations people in North America. One Pueblo person reported that Kateri's deathbed words were, "You must gather people from all different places and start having conferences." Another claimed she said, "The Catholic way and the Native American way can just build [together]" (96). Kateri has come to represent unity between the "Indian" way and the "Catholic" way and, moreover, unity among "her" people, that is, all the First Nations people of North America (94). For many of "her" people, she is already a saint.

FOOD FOR THOUGHT

Can you think of another important religious figure that unites a particular group of people?

---

with sacred natural sites, which were often unmarked (Mulk 1994). These sites included rock formations resembling humans, animals, or birds. The Saami sacrificed animals and fish at these sites until strong pressures from Christian missionaries forced them to repress their practices and beliefs. Although many Saami today still know where the sacred sites are, they will not reveal them to others.

Another important form of sacred space that has no permanent mark occurs in an important domestic ritual conducted by Muslim women throughout the world called the *khatam quran*, the "sealing" or reading of the holy book, the Qu'ran (Werbner 1988). A study of Pakistani migrants living in the city of Manchester, England, reveals that this ritual involves a gathering of mostly women who read the Qu'ran and then share a ritual meal. The reason for gathering can be to give thanks or to seek divine blessing. During the ritual, the otherwise non-sacred space of the house becomes sacred. A "portable" ritual such as this one is especially helpful in migrant adaptation, because it can be conducted without a formally consecrated ritual space. All that is required is a supportive group of kin and friends and the Qu'ran.

In another example the sacred space was clearly defined. A piece of land was a summer meeting ground for the Dunne-Za/Cree of the North River region of British Columbia. These hunting and gathering peoples spent part

of the summer round of activities, including important religious ceremonies, on what they called "the land where happiness dwells." This land was sold in 1945 to the Department of Indian Affairs at the instigation of the Indian agent. Many years later, in 1987, a suit to take back the land was initiated by the band, which argued that the land could not be alienated from the Dunne-Za/Cree because of responsibilities accepted by the government in an 1899 treaty with the band (Riddington 1990:186ff). Anthropologist Hugh Brody testified on behalf of the Dunne-Za/Cree as an expert witness. He tried to convey to the court how decisions were made in hunting and gathering groups where there is no leader, and how important a summer gathering place is for people who travel in smaller groups hunting and trapping elsewhere in the other seasons. Unfortunately, the judge never accepted this picture of the band life and decided against the Dunne-Za/Cree. The land was now valuable due to the discovery of oil and gas deposits. He did not see that the band had suffered a significant cultural and religious loss (see the Lessons Applied box for a similar case in Australia).

Ritual Practices

Rituals are patterned forms of behaviour that have to do with the supernatural realm. Many rituals are the enactment

Lessons Applied

ABORIGINAL WOMEN'S CULTURE, SACRED SITE PROTECTION, AND THE ANTHROPOLOGIST AS EXPERT WITNESS

A GROUP of Ngarrindjeri (prounounced NAR-en-jeery) women and their lawyer hired Diane Bell to serve as a consultant to them in supporting their claims to a sacred site in southern Australia (Bell 1998). The area was threatened by the proposed construction of a bridge that would cross sacred waters between Goolwa and Hindmarsh Island. The women claimed protection for the area and sought prevention of the bridge building on the basis of their secret knowledge of its sacredness—knowledge that had been passed down from mother to daughter over generations. The High Commission formed by the government to investigate their claim considered it to be a hoax perpetrated to block a project important to the country. Helping the women prove their case to a White, male-dominated court system was a challenging task for Diane Bell, an anthropologist teaching in the United States but also a White Australian by birth, with extensive fieldwork experience among Aboriginal women.

Bell conducted research over many months to marshall evidence for the validity of the women's claims—including newspaper archives, early recordings of ritual songs, and oral histories of Ngarrindjeri women. She prepared reports for the courtroom about women's sacred knowledge that were general enough to avoid violating the rule of women-only knowledge but detailed enough to convince the High Court judge that the women's sacred knowledge was authentic. In the end the judge was convinced, and the bridge project was cancelled in 1999.

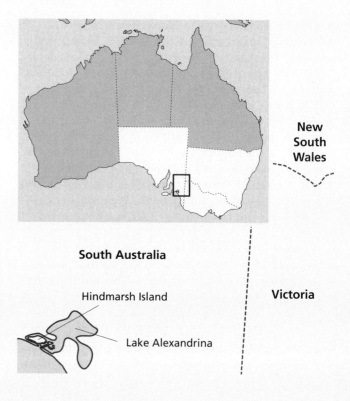

FOOD FOR THOUGHT

On the internet, learn more about this case and other disputes in Australia about sacred sites.

---

of beliefs expressed in myth and doctrine, such as the Christian ritual of communion. There are also secular rituals such as a sorority or fraternity initiation or a common-law wedding, all patterned forms of behaviour with no connection to the supernatural realm. It is not always easy to distinguish a religious ritual from a secular ritual. Consider the holiday of Thanksgiving, which originated as a sacred meal, with its primary purpose to give thanks to God for the first fruits of the harvest. Today, its original Christian meaning is not maintained by everyone who celebrates this holiday with a special meal of a roasted turkey.

Anthropologists and scholars of religion have categorized rituals in many ways. One division is based on how regularly the ritual is performed. Regularly performed rituals are called *periodic rituals*. Many periodic rituals are performed annually to mark a seasonal event like planting or harvesting, or to commemorate some important event. For example, an important periodic ritual in Buddhism, *Visakha Puja*, or Buddha's Day, commemorates the birth, enlightenment, and death of the Buddha (all on one day!). On this day, Buddhists gather at monasteries, hear sermons about the Buddha, and perform rituals such as pouring water over images of the Buddha. Calendrical events such as the shortest or longest day of the year, or the new moon or full moon, often shape ritual cycles. Non-periodic rituals, in contrast, occur irregularly, at unpredictable times, in response to unscheduled events such as a drought or flood, or to events in a person's life, such as illness, infertility, birth, marriage, or death.

A woman praying at a Buddhist pagoda in Ho Chi Minh City, Vietnam, is dwarfed by spiralled hanging incense. The temple is dedicated to Me Sanh, a fertility goddess. Both men and women, but especially women, come here to pray for children.

Life-Cycle Rituals

Belgian anthropologist Arnold van Gennep (1960 [1908]) first proposed the category of life-cycle rituals in 1908. **Life-cycle rituals**, or rites of passage, mark a change in status from one life stage to another of an individual or group. Victor Turner's (1969) fieldwork among the Ndembu, horticulturalists of Zambia, provided insights about the phases of life-cycle rituals. Among the Ndembu, and cross-culturally, life-cycle rituals have three phases: separation, transition, and reintegration. In the first phase, the initiate (the person undergoing the ritual) is separated physically, socially, or symbolically from normal life. Special dress may mark the separation; for example, a long white gown for a baby that is to be baptized in a church. In many cultures of the Amazon and in East and West Africa, adolescents are secluded for several years in separate huts or areas away from the village. The transition phase, or the "liminal phase," is the time when the person is no longer in their previous status, but is not yet a member of the next stage. Liminality often involves the learning of specialized skills that will equip the person for the new status. Reintegration, the last stage, occurs when the initiate emerges and is welcomed by the community in the new status.

How can we explain variations in the occurrence and amplification of such rituals? Here is an example of explanation related to the mode of reproduction. Ritual marking of a baby's entry into society as a human is a common practice, but it varies in terms of how soon after birth the ceremony is done. Where infant mortality rates are high, the ceremony tends to be done late, when the baby is a year old or older. Until the ceremony has been performed, the baby is not named and is not considered "human." This timing may be a way of ensuring that the baby has gotten through the most dangerous period and is likely to survive.

An Apache girl's puberty ceremony. Cross-cultural research indicates that the celebration of girls' puberty is more likely to occur in cultures in which adult women have valued productive and reproductive roles.

Differences in the distribution of puberty rituals for boys and girls have been interpreted as reflecting the value and status of males and females within society. Most societies have some form of puberty ceremony for boys, but puberty ceremonies for girls are less common. A cross-cultural analysis found that this difference is related to the mode of production and gender division of labour (J. K. Brown 1978). In societies where female labour is important and valued, girls have elaborate (and sometimes painful) puberty rites. Where their labour is not important, menarche is unmarked and there is no puberty ceremony. Female puberty rites function to socialize the female labour force. Girls going through initiations often receive training related to their expected adult economic roles. For example, among the Bembe of southern Africa, a girl learns to distinguish 30 or 40 different kinds of mushrooms and to know which ones are edible and which are poisonous.

Pilgrimage

Pilgrimage is round-trip travel to a sacred place or places for purposes of religious devotion or ritual. Prominent pilgrimage places are Varanasi in India (formerly called Banaras) for Hindus; Mecca in Saudi Arabia for Muslims; Bodh Gaya in India for Buddhists; Jerusalem in Israel for Jews, Christians, and Muslims; and Lourdes in France for Christians. Pilgrimage often involves hardship, with the implication that the more suffering that is involved, the more merit the pilgrim accumulates. Compared to a weekly trip to church or synagogue, pilgrimage removes a person further from everyday life, is more demanding, and is therefore potentially more transformative.

Victor Turner applied his three sequences of life-cycle rituals to pilgrimage as well: the pilgrim first separates from everyday life, then enters the liminal stage during the actual pilgrimage, and finally returns to be reintegrated into society in a transformed state. Indeed, in many pilgrimage traditions, a person who has done certain pilgrimages gains enhanced public status, for example, the status of *haji* (someone who has done the *haj*, or pilgrimage to Mecca) in the Islamic faith.

Connections between mythic sacred sites and pilgrimage are strong. For example, in the Hindu goddess tradition, the story of Sati is the basis for the sanctity of 4 major and 46 minor pilgrimage sites in India (Bhardwaj 1973). Because of an argument with her father over whether or not her husband Shiva was welcome at a big sacrifice her family was holding, the unhappy Sati committed suicide. When Shiva heard about her death, he was distraught. He picked up her body and carried it over his shoulder as he wandered across India, grieving. Along the way, parts of her body fell to the ground. The places where they dropped became holy. Some of these include her tongue at Jwala Mukhi and her throat at Vaishno

Devi, both in the Himalayas, and her genitals in the eastern state of Assam.

Pilgrimage, especially among Hindus in India, may involve bathing in a sacred river or in a pond near a temple, or even in the ocean (A. Gold 1988). Flowing water is believed to have great powers of purification in the Hindu tradition. Many of India's most famous pilgrimage sites are located on rivers, such as Varanasi (Banaras), the most prominent place of Hindu pilgrimage, which is located on the Ganges River.

Rituals of Inversion

In some rituals, normal social roles and order are temporarily inverted. Scholars say these rituals allow for social "steam" to be let off temporarily, and they also may provide a reminder about the propriety of normal, everyday roles and practices to which people must inevitably return once the ritual is over.

These **rituals of inversion** are common cross-culturally, with one of the most well-known in the West being Carnival. Carnival is celebrated throughout the northern Mediterranean region, North and South America, and the Caribbean. It is a period of riotous celebration before the Christian fast of Lent (Counihan 1985). Carnival begins at different times in different places, but always ends at the same time on Mardi Gras (or Shrove Tuesday), the day before Lent begins. The word *carnival* is derived from Latin and means "flesh farewell," referring to Lent.

A young Bosan man dressed as an over-sexualized woman, one of the most common costumes in the carnival street-theatre masquerades in the Sardinian town of Bosa.

In Bosa, a town in Sardinia, Italy, Carnival involves several aspects of social role reversal and relaxing of usual social norms: "The discotheques extend their hours, and mothers allow their daughters to attend more often and longer than at other times of the year. Men and women play sexually, fondling and flirting with each other in the discotheques and masquerades that are totally illicit at other times of the year" (14). Carnival in Bosa has three major phases. The first is impromptu street theatre and masquerades that take place over several weeks, usually on Sundays. The theatrical skits are social critiques of current events and local happenings. The masquerades mainly involve men dressing up as exaggerated women:

> Young boys thrust their padded breasts forward with their hands while brassily hiking up their skirts to reveal their thighs. . . . A youth stuffs his shirt front with melons and holds them proudly out. . . . The high school gym teacher dresses as a nun and lifts up his habit to reveal suggestive red underwear. Two men wearing nothing but bikinis, wigs, and high heels feign a stripper's dance on a table top. (15)

The second phase occurs during the morning of Mardi Gras, when hundreds of Bosans, mostly men, dress in black like widows and flood the streets. They accost passersby, shaking in their faces dolls and other objects that are maimed in some way or bloodied. They shriek at the top of their lungs as if mourning, and they say, "Give us milk, milk for our babies. . . . They are dying, they are neglected, their mothers have been gallivanting since St. Anthony's Day and have abandoned their poor children" (16). The third phase, called *Giolzi*, takes place during the evening. Men and women dress in white, wearing sheets for cloaks and pillow cases for hoods. They blacken their faces. Rushing into the street, they hold hands and chant the word "Giolzi." They storm at people, pretending to search their bodies for *Giolzi*, and then say "Got it!" It is not clear what *Giolzi* is, but whatever it is, it represents something that makes everyone happy. How does an anthropologist interpret these events? Carnival allows people to act out roles that are normally closed off to them, for a short time, before they have to go back to their normal positions. It also provides a time in which everyone has fun for a while. In this way, rituals of reversal can be seen to function as mechanisms of maintaining social order: After the allotted days of revelry, everyone returns to their original places for another year.

Sacrifice

Many rituals involve **sacrifice**, or offering of something for transference to the supernaturals. Sacrifice has a long history throughout the world and may be one of the oldest forms of ritual. It may involve the killing and offering of animals, or humans (offerings may be of a whole person, parts of a person's body, or blood), and the offering of vegetables, fruits, grains, flowers, or other products. One anthropologist has suggested that flowers are symbolic replacements for former animal sacrifices (Goody 1993).

Throughout the Aztec region of Mesoamerica, sacrifice (not just human sacrifice) has long been practised. State-level sacrifices were performed by trained priests, ostensibly to "feed" the gods on behalf of the welfare of the state. Apparently the gods were fond of human blood—as well as other items such as quails, crocodiles, jaguars, ducks, salamanders, and cakes made from the amaranth plant—because one of the most widely offered items for important events like a coronation or naming newborn babies was a limited amount of ritually induced bleeding. Symbolic anthropologists would accept the religious logic involved in pleasing the gods as a sufficient explanation for blood sacrifice. Cultural materialists would be inclined to propose an ecological explanation for the practice (see the Critical Thinking box).

Religious Specialists

Not all rituals require the presence of a religious specialist, or someone with special and detailed training, but all require some level of knowledge on the part of the performer(s) about how to do them correctly. Even the daily, household veneration of an ancestor requires some knowledge gained through informal learning. At the other extreme, many rituals cannot be done without a highly trained specialist.

Shamans and Priests

General features of the categories of shaman and priest illustrate some key differences between these two types of specialists (as with all types, many specialists fit somewhere in between). Shamans or shamankas (the female form with the -*ka* ending derives from the original Siberian usage) are part-time religious specialists who gain their status through direct relationships with the supernaturals, often by being "called." A potential shaman may be recognized by special signs, such as the ability to go into a trance. Anyone who demonstrates shamanic abilities can become a shaman; in other words, this is an openly available role. Shamans are more associated with pre-state societies, yet in many ways, faith healers and evangelists in North America could be considered to fit in this category. One of the most important functions of shamanic religious specialists is in healing, usually upon request from an afflicted individual, as described in Chapter 7 on medical anthropology.

In states, the more complex occupational specialization in religion means that there is a wider variety of types of specialists, especially what anthropologists refer to as

Critical Thinking

WHY DID THE AZTECS PRACTISE HUMAN SACRIFICE AND CANNIBALISM?

EVIDENCE OF state-sponsored human sacrifice and cannibalism of the victims among the Aztecs of Mexico comes from accounts written by the Spanish conquistadors (Harris 1977, 1989; Sanday 1986). The Aztec gods required human sacrifice—they "ate" human hearts and "drank" human blood. Most of the victims were prisoners of war, but many others were slaves, and sometimes young men and women, and even children.

The victims were marched up the steep steps of the pyramid, held lying on their backs over a stone altar, and slit open in the chest by a priest, who wrenched out the heart (said to be still beating), which was then burned in offering to the gods. The body was rolled down the other side of the temple, where it was retrieved by butchers and prepared for cooking. The skull was returned to the temple area to be put on display racks. Although no one knows for sure how many victims were sacrificed over all, estimates are in the hundreds of thousands. At a single site, a chronicler reported that the display racks contained more than 100 000 skulls (Harris 1977:106). At one especially grand event, victims were arranged in four lines, each three kilometres long. Priests worked for four days to complete the sacrifices.

Human sacrifice and cannibalism of any scale might seem to invite the question "Why?" Certainly one must ask "why" about sacrifice and cannibalism as practised on the grand scale of the Aztecs. Of the many attempted explanations, two perspectives are compared here: an etic view and an emic view.

Michael Harner (1977) and Marvin Harris (1977, 1989) propose an etic explanation based on references to factors in the regional ecology and the politics of Aztec expansionism. The region of the Aztec empire lacked sufficient amounts of animal sources of protein to satisfy its growing population. While the ruling classes managed to maintain their supply of delicacies such as dog, turkey, duck, deer, rabbit, and fish, little was available for the poor. Yet the rulers needed to support and retain the loyalty of their army in order to protect and expand the empire's boundaries, and they needed to keep the masses happy. Providing the gods with human hearts and blood was a powerful statement of the empire's strength. It had the additional benefit of yielding huge amounts of meat for soldiers and commoners. Such "cannibal redistribution" could be manipulated by the state to reward particular groups and to compensate for periodic shortages in the agricultural cycle.

Peggy Sanday (1986) rejects the etic perspective and provides an emic one based on texts describing the Aztec people's own rationale and motives. Sacrifice and cannibalism, she says, followed religious logic and symbolism and were practised to satisfy the gods' hunger, not human hunger. Aztec religion says that the gods require certain sacrifices in order for the universe to continue to operate. Human flesh was not consumed as an "ordinary meal," but as part of a religious identification with the gods, just as people would wear the skins of sacrificed victims in order to participate in their sacredness. Sanday says that the etic explanation, in focusing on the "business" aspects of Aztec sacrifice and cannibalism, has missed the tradition's religious meaning for the Aztecs.

CRITICAL THINKING QUESTIONS

How do the etic and emic interpretations differ in the data they use?

Which theory do you find more convincing, and why?

Is there any other way to explain Aztec human sacrifice and cannibalism?

"priests" (not the same as the specific modern role of the Catholic priest), and the development of religious hierarchies and power structures. The terms **priest** and **priestess** refer to a category of full-time religious specialists whose positions are based mainly on abilities gained through formal training. A priest may receive a divine call, but more often the role is hereditary, passed on through priestly lineages. In terms of ritual performance, shamans are more involved with non-periodic rituals. Priests perform a wider range of rituals, including periodic state rituals. In contrast to shamans, who rarely have much secular power, priests and priestly lineages often do.

Other Specialists

Certain other specialized roles are widely found. Diviners are specialists who are able to discover the will and wishes of the supernaturals through techniques such as reading animal entrails. Palm readers and tarot card readers fit into the category of diviners. Prophets are specialists who convey divine revelations usually gained through visions or dreams. They often possess charisma (a specially attractive and powerful personality) and may be able to perform miracles. Prophets have founded new religions, some long-lasting and others short-lived. Witches use psychic powers and affect people through emotion and thought. Mainstream society often condemns witchcraft as negative. Some scholars of ancient and contemporary witchcraft differentiate between positive forms that involve healing and negative forms that seek to harm people.

Even in cases where witchcraft or sorcery is interpreted as negative, the intent or result is not always that clear. Michael Lambek, in a study of a community on Mayotte Island off the east coast of Africa, discussed the implications of interpreting a death being caused by sorcery (1993). A woman was suspected of stealing another woman's bracelet. In retaliation, the victim and her husband declared they would curse the thief if the bracelet was not returned. The bracelet was not returned and some time later the suspected thief died. Lambek notes that not all people in the community agreed with the idea that the curse caused the

death. Moreover, this particular version of events developed years after the woman's death (388). Also, many in the community were not concerned with identifying the source of the sorcery for purposes of revenge. No one could be sure of the effects of such accusations (264).

WORLD RELIGIONS

The term **world religions** was coined in the nineteenth century to refer to religions with many followers that crossed national borders and had a few other specific features, such as a concern with salvation (the belief that human beings require deliverance from an imperfect world). At first, the term referred only to Christianity, Islam, and Buddhism. It was later expanded to include Judaism, Hinduism, Confucianism, Taoism, and Shintoism. The category of world religions is even less appropriate now because many more religions cross national boundaries and therefore have "world" reach. Nonetheless, since university religion courses teach entire semesters of material on these "world religions," this chapter provides an anthropological perspective on five of them. In addition, because of the global importance of the African diaspora that began with the European colonial slave trade, a sixth category of world religions is included that describes key elements shared among the diversity of traditional African belief systems.

Cultural anthropologists emphasize that no world religion exists as a single monolithic entity, but rather each is composed of many variants, such as regional and class variations, as well as doctrinal differences between reformist and fundamentalist interpretations. The world religions have long travelled outside their original borders through intentional attempts to expand and gain converts, or through migration of believers to new locales. European colonialism was a major force of expansion of Christianity, especially (but not exclusively) through missionary work of various Protestant sects. Now, the increased rate of population movements and the rapid expansion of television and the internet have given even greater impetus to religious movement and change. One anthropologist says that the world religions face a "predicament" in terms of how to maintain a balance between standardization based on core beliefs and the increasingly local variants emerging everywhere (Hefner 1998). From Christian televangelism to internet chat rooms, contemporary religion appears to be more dynamic and interactive than ever before, raising doubt about the validity of claims that modernity means the decline of religious belief and the rise of secularism.

The five world religions of long standing that are considered here are discussed first in terms of their general history, distribution, and teachings. Then examples are

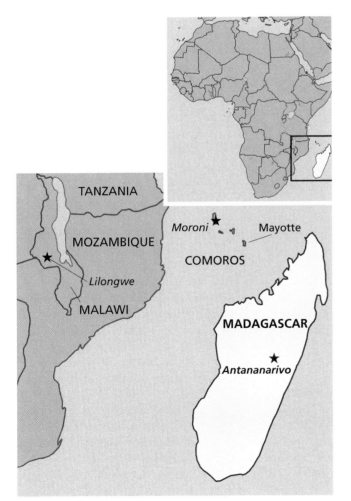

given of how they vary in different contexts to show how the same texts and teachings are localized. Often, when a world religion moves into a new cultural region, it encounters indigenous religious traditions. The two world religions that emphasize proselytizing, or seeking converts, are Christianity and Islam. Their encounters with indigenous religions have often been violent and have included physical destruction of local sacred places and objects (Corbey 2003). Common approaches include burning, overturning, dismantling, or cutting up things, dumping them into the sea, and hiding them in caves. European Christian missionaries in the 1800s often confiscated sacred goods and shipped them to Europe for sale to private owners or museums. Both Christian and Islamic conversion efforts frequently involved the destruction of local sacred sites and the construction of their own places of worship on top of the original site.

In many cases, incoming religions and local religions coexist as separate traditions, either as complements or as competitors, in what is called **religious pluralism**. In **syncretism**, elements of two or more religions blend together. Syncretism is most likely to occur when elements of two religions form a close match with each other. For example, if a local myth involves a hero who has something to do with snakes, there may be a syncretistic link with the Catholic belief in St. Patrick, who is believed to have driven snakes out of Ireland.

Many situations of non-fit can also be provided. Christian missionaries have had difficulty translating the Bible into indigenous languages because of lack of matching words or concepts, and because of differing kinship and social structures. Some Amazonian groups, for example, have no word that fits the Christian concept of "heaven" (Everett 1995, personal communication). In other cases, matrilineal peoples have found it difficult to understand the significance of the Christian construct of "god the father."

Hinduism

Over 650 million people in the world are Hindus (Hiltebeitel 1995). The majority live in India, where Hinduism accounts for about 80 percent of the population. The other 20 million, the Hindu diaspora, live in the United States, the United Kingdom, Canada, Malaysia, Fiji, Trinidad, Guyana, and Hong Kong. A Hindu is typically born a Hindu, and Hinduism does not actively seek converts. The four Vedas, composed in Sanskrit in northern India between 1200 and 900 BCE, are the core texts of Hinduism. Many other scholarly texts and popular myths and epics, especially the Mahabharata (the story of a war between two lineages, the Pandavas and the Kauravas) and the Ramayana (the story of king Rama and his wife Sita), also serve as unifying scriptures. Throughout India,

a multiplicity of local traditions exist, some of which carry forward elements from pre-Vedic times. Thus, Hinduism incorporates a diversity of ways to be a Hindu. It offers a rich polytheism and at the same time a philosophical tradition that reduces the multiplicity of deities into oneness. Deities range from simple stones (in Hinduism, stones can be gods) placed at the foot of a tree to elegantly carved and painted icons of gods such as Shiva, Vishnu, and the goddess Durga. Everyday worship of a deity involves lighting a lamp in front of the god, chanting hymns and mantras (sacred phrases), and taking *darshan* (sight of) the deity (Eck 1985). These acts bring blessings to the worshipper.

Although certain standard features of Hinduism exist, such as acceptance of key texts and worship of important, well-known deities, many localized versions of Hinduism throughout India involve the worship of deities and practice of rituals unknown elsewhere. For example, firewalking is an important part of goddess worship in southern and eastern India (J. Freeman 1981; Hiltebeitel 1988) and among some Hindu groups living outside India, notably Fiji (C. Brown 1984). Besides regional variations, caste differences in beliefs and practices even within the same area or village are marked. Lower-caste deities prefer offerings of meat sacrifices and alcohol, while upper-caste deities prefer offerings of flowers, rice, and fruit. Temple structures range from magnificent buildings to a simple canopy placed over the deity for shade. Yet the "unity in diversity" of Hinduism has long been recognized as real, mainly because of the shared acceptance of elements of Vedic thought.

A Nayar Fertility Ritual

The matrilineal Nayars of Kerala, South India, perform a non-periodic ritual as a remedy for the curse of the serpent deities who cause infertility in women (Neff 1994). This ritual exemplifies the unity of Hinduism in several ritual elements, such as the use of camphor and incense, the importance of serpent deities, and offering flowers to the deity. The all-night ritual includes, first, women painting a sacred design of intertwined serpents on the floor. Several hours of worshipping the deity follow. Ritual elements include a camphor flame, incense, and flowers. Music comes from drumming, cymbals, and singing. All of these please the deity. The presence of the deity, though, is fully achieved when a Nayar woman goes into trance. Through her, matrilineal family members may speak to the deity and be blessed.

Thus, along with universal elements of Hindu ritual, we find that the role of matrilineal kin among the Nayars provides local variation in ritual. Among the Nayars, a woman's matrilineal kin—mother, uncles, brothers—are responsible for ensuring that her desires for motherhood are fulfilled. They share her interest in her reproductive success in continuing the matrilineage. What the women say during the trance is important. They typically draw attention to family disharmonies or neglect of the deities. This message diverts blame from the infertile woman for whom the ritual is being held. It reminds family and lineage members of their responsibilities for each other.

Hindu Women and Karma in Great Britain

One of Hinduism's key concepts is that of *karma*, translated as "destiny" or "fate." A person's karma is determined at birth on the basis of his or her previous life and how it was conducted. The karma concept has prompted many outsiders to judge Hindus as fatalistic, that is, lacking a sense of agency. But anthropological research on how people actually think about karma in their everyday lives reveals much individual variation from fatalism to a strong sense of being in charge of one's destiny. One study looked at women's perceptions of karma among Hindus living in Britain (Knott 1996). Some Hindu women are fatalistic in their attitudes and behaviour, while others are not. One woman who had a strongly fatalistic view of karma said,

[W]hen a baby's born . . . we have a ritual on the sixth day. That's when you name the baby, you know. And on that day, we believe the goddess comes and writes your future . . . we leave a blank white paper and a pen and we just leave it [overnight], and a pair of brand new clothes. . . . So I believe that my future—whatever happens—is what she has written for me. That tells me [that] I have to do what I can do, and if I have a mishap in between I have to accept that. (24)

Yet another woman said that her sufferings were caused by the irresponsibility of her father and the "bad husband" to whom she had been married. She challenged her karma and left her husband: "I could not accept the karma of being with Nirmal [her husband]. If I had done so, what would have become of my children?" (25). Since Hindu women's karma dictates being married and having children, leaving one's husband is a major act of resistance. For some young women informants, questioning the role of karma was the same as questioning their parents' authority. Such intergenerational conflicts create feelings of ambiguity and confusion.

Options for women seeking support for their struggle to sort out their roles can be either religious (praying more and fasting) or secular (seeking the advice of a psychological counsellor or social worker). Some Hindu women in Britain have themselves become counsellors and help support other women's independence and self-confidence. This work involves clear subversion of the traditional rules of karma for women.

Buddhism

Buddhism originated in a founding figure, Siddhartha Gautama (*c*. 566–486 BCE), revered as the Buddha or Awakened One (Eckel 1995:135). It began in northern India, where the Buddha grew up. From there, it spread throughout the subcontinent, into Inner Asia and China, to Sri Lanka and on to Southeast Asia. In the past 200 years, Buddhism has spread to Europe and North America. Buddhism's popularity subsequently faded in India, and Buddhists now constitute less than 1 percent of India's population. Its global spread is matched by a great diversity of doctrine and practice, to the extent that it is difficult to point to a single essential feature (for example, no single text is accepted as authoritative for all forms of Buddhism), other than the importance of Gautama Buddha. Many Buddhists worship the Buddha as a deity, while others do not—they honour his teachings and follow the pathway he suggested for reaching nirvana, or release from worldly life.

Buddhism first arose as a protest against certain features of Hinduism, especially caste inequality, yet it retained and revised several Hindu concepts, such as karma. In Buddhism, everyone has the potential for achieving nirvana (enlightenment and the overcoming of human suffering in this life), the goal of Buddhism. Good deeds are one way to achieve a better rebirth with each incarnation until, finally, release from *samsara* (the cycle of birth, reincarnation, death, and so on) is achieved. Compassion toward others, including animals, is a key virtue. Branches of Buddhism have different texts that they consider their canon. The major division is between the Theravada Buddhism practised in Southeast Asia and the

Buddhism gained an established footing in Japan in the eighth century. The city of Nara was an important early centre of Buddhism. Here, the emperor sponsored the casting of a huge bronze statue of the Buddha, housed in the Todaiji, the "Great Eastern Temple."

Mahayana Buddhism of Tibet, China, Taiwan, Korea, and Japan. Buddhism is associated with a strong tradition of monasticism through which monks and nuns renounce the everyday world and spend their lives meditating and doing good works. Buddhists have many and varied annual festivals and rituals. Some events bring pilgrims from around the world to India—to Sarnath, where the Buddha gave his first teaching, and Gaya, where he gained enlightenment.

Buddhism and Indigenous Spirits in Burma

One theory says that wherever Buddhism exists outside India, it is never the exclusive religion of the devotees because it arrived to find established religions already in place (Spiro 1967). In any particular context, Buddhism and the local traditions may have blended (such blending is called religious syncretism), both may coexist in a pluralistic fashion, or Buddhism may have taken a major role and incorporated the indigenous traditions. The situation in Burma (Myanmar) fits in the second category. Indigenous Burmese beliefs remained strong because they offer a more satisfying way of explaining and dealing with everyday problems. According to Burmese Buddhism, a person's karma is a result of action in previous lives and determines his or her present condition. If something bad happens, it's because of karma and the person can do little but suffer through it. Burmese supernaturalism, on the other hand, says that the bad thing happened because of the actions of capricious spirits called *nats*. Ritual actions can combat the influence of *nats*. In other words, *nats* can be dealt with, karma cannot.

Buddhism, however, became an important cultural force and the key basis for social integration in Burma. One village, for example, had three Buddhist monasteries, with four resident Buddhist monks and several temporary monks. Every male child was ordained as a temporary member of the monastic order. Almost every villager observed Buddhist holy days. While Buddhism is held to be the supreme truth, spirits are called upon when it comes to dealing with everyday problems such as a toothache or a monetary loss.

Buddhism and Religious Roles for Women

In Theravada Buddhism, there are limited religious roles for women. However, women in many parts of Southeast Asia have created roles for the pursuit of a religious path. One possible route in Thailand is to begin wearing white robes, following the eight precepts or Buddhist commandments (which forbid taking life, stealing, lying, and taking intoxicants, among others), and living in a monastic establishment. In urban Thailand there are several such centres for "women in white." A growing trend is for young women who are dissatisfied with the demands of village life to go to the city and take up the white robe, spending their days in meditation and religious study (P. Van Esterik 2000). Another possibility for women is to intensify religious activity, especially meditation, while continuing their normal everyday activities. A very few of these women become meditation teachers educating their followers, both lay and monastic, in the intricacies of Buddhist thought and the techniques of meditation that can eventually lead to nirvana (J. Van Esterik 1996).

Buddhism and Abortion in Japan

Buddhist teachings about the "fluidity" of the supernatural and human realms are important in contemporary Japan, especially in relation to the widespread practice of abortion there. In Japanese Buddhism, fetuses, like newborn infants, are not considered to be full-fledged, solid lives (LaFleur 1992). They are fluid creatures who can be "returned" through abortion (or, in previous centuries, infanticide) to the supernatural realm. People believe that a "returned" fetus may come back at a more convenient time. Women who have had an abortion commonly go to a Buddhist temple and perform a special ritual in which they pray for the good fortune of the rejected fetus. They dedicate a small statue to it that may be placed, along with hundreds of other such statues, in a cemetery-like setting (refer to the photo on page 110 in Chapter 5). It is periodically adorned with clothing, cheap jewellery, and trinkets. These practices may have a positive psychological effect on the parents by diverting feelings of sadness. Thus doctrine and ritual fit with the reproductive goal of many Japanese families to have few children, within the context of abortion being the predominant way of limiting the number of offspring.

Judaism

The first and basic Judaic religious system was defined around 500 BCE, following the destruction of the Temple in Jerusalem by Babylonians in 586 BCE (Neusner 1995). The early writings, called the Pentateuch, established the theme of exile and return as a paradigm for Judaism that endures today. The Pentateuch is also called the Five Books of Moses, or the Torah.

Followers of Judaism share in the belief in the Torah (the Five Books of Moses, or Pentateuch) as the revelation of God's truth through Israel, a term for the "holy people." The Torah explains the relationship between the supernatural and human realms and guides people in how to carry out the world view through appropriate actions. A key feature of all forms of Judaism is the identification of what is wrong with the present and how to escape, overcome, or survive that situation. Jewish life is symbolically interpreted as a tension between exile and return, given its foundational myth in the exile of the Jews from Israel and their period of slavery in Egypt.

Judaism is monotheistic, teaching that God is one, unique, and all-powerful. Humans have a moral duty to follow Jewish law, to protect and preserve life and health, and to follow certain duties such as observing the Sabbath. The high regard for human life is reflected in the general opposition to abortion within Jewish law and in opposition to the death penalty. Words, both spoken and written, have unique importance in Judaism: There is an emphasis on truth-telling in life and on the use of established literary formulas at precise times during worship. These formulas are encoded in a *siddur*, or prayer book. Dietary patterns also distinguish Judaism from other religions; for example, rules of kosher eating forbid the mixing of milk or milk products with meat.

Contemporary varieties of Judaism range from conservative Hasidism to Reform Judaism, which emerged in the early 1800s. One difference between these two perspectives concerns the question of who is Jewish. Jewish law traditionally defined a Jewish person as someone born of a Jewish mother. In contrast, reform Judaism recognizes as Jewish the offspring of a Jewish father and a non-Jewish mother. Currently the Jewish population numbers about 18 million worldwide, with about half living in North America, a quarter in Israel, and another 20 percent in Europe and Russia. Smaller populations are scattered across the globe.

Who's Who at the Kotel

The most sacred place to all Jews is the *Kotel*, or Western Wall in Jerusalem. Since the 1967 war, which brought Jerusalem under Israeli rule, the *Kotel* can be considered the most important religious shrine and pilgrimage site of Israel. The *Kotel* is located at one edge of the Temple Mount (or Haram Sharif), an area sacred to Jews, Muslims, and Christians. According to Jewish scriptures, God asked Abraham to sacrifice his son Isaac on this hill. Later, King Solomon built the First Temple here in the middle of the tenth century BCE. It was destroyed by Nebuchadnessar in 587 BCE, when the Jews were led into captivity in Babylon. Around 500 BCE, King Herod built the Second Temple on the same site. The *Kotel* is a remnant of the Second Temple. Jews of all varieties and non-Jews come to the *Kotel* in vast numbers from around the world. The *Kotel* plaza is open to everyone, pilgrims and tourists. The wall is made of massive rectangular stones weighing between two and eight tonnes each. At its base is a synagogue area, partitioned into men's and women's sections.

An ethnographic study of what goes on at the *Kotel* reveals how this single site brings together a variety of Jewish worshippers and more secular visitors. There is great diversity among the visitors, evident in the various styles of dress and gesture:

The *Kotel* (or Western Wall) in Jerusalem is a sacred place of pilgrimage especially for Jews. Males pray at a section marked off on the left while women keep to the area on the right. Both men and women should cover their heads, and women should take care when leaving the wall area to keep their faces toward it and avoid turning their backs to it.

The Hasid . . . with a fur shtreimel on his head may enter the synagogue area alongside a man in shorts who utilizes a cardboard skullcap available for "secular" visitors. American youngsters in jeans may ponder Israeli soldiers of their own age, dressed in uniform, and wonder what their lot might have been if they were born in another country. Women from Yemen, wearing embroidered trousers under their dresses, edge close to the Wall as do women accoutred in contemporary styles whose religiosity may have been filtered through a modern education. . . . The North African-born Israeli, uttering a personal prayer with his forehead against the Wall becomes an object of comment for a European tourist. Pious women, with their heads covered for modesty, instruct their children in the decorum appropriate to the prayer situation. People from many parts of the country, nay the world, meet unexpectedly. (Storper-Perez and Goldberg 1994:321)

In spite of plaques that state the prohibition against begging, there are beggars who offer to "sell a blessing" to visitors. They may remind visitors that it was the poor who built the wall in the first place. Another category of people is young Jewish men in search of prospective "born again" Jews who "hang around" looking for a "hit" (in their words). Most of the hits are young Americans who are urged to take their Jewishness more seriously and, if male, to be sure to marry a Jewish woman. Other regulars are Hebrew-speaking men who are available to organize a prayer service. One of the most frequent forms of religious expression at the *Kotel* is the insertion of written prayers into the crevices of the wall.

The social heterogeneity of the Jewish people is thus brought together in a single space, creating some sense of what Victor Turner (1969) called *communitas*, a sense of collective unity out of individual diversity.

Passover in Kerala

The Jews of the Kochi area (formerly called Cochin) of Kerala, South India, have lived there for about 1000 years (Katz and Goldberg 1989). The Maharaja of Kochi had good relations with and respect for the Jewish people, who were mainly merchants. He relied on them for external trade and contacts. In recognition of this, he allowed a synagogue, which is still standing, to be built next to his palace. Syncretism is apparent in Kochi Jewish lifestyle, social structure, and rituals. Crucial aspects of Judaism are retained, along with adoption of many aspects of Hindu practices. Three aspects of syncretism with Hinduism are apparent in Passover, one of the most important annual rituals of the Jewish faith. First, compared to the typically joyous Western/European Passover celebration, the Kochi version has adopted a tone of austerity and is called "the fasting feast." Kochi Passover, second, allows no roles for children who, at a traditional *Seder* (ritual meal) usually ask four questions as a starting-point of the narrative. The Kochi Jews chant the questions in unison. This change relates to the fact that in Hinduism, children do not have solo roles in rituals. Third, a Kochi Seder stresses purity even more than standard Jewish requirements. Standard rules about maintaining the purity of kosher wine usually mean that no gentile (non-Jew) should touch it. But Kochi Jews say that if the shelf or table on which the wine sits is touched by a gentile, the wine is impure. This extra level of "contagion" is influenced by Hindu concepts of pollution.

Christianity

Christianity has many ties with Judaism, from which it sprang, especially in terms of the Biblical teachings of a coming saviour, or messiah. It began in Palestine and the eastern Mediterranean in the second quarter of the first century (Cunningham 1995:240–253). Most of the early believers were Jews, who took up the belief in Jesus Christ as the "messiah" (anointed one) who came to earth in fulfillment of prophesies contained in the Hebrew scriptures. Today, Christianity is the largest of the world's religions with about 1.5 billion adherents, or nearly one-third of the world's population. It is the majority religion of Australia, New Zealand, the Philippines, Papua New Guinea, most countries of Europe, and North and South America, and about a dozen southern African countries. Christianity is a minority religion throughout Asia, but

A celebration of the Christian holy day of Palm Sunday in Port-au-Prince, Haiti. European colonialism brought thousands of Africans as slaves to the "New World," and it also exported Christianity through missionary efforts. Many forms of Christianity are now firmly entrenched in the Caribbean region as well as in Central and South America.

Asian Christians constitute 16 percent of the world's total Christians and are thus a significant population.

Christians accept the Bible (Old and New Testaments) as containing the basic teachings, the belief that a supreme God sent his son to earth as a sacrifice for the welfare of humanity, and the importance of Jesus as the model to follow for moral guidance. The three largest branches of Christianity are Roman Catholic, Protestant, and Eastern Orthodox. Within each of these branches, various denominations exist. Christianity has existed the longest in the Near East and Mediterranean regions. In contemporary times, the greatest growth in Christianity is occurring in sub-Saharan Africa, parts of India, and Indonesia. It is currently experiencing a resurgence in Eastern Europe.

Protestantism among White Appalachians

Studies of variants of Protestantism in Appalachia describe local traditions that outsiders who are accustomed to standard, urban versions may view as "deviant." For example, churches in rural West Virginia and North Carolina, called Old Regulars, emphasize in their worship three obligatory rituals: foot washing, communion (a ritual commemorating the "Last Supper" that Jesus had with his disciples), and baptism (Dorgan 1989). The foot-washing ceremony occurs once a year in conjunction with communion, usually as an extension of the Sunday service. An elder is called to the front of the church, and he "introduces" the service. He preaches for about 10 to 20 minutes, and then there is a round of handshaking and embracing. Two deaconesses come forward to "prepare the table" by uncovering the sacramental elements placed there earlier under a white table-cloth (unleavened bread, serving plates for the bread, cups for the wine, a decanter or quart jar or two of wine). The deacons come forward to prepare the bread by breaking it into small pieces while the moderator pours the wine into the cups. By now, the men and women have formed separate groups as the deacons serve the bread and wine (a few groups have allowed deaconesses to serve the women's side; this issue has caused conflicts and splits among traditional groups). After the deacons serve each other, it is time for the foot washing. The moderator may begin this part of the service by quoting from the New Testament (the book of John, chapter 13, verse 4): "He riseth from supper, and laid aside his garments; and he took a towel and girded himself." While speaking these lines, he removes his coat and then ties a long towel around his waist. He takes a basin from the piles of basins by the communion table and puts water in it, selects a senior elder and removes his shoes and socks, then washes his feet slowly and attentively. Other members come forward and take towels and basins. Soon "the church is filled with crying, shouting, and praising as these highly poignant exchanges unleash a flood of emotions. A fellowship that may have remained very solemn during the communion will now participate in a myriad of intense expressions of religious enthusiasm and literally scores of high-pathos scenes will be played out" (106). Participants take turns washing and being washed. A functional interpretation of the ritual of foot washing is that it helps maintain interpersonal harmony in small religious communities.

Another feature of worship in some small, Protestant subdenominations in West Virginia involves the handling of poisonous snakes. This practice also finds legitimation in the New Testament (Daugherty 1997). According to a passage in Mark (16:15–18), "In my name shall they cast out devils; they shall speak with new tongues; they shall take up serpents; and if they drink any deadly thing, it shall not hurt them; they shall lay hands on the sick, and they shall recover." Members of "Holiness-type" churches believe that the handling of poisonous snakes is the supreme act of devotion to God. They are Biblical literalists and have chosen serpent handling as their way of celebrating life, death, and resurrection, and proving that only Jesus has the power to deliver them from death. During their services, the Holy Ghost (not the Holy Spirit) enables them to pick up serpents, speak in tongues, testify to the Lord's greatness, and drink strychnine or lye. Most serpent handlers have been bitten many times, but few have died. One interpretation says that the risks of handling poisonous rattlesnakes and copperheads mirrors the risks of the environment. The people are poor, with high rates of unemployment and few prospects for improvement. Are these people psychologically troubled?

Apparently not. Psychological tests indicate they are more emotionally healthy than members of mainline Protestant churches.

The Last Supper in Fiji

Among Christians in Fiji, the image of the "Last Supper" is a dominant motif (Toren 1988). This scene, depicted on tapestry hangings, adorns most churches and many houses. People say, "Christ is the head of this household, he eats with us and overhears us" (697). The image's popularity is the result of its fit with Fijian notions of communal eating and kava drinking. Seating rules at such events place the people of highest status, such as the chief and others close to him, at the "above" side of the room, away from the entrance. Others sit at the "lower" end, facing the highly ranked people. Intermediate positions are located on either side of the person of honor, in ranked order. Da Vinci's rendition of the Last Supper places Jesus Christ in the position of a chief, with the disciples in an ordered arrangement around him. "The image of an ordered and stratified society exemplified in people's positions relative to one another around the kava bowl is encountered virtually every day in the village" (706). The disciples and the viewers "face" the chief and eat and drink together, as is appropriate in Fijian society.

Islam

Islam is based on the teachings of the prophet Muhammad (570–632 CE), and is thus the youngest of the world religions (R. Martin 1995:498–513). The Arabic word *Islam* means "submission" to the will of the one god, Allah, through which peace will be achieved. Islam also implies acceptance of Muhammad as the last and final messenger of God, "the seal of the prophets." Muslim majority nations are located in northern Africa; the Middle East, including Afghanistan, Pakistan, and Bangladesh in South Asia; and several nations in Central Asia and Southeast Asia. In fact, the majority of the world's Muslims (60 percent) live either in South Asia or Southeast Asia. Although Islam originally flourished among pastoral nomads, only 2 percent of its adherents now are in that category.

A common and inaccurate stereotype of Islam among many non-Muslims is that, wherever it exists, it is the same. This erroneously monolithic model tends to be based on some imagined version of Arab Islam as practised in Saudi Arabia. In recent years, features of Arab-defined Islam are spreading globally, specifically guidelines about dress such as head-veiling for women and long robes for men (Nagata 1984). Yet not everyone in global Islamic cultures accepts these rules. In Malaysia, young people seem more willing to become part of the *dakwah* movement (call to faith), while their parents are more likely to be skeptical of the new practices and seek to have their children "deprogrammed" by a religious practitioner they trust. A comparison of Islam in highland Sumatra, Indonesia, and Morocco in North Africa reveals culturally constructed differences (J. Bowen 1992). The annual Feast of Sacrifice is celebrated by Muslims around the world. It commemorates God's sparing of Abraham's son Ishmael (Isaac in Christian and Jewish traditions). It takes place everywhere on the tenth of the last month of the year, also called Pilgrimage Month. The ritual reminds Muslims of their global unity within the Islamic faith. One aspect of this event in Morocco involves the king publicly plunging a dagger into a ram's throat, a re-enactment of Muhammad's performance of the sacrifice on the same day in the seventh century. Each male head of a household follows the pattern and sacrifices a ram. Size and virility of the ram are a measure of the man's power and virility. Other men of the household stand to witness the sacrifice, while women and children are absent or in the background. After the ram is killed, they come forward and dab its blood on their faces. In some villages, women play a more prominent role before the sacrifice by daubing the ram with henna (red dye), thus sanctifying it, and using its blood afterwards in rituals to protect the household. These national and household rituals are highly symbolic of male power in the public and private domains—the power of the monarchy and the power of patriarchy.

The degree of local adaptation to Moroccan culture becomes clear when compared with the ritual's enactment in Sumatra, which has a less patriarchal culture and a political structure that does not emphasize monarchy. In Isak, a traditionalist Muslim village, people have been Muslims since the seventeenth century. They sacrifice all kinds of animals, including chickens, ducks, sheep, goats, and water buffalo. As long as the throat is cut and the meat is eaten, it satisfies the demands of God. Before cutting the victim's throat, the sacrificer dedicates it to one or more relatives. In contrast to Morocco, most sacrifices receive little notice and are done mainly in the back of the house with little fanfare. Both women and men of the household refer to it as "their" sacrifice, and there are no signs of male dominance. Women may sponsor a sacrifice, as did one wealthy woman trader who sacrificed a buffalo (the actual cutting, however, is done by a man). The Moroccan ritual emphasizes fathers and sons. The Isak ritual includes attention to a wider range of kin on both the husband's and wife's side, daughters as well as sons, and dead relatives, too. In the Indonesian context, no centralized dynastic meanings are given to the ritual.

The differences in the way the same ritual is practised in two cultural contexts do not arise because Moroccans know the scriptures better than Sumatrans. The Isak area has many Islamic scholars who consult the scriptures and discuss issues. Rather, the cultural context, including kinship and politics, into which the same scriptural tradition is placed shapes it to local interests and needs.

African Religions

The distinction between the world religions and "local religions" is blurry because many local religions are now practised by people who have migrated to other nations, so they aren't just "local." This is true for African religions, many of which spread outside Africa through the enforced movements of people as slaves, and for other religions such as Confucianism, which have been diffused by voluntary migration. This section attempts to summarize some key features of African religions and then provides an example of a new religion with African roots, Ras Tafari.

Features of African Religions

As of 1994, Africa's total population comprised 341 million Christians, 285 million Muslims, and about 70 million practising indigenous religions (J. Smith 1995:15–16). With its diverse geography, cultural variation, and history, Africa encompasses a wide range of indigenous religions. Some common, but not universal, features of indigenous African religions include the following:

- myths about a rupture that once occurred between the creator deity and humans;
- a pantheon that includes a high god and many secondary supernaturals ranging from powerful gods to lesser spirits;
- elaborate initiation rituals;
- rituals involving animal sacrifices and other offerings, meals, and dances;

A sacred altar in a local African religion in Togo, West Africa.

- altars within shrines as focal places where humans and deities meet; and
- close links between healing and divination.

While these general features are fairly constant, African indigenous religions are rethought and reshaped with variable results (Gable 1995). Furthermore, as African religions have moved around the world to new locations with the movement of African peoples, they have been adapted in various ways to their new contexts, as discussed in the following section on the Ras Tafari religion.

Ras Tafari

Also called Rastafarianism, Ras Tafari is a relatively new religion—it was first enunciated in the 1930s—of the Caribbean, North America, and Europe. Numbers of Rastafarians are unknown because they refuse to be counted (J. Smith 1995:23). Ras Tafari is an unorthodox, protest religion that shares few of the features of African religions mentioned above. Ras Tafari traces its history to several preachers of the early twentieth century who taught that Ras ("Prince") Tafari, then the Ethiopian Emperor Haile Selassie I, was the "Lion of Judah" who would lead Blacks to the African promised land. Rastafarianism does not have an organized set of doctrines, and there are no written texts or enforced orthodoxy. However, Yawney and Homiak report that a Ras Tafari assembly in 1983 declared that one group in the movement, the House of Nyahbinghi, be accepted as the foundational Ras Tafari orthodoxy (2001:256). This orthodoxy includes such shared beliefs of the many diffuse groups that Ethiopia is Zion, or heaven on earth, and Emperor Haile Selassie I of Ethiopia is a living god, and that all African people are one and have the right of return to Africa. Since the death of Haile Selassie in 1975, a greater emphasis has been placed on pan-African unity and Black power, and less on Ethiopia. Rastafarianism is particularly strong in Jamaica, where it first emerged. It is associated with reggae music, dreadlocks, and *ganja* (marijuana) smoking. Variations within the Rastafarian movement in Jamaica range from beliefs that one must fight oppression to the position that living a peaceful life brings victory against evil.

DIRECTIONS OF CHANGE

All religions have established mythologies and doctrines that provide a certain degree of continuity and, often, conservativism in religious beliefs and practices. Yet, nowhere are religions frozen and unchanging. Cultural anthropologists have traced the resurgence of religions that seemed to have been headed toward extinction through colonial forces, and they have documented the emergence of seemingly new religions. Likewise, they are observing the contemporary struggle of once-suppressed religions in socialist states to find a new position in the post-socialist world. Religious icons, once a prominent part of Russian Orthodox churches, were removed and placed in museums. Now, the churches want them back. Indigenous people's beliefs about the sacredness of their land are an important part of their attempts to protect their territory from encroachment and development by outside commercial interests. The world of religious change offers these examples, and far more, as windows into wider cultural change.

Revitalization Movements

Revitalization movements are organized movements that seek to construct a more satisfying culture, either through re-establishing all or parts of a religion that has been threatened by outside forces or by adopting new practices and beliefs. Such movements often arise in the context of rapid cultural change and appear to represent a way for people to try to make sense of their changing world and their place in it. One such movement that emerged as a response of First Nations to the invasion of their land by Europeans and Euro-Americans was the Ghost Dance movement (J. Smith 1995:385). In the early 1870s, a shaman of the Paiute tribe named Wodziwob declared that the world would soon be destroyed and then renewed: First Nations peoples, plants, and animals would come back to life. He instructed people to perform a circle dance, known as the "Ghost Dance," at night.

This movement spread to other tribes in California, Oregon, and Idaho, but ended when the prophet died and his prophecy was unfulfilled. A similar movement emerged in 1890, led by another Paiute prophet, Wovoka, who had a vision during a total eclipse. His message was the same: destruction, renewal, and the need to perform circle dances in anticipation of the impending event. The dance spread widely and with differing effects. Among the Pawnee, it provided the basis for a cultural revival of old ceremonies that had fallen into disuse. The Sioux altered Wovoka's message and adopted a more overtly hostile stance toward the United States government and White people. Newspapers began to carry stories about the "messiah craze," referring to Wovoka. Ultimately, the government took action against the Sioux, killing Chief Sitting Bull and Chief Big Foot and about 300 Sioux at Wounded Knee. In the 1970s, the Ghost Dance was revived by the American Indian Movement, an activist organization seeking to improve First Nations rights.

Cargo cults are a variety of revitalization movement that emerged in much of Melanesia (including Papua New Guinea and Fiji) and in New Zealand among the indigenous Maori peoples, in response to Western influences. Most prominent in the first half of the nineteenth century, they are characterized by their emphasis on the acquisition of Western trade goods, or "cargo" in local terms. It was difficult for many island people to understand why Western people in their midst sat around in an office all day doing very little work but receiving large deliveries of goods by ship from abroad. The islander worked hard every day in his or her yam garden but never received these wonderful goods from afar. As a consequence, a prophetic leader emerges with a vision of how the cargo will arrive for the islander. In one instance, the leader predicted that a ship would come, bringing not only cargo, but also the dead ancestors. Followers set up tables for the expected guests, complete with flower arrangements.

Later, after World War II and the islanders' experiences of aircraft arrivals bringing cargo, the mode of arrival changed to planes. Once again, people would wait expectantly for the arrival of the plane. The cargo cults emerged as a response to the disrupting effects of new goods being suddenly introduced into indigenous settings. The outsiders imposed a new form of exchange system that emphasized the importance of Western goods and denied the importance of indigenous valuables, such as shells and pigs. This transformation undermined traditional patterns of status-gaining through the exchange of indigenous goods. Cargo cult leaders sought help, in the only way they knew, in obtaining Western goods so they could gain social status in the new system.

Contested Sacred Sites

Religious conflict often becomes focused on sacred sites. One place of recurrent conflict is Jerusalem, where many religions and sects within religions compete for control of sacred terrain. Three major religions claim they have primary rights: Islam, Judaism, and Christianity. Among the Christians, several different sects vie for control of the Church of the Holy Sepulchre. In India, frequent conflicts occur between Hindus and Muslims over sacred sites. Hindus claim that Muslim mosques have been built on sites sacred to Hindus. On some occasions, the Hindus have proceeded to tear down the mosques. Many conflicts that involve secular issues surrounding sacred sites also exist worldwide. In Israel, some Jewish leaders object to archaeological research because the ancient Jewish burial places should remain undisturbed. The same situation exists for First Nations peoples, whose burial grounds have often been destroyed for the sake of urban development in North America. Around the world, large-scale development projects such as dams and mines have destroyed indigenous sacred areas. Resistance to such destruction is growing—for example, among Australian Aborigines, as discussed earlier in this chapter.

Religious Freedom as a Human Right

According to a United Nations Declaration, freedom from religious persecution is supposed to be a universal human right. Yet, violations of this right by nations and by competing religions are common. Sometimes people who are being persecuted on religious grounds can seek and obtain sanctuary in other places or nations. Thousands of Tibetan Buddhist refugees, including their leader the Dalai Lama, fled Tibet after it was taken over by the Chinese. Several Tibetan communities have been established in exile in India, the United States, and Canada, where the Tibetan people attempt to keep their religion, language, and heritage alive.

Supporters of the John Frum Movement, a cargo cult, stand guard around one of the cult's flag poles at Sulphur Bay village (Tanna, Vanuatu).

The post-9/11 policy enactments, particularly in the United States, Canada, and the United Kingdom related to the "campaign against terrorism," are seen by many as dangerous steps against constitutional principles of personal liberty—specifically, as infringements on the religious rights of practising Muslims. The prevalent mentality in these governments, and in much of the general populace, links the whole of Islam with terrorism and thereby stigmatizes all Muslims as potential terrorists. Physical attacks against people assumed to be Muslim were another aspect of such extreme thinking. Many anthropologists (for example, Mamdani 2002) have spoken out against the wrong-headedness and indecency of labelling an entire religion dangerous and putting all its members under the shadow of suspicion.

WHAT is religion and what are the basic features of religions cross-culturally?

Early cultural anthropologists defined religion in contrast to magic and suggested that religion was a more evolved form of thinking about the supernatural realm. They collected information on religions of non-Western cultures and constructed theories about the origin and functions of religion. Since then, ethnographers have described the basic features of religious systems and documented a rich variety of beliefs, many forms of ritual behaviour, and different types of religious specialists. Beliefs are expressed either in myth or doctrine, and they often are concerned with defining the roles and characteristics of supernatural beings and how humans should relate to them. Rituals, or the action side of beliefs, include life-cycle rituals, pilgrimages, cleansing rituals, rituals of reversal, and sacrifice. In some sense, all rituals are transformative for the participants. Many rituals, but not all, require the participation of a trained religious specialist such as a shaman/shamanka or priest/priestess. Religious specialist roles are fewer, less formalized, and carry less secular power and status in non-state societies. In states, religious specialists are often organized into hierarchies, and many specialists gain substantial secular power.

HOW do world religions reflect globalization and localization?

The five world religions are based on a coherent and widely agreed-upon set of teachings, but as members of these religions move around the globe, the religious beliefs and practices are contextualized into localized variants. When a new religion moves into a culture, it may be blended with indigenous systems (syncretism), coexist with indigenous religions in a pluralistic fashion, or may take over and obliterate the original beliefs.

WHAT are some important aspects of religious change in contemporary times?

Cultural anthropologists have documented and sought to explain why and how religious change occurs. Religious movements of the past two centuries have often been prompted by colonialism and other forms of social contact. In some instances, indigenous religious leaders and cults arise in the attempt to resist unwanted outside forces of change; in other instances, they arise as ways of incorporating new ideas and values from the outside.

KEY CONCEPTS

SUGGESTED READINGS

Nadia Abu El-Haj, *Facts on the Ground: Archaeological Practice and Territorial Self-Fashioning in Israeli Society.* Chicago: University of Chicago Press, 2001. A cultural anthropologist writes about the political aspects, specifically nation-building, of archaeology in Israel. Attention is focused on contested sacred sites, how secular interests are linked to sacred site archaeology, and debates about excavation of grave sites.

Diane Bell, *Ngarrindjeri Wurruwarrin: A World That Is, Was, and Will Be.* North Melbourne, Australia: Spinifex Press, 1998. This is an ethnography about Australian Aboriginal struggles to protect their sacred land from encroachment by developers, with attention to the people's own voices, the perspective of the Australian government, the media, and even disputes among anthropologists about what constitutes truth and validity.

Thomas D. Blakely, Walter E. A. van Beek, and Dennis L. Thomson, *Religion in Africa: Experience and Expression.* Portsmouth, NH: Heinemann, 1994. This book contains an introductory overview and 20 chapters on topics including the impact of Islam and Christianity on African religious systems, women's spirit cults, myth and epic, and new religious movements.

Karen McCarthy Brown, *Mama Lola: A Vodou Priestess in Brooklyn.* Berkeley: University of California Press, 1991. The life story of Mama Lola, a Vodou practitioner, is set within an ethnographic study of a Haitian community in New York.

Susan Greenwood, *Magic, Witchcraft and the Otherworld: An Anthropology.* New York: Berg, 2000. This book examines modern magic as practised by Pagans in Britain, focusing on the Pagan view of the essence of magic as communication with an otherworldly reality. Chapters address witchcraft, healing, Goddess worship, and the relationship between magic and morality.

Klara Bonsack Kelley and Harris Francis, *Navajo Sacred Places.* Bloomington: Indiana University Press, 1994. The authors report on the results of a research project to learn about Navajo cultural resources, especially sacred sites, and the stories associated with them in order to help protect these places.

Gregory Forth, *Beneath the Volcano: Religion, Cosmology and Spirit Classification among the Nage of Eastern Indonesia.* Leiden, Netherlands: KITLV Press, 1998. This ethnography focuses on Nage ideas about spirits and how these influence ritual practice and relations with humans. This is an important addition to scholarship; it examines the religion of a people not previously investigated in the anthropological literature.

Michael Lambek, *Knowledge and Practice in Mayotte: Local Discourses of Islam, Sorcery, and Spirit Possession.* Toronto: University of Toronto Press, 1993. This reflexive study of religious practice among an Islamic people on an island off the east coast of Africa probes the meanings of sorcery and spirit possession.

Anna S. Meigs, *Food, Sex, and Pollution: A New Guinea Religion.* New Brunswick, NJ: Rutgers University Press, 1984. This book provides an analysis of taboos surrounding food, sex, and vital bodily essences among the Hua people of Papua New Guinea.

Fatima Mernissi, *Beyond the Veil: Male–Female Dynamics in Modern Muslim Society.* Bloomington: Indiana University Press, revised edition, 1987. The author considers how Islam perceives female sexuality and seeks to regulate it on behalf of the social order. This edition contains a new chapter on Muslim women and fundamentalism.

WEBLINKS

The Companion Website (**www.pearsoned.ca/miller**) that accompanies *Cultural Anthropology,* Third Canadian Edition, includes a destinations module containing links to many websites relevant to the content of this chapter. Use it to investigate the Web and expand your understanding of anthropology.

KEY QUESTIONS

- **WHAT** are the major features of human verbal language?
- **HOW** do language, thought, and society interact?
- **WHAT** is human paralanguage?

13

COMMUNICATION

Indigenous language dictionaries and usage guides
are available on the Web and may help indigenous
people preserve their culture (check out The Internet
Guide to Australian Languages).

Many animals and insects such as chimpanzees, lions, and bees have sophisticated ways of communicating about where food is available or warning about an impending danger. People are in almost constant communication with other people, with supernaturals, and pets or other domesticated animals.

Communication refers to the conveying of meaningful messages from one person or animal or insect to another. Means of communication among humans include eye contact, body posture, position and movements of limbs, and language. **Language** refers to a form of communication based on a systematic set of arbitrary symbols shared among a group and passed on from generation to generation. It may be spoken, signed, or written.

This chapter discusses culture and communication, drawing on work in linguistic anthropology, one of general anthropology's four fields. It discusses characteristics of human language that set it apart from communication among other animals and considers what we know about the origins of languages. Then the role of language in our multicultural worlds is explored, including how language relates to thought in general, different styles and patterns of languages used by different groups of people, and the growing importance of communication through the mass media.

Linguistic anthropology is devoted to the study of communication, mainly, but not exclusively, among humans. Some of the earliest research in linguistics was carried out by Franz Boas; he recorded many of the languages, myths, and rituals of First Nations groups, particularly those on the Northwest Coast and in the Canadian Arctic. Another force driving the development of linguistic anthropology was the discovery through cross-cultural fieldwork that many existing non-Western languages had never been written down. Study of non-Western languages revealed a wide range of different phonetic systems (pronunciation of various sounds) and exposed the inadequacy of Western alphabets to represent such sounds. This gap prompted the development of the International Phonetic Alphabet, which contains symbols to represent all known sounds, such as the symbol "!" to indicate a click sound common in southern African languages.

Many anthropologists are designing practical applications for research findings to promote improved language learning among school children, migrants, and refugee populations. The modification of standardized tests to reduce bias against children from varied cultural backgrounds is an area where applied linguistic anthropologists are increasingly active. Linguistic anthropologists also study language use in deaf communities, including research on cross-cultural differences in sign language. This work helps to promote greater public understanding of the cultures of people who are deaf and contributes to improved teaching of sign language (see the Lessons Applied box).

HUMAN VERBAL LANGUAGE

This section begins with a discussion of some of the challenges facing researchers in linguistic anthropology (review Chapter 2 on research methods) and then discusses two distinctive features of human language

Lessons Applied

ANTHROPOLOGY AND PUBLIC UNDERSTANDING OF THE LANGUAGE AND CULTURE OF PEOPLE WHO ARE DEAF

ETHNOGRAPHIC STUDIES of the communication practices and wider culture of people who are deaf have great importance and practical application (Senghas and Monaghan 2002). First, this research demonstrates the limitations and inaccuracy of the "medical model" that construes deafness as a pathology or deficit and sees the goal as curing it. Instead, anthropologists propose the "cultural model," which views deafness simply as one possibility in the wide spectrum of cultural variation. (In the context of using this cultural model, a capital D is often used: Deaf culture.) Studies clearly show that deafness leaves plenty of room for human agency. The strongest evidence of agency among people who are deaf is sign language itself, which exhibits adaptiveness, creativity, and change. This new view helps to promote a

non-victim, non-pathological identity for people who are deaf and to reduce social stigma related to deafness. Third, anthropologists working in the area of Deaf culture studies are examining how people who are deaf become bilingual—for example, fluent in both English and Japanese sign languages. Their findings are being incorporated in markedly improved ways of teaching sign language.

FOOD FOR THOUGHT

Learn the signs for five words in English sign language, and then learn the signs for the same words in another sign language. Are they the same or different, and how might one explain the similarity or difference?

that separate it from other animals' communication. A brief review of formal properties of language is followed by consideration of historical linguistics and language change.

Fieldwork Challenges

Research in linguistic anthropology shares the basic methods of cultural anthropology (fieldwork and participant observation), but its more specialized areas require unique approaches to data gathering and analysis. The study of language **pragmatics**, or language in use, relies on tape recordings or video recordings of people and events. The tapes are then analyzed qualitatively or quantitatively. Video recordings, for example, may be subjected to a detailed "frame analysis" that can pinpoint when communication breaks down or misunderstandings occur.

Linguistic anthropologists argue that the analysis of recorded data is best done when it is informed by broader knowledge about the culture. This approach derives from Malinowski's view that communication is embedded in its social context and must therefore be studied in relation to that context. An example of such a contextualized approach is a study of speech in Western Samoa that gathered many hours of tape-recorded speech as well as conducting participant observation (Duranti 1994). Analysis of the transcriptions of the recorded talk revealed two major findings about how speech used in village council

meetings is related to social status. First, turn-taking patterns reflected and restated people's power positions in the group. Second, people used particular grammatical forms and word choices that indirectly either praised or blamed others, thus shaping and reaffirming people's moral roles and status relations. Non-linguistic data that assisted the researchers in forming these interpretations included observation of seating arrangements and the order of the distribution of *kava* (a ritually shared intoxicating beverage). The findings about the role of language in creating and maintaining social and moral order contribute to a richer understanding of the wider social context of status formation in Samoa.

Most cultural and linguistic anthropologists face the challenge of translation. One has to understand more about a language than just vocabulary in order to provide a reliable and meaningful translation. An anthropologist once translated a song that occurred at the end of a play in Zaire (Fabian 1995). The play was presented in the Swahili language, so he assumed that the final song was, too. Thus, he assumed that the repeated use of the word *tutubawina*, a Swahili word, indicated that it was a fighting song. A Swahili speaker assisting the anthropologist said, no, it was a soccer song. The puzzled anthropologist later learned, by writing to the theatre performers, that the word *tutubawina* as used in this song was not a Swahili word, but from another language and that it indicates a marching song.

Linguistic anthropologists who study ordinary language use face the problem of the **observer's paradox**, the impossibility of doing research on "natural" communication events without affecting the "naturalness" sought (McMahon 1994:234). The mere presence of the anthropologist with a tape recorder makes the speaker concentrate on speaking "correctly" and more formally. Several options exist for dealing with the paradox: recording informants in a group, observing and recording speech outside an interview situation, or using structured interviews in which the informant is asked to perform various speech tasks at varying levels of formality. In this last technique, the informant is first asked to read a word list and a short passage. The next stage is a question-and-answer session. Last, the interviewer encourages the informant, who may be more relaxed by now, to produce informal conversational speech by asking about childhood rhymes and sayings, encouraging digressions to get the informant to talk for longer periods, and posing questions that are likely to prompt an emotional response. Another strategy is to use "role playing" in which informants are asked to act out a particular scene, such as arguing about something. Data from such semi-structured techniques can be compared with the more casual styles of "natural" speech to assess the possible bias created.

Key Characteristics: Productivity and Displacement

Most anthropologists agree that non-human primates share with humans some abilities to communicate through sounds and movements, and that some can be trained to recognize and use arbitrary symbols that humans use. Whatever progress will be made in teaching non-human primates aspects of sign language, it is unlikely that they could ever develop the range of linguistic ability that humans possess because human verbal language depends on the richness of arbitrary symbols.

Human language is said to have infinite **productivity**, or the ability to communicate many messages efficiently. In contrast, consider gibbon communication in the wild. Gibbons have nine calls that convey useful messages such as "follow me," "I am angry," "here is food," "danger," and "I am hurt." If a gibbon wants to communicate particular intensity in, say, the danger at hand, the only option is to repeat the "danger" call several times and at different volumes: "danger," "*danger*," "DANGER," and so on. This variation allows some productivity, but with greater degrees of danger, the system of communication becomes increasingly inefficient. By the time 20 danger calls have been given, it may be too late. In comparison, human language's capacity for productivity makes it extremely efficient. Different levels of danger can be conveyed in these ways:

Chimpanzees have demonstrated a remarkable ability to learn aspects of human language. Here, trainer Joyce Butler signs "Nim" and Nim signs "Me."

"I see a movement over there."
"I see a leopard there."
"A leopard—help!"
"Help!"

Human language also uses the feature of **displacement**, which allows people to talk about displaced domains—events in the past and future—as well as the immediate present. According to current thinking, displacement is not a prominent feature of non-human primate communication. A wild chimpanzee is unlikely to be able to communicate the message "Danger: there may be a leopard coming here tonight." Instead, it communicates mainly what is experienced in the present. Even if non-human primates can learn to use displacement, its use among humans is far more prevalent. Among humans, the majority of language use relates to displaced domains, including reference to people and events that may never exist at all, as in fantasy and fiction.

Formal Properties of Verbal Language

Besides the above general characteristics, human language can be analyzed in terms of its formal properties: sounds, vocabulary, and grammar—all features that lie within formal or "structural" linguistics (Agar 1994). Learning a new language usually involves learning different sets of sounds. The sounds that make a difference for meaning in a language are called **phonemes.**

Anthropologist Diamond Jenness, who learned several First Nations languages, considered the Algonquian languages the most musical because of their richness of vowel sounds, avoidance of harsh consonants, and use of whispered syllables. He found the Salish languages very harsh because of consonant clusters that English speakers find hard to pronounce, and found the Athapascan languages the most difficult to learn (J. Price 1979:23). Similarly, Sharon Hutchinson (1996) was attracted to the rich, melodic qualities of the Nuer language, but found it difficult to hear and control the heavy aspiration (audible release of breath). These subjective judgments about other languages reflect our experience using different phonemes.

A native English speaker trying to learn the North Indian language called Hindi is challenged to learn to produce and recognize several new sounds. For example, four different *d* sounds exist. None are the same as an English *d*, which is usually pronounced with the tongue placed on the ridge behind the upper front teeth (try it). One *d* in Hindi, which linguists refer to as a "dental" sound (see Figure 13.1), is pronounced with the tongue pressed firmly behind the upper front teeth (try it). Next is a dental *d* that is also aspirated (pronounced "with air"); making this sound involves the tongue being in the same position and a puff of air expelled during pronunciation (try it, and try the regular dental *d* again with no puff of air at all). Next is what is referred to as a "retroflex sound," accomplished by flipping the tongue back to the central dome of the roof of the mouth (try it, with no puff of air). Finally, there is the aspirated retroflex *d* with the tongue again in the centre of the roof of the mouth and a puff of air. Once

you can do this, try the whole series again with a *t*, because Hindi follows the same pattern with this letter as with the letter *d*. Several other sounds in Hindi require careful use of aspiration and placement of the tongue for communicating the right word. A puff of air at the wrong time can produce a serious error, for example, saying the word for "breast" when you want to say the word for "letter."

Grammar refers to the patterns and rules for combining sounds into word sequences that carry meaning. All languages have a grammar, although they vary in form. Even within the languages of contemporary Europe, German is characterized by its placement of the verb at the end of the sentence (try to compose an English sentence with the verb at the end). Phonemes, vocabulary, and grammar are the formal building blocks of language.

Origins and History

When did language capacity evolve, and what were the first human languages like? Did grunts and exclamations evolve into words and sentences? Did early humans attempt to imitate the sounds of nature? How did people decide to put together a set of arbitrary symbols with meanings that everyone would accept? No one knows,

FIGURE 13.1 Dental and Retroflex Tongue Positions

When making a dental sound, the speaker places the tongue against the upper front teeth (position A on the diagram), while for making a retroflex sound, the speaker places the tongue up against the back of the palate (position B on the diagram).

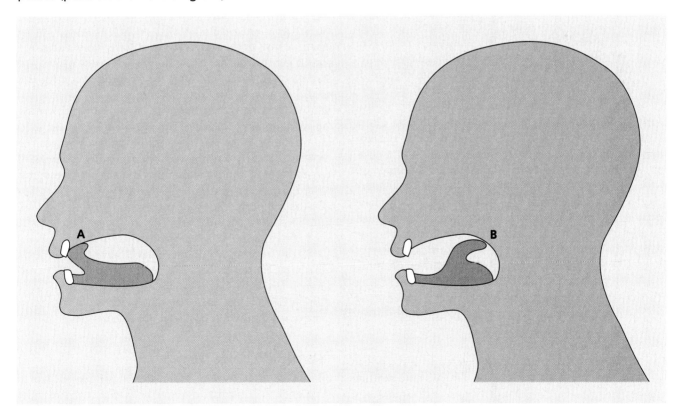

nor will we ever know, how language started in the first place. The prevailing view is that early humans began to develop language around 50 000 years ago, using calls, body postures, and gestures. Human **paralanguage** (a category that includes all forms of non-verbal communication, such as body posture, voice tone, touch, smells, and eye and facial movements) is thus a continuation of the earliest phase of human language.

No contemporary human language can be considered a "primitive" model of early human language. That would defy the principle of **linguistic relativism**, which says that all languages have passed through thousands of years of change, and all are equally successful forms of communication. Languages differ in their structure and in the meaning they attribute to various concepts (or "semantics"), but all are equally capable of conveying subtle meanings and complex thoughts. There is no such thing as a "simple" language—one that is easy to learn because it is less complex than others. Early scholars of comparative linguistics were sometimes misled by ethnocentric assumptions that language structures of European languages were normative and that languages that did not have the same structure were somehow deficient. Chinese was thus considered to be "primitive" on these grounds, as were many First Nations languages. Now we know that different languages have complexity in different areas—sometimes verb forms, sometimes noun forms.

Writing Systems

Gesture and speech are not recorded in the archaeological record. Attempts to trace the beginnings of language are thus limited to working with records of written language. Evidence of the earliest written languages comes from Mesopotamia, Egypt, and China, with the oldest writing system in use by the fourth millennium BCE in Mesopotamia (Postgate, Wang, and Wilkinson 1995). Some scholars say that symbols found on pottery in China dated at 5000 to 4000 BCE should be counted as the earliest writing. At question here is the definition of a writing system: Does the presence of symbolic markings on pots constitute a "writing system" or not? Most scholars say that a symbolic mark that could refer to a clan name is not necessarily evidence of a writing system that involves the use of words in relation to each other in a systematic way. A similarity of forms in all early writing systems is the use of **logographs**, or symbols that convey meaning through a form or picture that resembles what is being referred to. Over time, some logographs retained their original meaning, others were kept but given more abstract meaning, and other non-logographic symbols were added (see Figure 13.2).

The emergence of writing is associated with the political development of the state. Some scholars take writing as a key diagnostic feature that distinguishes the state from

FIGURE 13.2 Logographic and Current Writing Styles in China

Source: Courtesy of Molly Spitzer Frost.

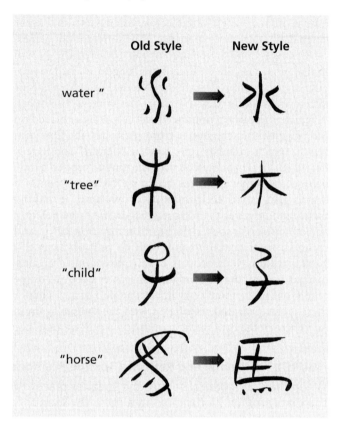

earlier political forms because record keeping was an essential task of the state. The Inca state is one exception to this generalization; it used *quipu,* or cords of knotted strings of different colours, for keeping accounts and recording events. Two interpretations of early writing systems exist. One is that the primary use of early writing was ceremonial because of the prevalence of early writing on tombs, bone inscriptions, or temple carvings. The other is that early writing was utilitarian, for government record keeping and trade. In this view, the archaeological record is biased toward durable substances, and this bias favours the preservation of ceremonial writing (because durable substances such as stone were more likely to be used for ceremonial writing that was intended to last.) Utilitarian writing would more likely have been done on perishable materials because people would be less concerned with permanence—somewhat like the way we treat shopping lists. Thus, no doubt much more utilitarian writing existed than what has been preserved.

Historical Linguistics

Historical linguistics is the study of language change through history using formal methods that compare shifts

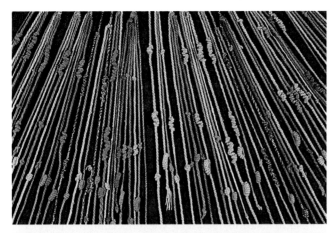

Quipu, or knotted strings, were the basis of state-level accounting in the Incan empire. The knots conveyed substantial information for those who could interpret their meaning.

over time and across space in formal aspects of language such as **phonetics** (the study of the production of speech sounds), grammar, and semantics. This approach originated in the eighteenth century with a discovery made by Sir William Jones, a British colonial administrator working in India. During his spare time in India, he studied Sanskrit, the ancient language of India. He was the first to notice strong similarities between Sanskrit, Greek, and Latin in vocabulary and grammar. For example, the Sanskrit word for "father" is *pitr,* in Greek it is *patér,* and in Latin, *pater.* This was an astounding discovery for the time, given the prevailing European mentality that placed its cultural heritage firmly in the classical Greco-Roman world and depicted the "Orient" as completely separate from Europe (Bernal 1987).

Following Jones's discovery, other scholars began comparing lists of words and grammatical forms in different languages; for example, the French *père,* the German *Vater,* the Italian *padre,* the Old English *faeder,* the Old Norse *fadhir,* the Swedish *far.* With these lists, scholars could also determine degrees of closeness and distance in their relationships; for example, that German and English are closer to each other, and French and Spanish are closer to each other. Later scholars contributed the concept of "language families," or clusters of related languages. Attempting to reconstruct the ancient ancestral languages of family trees was a major research interest of the nineteenth century. Comparison of contemporary and historic Eurasian languages and shifts in sound, vocabulary, and meaning yielded a model of a hypothetical early parent language called Proto-Indo-European (PIE). For example, the hypothetical PIE term for "father" is p#ter (the "#" symbol is pronounced like the *u* in "mutter"). The PIE homeland has not been located and may never be, since PIE speakers were probably pastoralists whose lifestyle left few remains in the archaeological record. Linguistic evidence suggests that the PIE homeland was located somewhere in Eurasia, either north or south of the Black Sea. From its area of origin, PIE speakers subsequently spread out in waves toward Europe, central and eastern Asia, and South Asia. The farther they moved from the PIE centre in terms of time and space, the more their language diverged from original PIE.

Colonialism, Globalization, and Language Change

Languages change constantly, sometimes slowly and in small ways, other times rapidly and dramatically. Most of us are scarcely conscious of such changes. Colonialism was a major force of change. Not only did colonial powers declare their own language as the language of government, business, and higher education, but they often took direct steps to suppress indigenous languages and literatures.

A **pidgin** is a contact language that emerges when different cultures with different languages come to live in close proximity and therefore need to communicate (McMahon 1994:253). Pidgins are generally limited to highly functional domains, such as trade, because that is what they were developed for. A pidgin therefore is no one's first language. Many pidgins of the Western hemisphere developed out of slavery, where owners needed to communicate with their slaves. A pidgin is always learned as a second language.

Current methods of linguistic analysis support the possibility of the original homeland of Proto-Indo-European either among pastoralists in an area north of the Black Sea about 6000 years ago, or in central Turkey among farmers over 8000 years ago.

Tok Pisin, the pidgin language of Papua New Guinea, consists of a mixture of many languages: English, Samoan, Chinese, and Malayan. Tok Pisin has been declared one of the national languages of Papua New Guinea, where it is transforming into a **creole**, or a language that is descended from a pidgin, has its own native speakers, and involves linguistic expansion and elaboration. About 200 pidgin and creole languages exist today, mainly in West Africa, the Caribbean, and the South Pacific.

National policies of cultural assimilation of minorities have also led to the extinction of many ethnic languages. One motivation for the establishment of residential schools for First Nations children was to eradicate Aboriginal languages. For example, residential schools were run in British Columbia from 1880, and lasted into the 1960s. Conditions were harsh; punishment was most severe for using Aboriginal languages (Tennant 1990:78). Yet Aboriginal languages in Canada were not obliterated. Of those who identify an Aboriginal language as their first language, 43 percent speak Cree, 14 percent speak Inuktitut, 13 percent speak Ojibwa, 3 percent speak Athabaskan, and 1 percent speak Sioux; but the average age of the speakers is over 40 (Frideres 1998:136). There are policies in place to revive and maintain these languages. While Inuit residential schooling used to be English or French based, grades 1 to 3 are now taught in Inuktitut, even for non-Inuit children (Frideres 1998:400). Native-as-a-Second-Language (NSL) programs in Ontario aim to develop literacy and encourage the functional use of Aboriginal languages such as Cree, Delaware, Ojibwa, Cayuga, Oneida, and Mohawk. The 2001 Aboriginal Peoples Survey reported that 63 percent of Inuit children and 80 percent of those over the age of 15 could speak Inuktitut relatively well, but only 15 percent of off-reserve Aboriginal people indicated they could speak their language well or relatively well.

Because language is such a vital part of culture, language rights and political rights are closely intertwined. One of the most complex examples of language politics and identity concerns the relation between French and English in Canada. Many of the language policies of Quebec, such as Bill 101, reflect the fear that without protection, the French language in Quebec will be contaminated by English, become corrupted and degenerate, with a resulting loss in cultural identity. Others argue that only in a bilingual Canada will French be protected, and that separation would result in a loss of French language in anglophone North America, particularly in the era of NAFTA.

National policies of cultural assimilation of minorities have also led to the extinction of many indigenous and minority languages. The Soviet attempt to build a USSR-wide commitment to communism after the 1930s included mass migration of Russian speakers into remote areas, where they eventually outnumbered indigenous peoples (Belikov 1994). In some cases, Russian officials visited areas and burned books in local languages. Children were forcibly sent away to boarding schools, where they were taught in Russian. The Komi, an indigenous group who spoke a Finno-Ugric language, traditionally formed the majority population in their area north of European Russia on the banks of the lower Pechora River. Russian immigration brought in greater numbers of people than the original population—and the use of Russian in schools. All Komi became bilingual. The Komi language was so heavily influenced by Russian that it now may be extinct.

Anthropologists are concerned about the rapid loss of languages throughout the world—one result of accelerated globalization, including Western economic and media expansion (Hill 2001). **Language decay** occurs when speakers use, in some contexts, a new language in which they may be semifluent and when they have limited vocabulary in their native language. **Language extinction** occurs at the point when language speakers abandon their language in favour of another language, and the original language no longer has any competent users. Language extinction is a serious problem in Australia and North and South America and is becoming more serious in Siberia, Africa, and South and Southeast Asia. As discussed in Chapter 3 (the Lessons Applied box), anthropologists are playing an important role in documenting decaying and dying languages.

Languages that are gaining currency over decaying and dying languages are called **global languages**, or world languages. They are languages that are spoken worldwide in diverse cultural contexts, notably English and Spanish. As these global languages spread to areas and cultures beyond their home area and culture, they take on new, localized identities. One scholar says that there are now many "Englishes," or plural English languages (Bhatt 2001). England's English was transplanted through colonial expansion to Canada, the United States, Australia, New Zealand, South Asia, Africa, Hong Kong, and the Caribbean. English became the dominant language in the colonies; it was used in government and commerce and was taught in schools. Over time, regional and subregional varieties of English have developed, often leading to a form of English that a native speaker from England cannot understand at all.

Efforts to revive or maintain local languages face a difficult challenge. Political opposition often comes from national governments that may fear local identity movements and may not wish to support administratively or financially bilingual or multilingual policies and programs. The English-only movement among political conservatives in the United States is an example of attempts at suppressing linguistic diversity (Neier 1996). Because language is such a vital part of culture, linguistic suppression can be equivalent to cultural suppression or ethnocide.

LANGUAGE, THOUGHT, AND SOCIETY

This section presents material that demonstrates the relationships among language, thought, and society. First, we discuss two theoretical approaches to these relationships. Then we look in greater depth at how different "levels" of language are also related to thought and society.

Two Models

During the twentieth century, two major theoretical perspectives were influential in defining how language, thought, and society are related. The first argues that language determines culture; the second reverses the causality, arguing that culture determines language. They are presented here as alternative models, but careful reading of all the writings of each founder and subsequent research would reveal that the contrasts are not really this simple (Hill and Mannheim 1992). Nonetheless, the "extreme" forms have persisted in the literature over several decades.

Edward Sapir and Benjamin Whorf formulated an influential model, called the **Sapir-Whorf hypothesis**, which claims that differences in language predetermine differences in thinking. For example, if a language has no word for what in English is called "snow," then a person who has been brought up in that language cannot think of "snow" as it is meant in English. Whorf first began developing this theory through study of different languages' vocabulary and grammar. He was so struck by the differences that he is often attributed with saying that people who speak different languages inhabit different "thought-worlds." This catchy phrase became the basis for what is called **linguistic determinism**, which states that language determines consciousness of the world and behaviour. Extreme linguistic determinism implies that the frames and definitions of a person's primary language are so strong that it is impossible to fully learn another language or understand another culture (Agar 1994:67).

An alternative model to the Sapir-Whorf hypothesis is proposed by scholars working in the area of **sociolinguistics**, the study of language in relation to society. These theorists argue that a person's society, culture, and social position determine the content and form of language. Linguists and anthropologists researched the reasons for linguistic variation within a speech community. William Labov's (1966) research of the 1960s established this approach to sociolinguistics. He conducted several famous studies of the use of particular speech sounds among people of different socioeconomic classes in New York City. He hypothesized that class differences would be reflected in the pronunciation of certain sounds in words. Class difference is not the only social factor affecting language use. For instance, researchers who study Montreal French (e.g., Sankoff and Laberge 1978) found that people's language use correlates with the linguistic demands of their job: people employed as lawyers, teachers, and receptionists tend to use more standard or prestigious speech variants than do those whose jobs require less public use of language, such as laboratory technicians, mechanics, and computer programmers. This variation cuts across class; for example a receptionist, whose job ranks lower than that of a laboratory technician, feels more pressure to use standard language.

Lisa Valentine (1995) conducted a sociolinguistic study of the discourse or language-in-use of the Severn Ojibwe people of northern Ontario, demonstrating how new speech forms are shaped by the liturgy and music of the Anglican Church, and the newspapers, radio, and television services provided by the Native Communications Society in the small, isolated community where everyone speaks Severn Ojibwe.

The topic of focal vocabulary illustrates the connections between the Sapir-Whorf hypothesis and sociolinguistics. **Focal vocabularies** are clusters of words that refer to important features of a particular culture. Studying focal vocabularies can contribute to understanding how language is both a thought-world (according to the Sapir-Whorf hypothesis) and a cultural construction responsive to a particular social context. Studying a culture's focal vocabularies provides useful comparative insights. For example, Inuktitut has a more amplified focal vocabulary related to cold weather precipitation, as do English speakers who are avid skiers; Arabic has many words for camels; and a horse breeder has a more elaborate focal vocabulary for kinds of horses.

Language socialization, or language learning through everyday interactions, is another area that links the two models described in this section. Language socialization includes two processes: socialization to *use* language and socialization *through* language (Ochs 1990:287). The first part of the definition refers to language acquisition, how children learn to be native speakers. Language acquisition concerns people in many fields, especially psychology and education. Anthropological study of language acquisition adds an important comparative element, showing how children acquire aspects of language such as storytelling, for example.

Language is also an important part of socializing children into a culture. Research shows again that culture shapes the content and process of such socialization. Language has the characteristic of **indexicality**; that is, certain linguistic features "index," or point to, the identities, actions, or feelings of the speaker and convey important social information. For example, two ways of making requests exist in Samoan (Ochs 1990). One, the imperative "Give it to me," uses the neutral form of "me" (*Mai ia te a'u*) and sets the meaning of the construction as a demand. The second uses the sympathy-marked form of "me" (*Mai taita*) and indexes that the speaker is begging. How do children gain knowledge of indexes? The answer lies in their participation in recurrent communicative events. In contrast to formal language learning in school, learning indexicality is indirect and unconscious.

Multiple Levels of Language

One characteristic of contemporary language use is the proliferation of people who speak more than one language. Much of this change is the result of colonialism and, now, increased migration related to economic globalization. Another characteristic is the existence of variation within a single language in such matters as word choice, intonation, and even grammar, which is tied to multicultural diversity and social differences of the users.

Bilingualism

Global cultural contact since the era of colonial expansion beginning in 1500 has meant that people have been increasingly exposed to more than one language. One result is that more people are bilingual. **Bilingualism** is simply the capacity to speak two languages. A true bilingual has "native" speaking abilities in two languages. Bilingualism is often the result of migration from one language area to another.

Many world populations are bilingual because their country was colonized and a second language was introduced. As a result of the close proximity and high exposure to many languages, Europeans often grow up learning more than one language. The emergence of large populations speaking multiple languages has led to debates about the value and cost of **linguistic pluralism** (the presence of linguistic diversity within a particular context). This is an important policy issue in Canada. The British North America Act of 1867, the Canadian Constitution, and the Official Languages Act of 1969 guarantee the equality of English and French as part of the national identity of Canada. Efforts of the federal government to promote bilingualism and of the Quebec provincial government to promote a unilingual French society are complicated by political opposition to Quebec separation, and the cost of maintaining bilingual policies and programs across Canada.

Bilingualism confers substantial advantages to people, giving them access to an alternative way of viewing the world and in some cases economic advantages. However, in a study conducted in the 1960s, monolingual French speakers in Quebec were found to have the lowest income, monolingual English speakers the highest income, and bilingual speakers intermediate incomes (Dorais 1979:165).

Bilingualism in Canada requires signs in both official languages.

Studies of the effects of differing degrees of bilingualism on the problem-solving abilities of children in grade 3 suggested that bilingual children had higher levels of control of attention when solving linguistic problems than monolingual children, and used the higher levels of control in more generalized situations (Bialystok and Majumder 1998).

Subtle differences in linguistic patterns between speakers of different languages or dialects can lead to serious miscommunication. For example, health care providers who speak standard English often misinterpret messages conveyed to them by speakers of other languages and dialects. Linguistic cues are words or phrases that preface a remark to give the speaker's attitude toward what is being said, especially the degree of confidence in it. Standard English includes cues such as "maybe" and "in my opinion."

Health care providers who speak standard English often misinterpret messages conveyed to them by speakers of Mohawk English (Woolfson et al. 1995). Three functions of cueing in Mohawk English indicate the speaker's unwillingness or inability to verify the certainty of a statement, respect for the listener, or the view of Mohawk religion that health is in the hands of the creator and any statement about health must acknowledge human limitations. The many cues may appear to health care practitioners as indecisiveness or non-cooperation. These interpretations are incorrect, given the rules that the speakers are following about the validity of statements, humility, and religious belief.

Cultural interpreters may be brought in when patients and healers have different cultural backgrounds. For example, Cree and Ojibwa interpreters assisted in obtaining informed consent from First Nations patients in Winnipeg

The presence of both French and Arabic cultural influences in Morocco results in the frequent use of bilingual shop signs.

hospitals. As in the Mohawk example, health professionals considered that these patients had limited ability to make informed consent decisions. Interpreters had to do more than provide accurate translations: They had to act as advocates during medical interviews (Kaufert and O'Neil 1990).

Dialects

A **dialect** is a way of speaking in a particular place, or, more precisely, a subordinate variety of a language arising from local circumstances (R. Williams 1983:105). Thus, there is standard English and there are dialects of English. For example, the British singing group the Beatles originated in the city of Liverpool, known for its distinct dialect called "Scouse." Cockney, spoken in London, is another prominent dialect. Speakers of both dialects would be able to understand each other, but with some difficulty.

Standard forms of a language will have the stamp of authority of the nation and will be taught using standardized textbooks. Dialects may appear in literature or films as a way of adding "local colour." It is often difficult for dialect speakers to avoid being considered somehow second class because they do not speak the standard language. Dialectical differences become a subject of debate in Canada particularly when they result in discrimination.

In the spirit of nationalistic pride in the 1970s, many writers in Quebec chose to write in *joual*, a form of French that incorporates many idiomatic expressions, anglicisms, and blasphemy. Some have argued, however, that *joual* is not the predominant dialect of Quebec French, but of

working-class francophones of Montreal. The dialectical difference between *joual*, Montrealais, and Parisian French reflect differences in identity with implications beyond language.

Newfoundland dialects are of great interest to linguists and folklorists. Studies of the regional dialects of one of the oldest overseas communities in the English-speaking world reflect features characteristic of their source dialects from the English West Country, including Dorset and Devon, and southeast Ireland. From the early seventeenth century, small enclaves of seasonal voyagers and settlers inhabited the bays and developed unique vocabularies; for example, classifications of water bodies by type of ocean floor, and names for seals at every stage of development, significant for coastal fishing and sealing (Story, Kirwin, and Widdowson 1982).

Language Codes

Within a single language, particular subcultures are likely to have distinctive **codes**, or ways of speaking, that may include marked vocabulary, grammar, and intonation depending on age, gender, occupation, class, region, and family role of the speaker and listener. Most people know more than one code and are able to **code-switch**, or move from one code to another as needed. For example, consider how you talk to your college friends when you are in a group, compared to how you might speak to a physician or potential employer. Code-switching can be an intentional strategy used to further the interests of the speaker. Generally, code-switching follows status lines, with a dominant language or code being used to make a statement of power or authority (see the Multiple Cultural Worlds box). In the decolonizing nations, people may wish to make a statement of resistance to the colonial powers by avoiding complete switching to the colonial language, but instead using code-mixing. In code-mixing, the speaker starts in the native language and then introduces strands of the colonial language (Myers-Scotton 1993:122).

Gender codes, or socially prescribed ways of speaking like a female or like a male, exist in most languages. In North America, women are widely regarded as being cooperative speakers, men as competitive speakers; women as indirect speakers, and men as direct speakers (Tannen 1990). However, such generalizations are suspect. Linguistic research shows that women and men vary their speech according to the particular context of the interaction, the degree of formality of the situation, and so on. Uniform use of stereotypically male or female speech probably exists only in parody, such as in situation comedies or in drag performances.

As for the idea that women are more cooperative speakers, researchers make the case that both women's and men's speech, if studied carefully and in sufficient detail,

Multiple Cultural Worlds

CODE-SWITCHING IN MARTINIQUE

MARTINIQUE IS an overseas department of France located in the eastern Caribbean. Martinicans are officially French citizens. As part of his ethnographic fieldwork in Martinique, David Murray (2002) had to learn to code-switch between Creole and French; learning to code-switch also socialized him into how the ambiguities of gender, race, and class are performed linguistically.

In Martinique, Creole and French have coexisted for centuries. French is generally the language of authority, prestige, legitimacy, and official discourse, and it is used for media and schooling. Creole is the language of subversion, marginality, and emotion. Locals know how to code-switch between French and Creole to reinforce gender distinctions, disrupt normative conduct, and mark outsiders from insiders. For example, while men switch freely between Creole and French, women are not encouraged to speak Creole, as it is considered vulgar. However, some men speak French exclusively, and women

vendors usually speak Creole to each other in the female-dominated space of the market (39).

Murray's ethnography explores the local complexities of identity formation made visible through language use. While French is considered necessary for economic reasons in a global economy, it reflects Martinique's colonial past. But Creole has not emerged as a symbol of Martinique separatism or identity. Both languages are central in public life.

As Martinique explores the politics of separation from and unity with a colonizing nation state, Quebec has emerged as a utopian destination of possible escape from the confines of the island. It is idealized as a French-speaking zone of racial and sexual freedom where people are friendlier and more tolerant than the French, a place like Martinique that has a shared colonial history with France. Thus, as Murray learned, the effects of colonialism are implicated in code-switching and language use in interesting and unpredictable ways (150).

bears features of both cooperative and competitive talk (D. Cameron 1997). This does not mean that the stereotype of what it means to "talk like a lady" (Lakoff 1973) does not exert an influence on the speech of girls and women, or that boys and men are not encouraged to conform to particular speech patterns.

Consider the power of male silence in North American culture. Girls and women who talk "too much" or too assertively may be judged aggressive or unfeminine; boys and men who display dynamic intonational patterns typically associated with North American English female speech may be judged effeminate. In reality, males and females make strategic use of speech features associated with "femininity" and "masculinity" within a culture, but gender stereotypes of language use are but one influence on males' and females' communicative behaviour.

Gender codes in spoken Japanese also reflect and reinforce gender differences and hierarchies (Shibamoto 1987). Certain words and sentence structures convey femininity, humbleness, and politeness. A common contrast between male and female speech is the attachment of the honorific prefix *o-* to nouns by females. This addition gives female speech a more refined and polite tone. Polite forms of speech, cross-culturally, are more associated with female gender codes than male gender codes. This gender differ-

ence carries over into related areas of speech. For example, a study of apologizing carried out on the Pacific Island of Vanuatu found that women apologize more frequently than men (Meyerhoff 1999).

Discourse, Identity, and Power

Some sociolinguists study **discourse** (or talk) in particular domains in order to learn about power dynamics, how people of different groups convey meaning, and how miscommunication occurs. Discourse styles and content provide clues about a person's social background, age, gender, and status. Consider what cultural information can be gleaned simply from the following bit of a conversation:

"So, like, you know, Ramadan?"

"Yeah."

"So I'm like talking to X, you know, and like she goes, 'Hey Ramadan starts next week.'"

"And I'm like, what do you say, Happy Ramadan, Merry Ramadan?" (Agar 1994:95)

If you thought that the speakers were college students, you were correct. They were young women who were probably born in North America, native English speakers likely to be White, and non-Muslim. Anthropologists have

Preschool children already know much about gender roles and strategies. A boy (centre) seeks to dominate a girl in the play area of a child-care centre.

studied such conversations in varied contexts to learn how people learn culturally appropriate discourse styles, from cursing someone out to telephone conversations to political speeches. The following examples illustrate how discourse is related to identity and power relationships in two domains: children's arguments and teenage girls' everyday talk.

Children's dispute styles in different cultures reveal how argumentation is learned and how power dynamics are played out. Cross-cultural research on children's disputes shows that argument style is culturally learned. For example, among Hindi-speaking Indian children of Fiji, overlapping is the norm, with little regard for strict turn-taking (Lein and Brenneis 1978). In other cultural contexts, offended feelings can arise when turn-takers try to converse with overlappers. The turn-taker feels that the overlapper is rude, and the overlapper feels that the turn-taker is distant and unengaged.

A study of how North American children argue identified stylistic strategies that include use of volume, speed, and stress and intonation (Brenneis and Lein 1977). Elevated volume was prominent, although sometimes an echo pattern of a soft statement followed by a soft response would occur. Acceleration of speed was common among older children, and less so among younger children. Strict adherence to turn-taking was followed, with no overlapping. Stress and intonation are used in rhythmical patterns, sometimes with a demand for rhyming echoes as in:

You're skinny.
You're slimmy.
You're scrawny.
You're . . . I don't know.

Many of the children's arguments involved insults and counter-insults. The voices of children in a downtown Toronto after-school program echo similar patterns:

As we sat together on the mat, Katie, Nadine and I discussed our favourite songs. The girls named popular songs that they had heard on the radio. Suddenly, the conversation shifted from music to focusing on other events in their lives. As we spoke, a boy named Julio wandered in. The girls immediately yelled at him to get out: "boys aren't allowed." Then they proceeded to compare the body sizes of several children. "Fat Amanda" occupied the conversation for the next few minutes. "Fat Amanda," Nadine chanted "Oh she's smelly too. She stunk up the whole laundry room. When my mother went down there, she had to plug her nose." (Caputo 2001:183)

The above comments about body appearance by eight- and nine-year-old girls anticipate the concern with body weight of older Euro-American adolescent girls (Nichter and Vuckovic 1994). A study of 253 girls in grades 8 and 9 in two urban high schools reveals the contexts and meanings of "fat talk." Fat talk usually starts with a girl commenting, "I'm so fat." The immediate response from her friends is, "No, you're not." Girls in the study say that fat talk occurs frequently throughout the day. The following representative conversation between two 14-year-olds was recorded during a focus-group discussion:

Jessica: I'm so fat.
Toni: Shut up, Jessica. You're not fat—you know how it makes you really mad when Brenda says she's fat?
Jessica: Yeah.

In North America, many teenage girls discuss body weight. The girl on the scale is pointing out the fat under her arm.

Toni: It makes me really mad when you say that cuz it's not true.

Jessica: Yeah, it is.

Toni: Don't say that you're fat. (112)

Yet girls who use fat talk are typically not overweight and are not dieting. The weight of the girls in the study was within "normal" range, and none suffered from a serious eating disorder. Fat talk sometimes functions as a call for positive reinforcement from friends that the initiator is an accepted group member. In other cases, it occurs at the beginning of a meal, "especially before eating a calorie-laden food or enjoying a buffet-style meal where an individual is faced with making public food choices" (115). In this context, fat talk is interpreted as functioning to absolve the girl from guilt feelings and to give her a feeling that she is in control of the situation.

Media Anthropology

Media anthropology is the cross-cultural study of communication through electronic media such as radio, television, film, and recorded music, and the print media of newspapers, magazines, and popular literature (Spitulnik 1993). In the 1960s, long before media anthropology became popular, Marshall McLuhan, the University of Toronto English professor who became the chief theorist and prophet of mass communications, examined how new technologies created new environments for communication (1964). He predicted the importance of the media using phrases such as the "global village" and "the medium is the message/massage." Media anthropologists study the media process and content, the audience response, and the social effects of media presentations. Media anthropology seeks to bring together the interests and goals of both anthropology and the media by promoting a contextualized view. In journalism, for example, media anthropology promotes going beyond the reporting of crises and other events to presenting a more holistic, contextualized story. Another applied goal is to disseminate more of anthropology's findings to the general public via radio, television, print journalism, magazines, and the internet. Critical media anthropology asks to what degree access to media messages is mind-opening and liberating or propagandizing and controlling, and whose interests the media are serving.

The Media Process: Studying War Correspondents

Mark Pedelty has studied who creates media messages and how they are disseminated. In *War Stories* (1995), he examines the culture of war correspondents in El Salvador. He finds that their culture is highly charged with violence and terror: "War correspondents have a unique relationship to terror, however, a hybrid condition that combines voyeurism and direct participation. . . . They need terror to realize themselves in both a professional and spiritual sense, to achieve and maintain their culture identity as 'war correspondents'" (2). Pedelty probes the psychological ambivalence of correspondents, who are often accused of making a living from war and violence and who become dependent on the continuation of war for their livelihood. (Even the Salvadoran correspondents, whose country was being racked by violence, worried that the end of the war would also mean the end of their ability to support their families.) He also addresses media censorship, direct and indirect, and how it affects what stories readers receive and the way events are described.

Nationalist media bias is clear in reports of sporting events. Canadian Donovan Bailey from Oakville, Ontario, won the 100-metre final at the 1996 summer Olympics in Atlanta. In the history of the modern Olympics, whoever won the 100-metre race was considered the "world's fastest man." However, the American press claimed that the title should go to American sprinter Michael Johnson on the basis of his record-breaking performance in the 200-metre race. Bailey complained that he did not get the respect he deserved from the American media because he was Canadian. The American magazine *Sports Illustrated* responded by calling Bailey a "whiner." To determine who was the "world's fastest man," Bailey and Johnson ran a 150-metre race at the SkyDome in Toronto on June 1, 1997. Johnson quit midway through the race, complaining of a strained quadriceps muscle, with Bailey well out in front. Not surprisingly, the event was reported very differently in the American and Canadian media. In addition to nationalist bias, racial bias is also evident in news reporting (see the Critical Thinking box).

Media Institutions and Gender: Inside a Japanese Television Studio

Ethnographic studies of television began in the 1980s. Along with related research done by scholars in English, comparative media studies, and communication studies, a substantial body of material is being amassed that situates television within its social context. A major question is how television both determines culture and reflects culture. The basic theoretical tension between structure and agency is of key importance in this area. Most anthropological and related studies of television treat television shows as "texts" that can be approached through analysis of content, dominant symbols, and plot, just as one would analyze a novel or play.

Ethnographic research within a Japanese television station provided one anthropologist with insights into the social organization of the workplace and how it mirrors the messages put forth through television programming

Critical Thinking

BIAS IN NEWS REPORTING

FRANCES HENRY and Carol Tator (2002) researched how mainstream Canadian media construct a view of Canadian society that silences, erases, or marginalizes a significant proportion of this country's population (226). They argue that mainstream media representations define dominant discourses (ways of talking about a topic). The way the media interpret events influences the way readers think about events, creating an ideological climate that seems natural, but in fact contains unchallenged assumptions about the world (26). As this study shows, images disseminated by the mainstream media of ethno-racial groups (African Canadians or Asian Canadians, for example), immigrants, and First Nations peoples are not the images these groups would present of themselves, and these images often reinforce negative stereotypes.

The authors document how the selection of news stories raises the public's anxiety about crime, keeps sensational stories in the news, over-reports crimes allegedly committed by people of colour—especially young Black males—and describes such crimes with emotional hyperbole. They analyzed the news reports about the murder in Toronto of a young White woman by several Black Jamaican men in the Just Desserts Café in Toronto in 1994 to reveal how the use of phrases such as "urban terrorism," "slaughter," "drug-crazed," and "gun-toting barbarians" helped create a moral panic about the need for law and order (202). By selection of stories, editorials, and specific rhetorical strategies, the mainstream media produce discourse that constructs immigrants as prone to criminality. News reports about Jamaicans and Vietnamese, for example, emphasized crime, immigration, and social problems. In an analysis of news stories from 1994 to 1997 on Jamaicans in Canada, 45 percent of the stories fell into the categories of sports or entertainment (Henry and

Tator 2002:167). Coverage of First Nations peoples in several newspapers represented them as pathetic victims, angry warriors, or noble environmentalists, stereotypes that could result in misunderstanding.

The problem, according to Henry and Tator, is lack of reflexivity and critical self-awareness among journalists who work for the mainstream media, few of whom are visible minorities, with the result that few oppositional and counter discourses are articulated in the mainstream media. But resistance to media stereotyping is growing. The Canadian Tamil community launched a lawsuit against the *National Post* for targeting its community and for labelling Tamils as "terrorists" and "criminals." The Canadian Islamic Congress continuously monitors the media for bias in the coverage of Islam and the representation of Muslim Canadians—a particularly important task following the events of September 11, 2001. Ethnic presses also have a critical role to play by challenging familiar stereotypes and providing the social, cultural, historical, and political context missing from the mainstream press (239).

CRITICAL THINKING QUESTIONS

Can you identify any differences in content or approach in two versions of the same story presented in different daily newspapers published on the same day?

Do the stories reveal any bias on the basis of culture, gender, or race?

Is there any difference in the way the same story is covered in the ethnic press and alternative press?

Can you identify any other dominant discourses that might influence the selection of articles and the content of editorials in the mainstream press?

(Painter 1996). The primary audience for Japanese television is the category of *shufu*, housewives. A Japanese television network classified housewives into six categories, ranging from the strongly self-assertive "almighty housewife" to the "tranquil and prudent" housewife. A popular form of programming for housewives is the *homu dorama*, the "home drama" or domestic serial. These serials consistently represent traditional values such as filial piety and the proper role of the daughter-in-law in regard to her mother-in-law. Caring for the aged has become a

prominent theme that supplies the central tension for many situations in which women have to sort out their relationships with each other.

In contrast, television representations of men emphasize their negotiation of social hierarchies within the workplace and other public organizations. While the dominant mode of representation puts women in traditional domestic roles, many women in contemporary Japan are rejecting such shows. In response, producers are experimenting with new sorts of dramas in which women are shown as active workers and aggressive lovers—anything but domesticated housewives. One such show is a 10-part serial aired in 1992 called *Selfish Women*. The story concerns three women: an aggressive single businesswoman who faces discrimination at work, a young mother who is raising her daughter alone while her photographer husband lives with another woman, and an ex-housewife who divorced her husband because she found home life empty and unrewarding. There are several male characters, but except perhaps for one, they are depicted as less interesting than the women. The show's title is ironic. In Japan, women who assert themselves are often labelled "selfish" by men. The lead women in the drama use the term in a positive way to encourage each other: "Let's become even more selfish!" Painter (1996) comments that, "though dramas like *Selfish Women* are perhaps not revolutionary, they are indicative of the fact that telerepresentations of gender in Japan are changing, at least in some areas" (69).

In Canada, the Canadian Broadcasting Corporation (CBC), a Crown corporation, was created in 1936 to enhance Canadians' sense of national identity through its emphasis on Canadian content, and to give Canadians an alternative to American programming.

Tuareg men in Niger, West Africa, greeting each other. Tuareg men's greetings involve lengthy handshaking and close bodily contact.

BEYOND WORDS: HUMAN PARALANGUAGE

Human communication involves a range of non-verbal forms, including tone of voice, silence, and the full gamut of body language from posture to dress to eye movements. Referred to as *paralanguage*, these ways of communication follow patterns and rules just as verbal language does. Like verbal language, they are learned—often unconsciously—and, without learning, one will be likely to experience communication errors, sometimes funny and sometimes serious. Like verbal language, they vary cross-culturally and intraculturally.

Silence

The use of silence can be an effective form of communication, but its messages and implications differ cross-culturally. In Siberian households, the lowest-status person is the in-marrying daughter, and she tends to speak very little (Humphrey 1978). However, silence does not always indicate powerlessness. In North American courts, comparison of speaking frequency between the judge, jury, and lawyers shows that lawyers, who have the least power, speak most, while the silent jury holds the most power (Lakoff 1990:97–99). While some First Nations groups value oratory, others value silence. For example,

the Kaska of northern British Columbia and the Yukon did not value verbal fluency or use baby talk, and they used silence as a response to pain or frustration. Knowing how and when to keep silent was highly valued (Darnell 1970).

Native Americans tend to be silent more often than Euro-American speakers. Many outsiders, including social workers, have misinterpreted this as either reflecting their sense of dignity, or, more insultingly, signalling a lack of emotion or intelligence. How wrong and ethnocentric such judgments are is revealed by a study of silence among the Western Apache of Arizona (Basso 1972). The Western Apache use silence in four contexts. First, when meeting a stranger (someone who cannot be identified), especially at fairs, rodeos, or other public events, it is considered bad manners to speak right away. That would indicate interest in something like money, or work, or transportation, which are possible reasons for exhibiting such bad manners. Second, silence is important in the early stages of courting. Sitting in silence and holding hands for several hours is appropriate. Speaking "too soon" would indicate sexual willingness or interest. That would be immodest. Third, when children come home after a long absence at boarding school, parents and children should meet each other with silence for about 15 minutes rather than rushing into a flurry of greetings. It may be two or three days before sustained conversations are initiated. Last, a person should be silent when "getting cussed out," especially at drinking parties. An underlying similarity of all these contexts is the uncertainty, ambiguity, and unpredictability of the social relationships. Rather than chattering to "break the ice," the Apache response is silence. The difference between the Apache style and the Euro-American emphasis on quick and continuous verbal interactions in most contexts can cause cross-cultural misunderstandings. Outsiders, for example, have misinterpreted Apache parents' silent greeting of their returning children as bad parenting or as a sign of child neglect.

Kinesics

Kinesics is the study of communication that occurs through body movements, positions, facial expressions, and spatial behaviour. This form of non-verbal language also has rules for correct usage, possibilities for code-switching, and cross-cultural variation. Misunderstandings of body language can easily happen because, like verbal language and international forms of sign language, it is based on arbitrary symbols. Different cultures may emphasize different "channels" more than others: some are more touch-oriented than others, for example, or use facial expressions more. Eye contact is something valued during Euro-American conversations, but in many Asian contexts, direct eye contact could be considered rude or possibly also a sexual invitation. Non-verbal communication is important in indexing social relationships, especially dominance and accommodation, or positive versus negative feelings.

Non-verbal communication in Japanese culture is especially marked by the frequent use of bowing. Two Japanese businessmen meet each other, bow, and exchange business cards.

Dress and Looks

Manipulation of the body is a way of sending messages. Marks on the body, clothing, and hair styles convey a range of messages about age, gender, sexual interest or availability, profession, wealth, and emotions. In North America, gender differentiation begins in the hospital nursery with the colour coding of blue for boys and pink for girls. In Japan, the kimono carries an elaborate system for

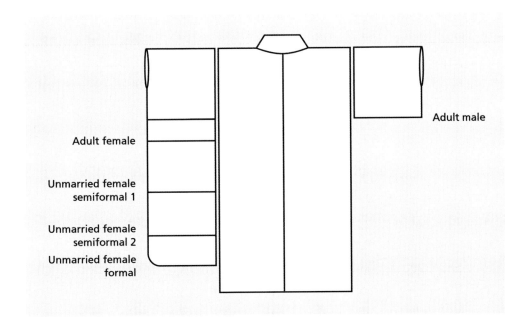

Adult male

Adult female

Unmarried female semiformal 1

Unmarried female semiformal 2

Unmarried female formal

FIGURE 13.3
The Meanings of Kimono Sleeve Length

Source: Liza C. Dalby, *Kimono: Fashioning Culture.* New Haven: Yale University Press, 1993. © Yale University Press. Used with permission.

coding gender, life-cycle stage, and formality of the occasion (see Figure 13.3). The more social responsibility and status one has (older males have most), the shorter the sleeve of one's kimono (Dalby 1993:195–196). An interesting contrast exists with the academic gown worn by professors for ceremonial occasions such as graduation. Professors with a doctorate (PhD) wear gowns with full length sleeves, whereas professors with a master's degree wear gowns with sleeves cut above the elbow.

Messages conveyed through hair (McCracken 1996) or dress, like other linguistic cues, have the property of arbitrariness. Consider the different meanings of the individual choice of young women in Egypt and Kuwait to wear veils (MacLeod 1992). The new veiling of Kuwaiti women distinguishes them as wealthy, leisured, and honourable, in contrast to poor, labouring, immigrant women workers. Veiling in Egypt is done mainly by women from the lower and middle economic levels, where it has been adopted as a way for working-class women to accommodate pressures from Islamic fundamentalism to veil, while preserving their right to keep working outside the home. The message of the head covering in Egypt is, "I am a good Muslim and a good wife/daughter." In Kuwait, the headscarf says, "I am a wealthy Kuwaiti citizen."

Human communication is a vast and exciting field. It includes verbal language and paralanguage. It varies across cultures and has rich and complex meanings. It touches every aspect of our lives from our hair styles to our jobs. A time allocation study of hours per day spent in some form of communication among the "Nacirema" would be quite revealing.

WHAT are the major features of human verbal language?

Linguistic anthropologists point to two features that appear to distinguish human verbal language from communication that other animals use: productivity and displacement. Some study the formal, or structural, properties of verbal language, especially the basic units of meaningful sound, or phonemes. Others focus on historical linguistics, including the emergence of writing as a distinctly human form of verbal communication. Early historical linguists such as Sir William Jones discovered the relationships among languages previously thought to be unrelated, such as German and Sanskrit, and this discovery contributed to greater insights about human history and settlement patterns across Asia and Europe. The recent history of language change has been influenced by the colonialism of past decades or centuries and by the Western globalization of the current era. Many indigenous and minority languages have become extinct, and many others are in danger of doing so. National policies of cultural integration sometimes involve the repression of minority languages. Western globalization supports the spread of English as an increasingly powerful global language with emerging localized variants that have their own distinctive character.

HOW do language, thought, and society interact?

Language, thought, and society are intimately connected in all cultural contexts. One model, the Sapir-Whorf hypothesis, places emphasis on how our language structures our cultural worlds. Another model, called sociolinguistics, emphasizes how our cultural and social worlds shape our language. Many anthropologists draw on both models. Linguistic anthropologists realize how arbitrary the boundaries are between languages, dialects, and even particular linguistic codes that gain prominence. More important than hard and fast definitions of these categories is the context within which modes of communication change and the way speech may be related to the social status and treatment of the speakers. Linguistic anthropologists increasingly study power issues in their attempt to understand how language is linked to dominance, agency, and identity. Media anthropology is an emerging area of interest in anthropology. Research in media anthropology sheds light on how culture shapes media messages and the social dynamics in media institutions.

WHAT is human paralanguage?

We use many forms of non-verbal language to communicate with each other. These include silence, body placement in relation to other people, and our physical appearance—the way we dress, hair styles, and body marking such as tattoos and other ornamentation. Like verbal language, paralanguage involves the use of arbitrary symbols, so speakers must learn it in order to communicate effectively in particular cultural contexts.

KEY CONCEPTS

bilingualism, p. 294
codes, p. 295
code-switch, p. 295
communication, p. 286
creole, p. 292
dialect, p. 295
discourse, p. 296
displacement, p. 288
focal vocabularies, p. 293
global languages, p. 292
grammar, p. 289
historical linguistics, p. 290
indexicality, p. 293
kinesics, p. 301
language, p. 286
language decay, p. 292

language extinction, p. 292
language socialization, p. 293
linguistic determinism, p. 293
linguistic pluralism, p. 294
linguistic relativism, p. 290
logographs, p. 290
observer's paradox, p. 288
paralanguage, p. 290
phonemes, p. 288
phonetics, p. 291
pidgin, p. 291
pragmatics, p. 287
productivity, p. 288
Sapir-Whorf hypothesis, p. 293
sociolinguistics, p. 293

SUGGESTED READINGS

John Edwards, *Language in Canada*. Cambridge: Cambridge University Press, 1998. This book examines bilingualism, multiculturalism, Aboriginal languages, and language issues in every province of Canada.

William Frawley, Kenneth C. Hill, and Pamela Munro, eds., *Making Dictionaries: Preserving Indigenous Languages of the Americas*. Berkeley: University of California Press, 2002. An introductory chapter by the editors presents 10 issues in the making of a dictionary, and 14 subsequent chapters address particular topics such as how to standardize spelling in formerly unwritten languages, and case studies of dictionary making in languages such as Hopi and Nez Perce.

Faye D. Ginsburg, Lila Abu-Lughod, and Brian Larkin, eds., *Media Worlds: Anthropology on New Terrain*. Berkeley: University of California Press, 2002. The editors offer an introductory chapter on media anthropology and new directions in the field. The remaining 19 chapters provide cultural examples organized in five themes: cultural activism and minority claims, the cultural politics of nation–states, transnational circuits, media industry and institutions, and media technology.

Marjorie H. Goodwin, *He-Said-She-Said: Talk as Social Organization among Black Children*. Bloomington: Indiana University Press, 1990. A study of everyday talk among children of an urban African American community in the United States, this book shows how children construct social relationships among themselves through verbal interactions including disputes, pretend play, and stories.

Jack Goody, *The Power of the Written Tradition*. Washington, DC: The Smithsonian Institution, 2000. This book focuses on how writing confers power on societies that have it, compared to those that rely on oral communication. Goody's analysis encompasses the changing power of books in the age of the internet.

Fadwa El Guindi, *Veil: Modesty, Privacy, and Resistance*. New York: Berg, 1999. El Guindi argues that veiling in Arab-Islamic states has many functions and is more complicated than most Western stereotypical views of shame and persecution suggest. The veil may signal group identity and resistance to Western values such as materialism.

Joy Hendry, *Wrapping Culture: Politeness, Presentation and Power in Japan and Other Societies*. New York: Oxford University Press, 1993. This book explores the pervasive idiom and practice of "wrapping" in Japanese culture, including verbal language, gift-giving, and dress. In verbal language, wrapping involves the use of various forms of respect, indicating social levels of the speakers, and the use of linguistic forms of beautification, which have the effect of adornment.

Robin Tolmach Lakoff, *Talking Power: The Politics of Language in Our Lives*. New York: Basic Books, 1990. Lakoff explores strategies of communication and language power-plays in English in the United States, providing examples from courtrooms, classrooms, summit talks, and joke-telling.

William L. Leap, *Word's Out: Gay Men's English*. Minneapolis: University of Minnesota Press, 1996. Fieldwork among gay men in the Washington, D.C., area produced this ethnography that addresses gay men's speech as a cooperative mode of discourse, bathroom graffiti, and discourse about HIV/AIDS.

Catherine A. Lutz and Jane L. Collins, *Reading National Geographic*. Chicago: University of Chicago Press, 1993. This study presents the way *National Geographic's* editors, photographers, and designers select text and images of Third World cultures and how middle-class American readers interpret the material.

Purnima Mankekar, *Screening Culture, Viewing Politics: An Ethnography of Television, Womanhood, and Nation in Postcolonial India*. Durham, NC: Duke University Press, 1999. This ethnographic study of mass media in India shows how modernity interacts with core cultural values, especially those related to the family and gender.

Daniel Miller and Don Slater, *The Internet: An Ethnographic Approach*. New York: Berg, 2000. This is the first ethnography of internet culture. Based on fieldwork in Trinidad, it offers an account of the political and social contexts of internet use, individual experiences of being online, and the impact of the internet on Trinidadian people and their culture.

Donna Patrick, *Language, Politics, and Social Interaction in an Inuit Community*. New York: Mouton De Gruyter, 2003. This book examines indigenous language maintenance among the Inuit of Arctic Quebec. The promotion and maintenance of Inuktitut has taken place through changes in language policy and Inuit control over institutions in a place where Inuktitut, Cree, French, and English are spoken.

Susan U. Philips, Susan Steele, and Christine Tanz, *Language, Gender, and Sex in Comparative Perspective*. New York: Cambridge University Press, 1987. An introductory essay, followed by 11 chapters, explores women's and men's speech in Japan, Western Samoa, and Mexico; children's speech in American preschools and in Papua New Guinea; and sex differences in how the brain is related to speech.

William A. Smalley, *Linguistic Diversity and National Unity: Language Ecology in Thailand*. Chicago: University of Chicago Press, 1994. This book describes levels of linguistic variation in Thailand, paying attention to standard Thai in relation to regional languages and local dialects. Also, the book provides a detailed analysis of changes in sounds and vocabulary as part of wider processes of social change such as migration and urbanization.

Lisa Philips Valentine, *Making It Their Own: Severn Ojibwe Communicative Practices*. Toronto: University of Toronto Press, 1995. This ethnographic study examines a variety of speech events in a small community of Ojibwe people in northern Ontario, Canada. It includes attention to speech variations among speakers, code-switching, and multilingualism as well as connections between spoken language and church music.

WEBLINKS

The Companion Website (www.pearsoned.ca/miller) that accompanies *Cultural Anthropology*, Third Canadian Edition, includes a destinations module containing links to many websites relevant to the content of this chapter. Use it to investigate the Web and expand your understanding of anthropology.

KEY QUESTIONS

- **HOW** is culture expressed through art?
- **WHAT** do play and leisure activities tell us about culture?
- **HOW** is expressive culture changing in contemporary times?

14

EXPRESSIVE CULTURE

The decorated façade of a domestic dwelling in Kano, northern Nigeria.

In the year 2004, the Louvre in Paris, one of the most well-known art museums in the world, opened a huge new museum in the shadow of the Eiffel Tower that displays so-called tribal art of Africa, Asia, the South Pacific, and the Americas (Corbey 2000). This project reflects the interest of France's President Jacques Chirac in non-Western art. It also reflects a new appreciation for the role of cultural anthropologists in helping museums to provide cultural context for objects that are displayed because Maurice Godelier, a specialist on New Guinea, is closely involved in planning the new exhibits.

This new museum elevates "tribal" objects to the level of art, rather than placing them in a museum of natural history, as is so often the case in North America. Yet, at the same time, it places "tribal" art in a museum that is clearly separate from the Louvre. The age-old conceptual division in European and Euro-American thinking, beginning with the Enlightenment, links the West with "civilization" and non-Western peoples with that which is uncivilized. It will prove most interesting to see how this new museum handles the challenge of moving beyond such a dichotomy.

In this chapter, we consider a vast area of human behaviour and thought called **expressive culture**, which consists of learned and patterned ways of creative endeavour that include art, leisure, and play (definitions of these terms are provided below). We start with a discussion of what the anthropology of art encompasses and some theoretical perspectives on cross-cultural art. Types of art discussed include sculpture, music, theatre, architecture, and interior design. The next section reviews findings from the field of museum studies, in which scholars are seeking appropriate ways of representing culture in a museum context. We then take a cross-cultural look at play and leisure activities. Last, we consider directions of change in expressive culture.

ART AND CULTURE

Compared to questions raised in art history classes you may have taken, you will find in this section that cultural anthropologists have a rather different view of art and how to study it. Their findings, here as in other cultural domains, stretch and subvert the Western concepts and categories and prompt us to look at art within its context. Thus anthropologists consider many products, practices, and processes to be art. They also study the artist and the artist's place in society. In addition, they ask questions about how art, and expressive culture more generally, is related to cultural variation, inequality, and power.

What Is Art?

Are ancient rock carvings art? Is subway graffiti art? An embroidered robe? A painting of a can of Campbell's soup? Philosophers, art critics, anthropologists, and art lovers have all struggled with the question of what art is. The question of how to define art involves more than mere word games. The way art is defined affects the manner in which a person values and treats artistic creations and those who create art. Anthropologists propose broad definitions of art to take into account emic definitions cross-culturally. One definition says that **art** is the application of imagination, skill, and style to matter, movement, and sound that goes beyond the purely practical (Nanda 1994:383). The anthropological study of art considers both the process and the products of such human skill, the variation in art and its preferred forms cross-culturally, and the way culture constructs and changes artistic traditions. The skill involved is recognized as such in a particular culture.

Rock paintings in Arnhemland, Australia, an important site for the Kunwinjku people. Arnhemland stretches across the northern part of the country and is the largest Aboriginal reserve in Australia.

Such culturally judged skill can be applied to any number of substances and activities and can be considered art: for example, a beautifully presented meal, a well-told story, or a perfectly formed basket. In this sense, art is a human universal, and no culture can be said to lack artistic activity.

Within the general category of art, subcategories exist, sometimes denoting certain eras such as paleolithic or modern art. Other subcategories are based on the medium of expression—for example, graphic or plastic arts (painting, drawing, sculpture, weaving, basketry, and architecture); the decorative arts (interior design, landscaping, gardens, costume design, and body adornment such as hairstyles, tattooing, and painting); performance arts (music, dance, and theatre); and verbal arts (poetry, writing, rhetoric, and telling stories and jokes). All these are Western, English-language categories.

Just as all cultures have art, all cultures have a sense of what makes something art versus non-art. The term *aesthetics* refers to agreed-upon notions of quality (R. Thompson 1971:374). Before anthropologists proved otherwise, Western art experts considered that aesthetics either did not exist or were poorly developed in non-Western cultures. We now know that aesthetic principles, or established criteria for artistic quality, exist everywhere regardless of whether they are written down and formalized. Franz Boas, from his wide review of many forms of art in pre-state societies, deduced principles that he claimed were universal for these cultures, especially symmetry, rhythmic repetition, and naturalism (Jonaitis 1995:37). These principles do apply in many cases, but they are not as universal as Boas thought.

Ethno-aesthetics considers local variations in aesthetic criteria. The set of standards concerning wood carving in West Africa illustrates the importance of considering cultural variation (R. Thompson 1971). Among the Yoruba of Nigeria, aesthetic guidelines include the following:

- Figures should be depicted midway between complete abstraction and complete realism so that they resemble "somebody," but no one in particular (portraiture in the Western sense is considered dangerous).

A carver of the Asmat culture in Northern Papua New Guinea, with a shield he carved.

Yoruba wood carving is done according to aesthetic principles that require clarity of line and form, a polished surface that creates a play of light and shadows, symmetry, and the depiction of human figures that are neither completely abstract nor completely realistic and that are shown as adults and never very young or very old.

- Humans should be depicted at their optimal physical peak, not in infancy or old age.
- There should be clarity of line and form.
- The sculpture should have the quality of luminosity achieved through a polished surface, the play of incisions, and shadows.
- The piece should exhibit symmetry.

Some anthropological studies have also documented intracultural differences in aesthetic standards. For example, one anthropologist showed computer-generated graphics to the Shipibo Indians of the Peruvian Amazon and learned that the men liked the abstract designs, whereas the women thought they were ugly (Roe in Anderson and Field 1993:257). If you are wondering why this difference would exist, consider the interpretation of the anthropologist: Shipibo men are the shamans and take hallucinogenic drugs that may give them familiarity with more "psychedelic" images.

STUDYING ART IN SOCIETY

The anthropological study of art seeks to understand not only the products of art, but also who makes it and why, its role in society, and its wider social meanings. Franz Boas was the first anthropologist to emphasize the importance of studying the artist in society. A significant thread in anthropology's theoretical history—functionalism—also dominated work of the early twentieth century on art. Anthropologists wrote about how paintings, dance, theatre, and songs serve to socialize children into the culture, provide a sense of social identity and group boundaries, and promote healing. Art may legitimize political leaders and enhance efforts in war through magical decorations on shields and weapons. Art may serve as a form of social control, as in African masks worn by dancers who represent deities visiting humans to remind them of the moral order. Art, like language, can be a catalyst for political resistance or grounds for ethnic solidarity in the face of the state.

With its breadth of topical interest, the anthropology of art relies on a range of methods in data gathering and analysis. For some research projects, participant observation provides most of the necessary data. In others, participant observation is complemented by collecting and analyzing oral or written material such as video and tape recordings. Some anthropologists have become apprentices in a certain artistic tradition. For example, in undertaking one of the earliest studies of Native American potters of the Southwest, Ruth Bunzel (1929) learned how to make pottery and thereby gained important data on what the potters thought constituted good designs. Kathy M'Closkey's (1996) experience as a weaver facilitated her research on Navajo rugs (see the Critical Thinking box).

In contrast, anthropologists who study past traditions, such as paleolithic art, cannot do participant observation or talk to the artists. They have to rely on indirect interpretation of silent symbols, shapes, colours, and contexts. Ethno-archaeology helps in this endeavour by providing clues about the past from the present. One example of this is a recent interpretation of the "Venus" figurines, the first human images from the European Upper Paleolithic period between 27 000 and 21 000 BCE (McDermott 1996). Little is known about why these palm-sized statuettes were made or who made them. Stylistically, each figurine has large breasts, abdomen, and buttocks, and small head, arms, and legs. Past interpretations of this characteristic shape have seen it as an intentional distortion to emphasize sexuality and fertility. A new theory proposes that women, especially pregnant women, sculpted these figurines as self-

Critical Thinking

NAVAJO TEXTILES: BACK TO THE REZ

THE BLANKETS and rugs woven by thousands of Navajo women living in the Southwest United States are highly desired by North American art collectors. Pre-1940 textiles typically sell for thousands of dollars at international auctions and galleries. Anthropologist/weaver Kathy M'Closkey of the University of Windsor spoke at a conference about the difficulties faced by contemporary Navajo weavers unable to receive adequate compensation for their rugs. The investment potential of historic weaving diminished the demand for contemporary textiles. However, the recent popularity of the southwest look in fashion and home furnishings created a demand for Navajo-like patterns. Entrepreneurs appropriated the designs using illustrations of historic textiles as models for copyweaving, or knockoffs, made in Mexico and other countries. Navajo patterns remain unprotected by copyright, as the designs have been part of the public domain for decades.

After hearing M'Closkey's presentation, a conference participant donated the century-old Navajo blanket pictured here to the Navajo Nation Museum and Cultural Center in Window Rock, Arizona. He found it in his mother's cedar chest, where she had carefully stored it away after purchasing it in Arizona during the 1920s. Navajo weavers were thrilled with the gift, as they seldom see the old textiles. Their ancestors had to exchange textiles for groceries at reservation trading posts in order to survive. Averaging two cents per hour in credit, Navajo women's weaving was treated as raw wool by the traders, ignoring the hours of work Navajo women put into creating the rugs.

Well-known American abstract artists collected historic Navajo textiles for more than 50 years. Several artists were greatly influenced by Navajo blanket weavers' use of colour and design. The first international touring exhibition of historic Navajo blankets (1972–1974) featured

Anthropologist/weaver Kathy M'Closkey displays a century-old Navajo blanket.

many examples from the collections of famous artists. Almost immediately the demand for the rare textiles escalated, culminating in a $522 000 sale of a historic Navajo blanket at Sotheby's in 1989. Formerly referred to as "craft," these old blankets are now revered as "art" (M'Closkey 1994). The blanket shown could have been sold as art on the auction block; instead, it went back home.

CRITICAL THINKING QUESTIONS

Since many languages lack a term that translates as "art," how can art be defined cross-culturally?

Why are textiles and weavings more likely to be exhibited in museums rather than art galleries?

---

representations. A woman who used herself as a model would have a view of her body very much like that of the figurines (McCoid and McDermott 1996).

This section presents findings in two important areas of the anthropological study of art: first, the artist, and then how art, gender, ethnicity, and power are related.

Focus on the Artist

In the early twentieth century, Boas urged his students to go beyond the study of the products of artistic endeavour and study the artists. The special role of the anthropologist is to add to the understanding of art by studying the process of creating art both within its social context and from the artist's perspective. Ruth Bunzel's (1972 [1929]) study of Pueblo potters is an example of this

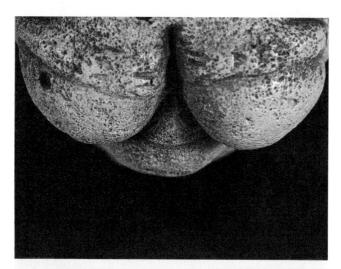

A top-down view of the "Venus" figurine, one of the first human images known. These small statues have often been interpreted as fertility goddesses on the basis of the large breasts, abdomen, and buttocks, and small head, arms, and legs. These features are said to be intentional distortions of the artist done to emphasize fertility.

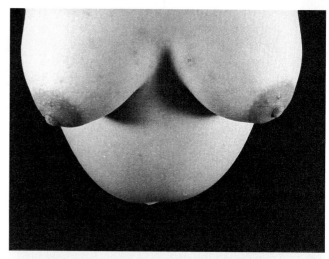

A new theory about the Venus figurines claims that they were self-portraits, crafted by women. A photograph of a pregnant woman looking down at herself presents a shape very much like that of the Venus figurines—but the shape is actual, not a distortion.

tradition. She paid attention to the variety of pot shapes and motifs employed and also interviewed individual potters about their personal design choices. One Zuni potter commented, "I always know the whole design before I start to paint" (49).

The social status of artists varies widely. Artists, individually or as groups, may be revered and wealthy, or stigmatized and economically marginal. In ancient Mexico, gold workers were a highly respected group. In First Nations groups of the Pacific Northwest Coast, male carvers and painters had to be initiated into a secret society, and they had higher status than other men. Often a gender division of artistic involvement exists. Among the Navajo, men do silversmithing, while women weave. In the Caribbean, women of African descent are noted for their carvings of calabashes (large gourds). Artists and performers often live outside the boundaries of mainstream society or challenge social boundaries.

In Morocco, a *shikha* is a female performer who sings and dances at festivities, including rites-of-passage ceremonies such as birth, circumcision, and marriage (Kapchan 1994). *Shikhat* (the plural ends with a *t*) usually appear in a group of three or four with accompanying musicians. Their performance involves suggestive songs and body movements, including reaching a state of near-possession when they loosen their hair buns. With their long hair waving, they "lift the belt," a special technique accomplished through an undulating movement that rolls the abdomen up to the waist. Their entertainment at these mixed-gender events creates a lively atmosphere as they dance, sing, and draw participants into dancing with them: "[S]hikhat dominate and dictate the emotional tenor of celebrations. Through the provocative movements and loud singing of the shikhat, the audience is drawn up and into a collective state of celebration, their bodies literally pulled into the dance" (93).

In their private lives, *shikhat* are on the social fringes, leading lives as single women who transgress limits applied to proper females. They own property, drink alcohol, smoke cigarettes, and may have several lovers. Most of the *shikhat* have been rejected by their natal families, and they live alone or in groups. Middle- and upper-class women consider them vulgar and generally distance themselves from them. Yet *shikhat* who become successful, widening their performance spheres to larger towns and cities, manage to save money and become landowners and gain economic status. Furthermore, the modern mass media is contributing to an increased status of *shikhat* as performers. Recordings of *shikha* music are popular, and the Moroccan term *mughanniyya* (singer) is being used to refer to them, implying more status. State-produced television broadcasts carry performances of regional *shikha* groups as a way of presenting the diverse cultures of the country. All of these forces are leading to a re-evaluation of the social standing of performers of this ancient art form.

As with other occupations, artists are more specialized in state-level societies. In foraging groups, some people may be singled out as especially good singers, storytellers, or carvers. Generally, however, among foragers, artistic activity is open to all, and artistic products are shared equally. With increasing social complexity and a market for art, specialized training is required to produce certain kinds of art and the products are sought after by those who can afford them. Class differences in artistic styles and preferences emerge along with the increasingly complex division of labour.

Art, Identity, and Power

Art forms and styles, like languages, are often associated with particular ethnic groups' identity and sense of pride. For example, the Berbers of highland Morocco are associated with carpets, the Navajo with woven blankets, and the Inuit with stone carving.

Cultural anthropologists provide many examples of linkages between various dimensions (ethnicity, gender, race) and power issues. In some instances, more powerful groups appropriate the art forms of less powerful groups. In others, forms of art are said to be expressive of resistance.

Gender relations are also played out in expressive culture. A study of a form of popular performance art in a Florida town, male strip dancing, shows how societal power relations between men and women are reinforced in this form of leisure activity (Margolis and Arnold 1993). Advertisements in the media tell women that seeing a male strip dancer is "their chance," "their night out." Going to a male strip show is thus presumably a time of reversal of traditional gender roles in which men are dominant and women submissive. The researchers asked whether gender roles are reversed in a male stripper bar, and their answer was no. Female customers and spectators are treated like juveniles, controlled by the manager who tells them how to tip as they stand in line waiting for the show to open, and symbolically humbled in relation to the dancers, who take on the role of lion-tamers, for example. The "dive-bomb" is further evidence that the women are not in charge. The dive-bomb is a particular form of tipping the dancer. The woman customer gets on her hands and knees and tucks a bill held between her teeth into the dancer's G-string.

However, not all forms of popular art and performance are mechanisms of social control and hierarchy maintenance. In North America, for example, urban Black youths' musical performance through rap music can be seen as a form of protest. Some hip-hop artists protest economic oppression, the danger of drugs, and men's disrespect for women through their lyrics and performances.

Performance Arts

The performance arts include music, dance, theatre, rhetoric (public speech-making) and narrative (such as storytelling). **Ethnomusicology**, an established subfield, examines musical traditions cross-culturally. Ethnomusicologists study a range of topics including the form of the music itself, the social position of musicians, how music interacts with other domains of culture, and change in musical traditions. This section provides a case study of the parallels between musical patterns and the gender division of labour in a foraging group in Malaysia. We next turn to an example of how anthropologists study theatre and, in this case, see how theatre and religion fit together.

Music and Gender: Balance among the Temiar

An important topic for ethnomusicologists is gender differences in access to performance roles in music (for readers interested in approaching this topic as a research question, see Table 14.1). For example, among the Temiar, a group of Orang Asli forager-hunters of highland Malaysia, musical traditions emphasize balance and complementarity between males and females (Roseman 1987). Kinship and marriage rules are relatively flexible and open. Temiar marriages are not arranged, but instead are based on the mutual desires of each spouse. Marriage may be either village endogamous or exogamous. Descent is bilateral, and marital residence follows no particular rule following a period of bride service. Marriages often end in separation, with the usual pattern for everyone being serial monogamy. Men, however, have a certain

TABLE 14.1 Ethnographic Questions about Gender and Music

If you were doing an ethnographic study of gender roles in musical performance, the following questions would be useful in starting the inquiry. But they would not exhaust the topic. Can you think of questions that should be added to the list?

1. Are men and women equally encouraged to use certain instruments and repertoires?
2. Is musical training available to all?
3. Do male and female repertoires overlap, where, and for what reasons?
4. Are the performances of men and women public, private, or both? Are women and men allowed to perform together? In what circumstances?
5. Do members of the culture give equal value to the performances of men and women? On what criteria are these evaluations based, and are they the same for men and women performers?

Source: From Carol E. Robertson, "Power and Gender in the Musical Experiences of Women," in *Women and Music in Cross-Cultural Perspective*, Ellen Koskoff, ed., pp. 224–225. Copyright © 1987. Reprinted by permission of Greenwood Publishing Group, Inc., Westport, CT.

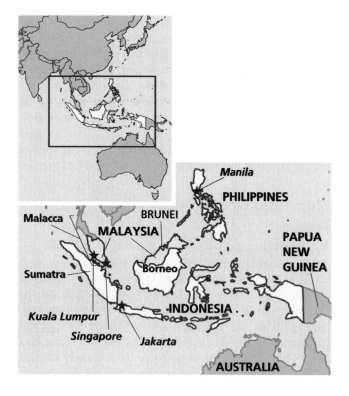

ritual dance-drama of southern India (Zarrilli 1990). Stylized hand gestures, elaborate makeup, and costumes contribute to the attraction of these dramas, which dramatize India's great Hindu epics, especially the Ramayana and the Mahabharata.

Costumes and makeup transform the actor into one of several well-known characters from Indian mythology. The audience can easily recognize the basic character types at their first entrance by "reading" the costuming and makeup. Six basic makeup types exist to depict characters, ranging from the most refined to the most vulgar, going along a continuum. Characters such as kings and heroes have green facial makeup, reflecting their high degree of refinement and moral uprightness. The most vulgar characters are associated with black facial makeup and occasionally black beards.

The teaching and performance of Hindu dance-dramas in Canadian cities offer opportunities to observe processes

Dance ethnologist Sarala Dandekar in Odissi costume represents the dancer/goddess of classical Indian dance.

edge over women in political and ritual spheres. Men dominate as headmen and as spirit mediums who sing the songs that energize the spirits (although historical records indicate that women have been spirit mediums in the past). In most performances, individual male singers are the nodes through which the songs of spirit-guides enter the community, but women's performance role is significant. For example, the delegation of gender roles as male initial singer and female chorus is sometimes varied when the female chorus itself transforms into a self-contained initiator-respondent unit. One woman sings, and the others respond chorally. Overall, the male spirit medium role is not necessarily of higher priority or status. The distinction between leader and chorus establishes "temporal" priority, but overall gender distinctions are blurred through substantial overlap between phrases and through repetition. The performance is one of intergender, community participation with integrated male and female complementary roles as in Temiar society in general.

Theatre and Myth: Ritual Dance-Drama in India and Canada

Theatre is a "form of enactment," related to other forms such as dance, music, parades, competitive games and sports, and verbal art (Beeman 1993). These forms seek to entertain through conscious forms of acting, movement, and words. One theatrical tradition that offers an exuberant blend of mythology, acting, and music is Kathakali of cultural change and adaptation. First-generation South Asian immigrants to Canada introduced Kathakali and other classical forms to immigrant and non-immigrant audiences, creating an appreciation for Indian dance-drama. Second-generation Indo-Canadian dancers recognize the need to preserve the integrity of the classical repertoire, but also use dance as a means of personal expression and seek opportunities for collaborative multicultural dance exchanges. "The Rebel Goddess," an experimental work performed in Toronto in 1999, draws attention to the crisis of the creative spirit of the dancer trapped within the elaborate rules of the classical Indian dance.

Architecture and Decorative Arts

Like other forms of art, architecture is interwoven with other aspects of culture. Architecture may reflect and protect social rank and class differences as well as gender, age, and ethnic differences (Guidoni 1987). Decorative arts—including interior decoration of homes and buildings, and external design features such as gardens—reflect people's social position and also stand as statements of their status and "taste." Local cultures have long defined preferred standards in these areas of expression, but global influences from the West as well as from Japan and, increasingly, non-Western cultures, have been adopted and adapted by other traditions.

Architecture and Interior Decoration

Foragers, being nomadic, build dwellings as needed, and then abandon them. Owning little and having few surpluses means that permanent storage structures are not needed. The construction of dwellings does not require the efforts of groups larger than the family unit. Foragers' dwellings are an image of the family and not of the wider society. The dwellings' positioning in relation to each other reflects the relations between families. More elaborate shelters and greater social cohesiveness in planning occur as foraging is combined with horticulture, as in the semi-permanent settlements in the Amazon rainforest. People live in the settlement for part of the year, but break up into smaller groups that spread out into a larger area for foraging. Important decisions concern location of the site in terms of weather, availability of drinking water, and defensibility. The central plaza must be elevated for drainage, and drainage channels must be dug around the hearths. The overall plan is circular. In some groups, separate shelters are built for extended family groups; in others, they are joined into a continuous circle with connected roofs. In some cases, the headman has a separate and larger shelter.

Pastoralists have designed ingenious portable structures such as the teepee and yurt. The teepee is a conical tent

Yurts in Pamir, Afghanistan. The yurt form of domestic architecture is widespread across Asia among pastoralists.

made with a framework of four wooden poles tied at the top with thongs, to which are joined other poles to complete the cone; this frame is then covered with buffalo hide. A yurt is also a circular, portable dwelling, but its roof is flatter than that of a teepee. The covering is made of cloth. This extremely lightweight structure is easy to set up, take down, and transport, and is highly adaptable to all weather conditions. Encampments often involved the arrangement of the teepees or yurts in several concentric circles, with social status as the structuring principle, placing the council of chiefs and the head chief in the centre.

In settled agricultural communities where permanent housing is the norm, decoration is more likely to be found in homes. Wall paintings, sculptures, and other features may distinguish the homes of more wealthy individuals. The great wooden houses with their painted facades and carved totem poles made by First Nations communities on the Northwest Coast of North America reflected the stability of their resource base and the high value placed on displaying rank. With the development of the state, around 4000 BCE, urban areas grew larger and showed the effects of centralized planning and power (for example, in grid-style street planning rather than haphazard street placement). The symbolic demonstration of the power, grandeur, and identity of states was—and still is—expressed architecturally through the construction of

Worldwide, Hilton hotels look much like each other and do not reflect local cultural architectural styles.

impressive monuments: temples, administrative buildings, memorials, and museums.

Universities also exhibit their own unique use of space, from the ivy-covered walls of Canada's oldest universities to the modern suburban high-rise campuses. York University's Anthropology Department is housed in Vari Hall, a new building whose open rotunda space has become a focal point for a university lacking ivy-covered walls and a central quadrangle. The space has been used for university ceremonies and has become a symbol of the university. However, the round, light, three-storey space is also used by students for studying, sleeping, talking, cuddling, and watching others from the higher floors. It has become a contested space as it has also been appropriated for student and faculty protests (Rodman, Hawkins, and Teramura 1998).

Studying the way people design and decorate the interior of buildings and homes links cultural anthropologists with people working in other professions and disciplines, including interior design, advertising, and consumer studies. One study of interior decoration in Japan used as data the contents of home decorating magazines and observations within homes to see what decorative choices people made (Rosenberger 1992). A recurrent thread was the way certain aspects of Western decorating styles were incorporated and localized (given a particularly Japanese flavour). Home decorating magazines target middle- and upper-class housewives who seek to identify their status through new consumption styles. A general trend was the abandonment of three key features of traditional Japanese design: *tatami*, *shoji*, and *fusuma*. *Tatami* are 5-cm-thick mats, about 1 metre by 2 metres. *Shoji* are the sliding screen doors of *tatami* rooms, one covered with glass and the other with translucent rice paper often printed with a design of leaves or waves. *Fusuma* are sliding wall panels made of thick paper; they are removable so that rooms can be enlarged for gatherings. The *tatami* room usually contains a low table with pillows for seating on the floor. A special alcove may contain a flower arrangement, ancestors' pictures, and a Buddhist altar. Futons are stored in closets around the edges and brought out at night for sleeping.

In seeking to distance themselves from the old style, the Japanese have made several changes, including giving the kitchen a more central location and displaying objects such as furniture, VCRs, and stereos. According to Rosenberger, these changing surfaces accompany deeper social changes involving new aspirations about marriage and family relationships. The home decorating magazines promote the idea that the new style brings with it happier children with better grades, and closer husband–wife ties. Tensions exist, however, between these ideals and the realities of middle- and upper-class life in Japan. Women feel compelled to work either part time or full time to be able to contribute to satisfying their new consumer needs. Simultaneously, Japanese women are discouraged from pursuing careers and are urged to devote more time to domestic pursuits, including home decorating and child care, in order to provide the kind of life portrayed in the magazines. Furthermore, the Western-style happy nuclear family image contains no plan for the aged. The wealthiest Japanese families manage to satisfy both individualistic desires and filial duties because they can afford a large house in which they dedicate a separate floor for the husband's parents, complete with traditional *tatami* mats. Less wealthy people have a more difficult time dealing with this complex and conflicting set of values.

Gardens and Flowers

Gardens for use, especially for food production, can be differentiated from gardens dedicated to decoration and beauty. Not all cultures have developed the concept of the decorative garden. Inuit peoples cannot construct gardens in the snow. Purely nomadic peoples have no gardens since they are on the move. The decorative garden seems to be a product of state-level societies, especially

Women practising the art of flower arrangement in Japan.

in the Middle East, Europe, and Asia (Goody 1993). Variation exists in what is considered to be the appropriate contents, design, and purpose of a garden. A Japanese garden may contain no blooming flowers, focusing instead on the shape and placement of trees, shrubs, stones, and bodies of water (Moynihan 1979). Elite Muslim culture, with its core in the Middle East, has long been associated with formal decorative gardens. A garden, enclosed with four walls, is symbolically equivalent to the concept of "paradise." The Islamic garden pattern involves a square design with symmetrical layout, fountains, waterways, and straight pathways, all enclosed within walls through which symmetrically placed entrances allow access. Islamic gardens were often used to surround the tombs of prominent people, with the usual plan placing the tomb in the centre of the garden. India's Taj Mahal, built by Muslim Emperor Shah Jahan, follows this pattern, with one modification in the landscaping: The tomb was placed at one edge of the garden rather than in the centre. The result is a dramatic stretch of fountains and flowers leading up to the monument from the main gate.

The contents of a garden, like a fancy dinner menu with all its special ingredients or a personal collection of souvenirs from around the world with all their memories and meanings, makes a statement about its owner's identity and status. For example, in Europe during the heyday of colonialism, imperial gardens contained specimens from remote corners of the globe, collected through scientific expeditions. Such gardens are created through the intentional collection and placement of otherwise diverse plants in one place, creating a *heterotopia,* or the pulling together of different "places" into one (Foucault 1970). These gardens expressed the owner's worldliness and intellectual status.

Cut flowers are now important economic products, as they provide income for gardeners throughout the world. They are also exchange items. In France, women receive flowers from men more than any other kind of gift (Goody 1993:316). In much of the world, "special occasions" require gifts of flowers. In the West, as well as in East Asia, funerals are times for special displays of flowers. Ritual offerings to the deities in Hinduism may be single flowers or flowers such as marigolds woven into a chain or necklace. Individual flowers also acquire local meanings, as in Canada, where poppies are associated with Remembrance Day (commemorating the world wars), and daffodils with the Canadian Cancer Society. Flowers are often important as motifs in Western and Asian secular and sacred art, although less so in African art. In his comparative study of the use of flowers in ritual and art, Jack Goody (1993) tried to understand the relative absence of flowers in the religion and graphic arts of Africa (except for Islamicized cultures of Africa where flowers are prominent). Some possible answers include ecological and economic factors. Eurasia possesses a greater variety of blooming plants than Africa. African gardens produce food, not flowers. In many African kingdoms, luxury goods included fabrics of various design, gold ornaments, and wooden carvings rather than flowers.

Museums and Culture

In this section we consider the concept of the museum and the debates about the role of museums in exhibiting and representing culture. Museum anthropology developed in the 1980s, and includes both anthropologists who work in museums helping to prepare exhibits and anthropologists who study museums—what they choose to display and how they display it—as important sites of culture itself (M. Ames 1992; A. Jones 1993; Stocking 1985).

What Is a Museum?

A museum is an institution that collects, preserves, interprets, and displays objects on a regular basis (Kahn 1995:324). Its purpose may be aesthetic or educational. Museums have played and continue to play a key role in Canadian anthropology. The term comes originally from a Greek word referring to a place for the muses to congregate, where one would have philosophical discussions or see artistic performances. In Europe, the concept of the museum developed into a place where art objects were housed and displayed. Ethnographic and science museums came later, inspired by Europe's emerging interests in exploration in the 1500s and the accompanying scientific urge to gather specimens from around the world and classify them into an evolutionary history.

Multiple Cultural Worlds

EXHIBITING RACISM

"INTO THE HEART" of Africa" was the Royal Ontario Museum's (ROM) most controversial exhibit. From November 1989 until its premature closing in August 1990, the temporary exhibition displayed photographs and objects such as masks, jewellery, and sculptures collected between 1870 and 1925 by Canadian missionaries to Africa, soldiers serving in the British Army, and explorers. These artifacts were not presented to the public as a traditional museum exhibit. Canadian anthropologist Jeanne Cannizzo designed the exhibit to encourage audiences to actively engage with and interpret the displays rather than passively observe them. As an example of reflexive museology, viewers were expected to critique British colonial ideology and the complicity of Canadians in sustaining it. For example, Cannizzo highlighted racist colonial language by using such phrases as the "unknown continent" and "barbarous customs" in the explanatory panels of the exhibits. She placed these terms in quotation marks to encourage viewers to challenge and critique their use.

Unfortunately, many visitors to the ROM did not recognize the reflexive and ironic nature of the exhibits. Instead, they thought the exhibit glorified imperialism and was racist in its portrayal of Africans. In March 1990, a group called the Coalition for the Truth about Africa (CFTA) began weekly protests outside the ROM. The CFTA and others challenged the authority of the ROM to represent Africa, and criticized the ROM's failure to consult Black community members about the exhibit.

While the media portrayed the controversy as a conflict between the ROM and the CFTA, Shelley Butler's ethnographic analysis of the exhibit (1999) reveals the many differing views and understandings of both the exhibit and the controversy. The ROM was accused by the CFTA of being elitist and representing the interests of only a small portion of Toronto's population. Nevertheless, the exhibit provided a forum for highlighting contemporary issues of racism in Canada and the authority of the museum to represent the "truth" about other peoples, cultures, and objects (Butler 1999).

FOOD FOR THOUGHT

Is an "ironic stance" appropriate for exhibits in a public institution? Where would an "ironic stance" be acceptable and even expected?

The concept of the museum and its several forms has now diffused to most parts of the world. Contemporary versions include children's museums, heritage parks, and local museums. The Saputik ("The Weir") Museum in Puvirnituq, Quebec, is an example of a community museum created by an Inuit elder. Aptly named, "The Weir" is a place to catch and hold personal objects before they pass out to sea to be lost forever (Graburn 1998). The Canadian Museum of Civilization and many other museums have shifted from an exclusively object-oriented approach to one that stresses cultural performances and interactive media experiences using new information and communication technologies (McDonald and Alsford 1989).

The Politics of Exhibits

Museum anthropologists are now at the forefront of serious debates about who gets to represent whom, the ownership of particular objects, and the public service role of museums versus their possible elitism. The political aspects of museums have always existed, but now they are part of explicit discussion (see the Multiple Cultural Worlds box). A major area of debate is whether objects from non-Western cultures should be exhibited, like Western art objects, with little or no ethnographic context (Clifford 1988; Watson 1997). Most anthropologists would support the need for context, not just for non-Western objects but for all objects on display. But the important point that all forms of expressive culture are context-bound and can be better understood and appreciated within their social context is unfortunately a rare view among Western art historians and critics (Best 1986). For example, the museum label of Andy Warhol's hyperrealistic painting of a can of Campbell's soup should include information on the social context in which such art was produced and some background on the artist.

Debates also exist about who should have control of objects in museums that may have been claimed through colonial and neocolonial domination. The issue of **repatriation**, or returning objects to their original homes, is a matter of international and national concern. The complexity of this process can be seen in the repatriation of objects confiscated by the Canadian government in 1922 following a large "illegal" potlatch held in Alert Bay,

British Columbia. The local Indian Agent alerted the RCMP about the potlatch, and authorities confiscated over 450 ritual items such as coppers, masks, rattles, head-dresses, blankets, and boxes, paying their owners a small price for them. The regalia ended up in major Canadian and American museums. The Canadian Museum of Civilization and the Royal Ontario Museum (ROM) agreed to return their collections not to individual families, but to two local museums that would be built to preserve and display the items. The Kwagiulth Museum and Cultural Centre on Quadra Island (opened in 1979) and the U'mista Cultural Centre in Alert Bay, Cormorant Island (opened in 1980), stress the family ownership of the items, and the local histories of the objects. The U'mista Cultural Centre displays large white cards with texts and quotations about the confiscation of the regalia that has been repatriated. In contrast, the University of British Columbia Museum of Anthropology provides brief labels with a small drawing of the object in its original setting (Clifford 1997; D. Cole 1985).

In 1999, museum officials returned four intricate wampum belts more than 500 years old to an assembly of Iroquois chiefs at a ceremony at the Six Nations Grand River Territory near Brantford, Ontario. They had been stored in the ROM since 1922, when they had been given to the museum by a Mohawk woman for safekeeping. The belts were repatriated after the Six Nations reserve approached the museum to return the wampum records. They received similar ones from other museums around North America. Wampum served as a record of laws, treaties, and promises, and it helps the Iroquois remember their oral history. One member of the reserve commented, "The last person we had who could recite the entire Great Law passed away . . . Getting the wampum back may help stop the erosion" (*Toronto Star*, November 12, 1999).

In the United States and Canada, many Aboriginal groups are lobbying successfully for the return of ancestral bones, grave goods, and potlatch goods. In 1990, the United States passed the Native American Graves Protection and Repatriation Act (NAGRPA), opting for legislation requiring inventories of archaeological and ethnographic holdings. Tensions between museums and First Nations peoples in Canada came to a head over "The Spirit Sings" exhibit developed by the Glenbow Museum to celebrate the 1988 Calgary Winter Olympics. The Lubicon Cree of northern Alberta called for an international boycott of the exhibit because they were engaged in a land claim dispute with the provincial and federal governments. The exhibit was sponsored by Shell Oil, the company drilling on the land they claimed. The confrontation resulted in the formation of a Task Force on Museums and First Peoples in 1989, under the joint sponsorship of the Assembly of First Nations and the Canadian Museums Association. The task force, which included Native and non-Native members, opted to develop a cooperative model of equal partnerships guided by moral, ethical, and professional responsibilities, rather than by legislation such as NAGRPA. The task force developed principles to serve as a basis for recommendations, including acknowledging that both museums and First Nations peoples share a mutual interest in the cultures and histories of Aboriginal peoples; that museums should recognize the authority of First Nations peoples to speak for themselves and that First Nations peoples should recognize the professional knowledge of museum academics; and that both should work together as equal partners to meet their differing needs and interests (Nicks 1992).

Other parts of the world face different repatriation problems. The breakup of the Soviet Union prompted claims from several independent states that wish to retrieve artistic property that originated in their locale but was taken to Soviet national museums in Moscow and St. Petersburg. For example, Central Asian republics lost medieval carpets to Moscow and St. Petersburg museums; there are Georgian arms in the Armory of the Moscow Kremlin; and Ukrainians seek the return of objects of historical interest, such as the ceremonial staff of their national hero, the *hetman* (headman) Mazepa, who fought for Ukrainian independence against Peter the Great (Akinsha 1992a). In all, Ukraine is demanding the return of about two million art objects that originated in Ukrainian territory and are currently housed in Russian museums (Akinsha 1992b). Many of these objects are the pride of Russian museums, such as the Hermitage in St. Petersburg, which now faces the loss of many key objects.

Another dimension of dispute about art in Russia concerns the state and the church. The Soviet state put many icons and other religious objects in museums and turned churches into museums. Now the Russian Orthodox Church is campaigning for the return of church property. Churches are demanding that "all sacred objects of the church, all church buildings, and masterpieces of church art that were confiscated by the state after 1917 must be returned without exception to the ownership of the Russian Orthodox Church" (Akinsha 1992a:102). Art historians and museum officials protest that the churches have neither the resources nor the experience to care for these treasures. On the other hand, there are threats of theft and violence from those who wish to return the icons to churches and monasteries. In response, some museums have removed certain pieces from display. Furthermore, a number of museums have posted on their websites artworks whose ownership prior to and during World War II cannot be certified, in the hopes of returning artwork stolen from the Jewish people by the Nazis.

PLAY, LEISURE, AND CULTURE

This section turns to another area of expressive culture: what people do "for fun." It is, however, impossible to draw clear lines between the concepts of play, leisure, art, and performance since they often overlap. For example, a person could paint watercolours in her leisure time, yet simultaneously be creating a work of art. In most cases, though, play and leisure can be distinguished from other activities by the fact that they have no direct, utilitarian purpose for the participant.

In the 1930s, Dutch historian Johan Huizinga offered some features of play: It is unnecessary and thus free action, it is outside of ordinary life, it is closed and limited in terms of time, it has rules for its execution, and it contains an element of tension and chance (as summarized in Hutter 1996).

Leisure activities often overlap with play, but many leisure activities, such as reading or lying on a beach, would not be considered play because they lack rules, tension, and change. Often, the same activity, depending on the context, could be considered work instead of play. For example, gardening as a hobby would be classified as a leisure activity, even though weeding, pruning, and watering are the same activities that could be considered work for someone else. Playing a game with a child might be considered recreational, but if one has been hired as the child's babysitter, then it is work. Professional sports is an area where the line between play and work breaks down completely since the "players" are paid to "play." Further, while play and leisure may be pursued from a non-utilitarian perspective, they are often surrounded by a wider context of commercial and political interests. For example, non-professional athletes competing in the Olympic Games are part of a wider set of powerful interests, from advertisers to host cities to athletic equipment companies.

Within the broad category of play and leisure activities, several subcategories exist, including varieties of games, hobbies, and recreational travel. Cultural anthropologists study play and leisure within their cultural contexts and as part of social systems. They ask, for example, why some activities involve teams rather than individuals; what are the social roles and status of people involved in particular activities; what are the "goals" of the activities and how are they achieved; how much danger or violence is involved in the activities; how are certain activities related to group identity; and how do such activities link or separate different groups within or between societies or nations.

Games and Sports

Games and sports, like religious rituals and festivals, can be interpreted as reflections of broader social relationships and cultural ideals. In Clifford Geertz's terms (1966), they are both "models of" a culture, depicting in miniature, key ideals, and "models for" a culture, through socializing people into certain values and ideals. American football can be seen as a model for corporate culture in that it relies on a clear hierarchy with leadership vested in one key person (the quarterback), and the major goal is to expand territorially by taking over areas from the competition. Canadian football carries less mythic value as a symbol of national identity, as it is more of a historical compromise between British rugby and American football. In spite of the importance of the Grey Cup, it is hockey that inspires a shared national identity.

Hockey in Canada, both casual street hockey and professional sport spectacle, has deeply rooted meanings linked to images of national character and identity (Gruneau and Whitson 1993). Hockey is part of the collective memory of many English and French Canadian men who grew up in towns with community hockey leagues. The organized, rule-governed professional game emerged in Montreal in the 1870s, as an event with spectators. In 1892, Canada's Governor General Lord Stanley donated a trophy cup to recognize the Dominion's best hockey team. By 1917, the National Hockey League (NHL) had added American franchises, as Canada's national winter pastime became a continental business, fuelling fears that the NHL would no longer be Canadian, and that it would be taken over by American business interests. By the 1930s, radio broadcasts of *Hockey Night in Canada* could be heard across the country and became a national symbol in spite of American money, influence, and teams in the NHL. Later, television provided the same unifying national entertainment.

Hockey continues to be part of a collective representation of what it means to be Canadian—a representation that ignores differences of race, ethnicity, class, and gender in participation, as if hockey emerged as a natural adaptation to ice and cold winters. Yet the game has deep roots in both rural and urban communities. Games between the Toronto Maple Leafs and the Montreal Canadiens dramatized the rivalry between the two solitudes, much as other NHL games bring out fears of selling out to American interests and losing a piece of distinctive national culture. Canada's 1972 win over the Soviet hockey team is still celebrated as a reflection of national identity and national character (Gruneau and Whitson 1993).

Sports and Spirituality: Male Wrestling in India

In many non-Western settings, sports are closely tied with aspects of religion and spirituality. Asian martial arts, for example, require forms of concentration much like meditation, leading to spiritual self-control. Male wrestling in India, a popular form of entertainment at rural fairs and other public events, also involves a strong link with spiritual development and asceticism (Alter 1992). A wrestler's daily routine is one of self-discipline. Every act—defecation, bathing, comportment, devotion—is integrated into a daily regimen of discipline. Wrestlers come to the *akhara* (equivalent to a gymnasium) early in the morning for practice under the supervision of a guru or other senior *akhara* member. They practise moves with different partners for two to three hours. In the early evening, they return for more exercise, which consists of two primary exercises. In all, a strong young wrestler will do around 2000 pushups and 1000 deep knee bends a day in sets of 50 to 100.

The wrestler's diet is prescribed by the wrestling way of life. Wrestlers are mainly vegetarian and avoid alcohol and tobacco, although they do consume *bhang*, a beverage made of blended milk, spices, almonds, and concentrated marijuana. In addition to regular meals, wrestlers consume large quantities of milk, *ghee* (clarified butter), and almonds. These substances are considered sources of strength as they help to build up the body's semen, according to traditional dietary principles.

Several features about the wrestler's life are similar to those of a Hindu *sannyasi*, or holy man who renounces

Wrestlers in the village of Sonepur, India. These wrestlers follow a rigorous regimen of dietary restrictions and exercise in order to keep their bodies and minds under control. Like Hindu ascetics, they seek to build up and maintain their inner strength through such practices.

life in the normal world. The aspiring *sannyasi* studies under a guru and learns to follow a strict routine of discipline and meditation called *yoga*, and has a restricted diet to achieve control of the body and its life force. Both wrestler and *sannyasi* as chosen life roles focus on discipline as a way of achieving a controlled self. Indian wrestling does not involve the stereotype of the "dull-witted sportsman" as it sometimes does in North America; rather, the image is of perfected physical and moral health.

Play, Pleasure, and Pain

Many leisure activities combine pleasure and pain because they may involve physical discomfort. Serious injuries may result from mountain climbing, horseback riding, or playing touch football in the backyard. Hockey, both recreational and professional, has increasingly incorporated violence in what is undeniably a forceful, physical game. A more intentionally dangerous category of sports is **blood sports**, competition that explicitly seeks to bring about a flow of blood or even death, either between human contestants or with animal competitors, or in animal targets of human hunting (Donlon 1990). In North America and Europe, professional boxing is an example of a highly popular blood sport that has not been analyzed yet by anthropologists. Cultural anthropologists have looked more at the use of animals in blood sports such as cockfights and bullfights. Interpretations of these sports range from seeing them as forms of sadistic pleasure or vicarious self-validation (usually of males) through the triumph of their representative pit bull or fighting cock, or as the triumph of culture over nature in the symbolism of bullfighting.

Even the seemingly pleasurable experience of a Turkish-style bath can involve discomfort and pain. One phase involves scrubbing the skin roughly several times with a rough natural sponge, a pumice stone, or a piece of cork wood wrapped in cloth (Staats 1994). The scrubbing removes layers of dead skin and "opens the pores" so that the skin will be beautiful. In Turkey, an option for men is a massage that can be quite violent, involving deep probes of leg muscles, cracking of the back, and being walked on by the (often hefty) masseur. In Ukraine, being struck repeatedly on one's bare skin with birch branches is the final stage of the bath. However, violent scrubbing, scraping, and even beating of the skin, combined with radical temperature changes in the water, are combined with valued social experiences at the bathhouse.

Leisure Travel

Anthropologists who study leisure travel, or tourism, have often commented that their work is taken less seriously than it should be because of the perspective that they are just "hanging out" at the beach or at five-star hotels. Anthropological research on tourism and its impact is an important subject. Tourism is now one of the major economic forces in the world; it is growing, and it has dramatic effects on people and places in tourist destination areas. Expenditure of money, time, and effort for nonessential travel is nothing new. In the past, pilgrimage to religious sites has been a major preoccupation of many people (see Chapter 12). A large percentage of worldwide tourism involves individuals from the industrialized nations of Europe, North America, and Japan travelling to the less industrialized nations. Ethnic tourism, cultural tourism, and off-the-beaten-path tourism are attracting increasing numbers of travellers. Julia Harrison (2003) has interviewed Canadian tourists to learn more about how they interpret their experiences of travel.

These new kinds of tourism are often marketed as providing a view of "authentic" cultures. Images of indigenous people as the "Other" figure prominently in travel brochures and advertisements. Tourist promotional literature often presents a "myth" of other peoples and places (Silver 1993:304) and offers travel as a form of escape to a mythical land of wonder. The travel industry promotes images that are likely to be verified during travel—people want to see what the brochures show. For example, tourist promotional literature presents the Kenyan safari as a particular kind of imaginative representation of the wild (Little 1991). In fact, research on Western travel literature shows that, from the time of the earliest explorers to the present, it has been full of "primitivist" images about indigenous peoples (Pratt 1992). They are portrayed as having static or "stone age" traditions and remaining largely unchanged by the forces of Western colonialism, nationalism, economic development, and tourism itself (Bruner 1991). Tourists often seek the culture that the tourist industry defines rather than gaining a genuine, more complicated, and perhaps less photogenic version of the culture (K. Adams 1984). For the traveller, obtaining these desired cultural images through mass tourism involves packaging the "primitive" with the "modern" because most tourists want comfort and convenience along with their "authentic experience." Thus, advertisements may minimize the foreignness of the host country, noting, for example, that English is spoken and that the destination is remote yet accessible. Primitivist imagery attracts tourists, while a dash of similarity offers enough of the comforts of home to make it all acceptable. For example, "The Melanesian Discoverer" is a ship that cruises the Sepik River in Papua New Guinea, providing a way for affluent tourists to see the "primitive" while travelling in luxury.

So far, the anthropology of tourism has focused most of its attention on the impact of global and local tourism on indigenous peoples and places. Such impact studies are important in exposing the degree to which tourism helps or harms local people. For example, the formation of Amboseli National Park in Kenya affected the access of the Maasai to strategic water resources for their herds (Honadle 1985, as summarized in Drake 1991). The project staff promised certain benefits to the Maasai if they stayed off the reserve, but many of those benefits (including shares of the revenues from the park) never materialized. In contrast, local people in Costa Rica were included in the early planning stages of the Guanacaste National Park and have played a greater role in the park management system there.

Other studies, discussed in the following section of this chapter, document how local residents are exercising agency and playing an active role in transforming the effects of tourism to their advantage, as well as localizing outside influences to make them relevant to local conditions and frameworks of meaning.

CHANGE IN EXPRESSIVE CULTURE

Nowhere are forms and patterns of art, play, and leisure frozen in time. Change is universal, and much change is influenced by Western culture through globalization. However, influence does not occur in only one direction. African musical styles have transformed the American musical scene since the days of slavery. Japan has provided a strong influence on upper-class garden styles in North America. Cultures in which tradition and conformity have been valued in pottery-making, dress, or theatre may find themselves having to make choices about whether to innovate, and if so, how. Many contemporary artists (including musicians and playwrights) from Latin America to China are fusing ancient and "traditional" motifs and styles with more contemporary themes and messages.

Western interest in indigenous arts as "art" is quite recent, since their aesthetic value was not widely recognized until the early twentieth century. Before that, the typical Western reaction to non-Western art was often one of either horror or curiosity (Mitter 1977). Graburn (1993) has analyzed the range of indigenous art in Canada and found a range from traditional activities and products made for internal consumption to those made for external markets.

Given current global exchanges and influences in art and play (especially organized sports), it is not surprising that leisure activities and artistic products and processes have changed to reflect new ideas and tastes as a result of past and present transnational processes.

Classical dancers perform in Thailand. The intricate hand motions, with their impact augmented by the wearing of metal finger extenders, have meanings that accompany the narrative being acted out. International tourism is a major support for such performance arts in Thailand.

Colonialism and Syncretism

Western colonialists had dramatic effects on the expressive culture of indigenous peoples with whom they came into contact. In some instances, colonial disapproval of particular art forms and activities resulted in their extinction. For example, when colonialists banned headhunting in various cultures, this change also meant that body decoration, weapon decoration, and other related expressive activities were abandoned. This section provides an in-depth example of how colonial repression of indigenous forms succeeded only temporarily.

Western colonialist powers often acted directly to change certain indigenous art and leisure practices. In the Trobriand Islands, now part of Papua New Guinea, British administrators and missionaries sought to eradicate the frequent tribal warfare as part of its pacification process. One strategy was to replace it with intertribal competitive sports (Leach 1975). In 1903, Reverend Gilmore, a British missionary, introduced the British game of cricket in the Trobriands as a way of promoting a new morality, separate from the former warring traditions. As played in England, cricket involves particular rules of play and a very "proper" look of pure-white uniforms. In the early stages of the adoption of cricket in the Trobriands, the game followed the British pattern closely. As time passed and the game spread into more regions, it became increasingly localized. Most importantly, it was merged into indigenous political competition between big-men. Big-men leaders would urge their followers to increase production in anticipation of a cricket match since the matches were followed by a redistributive feast. The British missionaries had discouraged traditional magic in favour of Christianity, but the Trobriand Islanders transferred war-related magic into cricket. For example, spells are used to help one's team win, and the bats are ritually treated in the way that war weapons were. Weather magic is also important. If things are not going well for one's team, a spell to bring rain and force cancellation of the game may be invoked.

In Bermuda, as elsewhere in the West Indies, cricket is "played with elegant skill, studied with scholarly intensity, argued with passionate conviction, and revered with patriotic pride" (F. Manning 1981:617). Participation in cricket festivals is marked by indulgence and festive sociability. These are cultural performances where Blacks dress in "whites" to play a White game they have transformed into a celebration of Black culture. But in Bermuda, where economic power is very much in White hands, the cricket games and related festivals reveal tensions between celebrations of Black culture and economic dependency.

Tourism's Complex Effects

Global tourism has had varied effects on indigenous arts. Often, tourist demand for ethnic arts and souvenirs has led to mass production of sculpture or weaving or jewellery of a lesser quality than was created before the demand. Tourists' preferences for certain colours have sometimes had an effect on an indigenous art form. For example, red and green are prominent combinations in the textiles of India, but for too many European and North American consumers, these colours signify "Christmas." Also, tourists' interests in seeing an abbreviated form of a traditionally long dance or theatre performance has led to the presentation of "cuts" rather than an entire piece. Some scholars suggest, therefore, that tourism leads to the decline and transformation of indigenous arts in a negative sense. While evidence exists to support this position, evidence exists to support an alternative argument, too.

Often, tourist support for indigenous arts is the sole force maintaining them, since local people in a particular culture may be more interested in foreign music, art, or sports themselves. Vietnamese water puppetry is an ancient performance mode, dating back at least to the Ly Dynasty of 1121 CE (Contreras 1995). Traditionally, water puppet shows took place in the spring during a lull in the farm work, or at special festival times. Now, water puppet

A water puppet performance in Hanoi, Vietnam. Water puppet shows are far more popular among international tourists than among the Vietnamese.

shows are performed mainly for foreign tourists in large cities. Vietnamese people tend to prefer imported videos (Brownmiller 1994).

One positive side effect of global tourism is the growing support for preservation of material cultural heritage, sometimes referred to as simply "cultural heritage," which includes entire sites (for example, an ancient city), monuments (buildings as well as monumental sculpture, painting, and cave temples), and movable objects considered of outstanding value in terms of history, art, and science (Cernea 2001). UNESCO proposed the basic definition of material cultural heritage in 1972. Since then, many locations worldwide have been placed on its World Heritage List for preservation. In the Middle East and North Africa alone, 60 places are on UNESCO's list. Many invaluable sites and other aspects of material cultural heritage are lost to public knowledge through destructive engineering projects, war, looting, and private collecting. Applied anthropologists are involved in promoting better stewardship of material cultural heritage. Some are motivated by a desire to preserve the record of humanity for future generations, or for science. Others see that material cultural heritage, especially in poorer countries, can serve to promote improvements in human welfare, and they endorse forging a link between material cultural heritage and development (see the Lessons Applied box).

The preservation of indigenous forms of expressive culture can also occur as a form of resistance to outside development forces. One example of this phenomenon is the resurgence of the hula, or Hawaiian dance (Stillman 1996). Beginning in the early 1970s, the "Hawaiian Renaissance" grew out of political protest. Hawaiian youth began speaking out against encroaching development from the outside that was displacing the indigenous people from their land and their resources. They promoted a concerted effort to revive the Hawaiian language, the hula, and canoe paddling, among other things. Since then, hula schools have proliferated, and hula competitions among the islands are widely attended. The 1990s saw the inauguration of the International Hula Festival in Honolulu, which attracts competitors from around the world. The hula competitions have helped ensure the continued survival of this ancient art form, although some Hawaiians have voiced concerns. First, they feel that allowing non-Hawaiians to compete is compromising the quality of the dancing. Second, the format of the competition violates traditional rules of style and presentation, which require more time than is allowed, so important dances have to be cut.

Post-Communist Transitions

Major changes are occurring in the arts in the post-communist states for two reasons: loss of state financial support and removal of state controls over subject matter and creativity. "A new generation of talented young artists has appeared. Many are looking for something new and different—art without ideology" (Akinsha 1992c:109). Art for art's sake—art as independent from the socialist project—is now possible. A circle of artists called the Moscow Conceptualists has been the dominant "underground" (nonofficial) school of art. These artists focused on political subject matter and poverty. In contrast, the new underground finds its inspiration in nostalgia for the popular culture of the 1950s and 1960s, a pack of Yugoslav chewing gum, or the cover of a Western art magazine. Commercial galleries are springing up, and a museum of modern art in Moscow may become a reality in the near future.

Theatre in China is passing through a difficult transition period with the recent development of some features of capitalism. Since the beginning of the People's Republic in 1949, the arts have gone through different phases, from being suppressed as part of the old feudal tradition to being revived under state control. In the mid-1990s, nearly all of China's theatre companies were in financial crisis (Jiang 1994:72). Steep inflation has meant that actors can no longer live on their pay. Theatre companies are urging their workers to find jobs elsewhere, such as making movies or videos, but this is not an option for provincial troupes. Traditional theatre troupes are surviving by going on tours. Foreign tourist audiences are one source of support for traditional theatre. Another factor is that audience preferences have changed: "People are fed up with shows that 'educate,' have too strong a political flavor, or convey 'artistic values.' They no longer seem to enjoy love

Lessons Applied

A STRATEGY FOR THE WORLD BANK ON CULTURAL HERITAGE

THE WORLD Bank, with headquarters in Washington, D.C., and offices throughout the world, is an international organization funded by member nations that works to promote and finance economic development in poor countries. Even though most of its permanent professional staff are economists, the Bank has begun to pay more attention to non-economic factors that affect development projects. One of the major moves in that direction occurred in 1972 when the Bank hired its first anthropologist, Michael Cernea. For three decades, Cernea has drawn attention to the cultural dimensions of development, especially in terms of the importance of local participation in development projects and people-centred approaches to project-forced resettlement (when, for example, large dams are being planned). His most recent campaign is to convince top officials at the World Bank that the Bank should become involved in supporting cultural heritage projects as potential pathways to development.

The World Bank already has in place a "do no harm" rule when it approves and financially supports construction projects. Cernea agrees that a "do no harm" rule is basic to preventing outright destruction, but it is a passive rule and does nothing to provide resources to pre-

serve sites. He wants the Bank to move beyond its "do no harm" rule. He has written for the World Bank a strategy that is active, not passive. The strategy has two major objectives: (1) The World Bank should support cultural heritage projects that promote poverty reduction and cultural heritage preservation by creating employment and generating capital from tourism. (2) These projects should emphasize the educational value to both local people and international visitors on the grounds that cultural understanding has value for good will and relations at all levels—local, national, and international.

Cernea also offers two suggestions for better management of cultural heritage projects: (1) selectivity in site selection on the basis of the impact in reducing poverty, and (2) building partnerships for project planning and implementation among local, national, and international institutions.

FOOD FOR THOUGHT

Find, on the internet, the UNESCO World Heritage Site that is nearest to where you live. What does the site contain, and what can you learn about its possible or potential role in generating income for the local people?

stories, old Chinese legends, or Western-style theater. Most of the young people prefer nightclubs, discos, or karaokes. Others stay at home watching TV" (73). The new materialism in China means that young people want to spend their leisure time having "fun." For the theatre, too, money now comes first. One trend is toward the production of Western plays.

For example, Harold Pinter's *The Lover* was an immediate success when it was performed in Shanghai in 1992. Why was it so successful?

> Sex is certainly a big part of the answer. Sex has been taboo in China for a long time; it is still highly censored in theater and films. The producers warned, "no children," fuel-

ing speculation about a possible sex scene. . . . Actually, *The Lover* contains only hints of sexuality, but by Chinese standards the production was the boldest stage show in China. The actress's alluring dress, so common in the west, has seldom, if ever, been seen by Chinese theatregoers. Also, there was lots of bold language—dialogue about female breasts, for example. (75–76)

Another important feature is the play's focus on private life, on interiority, thoughts, and feelings. This emphasis corresponds with increasing interest in private lives in China. Change in the performing arts in China is being shaped by underlying changes in the global and local political economy.

HOW is culture expressed through art?

Cultural anthropologists question the narrowness of Western definitions of art. Anthropologists choose a broad definition that takes into account cross-cultural variations. In the anthropological perspective, therefore, all cultures have art and all cultures have a concept of what good art is. Ethnographers document the ways art relates to many aspects of culture: economics, politics, human development and psychology, healing, social control, and entertainment. Art may serve to reinforce social patterns, but it may also be a vehicle of protest and resistance. In state societies, people began collecting art objects in museums. Later, ethnographic museums were established in Europe as the result of scientific and colonial interest in learning about other cultures. Anthropologists study museum displays as yet another reflection of cultural values as well as sites where perceptions and values are formed.

WHAT do play and leisure activities tell us about culture?

Anthropological studies of play and leisure examine these activities within their cultural context. Games reinforce dominant social values and have thus been analyzed as reflections of culture. Sports and leisure activities, while engaged in for non-utilitarian purposes, are often tied to economic and political interests. In some cultures, sports are also related to religion and spirituality.

HOW is expressive culture changing in contemporary times?

Major forces of change in expressive culture include Western colonialism and international tourism. In some cases, outside forces have led to the extinction of local forms, while in other cases outside forces have promoted continuity or the recovery of practices that had been lost. The effects of change are not always on the "receiving" culture's side, however, because art and play in former colonial powers have also changed through exposure to other cultures.

KEY CONCEPTS

SUGGESTED READINGS

Michael Ames, *Cannibal Tours and Glass Boxes: The Anthropology of Museums.* Vancouver: University of British Columbia Press, 1992. Written by the director of the Museum of Anthropology at UBC, this book wrestles with the role of anthropology in creating concepts of natives, native art, and the use of museums in these constructions.

Eugene Cooper and Yinho Jiang (contributor), *The Artisans and Entrepreneurs of Dongyang County: Economic Reform and Flexible Production in China.* Armonk, NY: M. E. Sharpe, 1998. This ethnography links attention to economic change and artistic change in China through its description of traditional and contemporary woodcarving in two villages and one town.

Noel Dyck and Eduardo Archetti, *Sport, Dance, and Embodied Identities.* Oxford: Berg Press, 2003. This edited volume provides ethnographic examples of how social life is reshaped through sport and dance.

Nelson H. H. Graburn, ed., *Ethnic and Tourist Arts: Cultural Expressions from the Fourth World.* Berkeley: University of California Press, 1976. Organized regionally, 20 chapters explore the survival, revival, and reinvention of the arts of indigenous peoples in North America, Mexico and Central America, South America, Asia, Oceania, and Africa. Graburn's introduction to the book and his intro-

ductory essays preceding each section provide theoretical and comparative insights.

Jay R. Mandle and Joan D. Mandle, *Caribbean Hoops: The Development of West Indian Basketball.* Amsterdam: Gordon and Breach Publishers, 1994. This concise description and analysis of the emergence of basketball (mainly men's basketball) as a popular sport in several Caribbean nations also explores regional differences within the Caribbean.

Timothy Mitchell, *Blood Sport: A Social History of Spanish Bullfighting.* Philadelphia: University of Pennsylvania Press, 1991. Based on fieldwork and archival study, this book presents a well-rounded view of bullfighting within the context of annual Spanish village and national fiestas, consideration of the role of the matador in society, and a psychosexual interpretation of the bullfight, with comparison to blood sports in ancient Rome.

Stuart Plattner, *High Art Down Home: An Economic Ethnography of a Local Art Market.* Chicago: University of Chicago Press, 1996. Based on participant observation and interviews with artists, art dealers, and collectors in St. Louis, Missouri, this book explores concepts of value related to contemporary art and constraints that the market places on artists.

WEBLINKS

The Companion Website (www.pearsoned.ca/miller) that accompanies *Cultural Anthropology,* Third Canadian Edition, includes a destinations module containing links to many websites relevant to the content of this chapter. Use it to investigate the Web and expand your understanding of anthropology.

KEY QUESTIONS

- **WHAT** are the reasons for migration?
- **WHAT** is a displaced person?
- **HOW** are new immigrants contributing to transnational connections and multiculturalism?

15

PEOPLE ON THE MOVE

The so-called Marsh Arab people, under the rule of Saddam Hussein, suffered from government projects that drained their region as well as from political repression. Many who fled the country as refugees are now returning.

The current generation of North American youths will experience more moves during their lives than previous generations. University graduates are likely to change jobs an average of eight times during their careers, and these changes may require relocation.

Ecological, economic, familial, and political factors are causing population movements at seemingly all-time high levels. Research in anthropology has shown, however, that frequent moves during a person's life and mass movements of peoples are nothing new; they have occurred throughout human evolution. Foragers and pastoralists relocate frequently as a normal part of their lives. Population movements account for the past and present dispersion of the world's cultures:

> When we look at population maps of any part of the world, we are looking at the results of migration. Some maps represent major permanent moves, such as the spread of Native Americans from the Bering Sea to Tierra del Fuego, or the spread of Bantu-speaking peoples into the southern half of the African continent. Major moves may be brought on by necessity (the potato famine in Ireland), by population pressure (as befell the San and the Khoi), or by extreme force (the African diaspora in which ten million people were removed from their home communities and scattered throughout the New World). (du Toit 1990:305)

Migration is the movement of a person or people from one place to another (Kearney 1986:331). It is related to other aspects of life such as job and family status, and it may also affect mental health and social relationships. Thus, many academic subjects and professions are relevant here. Historians, economists, political scientists, sociologists, and scholars of religion, literature, art, and music have studied migration. Migration is one of three core areas of demography, along with fertility and mortality. The professions of law, medicine, education, business, architecture, urban planning, public administration, and social work have specialties that focus on the process of migration and the period of adaptation following a move. Experts working in these areas share with anthropologists an interest in such issues as people who migrate, causes of migration, processes of migration, psychosocial adaptations to new locations, and implications for planning and policy.

Cultural anthropologists have addressed a wide range of issues surrounding migration. They have studied how migration is related to economic and reproductive systems, health and human development over the life cycle, marriage and household formation, politics and social order, and religion and expressive culture. There is no domain of human life that is not affected by migration; hence this topic pulls together much of the earlier material in this book. Given the breadth of migration studies, cultural anthropologists have used the full range of methods available, from individual life histories to large-scale surveys.

Three differences distinguish migration studies in cultural anthropology. First, anthropologists studying migration are more likely to have fieldwork experience in more than one location in order to understand the places of origin and destination. Maxine Margolis (1994), for example, first did fieldwork in Brazil, and then later studied Brazilian immigrants in New York City. Second, a greater emphasis on using macro and micro perspectives characterizes anthropology's approach to migration studies. Studying migration has challenged traditional cultural anthropology's focus on one village or neighbourhood and created the need to take into account national and global economic, political, and social forces (Basch, Glick Schiller, and Szanton Blanc 1994; Lamphere 1992). Third, anthropologists who work with migrants are more likely to be involved in assisting them, often in resettlement work. Doreen Indra became the director of a large agency for Southeast Asian refugees because of her interest in refugee resettlement; as a professor of anthropology at the University of Lethbridge, she also published extensively on refugee research (Indra 1988).

This chapter first presents information on the most important categories of migrants and the opportunities and challenges they face. The second section provides descriptions of several examples of immigrants to the United States and Canada. The last section considers urgent issues related to migration, such as human rights and risk assessment and prevention programs.

CATEGORIES OF MIGRATION

Migration encompasses many categories depending on the distance of the move, its purpose, duration, degree of voluntarism (was the move forced or more a matter of choice?), and the migrant's status in the new destination. There is a major difference between **internal migration** (movement within national boundaries) and **international migration**. Moving between nations is likely to create more challenges both in the process of relocation and in adjustment after arrival.

Categories Based on Spatial Boundaries

This section reviews the basic features of three categories of population movement defined in terms of the spatial boundaries crossed: internal migration, international migration, and the new category of transnational migration. **Transnational migrants** are migrants who regularly move back and forth between two or more countries and form a new identity that transcends a single geopolitical unit (recall the discussion of transnationalism in Chapter 11).

Internal Migration

Rural-to-urban migration was the dominant stream of internal population in most countries during the twentieth century. A major reason for people migrating to urban areas is the availability of work. According to the **push–pull theory** of labour migration, rural areas are increasingly unable to support population growth and rising expectations about the quality of life (the push factor). At the same time, cities (the pull factor) attract people, especially youth, for employment and lifestyle reasons. The push–pull model makes urban migration sound like a simple function of the rational decision making of freely choosing human agents who have information on the costs and the benefits of rural versus urban life, weigh that information, and then opt for going or staying (recall the approach to understanding culture that emphasizes human agency, Chapter 1). But many instances of urban migration are more the result of structural forces (economic need or political factors such as war) that are beyond the control of the individual.

Chinese Canadians mainly live in urban areas such as Vancouver and Toronto. In Vancouver, they constitute about 16 percent of the population. Vancouver's Chinatown is a vibrant tourist site as well as a place where Chinese Canadians reaffirm their cultural heritage as in the celebration shown here of Chinese New Year.

The anonymity and rapid pace of city life and the likelihood of "psychosocial discontinuity" caused by relocation pose special challenges for migrants from rural areas. Research has shown that urban life increases the risk of *hypertension* (elevated blood pressure through stress or tension), and hypertension is related to coronary heart disease. For example, an anthropological study of urban migrants in comparison to rural dwellers in the Philippines found that hypertension, as defined by high blood pressure, is more prevalent in urban migrant populations than in settled rural groups (Hackenberg et al. 1983). This finding applied to both men and women. (Other social factors such as income level, education, age at migration, and social support systems can be important in affecting health outcomes of migration.) The relationship between elevated health risks resulting from psychosocial adjustment problems in rural–urban migration exists among international immigrant groups as well, for example, among Samoans living in California (Janes 1990).

International Migration

International migration has grown in volume and significance since 1945, especially since the mid-1980s (Castles and Miller 1993). No one knows how many international migrants there are, although it is estimated that nearly 2 percent of the world's population lives abroad (thus, the vast majority resides in their home countries). This amounts to about 100 million people, including legal and illegal immigrants. Migrants who move for work-related reasons constitute the majority of people in this category. At least 35 million people from developing countries have migrated to the industrialized countries in the past three decades. International migration is likely to be one of the key factors in global social change through the first decade of the twenty-first century. Driving forces behind this trend are economic and political changes that affect labour demands and human welfare.

The "classic" countries of early international immigration are the United States, Canada, Australia, New Zealand, and Argentina. The first waves of European immigrants largely destroyed and dispossessed the indigenous peoples in each case. These countries' populations are now formed mainly of descendants of the European immigrants. The immigration policies of these nations in the early twentieth century have been labelled "White immigration" because they explicitly limited non-White immigration (Ongley 1995). In the 1960s in Canada, for instance, changes made immigration policies less racially discriminatory and more focused on skills and experience. Through the 1980s, further liberalization occurred and family reunification provisions were widened. In Canada, a combination of changing labour needs and interest in improving its international image prompted these reforms. During the 1980s, increased refugee flows inspired greater attention to humanitarian concerns.

Long-time areas of out-migration of northern, western, and southern Europe are now receiving many immigrants (often refugees from Asia). Some Central European states, such as Hungary, Poland, and Czechoslovakia, are new migrant destinations. Population flows in the Middle East are complex, with some nations such as Turkey experiencing substantial movements in both directions. Millions of Turks have emigrated to Germany, while ethnic Turks in places such as Bulgaria have returned to Turkey. Turkey has also received Kurdish and Iranian refugees. Several million Palestinian refugees now live mainly in Jordan and Lebanon. Israel has attracted Jewish immigrants from Europe, northern Africa, the United States, and Russia.

Turkish people migrated to Germany in substantial numbers in the 1960s and 1970s as "guest workers" to fill jobs in German factories. German leaders expected them to work, save money, and return to Turkey. Most stayed, and their children are now growing up in Germany, speaking German and having only a distant relationship with Turkey. Many incidents of violence between so-called neo-Nazis and Turkish people have occurred, including the murder of five Turkish youths in Solingen in 1993.

Transnational Migration

Transnational migration appears to be increasing along with other aspects of globalization. We must keep in mind, however, that transnationalism is a function of the creation of nation–state boundaries. Pastoralist people with extensive seasonal herding routes were "transnational" migrants long before national boundaries cut across their pathways.

Much contemporary transnational migration is motivated by economic factors. The spread of the global corporate economy is the basis for the growth of one category of transnational migrants nicknamed "astronauts," businesspeople who spend most of their time flying among different cities as investment bankers or corporate executives. At the lower end of the income scale are transnational migrant labourers who spend substantial amounts of time working in different places and whose movements depend on the demand for their labour.

An important feature of transnational migration is how it affects the migrant's identity and sense of citizenship. Constant movement among different places weakens the sense of having one home and promotes instead a sense of belonging to a diffused community of similar transnational migrants whose lives "in between" locations take on a new transnational cultural reality.

As a response to the increased rate of transnational migration, many of the "sending" countries (countries that are the source of emigrants) are making explicit efforts to redefine themselves as transnational nations (Glick Schiller and Fouron 1999). These countries, which have high proportions of emigrants, include Haiti, Colombia, Mexico, Brazil, the Dominican Republic, Portugal, Greece, and the Philippines. They confer continuing citizenship on emigrants and their descendants in order to foster a sense of belonging and willingness to continue to provide financial support in the form of remittances, or economic transfers of money or goods from migrants to their family back home. For example, at least 60 percent of the gross domestic product of the small Pacific island country of Tonga comes from remittances (H. Lee 2003:32).

Categories Based on Reason for Moving

In this section, we consider categories of migrants that are based on the reason for relocating. Readers should keep in mind that the spatial categories that we have already discussed overlap with the categories based on reason for moving. An international migrant, for example, may also be a person who moved for employment reasons. Displaced persons can be either internal or international. In other words, migrants experience different kinds of spatial change and, at the same time, have different reasons for moving.

Labour Migrants

Thousands of people migrate to work for a specific period of time. They do not intend to establish permanent residence and are often explicitly barred from doing so. This form of migration, when legally contracted, is called **wage labour migration**. The period of work may be brief or it may last several years, as among rural Egyptian men who go to other Middle Eastern countries to work for an average period of four years (Brink 1991).

Asian women are the fastest-growing category among the world's 35 million migrant workers (International Labour Office 1996:16–17). About 1.5 million Asian women are working abroad; most are in domestic service jobs, and some work as nurses and teachers. Major sending countries are Indonesia, the Philippines, Sri Lanka, and Thailand. Main receiving countries are Saudi Arabia and Kuwait, and to a lesser degree, Hong Kong, Japan, Taiwan, Singapore, Malaysia, and Brunei. Such women are usually alone and are not allowed to marry or have a child in the country where they are temporary workers. International migrant workers are sometimes illegally recruited and thus have no protection in their working conditions. The illegal recruitment of female prostitutes, a growing problem worldwide, is especially serious in Thailand, where young women are offered the prospect of migrating to Europe and North America under pretenses of receiving work, for example, as restaurant hostesses.

Circular migration refers to a common form of labour migration involving movement in a regular pattern between two or more places. Circular migration may occur either within or between nations. In the latter case, it is also referred to as transnational migration. Internal circular migrants include, for example, female domestic workers throughout Latin America and the Caribbean. These women have their permanent residence in rural areas, but work for long periods of time in the city for better-off people. They tend to leave their children in the care of their mother in the country and send regular remittances for their support.

Displaced Persons

Displaced persons are people who, for one reason or another, are "evicted from their houses, farms, and communities and forced to find a living elsewhere" (Guggenheim and Cernea 1993:1). Colonialism, slavery, war, persecution, natural disasters, and large-scale mining and dam-building are major causes of population displacement.

Refugees, a category of displaced persons, are forced to relocate because they are victims or potential victims of persecution because of race, religion, nationality, ethnicity, gender, or political views (Camino and Krulfeld 1994:vii). Refugees constitute a large and growing category of displaced persons. An accurate count of all categories of refugees globally is unavailable, but it probably exceeds 10 million people. As of 2000, about 1 of every 500 people was a refugee (Lubkemann 2002). The lack of accurate data is compounded by political interests, which, in some cases, inflate numbers and, in others, deflate numbers.

Internally displaced persons (IDPs) is the fastest-growing category of displaced people. IDPs are people who are forced to leave their home and community but who remain within their country. Current estimates are that the number of IDPs is double that of refugees, over 20 million people (R. Cohen 2002). Africa is the continent with the most IDPs, and within Africa, Sudan is the country with the highest number (around 4.5 million). Because IDPs do not cross national boundaries, they do not come under the purview of the United Nations or any other international body. These institutions deal with international problems and have limited authority over problems within countries. Francis Deng, former Sudanese ambassador, has taken up the cause of IDPs and is working to raise international awareness of the

Dr. Francis Deng (right), who earned a doctor of law degree from Yale University, is Representative of the United Nations Secretary-General on Internally Displaced Persons and directs a program on displaced persons at the Brookings Institution in Washington, D.C. He has been instrumental in gaining international recognition of the plight of internally displaced persons.

immensity of the problem. His efforts led to the formal definition of IDPs and to legal recognition of their status. In his role as UN Secretary-General for Internally Displaced Persons, Deng coordinates a global coalition of institutions (including the UN, governments, and nongovernmental organizations) to provide more timely and effective assistance for IDPs. Many IDPs, like refugees, live for extended periods in camps under miserable conditions with no access to basic supports such as health care and schools.

Development projects are often the reason why people become IDPs. Large dam construction, mining, and other projects have displaced millions in the past several decades. Dam construction alone is estimated to have displaced perhaps 80 million people in the past 50 years (Worldwatch Institute 2003). Forced migration due to development projects is termed **development-induced displacement** (DID). Development-induced displacement is usually internal displacement and thus has typically fallen outside international legal frameworks. Mega-dam projects are now attracting the attention of concerned people worldwide who support local resistance to massive relocation. One of the most notorious cases is India's construction of a series of high dams in its Narmada river valley, which cuts across the middle of the country from the west coast. This massive project involves relocating hundreds of thousands of people—no one has a reliable estimate of the numbers. The relocation is against the residents' wishes, and government compensation to the "oustees" for the loss of the homes, land, and livelihood is completely inadequate. Thousands of people in the Narmada valley have organized protests over the many years of construction, and international environmental organizations have lent their support. A celebrated Indian novelist, Arundhati Roy, joined the cause by learning everything she could about the 20 years of government planning for the Narmada dam projects, interviewing people who have been relocated, and writing a passionate statement called *The Cost of Living* (1999) against this massive project. A man now living in a barren resettlement area told how he used to pick fruit in the forest, 48 kinds. In the resettlement area he and his family have to purchase all their food, and they cannot afford any fruit at all (pp. 54–55). In the other Asian giant, China, the equally infamous Three Gorges Dam project will, when completed, have displaced perhaps two million (McCully 2003). Mega-dam projects are always promoted by governments as important to the national interest. But costs are always high for the local people who are displaced, and the benefits are always skewed toward corporate profits, energy for industrial plants, and water for urban consumers who can pay for it.

Canada became a signatory to the United Nations Convention on Refugees in 1969, some 18 years after it was drawn up. The Immigration Act of 1976 incorporated into law Canada's responsibility toward the humane treatment of refugee claimants. Since that time, thousands of refugees resettle in Canada each year. Some arrive at the border claiming refugee status and are given a hearing to determine whether they meet the criteria as refugee claimants. Some are resettled directly from refugee camps, as UNHCR-defined convention refugees or members of a designated class identified on humanitarian grounds. Some are government sponsored; others are sponsored by groups. Privately sponsored refugee resettlement is organized by sponsorship agreements between a consortium of interested groups, often including religious institutions. Both government and private sponsorships offer advantages and disadvantages to the newcomer. Canada's record of upholding its international obligations to refugees was recognized in 1986, when the United Nations awarded the Nansen medal for efforts on behalf of refugees to Canada, an honour that previously had only been given to individuals (Beiser 1999:41).

The manner in which displaced persons are relocated affects how well they will adjust to their new lives. Displaced persons in general have little choice about when and where they move; refugees typically have the least choice of all. Cultural anthropologists have done substantial research with refugee populations, especially those related to war (Camino and Krulfeld 1994; Hirschon 1989; Manz 1988). They have helped discover the key factors that ease or increase relocation stresses. One major issue is the extent to which the new location resembles or differs from the home place in several features such as climate, language, and food (Muecke 1987). Generally, the more different the places of origin and destination are, the greater the adaptational demands and stress. Other major factors are the refugee's ability to get a job commensurate with his or her training and experience, the presence of family members, and whether people in the new location are welcoming or hostile to the refugees.

Institutional Migrants

Institutional migrants are people who move into a social institution, either voluntarily or involuntarily. They include monks and nuns, the elderly, prisoners, and boarding school or university students. This section considers examples of students and soldiers within the category of institutional migrants.

Studies of student adjustment reveal similarities with many other forms of migration, especially in terms of risks for mental stress. Ethnographic research conducted among adolescent boarding school children in Ambanja, a town in Madagascar, showed that girls experience more adjustment strains than boys (Sharp 1990). Ambanja is a "booming migrant town" characterized by rootlessness and anomie. Boarding school children in this town constitute a vulnerable group because they have left their families and come alone to the school. Many of the boarding school girls, who were between the ages of 13 and 17, experienced bouts of spirit possession. Local people say that it is the "prettiest" girls that become possessed. The data on possession patterns showed, instead, that possession is correlated with a girl's being unmarried and pregnant. Many of these school girls become the mistresses of older men, who shower them with expensive gifts such as perfume and gold jewellery. Such girls attract the envy of both other girls and school boys, who are being passed over in favour of adult men. Thus, the girls have little peer support among their schoolmates. If a girl becomes pregnant, school policy requires that she be expelled. If the baby's father refuses to help her, she faces severe hardship. Her return home will be a great disappointment to her parents. Within this context, a girl's spirit possession may be understood as an expression of distress. Through the spirits, girls act out their difficult position between country and city and girlhood and womanhood.

International students also face serious challenges of spatial and cultural relocation. Like the school girls of Madagascar, they are at greater risk of adjustment stress than are local students. Many international students

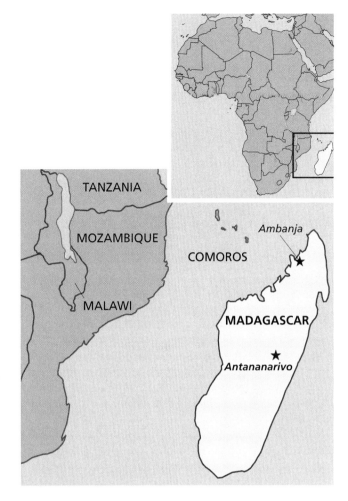

report mental health problems to varying degrees depending on age, marital status, and other factors. Spouses who accompany international students also suffer the strains of dislocation. The issue of international student adjustment is of increasing importance in Canada, where about 100 000 international students are enrolled in institutions of higher education, and that number is growing (Shik 1995).

Soldiers are often sent on distant assignments for lengthy periods of time. Their destination may have negative physical and mental health effects on them, in addition to the fact that they may face combat. During the British and French colonial expansion, thousands of soldiers were assigned to tropical countries (Curtin 1989). Colonial soldiers faced new diseases in their destination areas. Their death rates from disease were twice as high as those of soldiers who stayed home, with two exceptions—Tahiti and Hawaii—where soldiers experienced better health than soldiers at home. Most military personnel were male, but in some colonial contexts, many wives accompanied their husbands. In India, mortality rates were higher for females than for males. This finding may be explained by the fact that the men had to pass a

United States marines wearing gas masks as protection from oil fumes during the 1990–1991 Gulf War. Many poorly understood illnesses afflict veterans of "Desert Storm," including skin conditions, neurological disorders, chronic fatigue, and psychological-cognitive problems.

physical exam before enlistment, whereas their dependents did not.

Little has been published by anthropologists on how military migration affects people's lives and sense of identity. One thing that is clear, however, is that U.S. military people on assignment lack in-depth training in how to communicate with local people and in the importance of respecting local people's cultures. A pocket-size handbook on Iraqi etiquette used by some U.S. troops in Iraq provides some extremely basic guidelines (Lorch 2003). For example, one should avoid arguments and should not take more than three cups of coffee or tea if you are someone's guest. One should also avoid the "thumbs up" gesture (it's obscene in the Middle East) and should not sit with one's feet on a desk. Such basics are helpful, but they do little to provide the cultural understanding that is critical in conflict and post-conflict situations. Soldiers during wartime are trained primarily to seek out and destroy the enemy, not to engage in cross-cultural communication. Winning a war in contemporary times often hinges on what the conquerors do following the outright conflict, and that often means keeping troops stationed in foreign cultures for extended periods of time. Such extended assignments take a heavy toll on military personnel's mental health.

THE NEW IMMIGRANTS TO THE UNITED STATES AND CANADA

The term **new immigrants** refers to international migrants who have moved after the 1960s. New immigrants worldwide include increasing proportions of refugees, many of whom are destitute and desperate for asylum. Three trends are apparent in the new international migration of the last decade, and they are likely to continue:

- *Globalization:* More countries are involved in international migration, leading to increased cultural diversity in sending and receiving countries.

Every year the "Taste of the Danforth" celebrates Greek culture and cuisine in multicultural Toronto.

Multiple Cultural Worlds

THE NEW IMMIGRANTS AND FEMALE CIRCUMCISION IN CANADA

CANADA RECOGNIZES the principle that fear of the practice of female circumcision (see Chapter 6) is a reason for being given refugee status (Berg 1997). In 1994, a woman from Somalia was given refugee status in Canada because of the fear she had for her daughters. If the family returned to Somalia, her children would have been subjected to this practice. Estimated rates of female circumcision in Somalia and Ethiopia are 90 percent; in Egypt, 50 percent. This suggests that many young girls would undergo this invasive operation if they remained in countries where this is a common practice.

Canada along with England, France, Belgium, Denmark, Switzerland, and Sweden have made female circumcision illegal. Under Canadian law, it is considered a form of child abuse and aggravated assault (Berg 1997:21). Medical associations in most Canadian provinces have strict penalties for practitioners who perform

female circumcision and infibulation after childbirth. They have also begun educational efforts in communities where it is most likely, in the hopes of discouraging the practice rather than punishing parents.

The World Health Organization called for an eradication of the practice by 2000, and UNICEF identifies it as a violation of the rights of the child. No one expected these pronouncements to end female circumcision, but advocacy groups may use these statements as a guide for changing a long-established practice. Advocacy groups are active in both the countries of origin and among immigrant groups in Canada.

FOOD FOR THOUGHT

Should people be allowed to practise female circumcision when they immigrate in spite of the disapproval of the medical community in their new country?

- *Acceleration:* Quantitative growth of migration has occurred in all major regions of the world. In the 1990s the majority of new immigrants came to Canada from Europe and South and Southeast Asia.

- *Feminization:* Women are playing a greater role in migration to and from all regions and in all types of migration, with some forms having a majority of women.

These three trends merit scholarly attention and raise new issues for policy-makers and international organizations as the cultural practices of immigrant groups and the areas of destination increasingly come in contact and, sometimes, in conflict, with each other (see the Multiple Cultural Worlds box).

In Canada, the category of "new immigrants" refers to people who arrived following the development of the Immigration Regulations of 1967. The regulations made it possible for far more people from developing countries to enter Canada, especially if they were professionals or trained in some desired skill. Later, the "family reunification" provision allowed permanent residents and naturalized citizens to bring in close family members. Most of the new immigrants to Canada are from Asia, Latin America, and the Caribbean, although increasing numbers are from Eastern Europe, especially Russia.

Canada provides temporary employment visas to allow migrant labourers to work in Canada for up to 12 months.

Visas are also required by international students studying in Canada, who may stay for the period of their studies. Visa students may work in some limited contexts associated with their studies. Persons immigrating to Canada apply for landed immigrant status or permanent residence leading to citizenship after three years in the country. Canada's immigration policy tries to balance humanitarian concerns for refugee claimants, family reunification, and the perceived need to attract highly skilled and educated persons.

The New Immigrants from Latin America and the Caribbean

Since the 1960s, substantial numbers of people from Mexico, Central and South America, and the Caribbean have come to Canada. Major flows come from the Caribbean islands of Jamaica, Barbados, Cuba, and Haiti, among others. This is partly a result of the change in Canada's immigration policy in the 1960s, which had previously excluded people from areas outside Europe (Avery 1995:197). In addition to immigrant and refugee flows, many people came from Mexico and the Caribbean as seasonal farm labourers working in deplorable conditions for little pay. Some of these people work in the tobacco and fruit orchards of southern Ontario.

A Dominican Day parade in New York City.

Chain Migration of Dominicans

The Dominican Republic has ranked among the top 10 source countries of immigrants to the United States since the 1960s (Pessar 1995). Dominicans are one of the fastest-growing immigrant groups in the United States. They are found in clusters in a few states, with their highest concentration in New York State. Within New York City, Washington Heights is the heart of the Dominican community. Unlike many other new-immigrant streams, the Dominicans are mainly middle and upper class. Most have left their homeland "in search of a better life." Many hope to return to the Dominican Republic, saying that in New York, "There is work but there is no life."

Patricia Pessar conducted fieldwork in the Dominican Republic and in New York City, and thus she has a transnational view. She studied the dynamics of departure (such as getting a visa), the process of arrival, and adaptation in New York. Like most anthropologists who work with immigrant groups, she became involved in helping many of her informants: "Along the way I also endeavored to repay people's help by brokering for them with institutions such as the Immigration and Naturalization Service, social service agencies, schools, and hospitals" (xv).

For Dominican immigrants, as for most other immigrant groups, the *cadena,* or chain, links one immigrant to another. **Chain migration** is the process by which a first wave of migrants then attracts relatives and friends to join them in the destination place. Most Dominicans who are legal immigrants have sponsored other family members, so most legal Dominicans have entered through the family unification provision. The U.S. policy defines a family

as a nuclear unit, and thus, it excludes important members of Dominican extended family networks such as cousins and ritual kin (*compadres*). To overcome this barrier, some Dominicans use the technique of the "business marriage." In a business marriage, an individual pays a legal immigrant or citizen a fee of perhaps $2000 to enter into a "marriage." He or she then acquires a visa through the family unification provision. Such a "marriage" does not involve cohabitation or sexual relations; it is meant to be broken.

Dominicans have found employment in New York's manufacturing industries, including the garment industry. Dominicans are more heavily employed in these industries than any other ethnic group. Recent declines in the numbers of New York City's manufacturing jobs and the redefining of better positions into less desirable ones through restructuring have disproportionately affected them. Dominicans also work in retail and wholesale trade, another sector that has declined since the late 1960s. Others have established their own retail businesses, or *bodegas.* A problem with this line of work is that many bodegas are located in unsafe areas and some owners have been assaulted or killed. Declining economic opportunities for Dominicans have also been aggravated by arrivals of newer immigrants, especially from Mexico and Central America, who are willing to accept even lower wages and worse working conditions.

Although many families of middle and high status in the Dominican Republic initially secured fairly solid employment in the United States, they have declined economically since then. Dominicans now have the highest poverty rate in New York City, 37 percent, compared with an overall city average of 17 percent. Poverty is concentrated among women-headed households with young children.

The gender gap in wages is high, and women are more likely than men to be on public assistance. On the other hand, Dominican women in the United States are more often regularly employed than they would be in the Dominican Republic. This pattern upsets a patriarchal norm in which the nuclear family depends on male earnings and female domestic responsibilities. A woman's earning power means that husband–wife decision making is more egalitarian. A working Dominican woman is likely to obtain more assistance from the man in doing household chores. All of these changes help explain why Dominican men are more interested in returning to the Dominican Republic than women are. As one man said, "Your country is a country for women; mine is for men" (81).

Caribbean Women: Strategies for Survival

A large portion of recent immigration to Canada was from the Caribbean in the 1980s. Yvonne Bobb Smith (1999) describes how many Caribbean women never lose the sense that "home" is in the islands, whether Jamaica, St. Lucia, or Trinidad. Smith posits three strategies for their survival in a society where racist insults are a constant part of the social environment for people from the Caribbean (Henry 1987). They see education as the first strategy in opening the door to better employment and a more satisfying role in the community. The second strategy is networking, building links with other men and women of the diaspora—the movement of Black Caribbean people to industrial nations like Canada, the United States, and the United Kingdom. The links may be established though casual meetings that eventually develop into strong, warm friendships. The third strategy is community activism. Caribbean women in Canada have founded or are involved in several community organizations that support and promote causes important to Caribbean immigrant groups and other minorities, including the National Congress of Black Women of Canada, Black Theatre Canada, and the Coalition of Visible Minority Women of Ontario (Y. Smith 1999:163).

The New Immigrants from East Asia

Changing Patterns of Consumption among Hong Kong Chinese

Studies of how international migrants change their behaviour in the new destination have addressed, among other things, the question of whether consumption patterns change and, if so, how, why, and what effects such changes have on other aspects of their culture.

A study in Canada focused on the topic of consumption patterns among four groups: Anglo-Canadians, new Hong Kong immigrants (who had arrived within the previous seven years), long-time Hong Kong immigrants, and Hong Kong residents (W. Lee and Tse 1994). Since 1987, Hong Kong has been the single largest source of migrants to Canada. The new immigrant settlement pattern in Canada is one of urban clustering. The Hong Kong Chinese have developed their own shopping centres, television and radio stations, newspapers, and country clubs. Because of generally high incomes, the Hong Kong immigrants have greatly boosted Canadian buying power.

For most migrants, however, the move brought a lowered economic situation, reflected in consumption patterns. New immigrants may have to reduce spending on entertainment and expensive items. Primary needs of the new immigrants include items that only about half of all households owned: car, VCR, carpets, microwave oven, family house, and multiple TVs. Items in the second-needs category were dining room set, barbecue stove, deep freezer, and dehumidifier. Long-time immigrants tend to own more secondary products, suggesting that, with time and increased economic standing, expanded consumption of Anglo-Canadian products occurs.

Among the Chinese ethnic population in Canada, the majority come from Hong Kong, with much smaller proportions from Taiwan and China. The Hong Kong Chinese immigrants tend to be well-off in economic terms. Many of the male heads of household are "astronauts," leaving their families in Canada while they fly back and forth from Hong Kong to Canada.

At the same time, businesses in Canada have responded to immigrant tastes by providing Hong Kong style restaurants, Chinese branch banks, and travel agencies. Supermarkets have specialized Asian sections. Thus traditional patterns and ties are maintained to some extent. Two characteristics of Hong Kong immigrants distinguish them from other groups discussed in this section: their relatively secure economic status and their high level of education. Still, in Canada, they often have a difficult time finding suitable employment. Some have named Canada "Kan Lan Tai," meaning a difficult place to prosper, a fact that leads many to become "astronauts," or transnational migrants. Many saw Canada as a safe haven, not as a place to make great economic progress (J. Smart 1994).

The New Immigrants from Southeast Asia

Three Patterns of Adaptation among the Vietnamese

Over one and a quarter million refugees have left Vietnam since the 1970s. Although most were relocated to the United States, many went to Canada, Australia, France, Germany, and Britain (S. Gold 1992). For example, in the period between 1979 and 1981, Canada accepted 60 000 Southeast Asian refugees. Vietnamese immigrants in Canada constitute a significant Asian minority. Three distinct subgroups are the 1975-era elite, the boat people, and the ethnic Chinese. While they interact frequently, they have retained distinct patterns of adaptation.

The first group avoided many of the traumatic elements of flight. They were U.S. employees and members of the South Vietnamese government and military. They left before having to live under the communist regime, and they spent little time in refugee camps. A few of these came to Canada, especially to Quebec.

The boat people began to enter Canada after the outbreak of the Vietnam–China conflict of 1978. Mainly of rural origin, they lived for three years or more under communism, working in re-education camps or "new economic zones." Their exit, either by overcrowded and leaky boats or on foot through Cambodia, was dangerous and difficult. Over 50 percent died on the way. Those who survived faced many months in refugee camps in Thailand, Malaysia, the Philippines, or Hong Kong before being admitted to Canada. Many more males than females escaped as boat people; thus, they are less likely to have arrived with intact families. They were less well educated than the earlier wave, half had no competence in English or French, and they faced a depressed economy. They have had a much more difficult time adjusting to life in Canada than the 1975-era elite.

The Sino-Vietnamese, traditionally a distinct and socially marginalized class of entrepreneurs in Vietnam, arrived mainly as boat people. Many of these immigrants have successfully used contacts in the overseas Chinese community and have been able to re-establish their roles as entrepreneurs.

No Vietnamese had lived in the prairie city of Lethbridge, Alberta, before 1979 (Indra 1988). The adaptation of Vietnamese and Sino-Vietnamese to this environment has been relatively successful. The Sino-Vietnamese are able to connect with other Chinese in the community and therefore maintain their cultural identity. In addition, the Sino-Vietnamese have been better able to reconstitute their core families. The Vietnamese in Lethbridge have been less able to adjust, finding it more difficult to re-establish families and feeling a strong attachment to Vietnam as it once was. Despite their being marginally employed, all Vietnamese in Lethbridge had a positive self-concept and even after 10 years, people had kept contact with their sponsors in the community.

Khmer Refugees' Interpretation of Their Suffering

Since the late 1970s, approximately 20 000 people from Cambodia have come to Canada as refugees from the Pol Pot regime. These people survived years of political repression, a difficult escape, and time in a refugee camp before arriving in Canada. One question anthropologists ask is how people who have been through such terror and loss reconstruct their understanding of how the world works and their place in it. In Canada, many Cambodians, or Khmer, are from rural backgrounds and have beliefs in spirits called *neak ta*. Physical complaints are often blamed on these spirits. Some women refugees were possessed by the spirits of those who were murdered or not given proper burial rites, a common occurrence during the Pol Pot years. One cure for this state is giving food to Buddhist monks on behalf of the distressed spirit. Or consultation may be sought with a traditional healer, known as a *Khmer kru*. In this way, the possession can be resolved; but if monks or a traditional healer are not available, the suffering may be expressed in "physical ailments, social withdrawal and mental illness" (McLellan 1996:246). In Ontario, where most Khmer live in Canada, no programs have focused on the particular problems suffered by this population, despite widespread knowledge about the nature of the Pol Pot regime and the stresses this population has endured.

The New Immigrants from South Asia

The Sikhs in British Columbia: Maintaining Their Religious Identity

Sikhs began coming to British Columbia in the early twentieth century, but they did not arrive in large numbers until the 1960s and 1970s, when Canada's immigration laws were relaxed. Annamma Joy studied the Sikhs in the Okanagan Valley in the interior of British Columbia, an area famous for apple growing (1989). Many of the Sikhs had come to the valley on the recommendation of friends and relatives, an example of chain migration. Most had been successful farmers in India and hoped to be able to live well in Canada, purchasing houses and cars. Many worked in the sawmills of the northern Okanagan. Male Sikhs suffered severe criticism from non-Sikh co-workers because of the visible symbols of their religion—beards and turbans. Even when Sikhs gave in to pressure, by shaving their beards and no longer wearing the turban, they were still subject to prejudice. The Sikhs were recognized as good workers by management, but were seen as a threat by other community members.

The male practices of wearing the turban, having unshorn hair, and carrying the *kirpan* (sword) are important features of the Sikh religion. The bangle, the breeches, and the comb symbolize maintaining a balance between the uncontrollable nature of power and sexual virility and discipline and restraint. The unshorn hair is a symbol of power and virility, which is restrained by the comb, while the *kirpan* is restrained by the bangle. The *kirpan* is also important in the baptism of Sikhs. It is usually kept in the home, but some Sikhs feel they have the right to carry it, a practice which sometimes causes difficulties with various jurisdictions. Since 1976, Canadian law has allowed Sikhs to carry the *kirpan*, provided it is for religious purposes.

The New Immigrants from Eastern Europe

The breakup of the Soviet Union into 15 separate countries spurred the movement of over nine million people throughout Eastern Europe and Central Asia. Many of these immigrants are people of Slavic descent who had lived in Central Asia during the time of the former Soviet Union and are seeking to return to their homelands. Another large category includes people who were forcibly relocated to Siberia or Central Asia. Many Soviet Germans have migrated from Siberia to Germany, and Crimean Tatars are shifting from Uzbekistan back to Crimea. Since 1988, people from the former Soviet Union have been the largest refugee nationality to enter the United States (Littman 1993, cited in S. Gold 1995).

Soviet Jews: Refugees Fleeing Religious Persecution

A sizable proportion of the refugees from the former Soviet Union are Soviet Jews. They have relocated to Israel, some countries of Western Europe, and North America. The largest number of Soviet Jews live in Israel; since the mid-1960s, about 325 000 have settled in the United States and over 60 000 in Canada. Steven Gold (1995) has studied different refugee groups in California for many years and speaks from a comparative perspective when he points out unique features of the experience of Soviet Jewish refugees. First, their origins in the Soviet Union accustomed them to the fact that the government controlled almost every aspect of life, "from the production of butter and the administration of summer camps to the shaping of ideology" (xi). These émigrés are used to a wide range of government services, including jobs, housing, daycare, and other basic needs. They have had to find new ways of meeting these needs in a market economy. Second, Soviet Jews, as White Europeans, are members of the dominant racial majority group in the United States. While Soviet Jews have suffered centuries of discrimination in Eastern Europe, they are much closer to the racial mainstream in the United States. Third, they have access to established and prosperous communities of American Jews. They have well-connected sponsors when they arrive. Most other new immigrant groups do not have these advantages.

The economic downturn of the 1990s, however, prompted a wave of anti-immigrant sentiment of which Soviet Jewish immigrants are "keenly aware" (xiii). Soviet Jewish immigrants face other challenges as well. Depending on their area of relocation, many have a difficult time finding a job commensurate with their education and previous work in the Soviet Union. In Canada, many Soviet Jewish immigrants who were highly skilled professionals, such as doctors and dentists, are unable to pass their licensing exams and are forced to accept menial labour jobs far beneath their qualifications. This is especially true for women émigrés who were employed, often as professionals, in the Soviet Union, but who can find no work other than housecleaning or babysitting. Another major challenge relates to marriage options. Cultural norms promote interethnic marriage; however, the number of Soviet Jews in the marriage pool is small. As a result, marriage brokerage businesses have developed that pair young women in Russia with established émigrés in North America.

Immigrants learning English at an adult school.

MIGRATION POLICIES AND POLITICS IN A GLOBALIZING WORLD

Globalization and the increase in migration have attracted more attention to this issue on the part of anthropologists and other social scientists. The major questions raised concern national and international policies of inclusion and exclusion of particular categories of people. The human rights of various categories of migrants vary dramatically. Migrants of all sorts, including long-standing migratory groups such as pastoralists and horticulturalists, seek to find ways of protecting their lifestyles, maintaining their health, and building a sense of the future.

Inclusion and Exclusion

National immigration policies that set quotas on the quantity and types of immigrants welcomed and determine how they are treated are largely dictated by political and economic interests. Even in the cases of seemingly humanitarian quotas, governments undertake a cost–benefit analysis of how much will be gained and how much will be lost. Politically, governments show either their support or disapproval of other governments through their immigration policies. One of the most obvious economic factors affecting policy is labour flow. Cheap, even illegal, immigrant labour is used around the world to maintain profits for businesses and services for the better-off. Flows of such labour undermine labour unions and the status of established workers.

In Canada, immigration law determines who will be allowed entry and what benefits the government will allow them. The focus on cheap labour was dominant at the beginning of the twentieth century in Canada. The large extraction industries of lumbering and mining, along with the railroads, demanded large numbers of cheap labourers. Business in Canada overrode government concerns about foreign labour even when many residents of Canada complained about the influx of foreigners, mainly southern and eastern Europeans (Avery 1995). Government regulations on immigrants from Asia were more restrictive. For example, the Chinese were subject to an entry tax in 1885, and in 1923 were specifically forbidden to enter Canada. Canada still continues some restrictive policies. In 1995, the government introduced a $975 landing fee for every adult immigrant and refugee applying for permanent residence (in 2002 the fee for refugees was discontinued). Officially, this policy was put in place to offset the costs to the government of settlement programs. But many immigrant and refugee advocates perceive it as an unfair burden on immigrants and refugees struggling to become established in a new country.

National immigration policies are played out in local communities. In some instances, local resentments are associated with a so-called **lifeboat mentality**, which seeks to limit enlarging a particular group because of perceived resource constraints. Influxes of immigrants who compete for jobs have led to hostility in many parts of Europe and North America. Some observers have labelled this *working-class racism* because it emerges out of competition with immigrants for jobs and other benefits (J. Cole 1996).

The number of immigrants has grown substantially in southern Italy since the early 1980s. In the city of Palermo, with a total population of 800 000, there are now between 15 000 and 30 000 immigrants from Africa, Asia, and elsewhere. Does the theory of working-class racism apply to the working class in Palermo? Two conditions seem to predict that it would: large numbers of foreign immigrants and a high rate of unemployment.

However, instead of expressing racist condemnation of the immigrants, working-class residents of Palermo accept the immigrants as fellow poor people. One critical factor may be the lack of competition for jobs, which

derives from the fact that working Palermitans and immigrants occupy different niches. Immigrant jobs are less desirable, more stigmatized, and less well-paying. African immigrant men work in bars and restaurants, as building cleaners, or as itinerant street vendors. African and Asian women work as domestic servants in the better-off neighbourhoods. Sicilians do refer to immigrants by certain racial/ethnic names, but they seem to be used interchangeably and imprecisely. For example, a common term for all immigrants, Asian or African, is *turchi*, which means *Turks*. The word can be applied teasingly to a Sicilian as well and in conversation may connote alarm as in "Mom, the Turks!" Other loosely applied terms are the Italian words for Moroccans, Blacks, and Tunisians. In a questionnaire given to school children, the great majority agreed with the statement that "a person's race is not important." The tolerance among Palermo's working class may be only temporary. Nonetheless, it suggests that researchers take a closer look at cases elsewhere that assume working-class racism against immigrants.

Recent politically conservative trends in the United States have succeeded in rolling back more progressive policies about immigration and minorities. Police raids in areas known to have many undocumented migrants have brought mass expulsion. Reversals of affirmative action in college admissions, initiated in California in the late 1990s, have gained widespread support among "nativist" Americans. This lifeboat mentality of exclusiveness and privilege is held mainly by the dominant White majority and others who have "made it."

However, political and economic considerations about immigration exist within broad frameworks, such as "melting pot ideology" or "multiculturalism." While the United States refers to the melting pot that assimilates newcomers, Canada's official multiculturalism policy, incorporated into law by the Multiculturalism Act of 1988, encourages individuals and communities to maintain linguistic and cultural diversity.

Migration and Human Rights

Several questions arise in the context of anthropological inquiry about migration and human rights. One important question is whether migration is forced or voluntary (see the Critical Thinking box on pages 344–345). Forced migration itself may be considered a violation of a person's human rights.

Another question concerns whether members of a displaced group have a guaranteed **right of return**, or repatriation, to their homeland. The right of return, which has been considered a basic human right in the West since the time of the Magna Carta, is included in the United Nations General Assembly Resolution 194 passed in 1948. It was elevated by the UN in 1974 to an "inalienable right."

Lessons Applied

STUDYING PASTORALISTS' MOVEMENTS FOR RISK ASSESSMENT AND SERVICE DELIVERY

PASTORALISTS ARE often vulnerable to malnutrition as a consequence of climate changes, fluctuations in food supply, and war and political upheaval. Because of their spatial mobility, they are difficult to reach with relief aid during a crisis. Cultural anthropologists are devising ways to gather and manage basic information about pastoralists' movements and nutritional needs in order to provide improved service delivery (Watkins and Fleisher 2002). The data required for such proactive planning include the following:

1. Information on the number of migrants and the size of their herds in a particular location and at a particular time. Such data can inform planners about the level of services required for public health programs, educational programs, and veterinary services. This information can be used to assess the demand on particular grazing areas and water sources and is therefore important in predicting possible future crises.

2. Information on patterns of migratory movements. This information can enable planners to move services to where the people are rather than expecting people to move to the services. Some NGOs, for example, are providing mobile banking services and mobile veterinary services. Information about pastoralist movements can be used as an early warning to prevent social conflicts that might result if several groups arrived in the same place at the same time. And

conflict resolution mechanisms can be put in place more effectively if conflict does occur.

The data collection involves interviews with pastoralists, often with one or two key informants, whom the anthropologists select for their specialized knowledge. Interviews cover topics such as the migratory paths followed (both typical and atypical), population levels, herd sizes, and the nutritional and water requirements of people and animals. Given the complex social systems of pastoralists, the data gathering must also include group leadership, decision-making practices, and concepts about land and water rights.

The anthropologists organize this information into a computerized database, linking the ethnographical data with geographic information systems (GIS) data on the environment and climate information from satellites. The anthropologists can then construct various scenarios and assess the relative risks that they pose to the people's health. Impending crises can be foreseen, and warning can be provided to governments and international aid agencies.

FOOD FOR THOUGHT

The tracking system described here remains outside the control of the pastoralists themselves. How might it be managed so that they participate more meaningfully and gain greater autonomy?

The right of return is an enduring issue for Palestinian refugees, of whom hundreds of thousands fled or were driven from their homes during the 1948 war (Zureik 1994). They went mainly to Jordan, the West Bank/East Jerusalem, Gaza, Lebanon, Syria, and other Arab states. Jordan and Syria have granted Palestinian refugees rights equal to those of their citizens. In Lebanon, where estimates of the number of Palestinian refugees range between 200 000 and 600 000, the government refuses them such rights (Salam 1994). The lower number is favoured by Israel because it makes the problem seem less severe; the higher number is favoured by the Palestinians to highlight the seriousness of their plight and by the Lebanese government to emphasize its inability to absorb so many. Palestinians know that they are not welcome in Lebanon, but they cannot return to Israel because Israel denies them the right of return. Israel

responds to the Palestinians' claims by saying that their acceptance of Jewish immigrants from Arab countries constitutes an equal exchange.

Protecting Migrants' Health

The health risks to migrants are many and varied because of the wide variety of migrant types and situations. Migrants whose livelihood depends on long-standing migratory economic systems, such as foraging, horticulture, and pastoralism, constitute one area of concern. Given the frequency in recent decades of drought and food shortages in the Sahel region of Africa, anthropologists are conducting studies to see how such conditions can be prevented, monitored, and more effectively coped with through humanitarian aid (see the Lessons Applied box).

Critical Thinking

HAITIAN CANE-CUTTERS IN THE DOMINICAN REPUBLIC— TWO VIEWS ON HUMAN RIGHTS

THE CIRCULATION of male labour from villages in Haiti to sugar estates in the Dominican Republic is the oldest and perhaps the largest continuing population movement within the Caribbean region (Martínez 1996). Beginning in the early twentieth century, Dominican sugar cane growers began to recruit Haitian workers, called *braceros*. Between 1952 and 1986, an agreement between the two countries' governments regulated and organized labour recruitment. Since then, recruitment became a private matter, with men crossing the border on their own or with recruiters working in Haiti without official approval.

Many studies and reports have addressed the system of labour recruitment from Haiti to the Dominican Republic. Two competing views exist. The human rights activists (View 1) focus on evidence of forced and fraudulent labour recruitment and take the position that this system violates the human rights of the Haitian labourers and is neo-slavery. The academics (View 2), while not completely unified in their views, use ethnographic data to support their position that it is inaccurate to consider the *braceros* as slaves because they have evidence that, more often, *braceros* migrate voluntarily.

View 1

Interviews with Haitian *braceros* in the Dominican Republic have exposed a consistent pattern of labour rights abuses:

> Men and boys as young as seven in rural Haiti are accosted by Haitian Creole-speaking recruiters making promises of easy, well-paid employment in the Dominican Republic. Those who agree are taken to the frontier on foot and are either taken directly to a farm in the Dominican Republic or perhaps more often are turned over by the recruiter to Dominican soldiers for a fee of a few pesos per recruit. Inside the Dominican Republic, soldiers and policemen also detain undocumented Haitians at highway checkpoints and in roundups conducted mostly in rural areas. Contrary to common international practice, the Dominican authorities generally do not deport undocumented Haitian entrants but hand them over, again for a fee, to agents of state-owned sugar estates, for shipment to company compounds. The recruits are transported from the frontier under armed military guard in buses that stop infrequently on the way east to minimize the risk of their Haitian passengers absconding.
>
> Once on the sugar estates, the recruits are given only one means of earning money for survival, cutting sugar cane.

Cutting cane is very physically debilitating labour, and in the Dominican Republic only the strongest and most experienced cane cutters can earn more than the equivalent of US$2 a day. Given the horrible labour conditions on the estates and the availability of lighter and better-paying work elsewhere in the Dominican Republic, it is not surprising that cane growers take measures to try to prevent their Haitian recruits from leaving. For example, armed guards patrol estate grounds on the lookout for any bracero who tries to leave in the night.

At work, too, the braceros are subjected to open coercion. On ordinary work days, they are obliged to go out to the cane fields before dawn, sometimes even if they are too sick to work. Company overseers may also force them to work on Sundays or after dark, to help ensure a constant supply of cane to the mill. . . . As if all these abuses were not bad enough, a many-branched system of pay reductions and petty corruption deprives the braceros of a large fraction of the wages to which they are legally entitled. Many Haitians on the sugar estates say they have never been able to save enough money to return home. (19–29)

View 2

Anthropological studies based on long-term fieldwork in Haiti provide observations that appear to contradict the neo-slavery interpretation. They find instead that most Haitian labour migrants cross the border to the Dominican Republic of their own volition. Samuel Martínez comments that "Recruitment by force in Haiti seems virtually unheard of. On the contrary, if this is a system of slavery, it may be the first in history to have to turn away potential recruits" (20). Some recruits have even paid bribes to be hired. Most people, even young people, are aware of

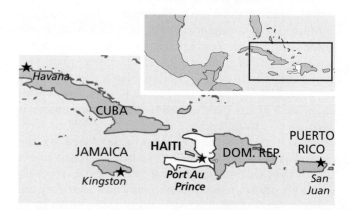

A Haitian migrant labourer. It is a matter of academic debate as to how much choice such a labourer has in terms of whether he will migrate to the neighbouring Dominican Republic for short-term work cutting cane, given the fact that he cannot find any kind of work in Haiti.

how terrible the working conditions are in the Dominican Republic. They therefore choose to go, understanding what they will face. Repeat migration is common and is also taken as evidence of free choice. In the cane fields, the major means of maintaining labour discipline is not force but wage incentives: The piece-work system ensures long and hard work. The life histories of *braceros* show that many of them move from one sugar estate to another, discrediting the view of the estates as being like "concentration camps."

Martínez adds a more focused understanding to View 2 by giving emphasis to the importance of the driving force of poverty in shaping the *braceros'* decisions to migrate. In this way, we can see, perhaps, a link between View 1 and View 2, since "neo-slavery" could be defined to include economic systems in which choice is so severely limited by economic needs that "freedom" is scarcely a factor in decision making:

> Both economically and legally, the bracero finds his freedoms narrowly restricted . . . poverty and the dearth of income opportunities and credit at home for the young, land-poor, and the unskilled leave many rural Haitians little or no choice about whether to emigrate. For example, the prevailing wage for a six-to-eight hour "day" of farm labor in rural Haiti is less than one dollar. Even at this wage, paid employment for poorer folk is scarce, because few Haitian farmers have the means to hire much labor. . . . Faced with such daunting obstacles to economic advancement at home, a man who lacks money, social support, and human capital to go to a more desirable urban or overseas destination may turn to the Dominican Republic, in hope of bringing home at least a small cash surplus. The typical migrant brings home savings of US$25 to $75, but many fail to save even this much. The fact that such meagre and uncertain rewards exert an important attraction suggests that most migrants leave home not so much to optimize their incomes as to grasp at any chance that may present itself . . . poverty drives dependent young men and male heads of poorer households to go to the Dominican Republic and thus opens the door to the labour rights abuses so amply documented. (21–22)

CRITICAL THINKING QUESTIONS

How might the research methods of the activists and the academic anthropologists differ?

How do these differences influence their results? Is either perspective more "biased" than the other in terms of presenting an accurate picture of the *bracero* system?

What does each view offer in terms of policy reform?

Source: Samuel Martínez 1996. Reproduced by permission of the American Anthropological Association from *American Anthropologist* 98:1, March 1996. Not for further reproduction.

WHAT are the reasons for migration?

Reasons for migration include the search for productive resources, for marriage and other domestic partnerships, or because of "push" factors such as warfare or natural disasters. People's adjustment to their new situations depends on the degree of voluntarism involved in the move, the degree of cultural difference between the place of origin and the destination, and how closely expectations about the new location are met, especially in terms of making a living and establishing social ties.

WHAT is a displaced person?

Displaced persons are one of the fastest growing categories of migrants. Refugees fleeing from political persecution, warfare, displacement by development projects, and ecological problems constitute an increasing number of all migrants. They face the most serious adjustment challenges since they often leave their home countries with few material resources and frequently have experienced much psychological suffering.

HOW are new immigrants contributing to transnational connections and multiculturalism?

Worldwide, new immigrants are contributing to growing transnational connections and the formation of increasingly multicultural populations within states. In Canada, the three largest non-European immigrant groups in the 1990s were from Hong Kong, India, and the Philippines. In 2004, 20 percent of Canada's population were visible minorities, most of them making up half the population of Canada's three largest cities, Toronto, Montreal, and Vancouver. Immigrant groups throughout the world are likely to face certain forms of discrimination in their new destinations, although the degree to which it occurs varies depending on perceived resource competition from already settled residents.

KEY CONCEPTS

chain migration, p. 338
circular migration, p. 333
development-induced displacement, p. 334
displaced persons, p. 333
internal migration, p. 331
internally displaced persons, p. 333
international migration, p. 331
lifeboat mentality, p. 342

migration, p. 330
new immigrants, p. 336
push–pull theory, p. 331
refugees, p. 333
right of return, p. 342
transnational migration, p. 331
wage labour migration, p. 333

SUGGESTED READINGS

Rogaia Mustafa Abusharaf, *Wanderings: Sudanese Migrants and Exiles in North America*. Ithaca, NY: Cornell University Press, 2002. This book explores the topic of Sudanese migration to the United States and Canada. The author provides historical background on the first wave, information on various Sudanese groups who have migrated, and an interpretation of Sudanese identity in North America as more unified than it is in the homeland.

Linda Basch, Nina Glick Schiller, and Christina Szanton Blanc, *Nations Unbound: Transnational Projects, Postcolonial Predicaments, and Deterritorialized Nation-States*. Langhorne, PA: Gordon and Breach Science Publishers, 1994. Eight chapters explore theoretical issues in transnational migration and present detailed analysis of cases of migration from the Caribbean, including St. Vincent, Grenada, and Haiti.

Morton Beiser, *Strangers at the Gate: The "Boat People's" First Ten Years in Canada*. Toronto: University of Toronto Press, 1999. This volume aims to inform the Canadian public about the impact of refugees on Canada, and shows how these newcomers have struggled, without making extensive use of health and social services.

Colin Clarke, Ceri Peach, and Steven Vertovec, eds., *South Asians Overseas: Migration and Ethnicity*. New York: Cambridge University Press, 1990. The text includes 15 chapters plus introductory essays that place the case studies in a broader context. Chapters are divided into two sections: South Asians in colonial and post-colonial contexts and South Asians in contemporary Western countries and the Middle East.

W. Giles, H. Moussa, and P. Van Esterik, eds., *Development and Diaspora: Gender and the Refugee Experience*. Dundas, ON: Artemis Enterprises, 1996. Chapters in this edited volume explore the relation among gender, development, and the movements of refugees, and include an examination of the resettlement process.

Sherri Grasmuck and Patricia R. Pessar, *Between Two Islands: Dominican International Migration*. Berkeley: University of California Press, 1991. Based on fieldwork in the Dominican Republic and New York City, this volume focuses on social ties and networks facilitating migration from rural areas in the Dominican Republic to Santo Domingo and from the Dominican Republic to the United States, and how employment opportunities shape the migration experience.

P. Magocsi, ed., *Encyclopedia of Canada's Peoples*. Toronto: University of Toronto Press, 1999. Edited by the director of the Multicultural History Society of Ontario, this massive book gathers complex information on about 130 peoples that make up Canadian society, including details about their origins, settlement, and intergroup dynamics.

Beatriz Manz, *Refugees of a Hidden War: The Aftermath of Counterinsurgency in Guatemala*. Albany: State University of New York Press, 1988. This study was conducted to assess whether conditions would allow the return to Guatemala of 46 000 Indian peasant refugees living in camps in Mexico. It gives attention to aspects of family and community life in the camps and in resettled villages in Guatemala, where the Indians face discrimination and harassment from the military.

Jennifer Robertson, *Native and Newcomer: Making and Remaking a Japanese City*. Berkeley: University of California Press, 1991. This text studies the social and symbolic adjustments of native residents of Kodaira city and the many residents who moved to Kodaira beginning in the 1950s. Detailed attention is given to the role of a community festival in expressing links between the natives and newcomers, while also stating and maintaining group boundaries.

Archana B. Verma, *The Making of Little Punjab in Canada: Patterns of Immigration*. Thousand Oaks, CA; Sage Publications, 2002. This book traces the historical connections between Hindu migrants from Paldi village, in India's northern state of Punjab, to Vancouver Island, British Columbia. Strong family and kinship ties continue to link the migrants to their home area. Caste group solidarity among the migrants provides support in the face of discrimination on the part of the wider Canadian society.

WEBLINKS

The Companion Website (www.pearsoned.ca/miller) that accompanies *Cultural Anthropology*, Third Canadian Edition, includes a destinations module containing links to many websites relevant to the content of this chapter. Use it to investigate the Web and expand your understanding of anthropology.

KEY QUESTIONS

- **HOW** do cultural anthropologists study change?

- **WHAT** are the most common approaches to development?

- **WHAT** does cultural anthropology contribute to understanding some major issues in development?

16

DEVELOPMENT ANTHROPOLOGY

International tourism is a huge and growing part of the global and local economies of many countries. Tourists are increasingly interested in "cultural" tourism through which they are able to see and participate in certain aspects of the culture they visit. Safari tour groups in Africa, as in the case of a trip to Maasailand shown here, combine exposure to wildlife and Maasai culture.

We have had many visitors to Walpole Island since the French "discovered us" in the seventeenth century in our territory, Bkejwanong. In many cases, these visitors failed to recognize who we were and to appreciate our traditions. They tried to place us in their European framework of knowledge, denying that we possessed our indigenous knowledge. They attempted to steal our lands, water, and knowledge. We resisted. They left and never came back. We continued to share our knowledge with the next visitors to our place. . . . It was a long-term strategy that has lasted more than three hundred years. (Dr. Dean Jacobs, Executive Director of Walpole Island First Nation, from his Foreword in VanWynsberghe 2002:ix)

The Walpole Island First Nation, located in southwestern Ontario, near Sarnia, has taken strong action in recent decades to protect its culture and environment. They organized themselves and successfully fought to control industrial waste that was polluting local water sources and land. Through their community-based research and advocacy, they have sought to safeguard their resources and gain environmental justice.

All cultures go through change, but the causes, processes, and outcomes are varied. Cultural change can be intentional or accidental, forward-looking or backward-looking, rapid or gradual, obvious or subtle, beneficial or harmful.

Anthropologists contribute to the understanding of how humanity has changed and how it continues to change. Biological anthropologists who study human evolution and humanity's relationship with non-human primates have the longest view. They look back many thousands—even millions—of years to learn how human biology and culture emerged. Archaeologists examine human cultural remains, from both prehistory and history, to discover how and when people migrated throughout the world and how social complexity developed. Linguistic anthropologists study the evolution of communication patterns and capabilities in prehistoric times, the spread and change in verbal and written languages with the emergence of settled life and of the state, and change in contemporary patterns of communication, including the effects of mass media.

In contrast to these three fields of anthropology, cultural anthropology's roots lie in the **synchronic** study of culture, or a "one-time" snapshot view of culture with minimal or no attention to the past. This early approach led to a static view of culture, perpetuating the images of cultures presented by ethnographers of, say, the 1960s or 1970s as though they had continuing validity decades later. Cultural anthropologists are currently moving away from such time-static approaches. They are paying more attention to cultural history and to studying cultures through time, replacing the synchronic approach with a **diachronic** (across-time) approach.

This chapter focuses on the topic of contemporary cultural change as shaped by development, which is directed change to achieve improved human welfare. The subject matter constitutes the important subfield of *development anthropology,* or the study of how culture and development interact. We consider general processes of cultural change in the first part of the chapter and contemporary theories and models in the second part. In the last section, we look in detail at three major issues in development anthropology: women and development, indigenous people, and human rights.

Critical Thinking

SOCIAL EFFECTS OF THE GREEN REVOLUTION

AGRICULTURAL SCIENTISTS of the 1950s, inspired by the laudable goal of eliminating world hunger, developed genetic variations of wheat, rice, and corn. These high-yielding varieties (HYV) of seeds were promoted to farmers throughout the developing world as part of the "Green Revolution" that would feed the world by boosting food production. In most places where Green Revolution agricultural practices were adopted, grain production did increase. Was world hunger conquered? The answer is no, because world hunger is not merely a problem of production; it also involves distribution.

Analyses of the social impact of the Green Revolution in India reveal that one of its results was to increase disparities between the rich and the poor (Frankel 1971). How did this happen? Green Revolution agriculture requires several expensive inputs: purchased seeds (HYV seeds cannot be harvested from the crop and saved until the next year because they are hybridized), the heavy use of commercial fertilizers, and the need for dependable irrigation sources. Thus, farmers who could use HYV seeds successfully tended to be those who were already better off because they could afford such inputs. Small farmers who tried planting HYV seeds but could not provide these inputs experienced crop failure, went deeper into debt, and ended up having to sell the small amounts of land they had. Larger and better-off farmers took advantage of these new openings in the land market to accumulate more land and expand their holdings. With the acquisition of tractors and other mechanized equipment, large farmers became even more productive. Small farm-

ers were unable to compete and continued to be squeezed out financially. They became hired day labourers, dependent on seasonal employment by large farmers, or they migrated to cities where they became part of the urban underclass.

Looking at the Green Revolution from a critical thinking perspective, we may see more clearly whose interests were served, whether this was the original intention or not. The big winners included the companies involved in selling chemical fertilizers (largely petroleum-based) and HYV seeds, companies that manufacture and sell mechanized farm equipment, the larger farmers whose income levels improved, and the research scientists themselves who gained funding for their research and world fame for their discoveries. In retrospect, it is difficult to imagine that early planners in the 1950s could have been so naive as to not realize who they would be helping and who they might end up hurting.

CRITICAL THINKING QUESTIONS

Is it likely that the original innovators of HYV grains considered what social transformations might occur in developing country agriculture as a result of their invention?

Would they have been likely to stop their research if they had realized that it would lead to the "rich getting richer and the poor getting poorer"? Should they have done so?

How does this example shed light on current debates about genetically modified food?

TWO PROCESSES OF CULTURAL CHANGE

All cultures change, but the causes and processes of change are varied. Basically, two processes drive all cultural change. The first is internal: the discovery of something new. The second is external: incorporation of something new from the outside. In this section, we consider some examples of cultural change brought about by each of these processes.

Invention

The invention of something new may prompt cultural change. Inventions usually evolve gradually, through stepwise experimentation and accumulation of knowledge, but some appear rather suddenly. We can all name many technological inventions that have created cultural change—for example the printing press, gun powder, polio vaccine, and satellite communication. (See the Critical Thinking box.)

Diffusion

Diffusion is the spread of cultural innovations, such as technology and ways of behaving and thinking, through

Lessons Applied

THE SAAMI, SNOWMOBILES, AND THE NEED FOR SOCIAL IMPACT ANALYSIS

HOW WILL adoption of a new belief or practice benefit or harm a particular culture and its various members? This question is difficult to answer, but it must always be asked. A classic study of the "snowmobile disaster" among a Saami group in Finland offers a careful response to this question in a context of rapid technological diffusion (Pelto 1973). In the 1950s, the Saami of Finland (previously referred to by outsiders as Lapps, which, in the Saami language, is a derogatory term) had an economy based on fishing and reindeer herding, which provided most of the diet. Reindeer had several other important economic and social functions. They were used as draft animals, especially for hauling wood for fuel. Their hides were made into clothing and their sinews used for sewing. Reindeer were key items of exchange, both in external trade and internal gift-giving. A child was given a reindeer to mark the appearance of his or her first tooth. When a couple became engaged, they exchanged a reindeer with each other to make the commitment. Reindeer were the most important wedding gift. Each summer the herds were let free and then rounded up in the fall, a time of communal festivity.

By the 1960s, all this had changed because of the introduction of the snowmobile. Previously, the men had tended the reindeer herds on skis. Introduction of snowmobiles in herd management had several results. The herds were no longer kept closely domesticated for part of the year, dur-

ing which they became tame. Instead they were allowed to roam freely all year and thus became wilder. On snowmobiles, the men would cover larger amounts of territory at roundup time to bring in the animals, and sometimes several roundups occurred instead of one.

Herd size declined dramatically. Reasons for the decline included the stress caused to the reindeer by the extra distance travelled during roundups, the multiple roundups instead of a single one, and the fear aroused by the noisy snowmobiles. Roundups were now held at a time when the females were near the end of their pregnancy, another factor causing reproductive stress. As the number of snowmobiles increased, the number of reindeer decreased.

Another economic change involved dependence on outside resources through links to the cash economy. Cash was needed to purchase a snowmobile and gasoline, and to pay for parts and repairs. This delocalization of the economy led to social inequality, which had not existed before:

- The cash cost of effective participation in herding exceeded the resources of some families, who therefore had to drop out of serious participation in herding.
- The use of snowmobiles changed the age pattern of reindeer herding in favour of youth over age; thus, older herders were squeezed out.

contact between different groups of people. It is logically related to invention because useful new discoveries are likely to spread. Diffusion can occur in several ways. First, in mutual borrowing, two roughly equal societies exchange elements of their culture with each other. For example, the United States exported rock and roll music to England and England exported the Beatles to the United States. Second, diffusion may occur between unequal societies and involve a transfer from a dominant culture to a less powerful culture. This process may occur through force or more subtly through education or marketing processes that promote adoption of new practices and beliefs. For example, through volunteer groups such as CUSO or WUSC (World University Service of Canada), many North American products, practices, and beliefs are spread to developing countries. Third, a more powerful culture may appropriate

aspects of a less powerful culture (the latter process is called *cultural imperialism*). For example, the Tower of London in England is full of priceless jewels from India.

In each of these types of diffusion, the result is some degree of **acculturation**, or change in one culture as a result of contact with another culture. At one extreme, a culture may become so completely acculturated that it has become **assimilated**, no longer distinguishable as having a separate identity. In many cases, cultural change through diffusion has led to extreme change in the "receiving" culture, which becomes deculturated, or extinct. Such deculturation has occurred among many indigenous peoples as the result of the introduction of new technology (see the Lessons Applied box). Other responses to acculturative influences include resistance, rejection, or partial acceptance of something new with reformulation and reshap-

- The snowmobile pushed many Saami into debt.
- The dependence on cash and indebtedness forced many Saami to migrate to cities for work.

Pertti Pelto, the anthropologist who documented this case, terms these transformations a "disaster" for Saami culture. He offers some recommendations that might be helpful for the future: The lesson of the Saami, and of some other groups, should be presented to communities before they adopt new technology so that they will better understand the potential consequences; any group facing change should have a chance to weigh evidence on the pros and cons and make an informed judgment, something that the Saami had no chance to do. Pelto's work is thus one of the early warnings from anthropology about the need for **social impact assessments** to gauge the potential social costs and benefits of particular innovations before the change is undertaken.

FOOD FOR THOUGHT

Are there any parallels in the way snowmobiles influenced the subsistence patterns of the Inuit?

Can you suggest what technological and cultural changes might have accompanied the "Distant Early Warning" radar system in the Canadian Arctic following World War II? Or Nunavut's launch into self-government in 1999?

The Saami are an indigenous Nordic people currently living in the two countries of Norway and Finland. Since the 1980s they have been fighting for legal rights in the countries where they live and, more broadly, in the Nordic Council, a regional association in which they have no representation. Saami activists are working on many issues including land rights, water rights, natural resource rights, language rights, other cultural rights, and political representation.

ing, like cricket in the Trobriands (see Chapter 14). The study of international development is, in fact, concerned with the dynamics and results of a particular form of change—the adoption of Western goods, behaviour, and values through processes such as neocolonialism, globalization, and international assistance projects.

Services for photocopying and sending faxes, invented in the West, have been recently diffused to most parts of the world, including the formerly remote capital of India's Andaman Islands, Port Blair. A popular restaurant at the same location also demonstrates the diffusion of cuisine: South Indian, Chinese, and Continental.

APPROACHES TO DEVELOPMENT

In this section we consider the theories of and approaches to international development that are applied by various kinds of organizations—both large-scale organizations and small grassroots ones. We look closely at the development project as the main mechanism that development organizations use for bringing about change. Special methods used by anthropologists who work in the field of development are then discussed.

Theories and Models

This section discusses five theories or models of change that influence approaches to international development. They differ mainly in terms of the importance that they attach to economic growth versus equitable distribution of resources, in which measures of development they assume are most meaningful (for example, income versus health or education), and in the degree to which they take into account the environmental and financial sustainability of particular development goals.

Modernization

Modernization theory refers to change marked by industrialization, consolidation of the nation-state, bureaucratization, market economy, technological innovation, literacy, and options for social mobility. It derives from a period in Western European history beginning in the seventeenth century, which emphasized the importance of secular rationality and the inevitable advance of scientific thinking (Norgaard 1994). Modernization appears as almost an inevitable process that will, given the insights of science and rationality, spread throughout the world and lead to improvement in people's lives everywhere. Overall, the emphasis of modernization is on material progress and individual betterment.

Supporters and critics of modernization are found in both rich and poor countries. Supporters claim that the benefits of modernization (improved transportation; electricity; domestic comforts such as air conditioning; and technology such as washing machines, biomedical health care, and telecommunications) are worth the costs—whether those costs are environmental or social. Other scholars in many disciplines—from literary studies to anthropology—regard modernization as problematic. Most cultural anthropologists are critics of modernization as a general process of social change because it leads to increased social inequality, the destruction of indigenous cultures, ecological ruin, and the overall decline in global cultural diversity. Selected aspects of modernity, however, such as electricity and antibiotics, may be accepted as positive. In spite of strong cautionary critiques from anthropologists and environmentalists about the negative impacts of modernization, nations around the world have not slowed their attempts to achieve it.

Growth-Oriented Development

International development emerged as a prominent theory about change after World War II. By the middle of the twentieth century, most countries had obtained political independence, but many were in a state of economic dependence. One can think of development as the attempt, through conscious planning and intervention, to increase economic productivity in the developing world. Indeed, **international development**, as conceived by major development institutions such as the World Bank, is similar to modernization in terms of its ultimate goals. The process, however, emphasizes economic growth as the most crucial element in development. According to this theory, investments in economic growth in some sectors of the population will subsequently support (through the "trickle-down" effect) wider achievement of improved human welfare, such as health and education. Since the 1950s, many industrialized countries have emphasized economic development in their foreign aid packages, especially the transfer of Western economic expertise (in the form of advisers) and technology (such as agricultural equipment) to developing countries. Promoting growth-oriented development in poor nations, as practised by most large-scale development organizations, includes two major economic strategies:

- Increasing economic productivity and trade through, for example, new forms of agriculture, irrigation, and markets.
- Reducing government expenditures on public services such as schools and health in order to reduce debt and reallocate resources to uses perceived to be more directly related to increased production. This strategy, called **structural adjustment**, has been promoted by the World Bank since the 1980s.

The growth-oriented development model is being powerfully spread throughout the world under the current intensified pattern of economic and political globalization. As noted in Chapter 1, cultural anthropologists are now taking up the research challenge presented by intensified globalization to study its effects on local cultures—and the effects of those cultures on efforts at globalization.

Distributional Development

In contrast to the growth-oriented development approach, a distributional approach to development views poverty as the result of global economic and political factors, such as world trade imbalances between nations and unequal distribution of resources within nations and communities. This approach rejects the claim of other approaches that poverty is caused by some inadequacy on the part of poor people or poor countries themselves (Rahnema 1992). In terms of poverty reduction, its position is based on evidence that growth-oriented strategies applied without concern for distribution result in increased social inequality, with the "rich getting richer and the poor getting poorer."

The distributional approach takes a critical view of structural adjustment promoted in the growth-oriented approach because it further undermines the welfare of the poor by reducing public services. Advocates of the distributional approach insist on the need to readjust access to crucial resources such as food within countries in order to allow the poor to have a greater ability to produce and provide for their own needs. Within a particular country, the distributional approach involves the following strategies that differ markedly from the growth-oriented approach (Gardner and Lewis 1996). The first step—called *resource assessment*—is to do research on the social distribution of access to critical resources. The next step, called *cultural assessment*, involves research on the positive or negative effects of development projects on the culture, with special attention to internal social variation. The third step is *redistribution of critical resources*, especially land, to take into account inequities discovered in the first two steps. The last step is implementation of *assistance programs*, which are another way to achieve greater social equity through the targeted provision of services such as health care and education.

Many conservative economists argue on economic grounds that redistribution is not a realistic or a feasible strategy. Nevertheless, anthropologists have reported many cases in which the redistribution model has worked. Anthropological research in Nadur village, Kerala, posed the question of whether redistribution was an effective and realistic development strategy (Franke 1993). The answer was yes. Kerala's per capita income is low in comparison to the rest of India and to the rest of the world. Yet, although income remained low and stagnant, substantial material improvements occurred in many people's lives, including some of the poorest of the poor. How did this happen? Redistribution was not the result of a socialist revolution; it took place through democratic channels—protests and pressure on the government by people's groups and labour unions. These groups forced the state to reallocate land ownership, shifting some land to the landless and thereby reducing inequality (although not eradicating it completely). In other instances, people pressured government leaders to improve village conditions by improving the schools, providing school lunches for poor children, and increasing attendance by *dalit* children.

Throughout the 1960s and 1970s, Nadur village became a better place to live, for many people.

Human Development

Yet another alternative to the "growth-first" strategy is called **human development**, the strategy that emphasizes investing in human welfare. The United Nations adopted the phrase *human development* in order to emphasize the need for improvements in human welfare in terms of health, education, and personal security and safety. According to this approach, improvements in human welfare will lead to overall development of the nation. We know that the reverse is not true. The level of economic growth of a country (or region within a country) is not necessarily correlated with its level of human development. Obviously, the relationship between poverty and development is very complex. Some poor countries, and areas within countries such as India's Kerala state, have achieved higher levels of human development than their GNP or GDP would predict. Thus, in this view, economic growth is not an end in itself. The goal of development should be improved levels of human welfare.

Sustainable Development

Sustainable development questions the long-term financial and environmental viability of the single-minded pursuit of economic growth. According to this view, the economic growth achieved by the wealthy nations has occurred at great cost to the environment and cannot be sustained at its present level. Since the 1980s, **sustainable development**, or forms of development that do not destroy non-renewable resources and are financially supportable by the host country, has gained prominence in international development. This approach emphasizes meeting the needs of the present without compromising the ability of future generations to meet their needs. The Canadian International Development Agency (CIDA) sustainable development program stresses preserving biodiversity, avoiding environmental degradation, and considering equity and social justice issues.

Institutional Approaches to Development

Cultural anthropologists have become increasingly aware of the importance of examining the institutions and organizations involved in international development. This knowledge helps cultural anthropologists have a greater impact on how development is done. They have studied the management systems of large-scale institutions, such as the United Nations agencies and the World Bank, as well as "local" management systems found in diverse settings.

TABLE 16.1 Major Agencies within the United Nations Related to International Development

Agency	Headquarters	Function
UNDP (The United Nations Development Program)	New York City	UNDP provides many different services designed to help a country in planning and managing its own development through executing agencies: groundwater and mineral exploration, computer and satellite technology, seed production and agricultural extension, and research.
FAO (The Food and Agricultural Organization)	Rome, Italy	FAO implements agricultural field projects that receive funding from the UNDP as well as "host governments." It monitors global food stocks and factors affecting food prices to ensure food security.
WHO (The World Health Organization)	Geneva, Switzerland	WHO has four goals: developing and organizing personnel and technology for disease prevention and control; eradication of major tropical diseases; immunization of all children against major childhood diseases; and establishing primary health care services.
UNICEF (The United Nations Children's Emergency Fund)	Joint headquarters New York City and Geneva, Switzerland	UNICEF, with nearly 90 field offices in developing countries, is concerned with basic health care and social services for children. UNICEF receives about three-fourths of its funding from UN member governments and the other one-fourth from the general public.
UNESCO (The United Nations Educational, Scientific, and Cultural Organization)	Paris, France	UNESCO is dedicated to enhancing world peace and security through education, science, and culture, and to promoting respect for human rights, the rule of law, and fundamental freedoms. One of UNESCO's practical concerns is to promote literacy.
UNHCR (The United Nations High Commission for Refugees)	Geneva, Switzerland	UNHCR is dedicated to promoting the rights and safety of refugees. It coordinates international efforts to solve refugee dilemmas.
UNIFEM (The United Nations International Development Fund for Women)	New York City	UNIFEM promotes projects directed toward raising the status of women. It supports initiatives that promote the political, social, and economic empowerment of women, and gender equality, and it ensures that women's issues are coordinated within the UN development system.
UNFPA (The United Nations Fund for Population Activities)	New York City	UNFPA supports family planning projects and projects that improve reproductive health. It helps formulate policies related to global and national population issues.

Source: Hancock 1989.

They have also examined internal hierarchies and inequalities, social interactions, symbols of power, and development discourse within the institutions themselves. This section first describes some of the major development institutions and then discusses smaller grassroots organizations.

Large-Scale Institutions

Large-scale development institutions can be separated into the *multilaterals* (those that include several nations as donors) and the *bilaterals* (those that involve a relationship between only two countries, a donor and a recipient). The major multilaterals include the United Nations and the World Bank, each constituting a vast and complex social system. The United Nations, established in 1945, includes in 2005 some 191 member states, each contributing an amount of money according to its ability to pay, and each given one vote in the General Assembly. Table 16.1 shows the major agencies within the United Nations and their functions.

The World Bank is supported by contributions from over 150 member countries. Founded in 1944 at a conference called by U.S. President F. D. Roosevelt in Bretton Woods, New Hampshire, "the Bank" is dedicated to promoting the concept of economic growth and expanded purchasing power throughout the world (B. Rich 1994). The main strategy is to promote international investment through loans. The World Bank is guided by a board of governors made up of the finance ministers of member countries. Rather than following the United Nations' approach of one country–one vote, in the World Bank system, the number of votes is based on the size of a country's financial commitment: "There is no pretense of equality—the economic superpowers run the show" (Hancock 1989:51).

Two major units within the World Bank are the International Bank for Reconstruction and Development (IBRD) and the International Development Association (IDA). Both are administered at the World Bank headquarters in Washington, D.C. They both lend for similar types of projects and often in the same country, but their conditions of lending differ. The IBRD provides loans to the poorest nations, which are generally regarded as "bad risks" on the world commercial market. Thus, the IBRD is a source of interest-bearing loans to countries that otherwise would not be able to borrow. The IBRD does not allow rescheduling of debt payments. It has recorded a profit every year of its existence, so it is in the interesting position of being a profit-making aid institution. Most of its loans support large infrastructure projects and, more recently, sectoral development in health and education. The IDA is the "soft-loan" side of the World Bank because it provides interest-free loans (although there is a 0.75 percent annual "service charge") and a flexible repayment schedule averaging between 35 and 40 years (B. Rich 1994:77). These concessional loans are granted to the poorest countries for projects of high development priority. The International Monetary Fund (IMF), also created in 1944, monitors the monetary policies of member nations, and provides credit for member countries experiencing temporary balance of payments deficits.

Critics of the World Bank and the IMF come from many directions, including politicians, scholars, and people whose lives have been affected negatively by their projects. Politicians in the United States who oppose foreign aid to developing countries in any form point to the overlapping and wasteful organization of some United Nations institutions and the fact that they seem to have accomplished too little in comparison to the funds required of member countries to support them. Others argue that, too often, the projects supported by these institutions have failed to help the poor but, instead, provide thousands of jobs for the people in their employment and are good business investments for first-world countries. Such critics point especially to the biased lending and aid policies that are shaped more by political factors than by economic need.

Prominent bilateral institutions include the Japan International Cooperation Agency (JICA), CIDA, the United States Agency for International Development (USAID), the United Kingdom's Department for International Development (DfID), the Swedish Agency for International Development (SIDA), and the Danish Organization for International Development (DANIDA). These agencies vary in terms of the proportion of aid disbursed as loans that have to be repaid or as grants that do not require repayment. Another variation is whether the loans or grants are "tied" to supporting specific projects that also provide for substantial donor country involvement in providing goods, services, and expertise versus being "untied," or allowing the recipient country the freedom to decide how to use the funds. The USAID generally offers more aid in the form of loans than grants, and more in tied than untied aid, especially in comparison to aid from Sweden, the Netherlands, Canada, and Norway.

Another difference among the bilaterals is the proportion of their total assistance that goes to the poorest of countries. The United Kingdom's DfID sends more than 80 percent of its aid to the poorest countries, while the largest chunk of U.S. foreign aid goes to Egypt and Israel. Canada's Official Development Assistance (ODA) used to be motivated by a moral obligation to help those who are oppressed or live in poverty. However, around 1994, priorities shifted to projects that support trade rather than targeting the poorest countries. Nevertheless, Canada seldom uses ODA to secure support for foreign policy objectives (Morrison 2000:22). Table 16.2 lists CIDA's ODA priorities.

Emphasis on certain types of aid also varies from bilateral institution to bilateral institution. Cuba has long played a unique role in bilateral aid, although this fact is not well known. Rather than offering assistance for a wide range of development projects, Cuba has concentrated on aid for training health care providers and promoting preventive health care (Feinsilver 1993). Most of Cuba's development assistance goes to socialist countries, including many in Africa.

Grassroots Approaches

Many countries have experimented with what are sometimes called grassroots approaches to development, or locally initiated "bottom-up" projects. This alternative to "top-down" development as pursued by the large-scale agencies described in the previous section is more likely to be culturally appropriate, locally supported through participation, and successful. During the 1970s, Kenya sponsored a national program whereby the government committed itself to provide teachers to local communities that built schools (Winans and Haugerud 1977). This program was part of Kenya's promotion of *harambee*, or self-help, in many sectors, including health, housing, and

TABLE 16.2 CIDA's ODA Priorities

Canada's Official Development Assistance (ODA) program concentrates resources on the following six priorities:

- *Basic human needs:* To support efforts to provide primary health care, basic education, family planning, nutrition, water and sanitation, and shelter. Canada will continue to respond to emergencies with humanitarian assistance. Canada will commit 25 percent of its ODA to basic human needs as a means of enhancing its focus on addressing the security of the individual.

- *Gender equity:* To support the achievement of equality between women and men to ensure sustainable development.

- *Infrastructure services:* To help developing countries to deliver environmentally sound infrastructure services, with an emphasis on poorer groups and on capacity building.

- *Human rights, democracy, good governance:* To increase respect for human rights, including children's rights; to promote democracy and better governance; and to strengthen both civil society and the security of the individual.

- *Private sector development:* To promote sustained and equitable economic growth by supporting private sector development in developing countries.

- *Environment:* To help developing countries protect their environment and contribute to addressing global and regional environmental issues.

Source: CIDA 2004.

CIDA's project with a Montreal-based NGO investigates a 1982 massacre in Guatemala. This project reflects CIDA's development priorities concerning human rights, democracy, and good governance.

schooling. Local people's response to the schooling program, especially, was overwhelmingly positive. They turned out in large numbers to build schools, which was their part of the bargain. Given the widespread construction of schools, the government found itself hard pressed to respond to its end of the bargain: paying the teachers' salaries. This program shows that self-help movements can be highly successful in terms of mobilizing local contributions, if the target—in this case, children's education—is something that is highly valued.

Many non-governmental, grassroots organizations have existed for several decades. Prominent international examples include Oxfam, CARE, and Feed the Children. Churches also sponsor grassroots development. In Bangladesh, for example, the Lutheran Relief Agency has played an important role in helping local people provide and maintain small-scale infrastructure projects such as village roads and canals.

With the push toward privatization in the 1980s in North America and Britain, an emphasis on supporting development efforts through non-governmental organizations (NGOs) emerged. This trend prompted the formation of many NGOs in developing countries that often became partners with bilateral agencies to develop and support local projects. For example, the Canada Fund in Thailand supports Thai NGOs that give small seed grants to grassroots organizations in rural Thailand. In India, CIDA collaborated with government agencies and NGOs to support a Tree Grower's Cooperative in three states undergoing rapid deforestation.

The Development Project

Development organizations, whether they are large multilaterals or small, local NGOs, rely on the concept of the development project as the specific set of activities that put policies into action. For example, suppose a government sets a policy of increased agricultural production by a certain percentage within a certain period. Development projects put in place to achieve the policy goal might include the construction of irrigation canals that would supply water to a specified number of farmers.

Anthropologists and the Project Cycle

The details vary among organizations, but all development projects have a basic **project cycle**, or the full process of a project from initial planning to completion (Cernea 1985). These steps include:

- *Project identification:* Selecting a project to fit a particular purpose.

- *Project design:* Preparing the details of the project.
- *Project appraisal:* Assessing the project's budget.
- *Project implementation:* Putting the project into place.
- *Project evaluation:* Assessing whether the project goals were fulfilled.

Since the 1970s, anthropologists have been hired to offer insights into the project cycle at different stages, and with differing impacts. In the early phase of their involvement, anthropologists were hired primarily to do project evaluations, the last step in the project cycle, to determine whether the project had achieved its goals. Unfortunately, many evaluations reported the projects to be dismal failures. Some of the most frequent findings were (1) the target group, such as the poor or women, had not been "reached," but instead project benefits had gone to some other group; (2) the project was inappropriate for the context; and (3) the intended beneficiaries were actually worse off after the project than before (as in the case of dam construction, for example).

Jim Freedman (2000), a Canadian anthropologist who has worked as a consultant for bilateral (CIDA) and multilateral (United Nations) organizations, conducted a baseline study and an impact study of an irrigation and salinity control project in northern Pakistan. The project cycle provides part of the story about the results, but he goes beyond the project cycle to analyze the impact on the people most affected by the project—the freedom-loving Pathans, people whose ancestral roots lie in stateless, semi-nomadic life. Freedman summarizes the steps of the project cycle:

- *Project identification:* Renovate a water delivery system and reduce soil salination.

- *Project design:* An underground drainage system would be provided to control salination, which would increase food production and result in higher incomes for local farmers.

- *Project appraisal:* The budget was negotiated between CIDA, the World Bank, and the government of Pakistan.

- *Project implementation:* The drains were built, food production (wheat, sugarcane, and maize) increased modestly (around 5 percent over 10 years), but during the process of building the system, some small farmers were displaced.

- *Project evaluation:* The project assumed that the cost to small farmers was a small price to pay for the value of the improved technology to the more productive farmers (200–208).

Freedman drew much broader conclusions about the interconnections between prosperity and democracy from the experience of working with this project. He observed that economic growth undermined social equity, and social and economic inequities undermined economic growth, a condition for democracy. What was missing from the project was a consideration of the effect of widening income disparities in the project villages and resultant shifts in power relations. The improved irrigation allowed landlords to increase their power over land and over their tenants, who became even more dependent on the protection of their patrons. The resulting factions intensified the conflict between rival landlords. Although the landlords increased their personal wealth, this did not translate into increased well-being for the villages, where disparities in wealth doubled or tripled (Freedman 2000).

One reason development initiatives often failed was that projects were typically identified and designed by Western economists located in cities far from the intended project site. These experts applied a "universal" formula, with little or no attention to the local cultural context (J. Scott 1998). In other words, projects were designed by "people-distant" and culturally uninformed economists and planners, but were evaluated by "people-close" and culturally informed anthropologists. By demonstrating the weaknesses in project planning that led to failed projects, and the need to take local cultural context into account in projects, cultural anthropologists gained a reputation in development circles as troublemakers and "nay-sayers."

Cultural anthropologists worked during the 1980s and 1990s to find a greater role earlier on in the project cycle, especially at the project identification and design stages. Although they are still far less powerful than economists in defining development policy, many anthropologists have made important contributions in this direction, including having leadership roles in development organizations. Their role as watchdogs and critics should not be discounted because it draws attention to important problems.

Socio-cultural Fit

Through the years, anthropologists have provided many examples of projects that were culturally inappropriate, some amusing and others not. All were a waste of time and money. A comparative study (Kottak 1985) reviewed evaluations of 68 development projects to see if the economic success of projects was related to **socio-cultural fit**, or how well a project meshes with the local culture and population. Results showed a strong correlation between the two factors. A project to improve nutrition and health in the South Pacific involved the transfer of large quantities of American powdered milk to an island community. The inhabitants, however, were lactose intolerant (unable to digest raw milk) and everyone soon had diarrhea. Realizing what caused this outbreak, the people used the powdered milk to whitewash their houses. Beyond wasting resources, inappropriately designed projects can result in the exclusion of the intended beneficiaries, such as when a person's signature is required among people who cannot write, or a photo identification card is requested from Muslim women, whose faces should not be shown in public. One role for anthropologists is to expose areas of non-fit and provide insights about how to achieve socio-cultural fit and enhance project success rates.

The Anthropological Critique of Development Projects

The early decades of development anthropology were dominated by what can be called **traditional development anthropology (TDA)**. In TDA, the anthropologist accepts the role of helping to make development work better, a kind of "add an anthropologist and stir" approach to development. Economists and others realize that anthropologists can help make their projects more effective. For example, an anthropologist familiar with a local culture can provide information about what kinds of consumer goods would be desired by the people, or what might induce them to relocate with less resistance. This kind of participation by anthropologists could be either positive or negative for the local people, depending on the project being undertaken.

Anthropologists have expressed concern that helping make large-scale development projects work can be disastrous for local people and their environments (Bodley 1990; Horowitz and Salem-Murdock 1993). For example, a study of the welfare of local inhabitants of the middle Senegal valley (in the country of Senegal, West Africa) before and after the construction of a large dam shows that people's level of food insecurity increased (Horowitz and Salem-Murdock 1993). Formerly, the periodic flooding of the plain helped support a dense human population dependent on agriculture, fishing, forestry, and herding. Productivity of the wetlands had remained high for a long period of human occupation, with no signs of deterioration. The current practice of water control by the dam managers, however, does not provide periodic flooding. Instead, water is released less often and with disregard for the needs of the people downstream. In some years, they do not have enough water for their crops, and fishing has become a less secure source of food. At other times, a large flood of water is released, damaging crops. As a result, many residents have been forced to leave the area. They have become development refugees, people who must leave home because of the effects of a development project.

The awareness of the socially negative impact of many supposedly positive development projects has led to the emergence of **critical development anthropology (CDA)**. In this approach, the anthropologist does not simply accept a supportive role, but rather takes on a critical-thinking role. The question is not: What can we do to make this project successful? Instead, the anthropologist asks: Is this a good project from the perspective of the people affected? After long and careful thinking, if the answer is yes, then that is a green light for a supportive role. If careful thinking reveals areas where revisions in the project would make it beneficial, then the anthropologist can intervene with this information. If all evidence suggests that the project will harm the target population, either in the short run or the long run, then the anthropologist should assume the role of whistle-blower and either try to stop the project completely or substantially change the design. In the case of the Senegal Valley dam project, anthropologists working with engineers and local inhabitants devised an alternative management plan of regular and controlled amounts of released water that would reduce the harm done to people downstream and restore the area's former agricultural and fishing abundance.

Methods in Development Anthropology

Many full-scale anthropological studies of cultural change and development are based on long-term fieldwork and standard research methods as described in Chapter 2. However, often a development agency needs input from an anthropologist faster than what long-term fieldwork would allow. Specialized methods have emerged to respond to shorter time frames in order to provide useful answers to specific questions at hand. Compared to standard long-term fieldwork, the methods used in development anthropology are more focused with a less holistic research agenda, make more use of multidisciplinary research teams, and rely on such specialized approaches as rapid research methods and participatory research methods. These three differences relate to the need to gather dependable data within a relatively short time period.

Rapid Research Methods

Rapid research methods (RRMs) are research methods designed to provide focused cultural data in a short time period (Chambers 1983). They include strategies such as going to the field with a prepared checklist of questions, conducting focus group interviews (talking to several people at the same time rather than one by one), and conducting "transect" observations (walking through a specific area with key informants and asking for explanations along the way) (Bernard 1995:139–140). When used effectively, RRMs can provide useful data for assessing the problems and opportunities related to development, particularly when several methods are used together.

An effective mix of RRMs was used for development project planning in rural Bali (Mitchell 1994). The research sought to identify environmental and social stresses that might be caused by economic development and then make recommendations to the government in preparing its next five-year development plan. A Canadian university and an Indonesian university designed an eight-village study to provide data on ecological, economic, and social features. Each village was studied by a four-member team. Teams consisted of Indonesian and Canadian researchers, both men and women. All team members could speak Bahasa Indonesian (the national language) and at least one could also speak Bahasa Bali (the local language). Researchers lived in the village for four weeks. The teams used several methods for data collection: background data from provincial documents and village records; and interviews with key informants representing the village administration, religion, women, youth, school teachers, health clinic personnel, and agricultural extension workers. Household interviews were conducted with 15 men and 15 women from different neighbourhoods in the village, and with a sample of primary school children. Other observations included general conditions of the village and villagers' daily activities. For each village, the research generated a fairly rich profile of relevant biophysical features, production and marketing, local government, health and welfare, and expressive culture. Their findings offered a range of issues for the government's consideration, including the apparent environmental and social stresses being caused by external development such as urbanization and tourism.

Participatory Research Methods

Building on the RRM approach, in the late 1980s, a more recent method has emerged involving the local people, called **participatory research methods (PRMs)**. PRMs respond to the growing awareness that when the population is involved in a development project, it is more likely to be successful in the short run and sustainable over the long run (Kabutha, Thomas-Slayter, and Ford 1993:76). Participatory research rests heavily on the anthropological assumption that local knowledge should not be bypassed, but instead should be the foundation of development work. Participatory research involves key community members in all stages of the research.

The best PRM work teaches local people how to collect and analyze important kinds of data themselves. For example, local people know about such things as field size and soil quality. Barely literate villagers understand seasonal changes and can therefore participate in considering alternative strategies for improving food supplies during lean times. Such people can learn how to prepare maps and charts that will be used in project identification. Besides sheer data gathering and analysis, a crucial feature of PRM is feedback from community members in project selection and project evaluation. Local people can be trained to carry on data collection and analysis after the team has left the village. Two important effects of PRM

are the fostering of local autonomy in planning and a greater chance that the projects put in place will be maintained and adjusted to changing conditions.

EMERGING ISSUES IN DEVELOPMENT

In this section we consider three interrelated issues in international development: women and development, indigenous peoples, and human rights. The first two issues emphasize particular categories of people who have been affected by international development in various ways. They are discussed in more detail because they illustrate key concepts used throughout this book: gender and social inequality. The issue of human rights crosses all social categories including indigenous peoples, ethnic minorities, women, men, and children.

Women and Development

Women constitute about half of every population, yet many live as "subordinates" in household configurations with more dominant group members. In the mid-1970s, gender inequity was recognized as a serious constraint to development. Emphasis on women and development— and later gender and development (Rathgeber 1990)—in multilateral and bilateral assistance programs, national governments, and NGOs—encouraged policies that made gender equity a goal of development, a goal that should transform the concept of development itself. Development has also resulted in women losing power in their communities, as well as former rights to property. One reason is that matrilineal kinship, a system that keeps property in the female line, is in decline throughout the world, often as a result of Westernization and modernization. Another is that Western experts have chosen to deal with men in the context of development projects.

In this section, we consider evidence that much activity in international development has been biased in favour of men to the detriment of women. We then turn to examples in which some women's groups are taking development into their own hands and making it work for their welfare.

The Male Bias in Development

Women have been affected by development differently from men within the same community and even the same household, because development has been pursued in an androcentric (male-centred) way. In the 1970s, researchers began to write about the fact that development projects were male-biased (Boserup 1970; Tinker 1976). Many projects completely bypassed women as beneficiaries or targeted men for such new initiatives as growing cash crops or learning about new technologies (Boserup 1970; Tinker 1976). This male bias in development contributed to increased gender inequality and hierarchy by giving men greater access to new sources of income and depriving women of their traditional economic roles. The development experts' image of a farmer, for example, was male, not female. Women's projects were focused on the domestic domain. Thus, women's projects were typically concerned with infant feeding patterns, child care, and family planning, and, over time, this has led to what has been labelled the "domestication" of women worldwide (Rogers 1979). For example, University of Windsor anthropologist Lynne Phillips found in her research on rural Ecuadorian women (1998) that development discourses may inadvertently homogenize women's own interpretations of their situations. Terms such as the "feminization of agriculture" may flatten the complexity of women's lives. Her research is a reminder that women in societies exposed to development programs may not necessarily experience development in ways envisioned by policymakers or by development critics.

The male bias in development also created an increased rate of project failure. In the West African nation of Burkina Faso, for example, a reforestation project targeted men as the sole participants, whose tasks would include planting and caring for the trees. Unfortunately, cultural patterns there dictate that men do not water plants; women do. So the men planted the seedlings and left them. Since the women were not included as project participants, the new young trees that were planted died.

Exclusion of women from development continues to be a problem, in spite of many years of work attempting to place and keep women's issues on the development agenda. An example of a new development issue is gender-based violence. The problem is gaining attention even among the large multilaterals, where experts now realize that women cannot participate in a development program if they fear their husbands will beat them for leaving the house. The United Nations Commission on the Status of Women formed a working group that drafted a declaration against violence against women (Heise, Pitanguy, and Germain 1994). The declaration was adopted by the General Assembly in 1993. Article 1 of the declaration states that violence against women includes "any act of gender-based violence that results in, or is likely to result in, physical, sexual or psychological harm or suffering to women, including threats of such acts, coercion or arbitrary deprivations of liberty, whether occurring in public or private life" (Economic and Social Council 1992). This definition cites "women" as the focus of concern, but it includes girls as well (see Table 16.3). A weakness of programs that address issues of violence against girls and women is that they tend to deal with their effects, not the causes, often with disastrous results. For example, they

TABLE 16.3 Gender-Based Violence against Girls and Women throughout the Life Cycle

Prebirth	Sex-selective abortion, battering during pregnancy, coerced pregnancy
Infancy	Infanticide, emotional and physical abuse, deprivation of food and medical care
Girlhood	Child marriage, genital mutilation, sexual abuse by family members and strangers, deprivation of food and medical care, child prostitution
Adolescence	Dating and courtship violence, forced prostitution, rape, sexual abuse in the workplace, sexual harassment
Adulthood	Partner abuse and rape, partner homicide, sexual abuse in the workplace, sexual harassment, rape
Old Age	Abuse and neglect of widows, elder abuse

Source: Adapted from Heise, Pitanguy, and Germain 1994:5.

may seek to increase personal security of women and girls in refugee camps by augmenting the number of guards at the camp when, in fact, it is often the guards who abuse refugee females.

Women Organizing for Change

There is a growing global consensus on gender issues, partly based on the use of "international instruments" to push the agenda for gender equity at the national level. Both multilaterals and bilaterals have cooperated in projects such as the Decade for Women (1975–1985) with the United Nations Commission on the Status of Women. International meetings on women's issues (particularly Nairobi, 1985, and Beijing, 1995) helped national groups and NGOs to use international instruments for women's advancement, such as the Convention on the Elimination of all Forms of Discrimination against Women (CEDAW).

In many countries, women have made substantial gains in improving their status and welfare through forming organizations. These organizations range from "mothers' clubs" that provide communal child care to lending and credit organizations that provide women with the opportunity to start their own businesses. Some are local and small-scale; others are global in reach, such as Women's World Banking, an international organization that grew out of credit programs for poor working women in India.

In the 1990s, micro-finance became the leading development strategy adopted by governments and NGOs for

Grameen Bank, a development project that began in Bangladesh to provide small loans to poor people, is one of the most successful examples of improving human welfare through "micro-credit." Professor Muhammad Yunnus (centre) founded Grameen Bank and continues to be a source of charismatic leadership for it.

alleviating poverty and empowering the poor, especially women. As the limits of a welfare-oriented approach to development are now well recognized by large institutions, micro-finance initiatives similar to South Asia's Grameen Bank model promote income-generating projects for the poor by providing access to low-interest credit or loans, and organizing savings activities. Because of women's higher repayment rates and preference for spending on family welfare, many of these programs target women specifically to increase program cost efficiency and to achieve more effective poverty alleviation.

Lynne Milgram's ethnographic research in the upland provinces of northern Luzon, Philippines (1999), documents how Ifugao women meet their households' needs by combining different forms of wage work, such as agriculture, crafts, and trading. In 1997, a new micro-finance initiative developed a local system of village savings-and-loan groups and connected them to local banking cooperatives. Milgram's work analyzes how women use the opportunities and constraints offered by this new project. In the first year of operation, the micro-finance program was very popular, particularly among farmers and craftspeople who do not have access to the formal banking sector because of their lack of collateral. They welcome the opportunity to obtain loans at interest rates of 15 percent per year—well below rates offered by local moneylenders (120 percent per year) and those available through the formal banking sector (21 to 26 percent per year). Realizing the limitations of a credit-only approach that simply gives loans to raise household income, this program also encourages members to contribute to pooled group savings from which they can make small personal loans. Milgram cautions, however, that many women still hesitate to take loans from the banking cooperative, fearing they might fall behind in their repayments.

Another community-based credit system in Mozambique, southern Africa, helps farm women buy seeds, fertilizers, and supplies on loan (Clark 1992:24). When the loan program was first started, 32 farm families in the village of Machel formed themselves into seven solidarity groups, each with an elected leader. The woman-headed farmer groups managed irrigation more efficiently and conferred on how to minimize use of pesticides and chemical fertilizers. Through their efforts, the women quadrupled their harvests and were able to pay off their loans. Machel women then turned their attention to getting additional loans to improve their herds and to buy a maize mill. Overall, in the midst of poverty, military conflict, the lack of government resources, and a drought, the project and the organization it fostered allowed many women farmers to increase their economic and household security.

An informal system of social networks has emerged to help support poor women vendors in San Cristobal, Mexico (Sullivan 1992). Many of the vendors around the city square are women, and most of them have been expelled from highland Chiapas because of political conflicts there. The women vendors manufacture and sell goods to tourists and thereby provide an important portion of household income. In the city, they find support in an expanded social network that compensates for the loss of support from the extensive god-parenthood system of the highlands, which has broken down because of out-migration. Instead, the vendors have established networks encompassing relatives, neighbours, and church members, as well as other vendors, regardless of religious, political, economic, or social background.

These networks first developed in response to a series of rapes and robberies that began in 1987. The perpetrators were persons of power and influence, and so the women never pressed charges. Mostly single mothers and widows, they adopted a defensive strategy of self-protection: They began to group together during the slow period each afternoon. They travel in groups and carry sharpened corset bones and prongs: "If a man insults one of them, the group surrounds him and jabs him in the groin" (39–40). If a woman is robbed, the other women surround her, comfort her, and help contribute something toward her loss. The mid-afternoon gatherings have developed into support groups that provide financial assistance, child care, medical advice, and job skills. They have also publicly, and successfully, demonstrated against city officials' attempts to prevent them from continuing their vending. Through their organizational efforts, these women refugees from highland Chiapas have brought about important improvements in their lives.

Indigenous Peoples' Development

This section first raises the question of who indigenous peoples are. We next consider findings about how indigenous peoples have been victimized by many aspects of growth-oriented development (as they were with colonialism before it) and then look at examples of how many indigenous groups are taking development into their own hands.

Who Are Indigenous Peoples?

The term **indigenous peoples** refers to groups of people who are the original inhabitants of a particular territory. Often, indigenous peoples now take the name of "First Peoples," or in Canada, "First Nations peoples," as a way of self-definition as original claimants to a place. This naming practice highlights one of the major problems facing most indigenous peoples today: the fact that they have lost, and are losing, claim to their ancestral lands in the face of encroachment from outsiders.

Indigenous peoples are typically a numerical minority in the states that control their territory. The United Nations distinguishes between indigenous peoples and minority groups such as the Roma, the Tamils of Sri Lanka, or Sikhs in Canada, for example. Although this distinction is useful in some ways, it should not be taken as a hard-and-fast difference (Maybury-Lewis 1997; Plant 1994). It is most useful to think of all these groups as forming a continuum from more clearly indigenous groups, such as the Inuit, to minority/ethnic groups that may not be geographically "original" to a place but share many problems with indigenous peoples as a result of living within a more powerful majority culture.

Indigenous peoples differ from most national minorities by the fact that they often occupy (or occupied) remote areas and were, until the era of colonial expansion, less affected by outside interests. Now governments and international businesses have recognized that their lands often contain valuable natural resources, such as natural gas and timber in Canada and gold in Papua New Guinea and the Amazon. Different governments have paid varying degrees of attention to "integrating" indigenous peoples into "mainstream" culture in the interests of fostering nationalism at the expense of pluralism.

Accurate demographic statistics on indigenous peoples are difficult to obtain (Kennedy and Perz 2000). There are often questions about who should be counted as indigenous, and in some cases, there are political implications to the collecting of statistics. Governments may not bother to conduct a census of indigenous peoples, or if they do, they may underreport counts of indigenous peoples in order to downplay recognition of their very existence as a group (Baer 1982:12). A few island populations in India's Andaman Islands in the Bay of Bengal remain uncounted because Indian officials cannot gain access to them (Singh 1994). Given the difficulties involved in defining and counting indigenous peoples, therefore, it is possible only to provide very rough information on their number. It is estimated that, globally, indigenous peoples make up about 5 percent of the total world population. (Bodley 1990:365; Lee and Daly 1999). (See Table 16.4.)

Marginalization of Indigenous Peoples

Many indigenous peoples and their cultures have been exterminated as a result of contact with outsiders. Besides death and decline through contagious disease, political conflicts within indigenous peoples' territory often threaten their survival. In the Peruvian Andes, armed conflict between the Peruvian guerrillas called the Shining Path, drug traffickers, and U.S.-backed police and army units has taken a heavy toll on indigenous groups.

First Peoples have also suffered from intentional efforts to take over their land by force, to prevent them from practising their traditional lifestyle, including using their own languages, and to integrate them into the state. John Bodley (1988) has examined the effects of loss of autonomy for indigenous peoples that results from the unwill-

TABLE 16.4 Population Estimates of Indigenous Peoples

Western Hemisphere
  less than 1 million in Canada
  1.75 million in the United States
  less than 13 million in Mexico and Central America
  16 million in South America
Europe
  60 000 in Greenland
  60 000 in Norway, Sweden, and Finland
  28 million within the former Soviet Union
Middle East
  5 million
Africa
  14 million
Asia
  52 million in India
  31 million in China (the government terms them
    national minorities)
  26.5 million in Southeast Asia
  50 000 in Japan and the Pacific combined
  550 000 in Australia and New Zealand combined
Total: About 5 percent of the world's total population.

Source: Maybury-Lewis 1997:10–11.

ingness of the state to tolerate the presence of politically sovereign tribes within its boundaries. States intervene to prevent and quell armed resistance by indigenous peoples, even though such resistance may be critical to the maintenance of indigenous culture and the people's welfare. Indicators that an indigenous group has lost its autonomy include inability to expel outside intruders or use force to regulate its internal affairs; introduction of formal schooling and national court systems; appointment of state-sanctioned political leaders; the institution of compulsory military service; and enforcement of payment of taxes. These changes undermine the previous quality of life and set in motion changes that indirectly lead to the people's further impoverishment.

Anthropological analysis of government policies in Thailand for development of the highlands reveals the complex interplay between outside interests and the welfare of the *chao khao*, or "hill people" (Kesmanee 1994). The hill people include the Karen, Hmong, Mien, Lahu, Lisu, Akha, and others, totalling about half a million people or 1 percent of the total Thai population. There is international pressure for the hill people to replace opium cultivation with other cash crops. The Thai government's concerns are with political stability and national security in this area, which borders on Burma and Laos. It therefore has promoted development projects to establish more connections between the highlands and the lowlands through transportation and marketing. Thus far, efforts to find viable substitute crops especially among the Hmong, who have traditionally been most dependent on opium as a cash crop, have been unsuccessful. Crops that have been introduced have required extensive use of fertilizers and pesticides, which have greatly increased environmental pollution. Efforts have been made to relocate hill horticulturalists to the plains, but there they have been provided plots with poor soil and the economic status of the people has declined. In the meantime, commercial loggers have gained access to the hills and done more damage to the forests than the traditional patterns of shifting horticulture. Increased penetration of the hill areas by lowlanders, international tourism, and communications have also promoted the increase of HIV/AIDS rates, prostitution, and opium addiction throughout the area. As a result, hill people are threatened both with the loss of their land and with the loss of their cultural identity. Solving this problem requires a major change in how development is being approached by international agencies and the Thai government.

The situation in Thailand is not unique. In case after case, indigenous peoples have been subjected to loss of the rights they once had, increased impoverishment, and widespread despair. Active resistance to their disenfranchisement has taken place throughout history, but more effective and highly organized forms of protest and reclamation of rights have become prominent only since the

A Hmong woman and child, northern Thailand. The Hmong people of highland Southeast Asia have suffered decades of war in their homeland. Many Hmong have entered the United States and Canada as refugees.

1980s. Many indigenous groups have acquired legal advice and expertise and have confronted power-holders in world capitals, insisting on changes. One of the most basic claims of all groups is recognition of their land rights.

Indigenous Peoples' Advocacy

Much evidence attests to the value of "development from within," or efforts to increase peoples' welfare and livelihood promoted by indigenous organizations rather than exogenous organizations. Basic components of indigenous peoples' development include rights to resources, local initiatives in planning through local organizations, and local leadership. The following sections consider resource issues (especially land) and indigenous organizations for change.

The many land and resource claims being made by indigenous peoples are a direct response to their earlier losses and a major challenge to many states. Depending on how these disputes are resolved, they can be a basis for conflicts, ranging from fairly benign litigation to attempts at secession (Plant 1994).

No Latin American country government provides protection against encroachment on the land of farm families. Throughout Latin America, increasing numbers of indigenous peoples have been forced off the land and have had to seek wage labour. Those who remain live in extreme poverty. In response, a strong resurgence of activity by indigenous peoples and groups that support them has occurred in the 1990s (Plant 1994). Some of this activity has taken the form of physical resistance. Violence continues to erupt between indigenous peoples and state-supported power structures, especially in the southern Mexican state of Chiapas.

In Canada, the law distinguishes between two different types of Aboriginal land claims (Plant 1994). "Specific claims" concern problems arising from previous agreements or treaties, and are moving through the courts. "Comprehensive claims" are those made by Native peoples who have not been displaced and have made no treaties or agreements. Many of the former claims have led to monetary compensation. In the latter category, government interests in oil and mineral exploration have led to negotiations with indigenous peoples seeking to have their native claims either relinquished or redefined. So far, of the over 40 comprehensive claims filed, only 4 have been settled. In some provinces, especially British Columbia, current claims affect most of the province (Woolford 2005). One recent land claim case has been settled after 112 years of bargaining. A historic land-claim treaty gives the Nisga'a of British Columbia $235 million in cash, 2000 square kilometres of land, and self-government powers.

Anthropologists played a role in the 1975 James Bay and Northern Quebec Agreement. The James Bay Cree Project provided the Cree and the Quebec government with information that helped settle the land claim (Salisbury 1986). Traditional hunting and fishing lands of several thousand Cree and Inuit were to be affected by a large hydroelectric project. It was agreed that the indigenous peoples would receive $225 million in partial compensation for their original title. A reserve was set aside for hunting, fishing, and trapping, but the agreement said that the government of Quebec and several corporations had the right to develop resources on those lands. In 1989, the Quebec government renewed its interest in hydroelectric development. The Great Whale River project would have threatened the livelihood and environment of the Cree in the area, and they successfully opposed the project on the grounds of global concerns about pollution and the protection of natural environments (Adelson 1998).

Most Asian countries have been reluctant even to recognize the concept of special land rights of indigenous peoples (Plant 1994). In Bangladesh, for example, settlers from the crowded plains have encroached on the formerly

Hunting remains an important part of Cree subsistence activities. Here, meat dries over a slow fire at a hunting camp.

protected area of the Chittagong Hill Tracts. Non-indigenous settlers now occupy the most fertile land. A large hydroelectric dam built in 1963 displaced 100 000 hill dwellers because they could no longer practise horticulture in the flooded areas. A minority received financial aid, but most did not. Tribal opposition groups began emerging, and conflict, although suppressed in the news, has been ongoing for decades. Other sites of contestation with the state over land and resources in the Asia-Pacific region include the Moros of the southern Philippines, and the people of Irian Jaya in western Papua New Guinea. In these cases, the indigenous people's fight for succession from the state that controls them is costing many lives.

In Africa, political interests of state governments in establishing and enforcing territorial boundaries have created difficulties for indigenous peoples, especially pastoralists who are, for example, accustomed to moving their herds freely. Pastoralists in the Sahel region of Africa have been particularly affected by this process. Many formerly autonomous pastoralists have been transformed into refugees living in terrible conditions. The Tuareg people, for example, have traditionally lived and herded in a territory crossing what are now five different nations: Mali, Niger, Algeria, Burkina Faso, and Libya (Childs and Chelala 1994). Given political conflict in the region, thousands of Tuareg people live in exile in Mauritania, and their prospects are grim. As elsewhere, resistance movements spring up, but states and local power interests move quickly to quell them. The death of Ogoni leader Ken Saro-Wiwa in 1995 is a shocking example of the personal price of resistance (Sachs 1996). Saro-Wiwa, a Nigerian writer, Nobel Peace Prize nominee, and supporter of minority people's rights, was executed by Nigerian military rulers. He had vigorously spoken out against the Nigerian regime and the oil development being pursued in Ogoniland by Royal/Dutch Shell. As president and spokesperson for the Movement for the Survival of the Ogoni People (MOSOP), he had asked the government to respect the Ogoni people's right to self-determination. He also had asked Shell to clean up oil spills and toxic waste pits that had ruined Ogoni farming and fishing communities along the Niger River delta. His message is one that applies worldwide: States tend to impose the costs of their economic growth on the people least able to cope with it—impoverished minorities—and then apply violent means of repression if such people raise serious objections to their treatment.

Many indigenous peoples have formed their own organizations for change in order to promote "development from within." In Ethiopia, for example, many NGOs organized by local people have sprung up since the 1990s (Kassam 2002). One organization in the southern region is especially noteworthy, because it seeks to provide a model of development based on the oral traditions of the Oromo people. This new model thus combines elements of Western-defined "development" with Oromo values and laws and provides a new approach that is culturally appropriate and goes beyond external notions of development and usual Oromo life-ways. The indigenous Oromo NGO is called Hundee, which refers to "roots," or the origins of the Oromo people, and, by extension, to all Oromo people, their land, and their culture. Hundee uses a theory of development that is based in Oromo metaphors of fertility and growth and involves gradual transformation like the spirals in the horn of a ram. Hundee relies on Oromo legal and moral principles about the communal use of natural resources and the redistribution of wealth to provide a social welfare system. These are elements of "good development," as distinguished from the "bad development" that has inflicted hunger and dependency on the Oromo people.

Hundee's long-term goal is to empower Oromo communities to be self-sufficient. It takes the view the Oromo

Nigerian author and Nobel Peace Prize nominee, Ken Saro-Wiwa founded the Movement for Survival of Ogoni People (MOSOP) in 1992 to protest Shell's actions in Ogoniland and the Nigerian government's indifference. In 1995, he was arrested, tried for murder under suspicious circumstances, and executed by hanging. His execution brought about an international outcry while Shell's response is largely denial of any problem.

culture is a positive force for social and economic change, rather than a barrier. Hundee members use a participatory approach in all their endeavours. They consult with traditional legal assemblies to identify needs and then to shape projects to address those needs. Specific activities include the establishment of a credit association and a grain bank to help combat price fluctuations and food shortages.

The Assembly of First Nations, formed in Canada in 1982, has become the unofficial spokesperson for many First Nations groups, presenting a united front on constitutional issues and self-government (Frideres 1998). Skilled in lobbying and the law, this group fights for Aboriginal rights guaranteed under the Canadian constitution. First Nations groups are taken more seriously today because Aboriginal issues are viewed as a threat to national security (Tanner 1983). In this era of rapid internet access, many indigenous groups are taking advantage of new forms of communication in order to maintain links with each other over large areas. For example, the Inuit Tapiriit Kanatami of Canada, founded in 1971, is a national organization representing over 40 000 Inuit. The federal government provided them with funding to create a website designed to allow the "national voice" of the Inuit to reach an international audience, encourage understanding and learning about the Inuit, and provide a virtual community linking Inuit groups and organizations across the Arctic. The Grand Council of the Cree has collaborated with the Inuit Tapiriit Kanatami and other organizations over land issues.

In many cases, indigenous peoples' development organizations have been formed that link formerly separate groups (Perry 1996:245–246), as a response to external threats. In Australia, many indigenous groups have formed pan-Australian organizations and regional coalitions, such as the Pitjantjatjara Land Council, that have had success in land claim cases. Although it is tempting to see hope in the newly emerging forms of resistance, self-determination, and organizing among indigenous peoples, such hope cannot be generalized to all indigenous peoples. Many are making progress and their economic status is improving; others are suffering extreme political and economic repression.

Human Rights

Much of the preceding discussion of women and indigenous peoples is related to the question of human rights and development. Anthropologists' cross-cultural research and growing sense of the importance of advocacy as part of their role place them in a key position to speak to issues of global human rights. In considering what cultural anthropologists have to contribute to the issue of human rights, we must first ask some basic and difficult questions:

- What are human rights?
- Is there a universal set of human rights?
- Are local cultural definitions of human rights that clash with those of other groups defensible?

Defining Human Rights

For over 50 years, the United Nations has been promoting human rights through its Universal Declaration of Human Rights and other resolutions. Difficulty in coming to a consensus on defining these rights is based in one sense on a split between capitalist and socialist states. The former emphasize political and civil rights such as freedom of speech as universally important. The latter emphasize socio-economic rights such as employment and fair working conditions. Capitalist states do not always acknowledge such socio-economic rights as universal human rights and some socialist states do not recognize political rights as valid. People living in developing countries and indigenous peoples throughout the world have added their voices, insisting on group rights to self-determination, locally defined paths of social change, and in some African states freedom from hunger. As Ellen Messer (1993) says, "[N]o state would go on record as being opposed to human rights. . . . Yet those from different states, and from different political, cultural, and religious traditions, continue to disagree on which rights have universal force and who is protected under them" (223).

As culturally diverse groups seek to define and claim their rights around the increasingly globalized world, we are all faced with the challenge of considering contending positions. (See the Multiple Cultural Worlds box.)

Human Rights and Development

This section provides two illustrations of how development and human rights are linked. In the first, we find ties between large-scale development institutions and military control in the Philippines, through which violations of local people's human rights have occurred. The second case addresses the question of environmental destruction as a violation of human and cultural rights.

An in-depth study of social conditions among the Ifugao, indigenous peoples of the highland region of northern Luzon, the Philippines, reveals the important, negative role of the militarization of everyday life for the Ifugao (Kwiatkowski 1998). The military presence is felt everywhere—in schools, clinics, and, especially, at sites of large development projects such as dams. The military presence is there to ensure that people adhere to its principles and do not participate in what it would consider subversive activities. Military force has been used to suppress local resistance to dams funded by the World Bank, resulting in numerous human rights violations, including torture, killings, imprisonment, and harassment of Cordillera people for suspected subversive activities (Drucker 1987). Members of a local NGO that support more appropriate, small-scale forms of development that would benefit more people in the area have been harassed by the military. The case of the Ifugao in northern Luzon illustrates how the powerful interests of state governments and international development institutions join together to promote their plans and projects and violate human rights along the way.

Development that leads to environmental degradation, such as pollution, deforestation, and erosion, can also be considered a form of human rights violation. Slain Ogoni leader Ken Saro-Wiwa made this point eloquently in a 1992 speech to the United Nations Working Group on Indigenous Populations:

Multiple Cultural Worlds

HUMAN RIGHTS VERSUS ANIMAL RIGHTS: THE CASE OF THE GREY WHALE

HUMAN RIGHTS are often understood to include the right of people, as members of a cultural group, to practise their cultural traditions. This provision extends the notion of human rights from including mainly the right to fulfilling basic physical needs such as health and personal security to including practices such as animal sacrifice, female genital cutting, hunting certain animals, and girls wearing headscarves in school—all issues that have received recent attention from European and North American governments and media because they differ from cultural practices in those countries. In many countries, a debate about some cultural practices is carried out between human rights activists who support cultural rights and those who support animal rights.

In spring 1999, members of the Makah Nation, a Native American group living in Washington state, undertook a revival of their traditional practice of hunting grey whales (Winthrop 2000). Like many other Native people of the Pacific Northwest, the Makah's traditional economy depended on fish, shellfish, and marine mammals. A treaty of 1855 provides the Makah with the right to hunt whales and seals. The practice died out, however, in the twentieth century due to dwindling supplies as a result of commercial overhunting. In 1982, the International Whaling Commission (IWC) imposed a ban on all commercial whaling, but allowed continued whale hunting for subsistence purposes. In 1994, the grey whale population had recovered and it was taken off the endangered list. The IWC allocated the Makah the right to harvest 20 whales during the period from 1998 to 2002.

When, under this new plan, the Makah killed a 30 tonne, 10 metre whale in May 1999, the Makah watching the event cheered. The animal rights activists at the scene, in contrast, protested and said this occasion should have been one of mourning and not celebration.

The Nuu-chah-nulth of Vancouver Island saw the whaling as a potential treaty issue, but voiced concern that it would pit Aboriginal rights against environmental rights. While the Makah see the revival of whale hunting as a sign of cultural revival, some animal rights activists say that the way the hunt is being carried out is not culturally authentic (the Makah first harpoon the whale and then use a rifle to kill it, for example) and thus the claim of whale hunting as a traditional cultural right is not legitimate. Environmental groups argued that cultural rights to whaling could be the "thin wedge" that opens up commercial whaling in countries such as Japan and Norway that also claim cultural rights to whaling. Other protests are motivated by ecological concerns for preservation of the species against extinction, supporting a concept of animal, especially mammalian, rights to life. The First Nations Environmental Network, based in Tofino, Vancouver Island, is opposed to whale hunting, arguing that the act of killing whales cannot be justified spiritually or morally (Lamirande 1999).

FOOD FOR THOUGHT

What other examples in the media illustrate the tension between human rights and cultural rights? Compare this case with other examples of human versus animal rights. Where do you stand in these debates and what is the basis for your position?

Environmental degradation has been a lethal weapon in the war against the indigenous Ogoni people. . . . Oil exploration has turned Ogoni into a wasteland: lands, streams, and creeks are totally and continually polluted; the atmosphere has been poisoned, charged as it is with hydrocarbon vapors, methane, carbon monoxide, carbon dioxide, and soot emitted by gas which has been flared 24 hours a day for 33 years in close proximity to human habitation. . . . The rainforest has fallen to the axe of the multinational companies . . . the Ogoni countryside is no longer a source of fresh air and green vegetation. All one sees and feels around is death. (quoted in Sachs 1996:13–16)

Many social scientists now argue, along with Saro-Wiwa, that such forms of development violate human rights since they undermine a people's way of life and threaten their continued existence (Johnston 1994).

Cultural Anthropology and the Future

During the past few decades, cultural anthropologists have played an important role in defining and exposing a wide range of human rights abuses around the world. Although this "whistle-blowing" can promote positive change, it is

A farmer walks through an oil-soaked field. About 500 000 Ogoni people live in Ogoni, a region in Nigeria. The fertility of the Niger delta has supported farming and fishing populations at high density for many years. Since Shell discovered oil there in 1958, 100 oil wells were constructed in Ogoniland and countless oil spills have occurred.

also important that cultural anthropologists participate more actively in advocacy work directed toward the prevention of human rights abuses. Determining exactly how cultural anthropologists can contribute to prevention is a challenge to a discipline whose roots lie in studying what is—rather than what might be, or, in this case, what should not be. One path is toward promoting continued dialogue on human rights and cultural diversity, which should help promote greater understanding and tolerance

Since its beginning, cultural anthropology has been a product of the knowledge gained from studying "others." In the early years, this knowledge was taken to Western centres of power. As this chapter shows, indigenous peoples, women, and other groups that have suffered from lack or loss of resources and power, often as a result of external forms of economic and political change, are beginning to reclaim their knowledge and identity and rework international ideas of development and change into models that are culturally appropriate. Local redefinitions of development, and local approaches to achieving improved human welfare, are a powerful example of how global forces can sometimes be transformed and remade to the advantage of seemingly marginalized and powerless people. We live in a time of war, but also a time of hope, in which insights and strength often come from those with the least in terms of material wealth but with cultural wealth beyond measure.

As the only discipline concerned with both individual and collective rights and responsibilities, human interaction with the natural environment, people's patterns of production and consumption, family structures and political organizations, language, expressive culture, and religious beliefs, anthropology is a field of study that can speak and act to advocate for increased respect for this cultural wealth.

HOW do cultural anthropologists study change?

Cultural anthropologists have become seriously involved in the study of change mainly since the mid-twentieth century. Since that time, many cultural anthropologists have contributed to theoretical debates about how change occurs and what the role of anthropological knowledge should be in contributing to culturally appropriate forms of change. Major processes of change are invention and diffusion. In contemporary times, modernization has been a powerful model of change that involves diffusion of Western technologies and values to non-Western contexts. After World War II, *development* became increasingly important as a form of modernization that emphasizes improved living standards.

WHAT are the most common approaches to development?

Several approaches to development exist, including growth-oriented development, distributional development, human development, and sustainable development. Institutional approaches to development, whether pursued by large-scale or grassroots organizations, tend to rely on the development project as a vehicle of local change. Cultural anthropologists have been hired as consultants on development projects, typically at the end of the project cycle to provide evaluations. More recently, some anthropologists have pushed for their involvement earlier in the project cycle so that cultural knowledge can be used in project planning to avoid many of the common errors. In order to provide relevant information often in a short time frame, cultural anthropology has adapted its traditional methods of long-term participant observation. Rapid and participatory research methods are intended to maximize data gathering during a short period with awareness of the limitations involved.

WHAT does cultural anthropology contribute to understanding some major issues in development?

The role of women in development, the status of indigenous peoples, and the complex issue of defining and protecting human rights are three urgent and interrelated areas in international development that have attracted anthropological research and thinking. Research on the impact of growth-oriented, large-scale development shows that many indigenous peoples and women have suffered decline in their entitlements and level of living. Often, such losses are tied to violence and environmental degradation in their homelands. Such tragic occurrences lead directly to the question of what human rights are and how development affects them. Cultural anthropologists contribute insights from different cultures about perceptions of basic human and cultural rights and may be able to help prevent human rights abuses in the future.

KEY CONCEPTS

acculturation, p. 352
assimilated, p. 352
critical development anthropology (CDA), p. 360
diachronic, p. 350
diffusion, p. 351
human development, p. 355
indigenous peoples, p. 364
international development, p. 354
modernization theory, p. 354

participatory research methods (PRMs), p. 361
project cycle, p. 358
rapid research methods (RRMs), p. 360
social impact assessment, p. 353
socio-cultural fit, p. 359
structural adjustment, p. 354
sustainable development, p. 355
synchronic, p. 350
traditional development anthropology (TDA), p. 360

SUGGESTED READINGS

Thomas W. Collins and John D. Wingard, eds., *Communities and Capital: Local Struggles against Corporate Power and Privatization*. Athens, GA: University of Georgia Press, 2000. Nine case studies of local resistance against large capitalist forces follow an introductory chapter that sets the stage. Cases include clam farmers of North Carolina, a fishing community in Malaysia, and banana growers in Belize.

H. Dagenais and D. Piché eds., *Women, Feminism and Development/Femmes, Féminisme et Développement*. Montreal and Kingston: McGill-Queen's University Press, 1994. This book contains French and English language chapters on development issues in Canada and internationally. The papers were first presented at a conference for the Canadian Research Institute for the Advancement of Women (CRIAW), and highlight feminist contributions to the theory and practice of development.

Jim Freedman, ed., *Transforming Development: Foreign Aid for a Changing World*. Toronto: University of Toronto Press, 2000. Fourteen essays look at the changing context of Canadian aid arranged around seven themes. Most authors favour the redefinition of development assistance and criticize Canada's reduction in humanitarian-motivated aid to the poorest countries.

Dolores Koenig, Tieman Diarra, Moussa Sow, and Ousmane Diarra, *Innovation and Individuality in African Development: Changing Production Strategies in Rural Mali*. Ann Arbor: University of Michigan Press, 1998. This ethnography of change looks at the history of Malian rural production, agricultural resources, and crop production, and how lessons learned contribute to an improved anthropology of development.

David H. Lempert, Kim McCarthy, and Craig Mitchell, *A Model Development Plan: New Strategies and Perspectives*. Westport, CT: Praeger, 1995. A group of university students from different disciplines (including one anthropologist, Lempert) spent six weeks in Ecuador, visiting nearly every province and studying development issues there as the basis for their development plan for Ecuador. A preface explains the background of the project. The rest of the volume consists of a detailed presentation of the plan.

Richard J. Perry, *From Time Immemorial: Indigenous Peoples and State Systems*. Austin: University of Texas Press, 1996. This book provides a comparative examination of the history and status of indigenous peoples of Mexico, the United States, Canada, and Australia. The conclusion offers findings about state policies, state violence, resistance of the indigenous peoples, and efforts at self-determination.

Richard Reed, *Forest Dwellers, Forest Protectors: Indigenous Models for International Development*. Part of the Cultural Survival Studies in Ethnicity and Change Series. Boston: Allyn and Bacon, 1997. This is a fieldwork-based study of the Guaraní, indigenous peoples of Paraguay and Brazil, now occupying one of the world's largest remaining subtropical rain forests. Chapters consider social organization and production and consumption patterns. The text focuses on Guaraní practices and their ideas about use of forest resources.

Kalima Rose, *Where Women Are Leaders: The SEWA Movement in India*. Atlantic Highlands, NJ: Zed Books, 1992. Although not written by an anthropologist, this in-depth case study of a pioneering credit scheme for poor women of India stands as a useful contribution to the "success story" literature. The book provides a history of the Self-Employed Women's Association (SEWA) and chapters describing different strategies of SEWA and its expansion throughout India and globally.

Joan Ryan, *Doing Things the Right Way*. Calgary: University of Calgary Press, 1995. Using participatory action research, the research team documented Dogrib systems of traditional justice. The work has implications for native self-government, constitutional rights, and First Nations legal systems.

Michael French Smith, *Hard Times on Kairiru Island: Poverty, Development and Morality in a Papua New Guinea Village*. Honolulu: University of Hawaii Press, 1994. This is a fieldwork-based analysis of local understandings of poverty and development on a small island off the north coast of Papua New Guinea. Special attention is given to the stresses involved when the indigenous reciprocity economy meets up with profit-oriented capitalism.

Andrew Woolford, *Between Justice and Certainty: Treaty-Making in British Columbia*. Vancouver: UBC Press, 2004. Woolford explores the treaty process for resolving land claims of First Nations in British Columbia, with particular attention to the interplay between the Aboriginal and non-Aboriginal visions of justice.

WEBLINKS

The Companion Website (www.pearsoned.ca/miller) that accompanies *Cultural Anthropology*, Third Canadian Edition, includes a destinations module containing links to many websites relevant to the content of this chapter. Use it to investigate the Web and expand your understanding of anthropology.

absolute cultural relativism: a perspective that says a person from one culture should not question the rightness or wrongness of behaviour or ideas in other cultures because that would be ethnocentric.

acculturation: change in one culture as a result of contact with another culture.

achieved position: a person's standing in society based on qualities that the person has gained through action.

adaptation: a process of adjustment that plants and animals make to their environments that enhances their survival and their reproduction.

adolescence: a culturally defined period of maturation from the time of puberty until adulthood.

agency: the ability of humans to make choices and exercise free will.

age set: a group of people close in age who go through certain rituals, such as circumcision, at the same time.

agriculture: a mode of production that involves growing crops with the use of plowing, irrigation, and fertilizer.

amazon: a person who is biologically female but takes on a male gender role.

ambilineal descent: a kinship system in which a person is said to be descended from both parents but that allows the individual to choose with which descent group to have more affiliation.

animatism: a belief system in which the supernatural is conceived of as an impersonal power.

animism: the belief in souls.

anthropomorphic: a supernatural in the form of a human.

art: the application of imagination, skill, and style to matter, movement, and sound that goes beyond what is purely practical.

ascribed position: a person's standing in society based on qualities that the person attains through birth.

assimilation: a process of culture change through which one culture becomes completely incorporated into another and no longer has a separate identity.

authority: the ability to take action based on a person's achieved or ascribed status, moral reputation, or other basis.

avunculocality: a kinship rule that defines preferred marital residence with or near the husband's mother's brother.

balanced reciprocity: a form of exchange in which the goal is either immediate or eventual equality in value.

band: the political organization of foraging groups.

basic needs fund: a category of a personal or household budget that includes food, beverages, shelter, clothing, and the tools needed to obtain these items.

below-replacement-level fertility: a situation in which births are fewer than deaths, leading to population decline.

berdache: a blurred gender category, usually referring to a person who is biologically male but who assumes a female gender role.

big-man or big-woman system: a form of political organization midway between tribe and chiefdom involving reliance on the leadership of key individuals who develop a political following through personal ties and redistributive feasts.

bilateral descent: a kinship system in which a child is recognized as being related by descent to both parents equally.

bilingualism: the capacity to speak two languages.

bilocality: a marital residence pattern that offers a married couple the choice of living near or with the family of either the groom or the bride.

biological determinism: a theory that explains human behaviour and ideas mainly as a result of biological features such as genes, hormones, and drives.

blood sport: a form of competition that explicitly seeks to bring about a flow of blood, or even death, of human contestants, animal competitors, or in animal targets of human hunting.

brideprice: a form of marriage exchange involving a transfer of cash and goods from the groom's family to the bride's family.

bride-service: a form of marriage exchange in which the groom works for his in-laws for a certain period of time before returning home with the bride.

capital: wealth used to create more wealth.

cargo cult: a form of revitalization movement that sprang up in Melanesia, the South Pacific, in response to Western and Japanese influences.

caste: a ranked group, determined by birth, often linked to a particular occupation and to South Asian cultures.

ceremonial fund: a category of a personal or household budget used for public events such as a potlatch.

chiefdom: a political unit of permanently allied tribes and villages under one recognized leader.

circular migration: a common form of labour migration involving movement in a regular pattern between two or more places.

civil society: the collection of interest groups that function outside the government to organize economic and other aspects of life.

clan: a kinship-based group in which people claim descent from a common ancestor, although they may be unable to trace the exact relationship.

class: a way of categorizing people on the basis of their economic position in society, usually measured in terms of income or wealth.

clinical or applied medical anthropology: the application of anthropological knowledge to furthering the goals of health care providers.

code: a variant within a language that may include a distinct vocabulary, grammar, and intonation, associated with a particular microculture.

code-switch: moving from one code to another as needed.

communication: the conveying of meaningful messages from one person, animal, or insect to another.

community healing: healing that emphasizes the social context as a key component and is likely to be carried out within the public domain.

consumerism: a mode of consumption in which people's demands are many and infinite and the means of satisfying them are insufficient and become depleted in the effort to satisfy these demands.

consumption: using up goods or money.

consumption fund: a category of a personal or household budget used to provide for consumption demands.

cooperative: an economic group whose members share surpluses and who follow the democratic decision-making principle of one person, one vote.

corporate farm: a large agricultural enterprise that produces goods solely for sale and that is owned and operated by companies that rely entirely on hired labour.

couvade: a variety of customs applying to the behaviour of fathers during and shortly after the birth of their children.

creole: a language directly descended from a pidgin but possessing its own native speakers and involving linguistic expansion and elaboration.

critical cultural relativism: a perspective that prompts people in all cultures to raise questions about their own and others' cultural practices and ideas, especially regarding who accepts them and why, and whom they might be harming or helping.

critical development anthropology: an approach to international development in which the anthropologist takes on a critical-thinking role and asks why and to whose benefit particular development policies and programs are pursued.

critical legal anthropology: an approach within the cross-cultural study of law that examines how law and judicial systems serve to maintain and expand dominant power interests rather than protecting marginal and less powerful people.

critical medical anthropology: an approach within the cross-cultural study of health and illness involving the analysis of how economic and political structures shape people's health status, their access to health care, and the prevailing medical systems that exist in relation to them.

cross-cousin: the offspring of either one's father's sister or one's mother's brother.

cultural broker: a person who is familiar with the practices and beliefs of two cultures and can promote cross-cultural understanding to prevent or mediate conflicts.

cultural configuration: Ruth Benedict's theory that cultures are formed through the unconscious selection of a few cultural traits that interweave to form a cohesive pattern shared by all members of the culture.

cultural constructionism: a theory that explains human behaviour and ideas as being mainly the results of learning.

cultural imperialism: a situation in which a dominant culture claims supremacy over minority cultures and makes changes in its culture and the minority culture(s) in its own interests and at the expense of the minority culture(s).

cultural materialism: a theoretical position that takes material features of life, such as the environment, natural resources, and mode of production, as the bases for explaining social organization and ideology.

cultural relativism: the perspective that each culture must be understood in terms of the values and ideas of that culture and should not be judged by the standards of another.

culture: learned and shared human behaviours and ideas.

culture-bound syndrome: a collection of signs and symptoms that is restricted to a particular culture or a limited number of cultures; also called "folk illness."

culture of poverty: Oscar Lewis's theory that the personality characteristics of the poor trap them in poverty.

culture shock: persistent feelings of uneasiness, loneliness, and anxiety that often occur when a person has shifted from one culture to a different one.

dalit: the preferred name for the socially defined lowest groups in the Indian caste system, meaning "oppressed" or "ground down."

deductive research: a research method that involves posing a research question or hypothesis, gathering empirical data related to the question, and then assessing the findings in relation to the original hypothesis.

demographic transition: the change from the combined high fertility and high mortality of the agricultural mode of reproduction to the low fertility and low mortality characteristic of industrialized societies.

demography: the study of population dynamics.

descent: the tracing of kinship relationships through parentage.

development-induced displacement (DID): forced migration due to development projects, such as dam building.

diachronic: the analysis of culture across time.

dialect: a way of speaking in a particular place or a variety of a language arising from local circumstances.

diaspora population: dispersed group of people living outside their original homeland.

diffusion: the spread of culture through contact.

direct entitlement: the most secure form of entitlement to providing for one's needs; in an agricultural society, owning land that produces food is a direct entitlement.

direct infanticide: the killing of an infant or child through practices such as beating, smothering, poisoning, or drowning.

discourse: people's talk, stories, and myths.

disease of development: a health problem caused or increased by economic development activities that affect the environment and people's relationship with it.

displaced person: someone who is forced to leave his or her home and community, or country, and to settle elsewhere.

displacement: a feature of human language that allows people to talk about events in the past and future.

divination: a diagnostic procedure in which a specialist uses techniques to gain supernatural insights about the future.

doctrine: direct and formalized statements about religious beliefs.

domestication: the control and management of plants and animals by humans in terms of both their location and their reproduction.

dominant caste: one caste in a particular locale that controls most of the land and is often numerically preponderant.

double descent: systems (also called *double unilineal descent*) that combine patrilineal and matrilineal descent.

dowry: a form of marriage exchange involving the transfer of cash and goods from the bride's family to the bride and groom or to the groom's family.

ecological/epidemiological approach: an approach that considers how aspects of the natural environment and social environment interact to cause illness.

economic systems: the relations among economic production, consumption, and exchange.

emic: what insiders do and perceive about their culture, their perceptions of reality, and their explanations for why they do what they do.

enculturation: cultural learning; socialization.

endogamy: marriage within a particular group.

entertainment fund: a category of a personal or household budget used to provide for leisure activities.

entitlement: a culturally defined right to life-sustaining resources.

ethnicity: a sense of group affiliation based on features such as a distinct history, language, or religion.

ethno-aesthetics: cultural definitions of what is art.

ethnobotany: an area of inquiry exploring knowledge in different cultures of plants and their uses.

ethnocentrism: judging other cultures by the standards of one's own culture rather than by the standards of that particular culture.

ethnocide: destruction of a culture without physically killing its people.

ethnography: a first-hand, detailed description of a living culture, based on participant-observation techniques.

ethnology: the study of a particular topic in more than one culture using ethnographic material.

ethnomedicine: the medical system of a culture, including practices and ideas about the body, illness, and healing.

ethnomusicology: the cross-cultural study of music.

etic: an analytical framework used by outside analysts in studying culture. It may be based on a hypothesis or search for causal relationships.

exchange: the transfer of goods or money between people or institutions.

exogamy: marriage outside a particular group or locality.

expressive culture: behaviour and beliefs related to the arts and leisure.

extended household: a co-resident kinship group that comprises more than one parent–child unit.

faction: a politically oriented group that has strong ties to a leader and that vies with other factions for resources and rights.

family: a group of people who consider themselves related through a form of kinship, such as descent, marriage, or sharing.

female circumcision: a term used for a range of genital cutting procedures, including the excision of part or all of the clitoris, excision of part or all of the labia majora, and sometimes infibulation, the stitching together of the vaginal entry.

femicide: the murder of a person based on the fact of her being female.

fertility: the rate of births in a population.

feuding: long-term, retributive violence that may be lethal between families, groups of families, or tribes.

fieldwork: research in the field, which is any place where people and culture are found.

focal vocabulary: a cluster of related words referring to important features of a particular culture.

foraging: collecting food that is available in nature, by gathering, fishing, or hunting.

formal sector: salaried or wage-based work registered in official statistics.

gender: culturally constructed and learned behaviours and ideas attributed to males, females, or blended genders.

genealogy: a record of a person's relatives constructed beginning with the earliest ancestors.

generalized exchange system: exchange involving more than two groups and occurring in a more diffuse and delayed way.

generalized reciprocity: exchange involving the least conscious sense of interest in material gain or thought of what might be received in return.

genocide: the destruction of a culture and its people through physical extermination.

globalization: increased and intensified global interconnections related to the flow of capital, information, goods and people throughout the world.

global language: or world language, a language spoken widely throughout the world and in diverse cultural contexts often replacing indigenous languages; notably English and Spanish.

grammar: the patterns and rules for combining sounds into word sequences that carry meaning.

groomprice: a form of dowry involving transfer of large amounts of cash and goods from the bride's family to the groom's family; often called dowry.

hijira: term used in India to refer to a blurred gender role in which a person, usually biologically male, takes on female dress and behaviour.

historical linguistics: the study of language change using formal methods that compare shifts over time and across space in formal aspects of language such as phonetics, grammar, and semantics.

historical particularism: the view that individual cultures must be studied and described on their own terms and that cross-cultural comparisons and generalizations ignore cultural specificities and are invalid.

holism: the perspective in anthropology that cultures are complex systems that cannot be fully understood without paying attention to their different components, including economics, social organization, and ideology.

horticulture: a mode of production based on growing domesticated crops in gardens using simple hand tools.

household: a group of people, who may or may not be related by kinship, who share living space and budgeting.

household headship: the primary person (or people) in charge of supporting the household financially and making decisions.

human development: a model of change promoted by the United Nations that emphasizes improvements in human welfare such as health, education, and personal security.

humoral healing system: a medical model that emphasizes balance among natural elements within the body.

hypergyny: a marriage in which the groom is of higher status than the bride.

hypogyny: a marriage in which the bride is of higher status than the groom.

iatrogenic: an affliction caused by medical definition or intervention.

image of the limited good: George Foster's theory that in non-industrial cultures, people have a characteristic world view of finite resources or wealth such that if someone in the group increases his or her wealth, other people will necessarily lose out.

incest taboo: a strongly held prohibition against marrying or having sex with particular kin.

indexicality: certain linguistic features that point to the identities, actions, or feelings of the speaker and convey important social information.

indigenous knowledge: local knowledge about the environment, including plants, animals, and resources.

indigenous people: people who have a longstanding connection with their home territory that predates colonial or outside societies that prevail in that territory.

indirect entitlement: a way of gaining one's livelihood that depends on exchanging something, such as labour or goods.

indirect infanticide: the killing of an infant or child through practices such as food deprivation or failure to seek health care during illness.

inductive research: a research approach that avoids hypothesis formation in advance of the research and instead takes its lead from the culture being studied.

industrial agriculture: a form of agriculture that is capital-intensive, substituting machinery and purchased inputs for human and animal labour.

industrial collectivized agriculture: a form of industrialized agriculture that involves state control of land, technology, and goods produced.

industrialism: a mode of production in which goods are produced through mass employment in business and commercial operations.

infant mortality rate: the number of deaths of children under the age of one year per 1000 births.

infanticide: the killing of an infant or child.

influence: the ability to achieve a desired end by exerting social or moral pressure on someone or some group.

informal sector: work that is outside the formal sector, not officially registered, and sometimes illegal.

informed consent: an aspect of fieldwork ethics requiring that the researcher inform the research participants of the intent, scope, and possible effects of the study and seek their consent to be in the study.

infrastructure: in the framework of cultural materialism, the first and most basic level of culture, which includes the material factors of economy and reproduction.

in-kind taxation: a revenue system that involves non-cash contributions such as labour.

institution: enduring group setting formed for a particular purpose.

intensive strategy: a form of production that involves continuous use of the same land and resources.

intergenerational household: a residential group in which an "adult child" returns to live with his or her parents.

internal migration: movement within national boundaries.

internally displaced persons: people forced to leave their home and community but who remain within their country.

international development: directed change to achieve improved levels of human welfare in developing countries usually in terms of economic growth.

international migration: moving between nations.

interpretive anthropology: Ideas and theoretical approaches that consider how people negotiate meanings to make sense of the world around them.

interview: a research technique that involves gathering of verbal data through questions or guided conversation between at least two people.

***jajmani* system:** an exchange system of India in which landholding patrons (*jajmans*) offer food grains to service providers such as brahman priests, artisans (blacksmiths, potters), and agricultural labourers.

kinesics: the study of communication that occurs through body movements, positions, facial expressions, and spatial behaviour.

kinship: a sense of being related to another person or persons through descent, sharing, or marriage.

kinship diagram: a schematic way of presenting data on kinship relationships of an individual (called "ego") depicting all of ego's relatives, as remembered by ego and reported to the anthropologist.

kinship system: the predominant form of kin relationships in a culture and the kinds of behaviour involved.

language: a form of communication that is a systematic set of arbitrary symbols shared among members of a group and passed on from generation to generation.

language decay: condition of a language in which speakers adopt a new language for most situations, begin to use their native language only in certain contexts, and may be only semi-fluent and have limited vocabulary in their native language.

language extinction: a situation, either gradual or sudden, in which language speakers abandon their native language in favour of a new language to the extent that the native language loses functions and no longer has competent users.

language pragmatics: language in use.

language socialization: language learning through everyday interactions.

law: a binding rule created through enactment or custom that defines right and reasonable behaviour and is enforceable by threat of punishment.

legal pluralism: the existence, within a culture, of more than one kind of legal system.

lifeboat mentality: local resentment of an immigrant group because of perceived resource constraints.

life-cycle ritual: a ritual performed to mark a change in status from one life stage to another of an individual or group; also called *rite of passage*.

life history: a qualitative, in-depth portrait of a single life experience of a person as narrated to the anthropologist.

limited-purpose money: an item or items that can be exchanged only for specified things.

linguistic determinism: the theory that language determines consciousness of the world and behaviour.

linguistic pluralism: the presence of linguistic diversity within a particular context.

linguistic relativism: the position that all languages are equally successful forms of communication.

local culture: distinct patterns of learned and shared behaviour and ideas found in localized regions and among particular groups.

localization: cultural change in which global or macrocultures become adapted and transformed by local cultures.

logograph: a symbol that conveys meaning through a form or picture resembling that to which it refers.

macroculture: a distinct pattern of learned and shared behaviour and thinking that crosses local boundaries, such as transnational culture and global culture.

magic: the attempt to compel supernatural forces and beings to act in certain ways.

market exchange: the buying and selling of commodities under competitive conditions in which the forces of supply and demand determine value.

marriage: a union between two or more people that creates a new kind category: in-laws.

matrifocality: a household system in which a female (or females) is the central, stable figure around whom other members cluster.

matrilineal descent: a kinship system that highlights the importance of women by tracing descent through the female line, favouring marital residence with or near the bride's family, and providing for property to be inherited through the female line.

matrilocality: a kinship rule that defines preferred marital residence with or near the bride's kin.

mechanical solidarity: social bonding among groups that are similar.

medicalization: labelling a particular issue or problem as medical and requiring medical treatment when, in fact, that issue or problem is economic or political.

medical pluralism: the existence of more than one medical system in a culture, or a government policy to promote the integration of local healing systems into biomedical practice.

migration: the movement of a person or people from one place to another.

minimalism: a mode of consumption that emphasizes simplicity, is characterized by few and finite (limited) consumer demands, and involves an adequate and sustainable means to achieve them.

mode of consumption: the dominant way, in a culture, of using things up or spending resources in order to satisfy demands.

mode of exchange: the dominant pattern, in a society, of transferring goods, services, and other items between and among people and groups.

mode of production: the dominant way, in a culture, of providing for people's material needs.

mode of reproduction: the predominant pattern of fertility and mortality in a culture.

modernization theory: a model of change based on belief in the inevitable advance of science and Western secularism and processes including industrial growth, consolidation of the state, bureaucratization, market economy, technological innovation, literacy, and options for social mobility.

money: currency or items with recognized value that can be exchanged for other kinds of things.

monogamy: marriage between two people.

monotheism: the belief in one supreme deity.

mortality: deaths in a population, or rate of population decline in general or from particular causes.

multi-purpose money: a medium of exchange that can be used for all goods and services available.

multi-sited research: fieldwork conducted in more than one location in order to understand the behaviours and ideas of dispersed members of a culture or the relationships among different levels such as state policy and local culture.

myth: a narrative with a plot that involves the sacred.

narcissist: someone who constantly seeks self-attention and self-affirmation, with no concern for other people's needs.

nation: a group of people who share a language, culture, territorial base, political organization, and history.

national character study: a type of analysis in psychological anthropology that defined basic personality types and core values of entire countries.

neolocality: a kinship rule that defines preferred marital residence in a new location not linked to either the bride's or the groom's parents' residence.

new immigrants: international migrants who have moved since the 1960s.

norm: a generally agreed-upon standard for how people should behave, usually unwritten and learned unconsciously.

nuclear household: a domestic unit containing one adult couple (married or partners), with or without children.

observer's paradox: the logical impossibility of doing research on natural communication events without affecting the naturalness sought.

organic solidarity: social bonding among groups with different abilities and resources.

paralanguage: non-verbal communication such as body posture, voice tone, touch, smells, and eye and facial movements.

parallel cousin: offspring of either one father's brother or one's mother's sister.

participant observation: basic fieldwork method in cultural anthropology that involves living in a culture for a long period of time while gathering data.

participatory research method (PRM): a method in development anthropology that involves the local people in gathering data relevant to local development projects.

pastoralism: a mode of production based on keeping domesticated animal herds and using their products, such as meat and milk, for most of the diet.

patrilineal descent: a kinship system that highlights the importance of men in tracing descent, determining marital residence with or near the groom's family, and providing for inheritance of property through the male line.

patrilocality: a kinship rule that defines preferred marital residence with or near the groom's kin.

personality: an individual's patterned and characteristic way of behaving, thinking, and feeling.

phoneme: a sound that makes a difference for meaning in a language.

phonetics: the study of the production of speech sounds.

pidgin: a contact language that emerges where people with different languages need to communicate; a pidgin involves linguistic simplification and reduction.

placebo effect: a healing effect obtained through the positive power of believing that a particular method is efficacious.

policing: the exercise of social control through processes of surveillance and the threat of punishment related to maintaining social order.

political organization: the existence of groups for purposes of public decision making and leadership, maintaining social cohesion and order, protecting group rights, and ensuring safety from external threats.

politics: the organized use of public power, as opposed to the more private politics of family and domestic groups.

polyandry: marriage of one wife with more than one husband.

polygamy: marriage involving multiple spouses.

polygyny: marriage of one husband with more than one wife.

polytheism: the belief in many deities.

postmodernism: a view that questions various aspects of modernism, including the scientific method, human progress through scientific knowledge, urbanization, technological change, and mass communication.

potlatch: a grand feast in which guests are invited to eat and to receive gifts from the hosts.

power: the ability to bring about desired results, often through the possession or use of force.

priest/priestess: male or female full-time religious specialist whose position is based mainly on abilities gained through formal training.

primary group: a social group in which members meet on a face-to-face basis.

primogeniture: inheritance system whereby only the eldest son could inherit the family property.

privatization: transferring the collective ownership and provision of goods and services to a system of private ownership.

production: making goods or money.

productivity: a feature of human language that offers the ability to communicate many messages efficiently.

project cycle: the steps of a development project from initial planning to completion: project identification, project design, project appraisal, project implementation, and project evaluation.

pronatalism: an ideology promoting many children.

puberty: a time in the human life cycle that occurs universally and involves a set of biological markers and sexual maturation.

public/private dichotomy: gender division in society that emerged with agriculture, whereby men are more involved with the non-domestic domain and women are more involved in activities in or near the home.

pure gift: something given with no expectation or thought of a return.

push–pull theory: a theory that attributes rural-to-urban migration to the "push" of rural areas' decreasing ability to support population growth and the "pull" of cities that offer employment and a more appealing lifestyle.

qualitative research: research that emphasizes generating description.

quantitative research: research that emphasizes gathering and analyzing numerical information and using tables and charts when presenting results.

race: a scientifically invalid way of classifying people on the basis of selected biological traits such as skin colour and facial features.

rapid research method (RRM): fieldwork method designed for use in development anthropology that can yield relevant data in a short period of time.

rapport: a trusting relationship between the researcher and the study population.

reciprocity: an exchange of approximately equally valued goods or services, usually between people roughly equal in social status.

redistribution: a form of exchange that involves one person collecting goods or money from many members of a group who then, at a later time and at a public event, "returns" the pooled goods to everyone who contributed.

reflexive anthropology: anthropological research carried out and described with attention to the researcher's presence, role, and influence on the research, research informants, and research results. Also called reflexivity.

refugee: someone who is forced to leave his or her home country.

region: a distinct spatial area with a name and cultural characteristics that separate it from other areas.

religion: beliefs and actions related to supernatural beings and forces.

religious pluralism: when two or more religions co-exist as either complementary to each other or as competitive systems.

remittance: economic transfer of money or goods by a migrant to his or her family back home.

repatriation: returning art or other objects from museums to the people with whom they originated.

replacement-level fertility: situation when births equal deaths, leading to maintenance of current population size.

reproduction: the predominant patterns of fertility in a culture.

research methods: particular strategies and techniques cultural anthropologists use to learn about culture.

restricted exchange system: bride exchange system in which women are exchanged only between two groups.

revitalization movement: an organized movement, usually surrounding a prophetic leader, that seeks to construct a more satisfying culture, either by re-establishing all or parts of a religion that has been threatened by outside forces or by adopting new practices and beliefs.

revolution: a political crisis prompted by illegal and often violent actions of subordinate groups that seek to change the political institutions or social structure of a society.

right of return: United Nations guaranteed right of refugees to repatriation.

ritual: a patterned form of behaviour that has to do with the supernatural realm.

ritual of inversion: a ritual in which normal social roles and order are temporarily reversed.

role: the expected behaviour for someone of a particular status, with a "script" for how to behave, look, eat, and talk.

sacrifice: a ritual in which something is offered to the supernaturals.

Sapir-Whorf hypothesis: a theory that claims that language determines thought.

secondary group: people who identify with each other on some basis but may never meet with one another personally.

segmentary model: type of political organization in which smaller units unite in the face of external threats and then disunite when the external threat is absent.

sex-selective infanticide: the killing of offspring depending on their sex.

shaman/shamanka: male or female part-time religious specialist who gains his or her status through direct relationship with the supernaturals, often by being "called."

social control: processes that maintain orderly social life, including informal and formal mechanisms.

social group: a cluster of people beyond the domestic unit who are usually related on grounds other than kinship.

social impact assessment: a study conducted to gauge the potential social costs and benefits of particular innovations before change is undertaken.

social stratification: hierarchical relationships between different groups as though they were arranged in layers or "strata."

socio-cultural fit: concept that refers to how well a development project meshes with the "target" culture and population.

sociolinguistics: approach that says that culture and society and a person's social position determine the content and form of language; a field of study devoted to revealing such social effects on language.

state: a centralized political unit encompassing many communities and possessing coercive power.

status: a person's position, or standing, in society.

stem household: a co-residential group that contains only two married couples related through males, commonly found in East Asian cultures.

structural adjustment: an economic policy that has been pursued by the World Bank since the 1980s requiring that countries receiving World Bank loans pursue privatization of services such as health care and schools and reduce government expenditures in these areas.

structure: within the cultural materialist framework, the second level of culture, which comprises social organization, kinship, and political organization.

superstructure: within the cultural materialist framework, the third level of culture, which comprises ideology (communication, religion, and expressive culture).

sustainable development: a directed change that involves forms of development that are not environmentally destructive and are financially supportable by the host country and environmentally supportable by the earth as a whole.

symbol: something that stands for something else; symbols are arbitrary (bearing no necessary relationship with what is symbolized), unpredictable, and diverse.

synchronic: a "one-time" view of a culture that devotes little or no attention to its past.

syncretism: the blending of features of two or more cultures, especially used in discussion of religious change.

taboo: a rule of prohibition

tax/rent fund: a category of a person's or household's budget used as payment to a government as part of one's civic responsibilities or to a landlord for use of land or housing.

teknonymy: the practice of naming someone on the basis of his or her relationship to someone else, as in "The Mother of So and So."

theatre: a form of enactment, related to other forms such as dance, music, parades, competitive games and sports, and verbal art.

trade: the formalized exchange of one thing for another according to set standards of value.

traditional development anthropology: an approach to development in which the anthropologist accepts the role of helping to make development work better by providing cultural information to planners.

transnationalism: national identity that crosses nation-states and is created through the flow of people, goods, and ideas.

transnational migrant: a person who moves back and forth regularly between two or more countries and forms a new identity that transcends association of the self with a single political unit.

trial by ordeal: a way of determining innocence or guilt in which the accused person is put to a test that may be painful, stressful, or fatal.

triangulation: research technique that involves obtaining information on a particular topic from more than one person or perspective.

tribe: a political group that comprises several bands or lineage groups, each with similar language and lifestyle and occupying a distinct territory.

trope: key theme.

unilineal descent: a kinship system that traces descent through only one parent, either the mother or the father.

use rights: a system of property relations in which a person or group has socially recognized priority in access to particular resources such as gathering, hunting, and fishing areas and water holes.

wage labour migration: migration to work for a specific period of time.

war: organized and purposeful group action directed against another group and involving the actual or potential application of lethal force.

wet rice agriculture: highly labour-intensive way of growing rice that involves starting the seedlings in nurseries and transplanting them to flooded fields.

world religion: a term coined in the nineteenth century to refer to religions that had many followers, that crossed state borders, and that exhibited other specific features such as a concern with salvation.

world view: a way of understanding how the world came to be, its design, and people's place in it with or without reference to a supernatural realm.

youth gang: a group of young people, found mainly in urban areas, who are often considered a social problem by adults and law enforcement officials.

zoomorphic: a supernatural in the shape, or partial shape, of an animal.

REFERENCES

Abler, Thomas S. 1992. Scalping, Torture, Cannibalism, and Rape: An Ethnohistorical Analysis of Conflicting Cultural Values in War. *Anthropologica* 34:3–20.

Abu-Lughod, Lila. 1993. *Writing Women's Worlds: Bedouin Stories.* Berkeley: University of California Press.

Adams, Kathleen M. 1984. Come to Tana Toraja, "Land of the Heavenly Kings": Travel Agents as Brokers in Ethnicity. *Annals of Tourism Research* 11:469–485.

Adams, Vincanne. 1988. Modes of Production and Medicine: An Examination of the Theory in Light of Sherpa Traditional Medicine. *Social Science and Medicine* 27:505–513.

Adelson, Naomi. 1998 Health Beliefs and the Politics of Cree Well-Being. *Health* 2(1):5–22.

___. 2000 *"Being Alive Well": Health and the Politics of Cree Well-Being.* Toronto: University of Toronto Press.

Adlam, Robert. 2000. Fish Talk. *Anthropologica* 44(1):99–111.

Agar, Michael. 1994 *Language Shock: Understanding the Culture of Conversation.* New York: William Morrow.

Ahmadu, Fuambai. 2000. Rites and Wrongs: An Insider/Outsider Reflects on Power and Excision. In *Female "Circumcision" in Africa: Culture, Controversy, and Change.* Bettina Shell-Duncan and Ylva Hernlund, eds. Pp. 283–312. Boulder, CO: Lynne Reiner Publishers.

Akinsha, Konstantin. 1992a. Russia: Whose Art Is It? *ARTNews* 91(5):100–105.

___. 1992b. Whose Gold? *ARTNews* 91(3):39–40.

___. 1992c. After the Coup: Art for Art's Sake? *ARTNews* 91(1):108–113.

Allison, Anne. 1994. *Nightwork: Sexuality, Pleasure, and Corporate Masculinity in a Tokyo Hostess Club.* Chicago: University of Chicago Press.

Alter, Joseph S. 1992. The Sannyasi and the Indian Wrestler: Anatomy of a Relationship. *American Ethnologist* 19(2):317–336.

Ames, David. 1959 Wolof Co-operative Work Groups. In *Continuity and Change in African Cultures,* ed. William R. Bascom and Melville J. Herskovits, 224–237. Chicago: University of Chicago Press.

Ames, Michael. 1992. *Cannibal Tours and Glass Boxes: The Anthropology of Museums.* Vancouver: University of British Columbia Press.

Anagnost, Ann. 2004. Maternal Labor in a Transnational Circuit. In *Consuming Motherhood.* Janelle S. Taylor, Linda L. Layne, Danielle F. Wozniak, eds. Pp.139–167. New Brunswick, NJ: Rutgers University Press.

Anderson, Benedict. 1991[1983]. *Imagined Communities: Reflections on the Origin and Spread of Nationalism.* New York: Verso.

Anderson, Richard L., and Karen L. Field. 1993. Chapter introduction. In *Art in Small-Scale Societies: Contemporary Readings.* Richard L. Anderson and Karen L. Fields, eds. P. 247. Englewood Cliffs, NJ: Prentice Hall.

Andriolo, Karin. 2002. Murder by Suicide: Episodes from Muslim History. *American Anthropologist* 104:736–742.

Antze, Paul, and Michael Lambek, eds. 1996. *Tense Past: Cultural Essays in Trauma and Memory.* New York: Routledge.

Appadurai, Arjun. 1986. Introduction: Commodities and the Politics of Value. In *The Social Life of Things: Commodities in Cultural Perspective.* Arjun Appadurai, ed. Pp. 3–63. New York: Cambridge University Press.

Applbaum, Kalman D. 1995. Marriage with the Proper Stranger: Arranged Marriage in Metropolitan Japan. *Ethnology* 34(1):37–51.

Arnup, Katherine. 2000. Living in the Margins: Lesbian Families and the Law. In *Open Boundaries: A Canadian Women's Studies Reader.* Barbara A. Crow and Lise Gotell, eds. Pp. 205–214. Toronto: Prentice-Hall Canada.

Asad, Talal, ed. 1973. *Anthropology and the Colonial Encounter.* London: Ithaca Press.

Asch, Michael. 1997. *Aboriginal Treaty Rights in Canada: Essays on Law, Equality and Responsibility for Difference.* Vancouver: UBC Press.

Attwood, Donald W. 1992. *Raising Cane: The Political Economy of Sugar in Western India.* Boulder: Westview Press.

Avery, Donald H. 1995. *Reluctant Host: Canada's Response to Immigrant Workers, 1896–1994.* Toronto: McClelland & Stewart.

Awe, Bolanle. 1977. The Iyalode in the Traditional Yoruba Political System. In *Sexual Stratification: A Cross-Cultural View.* Alice Schlegel, ed. Pp. 144–160. New York: Columbia University Press.

Bachnik, Jane M. 1983. Recruitment Strategies for Household Succession: Rethinking Japanese Household Organisation. *Man* 18:160–182.

Baer, Lars-Anders. 1982. The Sami: An Indigenous People in Their Own Land. In *The Sami National Minority in Sweden.* Birgitta Jahreskog, ed. Pp. 11–22. Stockholm: Almqvist & Wiksell International.

Bardhan, Pranab. 1974. On Life and Death Questions. *Economic and Political Weekly* Special Number 9(32–34): 1293–1303.

Barfield, Thomas J. 1993. *The Nomadic Alternative.* Englewood Cliffs, NJ: Prentice-Hall.

___. 1994. Prospects for Plural Societies in Central Asia. *Cultural Survival Quarterly* 18(2 & 3):48–51.

___. 2001. Pastoral Nomads or Nomadic Pastoralists. In *The Dictionary of Anthropology.* Thomas Barfield, ed. Pp. 348–350. Malden, MA: Blackwell Publishers.

Barker, J. 1987. T. F. McIlwraith and Anthropology at the University of Toronto, 1925–1963. *Canadian Review of Sociology and Anthropology* 24:252–268.

Barkey, Nanette, Benjamin C. Campbell, and Paul W. Leslie. 2001. A Comparison of Health Complaints of Settled and Nomadic Turkana Men. *Medical Anthropology Quarterly* 15:391–408.

Barlett, Peggy F. 1980. Reciprocity and the San Juan Fiesta. *Journal of Anthropological Research* 36:116–130.

___. 1989. Industrial Agriculture. In *Economic Anthropology.* Stuart Plattner, ed. Pp. 253–292. Stanford: Stanford University Press.

Barnard, Alan. 2000. *History and Theory in Anthropology.* New York: Cambridge University Press.

Barnard, Alan, and Anthony Good. 1984. *Research Practices in the Study of Kinship.* New York: Academic Press.

Barndt, Deborah, ed. 1999. *Women Working the NAFTA Food Chain: Women, Food and Globalization.* Toronto: Second Story Press.

Barrett, Stanley R. 1987. *Is God a Racist?* Toronto: University of Toronto Press.

Barth, Frederik. 1993. *Balinese Worlds.* Chicago: University of Chicago Press.

Basch, Linda, Nina Glick Schiller, and Christina Szanton Blanc. 1994. *Nations Unbound: Transnational Projects, Postcolonial Predicaments, and Deterritorialized Nation-States.* Langhorne, PA: Gordon and Breach Science Publishers.

Basso, Keith. H. 1972[1970]. "To Give Up on Words": Silence in Apache Culture. In *Language and Social Context.* Pier Paolo Giglioni, ed. Pp. 67–86. Baltimore: Penguin Books.

Beals, Alan R. 1980. *Gopalpur: A South Indian Village.* Fieldwork edition. New York: Holt, Rinehart and Winston.

Beattie, Andrew. 2002. Changing Places: Relatives and Relativism in Java. *Journal of the Royal Anthropological Institute* 8:469–491.

Beatty, Andrew. 1992. *Society and Exchange in Nias.* New York: Oxford University Press.

Beck, Lois. 1986. *The Qashqa'i of Iran.* New Haven: Yale University Press.

Beeman, William O. 1993. The Anthropology of Theater and Spectacle. *Annual Review of Anthropology* 22:363–393.

Beiser, Morton. 1999. *Strangers at the Gate: The "Boat People's" First Ten Years in Canada.* Toronto: University of Toronto Press.

Belikov, Vladimir. 1994. Language Death in Siberia. *UNESCO Courier* 1994(2):32–36.

Benedict, Ruth. 1959[1934]. *Patterns of Culture.* Boston: Houghton Mifflin Company.

___. 1969[1946]. *The Chrysanthemum and the Sword: Patterns of Japanese Culture.* Rutland, VT: Charles E. Tuttle Company.

Berg, Karen. 1997. Female Genital Mutilation: Implications for Social Work. *The Social Worker* 65:16–25.

Berlin, Elois Ann, and Brent Berlin. 1996. *Medical Ethnobiology of the Highland Maya of Chiapas, Mexico: The Gastrointestinal Diseases.* Princeton: Princeton University Press.

Bernal, Martin. 1987. *Black Athena: The Afroasiatic Roots of Classical Civilization.* New Brunswick, NJ: Rutgers University Press.

Bernard, H. Russell. 1995. *Research Methods in Cultural Anthropology: Qualitative and Quantitative Approaches.* 2nd edition. Newbury Park, CA: Sage Publications.

Berreman, Gerald D. 1963. *Hindus of the Himalayas.* Berkeley: University of California Press.

___. 1979[1975]. Race, Caste, and Other Invidious Distinctions in Social Stratification. In *Caste and Other Inequities: Essays on Inequality.* Gerald D. Berreman, ed. Pp. 178–222. New Delhi: Manohar.

Best, David. 1986. Culture Consciousness: Understanding the Arts of Other Cultures. *Journal of Art & Design Education* 5(1&2):124–135.

Beyene, Yewoubdar. 1989. *From Menarche to Menopause: Reproductive Lives of Peasant Women in Two Cultures.* Albany: State University of New York Press.

Bhardwaj, Surinder M. 1973. *Hindu Places of Pilgrimage in India: A Study in Cultural Geography.* Berkeley: University of California Press.

Bhatt, Rakesh M. 2001. World Englishes. *Annual Review of Anthropology* 30:527–550.

Bialystok, Ellen, and Shilpi Majumder. 1998. The Relationship between Bilingualism and the Development of Cognitive Processes in Problem Solving. *Applied Psycholinguistics* 19(1):69–85.

Bigenho, Michelle. 1999. Sensing Locality in Yura: Rituals of Carnival and of the Bolivian State. *American Ethnologist* 26:957–980.

Billig, Michael S. 1992. The Marriage Squeeze and the Rise of Groomprice in India's Kerala State. *Journal of Comparative Family Studies* 23:197–216.

Bird, Sharon R. 1996. Welcome to the Men's Club: Homosociality and the Maintenance of Hegemonic Masculinity. *Gender & Society* 10(2): 120–132.

Blackwood, Evelyn. 1995. Senior Women, Model Mothers, and Dutiful Wives: Managing Gender Contradictions in a Minangkabau Village. In *Bewitching Women: Pious Men: Gender and Body Politics in Southeast Asia*, ed. Aihwa Ong and Michael Peletz, 124–158. Berkeley: University of California Press.

Blaikie, Piers. 1985. *The Political Economy of Soil Erosion in Developing Countries*. New York: Longman.

Blanchard, Ray, Kenneth J. Zucker, Susan J. Bradley, and Caitlin S. Hume. 1995. Birth Order and Sibling Sex Ratio in Homosexual Male Adolescents and Probably Prehomosexual Feminine Boys. *Developmental Psychology* 31(1): 22–30.

Blau, Peter M. 1964. *Exchange and Power in Social Life*. New York: Wiley.

Bledsoe, Caroline H. 1983. Stealing Food as a Problem in Demography and Nutrition. Paper presented at the annual meeting of the American Anthropological Association.

Bledsoe, Caroline H., and Helen K. Hirschman. 1989. Case Studies of Mortality: Anthropological Contributions. Proceedings of the International Union for the Scientific Study of Population, XXIst International Population Conference, 331–348. Liége: International Union for the Scientific Study of Population.

Blim, Michael. 2000. Capitalisms in Late Modernity. *Annual Review of Anthropology* 29:25–38.

Blood, Robert O. 1967. *Love Match and Arranged Marriage*. New York: Free Press.

Bodley, John H. 1988. *Tribal Peoples and Development Issues: A Global Overview*. Mountain View, CA: Mayfield Publishing Company.

___. 1990. *Victims of Progress*. 3rd edition. Mountain View, CA: Mayfield Publishing Company.

Bogin, Barry. 1988. *Patterns of Human Growth*. New York: Cambridge University Press.

Bohannan, Paul. 1955. Some Principles of Exchange and Investment among the Tiv. *American Anthropologist* 57(1):60–70.

Bollman, R., and P. Smith. 1988. Integration of Canadian Farm and Off-Farm Markets and the Off-Farm Work of Farm Women, Men, and Children. In *The Political Economy of Agriculture in Western Canada*. G. S. Basran and D. A. Hay, eds. Toronto: Garamond Press.

Borins, M. 1995. Native Healing Traditions Must Be Protected and Preserved for Future Generations. *Canadian Medial Association Journal* 7.153(9):1356–1357.

Boserup, Ester. 1970. *Woman's Role in Economic Development*. New York: St. Martin's Press.

Bourdieu, Pierre. 1984. *Distinction: A Social Critique of the Judgement of Taste*. Trans. Richard Nice. Cambridge: Harvard University Press.

Bourgois, Philippe I. 1995. *In Search of Respect: Selling Crack in El Barrio*. New York: Cambridge University Press.

Bourgois, P., and J. Bruneau. 2000. Needle Exchange, HIV Infection and the Politics of Science: Confronting Canada's Cocaine Infection Epidemic with Participant Observation. *Medical Anthropology* 18(4): 325–350.

Bowen, Anne M., and Robert Trotter II. 1995. HIV Risk in Intravenous Drug Users and Crack Cocaine Smokers: Predicting Stage of Change for Condom Use. *Journal of Consulting and Clinical Psychology* 63:238–248.

Bowen, John R. 1992. On Scriptural Essentialism and Ritual Variation: Muslim Sacrifice in Sumatra. *American Ethnologist* 19(4):656–671.

___. 1998. *Religions in Practice: An Approach to the Anthropology of Religion*. Boston: Allyn and Bacon.

Boyd, Monica, and Doug Norris. 1999. The Crowded Nest: Young Adults at Home. Statistics Canada, *Canadian Social Trends* Spring.

Bradley, Richard. 2000. An Archaeology of Natural Places. New York: Routledge.

Brana-Shute, Rosemary. 1976. Women, Clubs, and Politics: The Case of a Lower-Class Neighborhood in Paramaribo, Suriname. *Urban Anthropology* 5(2):157–185.

Brenneis, Donald, and Laura Lein. 1977. "You Fruithead": A Sociolinguistic Approach to Children's Dispute Settlement. In *Child Discourse*. Susan Ervin-Tripp and Claudia Methcell-Kernan, eds. Pp. 49–65. New York: Academic Press.

Briggs, Jean L. 1970. *Never in Anger*. Cambridge, MA: Harvard University Press.

Brink, Judy H. 1991. The Effect of Emigration of Husbands on the Status of Their Wives: An Egyptian Case. *International Journal of Middle East Studies* 23:201–211.

Brison, Karen J., and Stephen C. Leavitt. 1995. Coping with Bereavement: Long-Term Perspectives on Grief and Mourning. *Ethos* 23:395–400.

Brodkin, Karen. 2000. Global Capitalism: What's Race Got to Do with It? *American Ethnologist* 27:237–256.

Brooks, Alison S., and Patricia Draper. 1998. Anthropological Perspectives on Aging. In *Anthropology Explored: The Best of Smithsonian AnthroNotes*. Ruth Osterweis Selig and Marilyn R. London, eds. Pp. 286–297. Washington, DC: Smithsonian Press.

Broude, Gwen J. 1988. Rethinking the Couvade: Cross-Cultural Evidence. *American Anthropologist* 90(4):902–911.

Brown, Carolyn Henning. 1984. Tourism and Ethnic Competition in a Ritual Form: The Firewalkers of Fiji. *Oceania* 54:223–244.

Brown, Judith K. 1970. A Note on the Division of Labor by Sex. *American Anthropologist* 72(5):1073–1078.

___. 1975. Iroquois Women: An Ethnohistoric Note. In *Toward an Anthropology of Women*. Rayna R. Reiter, ed. Pp. 235–251. New York: Monthly Review Press.

___. 1978. The Recruitment of a Female Labor Force. *Anthropos* 73(1/2):41–48.

___. 1982. Cross-Cultural Perspectives on Middle-Aged Women. *Current Anthropology* 23(2):143–156.

___. 1992. Introduction: Definitions, Assumptions, Themes, and Issues. In *Sanctions and Sanctuary: Cultural Perspectives on the Beating of Wives*. Dorothy Ayers Counts, Judith K. Brown, and Jacquelyn C. Campbell, eds. Pp. 1–18. Boulder: Westview Press.

Brown, Peter J., Marcia C. Inhorn, and Daniel J. Smith. 1996. Disease, Ecology, and Human Behavior. In *Medical Anthropology: Contemporary Theory and Method*. Carolyn F. Sargent and Thomas M. Johnson, eds. Pp. 183–218. Connecticut: Praeger Publishers.

Browner, Carole H. 1986. The Politics of Reproduction in a Mexican Village. *Signs: Journal of Women in Culture and Society* 11(4):710–724.

Browner, Carole H., and Nancy Ann Press. 1995. The Normalization of Prenatal Diagnostic Screening. In *Conceiving the New World Order: The Global Politics of Reproduction*. Faye D. Ginsberg and Rayna Rapp, eds. Pp. 307–322. Berkeley: University of California Press.

___. 1996. The Production of Authoritative Knowledge in American Prenatal Care. *Medical Anthropology Quarterly* 10(2):141–156.

Brownmiller, Susan. 1994. *Seeing Vietnam: Encounters of the Road and Heart*. New York: HarperCollins.

Brumfiel, Elizabeth M. 1994 Introduction. In *Factional Competition and Political Development in the New World*. Elizabeth M. Brumfiel and John W. Fox, eds. Pp. 3–14. New York: Cambridge University Press.

Bruner, Edward M. 1991. The Transformation of Self in Tourism. *Annals of Tourism Research* 18:238–250.

Bunzel, Ruth. 1972[1929]. *The Pueblo Potter: A Study of Creative Imagination in Primitive Art*. New York: Dover Publications.

Butler, Shelley. 1999. *Contested Representations: Revisiting "Into the Heart of Africa."* Amsterdam: Gordon and Breach.

Calhoun, Craig, Donald Light, and Suzanne Keller. 1994. *Sociology*. 6th edition. New York: McGraw Hill.

Call, Vaughn, Susan Sprecher, and Pepper Schwartz. 1995. The Incidence and Frequency of Marital Sex in a National Sample. *Journal of Marriage and the Family* 57:639–652.

Cameron, Deborah. 1997. Performing Gender Identity: Young Men's Talk and the Construction of Heterosexual Masculinity. In *Language and Masculinity*. Sally Johnson and Ulrike Hanna Meinhof, eds. Oxford: Blackwell.

Cameron, Mary M. 1995. Transformations of Gender and Caste Divisions of Labor in Rural Nepal: Land, Hierarchy, and the Case of Women. *Journal of Anthropological Research* 51:215–246.

Camino, Linda A., and Ruth M. Krulfeld, eds. 1994. *Reconstructing Lives, Recapturing Meaning: Refugee Identity, Gender and Culture Change*. Basel: Gordon and Breach Publishers.

Cancian, Frank. 1989 Economic Behavior in Peasant Communities. In *Economic Anthropology*. Stuart Plattner, ed. Pp. 127–170. Stanford: Stanford University Press.

Caplan, Pat. 1987. Celibacy as a Solution? Mahatma Gandhi and Brahmacharya. In *The Cultural Construction of Sexuality*. Pat Caplan, ed. Pp. 271–295. New York: Tavistock Publications.

Caputo, Virginia. 2001. Telling Stories from the Field: Children and the Politics of Ethnographic Representation. *Anthropologica* 43(2):179–189.

Carneiro, Robert L. 1994. War and Peace: Alternating Realities in Human History. In *Studying War: Anthropological Perspectives*. S. P. Reyna and R. E. Downs, ed. Pp. 3–27. Langhorne, PA: Gordon and Breach Science Publishers.

Carroll, M. 1984. On the Psychological Origins of the Evil Eye: A Kleinian View. *Journal of Psychoanalytic Anthropology* 8(4):360–382.

Carstairs, G. Morris. 1967. *The Twice Born*. Bloomington: Indiana University Press.

Carsten, Janet. 1995. Children in Between: Fostering and the Process of Kinship on Pulau Langkawi, Malaysia. *Man* (N.S.) 26:425–443.

Carsten, Janet, ed. 2000. *Cultures of Relatedness: New Approaches to the Study of Kinship*. New York: Cambridge University Press.

Carter, William E., Mauricio Mamani P., and José V. Morales. 1981. Medicinal Uses of Coca in Bolivia. In *Health in the Andes*. Joseph W. Bastien and John M. Donahue, eds. Pp. 119–149. Washington, DC: American Anthropological Association.

Carver, Cynthia. 1981. The Delivers: A Woman Doctor's Reflections on Medical Socialization. In *Childbirth, Alternative to Medical Control*. S. Romalis, ed. Austin: University of Texas Press.

Cassell, Joan. 1991. *Expected Miracles: Surgeons at Work*. Philadelphia: Temple University Press.

Castles, Stephen, and Mark J. Miller. 1993. *The Age of Migration: International Population Movements in the Modern World*. New York: The Guilford Press.

Cátedra, María. 1992. *This World, Other Worlds: Sickness, Suicide, Death and the Afterlife among the Vaqueiros de Alzada of Spain*. Chicago: University of Chicago Press.

Cernea, Michael M. 1985. Sociological Knowledge for Development Projects. In *Putting People First: Sociological Variables and Rural Development*. Michael M. Cernea, ed. Pp. 3–22. New York: Oxford University Press.

Chagnon, Napoleon. 1992. *Yanomamö*. 4th edition. New York: Harcourt Brace Jovanovich.

Chambers, David L. 2000. Civilizing the Natives: Marriage in Post-Apartheid South Africa. *Daedalus* 129:101–124.

Chambers, Robert. 1983. *Rural Development: Putting the Last First*. Essex, United Kingdom: Longman.

Chanen, Jill Schachner. 1995. Reaching Out to Women of Color. *ABA Journal* 81 (May):105.

Chant, Sylvia. 1985. Single-Parent Families: Choice or Constraint? The Formation of Female-Headed Households in Mexican Shanty Towns. *Development and Change* 16:635–656.

Chavez, Leo R. 1992. *Shadowed Lives: Undocumented Immigrants in American Society.* New York: Harcourt Brace Jovanovich.

Cherlin, Andrew J. 1996. *Public and Private Families: An Introduction.* New York: McGraw-Hill.

Cherlin, Andrew, and Frank F. Furstenberg, Jr. 1992. The American Family in the Year 2000. In *One World, Many Cultures.* Stuart Hirschberg, ed. Pp. 2–9. New York: Macmillan Publishing Company.

Cheung, Sidney C. H. 1998. Being Here, Searching "There": *Hon Para* as a Virtual Community. In *On the South China Track: Perspectives on Anthropological Research and Teaching.* Sidney C. H. Cheung, ed. Pp. 131–148. Hong Kong: Hong Kong Institute of Asia-Pacific Studies, The Chinese University of Hong Kong.

Childs, Larry, and Celina Chelala. 1994. Drought, Rebellion and Social Change in Northern Mali: The Challenges Facing Tamacheq Herders. *Cultural Survival Quarterly* 18(4):16–19.

Chiñas, Beverly Newbold. 1992 *The Isthmus Zapotecs: A Matrifocal Culture of Mexico.* New York: Harcourt, Brace, Jovanovich.

Church, Jon, Vernon Curran, and Shirley Solberg. 2000. "Voices and Faces": A Qualitative Study of Rural Women and a Breast Cancer Self-Help Group via Audio Teleconferencing Network. *Centers of Excellence for Women's Health Research Bulletin* 1(1):22–23.

Clark, Gracia. 1992. Flexibility Equals Survival. *Cultural Survival Quarterly* 16:21–24.

Clark, Sam, Elizabeth Colson, James Lee, and Thayer Scudder. 1995. Ten Thousand Tonga: A Longitudinal Anthropological Study from Southern Zambia, 1956–1991. *Population Studies* 49:91–109.

Clay, Jason W. 1990. What's a Nation: Latest Thinking. *Mother Jones* 15(7):28–30.

Cleveland, David A. 2000. Globalization and Anthropology: Expanding the Options. *Human Organization* 59:370–374.

Clifford, James. 1988. *The Predicament of Culture: Twentieth-Century Ethnography, Literature and Art.* Cambridge: Harvard University Press.

___. 1997. Routes: *Travel and Translation in the Late Twentieth Century.* Cambridge: Cambridge University Press.

Cohen, Mark Nathan. 1989. *Health and the Rise of Civilization.* New Haven, CT: Yale University Press.

Cohen, Mark Nathan, and George J. Armelagos, eds. 1984. *Palaeopathology at the Origins of Agriculture.* New York: Academic Press.

Cohen, Mark Nathan, and Sharon Bennett. 1993. Skeletal Evidence for Sex Roles and Gender Hierarchies in Prehistory. In *Sex and Gender Hierarchies.* Barbara Diane Miller, ed. Pp. 273–296. New York: Cambridge University Press.

Cohen, Roberta. 2002. Nowhere to Run, No Place to Hide. *Bulletin of the Atomic Scientists* November/December:36–45.

Cohn, Bernard S. 1971. *India: The Social Anthropology of a Civilization.* New York: Prentice-Hall.

Cole, Douglas. 1985 *The Scramble for Northwest Coast Artifacts.* Seattle: University of Washington Press.

Cole, Douglas. 1991. *Chiefly Feasts: The Enduring Kwakiutl Potlatch.* Aldona Jonaitis, ed. Seattle: University of Washington Press/New York: American Museum of Natural History.

Cole, Jeffrey. 1996 Working-Class Reactions to the New Immigration in Palermo (Italy). *Critique of Anthropology* 16(2):199–220.

Comaroff, John L. 1987. Of Totemism and Ethnicity: Consciousness, Practice and Signs of Inequality. *Ethnos* 52(3–4):301–323.

Contreras, Gloria. 1995. Teaching about Vietnamese Culture: Water Puppetry as the Soul of the Rice Fields. *The Social Studies* 86(1):25–28.

Corbey, Raymond. 2000. *Arts premiers* in the Louvre. *Anthropology Today* 16:3–6.

___. 2003. Destroying the Graven Image: Religious Iconoclasm on the Christian Frontier. *Anthropology Today* 19:10–14.

Cornell, Laurel L. 1989. Gender Differences in Remarriage after Divorce in Japan and the United States. *Journal of Marriage and the Family* 51:45–463.

Cornia, Giovanni Andrea. 1994. Poverty, Food Consumption, and Nutrition during the Transition to the Market Economy in Eastern Europe. *American Economic Review* 84(2):297–302.

Counihan, Carole M. 1985. Transvestism and Gender in a Sardinian Carnival. *Anthropology* 9(1 & 2):11–24.

Coward, E. Walter, Jr. 1976. Indigenous Organisation, Bureaucracy and Development: The Case of Irrigation. *The Journal of Development Studies* 13(1):92–105.

___. 1979 Principles of Social Organization in an Indigenous Irrigation System. *Human Organization* 38(1):28–36.

Crapanzano, Vincent. 1980. *Tuhami: Portrait of a Moroccan.* Chicago: University of Chicago Press.

Crawford, C. Joanne. 1994. Parenting Practices in the Basque Country: Implications of Infant and Childhood Sleeping Location for Personality Development. *Ethos* 22(1):42–82.

Cronin, Michael P. 1995. The Love Hotel. *Inc. Technology* 17(4):116.

Cruickshank, Julia. 1990. *Life Lived Like a Story: Life Stories of three Yukon elders.* Vancouver: University of British Columbia Press.

Culhane Speck, Dara. 1987. *An Error in Judgement.* Vancouver: Talon Books.

Cunningham, Lawrence S. 1995. Christianity. In *The HarperCollins Dictionary of Religion.* Jonathan Z. Smith, ed. Pp. 240–253. New York: HarperCollins.

Curtin, Philip D. 1989. *Death by Migration: Europe's Encounter with the Tropical World in the Nineteenth Century.* New York: Cambridge University Press.

Dalby, Liza Crihfield. 1983. *Geisha.* New York: Vintage Books.

___. 1993 *Kimono: Fashioning Culture.* New Haven: Yale University Press.

Daly, Martin, and Margo Wilson. 1984. A Sociological Analysis of Human Infanticide. In *Infanticide: Comparative and Evolutionary Perspectives*. Glenn Haustafer and Sarah Blaffer Hrdy, eds. Pp. 487–502. New York: Aldine Publishing Company.

Dando, William A. 1980. *The Geography of Famine.* New York: John Wiley and Sons.

Danforth, Loring M. 1989. *Firewalking and Religious Healing: The Anestenaria of Greece and the American Firewalking Movement.* Princeton: Princeton University Press.

Dannhaeuser, Norbert. 1989. Marketing in Developing Urban Areas. In *Economic Anthropology.* Stuart Plattner, ed. Pp. 222–252. Stanford: Stanford University Press.

Darnell, Regna. 1970. The Kaska Aesthetic of Speech Use. *Western Canadian Journal of Anthropology* 1(1).

___. 1998 Toward a History of Canadian Departments of Anthropology: Retrospect, Prospect and Common Cause. *Anthropologica* xl(2):153–168.

Dasgupta, Satadal, Christine Weatherbie, and Rajat Subhra Mukhopadhaya. 1993. Nuclear and Joint Family Households in West Bengal Villages. *Ethnology* 32(4):339–358.

Daugherty, Mary Lee. 1997. Serpent-Handling as Sacrament. In *Magic, Witchcraft, and Religion.* Arthur C. Lehmann and James E. Myers, eds. Pp. 347–352. Mountain View, CA: Mayfield Publishing Company.

Davis, Dona. 1984. Medical Misinformation: Communication between Outport Newfoundland Women and Their Physicians. *Social Science and Medicine* 18(3):273–278.

___. 1989. The Variable Character of Nerves in a Newfoundland Fishing Village. *Medical Anthropology* 11:63–78.

Davis, Susan Schaefer, and Douglas A. Davis. 1987. *Adolescence in a Moroccan Town: Making Social Sense.* New Brunswick: Rutgers University Press.

Davis-Floyd, Robbie E. 1987. Obstetric Training as a Rite of Passage. *Medical Anthropology Quarterly* 1:288–318.

___. 1992. *Birth as an American Rite of Passage.* Berkeley: University of California Press.

Davison, Jean, and Martin Kanyuka. 1992. Girls' Participation in Basic Education in Southern Malawi. *Comparative Education Review* 36(4):446–466.

de Athayde Figueiredo, Mariza, and Dando Prado. 1989. The Women of Arembepe. *UNESCO Courier* 7:38–41.

De Koninck, Rodolphe. 1992. *Malay Peasants Coping with the World: Breaking the Community Circle?* Singapore: Institute of Southeast Asian Studies.

de la Cadena, Marisol. 2001. Reconstructing Race: Racism, Culture and Mestizaje in Latin America. *NACLA Report on the Americas* 34:16–23.

de la Gorgendiere, Louise 2005. Rights and Wrongs: HIV/AIDS Research in Africa. *Human Organization* 64(2): 166-178.

Deitrick, Lynn. 2002. Commentary: Cultural Brokerage in the Newborn Nursery. *Practicing Anthropology* 24:53–54.

Delaney, Carol. 1988. Mortal Flow: Menstruation in Turkish Village Society. In *Blood Magic: The Anthropology of Menstruation.* Timothy Buckley and Alma Gottlieb, eds. Pp. 75–93. Berkeley: University of California Press.

Devereaux, George. 1976. *A Typological Study of Abortion in Primitive Societies: A Typological, Distributional, and Dynamic Analysis of the Prevention of Birth in 400 Preindustrial Societies.* New York: International Universities Press.

Diamond, Jared. 1994. The Worst Mistake in the History of the Human Race. In *Applying Cultural Anthropology: A Reader.* Aaron Podolefsky and Peter J. Brown, eds. Pp. 105–108. Mountain View, CA: Mayfield Publishing Company.

Dikötter, Frank. 1998. Hairy Barbarians, Furry Primates and Wild Men: Medical Science and Cultural Representations of Hair in China. In *Hair: Its Power and Meaning in Asian Cultures.* Alf Hiltebeitel and Barbara D. Miller, eds. Pp. 1–74. Albany: State University of New York Press.

Divale, William T. 1974. Migration, External Warfare, and Matrilocal Residence. *Behavior Science Research* 9:75–133.

Divale, William T., and Marvin Harris. 1976. Population, Warfare and the Male Supremacist Complex. *American Anthropologist* 78:521–538.

Donlon, Jon. 1990. Fighting Cocks, Feathered Warriors, and Little Heroes. *Play & Culture* 3:273–285.

Dorais, Louis-Jacques. 1979. Language and Society. In *Challenging Anthropology.* D. Turner and G. Smith, eds. Toronto: McGraw-Hill Ryerson.

Dorgan, Howard. 1989. *The Old Regular Baptists of Central Appalachia: Brothers and Sisters in Hope.* Knoxville: The University of Tennessee Press.

Douglas, Mary. 1962. The Lele: Resistance to Change. In *Markets in Africa.* Paul Bohannan and George Dalton, eds. Pp. 211–233. Evanston: Northwestern University Press.

___. 1966 *Purity and Danger: An Analysis of Concepts of Pollution and Taboo.* New York: Penguin Books.

Douglas, Mary, and Baron Isherwood. 1979. *The World of Goods: Towards an Anthropology of Consumption.* New York: W. W. Norton and Company.

Downe, Pamela. 1997. Constructing a Complex of Contagion: The Perceptions of AIDS among Working Prostitutes in Costa Rica. *Social Science and Medicine* 44(10):1575–1583.

___. 1999. Laughing When it Hurts: Humor and Violence in the Lives of Costa Rican Prostitutes. *Women's Studies International Forum* 22(1):63–78.

___. 2001. Playing with Names: How Children Create Identities of Self in Anthropological Research. *Anthropologica* 43(2):165–177.

Drake, Susan P. 1991. Local Participation in Ecotourism Projects. In *Nature Tourism: Managing for the Environment.* Tensie Whelan, ed. Pp. 132–155. Washington, DC: Island Press.

Dreifus, Claudia. 2000. Saving the Orangutan, Preserving Paradise. *The New York Times,* March 21:D3.

Drucker, Charles. 1987. Dam the Chico: Hydropower, Development and Tribal Resistance. In *Tribal Peoples and Development Issues: A Global Overview.* John H. Bodley, ed. Pp. 151–165. Mountain View, CA: Mayfield Publishing Company.

Dube, S. C. 1967. *Indian Village.* New York: Harper & Row.

Dunk, Thomas W. 1991. *It's a Working Man's Town: Male Working Class Culture*. Montreal and Kingston: McGill-Queen's University Press.

Duranti, Alessandro. 1994. *From Grammar to Politics: Linguistic Anthropology in a Western Samoan Village*. Berkeley: University of California Press.

Durkheim, Émile. 1951[1897]. *Suicide: A Study in Sociology*. New York: The Free Press.

___. 1965[1895] *On the Division of Labor in Society*. Trans. G. Simpson. New York: The Free Press.

___. 1966[1895] *The Elementary Forms of the Religious Life*. New York: The Free Press.

Durning, Alan Thein. 1993. Are We Happy Yet? How the Pursuit of Happiness Is Failing. *The Futurist* 27(1):20–24.

Durrenberger, E. Paul. 2001. Explorations of Class and Class Consciousness in the U.S. *Journal of Anthropological Research* 57:41–60.

du Toit, Brian M. 1990. People on the Move: Rural-Urban Migration with Special Reference to the Third World: Theoretical and Empirical Perspectives. *Human Organization* 49(4):305–320.

Dyson, Tim, and Mick Moore. 1983. On Kinship Structure, Female Autonomy, and Demographic Behavior in India. *Population and Development Review* 9(1):35–60.

Earle, Timothy. 1991 The Evolution of Chiefdoms. In *Chiefdoms, Power, Economy, and Ideology*. Timothy Earle, ed. Pp. 1–15. New York: Cambridge University Press.

Eck, Diana L. 1985. *Darson: Seeing the Divine Image in India*. 2nd edition. Chambersburg, PA: Anima Books.

Eckel, Malcolm David. 1995. Buddhism. In *The HarperCollins Dictionary of Religion*. Jonathan Z. Smith, ed. Pp. 135–150. New York: HarperCollins.

Economic and Social Council. 1992. *Report of the Working Group on Violence against Women*. Vienna: United Nations. E/CN.6/WG.2/1992/L.3.

Edwards, Elizabeth, ed. 1992. *Anthropology and Photography 1860–1920*. New Haven: Yale University Press.

Edwards, John. 1998. *Language in Canada*. Cambridge: Cambridge University Press.

Eisler, Kim Isaac. 2001. *Revenge of the Pequots: How a Small Native American Tribe Created the World's Most Profitable Casino*. New York: Simon and Schuster.

Ember, Carol R. 1983. The Relative Decline in Women's Contribution to Agriculture with Intensification. *American Anthropologist* 85(2):285–304.

Entwisle, Barbara, Gail E. Henderson, Susan E. Short, Jill Bouma, and Zhai Fengying. 1995. Gender and Family Businesses in Rural China. *American Sociological Review* 60:36–57.

Eriksen, Thomas Hylland. 2001. Between Universalism and Relativism: A Critique of the UNESCO Concept of Culture. In *Culture and Rights: Anthropological Perspectives*. Jane K. Cowan, Marie Bénédicte Dembour, and Richard A. Wilson, eds. Pp. 127–148. New York: Cambridge University Press.

Ervin, Alexander M., Antonet T. Kaye, Giselle M. Marcotte, and Randy D. Belon. 1991. *Community Needs, Saskatoon—The 1990's: The Saskatoon Needs Assessment Project*. Saskatoon, Canada: University of Saskatchewan, Department of Anthropology.

Escobar, Arturo. 2002. Gender, Place, and Networks: A Political Ecology of Cyberculture. In *Development: A Cultural Studies Reader*. Susan Schech and Jane Haggis, eds. Pp. 239–256. Malden, MA: Blackwell Publishers.

Esman, Milton. 1996. Ethnic Politics. In *The Social Science Encyclopedia*. Adam Kuper and Jessica Kuper, eds. Pp. 259–260. New York: Routledge.

Estioko-Griffin, Agnes. 1986. Daughters of the Forest. *Natural History* 95:36–43.

Estioko-Griffin, Agnes, Madeleine J. Goodman, and Bion Griffin. 1985. The Compatibility of Hunting and Mothering among the Agta Hunter-Gatherers of the Philippines. *Sex Roles* 12: 1199–1209.

Estrin, Saul. 1996. Co-operatives. In *The Social Science Encyclopedia*. Adam Kuper and Jessica Kuper, eds. Pp. 138–139. New York: Routledge.

Etienne, Mona, and Eleanor Leacock, eds. 1980 *Women and Colonization: Anthropological Perspectives*. New York: Praeger.

Evans-Pritchard, E. E. 1951. *Kinship and Marriage among the Nuer*. Oxford: Clarendon.

___. 1965[1947]. *The Nuer: A Description of the Modes of Livelihood and Political Institutions of a Nilotic People*. New York: Oxford University Press.

Ewing, Katherine Pratt. 2000. Legislating Religious Freedom: Muslim Challenges to the Relationship between "Church" and "State" in Germany and France. *Daedalus* 29:31–53.

Fabian, Johannes. 1995 Ethnographic Misunderstanding and the Perils of Context. *American Anthropologist* 97(1):41–50.

Fabrega, Horacio, and Barbara D. Miller. 1995. Adolescent Psychiatry as a Product of Contemporary Anglo-American Society. *Social Science and Medicine* 40(7):881–894.

Fadiman, Anne. 1997. *The Spirit Catches You and You Fall Down: A Hmong Child, Her American Doctors, and the Collusion of Two Cultures*. New York: Farrar, Straus and Giroux.

Farmer, Paul. 1990. Sending Sickness: Sorcery, Politics, and Changing Concepts of AIDS in Rural Haiti. *Medical Anthropology Quarterly* 4:6–27.

Fedigan, L. 1992. *Primate Paradigms: Sex Roles and Social Bonds*. Chicago: University of Chicago Press.

Feinsilver, Julie M. 1993. *Healing the Masses: Cuban Health Politics at Home and Abroad*. Berkeley: University of California Press.

Feldman, Gregory. 2003. Breaking Our Silence on NATO. *Anthropology Today* 19:1–2.

Feldman-Savelsberg, Pamela. 1995. Cooking Inside: Kinship and Gender in Bangangté Idioms of Marriage and Procreation. *American Ethnologist* 22(3):483–501.

Ferguson, James. 1994. *The Anti-Politics Machine: "Development," Depoliticization, and Bureaucratic Power in Lesotho*. Minneapolis: University of Minnesota Press.

Ferguson R. Brian. 1990. Blood of the Leviathan: Western Contact and Amazonian Warfare. *American Ethnologist* 17(1):237–257.

Firestone, M. 1985. The "Old Hag": Sleep Paralysis in Newfoundland. *Journal of Psychoanalytic Anthropology* 8(1):47–66.

Fischer, Edward F. 2001. *Cultural Logics and Global Economies: Maya Identity in Thought and Practice*. Austin: University of Texas Press.

Fiske, John. 1994. Radical Shopping in Los Angeles: Race, Media and the Sphere of Consumption. *Media, Culture & Society* 16:469–486.

Fluehr-Lobban, Carolyn. 1994. Informed Consent in Anthropological Research: We Are Not Exempt. *Human Organization* 53(1):1–10.

Fonseca, Isabel. 1995. *Bury Me Standing: The Gypsies and Their Journey*. New York: Alfred A. Knopf.

Fortune, Reo F. 1959[1932] *Sorcerers of Dobu: The Social Anthropology of the Dobu Islanders of the Western Pacific*. New York: E. P. Dutton & Co.

Foster, George. 1965. Peasant Society and the Image of the Limited Good. *American Anthropologist* 67:293–315.

Foster, George M., and Barbara Gallatin Anderson. 1978. *Medical Anthropology*. New York: Alfred A. Knopf.

Foucault, Michel. 1970. *The Order of Things: An Archaeology of the Human Sciences*. New York: Random House.

Foucault, Michel. 1977. *Discipline and Punish: The Birth of the Prison*. New York: Pantheon Books.

Fox, Robin. 1995[1978]. *The Tory Islanders: A People of the Celtic Fringe*. Notre Dame: University of Notre Dame Press.

Franke, Richard W. 1993. *Life is a Little Better: Redistribution as a Development Strategy in Nadur Village, Kerala*. Boulder: Westview Press.

Frankel, Francine R. 1971. *India's Green Revolution: Economic Gains and Political Costs*. Princeton: Princeton University Press.

Fratkin, Elliot. 1998. *Ariaal Pastoralists of Kenya: Surviving Drought and Development in Africa's Arid Lands*. Boston: Allyn and Bacon.

Fratkin, Elliot, Kathleen Galvin, and Eric A. Roth, eds. 1994. *African Pastoralist Systems: An Integrated Approach*. Boulder: Westview Press.

Frazer, Sir James. 1978[1890]. *The Golden Bough: A Study in Magic and Religion*. New York: Macmillan.

Freed, Stanley A., and Ruth S. Freed. 1969. Urbanization and Family Types in a North Indian Village. *Southwestern Journal of Anthropology* 25:342–359.

Freedman, J. 2000. A Case for Equity. In *Transforming Development: Foreign Aid for a Changing World*. J. Freedman, ed. Pp. 192–208. Toronto: University of Toronto Press.

Freeman, Derek. 1983. *Margaret Mead and Samoa: The Making and Unmaking of an Anthropological Myth*. Cambridge, MA: Harvard University Press.

Freeman, James A. 1981. A Firewalking Ceremony That Failed. In *Social and Cultural Context of Medicine in India*. Giri Raj Gupta, ed. Pp. 308–336. New Delhi: Vikas Publishing House.

___. 1989. *Hearts of Sorrow: Vietnamese-American Lives*. Stanford: Stanford University Press.

Frideres, James S. 1998. *Aboriginal Peoples in Canada: Contemporary Conflicts*. 5th edition. Scarborough, Ontario: Prentice Hall Allyn and Bacon Canada.

Friedl, Ernestine. 1986. Fieldwork in a Greek Village. In *Women in the Field: Anthropological Experiences*. Peggy Golde, ed. Pp. 195–220. Berkeley: University of California Press.

Frisch, Rose. 1978. Population, Food Intake, and Fertility. *Science* 199:22–30.

Fuller, Christopher J. 1976. *The Nayars Today*. New York: Cambridge University Press.

Furst, Peter T. 1989. The Water of Life: Symbolism and Natural History on the Northwest Coast. *Dialectical Anthropology* 14:95–115.

Gable, Eric. 1995. The Decolonization of Consciousness: Local Skeptics and the "Will to Be Modern" in a West African Village. *American Ethnologist* 22(2):242–257.

Gage-Brandon, Anastasia J. 1992. The Polygyny-Divorce Relationship: A Case Study of Nigeria. *Journal of Marriage and the Family* 54:282–292.

Galdikas, Biruté. 1995. *Reflections of Eden: My Years with the Orangutans of Borneo*. Boston: Little, Brown.

Gardiner, Margaret. 1984. *Footprints on Malekula: A Memoir of Bernard Deacon*. Edinburgh: The Salamander Press.

Gardner, Katy, and David Lewis. 1996. *Anthropology, Development and the Post-Modern Challenge*. Chicago: Pluto Press.

Garland, David. 1996 Social Control. In *The Social Science Encyclopedia*. Adam Kuper and Jessica Kuper, eds. Pp. 780–783. Routledge: New York.

Geertz, Clifford. 1966. Religion as a Cultural System. In *Anthropological Approaches to the Study of Religion*. Michael Banton, ed. Pp. 1–46. London: Tavistock.

Gibb, Camilla. 2002. Deterritorialized People in Hyperspace: Creating and Debating Harari Identity over the Internet. *Anthropologica* 44(1):55–67.

Gill, Lesley. 1993. "Proper Women" and City Pleasures: Gender, Class, and Contested Meanings in La Paz. *American Ethnologist* 20(1):72–88.

Gilman, Antonio. 1991. Trajectories towards Social Complexity in the Later Prehistory of the Mediterranean. In *Chiefdoms: Power, Economy and Ideology*. Timothy Earle, ed. Pp. 146–168. New York: Cambridge University Press.

Ginsberg, Faye D., and Rayna Rapp. 1991. The Politics of Reproduction. *Annual Review of Anthropology* 20:311–343.

Glasser, Irene, and Rae Bridgeman. 1999. *Braving the Street: The Anthropology of Homelessness*. New York: Berghahn Books.

Glick Schiller, Nina, and Georges E. Fouron. 1999. Terrains of Blood and Nation: Haitian Transnational Social Fields. *Ethnic and Racial Studies* 22:340–365.

Glínski, Piotr. 1994. Environmentalism among Polish Youth: A Maturing Social Movement? *Communist and Post-Communist Studies* 27(2):145–159.

Gliotto, Tom. 1995. Paradise Lost. *People Weekly* 43(17):70–76.

Gluckman, Max. 1955. *The Judicial Process among the Barotse of Northern Rhodesia.* Manchester: Manchester University Press.

___. 1963. *Politics, Law and Ritual in Tribal Africa.* London: Cohen and West.

Gmelch, George. 1997/[1971] Baseball Magic. In *Magic, Witchcraft, and Religion.* Arthur C. Lehmann and James E. Myers, eds. Pp. 276–282. Mountain View, CA: Mayfield Publishing.

Godelier, Maurice. 1971. "Salt Currency" and the Circulation of Commodities among the Baruya of New Guinea. In *Studies in Economic Anthropology.* George Dalton, ed. Pp. 52–73. Anthropological Studies No. 7. Washington, DC: American Anthropological Association.

Gold, Ann Grodzins. 1988. *Fruitful Journeys: The Ways of Rajasthani Pilgrims.* Berkeley: University of California Press.

Gold, Stevan J. 1992. *Refugee Communities: A Comparative Field Study.* Newbury Park: Sage Publications.

___. 1995. *From the Workers' State to the Golden State: Jews from the Former Soviet Union in California.* Boston: Allyn and Bacon.

Golde, Peggy, ed. 1986. *Women in the Field: Anthropological Experiences.* 2nd edition. Berkeley: University of California Press.

Goldstein, Melvyn C. 1987. When Brothers Share a Wife. *Natural History* 96:38–49.

Goldstein, Melvin C., and Cynthia M. Beall. 1994. *The Changing World of Mongolia's Nomads.* Berkeley: University of California Press.

Goldstone, Jack. 1996 Revolutions. In *The Social Science Encyclopedia.* Adam Kuper and Jessica Kuper, eds. Pp. 740–743. New York: Routledge.

González, Nancie L. 1970. Toward a Definition of Matrifocality. In *Afro-American Anthropology: Contemporary Perspectives.* Norman E. Whitten, Jr. and John F. Szwed, eds. Pp. 231–244. New York: The Free Press.

Goodall, Jane. 1971. *In the Shadow of Man.* Boston: Houghton-Mifflin.

___. 1986. *The Chimpanzees of Gombe: Patterns of Behavior.* Cambridge, MA: Harvard University Press.

Goody, Jack. 1976. *Production and Reproduction: A Comparative Study of the Domestic Domain.* New York: Cambridge University Press.

___. 1977. *Cooking, Cuisine and Class: A Study of Comparative Sociology.* New York: Cambridge University Press.

___. 1993. *The Culture of Flowers.* New York: Cambridge University Press.

___. 1996 Comparing Family Systems in Europe and Asia: Are There Different Sets of Rules? *Population and Development Review* 22:1–20.

Goody, Jack, and Stanley J. Tambiah. 1973. *Bridewealth and Dowry.* New York: Cambridge University Press.

Gough, E. Kathleen. 1959. The Nayars and the Definition of Marriage. *Journal of the Royal Anthropological Institute* 89:23–34.

Graburn, Nelson. 1993. Ethnic Arts of the Fourth World: The View from Canada. In *Imagery and Creativity: Ethnoaesthetics and Art Worlds in the Americas.* D. Whitten and N. Whitten, eds. Tucson: University of Arizona Press.

___. 1998. Weirs in the River of Time: The Development of Historical Consciousness among Canadian Inuit. *Museum Anthropology* 22(1):18–32.

Graham, Elizabeth. 1998. Mission Archaeology. *Annual Review of Anthropology* 27:25–62.

Greenhalgh, Susan. 2003. Science, Modernity, and the Making of China's One-Child Policy. *Population and Development Review* 29:163–196.

Greenough, Paul R. 1982. *Prosperity and Misery in Modern Bengal: The Famine of 1943–44.* New York: Oxford University Press.

Gregor, Thomas. 1981. A Content Analysis of Mehinaku Dreams. *Ethos* 9:353–390.

___. 1982. No Girls Allowed. *Science* 82.

Gremillion, Helen. 1992. Psychiatry as Social Ordering: Anorexia Nervosa, a Paradigm. *Social Science and Medicine* 35(1):57–71.

Grenier, Guillermo J., Alex Stepick, Debbie Draznin, Aileen LaBorwit, and Steve Morris. 1992. On Machines and Bureaucracy: Controlling Ethnic Interaction in Miami's Apparel and Construction Industries. In *Structuring Diversity: Ethnographic Perspectives on the New Immigration.* Louise Lamphere, ed. Pp. 65–94. Chicago: University of Chicago Press.

Grinker, Roy Richard. 1994. *Houses in the Rainforest: Ethnicity and Inequality among Farmers and Foragers in Central Africa.* Berkeley: University of California Press.

Gross, Daniel R. 1984. Time Allocation: A Tool for the Study of Cultural Behavior. *Annual Review of Anthropology* 13:519–558.

Gross, Daniel R., George Eiten, Nancy M. Flowers, Francisca M. Leoi, Madeleine Lattman Ritter, and Dennis W. Werner. 1979. Ecology and Acculturation among Native Peoples of Central Brazil. *Science* 206(30):1043–1050.

Gross, Daniel R., and Barbara A. Underwood. 1971. Technological Change and Caloric Costs. *American Anthropologist* 73:725–740.

Gruneau, Richard S., and David Whitson. 1993. *Hockey Night in Canada: Sport, Identities, and Cultural Politics.* Toronto: Garamond Press.

Guggenheim, Scott E., and Michael M. Cernea. 1993. Anthropological Approaches to Involuntary Resettlement: Policy, Practice, and Theory. In *Anthropological Approaches to Resettlement: Policy, Practice, and Theory.* Michael M. Cernea and Scott E. Guggenheim, eds. Pp. 1–12. Boulder: Westview Press.

Gugler, Josef. 1988. The Urban Character of Contemporary Revolutions. In *The Urbanization of the Third World.* Josef Gugler, ed. Pp. 399–412. New York: Oxford University Press.

Guidoni, Enrico. 1987. *Primitive Architecture.* Robert Erich Wolf, trans. New York: Rizzoli.

Gulliver, P.H., and M. Silverman. 1995. *Merchants and Shopkeepers: A Historical Anthropology of an Irish Market Town, 1200–1991*. Toronto: University of Toronto Press.

Gupta, Akhil, and James Ferguson, eds. 1997. *Anthropological Locations: Boundaries and Grounds of Field Science*. Berkeley: University of California Press.

Haas, J., and W. Shaffir. 1982. Ritual Evaluation of Competence: The Hidden Curriculum of Professionalization in an Innovative Medical School Program. *Work and Occupations* 9(2):131–154.

Hackenberg, Robert A. 2000. Advancing Applied Anthropology: Joe Hill in Cyberspace-Steps Toward Creating "One Big Union." *Human Organization* 59:365–369.

Hackenberg, Robert A., et al. 1983. Migration, Modernization and Hypertension: Blood Pressure Levels in Four Philippine Communities. *Medical Anthropology* 7(1):45–71.

Hacker, Andrew.. 1992. *Two Nations: Black and White, Separate, Hostile, Unequal*. New York: Ballantine Books.

Hagey, Rebecca. 1984. The Phenomenon, the Explanations and the Responses: Metaphors Surrounding Diabetes in Urban Canadian Indians. *Social Science and Medicine* 18:265–272.

Hahn, Robert. 1995. *Sickness and Healing: An Anthropological Perspective*. New Haven, CT: Yale University Press.

Hakamies-Blomqvist, Liisa. 1994. Aging and Fatal Accidents in Male and Female Drivers. *Journal of Gerontology [Social Sciences]* 49(6):5286–5290.

Hale, Horatio. 1883. *Iroquois Book of Rites*. Philadelphia: D.G. Brinton.

Hammerlsey, Martyn. 1992. *What's Wrong with Ethnography: Methodological Explorations*. London: Routledge.

Hammond, Peter B. 1966. *Yatenga: Technology in the Culture of a West African Kingdom*. New York: The Free Press.

Hancock, Graham. 1989. *Lords of Poverty: The Power, Prestige, and Corruption of the International Aid Business*. New York: The Atlantic Monthly Press.

Hardman, Charlotte E. 2000. *Other Worlds: Notions of Self and Emotion among the Lohorung Rai*. New York: Berg.

Harner, Michael. 1977. The Ecological Basis of Aztec Sacrifice. *American Ethnologist* 4:117–135.

Harris, Marvin. 1974. *Cows, Pigs, Wars, and Witches: The Riddles of Culture*. New York: Random House.

___. 1975. *Culture, People, Nature: An Introduction to General Anthropology*. 2nd edition. New York: Thomas Y. Crowell Company.

___. 1977. *Cannibals and Kings: The Origins of Culture*. New York: Random House.

___. 1989. *Our Kind: Who We Are, Where We Came From and Where We Are Going*. New York: HarperCollins.

Harris, Marvin, and Eric B. Ross. 1987. *Death, Sex and Fertility*. New York: Columbia University Press.

Harrison, Julia. 2003. *Being a Tourist: Finding Meaning in Pleasure Travel*. Vancouver: UBC Press.

Harrison, Simon. 1993. The Commerce of Cultures in Melanesia. *Man* 28:139–158.

Hart, C. W. M., Arnold R. Pilling, and Jane C. Goodale. 1988. *The Tiwi of North Australia*. New York: Holt, Rinehart, and Winston.

Hart, Gillian. 2002. *Disabling Globalization: Places of Power in Post-Apartheid South Africa*. Berkeley: University of California Press.

Hartmann, Betsy. 1987. *Reproductive Rights and Wrongs: The Global Politics of Population Control and Reproductive Choice*. New York: Harper & Row.

Hastrup, Kirsten. 1992. Anthropological Visions: Some Notes on Visual and Textual Authority. In *Film as Ethnography*. Peter Ian Crawford and David Turton, eds. Pp. 8–25. Manchester: University of Manchester Press.

Hawn, Carleen. 2002. Please Feedback the Animals. *Forbes* 170(9):168–169.

Hefner, Robert W. 1998. Multiple Modernities: Christianity, Islam, and Hinduism in a Globalizing Age. *Annual Review of Anthropology* 27:83–104.

Heise, Lori L., Jacqueline Pitanguy, and Adrienne Germain. 1994. *Violence against Women: The Hidden Health Burden*. *World Bank Discussion Paper No. 255*. Washington, DC: The World Bank.

Helleiner, Jane. 2001. "The Right Kind of Children": Childhood, Gender and Race in Canadian Postwar Political Discourse. *Anthropologica* 43(2):143–152.

Henry, Francis. 1984. *Victims and Neighbors: A Small Town in Nazi Germany Remembered*. South Hadley, Mass.: Bergin and Garvey.

___. 1987. Caribbean Migration to Canada: Prejudice and Opportunity. In *The Caribbean Exodus*. Barry Levine, ed. New York: Greenwood Publishing Group.

Henry, Francis, and Carol Tator. 2002. *Discourses of Domination: Racial Bias in the Canadian English-Language Press*. Toronto: University of Toronto Press.

Herdt, Gilbert. 1987. *The Sambia: Ritual and Gender in New Guinea*. New York: Holt, Rinehart and Winston.

Hewlett, Barry S. 1991. *Intimate Fathers: The Nature and Context of Aka Pygmy Paternal Care*. Ann Arbor: University of Michigan Press.

Heyneman, D. 1984. Development and Disease: A Dual Dilemma. *Journal of Parasitology* 70:3–17.

Hiatt, Betty. 1970. Woman the Gatherer. In *Woman's Role in Aboriginal Society*. Fay Gale, ed. Pp. 2–28. Canberra: Australian Institute of Aboriginal Studies.

Higginbotham, N., D. Willms, and N. Sewankambo. 2001. Transdisciplinary Work in the Community. In *Health Social Science: A Transdisciplinary and Complexity Perspective*. N. Higginbotham, G Albrecht, and L. O'Connor, eds. South Melbourne, Australia: Oxford University.

Hill, Jane H. 2001. Dimensions of Attrition in Language Death. In *On Biocultural Diversity: Linking Language, Knowledge, and the Environment*. Luisa Maffi, ed. Pp. 175–189. Washington, DC: Smithsonian Institution Press.

Hill, Jane H., and Bruce Mannheim. 1992. Language and World View. *Annual Review of Anthropology* 21:381–406.

Hiltebeitel, Alf. 1988. *The Cult of Draupadi: Mythologies from Gingee to Kuruksetra*. Chicago: The University of Chicago Press.

___. 1995. Hinduism. In *The HarperCollins Dictionary of Religion*. Jonathan Z. Smith, ed. Pp. 424–440. New York: HarperCollins Publishers.

Hirschfelder, Arlene, ed. 1995. *Native Heritage: Personal Accounts by American Indians 1790 to the Present*. New York: Macmillan.

Hirschon, Renee. 1989. *Heirs of the Catastrophe: The Social Life of Asia Minor Refugees in Piraeus*. New York: Oxford University Press.

Hodge, Robert W., and Naohiro Ogawa. 1991. *Fertility Change in Contemporary Japan*. Chicago: University of Chicago Press.

Hollan, Douglas. 2001. Developments in Person-Centered Ethnography. In *The Psychology of Cultural Experience*. Carmella C. Moore and Holly F. Mathews, eds. Pp. 48–67. New York: Cambridge University Press.

Holland, Dorothy C., and Margaret A. Eisenhart. 1990. *Educated in Romance: Women, Achievement, and College Culture*. Chicago: University of Chicago Press.

Holmes, Paula Elizabeth. 2001. The Narrative Repatriation of Blessed Kateri Tekakwitha. *Anthropologica* 43(1):87–103.

Hopkins, Nicholas S., and Sohair R. Mehanna. 2000. Social Action against Everyday Pollution in Egypt. *Human Organization* 59:245–254.

Horowitz, Irving L. 1967. *The Rise and Fall of Project Camelot: Studies in the Relationship between Social Science and Practical Politics*. Boston: MIT Press.

Horowitz, Michael M., and Muneera Salem-Murdock. 1993. Development-Induced Food Insecurity in the Middle Senegal Valley. *GeoJournal* 30(2):179–184.

Hostetler, John A., and Gertrude Enders Huntington. 1992. *Amish Children: Education in the Family, School, and Community*. New York: Harcourt Brace Jovanovich.

Howell, Nancy. 1979. *Demography of the Dobe !Kung*. New York: Academic Press.

___. 1986. Feedbacks and Buffers in Relation to Scarcity and Abundance: Studies of Hunter–Gatherer Populations. In *The State of Population Theory: Forward from Malthus*. David Coleman and Roger Schofield, eds. Pp. 156–187. New York: Basil Blackwell.

___. 1990. *Surviving Fieldwork: A Report of the Advisory Panel on Health and Safety in Fieldwork*. Washington, DC: American Anthropological Association.

Hughes, Charles C., and John M. Hunter. 1970. Disease and "Development" in Africa. *Social Science and Medicine* 3:443–493.

Humphrey, Caroline. 1978. Women, Taboo and the Suppression of Attention. In *Defining Females: The Nature of Women in Society*. Shirley Ardener, ed. Pp. 89–108. New York: John Wiley and Sons.

Hunte, Pamela A. 1985. Indigenous Methods of Fertility Regulation in Afghanistan. In *Women's Medicine: A Cross-Cultural Study of Indigenous Fertility Regulation*. Lucile F. Newman, ed. Pp. 44–75. New Brunswick: Rutgers University Press.

Hutchinson, Sharon E. 1996. *Nuer Dilemmas: Coping with Money, War, and the State*. Berkeley: University of California Press.

Hutter, Michael. 1996. The Value of Play. In *The Value of Culture: On the Relationship between Economics and the Arts*. Arjo Klamer, ed. Pp. 122–137. Amsterdam: Amsterdam University Press.

Illo, Jeanne Frances I. 1985. Who Heads the Household? Women in Households in the Philippines. Paper presented at the Women and Household Regional Conference for Asia, New Delhi.

Indra, Doreen M. 1988. Self-Concept and Resettlement: Vietnamese and Sino-Vietnamese in a Small Prairie City. In *Ten Years Later: Indochinese Communities in Canada*. Louis-Jacques Dorais, Kwok B. Chan, and Doreen M. Indra, eds. Montreal: Canadian Asian Studies Association.

Inhorn, Marcia C. 2003. Global Infertility and the Globalization of New Reproductive Technologies: Illustrations from Egypt. *Social Science and Medicine* 56:1837–1851.

Inhorn, Marcia C., and Peter J. Brown, eds. 1997. *The Anthropology of Infectious Disease: International Health Perspectives (Theory and Practice in Medical Anthropology and International Health)*. Malaysia: Gordon and Breach Publishers.

International Labour Office. 1996. Female Asian Migrants: A Growing But Vulnerable Workforce. *World of Work* 15:16–17.

Janes, Craig R. 1990. *Migration, Social Change, and Health: A Samoan Community in Urban California*. Stanford: Stanford University Press.

___. 1995. The Transformations of Tibetan Medicine. *Medical Anthropology Quarterly* 9(1):6–39.

Jankowski, Martín Sánchez. 1991. *Islands in the Street: Gangs and American Urban Society*. Berkeley: University of California Press.

Jenkins, Gwynne L and Marcia C. Inhorn. 2003. Reproduction Gone Awry: Medical Anthropology Perspectives. *Social Science and Medicine* 56:1831–1836.

Jentoft, Sven, and Anthony Davis. 1993. Self and Sacrifice: An Investigation of Small Boat Fisher Individualism and Its Implication for Producer Cooperatives. *Human Organization* 52(4):356–367.

Jiang, David W. 1994. Shanghai Revisited: Chinese Theatre and the Forces of the Market. *The Drama Review* 38(2):72–80.

Jinadu, L. Adele. 1994. The Dialectics of Theory and Research on Race and Ethnicity in Nigeria. In *"Race," Ethnicity and Nation: International Perspectives on Social Conflict*. Peter Ratcliffe, ed. Pp. 163–178. London: University of College London Press.

Johnson, Walter R. 1994. *Dismantling Apartheid: A South African Town in Transition*. Ithaca: Cornell University Press.

Johnston, Barbara Rose. 1994. Environmental Degradation and Human Rights Abuse. In *Who Pays the Price?: The Sociocultural Context of Environmental Crisis*. Barbara Rose Johnston, ed. Pp. 7–16. Washington, DC: Island Press.

Jonaitis, Aldona. 1995. *A Wealth of Thought: Franz Boas on Native American Art.* Seattle: University of Washington Press.

Jones, Anna Laura. 1993. Exploding Canons: The Anthropology of Museums. *Annual Review of Anthropology* 22: 201–220.

Joralemon, Donald. 1982. New World Depopulation and the Case of Disease. *Journal of Anthropological Research* 38:108–127.

Jordan, Brigitte. 1983. *Birth in Four Cultures.* 3rd edition. Montreal: Eden Press.

Jordan, Mark. 1998. Japan Takes Dim View of Fertility Treatments. *New York Times,* July 5:A13.

Joseph, Suad. 1994 Brother/Sister Relationships: Connectivity, Love, and Power in the Reproduction of Patriarchy in Lebanon. *American Ethnologist* 21:50–73.

Jourdan, Christine. 1995. Masta Liu. In *Youth Cultures: A Cross-Cultural Perspective.* Vered Amit-Talai and Helena Wulff, eds. Pp. 202–222. New York: Routledge.

Joy, Annamma. 1989. *Ethnicity in Canada.* New York: AMS Press.

Judd, Ellen. 2002. *The Chinese Women's Movement: Between State and Market.* Stanford, CA: Stanford University Press.

Kaberry, Phyllis. 1952. *Women of the Grassfields: A Study of the Economic Position of Women in Bamenda, British Cameroons.* London: Her Majesty's Stationery Office.

Kabutha, Charity, Barbara P. Thomas-Slaytor, and Richard Ford. 1993. Participatory Rural Appraisal: A Case Study from Kenya. In *Rapid Appraisal Methods.* Krishna Kumar, ed. Pp. 176–211. Washington, DC: The World Bank.

Kahn, Miriam. 1995. Heterotopic Dissonance in the Museum Representation of Pacific Island Cultures. *American Anthropologist* 97(2):324–338.

Kapchan, Deborah A. 1994. Moroccan Female Performers Defining the Social Body. *Journal of American Folklore* 107(423):82–105.

Kassam, Aneesa. 2002. Ethnodevelopment in the Oromia Regional State of Ethiopia. In *Participating in Development: Approaches to Indigenous Knowledge.* Paul Sillitoe, Alan Bicker, and Johan Pottier, eds. Pp. 65–81. ASA Monographs No. 39. New York: Routledge.

Katz, Nathan, and Ellen S. Goldberg. 1989. Asceticism and Caste in the Passover Observances of the Cochin Jews. *Journal of the American Academy of Religion* 57(1):53–81.

Katz, Richard. 1982. *Boiling Energy: Community Healing among the Kalahari Kung.* Cambridge: Harvard University Press.

Kaufert, Patricia. 1986. The Menopausal Transition; the Use of Estrogen. *Canadian Journal of Public Health* 77(1):86–91.

Kaufert, P., and J. O'Neil. 1990. Cooptation and Control: The Reconstruction of Inuit Birth. *Medical Anthropology Quarterly* 4(4):427–442.

Kearney, Michael. 1986. From the Invisible Hand to Visible Feet: Anthropological Studies of Migration and Development. *Annual Review of Anthropology* 15:331–361.

Kelley, Heidi. 1991. Unwed Mothers and Household Reputation in a Spanish Galician Community. *American Ethnologist* 18:565–580.

Kelm, Mary-Ellen. 1999. *Colonizing Bodies: Aboriginal Health and Healing in British Columbia.* Vancouver: UBC Press.

Kennedy, David P., and Stephen G. Perz. 2000. Who Are Brazil's Indígenas? Contributions of Census Data Analysis to Anthropological Demography of Indigenous Populations. *Human Organization* 59:311–324.

Kerns, Virginia. 1992. Preventing Violence against Women: A Central American Case. In *Sanctions and Sanctuary: Cultural Perspectives on the Beating of Wives.* Dorothy Ayers Counts, Judith K. Brown, and Jacquelyn C. Campbell, eds. Pp. 125–138. Boulder: Westview Press.

Kesmanee, Chupinit. 1994. Dubious Development Concepts in the Thai Highlands: The Chao Khao in Transition. *Law & Society Review* 28:673–683.

Kideckel, David A. 1993. *The Solitude of Collectivism: Romanian Villagers to the Revolution and Beyond.* Ithaca: Cornell University Press.

Kirsch, Stuart. 2002. Anthropology and Advocacy: A Case Study of the Campaign against the Ok Tedi Mine. *Critique of Anthropology* 22:175–200.

Klass, Perri. 1987. *A Not Entirely Benign Procedure: Four Years as a Medical Student.* New York: Penguin Books.

Kleinman, Arthur. 1988. *Illness Narratives.* New York: Basic Books.

___. 1995. *Writing at the Margin: Discourse between Anthropology and Medicine.* Berkeley: University of California Press.

Kneen, B. 1999. *Farmageddon: Food and the Culture of Biotechnology.* Gabriola Island: New Society Publishers.

Knott, Kim. 1996. Hindu Women, Destiny and Stridharma. *Religion* 26:15–35.

Kolenda, Pauline M. 1968. Region, Caste, and Family Structure: A Comparative Study of the Indian "Joint" Family. In *Structure and Change in Indian Society.* Milton Singer and Bernard S. Cohn, eds. Pp. 339–396. New York: Aldine.

___. 1978. *Caste in Contemporary India: Beyond Organic Solidarity.* Prospect Heights, IL: Waveland Press.

Kondo, Dorinne. 1997. *About Face: Performing Race in Fashion and Theatre.* New York: Routledge.

Konner, Melvin. 1987. *Becoming a Doctor: The Journey of Initiation in Medical School.* New York: Penguin Books.

___. 1989. Homosexuality: Who and Why? *The New York Times Magazine,* April 2:60–61.

Kottak, Conrad Phillip. 1985. When People Don't Come First: Some Sociological Lessons from Completed Projects. In *Putting People First: Sociological Variables and Rural Development.* Michael M. Cernea, ed. Pp. 325–356. New York: Oxford University Press.

___. 1992. *Assault on Paradise: Social Change in a Brazilian Village.* New York: McGraw Hill.

Krantzler, Nora J. 1987. Traditional Medicine as "Medical Neglect": Dilemmas in the Case Management of a Samoan Teenager with Diabetes. In *Child Survival: Cultural Perspectives on the Treatment and Maltreatment of Children.* Nancy Scheper-Hughes, ed. Pp. 325–337. Boston: D. Reidel.

Kroeber, A. L., and Clyde Kluckhohn. 1952. *Culture: A Critical Review of Concepts and Definitions*. New York: Vintage Books.

Kubik, Wendee, and Robert J. Moore. 2003. Changing Roles of Saskatchewan Farm Women: Qualitative and Quantitative Perspectives. In *The Trajectories of Rural Life. New Perspectives on Rural Canada*. Raymond Blake and Andrew Nurse, eds Regina: Saskatchewan Institute of Public Policy.

Kuipers, Joel C. 1990. *Power in Performance: The Creation of Textual Authority in Weyéwa Ritual Speech*. Philadelphia: University of Pennsylvania Press.

___. 1991 Matters of Taste in Weyéwa. In *The Varieties of Sensory Experience: A Sourcebook in the Anthropology of the Senses*. David Howes, ed. Pp. 111–127. Toronto: University of Toronto Press.

Kumar, Sanjay. 1996. Largest-ever World Bank Loan Mistrusted in India. *The Lancet* 347(April 20):1109.

Kurin, Richard. 1980. Doctor, Lawyer, Indian Chief. *Natural History* 89(11):6–24.

Kwiatkowski, Lynn M. 1998. *Struggling with Development: The Politics of Hunger and Gender in the Philippines*. Boulder: Westview Press.

Labov, William. 1966. *The Social Stratification of English in New York City*. Washington, DC: Center for Applied Linguistics.

Lacey, Marc. 2002. Where 9/11 News Is Late, But Aid Is Swift. *New York Times*, June 3:A1, A7.

Ladányi, János. 1993. Patterns of Residential Segregation and the Gypsy Minority in Budapest. *International Journal of Urbana and Regional Research* 17(1):30–41.

LaFleur, William.1992. *Liquid Life: Abortion and Buddhism in Japan*. Princeton: Princeton University Press.

Lake, Amy, and Steven Deller. 1996. *The Socioeconomic Impacts of a Native American Casino*. Madison: Department of Agricultural and Applied Economics, University of Wisconsin.

Lakoff, Robin. 1973. Language and Woman's Place. *Language in Society* 2:45–79.

___. 1990. *Talking Power: The Politics of Language in Our Lives*. New York: Basic Books.

Lambek, Michael. 1993. *Knowledge and Practice in Mayotte: Local Discourses of Islam, Sorcery, and Spirit Possession*. Toronto: University of Toronto Press.

Lamirande, T. 1999. Whale for the Killing: Controversy Erupts after Washington Natives Pursue a Tradition. *First Perspectives* 8(6).

Lamphere, Louise. 1992. Introduction: The Shaping of Diversity. In *Structuring Diversity: Ethnographic Perspectives on the New Immigration*. Louise Lamphere, ed. Chicago: University of Chicago Press.

Landes, Ruth. 1938. The Abnormal among the Ojibwa Indians. *Journal of Abnormal and Social Psychology* 33:14–33.

Landy, David 1985. Pibloktoq (Hysteria) and Inuit Nutrition: Possible Implication of Hypervitaminosis A. *Social Science and Medicine* 21(2):173–185.

Lansing, J. Stephen. 1995. *The Balinese*. Toronto: Harcourt Brace College Publishers.

Larsen, Clark Spenser, and George R. Milner. 1994. Bioanthropological Perspectives on Postcontact Traditions. In *In the Wake of Contact: Biological Responses to Conquest*. Clark Spenser Larsen and George R. Milner, eds. Pp. 1–8. New York: Wiley-Liss.

Laughlin, C. 1989. Brain, Culture and Evolution: Some Basic Issues in Neuroanthropology. In *A Different Drummer: Readings in Anthropology with a Canadian Perspective*. B. Cox, J. Chevalier, and V. Blundell, eds. Ottawa: Department of Sociology and Anthropology.

Laumann, Edward O., John H. Gagnon, Robert T. Michael, and Stuart Michaels. 1994. *The Social Organization of Sexuality: Sexual Practices in the United States*. Chicago: The University of Chicago Press.

Leach, Jerry W. 1975. *Trobriand Cricket: An Ingenious Response to Colonialism*. Video. Berkeley: University of California Extension Media.

Leacock, Eleanor. 1993. Women in Samoan History: A Further Critique of Derek Freeman. In *Sex and Gender Hierarchies*. Barbara D. Miller, ed., Pp. 351–365. New York: Cambridge University Press.

Lebra, Takie. 1976. *Japanese Patterns of Behavior*. Honolulu: University of Hawaii Press.

Lee, Gary R., and Mindy Kezis. 1979. Family Structure and the Status of the Elderly. *Journal of Comparative Family Studies* 10:429–443.

Lee, Helen Morton. 2003. *Tongans Overseas: Between Two Shores*. Honolulu: University of Hawai'i Press.

Lee, Raymond M., and Claire M. Renzetti. 1993. *Researching Sensitive Topics*. Newbury Park, CA: Sage Publications.

Lee, Richard Borshay. 1969. Eating Christmas in the Kalahari. *Natural History* December.

___. 1979 *The !Kung San: Men, Women, and Work in a Foraging Society*. New York: Cambridge University Press.

Lee, Richard, and Richard Daly, eds. 1999. *The Cambridge Encyclopaedia of Hunters and Gatherers*. Cambridge: Cambridge University Press.

Lee, Wai-Na, and David K. Tse. 1994. Becoming Canadian: Understanding How Hong Kong Immigrants Change Their Consumption. *Pacific Affairs* 67(1):70–95.

Lein, Laura, and Donald Brenneis. 1978. Children's Dispute in Three Speech Communities. *Language in Society* 7:299–323.

Lempert, David. 1996. *Daily Life in a Crumbling Empire*. 2 volumes. New York: Columbia University Press.

Lepowsky, Maria. 1993. *Fruit of the Motherland: Gender in an Egalitarian Society*. New York: Columbia University Press.

Levine, Robert, Suguru Sato, Tsukasa Hashimoto, and Jyoti Verma. 1995. Love and Marriage in Eleven Cultures. *Journal of Cross-Cultural Psychology* 26:554–571.

Levinson, David. 1989. *Family Violence in Cross-Cultural Perspective*. Newbury Park, CA: Sage Publications.

Lévi-Strauss, Claude. 1967. *Structural Anthropology*. New York: Anchor Books.

___. 1968. *Tristes Tropiques: An Anthropological Study of Primitive Societies in Brazil*. New York: Atheneum.

___. 1969[1949] *The Elementary Structures of Kinship*. Boston: Beacon Press.

Levy, Jerrold E., Eric B. Henderson, and Tracy J. Andrews. 1989. The Effects of Regional Variation and Temporal Change in Matrilineal Elements of Navajo Social Organization. *Journal of Anthropological Research* 45(4):351–377.

Lew, Irvina. 1994. Bathing as Science: Ancient Sea Cures Gain Support from New Research. *Condé Nast Traveler* 29(12):86–90.

Lewin, Ellen. 1993. *Lesbian Mothers: Accounts of Gender in American Culture*. Ithaca: Cornell University Press.

Lewis, Oscar. 1966. The Culture of Poverty. *Scientific American*. 215:19–25.

Leynaud, Emile. 1961. Fraternités d'âge et sociétés de culture dans la Haute-Vallée du Niger. *Cahiers d'Etudes Africaines* 6:41–68.

Leyton, Elliot. 1996. *Men of Blood: Murder in Everyday Life*. Toronto: McClelland & Stewart.

Lindenbaum, Shirley. 1979. *Kuru Sorcery: Disease and Danger in the New Guinea Highlands*. Mountain View, CA: Mayfield Publishing Company.

Linnekan, Jocelyn. 1990. *Sacred Queens and Women of Consequence: Rank, Gender, and Colonialism in the Hawaiian Islands*. Ann Arbor: University of Michigan Press.

Little, Kenneth. 1991. On Safari; The Visual Politics of a Tourist Representation. In *The Varieties of Sensory Experience*. D. Howes, ed.. Toronto: University of Toronto Press.

Lloyd, Cynthia B. 1995. *Household Structure and Poverty: What Are the Connections?* Working Papers, No. 74. New York: The Population Council.

Lock, Margaret. 1993. *Encounters with Aging: Mythologies of Menopause in Japan and North America*. Berkeley: University of California Press.

___. 1996. Deadly Disputes: Ideologies and Brain Death in Japan. In *Organ Transplantation: Meanings and Realities*. S. Youngner, R. Fox and L. O'Connell, eds. Madison: University of Wisconsin Press.

Lock, M., and G. Bibeau. 1995. Healthy Disputes: Some Reflections on the Practice of Medical Anthropology in Canada. *Health and Canadian Society/Santé et Société Canadienne* 1(1):147–175.

Lock, Margaret, and Pamela Wakewich-Dunk. 1990. Nostalgia: Expression of Loss among Greek Immigrants in Montreal. *Canadian Family Physician* 36:253–258.

Lockwood, Victoria S. 1993. *Tahitian Transformation: Gender and Capitalist Development in a Rural Society*. Boulder: Lynne Reiner Publishers.

Loker, William. 1993 Human Ecology of Cattle-Raising in the Peruvian Amazon: The View from the Farm. *Human Organization* 52(1):14–24.

Lorch, Donatella. 2003. Do Read This for War. *Newsweek* 141(11):13.

Louie, Andrea. 2000. Re-territorializing Transnationalism: Chinese Americans and the Chinese Motherland. *American Ethnologist* 27:645–669.

Lovell, N., and P. Lai. 1994. Lifestyle and Health of Voyageurs in the Canadian Fur Trade. In *Strength in Diversity: A Reader in Physical Anthropology*. A. Herring and L. Chan, eds. Toronto: Canadian Scholars Press.

Lovisek, J., T. Holzkamm, and L. Waisberg. 1997. Fatal Errors: Ruth Landes and the Creation of the "Atomistic Ojibwa." *Anthropologica* 39(1–2):133–145.

Low, Setha M. 1995. Indigenous Architecture and the Spanish American Plaza in Mesoamerica and the Caribbean. *American Anthropologist* 97(4):748–762.

Lozada, Eriberto P. 1998. A Hakka Community in Cyberspace: Diasporic Ethnicity and the Internet. In *On the South China Track: Perspectives on Anthropological Research and Teaching*. Sidney C.H. Cheung, ed. Pp. 149–182. Hong Kong: Hong Kong Institute of Asia-Pacific Studies, The Chinese University of Hong Kong.

Lu, Hanchao. 1995. Away from Nanking Road: Small Stores and Neighborhood Life in Modern Shanghai. *Journal of Asian Studies* 54(1):93–123.

Lubkemann, Stephen C. 2002. Refugees. In *World at Risk: A Global Issues Sourcebook*. Pp. 522–544. Washington, DC: CQ Press.

Luhrmann, Tanya M. 1989. *Persuasions of the Witch's Craft: Ritual Magic in Contemporary England*. Cambridge: Harvard University Press.

MacDonald, M. 2001. Postmodern Negotiations with Medical Technology: The Role of Midwifery Clients in the New Midwifery in Canada. *Medical Anthropology* 20:245–276.

Maclachlan, Morgan. 1983. *Why They Did Not Starve: Biocultural Adaptation in a South Indian Village*. Philadelphia: Institute for the Study of Human Issues.

MacLeod, Arlene Elowe. 1992. Hegemonic Relations and Gender Resistance: The New Veiling as Accommodating Protest in Cairo. *Signs: The Journal of Women in Culture and Society* 17(3):533–557.

Malinowski, Bronislaw. 1929. *The Sexual Life of Savages*. New York: Harcourt, Brace & World.

___. 1961[1922]. *Argonauts of the Western Pacific*. New York: E. P. Dutton & Co.

___. 1962[1926]. *Crime and Custom in Savage Society*. Paterson, NJ: Littlefield, Adams & Co.

Mamdani, Mahmoud. 1972. *The Myth of Population Control: Family, Caste, and Class in an Indian Village*. New York: Monthly Review Press.

___. 2002. Good Muslim, Bad Muslim: A Political Perspective on Culture and Terrorism. *American Anthropologist* 104:766–775.

Manning, Frank. 1981. Celebrating Cricket: The Symbolic Construction of Caribbean Politics. *American Ethnologist* 8:616–632.

Manning, Frank, ed. 1983. *Consciousness and Inquiry: Ethnology and Canadian Realities*. Canadian Ethnology Service, Paper No. 89e, Ottawa: National Museum of Man.

Manz, Beatriz. 1988. *Refugees of a Hidden War: The Aftermath of Counterinsurgency in Guatemala*. Albany: State University of New York Press.

Marano, L. 1982. Windigo Psychosis: The Anatomy of an Emic–Etic Confusion. *Current Anthropology* 23(4):385–397.

March, Kathryn S., and Rachelle L. Taqqu. 1986. *Women's Informal Associations in Developing Countries: Catalysts for Change?* Boulder: Westview Press.

Margolis, Maxine. 1994. *Little Brazil: An Ethnography of Brazilian Immigrants in New York City*. Princeton: Princeton University Press.

Margolis, Maxine L., and Marigene Arnold. 1993. Turning the Tables? Male Strippers and the Gender Hierarchy in America. In *Sex and Gender Hierarchies*, Barbara D. Miller, ed. Pp. 334–350. New York: Cambridge University Press.

Marotz-Baden, Ramona, and Claudia Mattheis. 1994 Daughters-in-Law and Stress in Two-Generation Farm Families. *Family Relations* 43:132–137.

Marshall, Ingeborg. 1996. *A History and Ethnography of the Beothuk*. Montreal: McGill-Queen's University Press.

Marshall, Robert C. 1985. Giving a Gift to the Hamlet: Rank, Solidarity and Productive Exchange in Rural Japan. *Ethnology* 24:167–182.

Martin, M. Kay, and Barbara Voorhies. 1975. *Female of the Species*. New York: Columbia University Press.

Martin, Richard C. 1995. Islam. In *The HarperCollins Dictionary of Religion*. Jonathan Z. Smith, ed. Pp. 498–513. New York: HarperCollins.

Martínez, Samuel. 1996. Indifference with Indignation: Anthropology, Human Rights, and the Haitian Bracero. *American Anthropologist* 98(1):17–25.

Marx, Karl, and Friedrich Engels. 1964[1848] *The Communist Manifesto*. New York: Monthly Review Press.

Massiah, Joycelin. 1983. *Women as Heads of Households in the Caribbean: Family Structure and Feminine Status*. Paris: UNESCO.

Maybury-Lewis, David. 1997. *Indigenous Peoples, Ethnic Groups, and the State*. Boston: Allyn and Bacon.

___. 2002. Genocide against Indigenous Peoples. In *Annihilating Difference: The Anthropology of Genocide*. Alexander Laban Hinton, ed. Pp. 43–53. Berkeley: University of California Press.

Mayer, Adrian. 1960. *Caste and Kinship in Central India: A Village and Its Region*. Berkeley: University of California Press.

McCaghy, Charles H., and Charles Hou. 1994. Family Affiliation and Prostitution in a Cultural Context: Career Onsets of Taiwanese Prostitutes. *Archives of Sexual Behavior* 23:251–265.

McCoid, Catherine Hodge, and LeRoy D. McDermott. 1996. Toward Decolonizing Gender: Female Vision in the Upper Paleolithic. *American Anthropologist* 98(2):319–326.

McCracken, Grant. 1996. *Big Hair: A Journey into the Transformation of Self*. Woodstock, NY: The Overlook Press.

McCully, Patrick. 2003. Big Dams, Big Trouble. *New Internationalist* 354:14–15.

McDermott, LeRoy D. 1996. Self-Representation in Upper Paleolithic Female Figurines. *Current Anthropology* 37:227–275.

McDonald, G., and S. Alford. 1989. *Museum for the Global Village*. Hull, Quebec: Canadian Museum of Civilization.

McElroy, Ann, and Patricia K. Townsend. 1996. *Medical Anthropology in Ecological Perspective*. 3rd edition. Boulder: Westview Press.

McGrew, William C. 1998. Culture in Nonhuman Primates? *Annual Review of Anthropology* 27:301–328.

McIlwraith, T. F. 1948[1992]. *The Bella Coola Indians*. 2 Volumes. Toronto: University of Toronto Press.

McKenna, James. 1993. Rethinking Healthy Infant Sleep. *Breastfeeding Abstracts* 12(3):27.

M'Closkey, Kathy. 1994. Marketing Multiple Myths: The Hidden History of Navajo Weaving. *Journal of the Southwest* 36(3):185–220.

___. 1996. Art or Craft?: The Paradox of the Pangnirtung Weave Shop. In *Women of the First Nations: Power, Wisdom and Strength*. Christine Miller and Patricia Chuchryk, eds. Pp. 113–126. Winnipeg: University of Manitoba Press.

McLellan, Janet. 1996. Silent Screams and Hidden Pain: Barriers to the Adaptation and Integration of Cambodian Women Refugees in Ontario. In *Development and Diaspora: Gender and the Refugee Experience*. Wenona Giles, Helene Moussa, and Penny Van Esterik, eds. Dundas, ON: Artemis Enterprises.

McLuhan, Marshall. 1964. *Understanding Media: The Extensions of Man*. New York: McGraw-Hill.

McMahon, April M. S. 1994. *Understanding Language Change*. New York: Cambridge University Press.

Mead, Margaret. 1961[1928]. *Coming of Age in Samoa: A Psychological Study of Primitive Youth for Western Civilization*. New York: Dell Publishing Company.

___. 1963[1935]. *Sex and Temperament in Three Primitive Societies*. New York: William Morrow.

___. 1977 *Letters from the Field 1925–1975*. New York: Harper & Row.

___. 1986. Field Work in the Pacific Islands, 1925–1967. In *Women in the Field: Anthropological Experiences*. Peggy Golde, ed. Pp. 293–331. Berkeley: University of California Press.

Meigs, Anna S. 1984. *Food, Sex, and Pollution: A New Guinea Religion*. New Brunswick: Rutgers University Press.

Mencher, Joan P. 1965. The Nayars of South Malabar. In *Comparative Family Systems*. Meyer F. Nimkoff, ed. Pp. 163–191. Boston: Houghton Mifflin Company.

___. 1974. The Caste System Upside Down, or The Not-So-Mysterious East. *Current Anthropology* 15(4):469–49.

Mernissi, Fatima. 1987. *Beyond the Veil: Male–Female Dynamics in Modern Muslim Society*. Revised edition. Bloomington: Indiana University Press.

___. 1995. *Dreams of Trespass: Tales of a Harem Girlhood*. New York: Addison-Wesley.

Merry, Sally Engle. 1992. Anthropology, Law, and Transnational Processes. *Annual Review of Anthropology* 21:357–379.

Messer, Ellen. 1993. Anthropology and Human Rights. *Annual Review of Anthropology* 22:221–249.

Meyerhoff, Miriam. 1999. *Sorry* in the Pacific: Defining Communities, Defining Practice. *Language in Society* 28:225–238.

Michaelson, Evalyn Jacobson, and Walter Goldschmidt. 1971. Female Roles and Male Dominance among Peasants. *Southwestern Journal of Anthropology* 27:330–352.

Migliore, Sam. 1983. Evil Eye or Delusions: On the "Consistency" of Folk Models. *Medical Anthropology Quarterly* 14(2):4–9.

Milgram, B. Lynne. 1999. Crafts, Cultivation and Household Economies: Women's Work and Positions in Ifugao, Upland Philippines. In *Research in Economic Anthropology*. Barry Issac, ed. Greenwich, CT.: JAI Press.

Miller, Barbara D. 1997[1981]. *The Endangered Sex: Neglect of Female Children in Rural North India*. Ithaca, NY: Cornell University Press.

___. 1987a. Social Patterns of Food Expenditure among Low-Income Jamaicans. In *Papers and Recommendations of the Workshop on Food and Nutrition Security in Jamaica in the 1980s and Beyond*. Kenneth A. Leslie and Lloyd B. Rankine, eds. Pp. 13–33. Kingston, Jamaica: Caribbean Food and Nutrition Institute.

___. 1987b. Female Infanticide and Child Neglect in Rural North India. In *Child Survival: Anthropological Perspectives on the Treatment and Maltreatment of Children*. Nancy Scheper-Hughes, ed. Pp. 95–113. Boston: D. Reidel Publishing Company.

___. 1993. Surveying the Anthropology of Sex and Gender Hierarchies. In *Sex and Gender Hierarchies*. Barbara D. Miller, ed. Pp. 3–31. New York: Cambridge University Press.

Miller, Barbara D., and Showkat Hayat Khan. 1986. Incorporating Voluntarism into Rural Development in Bangladesh. *Third World Planning Review* 8(2):139–152.

Miller, Barbara D., and Carl Stone. 1983. The Low-Income Household Expenditure Survey: Description and Analysis. Jamaica Tax Structure Examination Project, Staff Paper No. 25. Syracuse, NY: Metropolitan Studies Program, Syracuse University.

Millett, Kate. 1994. *The Politics of Cruelty: An Essay on the Literature of Political Imprisonment*. New York: Norton.

Mills, Mary Beth. 1995. Attack of the Widow Ghosts: Gender, Death, and Modernity in Northeast Thailand. In *Bewitching Women, Pious Men: Gender and Body Politics in Southeast Asia*. Aihwa Ong and Michael G. Peletz, eds. Pp. 244–273. Berkeley: University of California Press.

Millward, Hugh. 1996. Greater Halifax: Public Policy Issues in the Post 1960 Period. *Canadian Journal of Urban Research* 5(1):1–17.

Milton, Katharine. 1992. Civilization and Its Discontents. *Natural History* 3/92:37–92.

Miner, Horace. 1965[1956]. Body Ritual among the Nacirema. In *Reader in Comparative Religion: An Anthropological Approach*. William A. Lessa and Evon Z. Vogt, eds. Pp. 414–418. New York: Harper & Row.

Mines, Mattison. 1994. *Public Faces, Private Voices: Community and Individuality in South India*. Berkeley: University of California Press.

Mir-Hosseini, Ziba. 1993. *Marriage on Trial: A Study of Islamic Family Law: Iran and Morocco Compared*. New York: I. B. Tauris & Co.

Mitchell, Bruce. 1994. Sustainable Development at the Village Level in Bali, Indonesia. *Human Ecology* 22(2):189–211.

Mitter, Partha. 1977. *Much Maligned Monsters: A History of European Reactions to Indian Art*. Chicago: University of Chicago Press.

Modell, Judith S. 1994. *Kinship with Strangers: Adoption and Interpretations of Kinship in American Culture*. Berkeley: University of California Press.

Moerman, Daniel E. 1979. Anthropology of Symbolic Healing. *Current Anthropology* 20:59–80.

___. 1983. General Medical Effectiveness and Human Biology: Placebo Effects in the Treatment of Ulcer Disease. *Medical Anthropology Quarterly* 14:13–16.

___. 1992 Minding the Body: The Placebo Effect Unmasked. In *Given the Body Its Due*. M. Sheets-Johnstone, ed. Pp. 69–84. Albany, NY: State University of New York Press.

Montesquieu. 1949[1748]. *The Spirit of the Laws*. T. Nugent, trans. New York: Hafner.

Montgomery, Heather. 2001. *Modern Babylon: Prostituting Children in Thailand*. New York: Bergahn Books.

Moore, Carmella C. and Holly F. Mathews, 2001. Introduction: The Psychology of Cultural Experience. In *The Psychology of Cultural Experience*. Carmella C. Moore and Holly F. Mathews, eds. Pp. 1–18. New York: Cambridge University Press.

Morgan, Lewis Henry. 1851. *The League of the [Ho-de-ne-sau, or] Iroquois*. New York: Russell Sage.

Morgan, William. 1977. Navaho Treatment of Sickness: Diagnosticians. In *Culture, Disease, and Healing: Studies in Medical Anthropology*. David Landy, ed. Pp. 163–168. New York: Macmillan.

Morris, Rosalind. 1994a. *New Worlds from Fragments: Film, Ethnography and the Representation of Northwest Coast Culture*. Boulder: Westview Press.

___. 1994b. Three Sexes and Four Sexualities: Redressing the Discourses on Gender and Sexuality in Contemporary Thailand. *Positions* 2:15–43.

Morrison, David. 2000. Canadian Aid: A Mixed Record and an Uncertain Future. In *Transforming Development: Foreign Aid for a Changing World*. J. Freedman, ed. Toronto: University of Toronto Press.

Morrison, L., S. Guruge, and K. Snarr. 1999. Sri Lankan Tamil Immigrants in Toronto: Gender, Marriage Patterns, and Sexuality. In *Gender and Immigration*. Gregory A. Kelson and Debra L. Delaet, eds. Pp. 144–162. London: Macmillan Press.

Moynihan, Elizabeth B. 1979. *Paradise as a Garden in Persia and Mughal India*. New York: George Braziller.

Muecke, Marjorie A. 1987. Resettled Refugees: Reconstruction of Identity of Lao in Seattle. *Urban Anthropology* 16(3–4):273–289.

Mulk, Inga-Maria. 1994. Sacrificial Places and Their Meaning in Saami Society. In *Sacred Sites, Sacred Places*. David L.

Carmichael, Jane Hubert, Brian Reeves, and Audhild Schanche, eds. Pp. 121–131. New York: Routledge.

Mull, Dorothy S., and J. Dennis Mull. 1987. Infanticide among the Tarahumara of the Mexican Sierra Madre. In *Child Survival: Anthropological Perspectives on the Treatment and Maltreatment of Children*. Nancy Scheper-Hughes, ed. Pp. 113–132. Boston: D. Reidel Publishing.

Murcott, Anne. 1993[1983]. "It's a Pleasure to Cook for Him": Food, Mealtimes and Gender in Some South Wales Households. In *Gender in Cross-Cultural Perspective*. Caroline B. Brettell and Carolyn F. Sargent, eds. Pp. 77–87. Englewood Cliffs, NJ: Prentice Hall.

Murdock, George Peter. 1965[1949]. *Social Structure*. New York: The Free Press.

Murphy, Yolanda, and Robert F. Murphy. 1985. *Women of the Forest*. New York: Columbia University Press.

Murray, David. 2002. *Opacity: Gender, Sexuality, Race and the Problem of "Identity" in Martinique*. New York: Peter Lang Publishing.

Myerhoff, Barbara. 1978. *Number Our Days*. New York: Simon and Schuster.

Myers, James. 1992. Nonmainstream Body Modification: Genital Piercing, Branding, Burning, and Cutting. *Journal of Contemporary Ethnography* 21(3):267–306.

Myers-Scotton, Carol. 1993. *Social Motivations for Code-Switching*. New York: Oxford University Press.

Nader, Laura. 1972. Up the Anthropologist-Perspectives Gained from Studying Up. In *Reinventing Anthropology*. Dell Hymes, ed. Pp. 284–311. New York: Vintage Books.

___. 1995. Civilization and Its Negotiations. In *Understanding Disputes: The Politics of Argument*. Pat Caplan, ed. Pp. 39–64. Providence, RI: Berg Publishers.

___. 2001. Harmony Coerced Is Freedom Denied. *The Chronicle of Higher Education*, July 13:B1.

Nag, Moni. 1972. Sex, Culture and Human Fertility: India and the United States. *Current Anthropology* 13:231–238.

___. 1983. Modernization Affects Fertility. *Populi* 10:56–77.

Nag, Moni, Benjamin N. F. White, and R. Creighton Peet. 1978. An Anthropological Approach to the Study of the Economic Value of Children in Java and Nepal. *Current Anthropology* 19(2):293–301.

Nagata, Judith. 1984. *The Reflowering of Malaysian Islam: Modern Religious Radicals and Their Roots*. Vancouver: University of British Columbia Press.

Nanda, Serena. 1990. *Neither Man Nor Woman: The Hijras of India*. Belmont, CA: Wadsworth Publishing Company.

___. 1994. *Cultural Anthropology*. Wadsworth, CA: Wadsworth Publishing Company.

Nasser, M, M. Katzman, and R. Gordon. 2001. *Eating Disorders and Cultures in Transition*. New York: Taylor & Francis.

Neale, Walter C. 1976. *Monies in Societies*. San Francisco: Chandler & Sharp Publishers.

Neff, Deborah L. 1994. The Social Construction of Infertility: The Case of the Matrilineal Nayars in South India. *Social Science and Medicine* 39(4):475–485.

Neier, Aryeh. 1996. Language and Minorities. *Dissent* (Summer):31–35.

Nelson, Sarah. 1993. Gender Hierarchies and the Queens of Silla. In *Sex and Gender Hierarchies*. Barbara D. Miller, ed. Pp. 297–315. New York: Cambridge University Press.

Netting, Robert McC. 1989. Smallholders, Householders, Freeholders: Why the Family Farm Works Well Worldwide. In *The Household Economy: Reconsidering the Domestic Mode of Production*. Richard R. Wilk, ed. Pp. 221–244. Boulder: Westview Press.

Neusner, Jacob. 1995. Judaism. In *The HarperCollins Dictionary of Religion*. Jonathan Z. Smith, ed. Pp. 598–607. New York: HarperCollins.

Ngokwey, Ndolamb. 1988. Pluralistic Etiological Systems in Their Social Context: A Brazilian Case Study. *Social Science and Medicine* 26:793–802.

Nichter, Mark. 1992. Of Ticks, Kings, Spirits and the Promise of Vaccines. In *Paths to Asian Medical Knowledge*. Leslie Charles and Allan Young, ed. Pp. 224–253. Berkeley: University of California Press.

___. 1996. Vaccinations in the Third World: A Consideration of Community Demand. In *Anthropology and International Health: Asian Case Studies*. Mark Nichter and Mimi Nichter, eds. Pp. 329–365. Amsterdam: Gordon and Breach Publishers.

Nichter, Mark, and Mimi Nichter, eds. 1996. *Anthropology and International Health: Asian Case Studies*. Amsterdam: Gordon and Breach Publishers.

Nichter, Mimi, and Nancy Vuckovic. 1994. Fat Talk: Body Image among Adolescent Girls. In *Many Mirrors: Body Image and Social Relations*. Nicole Sault, ed. Pp. 109–131. New Brunswick: Rutgers University Press.

Nicks, Trudy. 1992. Partnerships in Developing Cultural Resources: Lessons from the Task Force on Museums and First Peoples. *Culture* 12(1):87–94.

Nieves, Isabel. 1979. Household Arrangements and Multiple Jobs in San Salvador. *Signs: Journal of Women in Culture and Society* 5:134–142.

Nodwell, Evelyn, and Neil Guppy. 1992. The Effects of Publicly Displayed Ethnicity on Interpersonal Discrimination: Indo-Canadians in Vancouver. *The Canadian Review of Sociology and Anthropology* 29(1):87–99.

Norgaard, Richard B. 1994. *Development Betrayed: The End of Progress and the Coevolutionary Revisioning of the Future*. New York: Routledge.

Nyambedha, Erick Otieno, Simiyu Wandibba, and Jens Aagaard-Hansen. 2003. Changing Patterns of Orphan Care Due to the HIV Epidemic in Western Kenya. *Social Science and Medicine* 57:301–311.

Obeyesekere, Gananath. 1981. *Medusa's Hair: An Essay on Personal Symbols and Religious Experience*. Chicago: University of Chicago Press.

Ochs, Elinor. 1990. Indexicality and Socialization. In *Cultural Psychology: Essays on Comparative Human Development*. James W. Stigler, Richard A. Shweder, and Gilbert Herdt, eds. Pp. 287–308. New York: Cambridge University Press.

Ohnuki-Tierney, Emiko. 1994. Brain Death and Organ Transplantation: Cultural Bases of Medical Technology. *Current Anthropology* 35(3):233–242.

Oinas, Felix J. 1993. Couvade in Estonia. *Slavic & East European Journal* 37(3):339–345.

Okely, Judith. 1993[1984]. Fieldwork in the Home Counties. In *Talking about People: Readings in Contemporary Cultural Anthropology*. William A. Haviland and Robert J. Gordon, eds. Pp. 4–6. Mountain View, CA: Mayfield Publishing Company.

Omvedt, Gail. 1995. *Dalit Visions: The Anti-Caste Movement and the Construction of an Indian Identity*. New Delhi: Orient Longman/Tracts for the Times/8.

Ong, Aihwa. 1987. *Spirits of Resistance and Capitalist Discipline: Factory Women in Malaysia*. Albany: State University of New York Press.

___. 1995. State versus Islam: Malay Families, Women's Bodies, and the Body Politic in Malaysia. In *Bewitching Women, Pious Men: Gender and Body Politics in Southeast Asia*. Aihwa Ong and Michael G. Peletz, eds. Pp. 159–194. Berkeley: University of California Press.

Ongley, Patrick. 1995. Post-1945 International Migration: New Zealand, Australia and Canada Compared. *International Migration Review* 29(3):765–793.

Oxfeld, Ellen. 1993. *Blood, Sweat and Mahjong: Family and Enterprise in an Overseas Chinese Community*. Ithaca: Cornell University Press.

Painter, Andrew A. 1996. The Telerepresentation of Gender. In *Re-Imaging Japanese Women*. Anne E. Imamura, ed. Pp. 46–72. Berkeley: University of California Press.

Panter-Brick, Catherine, and Malcolm T. Smith, eds. 2000. *Abandoned Children*. New York: Cambridge University Press.

Pappas, Gregory. 1989. *The Magic City: Unemployment in a Working-Class Community*. Ithaca: Cornell University Press.

Park, Michael Alan. 1996. *Biological Anthropology*. Mountain View, CA: Mayfield Publishing Company.

Parry, Jonathan P. 1966. Caste. In *The Social Science Encyclopedia*. Adam Kuper and Jessica Kuper, eds. Pp. 76–77. New York: Routledge.

Patterson, Thomas C. 2001. *A Social History of Anthropology in the United States*. New York: Berg.

Paxson, Heather. 2003. With or Against Nature: IVF, Gender and Reproductive Agency in Athens, Greece. *Social Science and Medicine* 56:1853–1866.

Peacock, James L., and Dorothy C. Holland. 1993. The Narrated Self: Life Stories in Process. *Ethos* 21(4):367–383.

Peattie, Lisa Redfield. 1968. *The View from the Barrio*. Ann Arbor: University of Michigan Press.

Pechman, Joseph A. 1987. Introduction: Recent Developments. In *Comparative Tax Systems: Europe, Canada, and Japan*. Joseph A. Pechman, ed. Pp. 1–32. Arlington, VA: Tax Analysts.

Pedelty, Mark. 1995. *War Stories: The Culture of Foreign Correspondents*. New York: Routledge.

Peletz, Michael. 1987. The Exchange of Men in 19th-Century Negeri Sembilan (Malaya). *American Ethnologist* 14(3):449–469.

Pelto, Pertti. 1973. *The Snowmobile Revolution: Technology and Social Change in the Arctic*. Menlo Park, CA: Cummings.

Pelto, Pertti, Maria Roman, and Nelson Liriano. 1982. Family Structures in an Urban Puerto Rican Community. *Urban Anthropology* 11:39–58.

Pendergast, David M, Grant D. Jones, and Elizabeth Graham. 1993. Locating Spanish Colonial Towns in the Maya Lowlands: A Case Study from Belize. *Latin American Antiquity* 4(1):59–73.

Perry, Richard J. 1996. ... *From Time Immemorial: Indigenous Peoples and State Systems*. Austin: University of Texas Press.

Pessar, Patricia R. 1995. *A Visa for a Dream: Dominicans in the United States*. Boston: Allyn and Bacon.

Phillips, Lynne. 1998. Dissecting Globalization: Women's Space-Time in the Other America. In *Transgressing Borders: Critical Perspectives on Gender, Household, and Culture*. Susan Ilcan and Lynne Phillips, eds. Westport, CT.: Bergin & Garvey.

Piddocke, Stuart. 1969. The Potlatch System of the Southern Kwakiutl: A New Perspective. In *Environment and Cultural Behavior: Ecological Studies in Cultural Anthropology*. Andrew P. Vayda, ed. Pp. 130–156. Garden City, NY: The Natural History Press.

Pigg, Stacey. 1996. The Credible and the Credulous: The Question of Villagers' Beliefs in Nepal. *Cultural Anthropology* 11:160–201.

___. 2001. The Politics of Development and the Politics of Health: Contradictions of AIDS Prevention in Nepal. *Anthropologie -et- Societes* 25(1):43–62.

Pillsbury, Barbara. 1990. The Politics of Family Planning: Sterilization and Human Rights in Bangladesh. In *Births and Power: Social Change and the Politics of Reproduction*. W. Penn Handwerker, ed. Pp. 165–196. Boulder: Westview Press.

Plant, Roger. 1994. *Land Rights and Minorities*. London: Minority Rights Group.

Plattner, Stuart. 1989. Markets and Marketplaces. In *Economic Anthropology*. Stuart Plattner, ed. Pp. 171–208. Stanford: Stanford University Press.

Poirier, Sylvie. 1992. "Nomadic" Rituals: Networks of Ritual Exchange between Women of the Australian Western Desert. *Man* 27:757–776.

Ponting, J. Rick, and Jerilynn Kiely. 1997. Disempowerment: "Justice," Racism, and Public Opinion. In *First Nations in Canada: Perspectives on Opportunity, Empowerment, and Self-Determination*. J. Rick Ponting, ed. Toronto: McGraw-Hill Ryerson.

Postgate, Nicholas, Tao Wang, and Toby Wilkinson. 1995. The Evidence for Early Writing: Utilitarian or Ceremonial? *Antiquity* 69:459–480.

Pratt, Mary Louise. 1992. *Imperial Eyes: Travel Writing and Transculturation*. London: Routledge.

Preston, Richard. 1983. The Social Structure of an Unorganized Society: Beyond Intentions and Peripheral Boasians. In *Consciousness and Inquiry: Ethnology and Canadian*

Realities. Frank Manning, ed. Pp. 286–305. Canadian Ethnology Service Paper 89E. Ottawa: National Museums of Canada.

Price, David H. 1995. Water Theft in Egypt's Fayoum Oasis: Emics, Etics, and the Illegal. In *Science, Materialism, and the Study of Culture*. Martin F. Murphy and Maxine L. Margolis, eds. Pp. 96–110. Gainesville: University of Florida Press.

Price, John A. 1979. *Indians of Canada: Cultural Dynamics*. Scarborough, ON: Prentice-Hall of Canada.

Prince, Raymond. 1985. The Concept of Culture-Bound Syndromes: Anorexia Nervosa and Brain-Fog. *Social Science and Medicine* 21(2):197–203.

Purdum, Elizabeth D., and J. Anthony Paredes. 1989. *Facing the Death Penalty: Essays on Cruel and Unusual Punishment*. Philadelphia: Temple University Press.

Radcliffe-Brown, A. R. 1964[1922] *The Andaman Islanders*. New York: The Free Press.

Radin, Paul. 1963[1920]. *The Autobiography of a Winnebago Indian: Life, Ways, Acculturation, and the Peyote Cult*. New York: Dover Publications.

Raheja, Gloria Goodwin. 1988. *The Poison in the Gift: Ritual, Prestation, and the Dominant Caste in a North Indian Village*. Chicago: University of Chicago Press.

Rahnema, Majid. 1992. Poverty. In *The Development Dictionary: A Guide to Knowledge and Power*. Wolfgang Sachs, ed. Pp. 159–176. Atlantic Highlands, NJ: Zed Press.

Ramesh, A., C. R. Srikumari, and S. Sukumar. 1989. Parallel Cousin Marriages in Madras, Tamil Nadu: New Trends in Dravidian Kinship. *Social Biology* 36(3–4):248–254.

Ramphele, Mamphela. 1996. Political Widowhood in South Africa: The Embodiment of Ambiguity. *Daedalus* 125(1):99–17.

Rapp, Rayna. 1993. Reproduction and Gender Hierarchy: Amniocentesis in America. In *Sex and Gender Hierarchies*, Barbara D. Miller, ed. Pp. 108–126. New York: Cambridge University Press.

Rathgeber, Eva M. 1990. WID, WAD, GAD: Trends in Research and Practice. *Journal of Developing Areas* 24:489–502.

Rathje, William, and Cullen Murphy. 1992 *Rubbish! The Archaeology of Garbage*. New York: Harper & Row.

Ravaillon, Martin. 2003. The Debate on Globalization, Poverty and Inequality: Why Income Measurement Matters. *International Affairs* 79:739–753.

Reiner, R. 1996. Police. In *The Social Science Encyclopedia*. Adam Kuper and Jessica Kuper, eds. Pp. 619–621. New York: Routledge.

Reyna, Stephen P. 1994. A Mode of Domination Approach to Organized Violence. In *Studying War: Anthropological Perspectives*. S. P. Reyna and R. E. Downs, eds. Pp. 29–65. Langhorne, PA: Gordon and Breach Science Publishers.

Rich, Adrienne. 1980/ Compulsory Heterosexuality and Lesbian Existence. *Signs* 5:631–660.

Rich, Bruce. 1994. *Mortgaging the Earth: The World Bank, Environmental Impoverishment, and the Crisis of Development*. Boston: Beacon Press.

Riddington, Robin. 1990. *Little Bit Know Something: Stories in a Language of Anthropology*. Iowa City: University of Iowa Press.

Robertson, Carol E. 1987. Power and Gender in the Musical Experiences of Women. In *Women and Music in Cross-Cultural Perspective*. Ellen Koskoff, ed. Pp. 225–244. New York: Greenwood Press.

Robertson, Jennifer. 1991. *Native and Newcomer: Making and Remaking a Japanese City*. Berkeley: University of California Press.

Robins, Kevin. 1996. Globalization. In *The Social Science Encyclopedia*. 2nd edition. Adam Kuper and Jessica Kuper, eds. Pp. 345–346. New York: Routledge.

Robson, Colin. 1993. *Real World Research: A Resource for Social Scientists and Practitioner-Researchers*. Cambridge, MA: Blackwell Publishers.

Rodman, Margaret. 1992 Empowering Place: Multilocality and Multivocality. *American Anthropologist* 94(3):640–56.

Rodman, Margaret, Patti Hall Hawkins, and Daniel Teramura. 1998. It's Not Over: Vari Hall as Contested Academic Space at York University. *Canadian Journal of Urban Research* 7(1):47–71.

Rogers, Barbara. 1979. *The Domestication of Women: Discrimination in Developing Societies*. New York: St. Martin's Press.

Rohde, J. E. 1982. Mother's Milk and the Indonesian Economy: A Major National Resource. *Journal of Tropical Pediatrics* 28:166–174.

Romalis, Shelly, ed. 1981. *Childbirth, Alternative to Medical Control*. Austin: University of Texas Press.

Rosaldo, Renato. 1980 *Ilongot Headhunting 1883–1974: A Study in Society and History*. Stanford: Stanford University Press.

Roscoe, Will. 1991. *The Zuni Man-Woman*. Albuquerque: University of New Mexico Press.

Roseman, Marina. 1987. Inversion and Conjuncture: Male and Female Performance among the Temiar of Peninsular Malaysia. In *Women and Music in Cross-Cultural Perspective*. Ellen Koskoff, ed. Pp. 131–149. New York: Greenwood Press.

Rosenberg, Harriet G. 1988 *A Negotiated World: Three Centuries of Change in a French Alpine Community*. Toronto: University of Toronto Press.

Rosenberg, Lisa. 1996. Determination/Despair: Agunot Speak about Their Chains. *Canadian Woman Studies/Les Cahiers De La Femme* 16(4):69–73.

Rosenberger, Nancy. 1992. Images of the West: Home Style in Japanese Magazines. In *Re-made in Japan: Everyday Life and Consumer Taste in a Changing Society*. James J. Tobin, ed. Pp. 106–125. New Haven: Yale University Press.

Rosenblatt, Paul C., Patricia R. Walsh, and Douglas A. Jackson. 1976. *Grief and Mourning in Cross-Cultural Perspective*. New Haven: HRAF Press.

Rouland, Norbert. 1994. *Legal Anthropology*. Trans. Philippe G. Planel. Stanford: Stanford University Press.

Roy, Arundhati. 1999. *The Cost of Living*. New York: The Modern Library.

Rubel, Arthur J., Carl W. O'Nell, and Rolando Collado-Ardón. 1984. *Susto: A Folk Illness.* Berkeley: University of California Press.

Rubin, Gayle. 1975. The Traffic in Women: Notes on the "Political Economy" of Sex. In *Toward an Anthropology of Women.* Rayna R. Rapp, ed. Pp. 157–210. New York: Monthly Review Press.

Sachs, Aaron. 1996. Dying for Oil. *WorldWatch* June:10–21.

Saggers, Sherry, and Dennis Gray. 1998. *Dealing with Alcohol: Indigenous Usage in Australia, New Zealand and Canada.* New York: Cambridge University Press.

Sahlins, Marshall. 1963. Poor Man, Rich Man, Big Man, Chief. *Comparative Studies in Society and History* 5:285–303.

___. 1972. *Stone Age Economics.* Chicago: Aldine de Gruyter.

Said, Edward W. 1979[1978]. *Orientalism.* New York: Vintage Books.

Saitoti, Tepilit Ole. 1986. *The Worlds of a Maasai Warrior.* New York: Random House.

Salam, Nawaf A. 1994. Between Repatriation and Resettlement: Palestinian Refugees in Lebanon. *Journal of Palestine Studies* 24(1):18–27.

Salisbury, Richard 1983. The Social Structure of an Unorganized Society: Beyond Intentions and Peripheral Boasians. In *Consciousness and Inquiry: Ethnology and Canadian Realities.* F. Manning, ed. Canadian Ethnology Service, Paper No. 89e. Ottawa: National Museum of Man.

___. 1986. *A Homeland for the Cree: Regional Development in James Bay, 1971–1981.* Montreal: McGill-Queen's University Press.

Salzman, Philip Carl. 2002. On Reflexivity. *American Anthropologist* 104:805–813.

Sanday, Peggy Reeves. 1973. Toward a Theory of the Status of Women. *American Anthropologist* 75:1682–1700.

___. 1986. *Divine Hunger: Cannibalism as a Cultural System.* New York: Cambridge University Press.

___. 1990. *Fraternity Gang Rape: Sex, Brotherhood, and Privilege on Campus.* New York: New York University Press.

___. 2002. *Women at the Center: Life in a Modern Matriarchy.* Ithaca: Cornell University Press.

Sanders, William B. 1994. *Gangbangs and Drive-Bys: Grounded Culture and Juvenile Gang Violence.* New York: Aldine de Gruyter.

Sanjek, Roger. 1990. A Vocabulary for Fieldnotes. In *Fieldnotes: The Making of Anthropology.* Roger Sanjek, ed. Pp. 92–138. Ithaca: Cornell University Press.

___. 1994. The Enduring Inequalities of Race. In *Race.* Steven Gregory and Roger Sanjek, eds. Pp. 1–17. New Brunswick, NJ: Rutgers University Press.

___. 2000. Keeping Ethnography Alive in an Urbanizing World. *Human Organization* 53:280–288.

Sankoff, D., and S. Laberge. 1978. The Linguistic Market and the Statistical Explanation of Variability. In *Linguistic Variation: Models and Methods.* D. Sankoff, ed. Pp. 239–250. New York: Academic Press.

Saul, John Ralston. 1997. *Reflections of a Siamese Twin at the End of the Twentieth Century.* Toronto: Viking.

Sault, Nicole L. 1985. Baptismal Sponsorship as a Source of Power for Zapotec Women of Oaxaca, Mexico. *Journal of Latin American Lore* 11(2):225–243.

___. 1994. How the Body Shapes Parenthood: "Surrogate" Mothers in the United States and Godmothers in Mexico. In *Many Mirrors: Body Image and Social Relations.* Nicole Sault, ed. Pp. 292–318. New Brunswick, NJ: Rutgers University Press.

Savishinsky, Joel S. 1974. *The Trail of the Hare: Life and Stress in an Arctic Community.* New York: Gordon and Breach.

___. 1991. *The Ends of Time: Life and Work in a Nursing Home.* New York: Bergin & Garvey.

Scheper-Hughes, Nancy. 1990. Three Propositions for a Critically Applied Medical Anthropology. *Social Science and Medicine* 30(2):189–197.

___. 1992. *Death without Weeping: The Violence of Everyday Life in Brazil.* Berkeley: University of California Press.

___. 1993. *Death without Weeping: The Violence of Everyday Life in Brazil.* Reprint ed. Berkeley: University of California Press.

Schlegel, Alice. 1995. A Cross Cultural Approach to Adolescence. *Ethos* 23(1):15–32.

Schlegel, Alice, and Herbert Barry III. 1991. *Adolescence: An Anthropological Inquiry.* New York: Free Press.

Schmid, Thomas J., and Richard S. Jones. 1993. Ambivalent Actions: Prison Adaptation Strategies of First-Time, Short-term Inmates. *Journal of Contemporary Ethnography* 21(4):439–463.

Schneider, David M. 1968. *American Kinship: A Cultural Account.* Englewood Cliffs, NJ: Prentice-Hall.

Scott, Colin. 2001. *Aboriginal Autonomy and Development in Northern Quebec and Labrador.* Vancouver: UBC Press.

Scott, James C. 1985. *Weapons of the Weak: Everyday Forms of Peasant Resistance.* New Haven: Yale University Press.

___. 1998. *Seeing Like a State: How Certain Schemes to Improve the Human Condition Have Failed.* New Haven, CT: Yale University Press.

Scrimshaw, Susan. 1984. Infanticide in Human Populations: Societal and Individual Concerns. In *Infanticide: Comparative and Evolutionary Perspectives.* Glenn Hausfater and Sarah Blaffer Hardy, eds. Pp. 463–486. New York: Aldine Publishing Company.

Sen, Amartya. 1981. *Poverty and Famines: An Essay on Entitlement and Deprivation.* New York: Oxford University Press.

Senghas, Richard J., and Leila Monaghan. 2002. Signs of Their Times: Deaf Communities and the Culture of Language. *Annual Review of Anthropology* 31:69–97.

Sentumbwe, Nayinda. 1995. Sighted Lovers and Blind Husbands: Experience of Blind Women in Uganda. In *Disability and Culture.* Benedicte Ingstad and Susan Reynolds, eds. Pp. 159–173. Berkeley: University of California Press.

Shahrani, Nazif M. 2002. War, Factionalism, and the State in Afghanistan. *American Anthropologist* 104:715–722.

Shankman, Paul, and Tracy Bachrach Ehlers. 2000. The "Exotic" and the "Domestic": Regions and Representations in Cultural Anthropology. *Human Organization* 59:289–299.

Sharff, Jagna-Wojcicka. 1995. "We Are All Chickens for the Colonel": A Cultural Materialist View of Prisons. In *Science, Materialism and the Study of Culture*. Martin F. Murphy and Maxine L. Margolis, eds. Pp. 132–158. Gainesville: University Press of Florida.

Sharp, Lesley. 1990. Possessed and Dispossessed Youth: Spirit Possession of School Children in Northwest Madagascar. *Culture, Medicine and Psychiatry* 14:339–364.

Shell-Duncan, Bettina, and Ylva Hernlund. 2000. Female "Circumcision" in: Dimensions of the Practice and Debates. In *Female "Circumcision" in Africa: Culture, Controversy, and Change*. Bettina Shell-Duncan and Ylva Hernlund, eds. Pp. 1–40. Boulder, CO: Lynne Reiner Publishers.

Sheriff, Robin E. 2000. Exposing Silence as Cultural Censorship: A Brazilian Case. *American Anthropologist* 102:114–132.

Shibamoto, Janet. 1987. The Womanly Woman: Manipulation of Stereotypical and Nonstereotypical Features of Japanese Female Speech. In *Language, Gender, and Sex in Comparative Perspective*. Susan U. Philips, Susan Steel, and Christine Tanz, eds. Pp. 26–49. New York: Cambridge University Press.

Shifflett, Peggy A., and William A. McIntosh. 1986–1987. Food Habits and Future Time: An Exploratory Study of Age-Appropriate Food Habits among the Elderly. *International Journal of Aging and Human Development* 24(1):2–15.

Shik, Angela W.Y. 1995. Visa-00000 Students from Hong Kong: Adaptation and Mental Health. Master of Science dissertation. University of Toronto.

Shipton, Parker. 2001. Money. In *The Dictionary of Anthropology*. Thomas Barfield, ed. Pp. 327–329.

Shore, Bradd. 1998. Status Reversal: The Coming of Age in Samoa. In *Welcome to Middle Age! (And Other Cultural Fictions)*. Richard A. Shweder, ed. Pp. 101–138. Chicago: The University of Chicago Press.

Short, James F. 1996. Gangs. In *The Social Science Encyclopedia*. Adam Kuper and Jessica Kuper, eds. Pp. 325–326. New York: Routledge.

Shostak, Marjorie. 1981. *Nisa: The Life and Times of a !Kung Woman*. Cambridge, MA: Harvard University Press.

Shu-Min, Huang. 1993. A Cross-Cultural Experience: A Chinese Anthropologist in the United States. In *Distant Mirrors: America as a Foreign Culture*. Philip R. DeVita and James D. Armstrong, eds. Pp. 39–45. Belmont, CA: Wadsworth Publishing Company.

Shweder, Richard A. 1986. Storytelling among the Anthropologists. *The New York Times Book Review*, September 21:1, 38–39.

Silver, Ira. 1993. Marketing Authenticity in Third World Countries. *Annals of Tourism Research* 20:302–318.

Simmons, William S. 1986. *Spirit of the New England Tribes: Indian History and Folklore, 1620–1984*. Hanover, NH: University Press of New England.

Singh, K. S. 1994. The Scheduled Tribes. In *Anthropological Survey of India, People of India, National Series Volume III*. K. S. Singh, ed. Delhi: Oxford University Press.

Skinner, G. William. 1964. Marketing and Social Structure in Rural China (Part 1). *Journal of Asian Studies* 24(1):3–43.

___. 1993. Conjugal Power in Tokugawa Japanese Families: A Matter of Life or Death. In *Sex and Gender Hierarchies*. Barbara D. Miller, ed. Pp. 236–270. New York: Cambridge University Press.

Skocpol, Theda. 1979. *States and Social Revolutions: A Comparative Analysis of France, Russia, and China*. New York: Cambridge University Press.

Skrobanek, S., Nataya Boonpakdee, and Chutima Jantateero. 1997. *The Traffic in Women: Human Realities of the International Sex Trade*. London: Zed Press.

Slocum, Sally. 1975. Woman the Gatherer: Male Bias in Anthropology. In *Toward an Anthropology of Women*. Rayna R. Reiter, ed. Pp. 36–50. New York: Monthly Review Press.

Smart, J. 1994. Business Immigration in Canada: Deception and Exploitation. In *Reluctant Exiles: Migration from Hong Kong and the new Overseas Chinese*. R. Skeldon, ed. Armonk, NY: M.E. Sharpe.

Smith, Derek. 2001. "Policy of Aggressive Civilization" and Projects of Governance in Roman Catholic Industrial Schools for Native Peoples in Canada, 1870–95. *Anthropologica* 43(2):253–271.

Smith, Jonathan Z., ed. 1995. *The HarperCollins Dictionary of Religion*. New York: HarperCollins.

Smith, Yvonne Bobb. 1999. There Is No Place Like Home: Caribbean Women's Feminism in Canada. In *Emigre Feminism: Transnational Perspectives*. Alena Heitlinger, ed. Toronto: University of Toronto Press.

Soh, Chunghee Sarah. 1993. *Women in Korean Politics*. 2nd edition. Boulder: Westview Press.

Sperber, Dan. 1985. *On Anthropological Knowledge: Three Essays*. New York: Cambridge University Press.

Spiro, Melford. 1967. *Burmese Supernaturalism: A Study in the Explanation and Reduction of Suffering*. Englewood Cliffs, NJ: Prentice-Hall.

___. 1990 On the Strange and the Familiar in Recent Anthropological Thought. In *Cultural Psychology: Essays on Comparative Human Development*. James W. Stigler, Richard A. Shweder, and Gilbert Herdt, eds. Pp. 47–61. Chicago: University of Chicago Press.

Spitulnik, Deborah. 1993. Anthropology and Mass Media. *Annual Review of Anthropology* 22:293–315.

Srinivas, M. N. 1959. The Dominant Caste in Rampura. *American Anthropologist* 1:1–16.

Staats, Valerie. 1994. Ritual, Strategy or Convention: Social Meaning in Traditional Women's Baths in Morocco. *Frontiers: A Journal of Women's Studies* 14(3):1–18.

Stack, Carol. 1974. *All Our Kin: Strategies for Survival in a Black Community*. New York: Harper & Row Publishers.

Stambach, Amy. 2000. *Lessons from Mount Kilimanjaro: Schooling, Community, and Gender in East Africa*. New York: Routledge.

Stannard, David E. 1992. *American Holocaust*. New York: Oxford University Press.

Starr, June. 1978. *Dispute and Settlement in Rural Turkey: An Ethnography of Law.* Leiden, Netherlands: E. J. Brill.

Statistics Canada. 2002. *Population and Dwelling Counts, for Canada, Provinces and Territories, 2001 and 1996 Censuses.* Electronic document, http://www12.statcan.ca/english/census01/products/standard/popdwell/Table-PR.cfm, accessed November 16, 2005.

Statistics Canada. 2004. *Farm Population, by Provinces (2001 Censuses of Agriculture and Population).* Electronic document, http://www40.statcan.ca/l01/cst01/agrc42a.htm?sdi=rural%20population, accessed November 7, 2005.\Nasser, M, M. Katzman and R. Gordon2001 Eating Disorders and Cultures in Transition.New York:Taylor &Francis Inc.

Stein, Gertrude. 1959. *Picasso.* Boston: Beacon Press.

Stephen, Lynn. 1995. Women's Rights are Human Rights: The Merging of Feminine and Feminist Interests among El Salvador's Mothers of the Disappeared (CO-MADRES). *American Ethnologist* 22(4):807–827.

Stephenson, P. 1991. *The Hutterian People.* Lantham: University Press of America.

Stillman, Amy Ku'uleialoha. 1996. Hawaiian Hula Competitions: Event, Repertoire, Performance and Tradition. *Journal of American Folklore* 109(434):357–380.

Stivens, Maila, Cecelia Ng, and Jomo K. S., with Jahara Bee. 1994. *Malay Peasant Women and the Land.* Atlantic Highlands, NJ: Zed Books.

Stocking, George W. Jr., ed. 1985. *Objects and Others: Essays on Museums and Material Culture.* History of Anthropology Series, 3. Madison: University of Wisconsin Press.

Stoler, Ann Laura. 1985. *Capitalism and Confrontation in Sumatra's Plantation Belt, 1870–1979.* New Haven: Yale University Press.

___. 1989. Rethinking Colonial Categories: European Communities and the Boundaries of Rule. *Comparative Studies in Society and History* 31(1):134–161.

Stone, Linda. 1998. *Kinship and Gender: An Introduction.* Boulder, Colorado: Westview Press.

Storper-Perez, Danielle, and Harvey E. Goldberg. 1994. The Kotel: Toward an Ethnographic Portrait. *Religion* 24:309–332.

Story, G., W. Kirwin, and J. Widdowson. eds., 1982. *Dictionary of Newfoundland English.* Toronto: University of Toronto Press.

Strathern, Andrew. 1971. *The Rope of Moka: Big-Men and Ceremonial Exchange in Mount Hagen, New Guinea.* London: Cambridge University Press.

Stringer, Martin D. 1999. Rethinking Animism: Thoughts from the Infancy of Our Discipline. *Journal of the Royal Anthropological Institute* 5:541–556.

Sullivan, Kathleen. 1992. Protagonists of Change. *Cultural Survival Quarterly* 16:4(Winter):38–40.

Sundar Rao, P. S. S. 1983. Religion and Intensity of In-breeding in Tamil Nadu, South India. *Social Biology* 30(4):413–422.

Suttles, Wayne. 1991. The Traditional Kwakiutl Potlatch. In *Chiefly Feasts: The Enduring Kwakiutl Potlatch.* Aldona Jonaitis, ed. Pp. 71–134. Washington, DC: American Museum of Natural History.

Tannen, Deborah. 1990. *You Just Don't Understand: Women and Men in Conversation.* New York: Morrow.

Tanner, A. 1983. *The Politics of Indianness.* St. John's, NF: Institute of Social and Economic Research, Memorial University of Newfoundland.

Tennant, Paul 1990. *Aboriginal Peoples and Politics: The Indian Land Question in British Columbia, 1849–1989.* Vancouver: University of British Columbia Press.

Thompson, Julia J. 1998. Cuts and Culture in Kathmandu. In *Hair: Its Meaning and Power in Asian Cultures.* Alf Hiltebeitel and Barbara D. Miller, eds. Pp. 219–258. Albany: State University of New York Press.

Thompson, Robert Farris. 1971. Aesthetics in Traditional Africa. In *Art and Aesthetics in Primitive Societies.* Carol F. Jopling, ed. Pp. 374–381. New York: E. P. Dutton.

Tice, Karin E. 1995. *Kuna Crafts, Gender, and the Global Economy.* Austin: University of Texas Press.

Tiffany, Walter W. 1979. New Directions in Political Anthropology: The Use of Corporate Models for the Analysis of Political Organizations. In *Political Anthropology: The State of the Art.* S. Lee Seaton and Henri J. M. Claessen, eds. Pp. 63–75. New York: Mouton.

Tinker, Irene. 1976. The Adverse Impact of Development on Women. In *Women and World Development.* Irene Tinker and Michele Bo Bramsen, eds. Pp. 22–34. Washington, DC: Overseas Development Council.

Toren, Christina. 1988. Making the Present, Revealing the Past: The Mutability and Continuity of Tradition as Process. *Man (N.S.)* 23:696–717.

Traphagan, John W. 2000. The Liminal Family: Return Migration and Intergenerational Conflict in Japan. *Journal of Anthropological Research* 56:365–385.

Trawick, Margaret. 1988. Death and Nurturance in Indian Systems of Healing. In *Paths to Asian Medical Knowledge.* Charles Leslie and Allan Young, eds. Pp. 129–159. Berkeley: University of California Press.

___. 1992. *Notes on Love in a Tamil Family.* Berkeley: University of California Press.

Trelease, Murray L. 1975. Dying among Alaskan Indians: A Matter of Choice. In *Death: The Final Stage of Growth.* Elisabeth Kübler-Ross, ed. Pp. 33–37. Englewood Cliffs, NJ: Prentice-Hall.

Trigger, Bruce. 1969. *The Huron: Farmers of the North.* New York: Holt, Rinehart and Winston.

___. 1976. *The Children of Aataentsic: A History of the Huron People to 1660.* 2 volumes. Montreal: McGill-Queens University Press.

___. 1996. State, Origins of. In *The Social Science Encyclopedia.* Adam Kuper and Jessica Kuper, eds. Pp. 837–838. New York: Routledge.

___. 1997. Loaves and Fishes: Sustaining Anthropology at McGill. *Culture* 17(1–2):89–100.

Trotter, Robert T., II. 1987. A Case of Lead Poisoning from Folk Remedies in Mexican American Communities. In *Anthropological Praxis: Translating Knowledge into Action.* Robert M. Wulff and Shirley J. Fiske, eds. Pp. 146–159. Boulder: Westview Press.

Trouillot, Michel-Rolph. 1994. Culture, Color, and Politics in Haiti. In *Race*. Steven Gregory and Roger Sanjek, eds. Pp. 146–174. New Brunswick: Rutgers University Press.

Tudiver, S. 1997. Depo-Provera. *Womanly Times* Summer/Fall:1–5,14.

Turner, Victor W. 1969. *The Ritual Process: Structure and Anti-Structure*. Chicago: Aldine Publishing Company.

Tylor, Edward Burnett. 1871. *Primitive Culture: Researches into the Development of Mythology, Philosophy, Religion, Art, and Custom*. 2 volumes. London: J. Murray.

Uhl, Sarah. 1991. Forbidden Friends: Cultural Veils of Female Friendship in Andalusia. *American Ethnologist* 18(1):90–105.

UNAIDS. 2004. AIDS Epidemic Update. Electronic document, http://www.unaids.org/wad2004/EPIupdate2004_html_en/epi04_00_en.htm, accessed November 8, 2005.

United Nations Development Programme. 1994. *Human Development Report 1994*. New York: Oxford University Press.

Uphoff, Norman T., and Milton J. Esman. 1984. *Local Organizations: Intermediaries in Rural Development*. Ithaca: Cornell University Press.

Valentine, Lisa Philips. 1995. *Making It Their Own: Ojibwe Communicative Practices*. Toronto: University of Toronto Press.

van der Geest, Sjaak, Susan Reynolds Whyte, and Anita Hardon. 1996. The Anthropology of Pharmaceuticals: A Biographical Approach. *Annual Review of Anthropology* 25:153–178.

Van Esterik, John. 1996. Women Meditation Teachers in Thailand. In *Women of Southeast Asia*. Penny Van Esterik, ed. Dekalb, IL: Northern Illinois University.

Van Esterik, Penny. 1989. *Beyond the Breast–Bottle Controversy*. New Brunswick: Rutgers University Press.

___. 1992. *Taking Refuge: Lao Buddhists in North America*. Program for Southeast Asian Studies: Arizona State University.

___. 1995. The Politics of Breastfeeding: An Advocacy Perspective. In *Breastfeeding: Biocultural Perspectives*. Patricia Stuart-Macadam and Katherine A. Dettwyler, eds. New York: Aldine de Gruyter.

___. 1996. Laywomen in Theravada Buddhism. In *Women of Southeast Asia*. Penny Van Esterik, ed. Dekalb, IL: Northern Illinois University.

___. 2000. *Materializing Thailand*. Oxford: Berg Press.

Van Gennep, Arnold. 1960[1908]. *The Rites of Passage*. Chicago: University of Chicago Press.

Van Maanen, John. 1988. *Tales of the Field: On Writing Ethnography*. Chicago: University of Chicago Press.

van Willigen, John. 1993. *Applied Anthropology: An Introduction*. Revised ed. Westport, CT: Bergin & Garvey.

VanWynsberghe, Robert M. 2002. AlterNatives: *Community, Identity, and Environmental Justice on Walpole Island*. Boston: Allyn & Bacon.

Velimirovic, Boris. 1990. Is Integration of Traditional and Western Medicine Really Possible? In *Anthropology and Primary Health Care*. Jeannine Coreil and J. Dennis Mull, eds. Pp. 751–778. Boulder: Westview Press.

Verdery, Katherine. 1996. *What Was Socialism, and What Comes Next?* Princeton: Princeton University Press.

Verdon, Michel. 1980. The Quebec Stem Family Revisited. In *Canadian Families: Ethnic Variations*. K. Ishwaran, ed. Toronto: McGraw-Hill Ryerson.

Vickers, Jeanne. 1993. *Women and War*. Atlantic Highlands, NJ: Zed Books.

Vincent, Joan. 1996. Political Anthropology. In *The Social Science Encyclopedia*. Adam Kuper and Jessica Kuper, eds. P. 624. New York: Routledge.

Wakin, E. 1992. *Anthropology Goes to War: Professional Ethics and Counterinsurgency in Thailand*. Center for Southeast Asian Studies, Monograph 7. Madison: University of Wisconsin.

Waldram, James. 2004. *Revenge of the Windigo: The Construction of the Mind and Mental Health of North American Aboriginal Peoples*. Toronto: University of Toronto Press.

Waldram, J., A. Herring, and K. Young. 1995. *Aboriginal Health in Canada: Historical, Cultural and Epidemiological Perspectives*. Toronto: University of Toronto Press.

Walker, Marilyn. 1984. *Harvesting the Northern Wild*. Yellowknife, NWT: The Northern Publishers.

Wallerstein, Immanuel. 1979. *The Capitalist World-Economy*. New York: Cambridge University Press.

Ward, Martha C. 1989. Once Upon a Time. In *Nest in the Wind: Adventures in Anthropology on a Tropical Island*. Martha C. Ward, ed. Pp. 1–22. Prospect Heights, IL: Waveland Press.

Warren, Carol A. B. 1988. Gender Issues in Field Research. *Qualitative Research Methods*, Volume 9. Newbury Park, CA: Sage Publications.

Warren, D. Michael. 2001. The Role of the Global Network of Indigenous Knowledge Resource Centers in the Conservation of Cultural and Biological Diversity. In *Biocultural Diversity: Linking Language, Knowledge and the Environment*. Pp. 446–461. Washington, DC: Smithsonian Institution Press.

Warren, Kay B. 1998. *Indigenous Movements and Their Critics: Pan-Maya Activism in Guatemala*. Princeton, NJ: Princeton University Press.

Watkins, Ben and Michael L. Fleisher. 2002. Tracking Pastoralist Migration: Lessons from the Ethiopian Somali National Regional State. *Human Organization* 61:328–338.

Watson, Rubie S. 1986. The Named and the Nameless: Gender and Person in Chinese Society. *American Ethnologist* 13(4):619–631.

___. 1997 Museums and Indigenous Cultures: The Power of Local Knowledge. *Cultural Survival Quarterly* 21(1):24–25.

Waxler-Morrison, N. J. Anderson, and E. Richardson. 1990 *Cross-cultural Caring: A Handbook for Health Professionals in Western Canada*. Vancouver: University of British Columbia Press.

Websdale, Neil. 1995. An Ethnographic Assessment of the Policing of Domestic Violence in Rural Eastern Kentucky. *Social Justice* 22(1):102–122.

Webster, Gloria Cranmer. 1991. The Contemporary Potlatch. In *Chiefly Feasts: The Enduring Kwakiutl Potlatch*. Aldona Jonaitis, ed. Pp. 227–250. Washington, DC: American Museum of Natural History.

Weiner, Annette. 1976. *Women of Value, Men of Renown: New Perspectives in Trobriand Exchange*. Austin: University of Texas Press.

Weismantel, M. J. 1989. The Children Cry for Bread: Hegemony and the Transformation of Consumption. In *The Social Economy of Consumption, Monographs in Economic Anthropology No. 6*. Henry J. Rutz and Benjamin S. Orlove, eds. Pp. 85–99. New York: University Press of America.

Werbner, Pnina. 1988. "Sealing the Koran": Offering and Sacrifice among Pakistani Labour Migrants. *Cultural Dynamics* 1:77–97.

White, Douglas R., and Michael L. Burton. 1988. Causes of Polygyny: Ecology, Economy, Kinship, and Warfare. *American Anthropologist* 90(4):871–887.

Whitehead, Tony Larry. 1986. Breakdown, Resolution, and Coherence: The Fieldwork Experience of a Big, Brown, Pretty-talking Man in a West Indian Community. In *Self, Sex, and Gender in Cross-Cultural Fieldwork*. Tony Larry Whitehead and Mary Ellen Conway, eds. Pp. 213–239. Chicago: University of Illinois Press.

Whitehead, Tony Larry, and Mary Ellen Conway, eds. 1986. *Self, Sex, and Gender in Cross-Cultural Fieldwork*. Chicago: University of Illinois Press.

Whiting, Beatrice B., and John W. M. Whiting. 1975. *Children of Six Cultures: A Psycho-Cultural Analysis*. Cambridge: Harvard University Press.

Whyte, Martin King. 1993. Wedding Behavior and Family Strategies in Chengdu. In *Chinese Families in the Post-Mao Era*. Deborah Davis and Stevan Harrell, eds. Pp. 89–218. Berkeley: University of California Press.

Wiber, M. 1997. *Erect Men, Undulating Women: The Visual Imagery of Gender, "Race" and Progress in Reconstructive Illustrations of Human Evolution*. Waterloo: Wilfred Laurier Press.

Wikan, Unni. 1977. Man Becomes Woman: Transsexualism in Oman as a Key to Gender Roles. *Man* 12(2):304–319.

___. 2000. Citizenship on Trial: Nadia's Case. *Daedalus* 129:55–76.

Wilde, James. 1988. Starvation in a Fruitful Land. *Time*, December 5:43–44.

Williams, Brett. 1988. *Upscaling Downtown: Stalled Gentrification in Washington, D.C.* Ithaca: Cornell University Press.

___. 1991. Good Guys and Bad Toys: The Paradoxical World of Children's Cartoons. In *The Politics of Culture*. Brett Williams, ed. Pp. 109–132. Washington, DC: Smithsonian Institution Press.

___. 1994. Babies and Banks: The "Reproductive Underclass" and the Raced, Gendered Masking of Debt. In *Race*. Steven Gregory and Roger Sanjek, eds. Pp. 348–365. Ithaca: Cornell University Press.

Williams, Raymond. 1983. *Keywords: A Vocabulary of Culture and Society*. New York: Oxford University Press.

Williams, Walter. 1992. *The Spirit and the Flesh: Sexual Diversity in American Indian Cultures*. 2nd edition. Boston: Beacon Press.

Wilson, Richard. 1995. *Maya Resurgence in Guatemala: Q'eqchi' Experiences*. Norman, OK: University of Oklahoma Press.

Winans, Edgar V., and Angelique Haugerud. 1977. Rural Self-Help in Kenya: The Harambee Movement. *Human Organization* 36:334–351.

Winland, D. 1992. The Role of Religious Affiliation in Refugee Resettlement: The Case of the Hmong. *Canadian Ethnic Studies* 24(1):96–119.

Winthrop, Rob. 2000. The Real World: Cultural Rights/Animal Rights. *Practicing Anthropology* 22:44–45.

Winzeler, Robert L. 1974. Sex Role Equality, Wet Rice Cultivation, and the State in Southeast Asia. *American Anthropologist* 76(3):563–565.

Wolf, Charlotte. 1996. Status. In *The Social Science Encyclopedia*. Adam Kuper and Jessica Kuper, eds. Pp. 842–843. New York: Routledge.

Wolf, Daniel R. 1991. *The Rebels: A Brotherhood of Outlaw Bikers*. Toronto: University of Toronto Press.

Wolf, Eric R. 1966. *Peasants*. Englewood Cliffs, NJ: Prentice-Hall.

___. 1969. *Peasant Wars of the Twentieth Century*. New York: Harper & Row.

Wolf, Margery. 1968. *The House of Lim: A Study of a Chinese Farm Family*. New York: Appleton-Century-Crofts.

Woodrick, Anne C. 1995. Mother-Daughter Conflict and the Selection of Ritual Kin in a Peasant Community. *Anthropological Quarterly* 68(4):219–233.

Woolford, Andrew J. 2005. *Between Justice and Certainty: Treaty Making in British Columbia*. Vancouver: UBC Press.

Woolfson, Peter, Virginia Hood, Roger Secker-Walker, and Ann C. Macaulay. 1995. Mohawk English in the Medical Interview. *Medical Anthropology Quarterly* 9(4):503–509.

Worldwatch Institute. 2003. *Vital Signs 2003: The Trends That Are Shaping Our Future*. Washington, DC: Worldwatch Institute/W.W. Norton.

Wright, Sue. 1998. The Politicization of "Culture." *Anthropology Today* 14:1, 7–15.

Wu, David Y. H. 1990. Chinese Minority Policy and the Meaning of Minority Culture: The Example of Bai in Yunnan, China. *Human Organization* 49(1):1–13.

Xenophanes. 1992. *Xenophanes of Colophon: Fragments: A Text and Translation with a Commentary*. Trans. James H. Lesher. Toronto: University of Toronto Press.

Xenos, Peter. 1993. *Extended Adolescence and the Sexuality of Asian Youth: Observations on Research and Policy*. East-West Center Reprints, Population Series No. 292. Honolulu: East-West Center.

Xizhe, Peng. 1991. *Demographic Transition in China: Fertility Trends Since the 1950s*. New York: Oxford University Press.

Yang, Mayfair Mei-hui. 1994. *Gifts, Favors and Banquets: The Art of Social Relationships in China*. Ithaca: Cornell University Press.

Yawney, Carole D., and J. Homiak. 2001. Rastafari. In *Encyclopedia of African and African-American Religions.* Stephen D. Glazier, ed. New York: Routledge.

Yinger, John. 1995. *Opening Doors: How to Cut Discrimination by Supporting Neighborhood Integration.* Center for Policy Research, Policy Brief No. 3.1995. Syracuse, NY: Syracuse University, Maxwell School of Citizenship and Public Affairs.

Young, Michael W. 1983. "Our Name Is Women; We Are Bought with Limesticks and Limepots": An Analysis of the Autobiographical Narrative of a Kalauna Woman. *Man* 18:478–501.

Young, Roger, and Caroline Van Bers. 1991. Death of the Family Farm. *Alternatives* 17(4):22–23.

Zaidi, S. Akbar. 1988. Poverty and Disease: Need for Structural Change. *Social Science and Medicine* 27:119–127.

Zarrilli, Phillip B. 1990. Kathakali. In *Indian Theatre: Traditions of Performance.* Farley P. Richmond, Darius L. Swann, and Phillip B. Zarrilli, eds. Pp. 315–357. Honolulu: University of Hawaii Press.

Zureik, Elia. 1994. Palestinian Refugees and Peace. *Journal of Palestine Studies* 24(1):5–17.

PHOTO CREDITS

Chapter 1

Page xxvi, Gilles Mingasson/Gamma Liaison; p. 4, Richard Wrangham/AnthroPhoto; p. 6, Spooner/Redmond-Callow/Gamma Liaison; p. 8, Bettmann/CORBIS; p. 9, University of Toronto Archives; p. 10, Michael Newman/PhotoEdit; p. 12, Barbara Miller; p. 14, Barbara Miller; p. 15, CRDPHOTO/CORBIS; p. 18, John Van Esterik.

Chapter 2

Page 24, Joel Savishinsky; p. 27, Pearson Education; p. 28, Penny Van Esterik; p. 33, Liza Dalby; p. 34, John Van Esterik; p. 37, Mel Konner/AnthroPhoto; p. 38, Gananath Obeyesekere; p. 39, Michael Horowitz.

Chapter 3

Page 48, Maxim Marmur/AFP/Getty Images; p. 52, Joel Savishinsky; p. 54, Reuters/George Mulala/Archive Photos; p. 56, Elliot Fratkin; p. 58, Barbara Miller; p. 61, Barbara Miller; p. 63, David Kideckel; p. 65, Sean Sprague/Stock Boston; p. 67, Reuters/Megan Lewis/Archive Photos; p. 68, Xinhua-Chine Nou/Gamma Liaison.

Chapter 4

Page 74, Wilson Melo/CORBIS; p. 76, J. Welsh/Royal British Columbia Museum 2307b; p. 78, Roshani Kothari; p. 79, Dick Loek/Canadian Press/Toronto Star; p. 81, Brennan Linsey/Canadian Press; p. 83, Edward Keller; p. 84, David Austen/Stock Boston; p. 87, © Douglas Mason/Woodfin Camp; p. 89, Chuck Fishman/Woodfin Camp; p. 90 (top & bottom), Barbara Miller; p. 95, Edward Keller; p. 96 (top), Bill Bachmann/PhotoEdit; p. 96 (bottom), Caroline Penn/CORBIS; p. 97, Lawrence Migdale.

Chapter 5

Page 100, Roshani Kothari; p. 103, David & Peter Turnley/CORBIS; p. 105, Stephanie Dinkins/Photo Researchers; p. 107, Rose Hartman/CORBIS; p. 108, Barry Iverson/Woodfin Camp; p.110 (top), Reza Webistan/CORBIS; p. 110 (bottom), Oliver Pichetti/Gamma Press; p. 113, Courtesy of UNICEF; p. 115, Lindsey Hebberd/CORBIS; p. 118 (top), The Rooms Corporation of Newfoundland and Labrador; p. 118 (bottom), Allan Tannenbaum/Image Works.

Chapter 6

Page 122, Kevin R. Morris/CORBIS; p. 125, Ken Heyman/Woodfin Camp; p. 129, Nancy Scheper-Hughes; p. 131, Roshani Kothari; p. 132 (left), Napoleon A. Chagnon/AnthroPhoto; p. 132 (right) Bill Varie/CORBIS; p. 133, Nichol Katz/Woodfin Camp; p. 134, Robert Caputo/National Geographic Image Collection; p. 138, National Anthropological Archive/Smithsonian Institution; p. 140, Barry Hewlett.

Chapter 7

Page 144, B. & C. Alexander, Photo Researchers; p.147, AFP/CORBIS; p. 148, Penny Van Esterik; p. 151, Mary Beth Mills/Colby College; p. 152, Irven DeVore/AnthroPhoto; p. 154 (top), Kevin Fleming/CORBIS; p. 154 (bottom), Courtesy of Ana Ning; p. 155, Peter Menzel/Stock Boston; p. 156, Laurel Kendall; p. 158, Lara Jo Regan/Getty Images; p. 161, Sean Sprague/Stock Boston; p. 164, Vincanne Adams.

Chapter 8

Page 168, Sa180oala, Liaison; p. 179, Reuters/Will Burgess; p. 182, Courtesy of Andrea and Nelia Camara; p. 183, Rick Smolan/Stock Boston; p. 184, Jack Heaton; p. 186, Naboro Komine/Photo Researchers.

Chapter 9

Page 190, Norbert Schiller/Image Works; p. 193, Keren Su/Stock Boston; p. 195, Barbara Miller; p. 197, Thomas L. Kelly/Woodfin Camp; p. 198, Ellen Oxfeld; p. 199, Reuters/Archive Photos; p. 201, David Wells/Image Works; p. 204, Andy Levin/Photo Researchers.

Chapter 10

Page 208, Barbara Miller; p. 213, Stephanie Maze/Woodfin Camp; p. 214, Jerome Sessini/In Visu/CORBIS; p. 215, Canadian Press EDMS; p. 216 (left), Charles & Josette Lenars/CORBIS; p. 216 (right), Royalty-Free/CORBIS; p. 218, Wolfgang Koehler; p. 220, David G. Houser/CORBIS; p. 223 (top), Bruno Barbey/Magnum; p. 223 (bottom), Barbara Miller; p. 227, Courtesy of Stuart Kirsch; p. 228, Peter Menzel/Stock Boston.

Chapter 11

Page 232, Robert Sorba/CORBIS; p. 235, Chunghee Sarah Soh; p. 237, Hank Wittemore/CORBIS SYGMA; p. 239, Kal Muller/Woodfin Camp; p. 240, North Wind Picture Archives; p. 241, Reuters NewMedia Inc./CORBIS p. 243, Roshani Kothari; p. 244, Daniel Simon/Gamma Liaison; p. 246, J.F.E. Bloss/AnthroPhoto; p. 248, Barbara Miller; p. 249, Giry Daniel/CORBIS SYGMA; p. 252, Reuters NewMedia Inc./CORBIS; p. 253, Bettmann/CORBIS; p. 254, Reuters/Fred Ernst.

Chapter 12

Page 258, Robert Frerck/Woodfin Camp; p. 261, Loring Danforth; p. 262, Simon Hiltebeitel; p. 263, AFP/Corbis; p. 267 (top & bottom), John Annerino/Liaison; p. 268, Lorenzo Pezzatini; p. 273, Jack Heaton; p. 275, Barbara Miller; p. 276, Edward Keller; p. 278, Gerd Ludwig/Woodfin Camp; p. 280, Lamont Lindstrom.

Chapter 13

Page 284, Robert Essel NYC/CORBIS p. 288, Susan Kuklin/Photo Researchers; p. 291, M. Vautier, Anthropological & Archaeological Museum, Lima, Peru/Woodfin Camp; p. 294, Michel Ponomareff/PONO-PRESSE; p. 295, Barbara Miller; p. 297 (top), Olympia/PhotoEdit; p. 297 (bottom), Richard Lord/PhotoEdit; p. 300, Charles O. Cecil; p. 301, Olympia/PhotoEdit.

Chapter 14

Page 306, Robert Frerck/Odyssey Productions, Inc.; p. 309 (top), Penny Tweedy/Panos Pictures; p. 309 (bottom), Roger Dashow/AnthroPhoto; p. 310, Peabody Museum, Harvard University; p. 311, Courtesy of Judy Chapman; p. 312 (left & right), Courtesy of Catherine H. McCoid and LeRoy D. McDermott. Reproduced by permission of the American Anthropological Association from American Anthropologist 98:2, June 1996. Not for further reproduction; p. 314, © Sarala Dandekar/photographer Arbindam Basu; p. 315, R. & S. Michaud/Woodfin Camp; p. 316, Paul Konklin/PhotoEdit; p. 317, Catherine Karnow/Woodfin Camp; p. 321, CORBIS. All rights reserved; p. 323, Dallas and John Heaton/CORBIS; p. 324, © John Elk III/Stock Boston.

Chapter 15

Page 328, Nick Wheeler/CORBIS; p. 331, Annie Griffiths Belt/CORBIS; p. 332, David Turnley/CORBIS; p. 334, AP/Wide World Photos; p. 336 (top), David Leeson/Image Works; p. 336 (bottom), Canadian Press STRGBS; p. 338, Stephen Ferry/Getty Images; p. 339, Annie Griffiths Belt/CORBIS; p. 341, David H. Wells/CORBIS; p. 345, Ed Keller.

Chapter 16

Page 348, Betty Press/Woodfin Camp; p. 353 (top), Staffan Widstrand/CORBIS; p. 353 (bottom), Barbara Miller; p. 358, William Rodman/CIDA; p. 363, Robert Nickelsberg/Gamma Liaison; p. 365, Roshani Kothari; p. 366, Naomi Adelson; p. 367, CORBIS; p. 370, CORBIS. All rights reserved.

INDEX

Note: Words in boldface type indicate key terms. Entries for tables and figures are followed by "*t*," and "*f*," respectively.

artist, focus on, 311–313
decorative arts, 315–317
definitions of, 308–310
ethno-aesthetics, 309–310
and identity, 313
museums, 317–319
performance arts, 313–315
and power, 313
repatriation, 318–319
study of, 310–311
subcategories, 309
theatre, 314–315
artists, 311–313
ascribed position
caste, 223–225
defined, 218
ethnicity, 221–222
race, 220–221
Asian women, as migrant workers,
333
Assembly of First Nations, 367
assimilated, 332
assistance programs, 355
authority, 235
autonomy, 236
avuncolocal, 177
awas, 149–151
the Aztecs, 269, 270

Baby-Friendly Hospital Initiative, 128
balanced reciprocity, 88
band leaders, 237
bands, 237
Bangladesh, family planning in,
108–109
Barberton, Ohio, 69–70
basic needs fund, 79
Bell, Diane, 266
below-replacement-level fertility, 103
berdache, 137
bias in news reporting, 299
big-man system, 238–239
big-woman system, 238–239
bilateral descent, 176–177
bilateral institutions, 357
bilingualism, 294
bilocal, 176
biological anthropology, 3–4
biological determinism
versus cultural constructionism, 19
described, 19
birth
cultural conflicts, 128
fertility. *See* fertility
identity, formation of, 127–128
personality, formation of, 127–128
reproduction. *See* reproduction
Western and non-Western practices,
127, 128
blood sports, 321

Boas, Franz, 7–8, 124, 310
the body, cultural perceptions of,
147–148
body modification groups, 215–216
bonding, 128–129
the *braceros*, 344–345
brahmans, 223
brain-dead, 147
breast milk, 178
bride-service, 185
brideprice, 114, 185
Buddhism
and abortion in Japan, 274
described, 273–274
and indigenous spirits in Burma,
274
religious roles for women, 274
bulimia, 149
Burma, indigenous spirits in, 274

Calcutta, household businesses in, 198
Canada
Aboriginal land claims, 366
bilingualism in, 294
descent patterns, 177
female circumcision in, 337
gay and lesbian rights, 137
legalized adoption, 179–180
racism, 221
ritual dance-drama, 314–315
sense of unity, 210
Canadian International Development
Agency (CIDA), 355, 357, 358f
Canadian museum timeline, 8t
cannibalism, 270
capital, 61
capital punishment, 246, 248
capitalism, 51, 70, 219
see also industrialism
cargo cults, 280
Caribbean, racial classifications in,
220
the Caribbean, new immigrants from,
338–339
carnival, 268–269
cash cropping, 94
caste, 223–225
celibacy, 253
ceremonial fund, 79
Cernea, Michael, 325
chain migration, 338
change. *See* cultural change
changing modes of production
described, 66
family farming, 68–69
foraging, 66–67
horticulture, 67
industrialism, 69–70
pastoralism, 67–68
chiefdoms, 239–240, 252

child care, 139
child rearing, and personality, 125
children
see also infants
adoption, 178–179
agricultural societies, 60
bread, demands for, 95
"the child," as special category, 130
dispute styles, 297
ethnographies of, 32
food stealing, 92
foraging, 53
formal schooling, 132–133
fostering, 178
horticulture, 55
infanticide, 103
informal learning, 131–132
legitimacy of, 181
modes of production and child
personality, 130–131
pastoralism, 57
pronatalism, 103
prostitution, 65
ritually defined sponsorship of, 180
socialization, 130–133
China
Chinese household businesses, 198
favours and gifts in, 86
household businesses, 197–198
logographic and current writing
styles, 290f
takeover of Tibetan medicine, 222
theatre, 324–325
transnational adoption of Chinese
infants, 179
women's movement in, 225–226
cholera, 156
Christianity
described, 276
Protestantism among White
Appalachians, 276–277
circular migration, 333
civil society
activist groups, 226–229
defined, 225
new social movements, 229
for the state, 225–226
clan, 237
class
as achieved status, 219
and consumption, 82–83
cultural differentiation and, 14
described, 13–14
and fieldwork, 31–32
meaning of, 219
and personality, 126
and social stratification, 219
"classic" nuclear household, 196–197
clearing, 55
clinical medical anthropology, 159

clubs, 213
CO-MADRES of El Salvador, 226–228
code-mixing, 295
code-switch, 295, 296
codes, 295–296
coercive harmony, 247
collaborative research, 45
collectivism, 62–63
college fraternities and sororities, 213
colonialism
and disease, 156
and expressive culture, 323
and indigenous systems, 248–249
and language change, 291–292
matrilineal descent, decline of, 176
Colville Lake community, 52
coming of age, 134–135
communication
human verbal language, 286–292
language. *See* language
meaning of, 286
media anthropology, 298–300
paralanguage, 290, 300–302
Communist Manifesto, 62
community-based credit system, 363
community healing, 152–153
computer-mediated communication
(CMC), 36
confederacies, 240
conflict. *See* social conflict
conflict mediation, 128
constant awareness, 35
consumerism, 78, 79
consumption, 77*f*
and age, 84
bread, 95
budgets, 80
cash cropping and declining nutrition, 94
categories of, 82–84
changing patterns of, 94–97
and class, 82–83
consumerism, 78, 79
consumption funds, 79–80
defined, 50
depersonalized consumption, 79
entitlements, 80–82
and equality, 92
and ethnicity, 83–84
forbidden consumption, 84–85
and gender, 83
inequalities, 80–84
market economies, 77
meaning of, 77–78
minimalism, 78, 79
modes of consumption, 78–79
non-market economies, 77
and privatization, 96
and race, 83–84

small-scale societies, 79
social organization of, 78
consumption funds, 79–80
contagious magic, 261
contemporary debates about cultural anthropology, 19–21
cooperatives, 217–218
corporate farms, 61–62
countercultural groups
body modification groups, 215–216
motorcycle gangs, 215
youth gangs, 214–215
courts, 247
couvade, 139
craft cooperatives, 218
credit card debt, 96–97
creole, 292
cricket, 323
critical cultural relativism, 18–19
critical development anthropology
(CDA), 360
critical legal anthropology, 245
critical medical anthropology
described, 157
poverty, role of, 157–158
Western medical training, 158–159
crop rotation, 56
cross-cousins, 182
cultural anthropology
agency, 21
biological determinism, 19–21
contemporary debates, 19–21
cultural constructionism, 19
cultural materialism, 21
cultural relativism, 18–19
culture. *See* culture
described, 4–5
diachronic approach, 350
distinctive features of, 16–19
diversity, valuing and sustaining, 19
ethnography, 16–17
ethnology, 16–17
founding fathers of, 7
and the future, 369–370
history of the field, 7–13
holism, 21
interpretive anthropology, 21
and participant observation, 26
research. *See* research methods
roots of Canadian anthropology, 8, 8*t*
structure, 21
synchronic approach, 350
cultural assessment, 355
cultural assimilation policies, 292
cultural change
acculturation, 352
assimilated, 332
deculturated, 352
described, 12–13

diffusion, 351–353
invention, 351
social impact assessment, 352–353
two processes of, 351–353
cultural configuration, 125
cultural constructionism
versus biological determinism, 19
described, 19
cultural heritage, 324, 325
cultural imperialism, 19
cultural knowledge, 128
cultural learning, 12
cultural materialism
adolescence, 134
described, 21
infrastructure, 21
versus interpretive anthropology, 21
structure, 21
superstructure, 21
cultural perceptions of the body, 147–148
cultural relativism
absolute cultural relativism, 18
critical cultural relativism, 18–19
described, 18
versus ethnocentrism, 18
female circumcision, 136
cultural resource management
(CRM), 5
culture
adaptation, 10
and change, 12–13
characteristics of, 9–13
and consumption, 77–85
Culture, with capital C, 9
and death, 111–119
definitions of, 9
and drinking, 11
and eating, 10–11
and elimination, 11
and exchange, 85–94
expressive culture. *See* expressive culture
and globalization, 12
human interaction levels, 244
and identity, 124–127
index culture, 13
integration of, 12
interaction, 12–13
learned nature of, 12
local culture, 9
localization, 12
macroculture, 9
multiple cultural worlds, 13–16
national character studies, 126
versus nature, 10
people who are deaf, 287
and personality, 124–127
recording culture, 39–41
and reproduction, 102–104

East Asia, new immigrants from, 339
Eastern Europe
  activism, 228–229
  new immigrants from, 341
  and privatization, 96
eating, and culture, 10–11
ecological/epidemiological approach,
  155–156
economic systems
  and adaptation, 10
  consumption. *See* consumption
  and cultural anthropology, 50–51
  described, 50
  exchange. *See* exchange
  and globalization, 51
  modes of production. *See* modes of
    production
  production, 50
  typologies, 50–51
economies, and political organization,
  236*f*
education, and socialization, 132–133
Egypt, environmental concern in, 228
elimination, and culture, 11
emergent nations, 243
emic, 34, 35, 148
emic perceptions of symptoms, 152
enculturation, 12, 124
endogamy, 182–183
the Enlightenment, 7
entertainment fund, 79–80
entitlements
  bundle of entitlements, 80–81
  described, 80
  direct entitlements, 80–81
  famine, 81–82
  global application, 81
  global level, 82
  household level, 82
  indirect entitlements, 80–81
  levels of, 81–82
  national level, 82
environmental degradation, 368–369
epics, 263
epidemics, 115
ethics
  in fieldwork, 44–45
  informed consent, 44
ethnic conflict, 250
ethnic pluralism, 250
ethnicity
  as ascribed class, 221–222
  and consumption, 83–84
  described, 14
  diaspora population, 221–222
  management of, by states, 221
  versus race, 14
  and social stratification, 221–222
ethno-aesthetics, 309–310
ethnobotany, 154

ethnocentrism, 18, 126
ethnocide, 118
ethnography
  children, 32
  described, 16–17, 42–43
  person-centred ethnography,
    126–127
  qualitative data, 41
  realist ethnographies, 43
  reflexive ethnographies, 43
  social violence in the field, 45
ethnology, 16–17
ethnomedicine
  see also medical anthropology
  cultural perceptions of the body,
    147–148
  culture-bound syndromes, 149
  defined, 146
  diagnosis, 151–152
  divination, 151
  emic perceptions of symptoms, 152
  healers, 154
  healing, 152–155
  healing substances, 154–155
  health problems, defining, 148–149
  preventive practices, 149–151
  use of term, 146–147
ethnomusicology, 313
ethnopsychology, 124
etic, 34, 35, 148
evil eye, 150
exchange, 77*f*
  changing patterns of, 94–97
  China, favours and gifts in, 86
  credit card debt, 96–97
  and culture, 85–94
  defined, 50
  described, 85
  exploitation, 92–93
  in fieldwork, 30–31
  gambling, 90–91
  items exchanges, 85–88
  of labour, 87
  market exchange, 89–90
  of material goods, 85–86
  modes of exchange, 88–93
  money, 87–88
  potlatch, 97
  rights in people, 88
  and risk aversion, 93
  and social inequality, 93–94
  symbolic goods, 86–87
  theft, 92
  theories of exchange, 93–94
  unbalanced exchange, 89–93
  Western goods, lure of, 95
  of women between men, 88
exclusion, 341–342
exogamy, 183
exploitation, 92–93

expressive culture
  architecture, 315–317
  art, 308–319
  change in, 322–325
  and colonialism, 323
  decorative arts, 315–317
  flowers, 316–317
  games, 320–321
  gardens, 316–317
  gender relations, 313
  leisure, 320–322
  leisure travel, 321–322, 323–324
  museums, 317–319
  performance arts, 313–315
  play, 320–322
  post-communist transitions,
    324–325
  sports, 320–321
  syncretism, 323
  theatre, 314–315
extended households, 192–193

factions, 242
fallowing, 55, 56
family
  current status and future trends,
    205
  meaning of, 192
  nuclear family, 192
family disaffiliation, 199
family farming, 58–61, 62, 68–69
family planning, 107, 108–109
famine, 81–82
farmers' cooperatives, 217
farming family businesses, 198–199
fatherhood, 139
female circumcision, 135, 136, 337
female genital cutting, 135, 136, 337
female infanticide, 113, 114
femicide, 117
fertility
  below-replacement-level fertility, 103
  daughter preferences, 106–107
  demographic transition, 104
  family-level decision making,
    106–107
  global-level decision making, 107
  meaning of, 102
  national-level decision making, 107
  politics of, 106–107
  replacement-level fertility, 103
  sexual intercourse restrictions and,
    106
  son preferences, 106–107
fertility control
  induced abortion, 109–110
  methods of, 108–109
  new reproductive technologies,
    110–111
  in vitro fertilization (IVF), 111

phonemes, 288
phonetics, 291
pidgin, 291–292
power, 296–298
pragmatics, 287
productivity, 288
rights, 292
Sapir-Whorf hypothesis, 293
sociolinguistics, 293
thought and society, 293–300
world languages, 292
writing systems, 290
language decay, 292
language extinction, 292
language socialization, 293–294
large-scale development institutions, 356–357
Last Supper in Fiji, 277
Latin America
    farm families, 366
    new immigrants from, 337–339
    racial classifications in, 220
law
    change in legal systems, 248–249
    colonialism and indigenous systems, 248–249
    and complexity, 249
    defined, 245
    international legal disputes, 253
    legal pluralism, 249
    and social inequality, 248
    study of, 245
law of similarity, 261
Leacock, Eleanor, 20
leadership
    see also political organization
    band leaders, 237
    chiefdoms, 239–240
    iyalode, 239–240
    state leadership, 242
    tribal headman or headwoman, 237
learned nature of culture, 12
legal anthropology. *See* law; social conflict; social order
legal pluralism, 249
legal systems, 248–249
legalized adoption in North America, 179–180
leisure, 320–322
leisure travel, 321–322, 323–324
lesbian mothers, 204
Lévi-Strauss, Claude, 19
life-cycle rituals, 267–268
life history, 37–38
life stages model, 127
lifeboat mentality, 342
limited-purpose money, 87
the Lin family of Taiwan, 173–174, 174*f*
linguistic anthropology, 4, 286

linguistic determinism, 293
linguistic pluralism, 294
linguistic relativism, 290
local culture, 9
local politics, 242
local religions, 278
localization, 12
Lock, Margaret, 27
logographs, 290
looks, 301–302
the Louvre, 308
Lozada, Eriberto, 36

the Maasai, 2
macroculture, 9
magic, 260–261
the Makah Nation, 369
mal ojo, 150
malaria, 156
male bias in development, 361–362
male-headed household, 194, 196
male wrestling in India, 321
Maliki law, 203
Malinowski, Bronislaw, 7, 27, 234, 244
"Man the Hunter" model, 53
mana, 264
Manu'a, 26
Mardi Gras, 269
marital satisfaction, 200
market exchange, 89–90
marriage
    arranged marriage, 185
    brideprice, 185
    change in marriage, 187
    cross-culturally valid definition, 180–181
    divine marriages, 264
    dowry, 185
    endogamy, 182–183
    exogamy, 183
    forms of marriage, 185–186
    generalized exchange systems, 182
    gift giving, 185
    group marriage, 186
    hypergyny, 183
    hypogyny, 183
    incest taboo, 182
    jati endogamy, 224
    legitimacy of children, 181
    monogamy, 186
    parallel-cousin marriage, 182
    patrilateral parallel-cousin marriage, 182
    polyandry, 186
    polygamy, 186
    polygyny, 186
    preference rules, 182–185
    remarriage, 204–205
    restricted exchange systems, 182

romantic love, 184–185
rules of exclusion, 182
spouse selection, 181–185
style changes in weddings, 187
teknonyms, 175
Martinique, code-switching in, 296
Marx, Karl, 70, 262
material cultural heritage, 324–325
material goods, 85–86
matrifocality, 177
matrilineal descent, 173, 174–176
matrilocality, 181
the Maya of Chiapas, Mexico, 68–69
McLuhan, Marshall, 298
Mead, Margaret, 20, 125, 134
measles, 156
mechanical solidarity, 219
media anthropology, 298–300
media institutions, 298–300
media process, 298
medical anthropology
    see also ethnomedicine
    approaches, 155–159
    clinical medical anthropology, 159
    critical medical anthropology, 157–159
    disease/illness dichotomy, 148
    diseases of development, 161
    ecological/epidemiological approach, 155–156
    globalization and change, 160–165
    health problems, defining, 148–149
    HIV/AIDS, 162–163
    infectious diseases, 160–161
    interpretive approaches to health systems, 156–157
    medical pluralism, 161–165
    nosology, 149
    structural suffering, 148
    vaccination programs, 160
medical pluralism
    conflict between explanatory models, 162–164
    meaning of, 161
    options and complications, 161–162
    selective pluralism, 164–165
medicalization, 157
medicines, 155
the Mehinaku, 124
men
    couvade, 139
    fatherhood, 139
    friendships in rural Spain, 212
    patrilineal descent, 173
    and urban gangs, 214–215
menopause, 140
men's clubs, 213
micro-finance, 362–363
middle age, 140

midwives, 127
migration
  acceleration, 337
  categories of, 331–336
  chain migration, 338
  circular migration, 333
  defined, 330
  development-induced displacement
    (DID), 334
  displaced persons, 333–335
  and family and household formation
    changes, 205
  feminization of, 337
  institutional migrants, 335–336
  internal migration, 331
  internally displaced persons (IDPs),
    333–334
  international migration, 331, 332
  labour migrants, 333
  male migration and women-headed
    households, 195–196
  meaning of, 102
  military migration, 335–336
  new immigrants, 336–341
  out-migration areas, 332
  push–pull theory, 331
  reason for moving, categories based
    on, 333–336
  refugees, 333
  right of return, 342
  spatial boundaries, categories based
    on, 331–333
  transnational migrants, 331
  transnational migration, 332–333
  wage labour migration, 333
migration policies and politics
  exclusion, 341–342
  human rights, 342–343
  inclusion, 341–342
  lifeboat mentality, 342
  protection of migrants' health, 343
  working-class racism, 342
military migration, 335–336
minerals, 155
minimalism, 78, 79
modernization theory, 354
modes of consumption, 78–79
modes of exchange
  exploitation, 92–93
  gambling, 90–91
  market exchange, 89–90
  reciprocity, 88–89
  redistribution, 89
  theft, 92
  unbalanced exchange, 89–93
modes of production, 77f
  agriculture, 58–63, 68–69
  changing modes of production,
    66–70
  and child personality, 130–131

foraging, 51–54, 66–67
horticulture, 54–56, 67
industrialism, 63–65, 69–70
pastoralism, 56–58, 67–68
and reproduction, 102–104
money
  limited-purpose money, 87
  meaning of, 87
  as medium of exchange, 87–88
  multi-purpose money, 87–88
  remittances, 199
Mongolia, herders of, 67–68
monogamy, 186
monotheism, 261
Montesquieu, Charles, 7
Morgan, Lewis Henry, 7, 27, 171
mortality
  demographic transition, 104
  epidemics, 115
  infant mortality rate, 113
  infanticide, 112–113
  meaning of, 102
  suicide, 113–115
  violence, 116–119
motherhood, 138–139
motorcycle gangs, 215
multi-purpose money, 87–88
multi-sited research, 27–28
multiple cultural worlds
  age, 15
  class, 13–14
  ethnicity, 14–15
  gender, 15
  institutions, 16
  race, 14
  region, 15–16
multiple levels of language, 294–296
the Mundurucu of the Brazilian
    Amazon, 67
museum timeline, 8t
museums, 317–319
music, and gender, 313–314, 313t
Muslim doctrine, 263
myths, 86, 262–263, 314–315

the Nacirema, 4–5
Nader, Laura, 247
naming systems, 172f, 175
narcissist, 131
nation, 243
nation-state, 243
national character studies, 126
national level of entitlement, 82
Native Americans
  see also First Nations; indigenous
    peoples
  amazon, 137
  berdache, 137
  casinos, 91
  confederacies, 240

genocidal destruction, 118–119
  potlatch, 76, 97
  silence, 300
  whale hunting, 369
nature, *versus* culture, 10
Navajo textiles, 311
Nayer fertility ritual, 272–273
needs assessment study, 40
negative reciprocity, 89
neo-colonialism, 176
neo-slavery, 344–345
neolocality, 176
nerves, 150
new immigrants
  and acceleration of migration, 337
  from the Caribbean, 337–339
  defined, 336
  from East Asia, 339
  from Eastern Europe, 341
  and female circumcision in Canada,
    337
  and feminization of migration, 337
  and globalization, 336
  from Latin America, 337–339
  from South Asia, 340
  from Southeast Asia, 339–340
new infectious diseases, 160–161
new reproductive technologies,
    110–111
new social movements, 229
news reporting, bias in, 299
the Ngarrindjeri, 266
niwa, 127
non-governmental organizations, 358
non-periodic rituals, 266
non-verbal communication. *See*
    paralanguage
nonviolent conflict, 253
norms, 245
nosology, 149
nuclear family, 192
nuclear household, 192
nurturant-responsible personalities,
    130
nutrition, and cash cropping, 94

observer's paradox, 288
obstetrical training, 158
Official Development Assistance (ODA)
    program, 358f
Old Hag, 150
open-ended interview, 35
orangutan research, 6
organic solidarity, 219
out-migration areas, 332
outcast, 223

paleopathology, 4
Palermo, Italy, 342
Palestinian refugees, 343

Panama, craft cooperatives, 218
Papua New Guinea
    and anthropologists as activists in,
        226–227
    big-men system, Mt. Hagen, 238
paralanguage
    described, 290, 300
    dress and looks, 301–302
    kinesics, 301
    silence, 300–301
parallel cousins, 182
parenthood, 138–139
participant observation
    see also fieldwork
    constant awareness, 35
    deductive research, 34
    described, 26
    emic approach, 34, 35
    etic approach, 34, 35
    as evolving method, 27–28
    inductive research, 34
    interviews, 35–36
    intuitive research, 34
    multi-sited research, 27–28
    "normal" life, 34–35
    qualitative research, 34
    quantitative research, 34, 35
    questionnaires, 35–36
    surveys, 35–36
    varieties of, 34–35
participatory research methods (PRMs),
    361
passive policing, 202
Passover in Kerala, 276
pastoralism
    architecture, 315
    described, 56
    division of labour, 57
    and domestication, 54
    herders of Mongolia, 67–68
    limits to, 56–57
    migration, and health issues, 343
    problems of, 57
    property relations, 57
    as sustainable system, 58
    variations in organization, 57
patrilateral parallel-cousin marriage,
    182
patrilineal descent, 173
patrilocal, 174
patrinomy, 177
peacekeeping, 254
performance arts, 313–315
periodic market, 90
periodic rituals, 266
permanent market, 90
perpetuity, 236
person-centred ethnography, 126–127
personality
    in adulthood, 138–141

birth context, 127–128
    and child rearing, 125
    and class, 126
    cultural configuration, 125
    cultural patterns in, 125–126
    and culture, 124–127
    Culture and Personality School,
        124–126
    defiant individualist, 214
    defined, 124
    dependent-dominant personalities,
        130
    formal schooling, 132–133
    formation of, at birth and infancy,
        127–130
    informal learning, 131–132
    modes of production and child
        personality, 130–131
    national character studies, 126
    niwa, 127
    nurturant-responsible personalities,
        130
    person-centred ethnography,
        126–127
    and poverty, 126
    sex-linked personality characteristics,
        130
    socialization during childhood,
        130–133
phonemes, 288
phonetics, 291
photography, 40–41, 42
physical ability, 184
physical anthropology, 3–4
physical features, 184
physical isolation, 202
pibloktoq, 150
pidgin, 291–292
pilgrimage, 268
placebo effect, 157
planting, 55
play, 320–322
policing, 246
political anthropology
    authority, 235
    changes in political systems,
        243–244
    described, 234
    globalization, and politics, 243–244
    influence, 235
    political organization and leadership,
        236–242
    politics, 235–236
political organization
    see also leadership
    bands, 237
    big-man system, 238–239
    big-woman system, 238–239
    chiefdoms, 239–240
    clan, 237

confederacies, 240
    defined, 236
    and economies, 236*f*
    features, 236
    states, 240–242
    tribes, 237–238
political systems
    changes in, 243–244
    emergent nations, 243
    transnational nations, 243
politics
    factions, 242
    and globalization, 243–244
    meaning of, 235
    of museum exhibits, 318–319
    universality of, 235–236
polyandrous household, 197
polyandry, 186
polygamy, 186
polygyny, 186
polytheism, 261
population puzzles, 102
post-communist transitions, 324–325
post-industrialism, 63–65
potlatch, 76, 97
poverty
    critical medical anthropology,
        157–158
    culture of poverty, 126
    in former Soviet Union, 96
    friendship among urban poor, 212
    image of the limited good, 126
    and personality, 126
    women-headed households,
        194–195
power, 235, 296–298, 313
practicing anthropology, 5
pragmatics, 287
premarital sexual activity, 105
preparation for the field, 29–30
preventive practices, 149–151
priest, 269–270
priestess, 270
primary group, 210
primogeniture, 181
prison friendships, 211–212
private violence, 116–117
privatization, 67–68, 96, 358
procedures, 236
processual analysis, 234
production
    defined, 50
    intensive strategy, 58
    modes of production. *See* modes of
        production
productivity, 288
project cycle, 358–359
project selection and funding, 28–29
pronatalism, 103
property relations

and privatization,   96
Soviet Jews,   341

the Saami,   352–353
sacred space,   264–266, 268, 280
sacrifice,   269
same-sex sexuality,   135–138
Sapir, Edward,   125, 293
Sapir-Whorf hypothesis,   293
sati,   115
secondary group,   210, 219
secondary research,   28
segmentary model,   250
selective pluralism,   164–165
senior years,   138–140
sex,   15
sex-linked personality characteristics,
   130
sex-selective infanticide,   106, 110
sexual activity,   200
sexual identity,   135–138
sexual intercourse,   104–106
shaman,   154, 269–270
sharing, and kinship,   178–180
shikhat,   312
shudra varna,   223
shudras,   223
sibling relationships,   200–201
the Sikhs in British Columbia,   340
silence,   300–301
site selection,   30
Six Cultures Study,   130–131
Skinner, William,   16
slavery
   as form of exploitation,   92–93
   institutionalized slavery,   88
   neo-slavery,   344–345
   women-headed households,   194
sleeping patterns,   129
smallpox,   156
snowmobiles,   352–353
social change and domestic life,   205
social class. *See* class
social conflict
   contested sacred sites,   280
   ethnic conflict,   250
   feuding,   250
   nonviolent conflict,   253
   processual analysis,   234
   revolution,   250–251
   study of,   244–245
   warfare,   251–252
social control
   change in legal systems,   248–249
   concept of,   245
   courts,   247
   defined,   245
   law,   245
   norms,   245
   policing,   246

punishment,   247–248
   small-scale societies,   245–246
   specialization,   246
   in states,   246–248
   trials,   247
social groups
   age set,   211
   body modification groups,   215–216
   clubs,   213
   cooperatives,   217–218
   countercultural groups,   214–216
   defined,   210
   fraternities,   213–214
   friendship,   211–212
   motorcycle gangs,   215
   primary group,   210
   rights and responsibilities of
      members,   210
   secondary group,   210, 219
   work groups,   216–217
   youth gangs,   214–215
social impact assessment,   352–353
social inequality
   see also social stratification
   and exchange,   93–94
   and the law,   248
social isolation,   202
social networks,   363
social order
   international legal disputes,   253
   international peacekeeping,   254
   maintenance of world order,
      253–254
   study of,   244–245
   systems of social control,   245–248
social stratification
   see also social inequality
   achieved position,   218
   ascribed position,   218
   caste,   223–225
   class,   219
   defined,   218
   ethnicity,   221–222
   race,   220–221
   status groups,   218–219
social violence in the field,   45
socialism,   62
socialization
   formal schooling,   132–133
   informal learning,   131–132
   language socialization,   293–294
   modes of production and child
      personality,   130–131
   women politicians in Korea,   235
socio-cultural fit,   359
sociolinguistics,   293
soldiers,   335–336
son preferences,   106–107
sororities,   213
South Africa

apartheid,   220–221
   Taiwanese in,   69
South Asia, new immigrants from,
   340–341
Southeast Asia, new immigrants from,
   339–340
Soviet Jews,   341
Spain, friendship patterns in,   212
specialization,   90, 246
spontaneous abortion,   103
sports,   320–321
spousal abuse,   116–117
spouse/partner relationships,   200
spouse selection
   arranged marriage,   185
   endogamy,   182–183
   hypergyny,   183
   hypogyny,   183
   physical ability,   184
   physical features,   184
   preference rules,   182–185
   romantic love,   184–185
   rules of exclusion,   182
state
   defined,   240
   evolution of,   240–241
   gender and leadership,   242
   local power and politics, democratic
      states,   242
   powers of,   241
   social control,   246–248
   symbols of state power,   241–242
status,   218
status groups,   218–219
stealing,   92
stem household,   193
stratificational model,   250
street gangs,   214
structural adjustment,   354
structural suffering,   148
structure
   versus agency,   21
   meaning of,   21
sugar cooperatives,   217
suicide,   113–115
suicide terrorism,   113–115
supernatural forces and beings,   264
superstructure,   21
surgical menopause,   140
surveys,   35–36
sustainability
   agriculture,   63
   foraging,   53–54
   horticulture,   56
   pastoralism,   58
sustainable development,   355
susto,   149
swapping system,   93
Swedish Agency for International
   Development (SIDA),   357